W9-ACS-125

THE HISTORY OF THE
PRIMITIVE CHURCH

THE MACMILLAN COMPANY
NEW YORK · BOSTON · CHICAGO · DALLAS
ATLANTA · SAN FRANCISCO

MACMILLAN AND CO., LIMITED
LONDON · BOMBAY · CALCUTTA · MADRAS
MELBOURNE

THE MACMILLAN COMPANY
OF CANADA, LIMITED
TORONTO

THE HISTORY OF THE
PRIMITIVE
✝ CHURCH ✝

by JULES LEBRETON, s.j., *Dean of the Faculty*

of Theology of the Institut Catholique, Paris,

and JACQUES ZEILLER, *Director of Studies*

at the Ecole des Hautes-Etudes (Sorbonne) ✝ ✝ ✝

with a Foreword by AUGUSTIN FLICHE,

Dean of the Faculty of Letters at Montpellier and

MGR. VICTOR MARTIN, *Dean of the Faculty of*

Catholic Theology at Strassburg ✝ *Translated from*

the French by ERNEST C. MESSENGER, PH.D.

VOLUME I   BOOKS I & II

New York · THE MACMILLAN COMPANY · *Mcmxlix*

TRANSLATOR'S PREFACE

The volumes here presented to the English reader constitute the first of a massive series of twenty-four volumes designed to cover the whole History of the Church from its beginning down to our own time. The General Editors, Monsieur Augustin Fliche, the Dean of the Faculty of Letters at Montpellier, and Mgr. Victor Martin, Dean of the Faculty of Catholic Theology at Strasburg, have entrusted each volume in the series to one or more specialists, thus ensuring that the whole work will have the highest scientific value. The present volumes, on the Primitive Church, are from the pen of Père Lebreton, Dean of the Faculty of Theology at the Institut Catholique in Paris, and Monsieur Jacques Zeiller, Director of Studies at the Ecole des Hautes Etudes (Sorbonne). Their work needs no further commendation than the mention of their names.

As to the work of translation, I have adhered to the original as faithfully as possible. Here and there I have added to the footnotes, or substituted references to English translations in the case of certain well-known works. Citations from Scripture are in the main quoted according to the version in common use amongst English Catholics, but I have not hesitated to modify this where the quotation is intended to express a sense not well brought out in the current text. For quotations from the Fathers and other ecclesiastical writers, I have followed the excellent versions given in the French, with an occasional glance at the original, or standard English translations.

I owe a debt of gratitude to my friend and former colleague, the Very Rev. Mgr. John M. Barton, D.D., Consultor to the Pontifical Biblical Commission, for so kindly reading through my translation, and for making many valuable suggestions, especially in matters of bibliographical detail.

It only remains for me to express the honour I feel it to be associated with a work of this kind, and my hope that it will be found possible to present the whole work to English readers as the several volumes appear.

ERNEST C. MESSENGER

FOREWORD

By the General Editors

OF all the branches of history, there is scarcely one which has made so much progress in the last half century as ecclesiastical history. Its growth has been favoured by a combination of favourable circumstances: the opening of the Vatican archives to all students by Pope Leo XIII, the creation at Rome, by various nations, of institutes for the study of archives or inscriptions, the founding almost everywhere of scientific societies dealing more especially with religious history, the development of auxiliary sciences, the publication of collections and catalogues which make easier the utilising of texts, the extension of historical studies in theology and canon law. Though much still remains to be done, it cannot be denied that important results have been obtained. In addition, besides the manifold works of scholarship which have elucidated or at least thrown light on so many obscure problems, great syntheses have been attempted, dealing with some special period, or the religious activity in a particular country in the East or West, or again a group of ecclesiastical institutions at a particular time. Lastly, some writers have endeavoured to give a general survey of the chief results obtained by contemporary scholarship, and to trace out, with more or less detail, the general history of the Church.

Among the last mentioned works, there are some which are deserving of all praise, and which have rendered real service. At the same time they have been criticised as being too condensed, or as not giving sufficiently numerous references, or more often, as not possessing the same scientific value in their various parts. Those who wrote them were qualified, by their personal researches, to deal with one period of ecclesiastical history; they could not be equally competent in others, and in spite of praiseworthy efforts, they have sometimes encountered obstacles which it was very difficult for them to overcome.

In fact, it seems clear at the present time that, in view of the ever

3

increasing number of books and articles appearing in all languages, one man cannot himself write a history of the Church from its most remote beginnings to the present day.

In contrast to what has happened in the domain of ecclesiastical history, the recent universal histories in course of publication, such as the *Histoire Générale* of G. Glotz, *Peuples et civilisations* by L. Halphen and C. Sagnac, *Histoire du monde* by E. Cavaignac, are collective works produced by groups of specialists who have been entrusted with one or two volumes at most, and hence they are of high scientific value.

We have decided to adopt a similar method here. The present work differs from the general histories of the Church which have preceded it, first in its size, for it will consist of no less than twenty-four double volumes, but still more because it will not be the work of one single historian or of a few collaborators.

More than thirty writers from various parts of Europe have agreed to take part in its production. Whether they belong to the laity or to the clergy, secular or regular, whether they be professors at Universities or State schools, in Catholic faculties, in seminaries, or Universities outside France, they are all men of learning and competence: some have already produced works which do honour to French scholarship; others who are younger have shown on many occasions that they are quite worthy of our hopes, and that it would not be rash to confide to them, along with their elders, a task for which they are certainly well prepared.

Thus we have been able, as in the already mentioned general histories, to entrust the various periods of Church history to specialists possessing a deep personal knowledge of the matters in question, and very capable of drawing from the works of scholarship which have already appeared the conclusions which must be accepted, and also of filling up, if necessary, the gaps which still exist.

This History of the Church from its origins to our own time, which begins with the present volume, aims above all at bringing fully to the light the general results acquired by the various researches in ecclesiastical history during recent years, and to put them at the disposition of all those who for various reasons desire to attain them in a speedy and easy way.

It is intended more particularly for students who, for purposes of their studies, require certain knowledge drawn from the best sources; for general readers desirous of instruction or of enlightenment, or to correct false statements; and lastly for workers of all kinds who, before specialising in the study of one subject, desire to envisage this in the framework of general history, in order not to go astray, and to avoid dangerous misinterpretations.

To all it will present an accurate statement, based on a critical knowledge of earlier works, or, where such do not exist, of the original sources, and it will, according to the case, be capable of satisfying all legitimate curiosity, or of giving direction for personal research.

From this general idea of the work there follow its distinctive characteristics.

Since it is a matter above all of initiation and of accurate statement, the various readers of this History of the Church should not only have at their disposition an accurate account of events, but should also be able constantly to refer to the works which have inspired it. Hence, besides the general bibliography at the end of the different volumes, each chapter will be preceded by a list of articles and works indispensable for anyone who wants to study more deeply the matters there treated. From these bibliographies we have deliberately eliminated works which are not altogether scientific in character, and retained exclusively those which may rightly be regarded as definitive, or at least as making an important contribution to the subject. Moreover, we have thus avoided recommending undeservedly those books and articles which so heavily encumber the literature of ecclesiastical history, and which for reasons which are not at all scientific, only too often give a wrong idea of the true character of the facts.

The text itself will be always accompanied by indispensable references. Original sources will be indicated wherever this seems necessary, but generally the reader will be referred to the most recent scientific works in which he will find these sources indicated. When dealing with questions which have given rise to diverse or contradictory opinions, we shall indicate briefly the reasons why one view has been adopted rather than another; at the same time, when the arguments in favour of the thesis enunciated have been set forth in a conclusive form in some book or article, we shall content ourselves with a reference to this. In every case, in one form or another, every affirmation, of whatsoever nature, will be justified, and the means of controlling it will be freely put at the disposition of all.

The same scientific preoccupations will inspire the utilisation of the materials thus tested and presented to the reader. We shall endeavour to banish personal considerations which prove nothing, and to give a picture as exact and complete as possible of the different forms of ecclesiastical activity through the ages, leaving aside no essential aspect. The fault of some publications similar to the present one is the almost exclusive consideration of what we may call the *external* history of the Church, that is to say, of its relations with States and with organised societies. Without wishing to sacrifice this aspect, we think it would be regrettable to relegate to the background, as is too often done, the *internal* activity of Catholicism which has enabled it to radiate its light, and to spread its influence through all the spheres of the lives of nations as well as of individuals. Everything is interconnected in the life of the Church through the ages, and if we want to discover its deep significance, we must endeavour to grasp the bond which exists at all times between the dogmatic conceptions and canonical rules on the one hand, and the social, political and economic structure on the other.

Accordingly, no source of information will be neglected. At the present time, scholars who are dealing with the history of the Church are not content to utilise literary and diplomatic documents, but direct their investigations more and more towards theology, canon law, and works of controversy, in which can often be found the explanation of events and of the direction these have taken. General history should profit by this orientation: it will thus be able to view facts from the correct angle, to grasp their real causes, establish the relations which unite them to the theological or canonical conceptions of a particular epoch, and thereby give them a wide and exact interpretation.

We may be allowed to hope that in this way there will appear in its full light the extraordinary universality of the Church's influence through the ages. Need we add that in order to arrive at a more complete and more solidly established historical truth, those who are collaborating in this work have decided to fulfil all the requirements of modern methods? Thirty-five years ago, the Chanoine Cauchie wrote in the first number of the *Revue d'histoire ecclésiastique*[1]: "Every Christian who is loyal to his faith accepts the government of the world by Providence, but this does not prevent him from studying scientifically the action of second causes." The distin-

[1] *Revue d'histoire ecclésiastique*, Vol. I, 1900, p. 141.

guished Louvain professor in writing these lines was but echoing the desire often expressed by Pope Leo XIII, who wanted to see a universal Church History brought into line with the progress of modern critical research.

The present work has no object other than that set forth by the Pontiff who did so much for the development of historical studies. Aiming as it does at being really scientific and synthetic, dealing equally with all the periods and all the forms of ecclesiastical activity, we trust that it will, thanks to the collaboration of historians all inspired by the same ideal, realise the programme laid down, to the greatest possible satisfaction of all.

CONTENTS

BOOK I

TRANSLATOR'S PREFACE 1
FOREWORD BY GENERAL EDITORS (AUGUSTIN FLICHE &
    VICTOR MARTIN) 3

INTRODUCTION

I. THE ROMAN WORLD AT THE
    COMMENCEMENT OF CHRISTIANITY
    By J. ZEILLER

Christianity Came from the East 25
It Develops First Within the Framework of the
    Roman Empire 26
It Became Organised as a Religion of Cities 26
The Organisation of the Roman Empire 28
Ethnical Elements 28
Oriental Colonies 29
Religious Aspect: Unification of Worship 29
Survival of the Ancient Local Cults 30
Penetration of Oriental Cults into the Roman
    Empire 31
Temporary Persistence of the Ethnic Character of
    the Eastern Religions 32
Judaism in the Roman Empire 33
The Philosophical Schools and their Varied Success 34
Persistence of Religious Aspirations 36

II. THE WORLD OF JEWRY
    By J. LEBRETON

§ 1. Palestinian Judaism

Palestine 38
The Last of the Hasmoneans 39
The Revolt of the Jews 41
The Procurators 43
Herod Antipas 44
The Jewish People 46
Hellenism and Judaism in Palestine 46
The Hellenic Penetration 47
The Jewish Reaction 49
Fidelity to God 51
The Religion of the Poor 52
Pride of Race 53

The Messianic Hope   55
The Servant of Jahveh, the Son of Man   55
The Son of David   56
Triumphal Messianism   57
The Scandal of the Cross   58
The Sadducees   60
The Pharisees   62
Jesus and the Pharisees   63
Dangers of Pharisaism   64
The Essenes   66

§ 2. *Judaism of the Dispersion*

The Origins of the Dispersion   69
Importance of the Jewish Population   71
Civil Condition of the Jews   72
Privileges of the Proselytes   74
Apostasies   74
Influence of Hellenism   75
Philo   76
The Logos   78
Influence of Philo   79
Proselytism   80

CHAPTER I

JESUS CHRIST AND THE BEGINNING OF THE CHURCH

By J. Lebreton

Christ in History   83
The Gospels   84
The Witness of the Church   85
The Forerunner   86
The Baptism of Jesus   88
The Temptation   89
The First Disciples   90
Christ's Ministry, and Its Aim   91
Jesus at Jerusalem and in Judea   93
Jesus in Galilee   96
The Preaching of the Kingdom of God   97
The Apostles   98
Jesus at Capharnaum   100
Jesus in the Synagogues   102
The Sermon on the Mount   104
The New Law   105
Interior Religion   107
Jesus and the Pharisees   109

The Parables of the Kingdom of Heaven   112
The Galilean Ministry   116
The Crisis in the Galilean Ministry   119
The Bread of Life   122
The Great Revelations   125
The Confession of St. Peter   125
The Prediction of the Passion   127
The Transfiguration   128
The Disciples   129
The Mission of the Disciples   130
The Preaching of Jesus at Jerusalem   133
Theological Character of these Discourses   135
The Last Weeks   137
The Raising of Lazarus   137
Palm Sunday   139
Holy Week   140
The Last Supper   143
The Discourse After the Supper   145
The Passion and Death of Jesus   147
The Agony in the Garden   148
Jesus before Annas and Caiphas   150
Jesus before Pilate and Herod   152
The Death on the Cross   154
The Resurrection   157
The Appearances to the Apostles   158
The Ascension   160

CHAPTER II

THE PREACHING OF THE APOSTLES, AND THE BEGINNINGS OF THE CHURCH

By J. LEBRETON

§ 1. *Pentecost*
    The Book of the Acts   162
    The First Years: Their Character   163
    The Apostles in Jerusalem   164
    Pentecost   166
    St. Peter's Sermon   168
    The First Expansion of the Church   169
    The Life of the Christians   172
    The Action of the Spirit   174
    The First Persecutions   175

§ 2. *The Martyrdom of St. Stephen and the Conversion*
       of St. Paul
    The Hellenists   176
    The Deacons   177

St. Stephen   178
St. Stephen's Discourse   179
Conversion of St. Paul   182
Baptism and First Preaching of St. Paul   185
St. Paul in Jerusalem   186
Philip the Deacon   187

§ 3. *Missions of St. Peter*
The Evangelisation of the Sharon   190
The Conversion of Cornelius   190
Peter in Jerusalem   193

§ 4. *Antioch and Jerusalem*
The Evangelisation of Antioch   194
Famine and Persecution in Jerusalem   196
Martyrdom of St. James the Great   198
The Deliverance of St. Peter   198
Persecutions and Growth of the Church   200

CHAPTER III

THE MISSIONS OF ST. PAUL

By J. Lebreton

The Sources: The Epistles and the Acts   201
§ 1. *First Mission of St. Paul. Cyprus, Pisidia, Lycaonia*
Cyprus   202
Anatolia   203
Antioch in Pisidia   203
Iconium   205
Lystra   205
Derbe   206

§ 2. *St. Paul and the Judaisers*
St. Paul's Narrative   207
The Account in the Acts   209
The Decree   211
The Dispute at Antioch   214
The Church and the Judaisers   216

§ 3. *The Second Mission of St. Paul (Autumn of A.D. 49
        to Autumn of A.D. 52)*
Paul and Barnabas   217
Timothy   219
Galatia   219
Macedonia   222
Philippi   222
Thessalonica   225

Berea 227
The Macedonian Churches 227
Athens 228
The Speech at the Areopagus 230
Corinth 232
Preaching and Charisms 234
Conversions and Persecutions 236

§ 4. *Third Mission (Spring, A.D. 53 to Summer, A.D. 57)*
Ephesus 238
Apollos 239
Preaching of St. Paul 239
Miracles 240
Apostolic Labours 241
First Letter to the Corinthians 242
The Divisions in Corinth 242
Immorality and Injustice 244
Marriage and Virginity 245
Idol Offerings 246
The Eucharist 246
Christian Life in Corinth 248
The Riot at Ephesus 250
The Departure from Ephesus 252

§ 5. *The Journey towards Jerusalem*
Paul in Macedonia 253
The Second Letter to the Corinthians 254
The Apostle's Defence 255
The Letter to the Galatians 257
The Letter to the Romans 259
The Reign of Sin 260
God's Mercy 261
God as Beginning and End 263
Paul Leaves for Jerusalem 264
Paul and the Church at Jerusalem 265
The Journey 268

§ 6. *The Captivity*
St. Paul in Jerusalem 269
St. Paul at Cæsarea 272
St. Paul in Rome 273
The Prisoner of Christ 274
The Epistles of the Captivity 276

§ 7. *The Last Years*
St. Paul in Asia 279
Prisoner in Rome 280
Paul's Death 282
The Epistle to the Hebrews 282

CHAPTER IV

ST. PETER AND THE BEGINNINGS OF THE ROMAN CHURCH

By J. ZEILLER

§ 1. *From Jerusalem to Rome*
St. Peter at Antioch 284
St. Peter in the Provinces of Asia Minor and in Macedonia 285
St. Peter in Corinth 286

§ 2. *The Coming of St. Peter to Rome*
Hypotheses and Certainties 286
Literary Testimonies 287
Archæological Testimony 290

§ 3. *St. Peter's Residence in Rome*
Duration of Peter's Stay in Rome 293
The Beginnings of the Roman Church 295

CHAPTER V

ST. JAMES AND ST. JOHN

By J. LEBRETON

§ 1. *St. James and the Church at Jerusalem*
St. James 299
The Bishop of Jerusalem 300
St. James and the Judaisers 302
The Epistle of St. James 303
The Martyrdom of St. James 305
The Fall of Jerusalem 306
St. Simeon and the Church of Jerusalem 307

§ 2. *St. John and the Churches of Asia*
St. John in Jerusalem 309
St. John in Asia 310
The Church and the Empire 310
The Letters to the Seven Churches 312
The Christian Church 314
The Gospel of St. John 315
The Son of God 318
The Word Made Flesh 320
The Influence of St. John 322
The Dispersion of the Apostles 323

GENERAL BIBLIOGRAPHY 325

BOOK II

CHAPTER VI

CHRISTIAN LIFE AT THE END OF THE FIRST CENTURY

By J. Lebreton

§ 1. *Christian Life and Worship*
The Religion of the Christ   336
The Sacraments   339
Baptism   341
The Eucharist   343

§ 2. *The Primitive Hierarchy*
Peter and the Twelve   346
Authority and the Spirit   347
The Deacons   349
The Presbyters   349

§ 3. *The Origins of Gnosticism*
Pagan Gnosticism   355
Simon Magus   357
Gnosticism in the Apostolic Churches   358

CHAPTER VII

THE PROPAGATION OF CHRISTIANITY

By J. Zeiller

§ 1. *The Evangelisation of the Roman World*
The First Propagation of Christianity in Italy   360
Illyria, Spain and Gaul   360
Christianity in Asia   363
Christianity in the Hellenic Peninsula   364
Christianity in Egypt   365
Progress of the Evangelisation of the West in the
Second Century: Gaul   366
Africa   367
Spain   367

§ 2. *Evangelisation beyond the Empire*
Christianity in Persia   368
Christianity in Osroene   369

CHAPTER VIII

THE FIRST PERSECUTIONS, AND IMPERIAL LEGISLATION CONCERNING THE CHRISTIANS

By J. ZEILLER

§ 1. *The Neronian Persecution*
The Martyrdom of St. Peter 371
The Burning of Rome and the Accusing of the Christians 371
The Martyrs 373

§ 2. *The Prohibition of Christianity*
Possible Extension of the Persecution to the Provinces 374
The Neronian Legislation against Christianity 375

§ 3. *Juridical Character of the Persecutions*
The persecutions were not the effect merely of the application of laws previously existing 376
Nor were they due merely to the coercive power of the magistrates 377
Special Legislation against the Christians 378
The Clarifications in Trajan's Rescript 378
Main Idea of the Legislation against the Christians 379
Juridical Origin and Form of this Legislation 380

CHAPTER IX

THE PERSECUTION UNDER THE FLAVIANS AND THE ANTONINES

By J. ZEILLER

§ 1. *The Church under the Flavians*
The Roman Church under the Flavian Emperors 382
Converts to Christianity from the Aristocracy 383
The Persecution in Rome under Domitian 384
The Persecution in the Provinces: Bithynia 386
Asia Minor 386
Palestine 387

§ 2. *The Persecution under Trajan*
Reign of Nerva 388
Trajan and the Christians 388
The Question of the Martyrdom of St. Clement 389
Martyrdom of St. Simeon of Jerusalem 389
Martyrdom of St. Ignatius of Antioch 390

The Persecution in Bithynia and Pontus ... 391
The Persecution in Macedonia ... 392
§ 3. *The Persecution under Hadrian*
The Emperor Hadrian and the Christians ... 393
Martyrs in Italy ... 394
The Jewish Rebellion of Bar Kokhba and the
Christians ... 395
§ 4. *The Persecution under Antoninus*
The Emperor Antoninus and the Christians ... 395
Martyrdom of St. Polycarp of Smyrna ... 396
§ 5. *The Persecution under Marcus Aurelius*
Marcus Aurelius and the Christians ... 397
Martyrs in Rome ... 398
Martyrs in Greece ... 398
Martyrs in Asia Minor ... 398
The Martyrs at Lyons in 177 ... 399
More Martyrs at Rome ... 402
The Episode of the "Thundering Legion" ... 402
§ 6. *Persecution and Peace under Commodus*
The Emperor Commodus and the Christians ... 403
African Martyrs ... 404
Martyrs in Asia Minor ... 405
Martyrdom of Apollonius at Rome ... 405
The Peace of the Church under Commodus ... 406

CHAPTER X

THE APOSTOLIC FATHERS AND THEIR TIMES

By J. LEBRETON

§ 1. *St. Clement of Rome*
St. Clement and his Letter ... 410
The Roman Primacy ... 412
The Ecclesiastical Hierarchy ... 413
The Christian Faith and the Christian Life ... 415
§ 2. *St. Ignatius of Antioch*
St. Ignatius and his Letters ... 420
The Church and the Churches ... 421
Authority and the Charisms ... 423
The Roman Primacy ... 424
The Flesh of Christ ... 426
The Eucharist ... 427
Life in Christ ... 427
Christ and Martyrdom ... 428
God the Father and Jesus Christ ... 430

§ 3. *St. Polycarp*
The Witness of Tradition 432
Letter to the Philippians 433
Witness of Irenæus 434
St. Polycarp in Rome 435
Martyrdom of St. Polycarp 436
The Lessons of the Martyrdom 438

§ 4. *The Controversy with the Jews and the Letter of*
Barnabas
Symbolical Interpretation of the Law 441
Theology 442

§ 5. *The Moral Reform and Penance in the Roman Church.*
The Shepherd of Hermas
The Book and the Author 443
Moral Reform 445
Strength and Weakness 446
Riches 447
Ambition 448
Persecution 449
The Hierarchy 450
The Church the Mother of the Christian 451
Penance 452
Theology 453

§ 6. *Prayer in the Primitive Church*
The Example and Teaching of Christ 456
Jewish and Christian Prayer 457
Prayer of St. Clement 459
Prayers to the Father and to Christ 461
The Eucharistic Liturgy 462
The Eucharistic Liturgy according to St. Justin 463
Origin and Development of this Liturgy 465
The Baptismal Liturgy 467

§ 7. *The Apostles' Creed*
Profession of Faith in Apostolic Times 469
The Baptismal Creed 471
The Roman Creed 473
The Rule of Faith 474

CHAPTER XI

ECCLESIASTICAL ORGANISATION IN THE FIRST TWO CENTURIES

By J. ZEILLER

§ 1. *The Primitive Church*
Charity and Fraternity 476
Unity 477

§ 2. *The Episcopate and the Presbyterate*
The Origins of the Episcopate 478
Collegiate or Unitary Episcopate 478
The Question of Alexandria 481
Priests 482

§ 3. *The Other Ecclesiastical Orders*
The Deacons 483
Deaconesses 483
Doctors 484
Prophets 484
Clergy and Laity 485
Choosing Clerics: Bishops elected by the Churches 486

§ 4. *Ecclesiastical Geography*
Episcopal Sees 486
The Future Metropolises 487

§ 5. *The Roman Church*
The Roman Church in the 1st Century 487
St. Clement 488
The Testimony of St. Ignatius of Antioch 490
The Testimony of St. Irenæus 490
The Epitaph of Abercius 491
The Roman Pontiffs as Guardians of Doctrine and
as Heads of the Church 491

CHAPTER XII

THE VARIOUS CHURCHES IN THE SECOND CENTURY

By J. ZEILLER

§ 1. *The Roman Church*
The Episcopal Succession in Rome established from
Apostolic Times 493
The Popes of the First Century 494
The Popes of the Second Century 494

§ 2. *The Other Churches in the West*
The Churches of Italy 495
Africa 496
Spain and Gaul 496
Britain 497

§ 3. *The Churches of the East*
Greece 497
Asia Minor 498
Syria and Palestine 499
Egypt 500

§ 4. *The Judeo-Christian Church*
  The Christian Community of Pella   500
  Characteristics of the Judeo-Christian Church 500

CHAPTER XIII

CHRISTIAN LIFE IN THE FIRST TWO CENTURIES

By J. ZEILLER

§ 1. *Christians and Ordinary Life*
  Christians Share in Civil Life   504
  Christians Did Not Object to Military Service 505

§ 2. *Christians and Social Life*
  Christians and the Life of the Ancient City 506
  Christian Asceticism   506

§ 3. *Christian Practices*
  Prayer   507
  Fasts   508
  Charity   508

§ 4. *Christianity and Humanity*
  Christianity and Slavery   509
  The Epistle to Philemon   511

§ 5. *The Pagan Attitude towards Christianity*
  Pagan Hostility   512
  The Accusations by the Populace   512
  The Prejudices of the Intellectuals   514

§ 6. *Martyrdom*
  The Frequency of Martyrdom   515
  The Number of the Martyrs   516

§ 7. *The Voluntary Effacement of Christians*
  Christians Compelled to Lead a Retired Life by Pagan
    Hostility   519
  Nevertheless Christians Were Still Found Everywhere 519

§ 8. *The Catacombs*
  Christian Worship in Private   520
  The Origin of Catacombs as Cemeteries   521
  The Catacombs become Places of Worship 523
  Development of the Catacombs   524

§ 9. *The Art of the Catacombs*
  The Decoration of the Catacombs   525
  Purely Decorative Paintings   525
  Religious Paintings   526
  The Sarcophagi   528

§ 10. *Christian Economy*
    The Contributions of the Faithful to the Material
        Life of the Church   529
    The End of the Second Century marks the End of
        an Epoch in the History of the Church   529

CHAPTER XIV

CHRISTIAN APOLOGETICS IN THE SECOND
CENTURY

By J. LEBRETON

§ 1. *The Origins of Christian Apologetics*
    The Pagan Calumnies   530
    Anti-Christian Literature   532
    Jewish Apologists and Pagan Controversialists   533
    Apologetic of the Martyrs   533
    The Apologies: Their Destination and Their Object   534
    Quadratus   535
    Aristides   536
    The Letter to Diognetus   538

§ 2. *St. Justin*
    Life of St. Justin   541
    His Conversion   541
    St. Justin in Rome   543
    The Schools of Rome   545
    Works of Justin   546
    The Knowledge of God   548
    Divine Revelation   550
    Christianity and Philosophy   551
    The Argument from Prophecy   553
    The Argument from Miracles   556
    Christian Morals   558
    Theology   560
    The Word in Creation   562
    The Divine Appearances   564
    Personality of the Word   566
    Divinity of the Word   567
    The Generation of the Son of God   569
    Martyrdom   570

§ 3. *The Greek Apologists of the End of the Second Century*
    Tatian   571
    Christian Doctrine   573
    The Defection of Tatian   574
    Athenagoras   575
    St. Theophilus   578

§ 4. *Minucius Felix*
    The Octavius   580
    The Apologetics of Minucius Felix   581
    Christian Apologetics in the Second Century   584

APPENDIX
    Chronological Table of Popes and Emperors   587

BOOK I

*The Church in the
New Testament*

NIHIL OBSTAT:

H. Franciscus Davis, S.T.D.
  Censor deputatus

IMPRIMATUR

✠ Thomas
  Archiepiscopus Birminghamiensis

Birmingamiae
die 3a Martii, 1942

INTRODUCTION

1. THE ROMAN WORLD AT THE COMMENCEMENT OF CHRISTIANITY [1]

Christianity Came from the East

THE Catholic Church is often called the Roman Church, because its head resides in Rome, and because the great empire of which Rome was the origin and centre was, in the early ages of its history, the chief sphere of its expansion. Nevertheless the cradle of Christianity was in Palestine, whence it penetrated into Syria in the first place. Thus the starting point of the development of Christianity is to be found practically on what we might call the dividing line between the Roman Empire or the Mediterranean world and the East. Judaism provided the original soil of Christianity, and the Jews of the Dispersion, the *Diaspora*, were found all the way from the Pillars of Hercules to the ancient Eastern boundaries of what had once been the empire of Alexander the Great. [2]

While Rome, and above all Alexandria, had become great Jewish centres by the end of the period of antiquity, Babylon was another centre, or at least it had been, so that the fact that Christianity was preached first of all in the synagogues of the Jewish colonies scattered throughout the world has even led some to suggest, though with little likelihood, that the "Babylon" of the First Epistle of Peter, so obviously a symbol, in our opinion, may have been the

[1] Bibliography.—A description of the state of the Roman world at the end of the ancient era will be found in E. Albertini, *L'Empire romain* (Vol. IV in series *Peuples et civilisations, Histoire générale,* published under the direction of L. Halphen and C. Sagnac, Paris, 1929). See especially ch. v and vi and bibliographies there given. On the conditions in which the first development of Christianity took place in the Roman Empire, see: Foakes Jackson and Kirsopp Lake, *The Beginning of Christianity,* London, 1920-33, 5 vols.; G. Kittel, *Die Religionsgeschichte und das Urchristentum,* Gütersloh, 1932; E. Meyer, *Ursprung und Anfänge des Christentums,* Stuttgart and Berlin, 1921-23, 3 vols.; W. Classen, *Eintritt des Christentums in die Welt. Der Sieg des Christentums auf dem Hintergrunde der undergehenden antiken Kultur,* Gotha, 1930. Other works dealing with particular questions occurring in this Introduction will be mentioned in the notes.

[2] On the *Diaspora* and the numerical importance of the Jews at the beginning of our era, see below, p. 68. Cf. J. Juster, *Les Juifs dans l'Empire romain,* Vol. I, Paris, 1914.

actual city on the banks of the Euphrates, instead of Rome, the spiritual Babylon.

In any case, Christianity in the earliest times spread over the two slopes of the mountainous mass of Judaism which stretched from Antioch through Jerusalem to Alexandria. It is none the less true, and of great importance, that it spread in the two directions with a very unequal intensity, rapidity, and success. Thus, while there seems to be little doubt that there was an early evangelisation of Persia in the Apostolic age, the results either remained invisible, or were effaced for about two centuries.[3] It was quite otherwise with the evangelisation of the Roman Empire.

It Develops First Within the Framework of the Roman Empire

The existence of a political frontier, the disparity between means of communication, and the unequal resistance of two distinct civilisations provide an easy explanation of this diversity of success. The contact which had already existed for a long time between Hellenism and Judaism, and the fact that Christianity very soon found defenders possessing at least some degree of Greek culture, account for the greater permeability of the Greco-Roman civilisation to the diffusion of Christianity. In addition, there were more facilities of communication between the Mediterranean world and Syria and Palestine than between the latter and the region of the Tigris and the Euphrates: on the one hand there was the sea, and the roads of Asia Minor, and on the other there was a desert to cross over or go round. Lastly, and this is perhaps the most important point, Palestine at the time of Our Lord was already part of the Empire, and the first preachers of the Gospel, the Apostles and other disciples, were Roman subjects. The first Christian teaching started out from a land already Roman, spread to the Roman Empire, and quite naturally tended at first to develop within the Empire rather than beyond it.

It Became Organised as a Religion of Cities

Thus, each great city visited by the first messengers of the Gospel which produced even a small number of converts became the seat of a Christian congregation which was called a church, ἐκκλησία. In this way Christianity manifested itself from the first as a religion

[3] C. J. Labourt, Le christianisme dans l'Empire perse, Paris, 1904, pp. 16-17. See Bk. II.

of cities [4] which adapted itself fairly closely in its external organisation to the imperial framework.

Being a city religion, its organisation developed and progressed along the same lines. Generally there was a distinct church corresponding to one city, and its head, the bishop, resided there, *chorepiscopi*, or country bishops, being sometimes found presiding over the rural congregations connected with the city. Later on, the city churches were themselves graded following the provincial organisation according to which simple cities were subject to the provincial metropolises, and these in turn were later on subordinated, at least in the East, to the higher metropolises, the chief towns of civil "dioceses" formed in the later Empire, exarchates or primacies, and later on still, patriarchates, Rome, the capital of the Empire, being the central and supreme see.

But there will never be an absolutely strict correspondence here, and the historical origin of a particular ecclesiastical condition is not always or only to be explained by its correspondence with a particular political situation. The religious supremacy of Rome is explained to a certain extent by its political supremacy, but its starting point is to be found in the arrival of St. Peter in Rome. Similarly, the dignity of various great Eastern sees such as Alexandria, Antioch, or Ephesus, though finally consolidated through their administrative status, had its origin in foundations which were apostolic, or were regarded as such. At the same time, these foundations were themselves to a certain extent connected with the political functions of the cities in question. Why did the first preachers of Christianity fix their dwelling places provisionally or definitely at Antioch, Ephesus or Alexandria, and St. Peter fix his see at Rome, if not because of the importance of these great cities, and in the case of Rome, because of its position as the capital city? Whatever may have been the prestige Jerusalem still enjoyed, Rome was bound to become the head, and to attract the first governors of a spiritual society which already before St. Peter's death had spread through a great part of the Empire. In other words, though the Church was not confined to the Imperial framework, and did not slavishly adopt its boundaries, it was nevertheless Roman from the first. In other words, the Roman Empire was, to use a phrase of Mgr. Duchesne's, the "fatherland of Christianity." [5]

[4] P. Batiffol, *Primitive Catholicism,* p. 33.
[5] L. Duchesne, *Histoire Ancienne de l'Eglise,* Vol. I, Paris, 1906, ch. i.

The Organisation of the Roman Empire

The organisation of the Empire, then, explains in a great measure the organisation of the Church. Although based upon conquest, which destroyed the independence of many conquered states— great kingdoms such as Macedonia or Egypt, quarrelsome tribes or cities, such as the Gauls or the cities of Greece—the Empire rested essentially on the maintenance or institution of a civic or municipal life, over which there was a central power which was almighty and unlimited in theory, but which tempered its action in practice in such a way as to leave the old or newly founded cities to conduct their own affairs. A civilisation mainly urban, local autonomy, and a supreme absolute power: such are the general characteristics of the Empire.

But the central power did not control directly the hundreds of cities, great or small, comprised in the Empire: between these and the centre there was interposed the regional administrative machine, the name of which became synonymous with that of a land subject to Rome, i.e. the "province." The governor of the province, whether called proconsul, legate of Augustus, prefect or procurator, was its real ruler under the sovereign control of the Emperor. But he did not possess an authority which could not be contested effectively in the details of local life.

Ethnical Elements

As local life thus remained almost autonomous, and as there were in addition vigorous ethnic tendencies operating,[6] we find more or less strong and consistent national or regional elements existing within the apparent uniformity of the provincial organisation. Gaul, Spain, Africa, or Greece (officially named Achaia) were not mere administrative terms. On the other hand, while the use of the old native tongues such as Celtic or Punic persisted with varying success in different countries, amongst the upper classes of the population in the West, Latin was constantly gaining ground. In this way there gradually came about a profound transformation in the domain of languages. In the end, there were only two languages which mattered: Latin, and Greek. At first the Church used prac-

---

[6] On these ethnical survivals, see S. Gsell, *Histoire ancienne de l'Afrique du Nord*, Vol. IV, p. 498, Paris, 1920.

tically only these two languages, at least inside the Roman boundaries, in its liturgy and its communications between its various communities. And of these two, the Greek language preponderated, because of the national origin of the first groups of the faithful.

Oriental Colonies

This survival of particular differences, even within an ever increasing uniformity, showed itself again in the Roman Empire by a social characteristic which manifests the former, and yet is also linked up with the latter: the development in numerous places in the Roman world, and especially in the great cities and maritime ports like Rome, Alexandria, Antioch, Carthage, Lyons, Aquileia and Salona, to name only a few, of ethnic "colonies" [7] originating from lands often far away. The members of these were closely linked together. Thus the Greeks of Alexandria, the Egyptians in Rome and Salona, the Syrians in Rome, Marseilles or Carthage, and the Asiatics of Lyons, for instance, are proofs at once of the mingling of populations within the bosom of the Empire, and of their instinctive resistance to complete fusion.

These colonies, oriental for the most part, played a great part in the religious evolution of the Roman world, and it was largely through them that were propagated the religions from Asia or Egypt which either prepared the way for Christianity, or else constituted so many obstacles to its later progress. [8]

Religious Aspect: Unification of Worship

Again, the religious evolution of the Roman Empire was inevitably bound up with its political and social history. The tendency towards unification was manifested in the adoption of the Roman

---

[7] On these colonies, and the part they played in the Roman world, see L. Bréhier, *Les colonies d'Orientaux en Occident au commencement du moyen âge*, in *Byzantinische Zeitschrift*, XII, 1903, pp. 1-39; F. Cumont, *Une dédicace de Doura Europos, colonie romaine*, in *Syria*, V, 1924, p. 345; *Les Syriens en Espagne et les Adonis à Séville*, in *Syria*, VIII, 1927, pp. 330 *et seq.*; H. Leclercq, *Colonies d'Orientaux en Occident*, in *Dictionnaire d'histoire et d'archéologie chrétiennes*, col. 2272; L. Bréhier and P. Batiffol, *Les survivances du culte imperial romain*, Paris, 1920; G. La Piana, *The Foreign Groups in Rome*, Cambridge, 1927.

[8] Cf. F. Cumont, *Les religions orientales dans le paganisme romain*, 4th edn., Paris, 1929.

deities by all the provinces. What city did not worship the Capitoline triad? The most popular sanctuary in Roman Gaul was consecrated to Mercury, and there were innumerable African dedications to Saturn. At the same time, underneath the names of the deities of the Greco-Roman Pantheon, local cults carried on the ancient worship. The Saturn of Carthage and of Cirta hid the old Punic Baal, and similarly the Mercury of the Auvergne Mountains concealed the Celtic Teutates.

Survival of the Ancient Local Cults

Even this opposition does not exhaust the complexity of the religious phenomena which we find during the first two centuries of the Roman Empire. At first, we find with Augustus an imperial attempt to bring about amongst the citizens of Rome a return to tradition, to the old beliefs, and the old morals. Though this did not meet with immediate obedience—that would have been impossible—the effects, aided by the progress of the Stoic philosophy, were felt in the following century. The second century was more moral and more religious than the first.

Apart from a return, more conventional perhaps than profound, to the old traditions, the manifestations of religious life in the same period take two different directions. Some, and those the most visible, but also the most superficial, are religious only in appearance, and merely constitute the most characteristic form of political loyalty. Such is the case with the cult of Rome and of Augustus, spontaneously begun by Eastern peoples accustomed for centuries to king worship, and imposed by the will of the prince upon Western countries without the least resistance, but rather the contrary.

This took almost everywhere a similar form, that of religious ceremonies during the provincial meeting, usually annual, of delegates from the civic aristocracies, under the presidency of a member promoted to the dignity of *sacerdos* of Rome and Augustus. Nothing shows better than the rites of this new official religion practised throughout the Empire the docility and even devotion to Rome and the Emperor on the part of subjected and externally unified peoples.[9]

[9] Cf. P. Guiraud, *Les assemblées provinciales dans l'Empire romain*, Paris, 1887; E. Beurlier, *Le culte impérial, son histoire et son organisation depuis Auguste jusqu'à Justinien*, Paris, 1891; L. R. Taylor, *The Divinity of the Roman Emperor*, Middleton Co., 1931.

Penetration of Oriental Cults into the Roman Empire

More profound was the movement which began in the first century though it became of much importance only in the second, and which inclined a growing part of the population of the Empire towards the religions emanating from the East, such as those of the Phrygian Great Mother, the Egyptian Isis, the Syrian Baals, or the Persian god Mithra. These religions made converts in ever increasing numbers amongst the various classes of society. They were open to all, and the slave might rub shoulders with his master during the sacred rites. It is none the less true that their spread tended to be confined by preference to some particular categories of followers, as also to certain parts of the territory of the Empire. Thus, the cult of Mithra, which excluded women,[10] at any rate from its hierarchy, recruited a great number of its followers from the army, and for this same reason flourished in the frontier provinces that were strongly occupied, such as those of the Rhine and the Danube, while it had little success in Africa.[11]

These religions, the sensual practices of which constituted at once their chief attraction and their danger, went through various phases in their relations with the Roman authority. Sometimes they experienced its mistrust, and even its rigour, and at other times its toleration or even its favour. The Republic had introduced into Rome already in 204 B.C.[12] the *Magna Mater Deum* from Phrygia, while surrounding her worship with precautions, and subjecting it to a strict control. It remained for a long time somewhat suspect, while passing as an official cult, and it was only under Claudius that the worship of Attis, which comes so close to that of the *Magna Mater*, received a recognised place in the Empire.[13] The religion of Isis met with prohibition under Tiberius, then a return of favour under Caligula. Mithra and the Syrian Baals made their entry into the Empire, or at any rate attracted attention there only at a time when the Eastern deities, far from arousing the

[10] On this exclusion, cf. J. Zeiller, *Sur les cultes de Cybèle et de Mithra*, in *Revue archéologique*, 1928 (2), pp. 209-19.

[11] Cf. F. Cumont, *Les religions orientales dans le paganisme romain*, 4th edn., Paris, 1929; J. Toutain, *Les cultes paiens dans l'Empire romain*, Paris, 1907, 1911, 1920, 3 vols.

[12] Cf. H. Graillot, *Le culte de Cybèle, Mère des dieux, à Rome et dans l'Empire romain*, Paris, 1912.

[13] Cf. J. Carcopino, *Attideia*, in *Mélanges d'archéologie et d'histoire publiés par l'Ecole française de Rome*, XL, 1923, pp. 135-99 and 237-324.

mistrust of the government, found it quite ready to accept them. This was the era of syncretism, tending to unify all beliefs in one broad religion, and finding places for various deities which by a process of assimilation or by ingenious interpretation gradually approached each other and melted into one, until the old Greco-Roman polytheism became transformed into a monotheistic cult, generally solar in form, which, towards the beginning of the later Empire, won the support of at least a great part of cultivated society.

Temporary Persistence of the Ethnic Character of the Eastern Religions

What is perhaps most important of all to notice here is that, suspect, tolerated or favoured, these various cults, Phrygian, Syrian, Egyptian or other, retained for a more or less long time in the Empire, and in any case until the second century, a very marked national character. Though destined eventually to be integrated into the great movement of syncretism which won over the higher classes of Roman society, they were at the beginning upheld above all by the local colonies consisting, in the great cities, of groups, usually of the middle or lower classes, of natives from the Eastern provinces or their descendants.

These local groups, which remained at first ethnically homogeneous, formed so many distinct religious units, independent of each other. No oriental religion—not even that of Mithra, the different communities of which possessed a certain solidarity,[14] was ever organised into a church. Their followers might salute each other by the title "brother," [15] but the only bond which united them was their common belief, not their organisation. The only organisation the Roman State allowed was its own, and it provided for religions of foreign origin an administrative system under the control of one of its great religious colleges, that of the *Quindecemviri sacris faciundis.*[16]

---

[14] Cf. F. Cumont, *Textes et monuments figurés relatifs aux mystères de Mithra,* Brussels, 1896-9, 2 vols, especially Vol. I, pp. 269-70.

[15] Cf. *ibid.,* Vol. II, p. 535. See also, for instance, the title "fratres carissimi" given to the worshippers of the Syrian Baal honoured in the Empire under the name of Jupiter Dolichenus, C.I.L., V, 406.

[16] Cf. G. La Piana, *The Foreign Groups in Rome,* pp. 330-40.

Judaism in the Roman Empire

But was there not one religion from the East which existed in the Empire under a different régime? Certain it is that the Jewish religion enjoyed throughout, in consequence of old agreements between Rome and the Jewish nation, a special toleration, and a particular status.

In the next section, which deals with the Jewish world at the time of Christ, we shall discuss in greater detail the situation of the Jews of the Dispersion in the Empire. Let it suffice here to say that the treaties concluded in former times gave to the Jews the right freely to practise their religion, although this latter forbade its members to perform acts such as those of the Imperial worship, the omission of which was punished by Roman Law once their performance had become obligatory. Judaism thus enjoyed a very real privilege. Doubtless some measures of control, natural in the case of an awkward race and one which was from some points of view undesirable, reminded the Jews from time to time that their religion was still only tolerated. But on the whole their situation was a favourable one.[17]

Privileged by reason of their situation in the Empire, did these Jewish communities, which were religious as well as ethnical, possess also an organisation which distinguished them from the other Oriental groups? It has been suggested that in the towns in which they were installed, the Jews possessed synagogues, comparable to Christian parish churches, meeting places for a particular portion of territory, and that these did not constitute so many distinct colleges:[18] the group of synagogues in one and the same town would constitute the whole synagogue, or Jewry, or again, to use the juridical language of Rome, the *corpus* or *universitas*[19] of the Jews of that town,[20] and the totality of the synagogues of the Diaspora

[17] Cf. E. Schuerer, *Geschichte des jüdischen Volkes im Zeitalter Jesu Christi*, 4th edn. (Leipzig, 1907-9, 3 vols. and Index, 1911), Vol. I, pp. 391-406, and J. Juster, *op. cit.*, Vol. I, pp. 179-242.

[18] G. La Piana, *La successione episcopale in Roma e gli albori del primato*, Rome, 1922. This is also the thesis of Juster, *op. cit.*, Vol. I, pp. 420-5.

[19] The *universitas* of the Jews of Antioch is mentioned in an edict of Caracalla in A.D. 213.

[20] On the Jewries in Rome, see G. La Piana, *Foreign Groups in Rome*, p. 350, n. 20; Juster, *op. cit.*, Vol. I, p. 432; J.-B. Frey, *Les communautés juives à Rome aux premiers temps de l'Eglise*, in *Recherches de science religieuse*, XX, 1930, pp. 269-97.

would be subject to the supreme authority which governed the whole Jewish world from the religious point of view, Sanhedrin or Patriarch. In such a case the analogy with what we find later on in the Christian Church would be striking, though not such as to obliterate important differences.

But in point of fact, the central organisation of the Jewry of a city such as Rome has not been proved with certitude, and the real obedience of the whole Jewish world to the Patriarch of Palestine, who incidentally did not exist before the second century, and who always had a rival in the exilarch of Babylon, is equally unproven. Even if the existence of this kind of a Jewish "Church" were proved, it would remain true on the one hand that the government of the Jewish communities rested in the hands of temporal authorities and that the clergy had no directing power, such as the Christian clergy possessed in the Church,[21] and on the other hand, that while for Christians there was "neither Jew nor Greek," [22] the religious unity of the Jews coincided with a very marked national unity.

Nevertheless, the religion of this particular and independent nation was addicted to making proselytes. It received and even attracted followers outside the Jewish race, "proselytes of the gate," provided these consented to accept the faith of Israel, and "proselytes of justice," i.e. assimilated to true Jews, if they submitted also to the rite of initiation, circumcision.

The Philosophical Schools and their Varied Success

More free from national attachments, and as universal in their programme for human reform, if not in their actual propaganda, which reached the circles of a cultivated aristocracy rather than the common people, whom speakers nevertheless endeavoured to reach, the schools of philosophy offered to men's minds a way of rising above the ephemeral contingencies of earthly life and of achieving union with the Godhead.

It was Stoicism which, in the beginnings of the Empire, became more and more fashionable. But its teaching was not very consoling: it merely taught men to accept universal necessity, and set

[21] J.-B. Frey, *op. cit.*, 2nd article, in *Recherches de science religieuse*, XXI, 1931, pp. 129-68, containing a very close criticism of the theories of Juster and La Piana.
[22] *Galatians*, iii, 28.

before them no participation in the divine life other than submission to fate, and did not give them any hope of a personal immortality.

The Alexandrine philosophy of Philo, with its conception of ecstasy, which will reappear in neo-Platonism, corresponds much more to the aspiration of the soul which desires to free itself from the conditions of the present life and to attain to God, but being a kind of synthesis of Hellenism and Judaism, the Alexandrine system of Philo belongs to religion as well as to philosophy.[23]

The same is true of a third teaching, the recent discoveries concerning which, and the fine works written thereon,[24] have only recently revealed its influence at the dawn of the imperial age, in circles which were doubtless fairly restricted, but which comprised some of the best sections of the social and intellectual élite of the time. We speak of neo-Pythagoreanism.

The hazardous thesis which has attempted to connect Christianity with neo-Pythagoreanism, by regarding the Gospels as mere imitations of the shadowy biography of Pythagoras,[25] has not won much acceptance, but nevertheless the temporary and relative importance of the renaissance of Pythagoreanism, modified by a Platonist influence, is quite certain. A contemporary of Cicero, Nigidius Figulus, has left an account of the doctrine as it was taught in his time.[26] The Fourth Eclogue of Virgil and some passages of Ovid [27] bear witness at least to the character of the support it won; a Roman inscription on the other hand leads one to suspect a certain penetration into humbler circles,[28] and the famous basilica of the Porta Major in Rome shows that neo-Pythagoreanism was something more than a school: it was also a church. But this church, free as it apparently was from the impurity of the more or less sensual religions of the East, alarmed the

[23] On Philo, see below, p. 55 et seq.

[24] See amongst others: J. Carcopino, La basilique pythagoricienne de la Porte Majeure, Paris, 1927; Virgile et le mystère de la IVe Eclogue, Paris, 1930.

[25] I. Levy, La légende de Pythagore de Grèce en Palestine, in Bibliothèque de l'Ecole des Hautes Etudes, Sciences historiques et philologiques, fasc. 250, Paris, 1927.

[26] E. Swoboda, Vienne, 1889.

[27] On the Fourth Eclogue, see above, n. 24. On Ovid, cf. J. Carcopino, Archéologie et philologie, in Revue des études latines, V, 1927, pp. 146-9.

[28] Inscription of a societas cantorum graecorum found in the Porta Major and published by R. Paribeni, Raccolta di Scritti in onore di Giacomo Lumbroso, Milan, 1925, pp. 287-92.

civil powers because of its thaumaturgy, and its secrecy annoyed the common people. It met with persecution at Rome from Augustus to Claudius, and perhaps hardly survived there, although the partly legendary account of Apollonius of Tyana,[29] whom Nero expelled from Rome, shows that it retained some disciples for some time. In any case, being a scholarly and ultimately an aristocratic religion, it could hardly hope to conquer the masses, without developing quite openly into theurgy, as neo-Platonism did later on.

Persistence of Religious Aspirations

The progress of the Stoic ethic and of neo-Platonist speculation doubtless had their influence on religious conceptions, but they never reduced religion to a mere morality or to a pure philosophy— far from it. The chances of success were on the side of the religions which appealed more to the senses: hence the growing influence of the Eastern cults, with their mysteries, which had been preceded on Greek soil by those of Eleusis and Orphism, to which, moreover, the neo-Pythagorean teaching was more or less related. They promised salvation to their initiates by means of trials and ritual purifications, without the accompanying obligation of a stricter morality.[30]

At the same time, at the beginning of the first century the great popularity of the mysteries had hardly begun in the Roman Empire. But on all sides we find aspirations, confused perhaps but convergent, to which Christianity was to bring a definite response. This response would not only give to those who adopt it the satisfaction of their soul's desires and a better rule for their individual life: there is no religion which has not also its social side. From the first, Christianity presents itself as a Church, a Society, and there is no society without organisation. That of the Christian Church can be satisfactorily explained only by a positive institution. For this organisation, at once necessary and intended, the Roman Empire, in which it rose and through which it spread during four centuries, provided a framework both solid and varied, and at that time still supple; and this framework had to be explained here before we begin the history of the propagation of Christianity.

[29] His life, or rather the uncritical romance which claims to narrate it, was written by Philostratus about A.D. 200 at the request of the Empress of Syrian origin, Julia Domna.
[30] See also on this subject, M. Rostovtzeff, *Mystic Italy*, New York, 1927.

II. THE WORLD OF JEWRY[1]

"Salvation comes from the Jews" (John iv, 22). Hence Judaism, the source of Christianity, must be studied here with particular care. We do not, of course, intend to trace out here the whole of Jewish history, but it is indispensable for us to know the nation in which Jesus was born, from which He chose His apostles, and in the midst of which He preached the Gospel.

At the time of Jesus Christ, the Jewish people was no longer wholly found in the land which God had allotted to them, the land of Israel: many of its sons were dispersed throughout the world. Jesus did not Himself carry the Gospel to these Jews of the Dispersion, nor to the Pagans; but His apostles on their journeys found everywhere their racial brethren who should have been the first disciples of the Messias. In point of fact, the Church found amongst them a few disciples, but also many enemies. In order to understand the support which the Church found, and the opposition it had to encounter, we must briefly describe the Judaism of the Dispersion, after a first glance at Palestinian Judaism.

§1. PALESTINIAN JUDAISM

Luke, the evangelist, in order to fix the date of the beginning of the ministry of St. John the Baptist, writes: "It was the fifteenth year of the reign of Tiberias Cæsar, Pontius Pilate being governor of Judea, Herod tetrarch of Galilee, Philip his brother tetrarch of Iturea and the country of Trachonitis, and Lysanias tetrarch of

[1] General Bibliography.—E. Schuerer, *Geschichte des jüdischen Volkes im Zeitalter Jesu Christi*, 4th edn., Leipzig, 1901-9, 3 vols.; J. Felten, *Neutestamentliche Zeitgeschichte*, 2nd edn., Regensburg, 1925, 2 vols. (the study of Judaism fills the first volume and pp. 3-271 of the second); J. Juster, *Les Juifs dans l'Empire romain*, Paris, 1914, 2 vols.; Wilhelm Bousset, *Die Religion des Judentums im späthellenistischen Zeitalter. in dritter, verbesserter Auflage herausgegeben von Hugo Gressmann*, Tübingen, 1926; M. J. Lagrange, *Le Judaisme avant Jésus-Christ*, Paris, 1931; J. Bonsirven, *Le judaisme palestinien au temps de J.-C.*, Paris, 1935, 2 vols.; E. Meyer, *Ursprung und Anfänge des Christentums*, Stuttgart, 1921-3, 3 vols. (Judaism is studied in the second volume). This bibliography and those which follow contain only the most important references; others will be given in notes. The Works of Josephus are quoted according to the edition by Naber, Leipzig, 1888-96; the translation is based upon that of Theodore Reinach. The works of Philo are quoted from the edition Cohn-Wendland-Reiter, Berlin, 1896-1915.

Abilina, under the high priests Annas and Caiphas." These few lines already give us an idea of what Judea was at that time, subject to the domination of many rulers who made claims to its government. The Roman power, the most recently established of all, was sovereign; the descendants of Herod still possessed some portion of the authority which the Idumean king had bequeathed to them; below these, but closer to the people, the high priests enjoyed the prestige of a priesthood which the Jews reverenced even when it was in unworthy hands.

Just as the various rules, Roman, Herodian and Jewish, overlapped, so also the land of Judea was inhabited by different peoples which had occupied the country one after another, and had superimposed their civilisations and cults. Does not Palestine present the same appearance to-day? Under the British domination, which in some respects resembles the Roman Imperialism, we have the Mahometan Arabs, the Jews, and Christians, schismatic or in union with Rome, of various rites. To understand this mixture of races and religions, we must recall, at least briefly, the history of the half century which preceded the birth of the Saviour.

Palestine

During many centuries, the Jews had lived their isolated life, which nevertheless had its greatness. The high plateau of Judea, where they were established, forms a rocky promontory to the south of Lebanon, and to the north of the Arabian Desert; [2] it descends towards the west by the rich plain of Sharon in the direction of the Mediterranean; to the East it is separated from the plateau of Moab by the deep depression of the Jordan; the Lake of Galilee, which the river enters to the north, is already more than 600 feet beneath the level of the Mediterranean; the Dead Sea into which it flows, about 55 miles to the south of the lake, is at a depth of 1,292 feet. The holy city of Jerusalem, built on a sharp rock, with Cedron at the east and Gehenna at the south dividing it from the surrounding mountains, towers over this land, now desolate but then covered with olives and vines. A short distance to the east we have the desert of Judea, which descends from plateau to plateau down to

[2] Cf. G. A. Smith, *Historical Geography of the Holy Land*, 25th edn., London, 1931; G. Dalman, *Les itinéraires de Jesus*, trans. by J. Marty, Paris, 1930 (Engl. trans. *Sacred Sites and Ways*, London, S.P.C.K., 1935); R. Koeppel, *Palästina*, Tübingen, 1930; F. M. Abel, *Géographie de la Palestine*, Vol. I, Paris, 1933.

the Dead Sea, some nineteen miles away. To the west, in the direction of the coast, the hills are steep, furrowed with ravines and precipices, difficult to climb and easy to defend. It was there, at Modin, near Lydda, that under Antiochus Epiphanes in 167 B.C., a priest Mathathias had placed himself at the head of a national revival which put the Jews in conflict with the Greeks. The Seleucids, successors of Alexander, had extended the Syrian domination over all the East, deprived Judea of its political independence, and worse still, had disturbed its religious faith. Mathathias and his five sons fell one after the other; they left Judea not only free from the Syrian yoke, but more powerful than it had been since the exile; for a century it was governed by the Hasmoneans, kings and high priests, descendants of the first Machabees.

The Last of the Hasmoneans

Sixty years before the birth of Christ, this last national dynasty fell, and with it Israel ceased to be independent. Then began the most tragic period in its history: carried away by an irresistible current, Judea was swept like a log into all the eddies of the Roman revolutions: the quarrels of Pompey and Cæsar, Brutus and the triumvirs, Antony and Augustus stained Palestine in turn with blood; the Parthians invaded it, and in the interior of the country, the most sacred authorities were overturned by foreigners, by Rome first and then by Herod.[3]

The invasion of Judea by Hellenism and then by the Roman Empire became irresistible under Herod, and it is this fact that gives to his brilliant and violent reign its real significance. Hence it is that historians pass such different judgments upon it: those who, like E. Meyer, view the spread of Hellenism with sympathy, acclaim Herod as its champion, and while not denying the violence of his passions or the hardness of his unscrupulous conscience, they like to regard him as one of the potentates of the time of the Diadochi or the Renaissance, a great politician, a redoubtable fighter and at the same time a protector of the arts and the promoter of a brilliant civilisation. On the other hand, the Jewish writers regard him as the scourge of Israel; they hate him not only because

[3] The reign of Herod does not belong to this history. Reference may be made to the following: M. J. Lagrange, Le judaisme, pp. 164-202; W. Otto, article Herodes in Pauly-Wissowa, Supplément II, 1918, col. 1-158; Schuerer, op. cit., Vol. I, pp. 360-418; E. Meyer, op. cit., Vol. II, pp. 319-29.

of his Idumean origin, but above all because of the help he accepted from foreigners and gave to them in return; here their hatred is clear-sighted and deliberate.

It is certain that the reign of Herod was not without its brilliance; he restored to the Holy Land for a few years its unity and a semblance of independence; he decorated it with sumptuous buildings, and above all with a new temple at Jerusalem; but this brilliance was ephemeral; at the death of Herod [4] the country found itself ruined, more divided and more enslaved than ever.

It was towards the end of this reign of violence, "in the days of Herod the King," that Jesus was born.

Herod's last testament divided his territories between his sons Archelaus, Philip, Antipas, and his sister Salome.[5] Archelaus took over the government as soon as his father was dead. He endeavoured to win the people by reducing taxes and making promises; encouraged by these concessions the Jews decided to avenge the torture of the two doctors Judas and Matthias who had been burnt alive under Herod's orders a few days before his death; they demanded the dismissal of Herod's counsellors, and the deposition of the high priest; the pilgrims who came together in great numbers on the occasion of the Pasch joined in the rising; Archelaus sent against them a company of hoplites; the soldiers were greeted with showers of stones, and killed or wounded. Then the king called out his whole army: "the horsemen slew about three thousand men; the remainder fled into the surrounding hills" (Josephus, *Antiquities of the Jews*, XVII, 19, 3). Such was, writes Nicholas of Damascus, the victory of the Greeks over the Jews.[6]

So bloody a repression in the Temple itself during the festival of the Pasch exasperated the Jews. They decided to ask for autonomy from Rome. Archelaus likewise hastened to Augustus, as did also the other princes of his family and representatives of the Greek

---

[4] In the month of Nisan (March-April), 4 B.C. The Christian chronology was fixed by Dionysius Exiguus in the Roman year 754, at least five years too late.

[5] "To Antipas, to whom he had first of all left the crown, Herod gave the tetrarchies of Galilee and Perea; Archelaus obtained the kingship; Philip, brother of Archelaus, had Gaulonitis, Trachonitis, Batanea and Panias as tetrarchy; Jamnia, Azotus, and Phasaelis were attributed to Salome, Herod's sister, with 500,000 drachmas of silver coins" (Josephus, *Antiquities of the Jews*, XVII, 8, 1, 188-9). Herod had put to death three other sons; also in the year 7, the two sons which he had had from Mariamne, herself put to death in 29. Five days before his death, Herod had his eldest son Antipater executed.

[6] Fragment 5 (*Fragmenta historicorum graecorum*, Didot, Vol. III, 353).

cities. The Jewish embassy comprised fifty members, and was supported by "more than eight thousand Jews in Rome." It was very violent in its accusations against Herod and his family, and ended by requesting "that the Jews might be delivered from kingly and the like forms of government, and might be added to Syria and put under the authority of legates" (*Antiquities of the Jews,* XVII, 314). Nicholas pleaded for Archelaus. Augustus settled the matter by awarding half the country to Archelaus, and the rest to the other sons of Herod; he named Archelaus ethnarch, promising to have him made king if he should show himself worthy of the title; his young brothers Philip and Antipas were named tetrarchs.[7]

The Revolt of the Jews

Rome rather than the Herods! While the Jews of Jerusalem, supported by the Jews of Rome, were passionately requesting Augustus to give them Roman government, the whole of Palestine was rising against the Roman agents.[8] As soon as Archelaus had departed, the Jews of Jerusalem had revolted. Varus, legate of Syria, had subdued the rebellion, and departed, leaving one legion to maintain order. But Sabinus, whom the emperor had sent as temporary procurator until such time as the succession to Herod should be settled, showed himself to be violent and rapacious. "He made a bitter search after the royal treasure, using for this purpose not only the Roman soldiers, but also the slaves" (Josephus, *Wars of the Jews,* II, ch. iii, 1). On Pentecost Day the Jews rose; a bloody fight took place in the Temple, the gates were burnt and the sacred treasury pillaged, Sabinus taking away four hundred talents as his own portion.

The revolt spread as a result of this catastrophe through the whole of Palestine. Galilee was led by Judas, son of Ezechias, an old opponent of Herod; Perea by Simon, once Herod's slave; and lastly in Judea a certain Athronges directed the struggle with his four brothers. All these leaders had themselves proclaimed kings by their followers.[9] To re-establish order, Varus had to return with his two legions; the Jews submitted, two thousand insurgents were crucified. All this took place during the early days of the life of Jesus. Galilee, where thirty years of His life were to be spent, suffered par-

[7] Nicholas, frag. 5, p. 354; Josephus, *Antiquities of the Jews,* XVII, 317.

[8] *Antiquities of the Jews,* XVII, 10, 250-98; *Wars of the Jews,* II, 3-5, 39-79.

[9] Josephus, always careful to hide Messianic aspirations, says nothing of these here, but we recognize their influence in these ephemeral kingships.

ticularly in consequence of the rising of Judas and its repression by Varus: the town of Sepphoris, quite close to Nazareth and the capital of the province, was first seized and devastated by the insurgents (*Antiquities of the Jews*, XVII, 271), then retaken by the Romans, who set fire to it and sold all its inhabitants into slavery.[10]

The new city, rebuilt by Antipas, was magnificent, and Josephus describes it as "the ornament of all Galilee." But it was no longer a centre of Jewish nationalism as the town destroyed by Varus had been; it was now a Herodian and Roman city.[11]

This campaign of Varus remained in the memory of the Jews as one of the greatest catastrophes which had afflicted their nation, a disaster comparable to the invasion by Pompey or that of Vespasian.[12] When Jesus told His disciples that they had to carry their cross, they would understand this without difficulty, having still before their eyes the spectacle of the two thousand Jews crucified by Varus.

The reign of Archelaus, so tragically begun, lasted only ten years; Augustus had promised the royal crown to the ethnarch, "if he merited it by his virtue." Archelaus did not merit it, and did not get it. His government was arbitrary and brutal,[13] the Jews complained about it to the Emperor; Augustus summoned the ethnarch to Rome, heard his defence, then sent him as an exile to Vienne in Gaul, and confiscated his goods (*Antiquities of the Jews*, XVII, 344).

Such was the end, at any rate in Judea, of the Herodian régime. The Jews themselves had clamoured for its abolition, and many greeted this as a deliverance. It was about this time that an unknown Pharisee wrote the *Assumption of Moses*. After recalling the reign of the Hasmoneans, he continues:

"An insolent king shall succeed them, who will not belong to the race of priests; a bold and impudent man, who will govern his subjects

---

[10] *Antiquities of the Jews*, XVII, 289. Herod Antipas built up the city and fortified it once more; he dwelt there as in a capital city until the year A.D. 18. Cf. Dalman, *Orte und Wege*, p. 86; Schuerer, *op. cit.*, Vol. II, pp. 212 et seq.; Otto. col. 175.

[11] Schuerer, *op. cit.*, Vol. II, p. 212.

[12] Josephus, *Contra Apion*, 1, 7.

[13] "He deprived Joazar, son of Boethos, of the pontificate," and replaced him by Eleazar, in turn supplanted by Jesus, son of Sie (*Antiquities of the Jews*, XVII, 13, 1, 339-41).

as they deserve. And he shall cause their leaders to perish by the sword, and shall make them disappear so that one shall not know even the place of their bodies. He shall slay the old and the young, sparing none. He shall spread a great terror throughout all the land; he shall ill-treat them as the Egyptians ill-treated them, for thirty-four years. And he shall have children who will succeed him and reign for less time. Then shall come from the west cohorts and a mighty king who shall dominate them, and he shall make them captives, and shall burn a part of their temple, and crucify men all around their colony." [14]

Behind the deliberate vagueness of this text we recognise without difficulty the reign of Herod and his children, then the Roman domination, the campaigns of Sabinus and Varus: all this is actual and real. What follows is imagined by the seer as a tragic era; the wicked flourish, the just are tormented, finally God appears, avenges His children, punishes the nations, and reigns.

God was indeed to appear; already the Son of God had been born and was now a growing child, but no one suspected it, and the writers of apocalypses continued to predict great catastrophes as the prelude to the reign of God.

The Procurators

In place of the deposed ethnarch, Rome had entrusted the administration of Judea to a magistrate chosen from amongst the Roman knights. This "procurator" was nominated by the emperor, and depended upon him. The legate of Syria, whose territory adjoined, and whose authority was greater, occasionally intervened and took in hand the government of Judea, but these interventions were exceptional. The procurator fixed his usual residence at Cæsarea, but went up to Jerusalem at the time of the great festivals to keep order there.

This Roman administration had been asked for by the Jews, but it did not bring them the peace they desired. Certainly it delivered them from the Herods; the tyranny of the Idumeans was very great, and almost without remedy; Rome left the princes a fairly wide autonomy, and intervened in their government only for grave reasons. The Roman magistrates were more under control, their subjects could have recourse to Cæsar, and did not hesitate to do so;

---

[14] *Assumption of Moses*, 6. On this passage see notes by Charles in *Pseudepigrapha*, pp. 418 *et seq.*; and Lagrange, *Judaisme*, p. 238.

the history of Pilate shows by more than one example that this appeal to Rome was a redoubtable menace;[15] the Jews, having powerful friends near the Emperor,[16] could make their complaints heard better than many other provincials. Nevertheless, Cæsar was far off; these appeals could not be made every day; in the ordinary course of affairs the Jews found themselves in presence of administrators less involved than Herod in their quarrels, but also more foreign to their traditions, and in consequence, more apt to hurt and wound their religious susceptibilities.

In the administration of the procurators, these incidents were not rare, and often involved brutality. Of these magistrates, the one who is by far the best known to us, and is most important for the history of Christianity, is Pontius Pilate;[17] the Gospel story makes him known to us, and the narratives of Josephus and Philo complete the Gospel data.[18] They reveal a magistrate who was suspicious, violent, always mistrustful of the Jews, and ready in case of alarm to harry and massacre. He had little understanding of his subjects and their religious scruples; he was suspicious, and not without reason, of their loyalty to Rome; in Palestine he felt himself in a hostile country, and regulated his conduct accordingly.

Herod Antipas

Pilate had under his administration only Judea and Samaria; Herod Antipas governed Galilee and Perea; Philip, Iturea and

---

[15] We see this already in the accounts of the Passion of Christ (John xix, 12). A little later, in the affair of the votive shields, Pilate was effectively denounced to Tiberius and disavowed by the Emperor (Philo, Leg. ad Caium, XXXVIII, 299-305). Lastly, in A.D. 35, after the cruel punishment inflicted by him on the Samaritans, he was denounced to the Syrian Proconsul, Vitellius, who sent him to Rome (Josephus, Antiquities of the Jews, XVIII, 4, 2, 88-9).

[16] The Jewish colony in Rome was large, and very devoted to the national interest. We have seen that against Archelaus, 8,000 Jews at Rome were joined to the fifty ambassadors. Sometimes, it is true, the Jews were out of favour. Such was the case under Caligula and also in the time of Sejanus under Tiberius, but these periods of disgrace were short and rare in the epoch we are studying.

[17] From the deposition of Archelaus to the coming of Agrippa there were seven procurators: Coponius (A.D. 6-9), Marcus Ambibulus (A.D. 9-12), Annius Rufus (A.D. 12-15), Valerius Gratus (A.D. 15-26), Pontius Pilatus (A.D. 26-36), Marcellus (A.D. 36-7), Marullus (A.D. 37-41). Cf. Schuerer, op. cit., Vol. I, pp. 487 et seq.

[18] Antiquities of the Jews, XVIII, 3, 1-2, 55-62; Wars of the Jews, II, 9, 2-4, 169-77; Antiquities of the Jews, XVIII, 4, 1-2, 85-98; Philo, De Leg. ad Caium, XXXVIII, 299-305.

Trachonitis. Of these two latter princes, the first alone is directly connected with the history of Christianity;[19] this "fox," as Jesus called him (*Luke* xiii, 32), was able in the year A.D. 6 to avoid the disgrace into which Archelaus fell, and instead ingratiated himself into the favour of Tiberius. But he was sensual, drunken, brutal, and had all the vices of his father without his strength.[20] Herodias, his brother's wife, to whom he was united in an adulterous marriage, was the cause of all his downfall, as also of his greatest faults; she persuaded him to cast John the Baptist into prison, and later on to put him to death; she caused the tetrarch to repudiate his first wife, the daughter of Aretas, King of the Arabs, and this provoked a war in which Herod's army was cut to pieces (*Antiquities of the Jews*, Book XVIII, ch. v, 1). Lastly, it was Herodias who finally succeeded in persuading her husband to take a step which was fatal to him: Agrippa, brother to Herodias, and nephew of Antipas, had received from the Emperor Caligula the title of king, and Antipas himself was only a tetrarch. This was for the princess a humiliation which was insupportable; she insisted that Herod should go to Rome and ask Caligula for the royal crown. Herod resisted for a long time, but "it was impossible for him to escape from what his wife had decided"; he set out for Rome. He was followed there by emissaries from Agrippa; he was accused of having plotted against the emperor; was condemned, and deported to Lugdunum (Lyons) in Gaul [21] in the year 39.[22] Shortly after he died, having possibly been condemned to death by Caligula.[23] His tetrarchy was given to his nephew and enemy, Agrippa; for the last time, and for just a little while, the whole of Palestine was under one king. The history of the Apostles will give us occasion to recall this brilliant but ephemeral fortune of Agrippa.

[19] Cf. Otto, *art. cit.*, col. 168-91.

[20] His vices appear clearly in the Gospel narrative: it suffices to recall his adulterous union with Herodias, the imprisonment and death of John the Baptist, the measures taken against Jesus, and lastly, the derisory judgment (*Luke* xxiii, 4-12). It would be easy to confirm this testimony by the narrative of Josephus.

[21] *Antiquities of the Jews*, XVIII, 7, 1-2, 240-56. According to *Wars of the Jews*, II, 183, Herod was exiled "to Spain." These two statements have been harmonised by the supposition that the Lugdunum here spoken of is Lugdunum Convenarum (St. Bertrand des Commings; Otto, *art. cit.*, col. 188). Reinach, note to *Wars of the Jews*, rejects this solution, abandons the text of *Wars of the Jews*, and gives Lyons as Herod's place of exile.

[22] On this date see Schuerer, *op. cit.*, Vol. I, p. 448, n. 46.

[23] Dic Cassius, LIX, 8.

The Jewish People

The Roman procurators and the tetrarchs were the rulers in whose hands was the government of Palestine during the life of Jesus. For that reason we had here to recall their history, but they form only the remote framework for the events which are going to take place. Of far greater interest to us, because much nearer to Christ, are the Jews among whom He lived, teaching them, healing them, and converting, or, at least, leading them towards the little flock which was to become the Church.

What we have said about the government of Judea has given us some idea of the state of the Jewish people, subjected to foreign masters, striving to defend against these its nationality, and, above all, its religion. Of this resistance it might well be proud. The Jewish nation alone in the Roman and Hellenic world found in its religious faith sufficient strength to enable it to purify itself from the pagan elements introduced in the preceding century by the Seleucids, and to defend itself against the pagan influences which were made still more dangerous by the Herodian and Roman governments. True this resistance was carried to extremes, and religious fidelity too often degenerated into political revolt, but the nationalism of the zealots ought not to lead us to forget the religion of the Jewish people; we stress this because we see therein the proximate preparation for the Gospel.

Hellenism and Judaism in Palestine

This fidelity to God and the Law seems all the more remarkable if we consider the population of Palestine. This was never altogether homogeneous; at the time of Christ it was still less so. Pompey had freed the Hellenic towns and had transferred them to the province of Syria; Herod reconstituted the unity of Palestine for a time, but that was in order to favour Hellenism,[24] and still more in order to manifest his devotion to Cæsar, as is shown above all by the foundation of Cæsarea and the transformation of Samaria into Sebaste. In these two cities he erected magnificent temples in honour of Rome and Augustus; but he did not stop there:

"There was not any place of his kingdom fit for the purpose in
[24] "Herod was avowedly more favourable to the Greeks than to the Jews . . ."
(*Antiquities of the Jews*, XIX, 7, 3, 29).

which he did not leave some mark of honour for Cæsar. When he had filled his own territory with temples, he poured out the like plentiful marks of his esteem in the whole province." [25]

The movement begun by Herod was carried on by his successors; Philip founded a new Cæsarea; Antipas rebuilt Sepphoris and made it a pagan city; he founded Tiberias and Julias.

All these efforts bore their fruit: in a good number of towns [26] the Hellenic and pagan population was as strong as the Jewish, or even stronger. We see this in the riots which often broke out in the course of the first century between Jews and pagans; e.g. in A.D. 44 at Cæsarea and Sebaste, on the occasion of the death of Agrippa I; [27] in 58-60 at Cæsarea under the government of Felix; [28] and above all in 66, when the great revolt broke out; twenty thousand Jews were then massacred at Cæsarea. As a reprisal, the Jewish colonies destroyed or burnt the Greek cities of the Decapolis and the coast, but when their bands had disappeared the pagans recovered; "they killed those whom they caught in their cities. . . . All Syria was subject to terrible disorders; all the cities were divided into two camps, and the preservation of the one party was in the destruction of the other." [29] We learn from this account of Josephus, not only the bitterness of the struggle, but also the respective strength of the opposing parties: the Jews, coming doubtless from Judea and Galilee, were able to invade and burn the towns of the Decapolis and the coast, but when these bands had passed on, the pagans regained the mastery and massacred the Jews.[30]

The Hellenic Penetration

This bloody conflict brings out the rivalry between the two populations, and their strength. It also shows their zones of influence:

[25] Wars of the Jews, I, 21, 4, 407.

[26] On the Hellenistic cities of Palestine, the most complete study is that of Schuerer, op. cit., Vol. II, pp. 94-222.

[27] Antiquities of the Jews, XIX, 9, 1, 354-9.

[28] Wars of the Jews, II, 13, 7, 266-7.

[29] The first riot, which was the cause of the war, broke out at Cæsarea, in the month of Artemisios (April-May) of the year 66 (Wars of the Jews, II, 14, 4-9, 284-308). The great massacre took place at Cæsarea on the 17th Gorpieios (August-September) 66 (Wars of the Jews, II, 18, 1, 457); the reprisals which followed are narrated ibid., 458-80.

[30] At Scythopolis, the Jews had made common cause with the pagans. Nevertheless they were massacred by the latter to the number of 13,000. At Ascalon 2,500 Jews were killed, at Ptolemais 2,000. Elsewhere only the leaders were killed: the others were imprisoned, e.g., at Tyre, Hippo, Gadara.

Hellenism was concentrated mainly on the coast and in the eastern parts of Palestine, Transjordan and Eastern Galilee. On the coast, we find the Jews destroying or burning [31] Gaza, Anthedon, Ascalon, Cæsarea, Gaba and Ptolemais; in Transjordan, Philadelphia, Hesbon, Gerasa, Pella, Gadara, and Hippo; in Galilee, Scythopolis; in Samaria, Sebaste. The eastern cities belonged for the most part to the league of the "ten towns," the Decapolis.[32] This confederation was, it seems, constituted[33] just after the freeing of these cities by Pompey; realising that their new liberty was threatened by the Semitic population which surrounded them, these Hellenic towns had united together for mutual defense.[34] They dominated the commercial routes which spread out from Galilee at the east of the Jordan, to Damascus in the north, and in the south as far as Philadelphia (Ammân).

If after this glance at the Decapolis we recall what we said just now about the diffusion of paganism in Galilee under Antipas at Sepphoris, Tiberias and Julias, we realise that the Galilee in which Jesus grew up and later on preached was, almost as greatly as the Phœnician coast, invaded or at least permeated by Hellenism. And nevertheless, Jesus never preached in any of these new and splendid towns so close to him: Tiberias and Julias were on the edge of the lake; Sepphoris was five miles from Nazareth; Scythopolis nineteen miles. The Gospel does not mention these towns; it mentions the district of Cæsarea Philippi, but not the town itself. This reserve, evidently intentional, shows that Jesus up to the last confined His ministry to the Jews; He gave the same command to His Apostles: "Go ye not into the way of the Gentiles, and into the city of the Samaritans enter ye not" (Matthew x, 5). It was not until after the Resurrection that He said to them: "Going therefore, teach ye all nations" (Matthew xxviii, 19).

This fact, the penetration of Hellenism into Palestine, will also help us to understand the first circumstances of the ministry of the Apostles. They were Jews, but from birth they had rubbed

[31] As Reinach notes on this text, it seems that the Jews had really taken only Gaza and Anthedon; in the case of the other cities, they had burnt the surrounding villages.

[32] On the Decapolis, see G. A. Smith, Historical Geography of the Holy Land, 25th edn., 1931, pp. 623-38.

[33] The title "Decapolis" first appears in the Gospels, Josephus, and Philo.

[34] The list of the ten towns in Pliny, Natural History, V, 16 (18), quoted by Smith, p. 629, comprises: Scythopolis, Pella, Dio, Gerasa, Philadelphia, Gadara, Raphana, Kanatha, Hippo, and Damascus.

shoulders with pagans; they fled from contact with them, but they knew them and must have understood their language. Of course, the fishermen from Galilee did not speak Greek like the poets or rhetoricians of the Greek cities, Philodemus or Meleager, who were the boast of Gadara, or Antiochus of Ascalon, who taught Cicero, but at least they must have known enough Greek to sell their fish to the inhabitants of Tiberias or Julias, and also sufficient to understand the orders of the Roman magistrates, as, for instance, the imperial decree made known to us recently by the Nazareth inscription.[35] And then, when the barriers fell down, and the vision at Joppa showed St. Peter that the way was open to the pagans, he found these first in Palestine, in the city of Cæsarea so often stained with the blood of the anti-Jewish riots.[36]

The Jewish Reaction

These considerations will help us to understand the ministry of Christ and His Apostles, but already they throw light on the religious state of the Jewish people. In the past, in the times of the kings, the paganism of Egypt and Assyria constituted a great temptation. Under the Seleucids, and now under Herod and the Romans, this temptation had become much more pressing. Isolated in the Roman Empire which dominated it, and in the Hellenic world which threatened to absorb it, Judaism maintained itself in Palestine only by struggling against an invasion which was penetrating it from all sides. It had been almost expelled from the coast; it was held in check in the valley of the Jordan; and the mountainous massif in the centre of the country, in which it was entrenched, was being battered by the rising sea which surrounded it, penetrated it, filtered into it, and tended to break it up.

[35] This inscription was published for the first time by Cumont in *Review historique*, CLXIII, 1930, pp. 241-66. It has often been studied; we shall have occasion to mention it later on.

[36] On the two languages, Aramaic and Greek, spoken in Judea in the time of Our Saviour, see G. Dalman, *Jesus-Jeschua*, Leipzig, 1922 (Engl. trans. by Levertoff: *Jesus-Jeshua: Studies in the Gospels*, London, S.P.C.K., 1929), especially pp. 1-6, and F. G. Kenyon, *The Two Languages of Palestine*, in *History of Christianity*, London, 1929, pp. 172-4. Dalman writes with reason: "He who knows the East is aware that familiarity with several languages is not necessarily proof of higher education, but is rather a state of things arising out of the conditions of intercourse between the different populations. He will not, therefore, have a different conception of the Palestine of the first century which was permeated with Hellenistic culture."

The whole strength of Judaism was being exerted to parry this threat: it drew itself closer together and isolated itself, and also the most healthy part of it attached itself more closely to God, His Law, and the promises.

To the Israelite, all the pagans were impure, and all contact with them was a stain. A symbolic dream three times repeated (*Acts* x, 10-16) was necessary to make Peter decide to go to the house of the centurion Cornelius and eat with him. When he presented himself to his host, he gave this explanation: "You know how abominable it is for a man that is a Jew, to keep company or to come unto one of another nation. But God hath shewed to me to call no man common or unclean" (*Acts* x, 28). A little while afterwards, when St. Peter went up to Jerusalem, he was questioned about his inexplicable conduct: "Why didst thou go into men uncircumcised, and didst eat with them?" (*Acts* xi, 3). He had once more to relate the vision which had enlightened him.

Outside Palestine also, the Jews held fast to this rule, even at the cost of grave inconveniences. Priests sent to Rome by the procurator Felix to plead their cause before Cæsar fed exclusively on figs and nuts, in order to avoid being made unclean by pagan food.[37] The holy books, moreover, gave them models to imitate: the three children at Babylon refused to eat anything that came from the royal table (*Daniel* i, 8).

In this land of Israel which pagans had invaded, and where there was in all parts the risk of being affected by contact with them, it was felt that the only method of defence was to surround the faithful with a hedge of precepts; the Pharisaic doctors, teachers of the people, did their best from generation to generation to make this hedge thicker and more prickly;[38] this jurisprudence very soon became so difficult not only to apply but even to know, that those who had not been initiated into it, the "common people," were always presumed to have violated it, and contact with them was likewise regarded as an impurity; this presumption created in those who regarded themselves as pure a haughty disdain: "this multitude, that knoweth not the Law" (*John* vii, 49); and the illiterate ones answered this disdain with hatred. Rabbi Akiba, who was one of the glories of second century Pharisaism, narrates that when

[37] Josephus, *Life*, 3.
[38] We need not here describe these endeavours by the Pharisees: they have often been studied, e.g. by Schuerer, *op. cit.*, Vol. II, pp. 560-6, and Billerbeck, *op. cit.*, Vol. I, pp. 695-702.

he was still outside this sect, he said: "If I had hold of one of these lettered folk, I would bite him as an ass bites, until I broke his bones." [39]

These conflicts, so painful to the conscience, must not be lost sight of by the historian of Christ and His Apostles. They help us to understand the preaching of Jesus, so patient, and so reserved when that was possible, but also, when necessary, so clear and decisive;[40] they enable one also to foresee the reception which such a preaching was bound to encounter: from the Pharisees, scandal (*Matthew* xv, 12); from the people, astonishment and admiration, sometimes also uneasiness; but lastly, from the most teachable and most faithful, the assurance that their Master had "the words of eternal life." [41]

Fidelity to God

The horror of every stain only too often led to a morbid fear, and also a spirit of caste. But at least it defended Israel against all contagion of idolatry. "There arose none in our age, neither is there any of us to-day, tribe or kindred or family or city, which worship gods made with hands, as it was in the former days" (*Judith*, viii, 18). This intransigeance was so strict that Herod had to reckon with it; his coins bore no image of man or animal, no emblem, in short, which might be suspected as idolatrous. True, he defied the popular faith in having a golden eagle erected on the pinnacle of the Temple. But some rabbis led a revolt; the eagle was beaten down; the rabbis were burnt alive, and the populace regarded them as martyrs. Pilate experienced a similar outburst of

[39] *Pesachim,* 49b.

[40] See especially *Mark* vii, 1-23.

[41] A Jewish writer has well understood that this deliverance from the yoke of the Pharisees led the people of Galilee to attach themselves to Christianity: ". . . Even the controversial methods of the Pharisees exasperated the 'common people.' While the Pharisees regarded the Sadducees as opponents who were their equals, they despised the 'common people' and regarded them as an inferior class. This isolation which cut off the learned from the simple people caused the latter to fall into a state of complete ignorance. . . . This separation helped greately to strengthen the new sect of Christians. Amongst them the 'common people' found a loving welcome, while from the learned they encountered only the most brutal repulsion. Christianity did not uphold the requirements of the Pharisees of fidelity to the Law on the part of those who came to it, and it took much more account of the conditions of life of the Galilean population." (S. Bialoblotzki, in *Encyclopædia Judaica,* Vol. II, 1928, art. *Am ha-arez,* cols. 537-41.)

indignation and revolt because he allowed his soldiers to march into Jerusalem carrying pictures of the emperors: after a long resistance he had to give way, and the pictures were taken back from Jerusalem to Cæsarea.[42]

If the Israelite thus repudiated all idolatry, it was in order to devote all his strength to his God. Each day, at the commencement of his prayer, he repeated the verse of *Deuteronomy* (vi, 4): "Hear, O Israel, the Lord our God is one Lord." That was the mainspring of the Jewish faith, it is also the starting point of the Christian belief. A scribe asked Our Lord what was the greatest commandment. Jesus replied (*Mark* xii, 29): "Hear, O Israel, the Lord thy God is one God. And thou shalt love the Lord thy God with thy whole heart, and with thy whole soul, and with thy whole mind, and with thy whole strength. And the second commandment is: Thou shalt love thy neighbour as thyself. There is no other commandment greater than these." And the scribe said to him: "Well, Master, thou hast said in truth, that there is one God, and there is no other besides him. And that he should be loved with the whole heart, and with the whole understanding, and with the whole soul and with the whole strength; and to love one's neighbour is a greater thing than all holocausts and sacrifices." And Jesus seeing that he had answered wisely, said to him: "Thou are not far from the kingdom of God" (*Mark* xii, 28-34).

This short dialogue belongs to the last week in the life of Jesus. It took place in the Temple, in the midst of so many controversies which brought out the opposition between the Master and the Pharisees. At the very time of all those conflicts which were so soon to cause the death of Jesus and the ruin of His people, it is pleasing to see manifested here the deep agreement which, even then, was able to unite the truly religious Scribes with the Messias.

The Religion of the Poor

And if we can find in a scribe this religion "in spirit and in truth," we shall find it still more easily amongst the poor and the humble who surrounded Jesus. There were still at this time Israelites such as Nathanael, "in whom there was no guile" (*John* i, 47); there were thousands of people who "hungered and thirsted after

[42] *Antiquities of the Jews*, XVIII, 3, 1, 55-9; *Wars of the Jews*, II, 9, 2-3, 169-74.

the word of God," who, in order to hear it, forgot to eat and drink, following Jesus into the desert without provisions. There were some who went further, and who, like the Apostles, abandoned all to follow the Master, or who, like Mary of Bethany, broke the box of alabaster to pour out the most precious perfumes upon His head. But as we shall see, those who during the lifetime of Jesus made a complete sacrifice for Him of all their possessions and of their life, were very few in number; in the case of the majority, the enthusiasm so keen at certain times, withered away quickly like the spring flowers on the rocks of Judea.

Why was it that these souls were so hard, and that the faith could not take deep root in them, but dried up and withered away? In many instances it was because of the care for earthly things; as in the case of the rich young man, to whom the Master addressed this severe sentence: "It is easier for a camel to pass through the eye of a needle, than for a rich man to enter into the kingdom of God" (*Mark* x, 25). Again, we find the same thing amongst those invited to the feast: "I have bought a farm, and I must needs go out and see it; I have bought five yoke of oxen, and I go to try them; I have married a wife, and therefore I cannot come" (*Luke* xiv, 16-20). Such things, says Our Lord, are thorns which choke the good seed. How can one observe the great commandment, and love God "with all one's strength," when the soul is absorbed in so many other cares? And how, again, can one love one's neighbour as oneself, if one is a fellow servant greedy for gain, or a pitiless creditor, towards whom God will in turn show himself pitiless? (*Matthew* xviii, 23-35).

Pride of Race

The supreme danger lies in the pride of race which tends to pervert all religion. John the Baptist already warned his hearers in the desert: "Think not to say within yourselves, 'We have Abraham for our father,' for I tell you that God is able of these stones to raise up children to Abraham" (*Matthew* iii, 9-10). Later on, when Jesus promised in the Temple to His followers that the truth should set them free, the Jews protested: "We are the seed of Abraham, and we have never been slaves to any man: how sayest thou, 'you shall be free'?" (*John* viii, 31-33). Similarly the Jews of Capharnaum quoted Moses against Jesus (*John* vi, 31 *et seq.*); the

Samaritan woman herself appealed to her "father Jacob." Could Jesus possibly be greater than he? (*John* iv, 12). In this woman the desire for the "living water" promised by Jesus was stronger than her pride, and she believed; but the Jews of Capharnaum and those in the Temple persisted in their opposition. The same pride was denounced by St. Paul in the unbelieving Jews: "Thou art called a Jew and restest in the Law, and makest thy boast of God, and knowest his will, and approvest the more profitable things, being instructed in the Law, art confident that thou thyself art a guide to the blind, a light of them that are in darkness, an instructor of the foolish, a teacher of infants, having the form of knowledge and of truth in the Law . . ." (*Romans* ii, 17-20).

Doubtless these prerogatives of Israel were real, but they belonged to them only as a talent which was meant to be used, while many of the Jews regarded them as a privilege of which they had the exclusive enjoyment. Thus Eleazar ben Azaria, interpreting a passage in *Deuteronomy* (xxvi, 7), puts these words in God's mouth: "Just as you recognise me as the sole God in the world, so I recognise you as the sole nation on the earth." [43] And Akiba, commenting on *Exodus* (xv, 2), represents all the peoples of the earth as disturbed by the praises with which Israel worships God, and saying: "Whither is thy Beloved gone? We wish to seek him with thee." But Israel answers them: "You have no part at all in him, but my Beloved belongs to me, and I to him." [44]

We must certainly recognise the passionate ardour of this religious faith, but we must also recognise the bitter jealousy to which it led, and which was so manifest in the whole history of Jesus and His Apostles. The patient condescension of the Master, confining during His lifetime His preaching to the children of Israel, did not succeed in dispelling their suspicions, or pacifying their anger. The prospect of the evangelisation of the pagans was enough to exasperate the people of Nazareth (*Luke* iv, 28 *et seq.*), and later on, those of Jerusalem (*Mark* xii, 1-12). The same anger burst out against St. Paul: they heard him quietly when he told them of his training by the Pharisees, and his conversion on the road to Damascus, but as soon as he narrated the vision which he had in the Temple, and the words of Jesus: "Go, for unto the Gentiles afar off will I send thee," the Jews cried out and demanded his death (*Acts* xxii, 22).

[43] Quoted by Bacher, *Die Agada der Tannaiten*, Vol. I, pt. ii, p. 226.
[44] Mekilta, on *Exodus* xv, 2 (tr. Winter-Wuensche, p. 122).

The Messianic Hope

Above all, the Messianic hope was disfigured by this national pride and hatred of the foreigner. This disfigurement was the chief obstacle to the preaching of Jesus. At the same time, it would not be just to the Jewish faith to reduce all the Messianism of this period to dreams of national independence and of revenge against the pagans: political passions often disfigured religious faith, but did not stifle it entirely.[45]

Jewish fidelity to the Messianic hope must be stressed in the first place. The national independence had been destroyed; the bright hopes aroused by the coming of the Machabees had been extinguished with their family; the Jews nevertheless did not despair, they still waited for "he who is to come."

We find this expectation mirrored in every page of the Gospel: in the question put to John the Baptist by the priests and levites sent from Jerusalem, "Who art thou?" which drew the reply, "I am not the Messias"; in the cry of joy when Andrew went to his brother Simon: "We have found the Messias!"; in the faith of the Samaritan woman: "I know that the Messias must come; when he comes, he will tell us all things" (*John* iv, 25); in the message of John the Baptist: "Art thou he who is to come, or look we for another?" (*Matthew* xi, 3).

Twenty-five or thirty years earlier, this Messianic hope inspired the rising of the Jews of Galilee, Perea, and Judea against Sabinus and Varus; an adventurer such as Judas, Simon, or Athronges had only to put himself at their head, and they rose up at once.

This "Messianism in action" reveals the warmth of the Messianic hope; it does not so well manifest its religious character; it is the literature of this epoch that best brings home to us the faith of the people.

The Servant of Jahveh, the Son of Man

The reading of the Gospels shows us that the Jewish nation at the time of Christ thought of the Messias as above all the Son of

[45] On Jewish Messianism at the beginning of the Christian era, see M. J. Lagrange, *Le messianisme chez les Juifs,* Paris, 1909; *Le Judaisme avant Jésus-Christ* (1931), pp. 363-87; L. de Grandmaison, *Jesus Christ,* Eng. tr., Vol. I, pp. 287-91, Vol. II, pp. 18-20; G. F. Moore, *Judaism,* 1927, Vol. II, pp. 323-76; J. Bonsirven, *Le judaisme palestinien,* Vol. I, pp. 341-67.

David and the King of Israel; but when Jesus directed His hearers towards higher hopes, towards the Servant of Jahveh, towards the Son of Man, He was understood, though not always followed. The prophecy of Isaias (xlii, 1-4) concerning the humble and gentle Messias, who "shall not break the bruised reed, and smoking flax he shall not quench," was constantly before the mind of Jesus; the text in *Daniel* (vii, 13) on "the Son of Man coming on the clouds of heaven" was quoted by Him before Caiphas when in answer to the High Priest He made His final claim.

This Son of Man, whom Daniel had contemplated, was never entirely forgotten by the Jews; [46] Jesus was able to recall Him to the mind of the Jews towards the end of His life, to bring out at once His humble nature, His redemptive suffering, and His glory. In the *Book of Enoch,* an apocalyptic compilation, the different parts of which were composed in the course of the first century B.C., the Son of Man appears in great majesty, surpassing all the holiness and greatness of those here below; He existed before the creation of the world, and dwells near to God; "he will be a staff for the just so that they may rest upon him and not fall; he will be the light of the peoples, and the hope of those who suffer in their hearts. All those who dwell on dry land will fall down and adore him; they will bless and glorify him, and sing to the Lord of spirits." [47]

The Son of David

The *Psalms of Solomon,* written by Pharisees shortly after the capture of Jerusalem and the Temple by Pompey, do not, like the *Book of Enoch,* contemplate the Son of Man in heaven, near to God, but they await the Son of David, and they beseech God to send Him here below. *Psalm* xvii especially describes this royal figure. [48]

This beautiful canticle reveals to us the aspirations of the Jews towards a reign of justice and holiness. The royal son of David will be almighty, but this power will not come from His arms, it

---

[46] Nevertheless, it was understood only with difficulty: "We have heard out of the Law that Christ abideth for ever; and how sayest thou 'The Son of man must be lifted up'? Who is this Son of Man?" (*John* xii, 34).

[47] *Enoch* xlviii, 4-5. On the *Book of Enoch,* see Martin, *Le livre d'Henoch,* Paris 1906; R. H. Charles, *Enoch,* in *Pseudepigrapha,* Oxford, 1913, pp. 163-281.

[48] *Psalms of Solomon,* cf. Charles, *op. cit.,* pp. 625-52; Lagrange, *Judaisme,* pp. 149-63.

will be a purely spiritual power, having its source in the divine gifts which the Lord will bestow on Him. We see here an echo of the prophecy of Isaias, but a feeble one; the "mighty God" spoken of by the prophet no longer appears, but we have a just and holy king, a good shepherd. This passage reminds us that on the eve of the Christian era, amongst the Pharisees there were still Israelites who were not affected by the warlike temper of the zealots, and who desired for their Messias holiness above all things.

Triumphal Messianism

At the same time, we must acknowledge that these religious aspirations towards the holiness of the Messianic Kingdom are less manifest in Jewish apocalypses than the dreams of victory, domination, and vengeance. For instance, the author of *The Assumption of Moses* thus announces the Kingdom of God:

". . . He arises, the most high and only everlasting God, and he will appear to punish the nations, and he will destroy all their idols. Then shalt thou be happy, O Israel, and thou shalt mount upon the neck and the wings of the eagle, and they shall be spread out (to fly). And God will draw thee up, and place thee in the starry heaven, in the place where they dwell, and thou shalt look down from on high. And thou shalt see thy enemies on the earth, and thou shalt recognise them, and rejoice, and give thanks and worship to thy Creator." [49]

This book, we must repeat, was written in Palestine at the time when Our Lord was a child. The Jews of the Dispersion frequently expressed in the Sibylline books the same ardent hopes.[50] And even after the great catastrophe of A.D. 70, and the ruin of the city and the Temple, they looked for and sang of the triumph of the Messias over all his enemies. About the year 100 a Pharisee writing at Rome composed a series of visions on this theme. The sixth is the most majestic:

"And lo, a violent wind rose from the sea, so strong that it lifted up all the waves thereof. And lo, the wind caused to come up from the bosom of the sea as it were a man. And this man flew with the clouds

[49] *Assumption of Moses*, X, 7-10, cf. Lagrange, *Messianisme*, p. 86. These verses are taken from a canticle which forms ch. x of this apocalypse. Cf. Charles, *Pseudepigrapha*, pp. 421 *et seq.*

[50] E.g. in the great apocalypse in Book III, which dates about 140 B.C. (Schuerer, *op. cit.*, Vol. III, pp. 571 *et seq.*; Lagrange, *Judaisme*, pp. 505-10.)

of heaven. And wherever he turned his face, all things trembled before his look. And wherever there was heard the sound of his mouth, all things melted as wax melts in the fire. And then lo, an immense multitude of men, that no man could number, assembled together from the four winds of heaven, to fight against the Man who had come up out of the sea. And lo, he graved out a great mountain, and flew up upon its summit. And I sought the place whence the mountain had been graven, and I could not find it.

"And then I beheld: all those who had gathered together to fight against him were troubled: and yet they continued their attack. But although he saw this great army coming to fight him, he lifted not up his hand, he took neither sword or any weapon. But I beheld, and lo, he sent forth from his mouth a flood of fire, from his lips a breath of fire, from his tongue a spark of fire, and all this mingled together, the wave of fire, the breath of fire, and the spark of fire, and it fell upon the multitude who were advancing to the attack, and it consumed them all, so that of that innumerable army there was seen nothing any more but a mass of ashes and of smoke. I saw and I awoke." [51]

This vision is very striking; this Man with a breath of fire is of a more than human greatness, but it is all very far from the Gospel. When we read these apocalypses, we understand the anxiety of the Pharisees who pressed upon Jesus and said to Him: "Show us a sign from heaven."

The Scandal of the Cross

But what must have disconcerted them most of all was the Passion. The Cross was to the Jews a great stumbling block. We could run through all the Messianic chants, but nowhere shall we find the suffering and redeeming Messias long ago foretold by Isaias.[52] These perspectives had become so foreign to the contemporaries of Jesus that although He multiplied on these points the clearest predictions, even His Apostles did not want to listen to them, and His Passion was for them a crushing blow.

This brings out the danger in the triumphal Messianism in which the Jews delighted; they could not recognise in the "humble

[51] IV Esdras, xiii, 2-11. (IV Esdras is known as II Esdras in non-Catholic works. Catholics give the names of I and II Esdras to the canonical books of the O.T. called "Ezra" and "Nehemiah" in Protestant versions.)

[52] Cf. Billerbeck, op. cit., Vol. II, pp. 273-99, 363-70; L. de Grandmaison, Jesus Christ, Eng. tr., Vol. I, p. 291; Lagrange, Judaisme, p. 386; J. Bonsirven, Le judaisme, Vol. I, pp. 381-6.

and gentle Jesus" the one who was to come, and when, after His death, the Temple, the Holy City, and all Israel was overthrown, the scandal reached its culmination:

"Thou hast said that thou didst create the world for us, and thou hast said that the other nations coming from Adam were as nothing, that they were as spittle, or the froth that overflows a vessel. But now, O lord, these nations which are nothing, make slaves of us and devour us. And we, thy people, whom thou hast chosen, whom thou hast called thy first-born, thy only child, thy love, we are delivered into their hands. If it was for us that thou didst create the world, why do we not possess the world as our inheritance? How long are we to wait for it?" [53]

When Jesus appeared, this great catastrophe had not yet taken place, but already for some considerable time Israel had been greatly oppressed. The Jewish historian, Klausner, reviewing the century which elapsed from the fratricidal war of Hyrcanus and Aristobulus until the end of the government of Pilate and the reign of Herod Antipas (67 B.C. till A.D. 39) writes: "There was hardly a single year during this century which was not rendered bloody by wars, revolts, risings, riots; this state of things afflicted the land of Israel during the whole period which preceded Jesus, it lasted on during his lifetime." The same historian estimates that, if we wish to count the number of Israelites who fell in these wars or were executed by Herod or by the Romans, we shall arrive at a total of at least two hundred thousand men, a terrible figure for a country which had hardly more than a million inhabitants, and still more terrible if we remember that those who thus perished were the *élite* of the nation.[54] And while these executions decimated the people, spying harassed them. We may recall what Josephus says of King Herod, who disguised himself and mingled with groups of Jews to listen to what they were saying (*Antiquities of the Jews*, Book XV, 367). This reign of terror made such an impression that we still find traces of it in the Talmud.[55]

All these sufferings were a trial which, if accepted in the proper spirit, would have prepared Israel for the coming of the Messias. Such was, in fact, the preparation of the poor, the humble, and the

[53] *IV Esdras*, vi, 55-9.
[54] Klausner, *Jésus de Nazareth*, p. 242.
[55] We read that Herod disguised himself and sought out Baba ben Buta, and began to criticise the government, in order to lead him on, but Baba ben Buta was on his guard: "The birds in the heavens would repeat what one said."

afflicted whom Jesus pronounces blessed.[56] But those who did not
know how to humble themselves under the hand of the Lord were
crushed by suffering or revolts. It had been promised to Judah
that all the nations would be subject to it, and Judah was dominated
by the nations. The "riches of the nations" had been promised, and
Pagan Rome imposed taxes and tributes upon it. It had been
promised that kings would be its foster fathers, and Pompey came
and conquered with his army. It had been said that pagans would
bend down their foreheads to the ground and kiss the prints of their
feet, and an insignificant Roman officer was the all-powerful master
of Judea. To Israel had been promised the Messias, the Son of
David, and there came to them Herod the Idumean. This was indeed too much.[57]

This terrible trial would have been better borne if the people
had possessed religious leaders worthy of their confidence, but at
this time there were none such; the Israelites were as "sheep without a shepherd" (*Mark* vi, 34). There were indeed some who were
in charge of the sheep, but these were hirelings or robbers (*John* x,
8 et seq.).

The Sadducees

At the time of Christ, two great parties vied for religious supremacy: the Sadducees and the Pharisees.[58] We find them in turn
opposing Him in the course of His ministry, and finally joining
together to destroy Him. Later on, St. Paul, appearing before the
Sanhedrin, in which Pharisees and Sadducees were represented,
set them against one another.

This last incident shows us that the Sadducees and Pharisees
both belonged to the Supreme Council of the nation, and con-
fronted each other. The Sadducees belonged to the priestly and lay
aristocracy; [59] the Scribes belonged for the most part [60] to the Phar-

[56] On this religious movement, see I. Loeb, *La littérature des pauvres dans la
Bible,* Paris, 1892; A. Causse, *Les pauvres d'Israel,* Strassburg, 1922.

[57] Klausner, *op. cit.,* p. 246.

[58] On these two sects see Schuerer, *op. cit.,* Vol. II, pp. 447-88; Moore, *op. cit.,*
Vol. I, pp. 56-71; Lagrange, *Judaisme,* pp. 271-306; L. de Grandmaison, *Jesus
Christ,* Eng. tr., Vol. I, pp. 266-75.

[59] The Sanhedrin was made up of three classes: the priests, the elders, and the
scribes. The elders, who represented the lay aristocracy, belonged like the priests to
the party of the Sadducees. Cf. J. Jeremias, *Jerusalem zur Zeit Jesu,* II Teil, 1
Lieferung, Leipzig, 1929, pp. 88-100.

[60] The leaders of the Pharisees were Scribes. But many Pharisees were not

isaic party. These two groups were distinguished by the social class to which they belonged, but still more by the religious tendencies they represented.

The Sadducees [61] were characterised above all by the exclusive importance which they attached to the written law, to the detriment of oral tradition; [62] they rejected the belief in the resurrection [63] and in the angels.[64] Josephus accuses them of behaving barbarously not only towards strangers, but also to each other.[65] In the administration of justice, this roughness went as far as cruelty.[66]

In the time of Christ, the Sadducees occupied a prominent position because of their social rank and the functions they exercised; they played a preponderating role in the trial of Jesus; they were entirely responsible for the first measures taken against the Apostles (*Acts* iv, 1), and later on for the death of James the Less (Josephus, *Antiquities of the Jews*, XX, 200). But though their authority was great, their religious influence was weak: "they succeeded in convincing only the rich, and were not followed by the people" (*Antiquities of the Jews*, XIII, 298). Their doctrine was characterised only by negations; their contempt for tradition and even for their masters [67] isolated them; their pride alienated the people from them: "Their teaching is received but by a few, yet by those of the greatest

Scribes, and conversely some Scribes were not Pharisees. Cf. Jeremias, *op. cit.*, p. 127. In the Gospel the Scribes and Pharisees usually appear together, either in the steps they take, or in the rebukes which Jesus addresses to them. But sometimes the two groups are distinguished: *Luke* xi, 39-44, and 46-52. Cf. our *Life and Teaching of Jesus Christ*, Eng. tr., Vol. II, p. 179, n. 2.

[61] By their name, the Sadducees are assimilated to sons of Sadoc, or priests, but, as we have said, they also included layfolk. We must add that in the first century the high priests belonged for the most part to the non-priestly families of Boethus, Hannas, and Phiabi. Cf. Jeremias, *op. cit.*, pp. 54-9.

[62] *Antiquities of the Jews*, XIII, 10, 6, 298; XVIII, 1, 4, 16.

[63] *Mark* xii, 18; *Acts* xxiii, 8; *Antiquities of the Jews*, XVIII, 1, 4, 16; *Wars of the Jews*, II, 8, 14, 166.

[64] *Acts* xxiii, 8.

[65] *Wars of the Jews*, II, 8, 14, 166.

[66] *Antiquities of the Jews*, XX, 9, 1, 199-200. We must be careful in reading these passages of Josephus: his exposition of the different doctrines is affected by the attempt to correlate them with Greek philosophy (the immortality of the soul is substituted for the resurrection of the body), and Josephus, very enthusiastic when speaking of the Essenes, and very benevolent with regard to the Pharisees (except when he copies Nicholas of Damascus, *Antiquities of the Jews*, XVII, 2, 4, 41), has no sympathy at all for the Sadducees.

[67] "Arguing against the masters of wisdom whom they follow is in their eyes a virtue" (*Antiquities of the Jews*, XVIII, 1, 4, 17).

dignity. They do almost nothing of themselves, so to speak, for when they become magistrates, as they are unwillingly and by force sometimes obliged to do,[68] they conform themselves to the propositions of the Pharisees, because the multitude would not otherwise bear with them" (*Antiquities of the Jews*, XVIII, 17). The Sadducees were influential less as a religious sect than as a caste; when the holy city was destroyed with the Temple, they lost their political authority, and with it all domination over the people.[69]

The Pharisees

We have just seen that religious influence never belonged to the Sadducees; it was completely in the hands of the Pharisees. The testimony of Josephus is in this connection confirmed by the texts and narratives of the Gospel: "The scribes and the Pharisees have sitten on the chair of Moses. All things therefore whatsoever they shall say to you, observe and do, but according to their works do ye not" (*Matthew* xxiii, 2-3). The discourse of Jesus from which these words are taken is the most severe in the whole Gospel. It is a terrible indictment of the Scribes and the Pharisees, and nevertheless, even there Christ is careful to safeguard their authority. The Pharisees abuse it; these abuses must be condemned, but the yoke must not be entirely rejected, for that could not be done without rejecting the yoke of the Law. The chair in which the Pharisees sit is the chair of Moses. St. Paul speaks in the same way: when he reminds the Philippians of his very close attachment to Judaism he tells them he was "an Hebrew of the Hebrews; according to the law, a Pharisee" (*Philippians* iii, 5).

The Gospel history tells us how the Pharisees made their influence serve their hatred; thereby they lost themselves in losing the people: they became blind guides of the blind. But so long as this decay was not complete they were the doctors of the Law, and had a right to be respected.

This authority enjoyed by the Pharisees in the time of Jesus was not based on their birth, or on their functions. They were

---

[68] This repugnance of the Sadducees to become magistrates is to be noted.

[69] Hence to-day Jewish writers and those who agree with their positions are very careful of the reputation of the Pharisees, and not interested in that of the Sadducees. Pharisaism exists still to-day, and defends itself (their defence may be seen in R. T. Herford's *The Pharisees*, 1923; Herford is not a Jew). The Sadducees have disappeared and have left no trace.

recruited from all classes of the people; we find some among the priests,[70] many amongst the scribes, but many also amongst the simple people.[71] What made a Pharisee was the traditional teaching received from a master, to whom he had devoted his life, and which he would in turn bequeath to his own disciples. The Sadducee recognised only the written law; the Pharisee was above all faithful to the tradition of the elders, and regarded this as binding, as much as and even more than the letter of Scripture.

The doctrines which the Sadducees rejected and which the Pharisees on the contrary held were the existence of angels and the resurrection of the body. But it was above all to moral theology and casuistry that they devoted themselves. They called themselves and claimed to be the "saints." Their holiness consisted above all in a scrupulous conformity with the law; the Pharisees were especially careful in the observance of the Sabbath and of legal purity.[72]

Jesus and the Pharisees

This scrupulous and devoted observance appears all through the Gospel story. Jesus cannot have been sent by God, for He does not keep the Sabbath (*John* ix, 16); His disciples break the Sabbath inasmuch as they pull a few ears of corn in passing, and this, for a Pharisee, was equivalent to working at the harvest, and was forbidden.[73] The paralytic at the pool of Bezatha broke the Sabbath by carrying his couch;[74] Jesus Himself infringed it in miraculously curing a sick man.[75] On the question of purity and impurity the

[70] E.g. the writer of the *Psalms of Solomon*.

[71] On the distinction between the Scribes and the Pharisees, see above, p. 60, n. 60.

[72] Cf. Lagrange, *op. cit.*, pp. 274-7.

[73] On the Sabbath Day "one may cut neither a branch nor a leaf, nor pluck fruit" (Philo, *Life of Moses*, II, 4). Cf. *Life and Teaching of Jesus Christ*, Vol. I, p. 105.

[74] *John* v, 10.

[75] *Mark* iii, 1-6; *Matthew* xii, 9-14. Jesus replies: "What man shall there be among you, that hath one sheep: and if the same fall into a pit on the sabbath day, will he not take hold on it and lift it up? How much better is a man than a sheep!" Some doctors at the time of Christ were still more severe than the Pharisees whom Jesus rebuked. We read in a Zadokite work: "If an animal fall into a pit or a ditch, it must not be taken out on the sabbath day." And again: "If a human being falls into the water . . . it is forbidden to get him out with the help of a ladder, a rope, or an instrument" (*Un écrit sadducéen*, tr. Israel Levi, in *Revue des études juives*, LXI, 1911, p. 198). Charles, in his note on this text (*Pseudepi-*

divergence was still deeper. "Why," asked the Pharisees, "do not thy disciples live according to the tradition of the elders? Why do they eat with unwashed hands?" And Jesus answers: "And why do you transgress the commandment of God for your tradition?" And calling the multitudes together, He said to them: "Hear ye and understand. Not that which goeth into the mouth defileth a man; but what cometh out of the mouth, this defileth a man. If any man have ears to hear, let him hear." [76]

Dangers of Pharisaism

"The rupture between Jesus and the Pharisees was complete." This statement of Professor Klausner [77] is true, but we must add that the rupture was a liberation for the disciples of Jesus. The aim of the Pharisees had been at the beginning legitimate and beneficial: in the land of Israel, invaded by so many foreigners, the Law could be observed only at the price of great vigilance; this fidelity had often been heroic, and under the Machabees it had had its martyrs. But the martyrs had been succeeded by the Scribes; to safeguard the Law they had multiplied around it the precautions of their jurisprudence, and in their anxiety to prepare for everything, to regulate everything, and to prescribe for all occasions, they had rendered the yoke of the Law so heavy that they themselves often avoided it: "They bind heavy and insupportable burdens, and lay them on men's shoulders, but with a finger of their own they will not move them" (*Matthew* xxiii, 4). And then, to make this burden tolerable, they indulged in quibbles which sacrificed religion to their meticulous requirements; [78] "they strained at a gnat and swallowed a camel."

Lastly, and this was one of the chief dangers of this sectarian

---

grapha, p. 827, n. 23), compares *Shabbat*, 128*b*, citing R. Jehuda: "If an animal falls into a well, it may be fed there; one may also put things under him so that he can raise himself and get out of the well by his own efforts." Cf. *Life and Teaching of Jesus Christ*, Vol. I, p. 109.

[76] *Mark* vii, 1-23; *Matthew* xv, 1-20.

[77] Klausner, *op. cit.*, pp. 246.

[78] E.g. in the question of the corban, in which they made little of filial piety (*Mark* vii, 10-13. Cf. *Life and Teaching of Jesus Christ*, Vol. I, p. 327), and in the question of oaths: "Woe to you, blind guides, that say 'Whosoever shall swear by the Temple, it is nothing, but he that shall swear by the gold of the temple, is a debtor'" (*Matthew* xxiii, 16; *Life and Teaching of Jesus Christ*, Vol. I, p. 161).

formation, by this plethora of precautions, and this exaggeration of legal purity, the Pharisees isolated themselves. They were, as their name indicates, the "separated ones." [79] This danger was so manifest that historians who are especially sympathetic towards them [80] have recognised it. It is this separatism that Jesus denounced in the parable of the Pharisee and the publican: "O God, I give thee thanks that I am not as the rest of men," says the Pharisee (*Luke* xviii, 11).

In spite of these terrible faults, the Pharisees were regarded by the Jews as the men of the Law. Many of the Israelites desirous of holiness went to them. In a passage which seems to be taken from Nicholas of Damascus, [81] Josephus narrates that six thousand of them had refused the oath to the emperor and King Herod.

This figure of six thousand is very far from representing the total number of adherents of the sect; they were numerous, not only in Jerusalem, where dwelt the great doctors who were their leaders, but in all Palestine and even in the Diaspora.

It was likewise the Pharisees who organised the fight against Jesus, and later on against St. Paul. If the Jewish people as a whole rejected the Messias, it was the Pharisees who were responsible.

[79] On this name, see Lagrange, *op. cit.*, p. 273 and n. 2. This appellation was given to the Pharisees and finally accepted by them. They preferred to call themselves the "holy ones" or "companions" (Haberim). The latter title, however, belonged only to those who had been regularly affiliated to the sect, not to its sympathisers.

[80] G. F. Moore, *Judaism,* Vol. II, p. 161, after condemning the lowering of moral values in this sectarian ethic, goes on: "Worse . . . is the self-complacency of the members of such a party or association and the self-righteousness that comes of believing that their peculiarities of doctrine or practice make them singularly well-pleasing to God. With this goes censoriousness towards outsiders, which often presumes to voice the disapprobation of God. The Pharisees and the Associates, who seem to have numbered among them in the second century most of the learned and their disciples, conspicuously illustrate these faults. It is not without detriment to himself that a man cherishes the consciousness of being superior to his fellows, and the injury to his character is not least when he has the best reason for his opinion."

[81] "There was a sect of Jews who boasted of observing very strictly the law of their fathers. . . . They were called Pharisees. They were able to hold their own before kings, far-seeing and planning openly to oppose and hurt them. In point of fact, whereas the whole Jewish people had confirmed its loyalty towards the Emperor and the royal government with oaths, these men had not sworn, to the number of more than six thousand. . . ." (*Antiquities of the Jews,* XVII, 2, 4, 41-2). Josephus himself was a Pharisee, and he everywhere speaks of the sect with a great veneration; the severity of this particular judgment is not due to him, but comes from a source transcribed without reflection.

At the same time, amongst the Pharisees as in the Jewish people, God had reserved some chosen ones: St. Paul himself is a proof of this.

The Pharisees aimed above all at being a religious sect. In political matters, their attitude was dictated by their beliefs. The majority thought above all else of the privileges of Israel, and like the six thousand of whom Josephus speaks, they rejected all foreign domination, all oaths given to strangers, and also all taxes levied by them (*Matthew* xxii, 17 *et seq.*). But some of them saw in the subjection imposed upon Israel a divine Judgment to which one ought to submit.[82] When the catastrophe of A.D. 70, and the still more terrible one of A.D. 134, had destroyed once and for all the political independence of Israel, the Sadducees and the Zealots disappeared,[83] but the Pharisees retained their influence over the faithful Jews; they retain it still to-day.

The Essenes

The Sadducees and the Pharisees were both closely mixed up with Christian origins, as is shown sufficiently by the *Gospels* and *Acts*. On the other hand, the Essenes are never mentioned in the New Testament, and they seem, in fact, to have remained completely outside the sphere of action of Jesus and His Apostles. Hence we shall not have much to say of them. For the rest, this sect is little known.[84] We have to guide us a brief mention in Pliny,[85] two texts of Philo,[86] and two in Josephus.[87]

Of all these, the most detailed by far is that in the *War of the Jews*. If we could regard this as the recollection of a man who had

[82] E.g. Pollio and Sameas; *Antiquities of the Jews*, XIV, 9, 4, 176; XV, 1, 1, 3-4.

[83] The Zealots are only indirectly connected with the history of Christianity: their religious position was that of the Pharisees, but their zeal for the Law took the form of an armed rebellion. They appeared in the first years of the first century in the troubles which followed the death of Herod and the Roman intervention (cf. above, p. 26), but they took the name of Zealots only just before the great revolt (*Wars of the Jews*, IV, 3, 9, 160-1). Cf. Lagrange, *op. cit.*, p. 214.

[84] Cf. Schuerer, *op. cit.*, Vol. II, pp. 651-80; E. Meyer, *op. cit.*, Vol. II, pp. 393-402; Bauer, art. *Essener* in Pauly-Wissowa, *Suppl.*, IV, pp. 386-430; Lagrange, *op. cit.*, pp. 307-30.

[85] *Hist. nat.*, V, 17.

[86] *Quod omnis probus liber*, XII, 75-91; *Apology*, apud Eusebius, *Praep. evang.*, VIII, 11.

[87] *Wars of the Jews*, II, 8, 2-13, 119-61; *Antiquities of the Jews*, XVIII, 1, 5, 18-21. These texts have been gathered together by Lagrange, *op. cit.*. pp. 307-18.

himself lived the life of the Essenes, it would be of great interest. Unfortunately, it is difficult to attribute it so great a value. If we compare the two passages in Josephus with one another, we find that the later one harmonises ill with the earlier, that it is much less detailed, and depends on Philo.[88] However careless Josephus may have been in transcribing his sources, it would be difficult to imagine that, knowing by personal experience the life of the Essenes and having already described it from his own recollections, he would have recourse in the second passage to the testimony of an earlier writer who had never seen them.

These considerations must lead an historian to be very reserved in making use of these passages. What we may learn from them is the existence of the Essenian sect in the first century of our era. Their chief centre was situated near Engaddi, on the western bank of the Dead Sea. There they lived in common a simple and frugal life, inspired by a great care for ritual purity. In this care, as in the exaggerated respect for the rest of the Sabbath day,[89] the Essenes exceeded even the Pharisees, and were poles apart from the teaching of Christ. In other respects, and above all by their community life and their celibacy,[90] they resembled externally the first Christians, but in spite of this external resemblance, the religious sentiment which inspired them was very different.[91]

The religion of the Essenes was differentiated from ordinary Judaism by some singular characteristics, which are, however, difficult to determine with precision. Philo praises their disciples

[88] Those who led a communal life were more than four thousand: *Antiquities of the Jews*, XVIII, 21; *Q. o. pr. lib.*, 75. According to *Antiquities of the Jews*, 21, their celibacy was undertaken, as by Philo (*Apol.*, 14) for fear of discord. According to *Wars of the Jews*, 121, its motive was the unfaithfulness of woman. The text of *Antiquities of the Jews* stresses above all the common life, the preference given to work in the fields, and the fact that the Essenes kept away from the Temple. In *Wars of the Jews*, the life of the Essenes is represented as dominated above all by a care for ritual purity.

[89] They were forbidden to go to stool on the Sabbath day (*Wars of the Jews*, 147).

[90] Celibacy was not imposed on all: there were married Essenes (*Wars of the Jews*, 160-1).

[91] A Christian prefers virginity to marriage in order to belong more completely to the Lord (*I Cor.* vii, 32); the Essene prefers it because of ritual purity, or again to avoid discord, or by mistrust of womenfolk. The communal life of the Christians at Jerusalem, again, had nothing in common with the Essenes. The former did not withdraw to the desert or separate themselves from the world, but in a great spirit of charity and detachment they put all things in common in order the better to serve God.

as being, amongst other things, "splendid servants of God, sacrificing no animals, but doing their best to make their thoughts such as were fitting to priests." Josephus writes in turn: "They send offerings to the Temple, but do not offer sacrifices, for they practise another kind of purification. That is why they keep away from the holy place, and sacrifice apart." [92]

We find amongst the Essenes some who foretold the future; Josephus especially mentions their prophecies.[93] He also says that the Essenes had an esoteric doctrine; when anyone was received into the sect, he took an oath "to hide nothing from the members of the sect, and to reveal nothing about them to the profane, even if tortured to death. He also swore to pass on the rules of the sect exactly as he had received them . . . and to guard with the same respect the books of the sect and the names of the angels" (*Wars of the Jews*, 141-2).

Finally, if we must understand literally a passage in Josephus, it would seem that the Essenes regarded the sun as a god.[94]

All these features give one the impression of a Jewish gnosis, affected not exactly by the Iranian religion, but by Oriental syncretism. The study of Christian origins will show us how virulent this Gnostic syncretism was during the first half of the second century.

§ 2. JUDAISM OF THE DISPERSION [1]

At the time of Christ, the Jews were much less numerous in Palestine than they were in the rest of the world. In the land of

---

[92] *Antiquities of the Jews*, 19. This text is much discussed: I reproduce it as it is translated by Reinach. The negation ("they do not offer sacrifice") is lacking in the Greek MS., but we find it in the old Latin translation and in the Epitome. Niese strikes it out, Naber retains it, as also Schuerer, *op. cit.*, Vol. II, p. 663, n. 50, and Meyer, *op. cit.*, Vol. II, p. 397, n. 4. On the other side are Bauer, *op. cit.*, p. 398, and Lagrange, *op. cit.*, p. 316, n. 5.

[93] "There are amongst them some who are strong in foretelling the future through close study of the holy books, various purifications, and the words of the prophets, and they are seldom wrong in their predictions" (*Wars of the Jews*, 159). Elsewhere he gives three instances of Essenian prophecies: *Wars of the Jews*, I, 78; II, 113; *Antiquities of the Jews*, XV, 372.

[94] "They dig a hole about a foot deep and there attend to their needs, covering themselves with their mantle in order not to soil the rays of God" (*Wars of the Jews*, 148).

[1] On the Diaspora, the two most complete studies are those of Juster, *Les Juifs dans l'empire romain*, 2 vols., Paris, 1914, and that of Schuerer, *op. cit.*, Vol. III,

Israel there were hardly more than a million;[2] in the other provinces of the Roman Empire they were at least four or five times as many.[3]

Nevertheless, Palestinian Judaism was more deserving of a detailed study than that of the Diaspora, because its influence until the fall of Jerusalem extended over all Jews everywhere. Moreover, we are concerned with Christian rather than with Jewish history, and it was in Palestine that Christianity arose, and it is there that its relations with Judaism must be studied. Later on, by reason of its triumphant expansion, the Church was in constant contact with the dispersed Jews. It made their synagogues the starting point of its propaganda, and when it had grown, these constituted centres of persecution. We must therefore study briefly the network of Jewries which in the first century extended throughout the world.

The Origins of the Dispersion

For a long time before this, the Jews had established themselves outside the land of Israel, either in the neighbouring kingdom of Syria, or in the two great empires of Assyria and Egypt. The conquests of Alexander opened all the East to the Jews, and the Roman conquests did the same for the countries surrounding the Mediterranean.

They spread everywhere, as soldiers, tradespeople, slaves, or exiles. Everywhere they established themselves with the tenacity of their race, and often enjoyed the protection of princes. At

pp. 1-187. On the origins of the Diaspora, consult: A. Causse, *Les Dispersés d'Israel*, Paris, 1929. On the religious tendencies, see Wendland, *Die Hellenistisch-Roemische Kultur*, Tübingen, 1912, pp. 192-211. Short but precise descriptions in T. Reinach, art. *Judaei* in the *Dictionnaire des antiquités grecques et romaines*, pp. 619-32 (English translation in the *Jewish Encyclopædia*), and in J. Guimann, art. *Diaspora* in *Encyclopædia Judaica*, Vol. V, pp. 1088-98.

[2] Harnack, *Mission und Ausbreitung*, Vol. I, p. 7, reckons this population at 700,000. So also E. Meyer, *Die Bevölkerung des Altertums*, in *Handwörterbuch der Staatswissenschaften herausg.* of J. Conra, Vol. II, p. 687, Jean, 1899. Juster, on the other hand, gives 5 millions, *op. cit.*, Vol. I, p. 210, n. 2; so also Felten, *op. cit.*, Vol. I, p. 32.

[3] Harnack (*ibid.*) gives a Jewish population of from 4 to 4½ millions, in a total population of 55 millions, which makes 7 per cent of the population of the empire. Juster gives the same proportion, but thinks the figures are too low: the Jews would be about 7 millions. Gutmann (*art. cit.*, p. 1091) gives 5 million Jews, representing 8 per cent of the population.

Alexandria, Alexander, in founding the city, had given them equal rights with those of the Macedonians; [4] the Lagidæ protected them in their turn; [5] the Seleucids, who acted as persecutors and tyrants in Palestine, were in Anatolia protectors of the Jews; [6] the Romans, who from the time of Judas Machabæus (161 B.C.) supported the Palestinian Jews, extended in the time of Simon (139) their protection to the Jews throughout the Empire.[7] Cæsar granted to Hyrcanus II (B.C. 63-40) a guarantee for the Jewish privileges, and allowed him the right to intervene in their favour.[8] Augustus, Tiberius, and above all Claudius, protected them efficaciously, while requiring from them respect for public peace and the rights of others.[9]

The Roman policy towards the Jews was such as to be easily adaptable to local circumstances. In Palestine it respected the Jewish cult, and caused it to be respected by others. But it kept a close watch on political tendencies, and restrained all manifestation of independence. In Rome itself, it was careful to maintain public peace, and as soon as the Jews seemed to disturb this, it took steps against them, and if necessary expelled them. We find the same severity at Alexandria, where the Jews were very numerous and powerful. But in the Hellenic cities of less importance, where they could not constitute a great danger, Rome regarded them as Roman subjects, loyal to the Empire, and putting its interests when necessary before the particular interests of cities. The Roman Emperors

[4] Josephus, *Contra Apion*, II, 4, 35-7; *Wars of the Jews*, II, 18, 7, 487-8; *Antiquities of the Jews*, XIV, 10, 1, 188; Philo, *In Flaccum*, 44. Cf. Juster, *op. cit.*, Vol. II, p. 6; Schuerer, *op. cit.*, Vol. III, pp. 35-6.

[5] Cf. Schuerer, *op. cit.*, pp 40-50.

[6] Cf. Ramsay, *Historical Commentary on the Galatians*, pp. 189-92.

[7] *I Mach.* viii, 17 *et seq.*; xiv, 24; xv, 15-22. Cf. Juster, *op. cit.*, Vol. I, p. 215.

[8] Cf. Juster, *op. cit.*, Vol. I, p. 216. We must note, however, that several of the documents attributed to Cæsar by Josephus and quoted here by Juster seem to be older, see notes by Reinach to *Antiquities of the Jews*, XIV, 145; XIV, 241, etc.

[9] Tiberius was hostile to the Jews as long as Sejanus was alive, but after that he was favorable to them. In the case of Claudius, we note in particular the edicts cited by Josephus, *Antiquities of the Jews*, XIX, 5, 2-3, 280-91. In A.D. 49 he expelled the Jews from Rome: Suetonius, *Claudius*, p. 25; *Acts* xviii, 2. At Alexandria he required the maintenance of peace. Cf. H. J. Bell, *Jews and Christians in Egypt*, London, 1924. The letter of Claudius (A.D. 42) is commented on by A. d'Alès in *Etudes*, Vol. CLXXXII, 1925, pp. 693-701. Two Alexandrians, Isidore and Lampo, were condemned to death by Claudius and executed as responsible for the massacre of Jews at Alexandria under Caligula in A.D. 38. On these papyri, cf. T. Reinach, *L'empereur Claude et les antisémites alexandrins* in *Revue des études juives*, XXXI, 1895, pp. 161-77, and XXXIV, 1897, pp. 296-8; Juster, *op. cit.*, Vol. I, p. 125.

recognised this fidelity,[10] and in return protected the Jews against the local authorities. In vain did the magistrates of Tralles openly declare to the proconsul C. Rabirius that they disapproved of this protection: the proconsul insisted and the magistrates had to submit. Similarly, the proconsul made known his wishes to those of Laodicæa: "by reason of their friendship and alliance with us Romans, they are not to be ordered about by anyone, or suffer anything from anyone in our province." [11] No one will think that this immunity of the Jews was accepted by the Greeks with a good grace, but they could but submit to the Roman ruling, and those who disobeyed could be delated to the Emperor, condemned by him to death, and executed, as Isidore and Lampo were under Claudius.[12]

Importance of the Jewish Population

It is not surprising that being thus protected by Alexander, the Lagidæ, Seleucids, and above all by the Roman Emperors, the Jews spread out in great numbers in the Mediterranean world. Already in the second century B.C. they make the Sibyl say (III, 271): "The earth is full of thy race, and the sea is full of it." Strabo, writing under Augustus, says of the Jews: "They have invaded all the cities, and it would be difficult to find a place where these people have not been received and become masters." [13] The Jewish writers do not stop there. Philo goes so far as to maintain that the Jews form one half of the human race,[14] and that in the countries in which they are established they are almost equal in number to the native population.[15] Speaking of Egypt which he knows well, he is more precise and at the same time more reserved, but his statements show that the Jews were very numerous: at Alexandria, two out of five sections had a majority of Jews, and were called Jewish quarters; [16] in the whole of Egypt Philo reckons

[10] The texts are collected by Juster, *op. cit.*, Vol. I, p. 220.

[11] Letters of the Laodicæan magistrates, *Antiquities of the Jews*, XIV, 10, 20, 241.

[12] Cf. above, p. 70, n. 9.

[13] Quoted by Josephus, *Antiquities of the Jews*, XIV, 7, 2, 115. Reinach wisely notes: "These last words seem to me suspect."

[14] *Legat. ad Caium*, 31.

[15] *De vita Mosis*, II, 27.

[16] *In Flaccum*, 8. Strabo said (*Antiquities of the Jews*, XIV, 117): "One whole quarter of Alexandria is reserved for this people." At the time of the massacre of Jews in A.D. 66, we gather from Josephus that they were concentrated in the Delta, or fourth quarter (*Wars of the Jews*, II, 18, 8, 495).

the Jewish population at one million,[17] that is, about one-eighth of the whole population. In Syria, and in Asia Minor also, the Jews seem to have been very numerous.[18] At Rome the importance of their colony is attested by many facts: the number of their synagogues,[19] their activity, feared by Cicero at the trial of Flaccus,[20] their mourning, noticed by all, at the funeral of Cæsar,[21] by the fact, again, that the Jewish ambassador who presented himself to Augustus in B.C. 4 was accompanied by eight thousand Jews of Rome.[22] Under Tiberius, a decree of the Senate enrolled and sent off to Sardinia four thousand young Jews who were freedmen.[23]

Civil Condition of the Jews

Great in numbers, the Jewish Dispersion was strong above all by reason of its cohesion; its members might rank as citizens of Rome,[24] or of the city in which they had been born,[25] but whether they were thus Romans, Alexandrians, Thessalonians, or Tarsiots, they were

[17] *In Flaccum*, 6.

[18] Juster, *op. cit.*, Vol. I, p. 210.

[19] Cf. J. B. Frey, *Les communautés juives à Rome aux premiers temps de l'Eglise*, in *Recherches de Science religieuse*, 1930, pp. 269-97; 1931, pp. 129-68.

[20] *Pro Flacco*, 28, 66.

[21] Suetonius, *Julius*, 84: "In summo publico luctu exterarum gentium multitudo circulatim suo quaeque more lamentata est, praecipueque Judaei, qui etiam noctibus continuis bustum frequentarunt."

[22] *Antiquities of the Jews*, XVII, 11, 1, 300; *Wars of the Jews*, II, 6, 1, 80.

[23] Tacitus, *Annals*, II, 85; Suetonius, *Tiberius*, 36.

[24] Many Jews became Roman citizens by enfranchisement; but there were also some who were not of servile origin, and who had obtained this right by privilege; e.g. the family of Philo; on Philo's nephew, Tiberius Julius Alexander, see Schuerer, *op. cit.*, Vol. I, p. 624, n. 85. On Roman citizenship, see Juster, *op. cit.*, Vol. II, pp. 15 *et seq.*

[25] Juster, Vol. II, *op. cit.*, p. 2 *et seq.* Hence the unusual situation of a Jew possessing citizenship of Rome and one or more Greek cities, and also regarding himself as a Jewish citizen. Thus St. Paul was a Roman citizen (*Acts* xvi, 37; xxii, 25), a citizen of Tarsus (xxi, 39) and a Jew (*Phil.* iii, 5; II *Cor.* xi, 22). Roman law in the time of the Republic did not allow a Roman citizen to belong to another city: "Duarum civitatum civis noster esse jure civili nemo potest" (Cicero, *Pro Balbo*, xi, 28); cf. Mommsen, *Droit public*, Vol. VI, 1, p. 51. After Augustus, on the other hand, "Roman citizenship is compatible with citizenship of all the cities of the Empire" (Mommsen, *op. cit.*, Vol. VI, 2, p. 331). Was a Jew possessing political rights outside Judea at the same time a Jewish citizen? Yes, from the standpoint of Jewish law; not, apparently, from the standpoint of Roman law. Cf. Juster, *op. cit.*, Vol. II, p. 11, n. 3.

above all Jews. As Philo says, they regarded as their own the city where their fathers or grandfathers had lived, but they venerated Jerusalem as their metropolis.[26]

Such a situation was tolerated with difficulty by the Greek cities in which the Jews were established. The Alexandrians bitterly opposed their citizenship;[27] at Cæsarea, the struggle was still more violent: it led to bloody riots, an appeal to Rome, where the Jews were condemned by Nero, and finally the massacre of the Jews of Cæsarea: "in one hour, more than twenty thousand were slain."[28]

But this resistance on the part of the Greek cities could not prevail against the Roman will, and Rome usually upheld the rights of the Jews, and thus ensured in the majority of Hellenic cities the presence of citizens habitually loyal to its political policy. Nevertheless, when the interest of the Jewish fatherland came in conflict with the service of Rome, the Jews of the Empire rose up at once: we see this on the occasion of the great revolt (A.D. 66-70); and again during the last years of the reign of Trajan (A.D. 115-117) and finally in the terrible war which ranged the whole nation against Hadrian (A.D. 132-135).

This unanimity in the national struggles reveals the profound feeling in the Jews of the Diaspora. Their religious faith, and above all their religious practices, might reflect their remoteness from Jerusalem, as we shall shortly point out, but in spite of everything they remained Jews, and in case of conflict, they preferred their race and religion to all else.

Several facts show this strong religious cohesion, and amongst them is the influence exerted by the Jews of Judea on those of Mesopotamia. The latter were descended from the Israelites deported by the Assyrians and Chaldeans; they had never returned to Palestine, but nevertheless they adopted all the reforms elaborated by the Scribes from the time of Esdras.[29] Of all the dispersed Jews, the most numerous and most powerful were those of Alexandria. These remained in close touch with the Jews of Judea; their literary output, which was considerable, aimed chiefly at

[26] *In Flaccum*, 46.
[27] This is still a matter of controversy. Cf. Schuerer, *op. cit.*, Vol. III, pp. 35 *et seq.*; Juster, *op. cit.*, Vol. I, p. 204.
[28] *Wars of the Jews*, II, 13, 7, 266-70; 13, 4, 284-92; 18, 1, 457. This massacre was immediately followed by the great rebellion of A.D. 66.
[29] Cf. Juster, *op. cit.*, Vol. I, p. 499, and n. 4.

making known to pagans the history and belief of the Jews, the Mosaic legislation, the great figures and martyrs of Judaism, and particularly those of the times of the Machabees.[30]

Privileges of the Proselytes

This religious fidelity was moreover protected by national feeling: race, worship and faith were all linked together in the attachment of the Jews to Israel, and to the pagans, were all one. By a strange departure from the ordinary tenor of their legislation, they refused the enjoyment of Jewish privileges to those Jews who did not practise their religion;[31] and conversely, they granted it to those who were not Jews by birth, but had adopted the Jewish religion.[32]

This derogation is understood without difficulty if we remember what were the Jewish privileges, and the reasons which had led the Romans to consent to them: they consisted in dispensations from certain civil or military duties, which all helped to give the Jews the right to live according to their conscience. Only those had a right to these privileges who regarded the Jewish faith as binding on their consciences, and in fact observed it.

Apostasies

Protected in this way by their attachment to the Jewish nation and by the Roman legislation itself, the Jews were almost unanimous in their fidelity to their religion. But there were apostasies in the Diaspora; Philo denounced them more than once; he knew people who "arrive at such a degree of madness that they do not even reserve the possibility of repentance, making themselves the slaves of idols, and professing this slavery by graving it, not on sheets of papyri, but, like animals, on their bodies, with red-hot iron, so as to make this mark ineffaceable."[33] Elsewhere he shows how "the apostates from the holy laws" fall into all the vices.[34]

[30] On this literature, see Schuerer, *op. cit.*, Vol. III, pp. 420-719; Lagrange, *Judaisme*, pp. 494-580; Wendland, *op. cit.*, pp. 192-211.

[31] Edict of May 21st, 49 B.C.: Lucius Lentulus, consul, says: "I exempt from service, for reasons of a religious nature, the Jews who are Roman citizens and who seem to me to observe and practise the Jewish rites at Ephesus" (*Antiquities of the Jews*, XIV, 10, 16, 234); cf. *ibid.*, 228.

[32] Juster, *op. cit.*, Vol. I, p. 232.

[33] *De special. leg.*, I, 8, 58. Cf. *Levit.* xix, 28.

[34] *De virtutibus* (*de paenit.*), II, 182.

Elsewhere again he denounces the wicked, in whom he sees the posterity of Cain: Greek sophistry has perverted them and led them to despise God and his law.[35] Others see nothing more in the biblical narratives than legends similar to those of the Greek mythology;[36] others, lastly, while adhering still to Judaism, elude its legislation by their allegorical exegesis: "they regard the written laws as symbols of intelligible realities, they study these realities with great care, but neglect the laws."[37]

Influence of Hellenism

We could find elsewhere other examples of these apostasies[38] and of this syncretism.[39] Such excesses, nevertheless, were rare in the Diaspora; they were felt to be scandalous. It was not by these complete defections that the Jews of the Dispersion differed from those of Judea, it was by their attachment to Hellenism, by their striving to be citizens of the world. To the Israelites of Palestine, Greek civilisation was regarded as the reign of the wicked, the Seleucids, the Herodians, the Romans; it was the wicked world, the kingdom of Satan. To the Jewish citizens of Alexandria, Smyrna, or Ephesus, Hellenism appeared under a different colour; it was a great temptation, doubtless, but also a great force, with a great attraction; one did not repudiate it, but one endeavoured to assimilate it. At this time, when the Greeks were everywhere fabricating apocryphal works, putting their dreams under the patronage of Pythagoras, Plato, Aristotle, Timæus, or Thucydides,

[35] De posteritate Caini, 33-48. Cf. our History of the Dogma of the Trinity, Vol. I, p. 134.

[36] De confus. ling., 2-3; ibid.

[37] De migrat. Abr., 89; ibid.

[38] In an inscription of the time of Hadrian (C.I.G., 3148, quoted by Schuerer, op. cit., Vol. III, p. 14), we find a list of people "previously Jews," who have made a gift to the city.

[39] In the Temple of Pan at Edfu, two inscriptions (Dittenberger, O.G.I., 73 and 74) express the gratitude of the "Jew Ptolemy" and of the "Jew Theodotus" to the god; the donors of these ex-voto offerings do not make it plain whether they mean thereby Pan or Jahveh.—The book On the Jews, written by Artapan before Alexander Polyhistor (80 B.C.) and which is known to us by quotations in Josephus and Eusebius, is more surprising still: all the institutions of the Egyptians, including their religion, are attributed to Jacob and his sons, and especially to Moses: Jacob and his sons founded the sanctuaries of Athos and Heliopolis (Eusebius, Praeparatio evangelica, IX, p. 23); Moses instituted the cult of Ibis and Apis (ibid., xxvii, 9 and 12), etc. Cf. Schuerer, op. cit., Vol. III, p. 478.

the Jews similarly professed to quote the Sibyls, Orpheus, Pho-
cylides, Menander. They translated the holy books into Greek;
the translators were hallowed with a glorious legend: they became
the seventy prophets inspired by God, dear to the king and dear
to the people.[40] The exegetes follow the translators; they make
the Bible the source of all philosophy and of all science.[41]

Philo

Of all the commentators on the Bible, the best known is Philo.[42]
Born about 20 B.C., in a rich and influential Jewish family, with
a brother an alabarch, and Tiberius Alexander as a nephew, he
is well qualified to represent Alexandrian Judaism in the time of
Christ. He has, moreover, the rare good luck to have survived not
only in some citations in Eusebius, but in numerous works of
exegesis or history which enable us to know him well.

He was a scholar and a learned philosopher, but nevertheless he
remained attached to his people and his faith. He made a pil-
grimage to Jerusalem to pray there and offer sacrifice. In his old
age, he undertook in A.D. 39-40 an embassy to the Emperor Caius
in defence of the Jews.[43] The date of his death is unknown. His
chief works form an allegorical commentary on the Pentateuch.[44]
To these we must add a few philosophical treatises,[45] two historical

[40] This story was told first in the letter of Aristeus in the second century B.C.
(Eng. tr. in Charles, *Pseudepigrapha*, pp. 83-122). It was later on embellished
with new additions. Cf. R. Tramontano, *La Lettera di Aristea*, Naples, 1931, p.
113-26.
[41] On all this see our *History of the Dogma of the Trinity*, Vol. I, p. 134.
[42] The works still extant in Greek have been edited many times. The best
edition until recently was that of Mangey, London, 1742, 2 vols., but now we
have that of Cohn-Wendland, 6 vols., with 2 vols. of tables by Leisegang (Berlin,
Reimer and De Gruyter, 1896-1930). The works existing in an Armenian translation have been edited with a Latin version by Aucher, Venice, 1822-6. Principal
studies: I. Heinemann, *Philos. griechische und jüdische Bildung*, Breslau, 1932;
J. Drummond, *Philo Judaeus*, London, 1888; E. Bréhier, *Les idées philosophiques
et religieuses de Philo d'Alexandrie*, Paris, 1908; W. Bousset, *Jüdisch-Christlicher
Schulbetrieb in Alexandria und Rom*, Goettingen, 1915 (on Philo: pp. 8-154);
Schuerer, *op. cit.*, Vol. III, pp. 633-716; Lebreton, *History of the Dogma of the
Trinity*, Vol. I, pp. 133-90; Lagrange, *Judaisme*, pp. 542-86.
[43] He himself gives the story of this embassy in his book, *On the Embassy to
Caius*. This, together with the book *Contra Flaccum*, is translated into French
with a long introduction by F. Delaunay, *Philon, Ecrits historiques*, Paris, 1870.
[44] One of these has been translated into French: *Le commentaire allégorique
des saintes lois*, by E. Bréhier, Paris, 1909.
[45] *De aeternitate mundi*, ed. Cumont, Berlin, 1891; *Quod omnis probus liber*;
this gives a description of the life of the Essenes (cf. *supra*, pp. 67-68); De

works,[46] and the book on the Contemplative Life, which describes and praises the life of the Therapeutæ.[47]

What his life reveals is fully developed in his books. Philo was a believing and pious Jew. This gives his theology a firmness and an authority which we do not find in Greek speculation; it also explains the truly religious ideas we find in his works: God is good, not in the purely metaphysical sense of Plato, but with a merciful goodness which spreads good around Him; He is peace and liberty, perfection and end. Supremely happy Himself, He is the principle of beatitude for all men; He invites each one of us to beatitude, draws us by His call, and leads us on by His action.

But while he was a faithful Jew, Philo was also a Greek philosopher.[48] His God is no longer the God of Israel, but the God of the world; Jewish history is transformed by his allegorical method into a doctrine of salvation;[49] Abraham is no longer the father of the faithful, but the first philosopher: he was the first to recognise that the world has a supreme cause, and that it is governed by Providence.[50] The divine transcendence is no longer regarded as having its source in holiness, as in Jewish thought, but it arises from God's ideal greatness, which renders Him superior to all determination.[51] All this directs the soul towards a natural theology rather than to a positive faith, and the soul, inspired with a desire of God, wonders how she may attain to Him.

Philo endeavours to solve this problem by his theology of intermediaries: between God and the world there are the powers. It is by these that God's action reaches the world, and it is by them that man's contemplation can rise up towards God. They are sometimes identified with the angels of Jewish theology, sometimes with the Platonic ideas, and at other times with the Stoic powers.

Providentia; Alexander, sive de eo quod rationem habeant bruta animalia. These two last works exist only in an Armenian version.

[46] *Supra,* p. 76, n. 43.

[47] This work was long regarded as doubtful or spurious, but is now generally regarded as authentic. Cf. Massebieau, in *Revue de l'histoire des religions,* XVI, 1887, pp. 170 *et seq.,* 284 *et seq.,* Conybeare's edition of the work, 1895.

[48] On this question of Judaism and Hellenism, see especially Heinemann, *op. cit.;* cf. *Recherches de Science religieuse,* 1933, pp. 331-4.

[49] Bréhier, *Les idées philosophiques de Philon,* pp. 48-9; 2nd edn., pp. 59-61.

[50] *De virtutibus,* 216.

[51] *Leg. alleg.,* II, 86; *De sacrif. Abel,* 92; *Quod Deus sit immut.,* 62, 55; *De poster. Caini,* 168.

Their personality is only apparent, and arises simply from the weakness of the perceiving mind.[52]

The Logos

Of all the powers, the highest and the nearest to God is the Logos. In Philo's theology, it plays a part similar to that of the other powers, but in an eminent degree: it is the intermediary which enables God to act upon the world, and men to elevate themselves towards God; it is the object of contemplation to those who are not able to attain to God Himself. Just as the powers are identified with the angels of the Bible, so also the Logos is symbolised by the Angel of the Lord, the High Priest, the Place, and the Dwelling. The Logos is sometimes called the elder son of God, the younger being the sensible world.[53] And just as the powers are identified with ideas, so also the Logos is regarded as the intelligible world, the exemplar of all beings and particularly of man; it is also, as for the Stoics, the support, the bond of union, the physical law and the moral law.

The Logos is not God.[54] Is it a person? What we know of the powers prepares us for the reply: the Logos, the supreme power, has, like the other powers, only a fugitive and vague personality, due above all to our infirmity. To the human mind, too feeble to gaze upon the divine sun, these intermediaries appear as distinct beings, and gradually, by contemplation and worship, the soul rises from one to the other and towards God. But this multiplicity

[52] "God then, in the midst of the two powers which assist Him, presents Himself to the mind which contemplates Him sometimes as one single object, sometimes as three: one only, when the mind is purified, and having gone beyond not only the multiplicity of numbers but also the neighbouring dyad of the monad, approaches the pure idea, simple and perfect in itself; three, when it has not yet been initiated into the great mysteries, and still studies the lesser ones, and when, being unable to grasp the Being by itself and without outside help, it attains to Him in his works, as creating or as governing" (De Abraham, 122). A little later on (131) Philo returns again to this "triple impression produced by one unique subject."

[53] Sometimes also the world is called "the only begotten and well beloved son of God" (De ebriet., 30).

[54] There are in Philo three passages in which, under the influence of the text on which he is commenting, he calls the Logos God: De somniis, I, 228-30; Leg. alleg., III, 207-8; Qu. in Gen., apud Eusebius, Praep. evang., VII, 13. But he is careful in these three passages to weaken the force of the expression, which he considers an improper one. Elsewhere, and with the same reservation, he gives the title of "God" to the world or to the stars.

is only apparent, and if the eye is healthy and the mind strong, and if it can fix its gaze upon the sun without seeing double or triple, then it will see God as He is, in His unity.[55]

Influence of Philo

This theology of Philo has for a long time enjoyed the advantage due to the state of the texts and the privileged situation resulting therefrom. Philo is one of the few survivors of that Jewish world; his isolation has increased his stature, and often to his speculations has been attributed an influence which they did not in fact exercise. The historical studies of the last twenty years have greatly reduced this influence. It was supposed that Philo had greatly influenced neo-Platonism and especially Plotinus;[56] the work of recent historians[57] has dispelled this illusion. In 1903 Loisy wrote: "The influence of Philo's ideas on John is unquestionable," but in 1921: "If there are manifold affinities between the doctrines of our Gospel and those of Philo, the differences are no less considerable, and, moreover, it is not likely that the Johannine gospel depends literally on the Philonian writings."[58] But it was thought that at any rate Philo's exegesis had exercised a great influence on that of St. Justin.[59] A more careful study of Justin, however, has led to the acknowledgment that the writings of the apologist are altogether independent of Philo.[60]

In reality, Philo's influence affected the Alexandrian exegetes, and chiefly Clement and Origen. On these it was considerable and often unfortunate, but outside Alexandria we may seek in vain for any trace of it. Even at Alexandria it affected only the exegetes;

[55] The above outline of the theology of Philo is based on the more complete study in our History of the Dogma of the Trinity, Vol. I, pp. 133-90. The reader will find there a more detailed study of texts and doctrines.

[56] E.g. Guyot, L'infinité divine depuis Philon le Juif jusqu'à Plotin, and Les reminiscences de Philon le Juif chez Plotin, Paris, 1906.

[57] Cf. Wendland, op. cit., p. 210, and above all the works of Bréhier on Philo and Plotinus.

[58] Le quatrième Evangile, 1st edn., p. 154; 2nd edn., p. 88. On this subject cf. our History of the Doctrine of the Trinity, Vol. I, n. vii, The doctrine of the Logos in Philo and St. John, pp. 447-50.

[59] P. Heinisch, Der Einfluss Philos auf die älteste Exegese (Barnabas, Justin und Clemens von Alexandria), Munster, 1908.

[60] Histoire du dogme de la trinité, Vol. II, pp. 663-77. Cf. Harnack, Judentum und Christentum in Justins Dialog. in Texte und Untersuchungen, XXXIX, p. 90.

the biblical texts interpreted by Philo often passed into their works
with the symbolical signification which Philo had given them. In
this way the Philonian theology spread into the books of Clement,
and into some of those of Origen. Pagans left Philo alone, and the
Jews did the same. Jerusalem remained the centre of Judaism until
the destruction of the city, and after that Lydda took its place.
Alexandria never had the same position.[61]

Proselytism

The Diaspora nevertheless played an important part in the
history of the origins of Christianity, not so much because of its
literature, but rather because of its proselytism. In the days of
Jesus, this proselytism was very ardent,[62] and its success considerable.[63]

Scattered throughout the world, the Jews were convinced that
their dispersion was providential: "He hath therefore scattered
you among the Gentiles who know Him not, that you may declare
His wonderful works, and make them know that there is no other
almighty God besides Him" (Tobias xiii, 4). This thought of old
Tobias was familiar to all Jews.[64] Not content to profit by their
dissemination, they "went round about the sea and the land to
make one proselyte" (Matt. xxiii, 15). Every Jew was "convinced
that he is the guide of the blind, a light of them that are in darkness, an instructor of the foolish, a teacher of infants, having the
form of knowledge and of truth in the Law." [65] After the great
catastrophe of A.D. 70 and, above all, in A.D. 134, Judaism, battered
and uprooted, took refuge in isolation. Then one could say that

[61] On Philo's influence, we may quote the very just reflections of Wendland,
Die hellenisch-römische Kultur, p. 210 *et seq.*: "The question of Philo's influence
seems to me to call for revision." He sets out to prove that in Christian literature
only the Alexandrians show a strong Philonian influence, and that so far as neo-
Platonism is concerned, the influence attributed to Philo is unlikely and unproven. This was written in 1912: nowadays the matter is still clearer.

[62] Cf. Schuerer, *op. cit.*, Vol. III, pp. 162-4; Juster, *op. cit.*, Vol. I, p. 253
and n. 11.

[63] On the proselytes, see Schuerer, *op. cit.*, Vol. III, pp. 150-187; Juster, *op. cit.*,
Vol. I, pp. 253-90.

[64] Rabbi Eleazer: "God has dispersed the Jews in order to facilitate proselytism" (*b. Pesachim*, 87*b*, quoted by Juster, *op. cit.*, Vol. I, p. 254, n. O).

[65] *Rom.* ii, 19-20. Already in the second century B.C. the Jewish Sibyl said:
"They (the Jews) will be to all men the guide of life."

proselytism was a disease in Israel: at the time of Jesus it was its glory.[66]

This propaganda so keenly carried on produced results: Josephus could write: "Many (pagans) have adopted our laws; some of them have remained faithful to them, others, lacking in courage, have apostatised." [67]

Courage was indeed required to adhere completely to Judaism and to remain attached to it: one had to adopt the Jewish doctrine, undergo circumcision, receive a baptism, and offer a sacrifice.[68] Of all these obligations, the most onerous was that of circumcision. Many pagans regarded it with repugnance, not only because of the rite itself, but above all because they regarded it as an enrolling in the Jewish nation, and consequently the abandonment of the city to which they had previously belonged. Tacitus echoes this mistrust: "The first instruction given to the circumcised is to despise the gods and to abjure the fatherland, to forget parents, children, brothers." [69]

Judaism was the faith and hope of Israel; one could not adhere to it completely without becoming an Israelite. This nationalist character was a great hindrance to its development and its propaganda. The majority of those who were attracted by the preaching of Jewish doctrines contented themselves with adopting Jewish beliefs, and often Jewish rites as well, but without submitting themselves to circumcision. They formed numerous groups of sympathisers round the synagogues, and were called "those fearing God." The Jews, who understood this repugnance in pagans, contented themselves with this half-adhesion; they knew that the first steps would often lead to others,[70] and they were proud to see the Hellenic world so widely won, almost unconsciously, to Jewish rites and

---

[66] On this change of attitude towards proselytes, cf. Billerbeck, *op. cit.*, Vol. I, pp. 924-31. The description of proselytes as "the lepers of Israel" is attributed to Rabbi Chelbo (about 300), and is quoted many times in the Talmud (*Quiddushin*, 70b; *Jebamoth*, 109b, 47b; *Nidda*, 13b).

[67] *Contra Apion*, II, 10.

[68] Cf. Dobschuetz, *Proselyten*, in *P.R.E.*, XVI, pp. 161-81; M. Friedlaender, *La propagande religieuse des Juifs avant l'ère chrétienne*, in *R.E.J.*, XXX, 1895, pp. 161-81; I. Lévi, *Le prosélytisme juif, ibid.*, L, 1905, pp. 1-9; LI, 1906, pp. 1-31; LIII, 1907, pp. 51-61; Juster, *op. cit.*, Vol. I, p. 255, n. 1.

[69] *History*, V, 5. This repugnance for circumcision was one of the reasons why women were more easily won to Judaism than men.

[70] Cf. the classic text of Juvenal, *Satire*, XIV, 96-106: the father keeps the Sabbath; the son has himself circumcised, despises the Roman laws, and reveres only the Jewish law.

ideas. "The multitude itself," writes Josephus, "is long since in-spired with a great zeal for our pious practices, and there is not a town amongst the Greeks, nor a people amongst the barbarians, where our custom of weekly rest has not spread, and where fasts, the lighting of lamps, and many of our laws concerning food are not observed. . . ."[71]

This wide diffusion of Jewish beliefs and rites very soon led to a sharp reaction,[72] which the national risings of the Jews made still more violent. Christian propaganda by its rapid and profound suc-cess stifled Jewish proselytism; the pagans could adhere to the true religion, and to the worship of the One God, without being compelled to abjure their nation and to enrol themselves in an-other: "There is neither Jew nor Greek, but all are one in Christ Jesus." But we must not forget that Christian propaganda had been prepared by Jewish preaching; the history of the missions of St. Paul shows us that his efforts were first directed to the Jews, the first beneficiaries of the Gospel, and then to the proselytes and those who feared God grouped round the Jews, and lastly to the pagan masses.[73] To Israel, the missionary people, God had offered through the prophets, and especially through Isaias, the magnificent work of conquering the world for God. Israel was too passionately jealous of its national greatness, had lost sight of its religious function and had fallen from it.[74] The proselytism of the dispersed Jews on the eve of the Christian era may be regarded as a rough attempt at this conquest: the task abandoned by Israel was confided to the Church.

[71] Contra Apion, II, 39, 282. Seneca, quoted by St. Augustine, De Civitate Dei, VI, 10-11, writes of the Jews: "Usque eo sceleratissimae gentis consuetudo valuit, ut per omnes jam terras recepta sit. . . . Illi tamen causas ritus sui noverunt; major pars populi facit quod cur faciat ignorat."

[72] Cf. Wendland, op. cit., p. 195 and n. 4. There was at this time a whole anti-Jewish literature (Schuerer, op. cit., Vol. III, pp. 528-45), and the anti-Semitic riots at Alexandria show that the people gladly sided against the Jews.

[73] Wendland, op. cit., p. 211, rightly notes the indefensible exaggeration of E. Havet (Le christianisme et ses origines, Vol. IV, p. 102, Paris, 1884), ac-cording to whom St. Paul converted no Pagan who had not already been affected by Jewish propaganda. Cf. Harnack, Mission und Ausbreitung, p. 59 and n. 3.

[74] This failure of Israel is one of the main themes in the preaching of Jesus.

CHAPTER I

JESUS CHRIST AND THE BEGINNING OF THE CHURCH[1]

Christ in History

WHEN St. Paul was a prisoner at Cæsarea in the year A.D. 60 and expounded to King Agrippa the mission of Jesus and his own Apostolate, he was able to say: "The king knoweth of these things, to whom also I speak with confidence. For I am persuaded that none of these things are hidden from him. For neither was any of these things done in a corner" (*Acts* xxvi, 26). All historians share this assurance: the life and death of Jesus, the beginnings of the Church at Jerusalem, the travels and preaching of St. Paul—all this is clear to us in the full light of history.

Born "in the days of Herod the king," put to death, as Tacitus records,[2] by the procurator Pontius Pilate, baptised by John, condemned by Annas and Caiphas, Jesus lived and preached in Judea in a period well known to us, and came up against those procurators, tetrarchs and high priests of whom we have written in the preceding chapter, utilising Josephus, Philo, and pagan historians. From the short life of Jesus the Church was born. Full of life and vigour, it flourished in Jerusalem, in Judea, then in Syria, and then in the whole Greco-Roman world. In A.D. 51, the proconsul of Achaia, Gallio, brother to Seneca, saw it spreading round him at

[1] Bibliography.—On this subject there is an immense bibliography. We confine ourselves to indicating the works which seem to us to be the most useful: L. de Grandmaison, *Jesus Christ*, Eng. tr. in 3 vols.; M. J. Lagrange, *The Gospel of Jesus Christ*, Eng. tr., London, 1938; J. Lebreton, *The Life and Teaching of Jesus Christ*, Eng. tr. in 2 vols.; F. Prat, *Jésus Christ, Sa vie, sa doctrine, son œuvre*, Paris, 1933, 2 vols.; A. Goodier, *The Public Life of Our Lord Jesus Christ*, London, 1931, 2 vols.; J. Sickenberger, *Leben Jesu nach den vier Evangelien, Kurzgefasste Erklärung*, Münster, 1932. These are Catholic works. Amongst non-Catholic works we may mention: A. C. Headlam, *Life and Teaching of Jesus the Christ*, 2nd edn., London 1927 (Anglican); M. Goguel, *La vie de Jésus*, Paris, 1932 (Liberal Protestant); J. Klausner, *Jésus de Nazareth*, Paris, 1933, translated from the Hebrew original published at Jerusalem in 1922 (Jewish); A. Loisy, *La naissance du christianisme*, Paris, 1933 (radical critic); C. Guignebert, *Jésus*, Paris, 1933 (*id.*). A history of the subject in the nineteenth century and the first years of the twentieth will be found in A. Schweitzer, *Geschichte der Leben Jesu Forschung*, Tübingen, 1931.

[2] *Annals*, III, 15, 44.

Corinth; in A.D. 64 Nero's persecution at Rome affected, according to Tacitus,[3] a "great multitude." That was only thirty-five years after the death of Jesus. All this has not the appearance of a dream, in an imaginary setting; all "takes its place in an historical setting of unquestioned continuity."[4]

The Gospels

These great events live again for us in writings in which we hear the voice of the primitive church and its leaders—the *Gospels, Epistles,* and *Acts.* That becomes apparent to us on the threshold of this history in the study of the life of Jesus. The Gospels are not just literary works which have resulted from the initiative of a few writers; they are not books created by the authors whose names they bear, Matthew, Mark, Luke, or even John: they are catecheses taught for some time previously, and finally put in writing.[5]

Certainly, these books bear the individual impress of the witnesses who have drawn them up or on whom they depend: in Matthew we recognise the Apostle of the Jews converted to Christianity, stressing the prophecies of the Old Testament, showing in the Gospel the fulfilment of the Law, warning the disciples against the leaven of the Pharisees. Mark is the interpreter of Peter, and this gives to his Gospel the freshness and charm of Galilean memories; Luke, the companion of St. Paul, did not know the Lord personally, but as a diligent historian he profited by his lengthy stay at Cæsarea to question the disciples of Jesus and to gather recollections of his infancy from Mary.[6] Of all the evangelists, John has most deeply impressed his own personality on his book. We shall describe it later on.[7]

These individual characteristics give to the witness of the evan-

[3] *Loc. cit.*

[4] L. de Grandmaison, *Jesus Christ,* Eng. tr., Vol. I, p. 4.

[5] These ideas are developed more at length in *The Life and Teaching of Jesus Christ,* Vol. I, pp. xiii *et seq.*

[6] How were these recollections transmitted to the evangelist? Orally or by writing? The question is a disputed one, and is of little importance to us here. Cf. *Life and Teaching of Jesus,* Vol. I, p. 4.

[7] *Infra,* ch. v. sec. 2. On the characteristics and origin of our four Gospels, cf. L. de Grandmaison, *Jesus Christ,* Eng. tr., Vol. I, pp. 56-190; Huby, *L'Évangile et les Evangiles,* 1929. The Gospel of St. Luke is earlier than the *Acts,* which most probably date to the end of St. Paul's captivity, about A.D. 63. The two other synoptic gospels are prior to Luke; the Gospel of St. John belongs to the very last years of the first century.

gelists a character which makes them nearer to us, and more persuasive. But at the same time, the testimony which these books bring us is above all the testimony of the Church. From the very first, this witness is presented as a collective one: it is not a number of isolated individuals but the entire group of Apostles who narrate the life and teaching of the Master whom they followed during the whole course of His public life and even after His death, until His Ascension. In one of His last appearances, Jesus had said to them: "You shall be witnesses to me"; this testimony, given in all fidelity and freedom, was their first duty, and to the Jewish magistrates who sought to impose silence upon them, they replied through Peter, their head and spokesman, "We cannot but speak the things which we have seen and heard" (*Acts* iv, 20; cf., v. 29).

The Witness of the Church

It was from this daily preaching by the Church that the Gospel arose, and its character and guarantee come from the same source. Its aim was not to satisfy the curiosity of its readers, but to uphold the faith of the believers. Towards the end of his gospel, St. John writes (xx, 30-31): "Many other signs also did Jesus in the sight of his disciples, which are not written in this book, but these are written that you may believe that Jesus is the Christ, the Son of God, and that believing you may have life in His name." The other evangelists have the same aim: the good news which they bring is salvation; their whole aim is to bring out the person of the Saviour, His teaching and His redemptive work.

The Church, then, did not aim at giving us a complete account of the life of Christ which would enable us to study and date all its development; in endeavouring to understand and interpret its testimony, we must respect its nature, and see in it a document of religious history rather than a biography of Jesus; its lacunæ must not surprise us, nor the difficulty which we often find in localising the incidents, or marking their date or succession.[8]

[8] We have set forth elsewhere (*Life and Teaching of Jesus Christ,* Vol. I, pp. xxii-xxxii) the chief chronological problems presented by the life of Christ. We will not reproduce the discussion here, but will recall the conclusions. As we have said above (p. 25, n. 2), the Christian era was fixed by Dionysius Exiguus a few years too late. Jesus was born at the latest in the year 5 B.C., and most probably in 7 or 8 B.C. The preaching of John the Baptist probably began in the autumn of A.D. 27; the baptism of Jesus a few months later; at the Pasch of A.D. 28 Jesus was at Jerusalem and expelled the merchants from the Temple. After a

On the other hand, this religious character of the testimony provides us with the most certain guarantee of its fidelity. It was by contemplating the miracles of Jesus that the first disciples were converted (*John* ii, 11); it was by hearing them or reading their account that the new Christians came in their turn to the Faith. The office of an Apostle was thus that of a faithful witness, attesting what he had seen, heard, and touched, and by his testimony putting his catechumens in contact with Christ. If the facts which he reported were not true, his witness would be a lie, and the faith of his converts would be vain.[9]

The Forerunner

In this Judea, invaded by so many foreigners, oppressed by so many tyrants, and in which the Jews themselves were so divided, and for the most part so little prepared for the Kingdom of God, a voice suddenly made itself heard in the desert: "Repent, for the kingdom of God is at hand" (*Matt.* iii, 2).

For a long time the words of the psalmist had been sadly repeated: "There is now no prophet" (*Ps.* lxxiii, 9). God remained silent, and the Messias held back. But now at last a prophet appeared in Israel: John. Who was he? No one knew; but his voice was so powerful, and he spoke with such authority that people asked themselves whether he was not indeed himself the Messias.

---

few weeks spent in Judea, Jesus went through Samaria and returned to Galilee; He preached there, gathered Apostles round Him, and sent them on a mission in the year A.D. 29. Just before the Pasch of A.D. 29 there took place the first multiplication of the loaves; a little after, Jesus went up to Jerusalem for the Pasch or the Pentecost, and there cured the paralytic in the pool of Bezatha. He returned to Galilee, passed through Phœnicia and the Decapolis, and went on to Cæsarea Philippi. Eight days after the event at Cæsarea, the Transfiguration took place; shortly afterwards Jesus finally left Galilee. In October He was at Jerusalem for the Feast of Tabernacles; in December He was there again for the Feast of the Dedication. In March A.D. 30 He raised Lazarus, withdrew to Ephrem, and then returned to Jerusalem by Jericho. He was put to death there on Friday the 14th Nisan, the great day of the Pasch. According to the foregoing chronological data, this 14th Nisan must have been April 7th in the year A.D. 30. A careful and detailed discussion of all these questions will be found in the work of U. Holzmeister, *Chronologia vitæ Christi*, Rome, 1933.

[9] We may recall the insistence with which St. Paul affirms his responsibility as a witness: "If Christ be not risen again, then is our preaching vain, and your faith is also vain. Yea, and we are found false witnesses of God, because we have given testimony against God, that he hath raised up Christ, whom he hath not raised up" (*I Cor.* xv, 14-15).

He denied this: "I am not worthy to loose the latchet of the shoes of the Messias." John was but a voice, the voice of the forerunner crying in the desert: "Prepare ye the way of the Lord."

All Israel was roused by this cry: towards the Jordan, where John was preaching, there came "all Judea and all they of Jerusalem" (*Mark* i, 5). The new Elias who appeared before them impressed them first by his austerity: he came from the desert, he had retained its vesture and food: he was clothed with a garment of camel's hair and a leathern girdle, he fed on locusts and wild honey. But though strict with himself, he imposed his asceticism on no one else. But he was merciless towards the Jewish pride of race, and the illusions to which it had given rise: "Do not begin to say 'We have Abraham for our Father.' For I say unto you that God is able of these stones to raise up children to Abraham. For now the axe is laid to the root of the trees. Every tree therefore that bringeth not forth good fruit, shall be cut down and cast into the fire." The people then asked him "What shall we do?" He answered: "He that hath two coats, let him give to him that hath none." Publicans and soldiers came to him: he did not tell them to renounce their profession, but only that they were to respect justice.

Those whom his words had touched confessed their sins and received from him a baptism of penitence which prepared them for the kingdom of God. The most zealous became his disciples, sharing his life and learning from him how to pray and to fast.

This religious activity did not last a year; [10] but it left a very deep and enduring impression. Two years later, in the last days of the life of Jesus, the Pharisees did not dare to maintain that John's baptism was from man, and not from God; "If we say so, the whole people will stone us" (*Luke* xx, 6). The story of Apollos and the Johannites of Ephesus (*Acts* xviii, 24; xix, 7) shows that John's influence persisted for long after his death, and extended to people who knew nothing of Christianity. [11]

This powerful movement which took place at the beginning of

[10] John's preaching began in the fifteenth year of Tiberius, shortly before the baptism of Jesus (*Luke* iii, 1). Three or four months after this baptism, John was thrown into prison (*Matt.* iv, 12).

[11] The insistence with which the apostolic preaching points out John's office as forerunner and witness to Jesus (*Acts* xiii, 25; *John* i, 8, 20, 26-7) shows the danger still present at that date, at least in certain circles, of recognising John only and of forgetting Jesus. Already in John's lifetime the jealousy of some of his disciples was a forecast of this danger (*John* iii, 26).

Christianity was directed by John towards Jesus: he himself was the Forerunner, and wanted to be only that.[12] This praiseworthy unselfishness was manifested, as we have seen, in the preaching of the Baptist; it was still more manifest when Jesus came back to the Jordan and John gave decisive testimony to Him, and transferred to Him his best disciples.

The Baptism of Jesus

Amongst the crowd which pressed around him, John noticed one day a man whom he knew not, but whose holiness struck him at once. This was Jesus of Nazareth: "I ought to be baptised by thee, and comest thou to me?" the Baptist cried. Jesus answered: "Suffer it to be so now. For so it becometh us to fulfil all justice." John gave way; Jesus went down into the water, and received baptism. As He came out of the water, He saw the heavens open, and the Spirit descend on Him as a dove, and a voice from heaven was heard, saying: "Thou art my beloved Son, in thee I am well pleased" (Mark i, 10-11).

This divine manifestation was the first public revelation of Jesus. Born of the Virgin Mary at Bethlehem, worshipped by a few shepherds, by Simeon and Anna in the Temple, and by the Magi, our Lord was, after a short exile in Egypt, taken while still quite a child by Joseph and Mary to Nazareth. It was there He had grown up, and yet no one in the little town or even amongst His relatives had divined the mystery known only to Mary and Joseph. In the eyes of all He was a carpenter and the son of a carpenter: that was all that was known of Him. Now He was thirty years old. He was about to begin His public ministry; the Heavenly Father bestowed His testimony upon his beloved Son, the object of His good pleasure, and the Holy Spirit descended visibly upon Him.

This revelation, like the most important manifestations in the life of Jesus,[13] was perceived only by a few witnesses.[14] The first to be enlightened was the Forerunner: "I knew him not," he says

---

[12] Such was the office which the Archangel Gabriel gave to John in his message to Zachary (Luke i, 17), and Zachary himself in his Canticle (Luke i, 76).

[13] Thus the Transfiguration had only three witnesses, and was kept secret until the death and resurrection of Jesus (Mark ix, 9). The Resurrection itself was witnessed not by the whole people but by those whom God had chosen beforehand (Acts x, 41).

[14] Cf. Life and Teaching of Jesus Christ, Vol. I, p. 44.

soon afterwards, "but he who sent me to baptise with water, said to me: 'He upon whom thou shalt see the Spirit descending, and remaining upon him, he it is that baptiseth with the Holy Ghost.' And I saw, and I gave testimony, that this is the Son of God" (*John* i, 33-34).

But it was above all to Jesus Himself that the voice was addressed; the well-beloved Son experienced the infinite sweetness of the good pleasure of His Father; He also felt the force of the Spirit which descended upon Him and sent Him forth upon His mission.

The Temptation

It was to the desert first of all that the Holy Spirit led Jesus. On the wild slopes which descend from the plateau of Judea towards the deep valley of the Jordan, alone amongst the animals, Christ passed forty days and forty nights in prayer and fasting. After these forty days of fast, He was hungry; the tempter approaching said to Him: "If thou be the Son of God, command that these stones be made bread." "Not in bread alone doth man live," Jesus replied, "but in every word that proceedeth from the mouth of God." Then the devil took Him up into the holy city, and set Him upon the pinnacle of the Temple, and said to Him: "If thou be the Son of God, cast thyself down, for it is written, 'He hath given his angels charge over thee, and in their hands shall they bear thee up, lest perhaps thou dash thy foot against a stone.' " Jesus said to him: "It is written again: 'Thou shalt not tempt the Lord thy God.' " Again the devil took Him up into a very high mountain, and showed Him all the kingdoms of the world, and the glory of them, and said to Him: "All these will I give thee, if falling down thou wilt adore me." Then Jesus saith to Him: "Begone, Satan, for it is written: 'The Lord thy God shalt thou adore, and him only shalt thou serve.' " Then the devil left Him, and angels came and ministered to Him (*Matthew* iv, 2-11).

This temptation had no other witness besides Jesus, and if He narrated it to His disciples it must have been because He regarded it as an instruction, and for the same reason the evangelists have narrated it with such care. For the incident is, as it were, a prologue to the Gospel history, and, we might even say, to the whole history of the Church. The battle fought by Christ and Christians "is not against flesh and blood, but against principalities and powers, against the rulers of the world of this darkness, against the spirits of wickedness in the high places" (*Ephes.* vi, 12). We also gather from this first conflict to what end the efforts of Satan are going to be directed: to the spiritual kingdom of God, which Jesus has come to institute, the tempter opposes a kingdom altogether earthly, a banquet, a universal domination, accompanied by brilliant prodigies. Jesus could not be led astray by these dreams, but did not His hearers, and the Apostles themselves, run the risk of being deceived by them? The history of Christ's ministry, His successes, brilliant indeed but fragile also until His death, His failures, and lastly, the supreme crisis of His Passion, bring out with painful evidence the danger of these temptations. Jesus triumphed over them finally only by His death.

The First Disciples

John the Baptist, doubtless because of the threat involved in the ill will of the Jews of Jerusalem, had passed over the Eastern bank of the Jordan into Perea, and was baptising at Bethany. Jesus went there. John said, when he perceived him: "Behold the Lamb of God, who taketh away the sins of the world!" The next day there was a similar meeting, and the same testimony. There stood close to John two of his disciples, John [15] and Andrew; moved by the testimony of the Baptist, they left him and followed Jesus. The next day, Andrew took his brother Simon to Jesus, who called him Peter, and the day after that Philip was won, and he brought Nathaniel in his turn.[16] This first call by Christ is narrated by the evangelist St. John with a charming freshness of memory. The historian also finds this of great interest: in reading it he gets a better understanding of the second calling on the borders of the lake: those whom Jesus then called finally belonged to Him already; when the time came, He took them away from their families and their boats: they were now His men. This first calling also brings out the importance of the office of the Forerunner: six [17] of

[15] Here, as in all his gospel, John does not name himself, but he describes himself sufficiently clearly.

[16] Nathaniel was from Cana in Galilee; he bears this name only in St. John's Gospel (i, 47, and xxi, 2). He is identified with great probability with the Apostle Bartholomew.

[17] James the son of Zebedee is not named in the account in St. John, who is always reserved where his own person or family is concerned; but it is very likely that the two brothers were together then as always.

the twelve Apostles, and these the most important, were chosen by
Jesus from the group of the disciples of the Baptist, and the first
invitation was given by John the Baptist himself: from that day
his whole delight was to see Jesus increase, and himself decrease
(*John* iii, 30).

Christ's Ministry, and Its Aim

Near the Jordan, Jesus called his first disciples, and it was then
that He began to preach and to act. A problem here presents itself
to the historian: did Jesus have a clearly defined plan, and did He
follow this in his public ministry?

One feature of this plan is manifest, and very clearly marked:
until His death, Jesus limited His ministry to the children of
Israel;[18] pressed by the Canaanite woman, He put her off, saying:
"I was not sent but to the sheep that are lost of the house of
Israel" (*Matt.* xv, 24). He had already laid down the same limits
when sending the Apostles on their mission: "Go ye not into the
way of the Gentiles, and into the city of the Samaritans enter ye
not. But go ye rather to the lost sheep of the house of Israel"
(*Matt.* x, 5-6). We have already remarked when describing the
state of Palestine in the time of Christ that these pagan and
Samaritan towns were scattered all over the land of Israel, and if
any did not enter them, it was because they intended to avoid
them.

This reserve appears still more clearly in the exceptions which it
allowed, and which were granted only for pressing reasons. The
centurion of Capharnaum did not dare to go to Jesus himself, but
had his request presented by Jews, who recommended him as a
benefactor of their nation: "He is worthy that thou shouldst
do this for him, for he loveth our nation, and he hath built us a
synagogue" (*Luke* vii, 5).

The Canaanite woman, at first sent away by the Apostles and
put off by Jesus, obtained only by her persistence the miracle which
she sought (*Matt.* xv). The Greeks who came to Jerusalem for the
Pasch and who wanted to see Jesus, did not dare to accost him
directly; they timidly expressed their desire to Philip, "who was of

---

[18] Cf. J. Lebreton, *Des origines de la mission chrétienne*, in *Histoire générale
comparée des Missions* of Baron Descamps, Brussels, 1932, pp. 15-103, especially
pp. 52 *et seq.*

Bethsaida of Galilee"; Philip told Andrew, and the two presented the request to Jesus (*John* xii, 20-22).

Doubtless this reserve was not absolute or final. Jesus already made this understood in connection with the incidents we have just recalled. To the Greeks He replied by this prophecy: "The hour is come that the Son of man should be glorified. Amen, amen I say to you, unless the grain of wheat falling into the ground die, itself remaineth alone. But if it die, it bringeth forth much fruit. . . . And I, if I be lifted up from the world, will draw all men to myself." [19] This universal fecundity was promised to Christ's ministry, but was gathered to Him only by His death. The grain of wheat had to fall to the ground and die; Jesus had to be lifted up on the cross. After His Passion, all the barriers fell down, and there was no limit to the mission of the Apostles: "All power is given to me in heaven and in earth. Going therefore teach ye all nations. . . ." (*Matt.* xxviii, 18-20).[20]

This triumphant expansion will be set forth in the history of the Apostles. We shall then point out that it was the will of Jesus which sent them through the world, and that it was His death which secured the wonderful fruitfulness of their activity. But during the two and a half years of the Lord's ministry,[21] the Jews alone, with a few very rare exceptions, were the hearers of His discourses and the beneficiaries of His miracles.

This feature of Christ's mission being understood, can we go further, and discover in His ministry to the Jews a plan drawn up in advance and followed out by Him? If we study the gospel narratives, and especially the earliest, this plan is not evident at first sight: we rather have the impression of a series of preachings and miracles, arising out of chance circumstances or rather Divine Providence, but not at all due to a deliberate plan, tracing out a

---

[19] *John* xii, 23-32. The same perspective appears in the other episodes mentioned above. Thus to the Canaanite woman Christ says, "Suffer first the children to be filled," which implies that after them the pagans will have their turn. And in connection with the centurion of Capharnaum: "Amen, I say to you, I have not found so great faith in Israel. And I say to you that many shall come from the east and the west, and shall sit down with Abraham and Isaac and Jacob in the kingdom of heaven, but the children of the kingdom shall be cast out into the exterior darkness" (*Matt.* xiii, 10-12).

[20] On the universal expansion of Christianity and Jesus' intention on this point, cf. M. Meinertz, *Jesus und die Heidenmission*, 2nd edn., Münster, 1925.

[21] On the length of Our Lord's ministry, see E. F. Sutcliffe, S. J., *A Two-Year Public Ministry*, Burns & Oates, 1939, 7s. 6d. (note by translator).

path mapped out by Jesus from the beginning. The evangelisation of Galilee by Christ and His Apostles would rather resemble the preaching of the first disciples of St. Francis through Italy and the world.

But a more careful reading leads us to see that this first impression is due above all to the manner of composition of the early Christian catechesis, which cared little for chronology, and was much more attentive to the religious import of each episode than to the connection or progress of the different phases in the ministry of Jesus. We very soon note another cause of this apparent confusion: the plan foreseen and adopted by Jesus may indeed be little evident in the early narratives, but it was in Christ's own lifetime upset and broken by the constant opposition of His enemies. The reading of St. John enables us to reconstitute the original plan of the Master, at least in its main outline: He aimed at the conquest of Israel, and primarily of Jerusalem the capital, the Holy City, whose adhesion or opposition would be decisive. This plan, adopted at the beginning and returned to several times in spite of an obstinate opposition, finally collapsed before the irreducible hostility of the Jews and especially of their leaders. And then another plan appeared: Israel had not been won, and it would not be as a whole the missionary people it should have been, but from it Jesus would draw a faithful élite, the little group of Apostles and disciples which would form the hierarchy of the Church and would conquer the world.

Jesus at Jerusalem and in Judea

Leaving the Jordan, Jesus returned to Galilee; it was only a short journey to Cana or Capharnaum. When the Pasch came round He went up to Jerusalem and there made His first effort. After His resurrection, He was to instruct His Apostles to remain at Jerusalem and there wait for the descent of the Holy Ghost (Acts i, 4), and these Galileans, whom nothing called to Jerusalem, would indeed stay there, obedient to the will of the Master, and conscious of the object in view: Jerusalem was the religious centre of Israel, and everything depended on it. Jesus knew that from the first, and accordingly went there, and the blow that He struck re-echoed through all Jewry: in the midst of the feast of the Pasch, in the sight of all the pilgrims, He expelled the merchants from the

Temple.[22] His most striking miracles were usually brought about by external circumstances, the supplications of the sick, or the needs of the people. But the expulsion of the merchants was a spontaneous act of authority and of religion. As Messias and Son of God, Jesus was jealous for the holiness of the Temple: "The zeal of thy house hath eaten me up"; this sacred oracle (*Psalm* lxix, 10) came back to the memory of the disciples, and it reveals indeed the sentiment which inspired Jesus; during the long years of His hidden life He had suffered this scandal in silence, now He acted authoritatively, as Messias.

During these feasts He performed miracles; many Jews were astonished at them, and believed in Him, but with a fragile faith. Jesus was not deceived: "he knew what was in man" (*John* ii, 25). The crowds at Jerusalem appeared in this first contact what they were to remain until Jesus' death: impressionable, rapidly won by the miracles or the words of the Master, but giving Him only a precarious and timid adhesion, shaken by the least incident, and disturbed by the opposition of their leaders.

These leaders were chiefly the Pharisees, who "sat in the seat of Moses." They imposed their authority upon the people, and each one watched the others. These "companions," as they called themselves, were, as it were, chained together. Christ could say to them: "How can you believe, who receive glory from one another, and the glory which is from God alone you do not seek?" (*John* v, 44).

During this first stay of Jesus at Jerusalem, one of these masters of Israel, Nicodemus, came to find Him, but at night-time, in secrecy. Jesus had a long conversation with him. From the outset, He taught him that to see the Kingdom of God a rebirth is necessary: these are spiritual things which can be understood only by those who are born of the spirit.

Nicodemus became a faithful disciple of Christ (*John* vii, 50, xix, 39). At his first visit he appears to have been timid, and to have remained such even when he intervened in the Sanhedrin in favour of Jesus, but the death of the Master strengthened his courage, and he followed his Lord to the tomb.

This gives us an example of something which appears rarely in

[22] This purification of the Temple is referred by the Synoptics to the last week in the life of Jesus; St. John, on the other hand, puts it at the very beginning of the public ministry. It is in that period that we must place it, and it does not seem necessary to admit a twofold purification. Cf. *Life and Teaching of Jesus Christ*, Vol. I, p. 54 n.

the evangelical narrative: individual conversions. There were in particular at Jerusalem some isolated disciples, sometimes unknown to the Apostles themselves, as seems to have been the case with the master of the house in which the Last Supper was celebrated (*Mark* xix, 13). The timidity of these converts and the discretion of the Master are easily understandable when we remember that during the last months of the life of Jesus, anyone who confessed to being His disciple was put under the ban of the synagogue.

We are still in the first weeks of the Ministry of Jesus. At this date the persecution has not yet broken out, but it can be foreseen. The Master had to leave Jerusalem, but at first He remained in Judea (*John* iii, 22). He preached, His disciples baptised, and soon the concourse of people round Him was so great that there was consternation in those who followed John the Baptist: "Rabbi, he that was with thee beyond the Jordan, to whom thou gavest testimony, behold he baptiseth, and all men come to him." But the Forerunner was incapable of jealousy: "You yourselves do bear me witness that I said 'I am not the Christ, but that I am sent before him.' He that hath the bride is the bridegroom: but the friend of the bridegroom, who standeth and heareth him, rejoiceth with joy because of the bridegroom's voice. This my joy therefore is fulfilled. He must increase, but I must decrease" (*John* iii, 28-30).

This testimony, so full of humility and love, was the last homage given by John to Jesus, the last gleam of the one who had been "a bright and shining light," whom imprisonment was to conceal, and soon death would extinguish. Herod Antipas, whom he rebuked for his adulterous union with Herodias, caused him to be arrested and imprisoned in the dungeons of Machaerus. Jesus himself felt no longer safe: He knew that the Pharisees were alarmed at the success of His preaching: they were saying that He had made more disciples even than John had made. He accordingly departed from Judea, and went through Samaria back to Galilee.

Thus this first attempt to gain the heart of Judaism failed: Jesus' preaching and His miracles attracted and moved many of the Jews, but the majority had only a wavering faith which could not resist the pressure of the Pharisees. Christ indeed did not abandon either Jerusalem or Judea for ever; more than once He would again essay to convert them, but then He would no longer be alone or surrounded by just a handful of disciples: He would be supported by all those whom He had won in Galilee, and who were gathered round Him at Jerusalem on the occasion of the great festivals of Tabernacles, the Dedication, and the Pasch. It was above all during the last six months of His life that Jesus was to make these decisive efforts, but even then He did not succeed in gathering and retaining around Him the children of Jerusalem as a hen gathers its chickens under its wings.

Jesus in Galilee

Galilee was to be for more than a year [23] the centre of the ministry of Jesus; his action there could not have on the whole of Judaism the influence which it would have had at Jerusalem, but it was less opposed there. Though the Pharisees were numerous in Galilee as everywhere in Palestine, they were not so strongly organised as at Jerusalem, where the Sanhedrin extended over the teaching in the synagogues and on the whole of religious life a daily supervision which very soon became tyrannical. The Sadducees, who had to take the initiative and the direction of the judicial steps against Jesus, were powerful at Jerusalem, but outside Judea had only a distant and occasional influence. The population of Galilee, less confined than that of Jerusalem, less involved in political intrigues, was more rustic and more violent, but more straightforward and more simple. When we remember the timid *démarche* of Nicodemus coming in the night time to find Jesus, and compare him with the immense crowds of people pressing to hear the Sermon on the Mount, or following Jesus into the desert, we realise that the Gospel, which the atmosphere of Jerusalem threatened to stifle, could expand freely in the fields of Galilee.

Very soon, nevertheless, this development, so full of promise, was to be hindered, and then crushed: that would be the work of emissaries from Jerusalem, but their tactics would meet with ample support from the passions of the Galilean crowds. In this frontier province, the Jews had been compelled in the time of Simon the

[23] According to the chronology we have set forth above (p. 85, n. 8) Jesus received the baptism of John in the first days of A.D. 28; after the forty days passed in the desert He returned to the Jordan, and after a short stay at Cana and Capharnaum, He went up to Jerusalem for the Pasch; He remained only a few weeks in Judea. In May He passed through Samaria and went to Galilee; He remained there during the whole of the following year. (But see Fr. Sutcliffe's work mentioned on p. 92, n. 21—Tr.)

Machabee to give place to the pagans and to leave the country; they returned in force and endeavoured to regain the mastery. Towards this end all their forces were directed. "Surrounded by so many foreign races," writes Josephus,[24] "they have to keep a perpetual look-out; they are warlike from their childhood." In Galilee more than elsewhere the preaching of the Kingdom of God ran the risk of arousing a nationalist echo which would give it a wrong direction. We shall not be surprised to see the Galileans after the first multiplication of the loaves, trying to put Jesus at their head and to make him king. Jesus withdrew from their homage, and their spirits were so sadly disillusioned by this fact that for the most part their faith vanished with their dreams.

This great crisis came about towards the Pasch of the year 29, and was a foretaste of the very similar but decisive defection which was to follow the triumphal entry in Jerusalem, and would end on Calvary.

Jesus had all this future before His eyes when He began to pass through the country of Galilee, preaching, healing and converting. He knew well that His work would be that of a sower, and that the seed would fall to the ground and die there, but He also knew that it would germinate, and that the Apostles would gather up the fruits.

The Preaching of the Kingdom of God

He preached. In the early days, He took up the theme constantly developed by John the Baptist: "Repent, for the Kingdom of Heaven is at hand" (*Matt.* iv, 17), but to this He added the decisive words: "The time is accomplished" (*Mark* i, 15). This cry had been awaited long since with a great and ardent desire, and often with a fever which could soon be exalted and impatient, but could equally speedily be discouraged. It should have been welcomed with enthusiasm, but on the contrary, it was hardly believed. The news was too good to be true, and then again, the Kingdom of Heaven did not change everything as one had hoped, but it mingled itself with and became one with one's daily life. The seed is put in the ground and will germinate there; the leaven is mixed with the paste and will make it rise, but this activity is still invisible: faith alone can detect it, illumined by the words of

[24] *Wars of the Jews*, III, 3, 2, 42.

Jesus. And so people hesitated to believe in it. Much later, towards the end of the Lord's ministry, this unbelief was to show itself in an incident narrated by St. Luke (xvii, 20-21): "Being asked by the Pharisees when the Kingdom of God should come, He answered them and said: 'The Kingdom of God cometh not with observation; neither shall they say: Behold here, or behold there. For lo, the Kingdom of God is amongst you.'"

Those who were the most ready to receive this modest preaching of a humble and gentle Messias were the little ones and the poor: "I thank thee, Father, Lord of heaven and earth, because thou hast hidden these things from the wise and prudent, and hast revealed them to little ones. Yea, Father, for so it hath seemed good in thy sight" (*Luke* x, 21). But these privileged ones, these little ones, themselves understood only imperfectly their good fortune. Jesus had to emphasise it: "Turning to his disciples, he said, 'Blessed are the eyes that see the things which you see. For I say to you, that many prophets and kings have desired to see the things that you see and have not seen them, and to hear the things that you hear and have not heard them'" (*ibid.*, 23-24). The Apostles themselves would arrive only gradually at a deeper understanding of the words of Jesus as the Holy Ghost recalled these words to them and revealed their meaning (*John* xiv, 26), and the whole Church would have to meditate upon our Lord's teaching until the last day, in order gradually to penetrate its mystery.

The Apostles

We have just mentioned the Apostles. From the commencement of the preaching in Galilee, Jesus called them to Him and attached them to His mission:

"Passing by the sea of Galilee, he saw Simon and Andrew his brother, casting nets into the sea (for they were fishermen). And Jesus said to them: Come after me, and I will make you to become fishers of men. And immediately leaving their nets they followed him. And going on from thence a little farther, he saw James the son of Zebedee, and John his brother, who also were mending their nets in the ship. And forthwith he called them. And leaving their father Zebedee in the ship with his hired men, they followed him" (*Mark* i, 16-20).

After this first group of four Apostles, eight others were called: Philip, Bartholomew, Thomas and Matthew, James the son of

Alphaeus, Lebbaeus, Simon, and Judas Iscariot. This list is given four times in the New Testament.[25] Judas Iscariot is always the last to be named, and St. Peter always the first. St. Matthew says expressly: "The names of the twelve apostles are these: the first, Simon who is called Peter. . . ."

This choice came from the free initiative of Christ: "He called unto him whom he would himself" (*Mark* iii, 13). On the last day of his life, Jesus reminded them of this: "You have not chosen me, but I have chosen you" (*John* xv, 16). He chose twelve, because they were to evangelise the twelve tribes of Israel, and to judge them on the last day (*Matt.* x, 28). The first mission of the Apostles, as we have already said, was only to Israel, like the preaching of Jesus Himself; but later on the Twelve were to be sent to "all nations," and St. John contemplates in heaven, together with the elect of the twelve tribes, "a great multitude which no man could number, of all nations and tribes and peoples and tongues" (*Apoc.* vii, 9).

From the beginnings of the ministry of Jesus, these twelve Apostles chosen by Him, grouped around Him and constantly following Him, already warn us of His design: the foundation of the Church, a visible and hierarchical society, of which they will be the heads and the pastors, and at their head "the first, Simon, who is called Peter." This design becomes more precise and determined as time goes on: when Our Lord preaches in parables, the Apostles are the only recipients of an interpretation which the multitude does not hear, and this they are later on to make known to all, crying on the housetops what was whispered into their ears. Then we have their first mission: they go forth in twos, preaching the kingdom of God, healing the sick, raising the dead, cleansing the lepers, casting out devils (*Matt.* x, 7). Next we have at Cæsarea Philippi the confession of St. Peter, and the reply of Christ conferring upon him the primacy:

"Blessed art thou, Simon Bar-Jona: because flesh and blood hath not revealed it to thee, but my Father who is in heaven. And I say to thee: That thou art Peter; and upon this rock I will build my church, and the gates of hell shall not prevail against it. And I will give to thee the

[25] *Matt.* x, 2-4; *Mark* iii, 16-19; *Luke* vi, 14-16; *Acts* i, 13. This list can be analysed into three groups of four Apostles; in each group the first name is always the same. The three others are always found in the same group, but the order is not constant.

keys of the kingdom of heaven. And whatsoever thou shalt bind upon earth, it shall be bound also in heaven: and whatsoever thou shalt loose on earth, it shall be loosed also in heaven" (*Matt.* xvi, 17-19).[26]

Then the other Apostles, in their turn, receive the power of binding and loosing (*Matt.* xviii, 18), and at the Last Supper they will be given the power to consecrate the body of Christ (*Luke* xxii, 19). After His resurrection, Jesus will confirm all these privileges, saying to the Apostles: "Receive the Holy Ghost; whose sins you shall forgive they are forgiven them; and whose sins you shall retain, they are retained" (*John* xx, 23), and to Peter in particular: "Feed my lambs, feed my sheep" (*John* xxi, 16-17); and finally on the occasion of the solemn appearance on the mountain of Galilee, He will say to the eleven: "All power is given to me in heaven and in earth. Going therefore, teach ye all nations, baptising them in the name of the Father, and of the Son, and of the Holy Ghost, teaching them to observe all things whatsoever I have commanded you: and behold I am with you all days, even to the consummation of the world" (*Matt.* xxviii, 18-20).

We have had to anticipate in the account of these events in order to give to the institution of the Apostles all its significance. The matter is indeed of supreme importance: at the beginning of a history of the Church it must first of all be pointed out that Jesus founded the Church, and that He gave to it from the first certain essential features. The Church is a society vivified by Christ who is its Head, and by the Holy Spirit who is its soul, but it also appears from the very first as a visible and hierarchical society, which will rest on St. Peter as an unshakable foundation, will depend on him as its supreme head here below, will be taught and governed under him by the Apostles, and will be aided constantly by Jesus Christ until the end of the world.

Jesus at Capharnaum

When Jesus began the evangelisation of Galilee, He did not fix his headquarters in the little town of Nazareth where he had grown up. Later on He would go and preach there, and be faced with the unbelief of his fellow citizens: "A prophet is not without honour but in his own country, and in his own house, and among

---

[26] On this text, see *Life and Teaching of Jesus Christ*, Vol. I, pp. 355-6, and the works there referred to.

his own kindred," said He to them. This unbelief strongly opposed Him: the people of Nazareth turned Him out of the synagogue where he was preaching, and tried to cast Him down from the top of the hill on which their town was built.[27]

At a day's journey from Nazareth, on the northern side of the Lake of Galilee, there was the little town of Capharnaum. This was not a Hellenic city like Tiberias or Julias, but a Jewish town. At the same time, it was quite open to strangers: some came from the rich plateaux of the Hauran, others from the Phœnician coast. It was in this busy town, amidst the numerous publicans [28] gathered there for the receipt of taxes, that Jesus, passing near the table where Levi was sitting, called him and made him an Apostle (*Matt. ix, 9-13*). It was also there that he found the rich centurion, the friend of the Jews, who had built them a synagogue.[29]

It was in this town of Capharnaum that St. Peter had married; Jesus was given hospitality there and remained there in the intervals between His missions through Galilee. During the whole of this period, Capharnaum was His city (*Matt. ix, 1*).

The evangelists, and especially St. Mark, the interpreter of the memoirs of St. Peter, enable us to accompany Jesus in one of His daily rounds (*Mark i, 21-34*). It was a Sabbath day; in the morning, Jesus went to the synagogue; "He taught them, and they were astonished at his doctrine, for he was teaching them as one having power, and not as the scribes." There was present a man possessed by an unclean spirit, who cried out: "What have we to do with thee, Jesus of Nazareth? Art thou come to destroy us? I know who thou art, the Holy One of God." Jesus commanded him: "Speak no more, and go out of the man!" And after a convulsion and a great cry, the devil went out. The crowd was amazed; "What thing is this? What is this new doctrine? For with power he commandeth even the unclean spirits, and they obey him!"

Protected by the Sabbath repose, Jesus withdrew. Peter and Andrew took Him to their home. They were followed by their

---

[27] *Mark vi, 1-6; Luke iv, 16-30.*

[28] *Luke v, 29*, mentions "a great company of publicans" around Levi. Cf. *Mark ii, 15; Matt. ix, 10.*

[29] At Tell-Hum, the ancient Capharnaum, the ruins of a very fine synagogue have been discovered. They have been described by P. G. Orfali, *Capharnaum et ses ruines*, Paris, 1922. According to P. Orfali, this synagogue dates back to the first century of our era; according to Père Lagrange, *Gospel of Jesus Christ*, Vol. I, p. 162 n., it belonged to the end of the second century.

friends and fellow fishermen, James and John; the four first Apostles thus passed the day with the Master. Peter's mother-in-law was ill: Jesus cured her. This new miracle redoubled the excitement in the little town: as soon as sunset had brought the Sabbath to a close, "they brought to him all that were ill and that were possessed with devils. And all the city was gathered together at the door. And he healed many that were troubled with divers diseases, and he cast out many devils, and he suffered them not to speak, because they knew him."

And after this day of teaching and working miracles, spent wholly with the Apostles and the multitude, Jesus "rising very early went out into a desert place, and there he prayed" (ibid., 25). Prayer was His repose. But He was not able to enjoy it for long: "Simon and they that were with him, followed after him, and when they had found him, they said to him: 'All seek for thee.' And he saith to them: Let us go into the neighbouring towns and cities, that I may preach there also, for to this purpose am I come. And he was preaching in their synagogues and in all Galilee, and casting out devils" (ibid., 37-39).

Such was henceforth the life of Jesus: accompanied always by the Apostles, with the crowd pressing upon Him and following Him, He no longer belonged to Himself: His miracles drew to Him all those who were sick, His teaching attracted all those who were athirst for the word of God, and who for the first time recognised its sound upon human lips. This Master was so different from the Scribes. That was the impression of the people of Capharnaum, as also of those who heard Christ on the Mountain (Matt. vii, 28-29), and it is experienced still to-day by every reader of the Gospel.

Jesus in the Synagogues

Jesus preached by preference in the synagogues; there He would find the Jews assembled together to pray to God, and to hear and comment upon the readings from the Pentateuch and the prophets. So long as the break with the Jewish authorities was not complete, He was invited to give a homily. The preaching at Nazareth, narrated with such detail by St. Luke (iv, 16-30), puts before our eyes this touching scene: Jesus took up the Book of Isaias, and read from it:

"The Spirit of the Lord is upon me. Wherefore he hath anointed me to preach the gospel to the poor; he hath sent me to heal the contrite of heart, to preach deliverance to the captives, and sight to the blind, to set at liberty them that are bruised, to preach the acceptable year of the Lord, and the day of reward."

He closed the book, gave it back to the minister, and sat down. All eyes in the synagogue were fastened upon Him. He began to speak: "To-day is fulfilled this scripture in your ears."

We cannot read this page without once more feeling some emotion. But what must have been that of the hearers! They had so often repeated the complaint of the psalmist: "Lord, where are thy ancient mercies, to which thou didst swear to David in thy truth?" (*Psalm* lxxxviii, 50), and now they heard this majestic voice: "To-day this scripture is fulfilled!"

As long as Jesus was able, He preached in the synagogues and in the Temple, as He affirmed on the last day of His life before the High Priest (*John* xviii, 20). More than once the hatred of His enemies caused His expulsion; more often still the concourse of hearers obliged Him to leave the narrow walls of the synagogue and to preach in the open air, sitting on the mountain side (*Matt.* v, 1) or in the desert (*Mark* vi, 35), or in Peter's boat, while the crowd was massed on the edge of the lake (*Matt.* xiii, 2).

Of these long discourses many have not been recorded for us; [30] but the evangelists describe the preaching of the Master in sufficient detail to enable us to grasp His method of teaching and the progressive development of His doctrine.

What impressed the multitude in the first place was, as we have said, the authority with which Jesus spoke. The Scriptural commentary as set forth by the Scribes was usually a scholastic discussion, encumbered with the contradictory testimonies of the elders, exegetical subtleties, and the requirements or concessions of a wholly human casuistry. There was nothing of that sort here: a simple, direct speech, imposing itself authoritatively as the very word of God, and going straight to the conscience. Its appeal was an intimate one, it penetrated to the centre of the soul, but it never shocked it: it set forth to human life the highest moral ideal, the very perfection of God, but it did so without effort, or excited

[30] E.g. the preaching in the desert, before the first multiplication of the loaves: St. Matthew does not mention it; St. Mark says: "he began to teach them many things"; St. Luke: "he spoke to them of the kingdom of God."

speech: the Master did not have to raise Himself up to those heights: He lived there: "You are from beneath, I am from above" (*John* viii, 23).

The Sermon on the Mount

It is above all in the Sermon on the Mount [31] that we can grasp this characteristic in the teaching of Jesus: less reserved than in the parables, less intimate than in the discourse after the Last Supper, it is so limpidly clear and deep that we can never grow weary of studying it.

It begins with the beatitudes: [32] the poor, the afflicted, the meek, those who hunger and thirst after justice, the merciful, the pure, the peacemakers, the persecuted—these are the blessed ones, and it is to them that the Kingdom of God belongs.

To some modern readers this preaching has the appearance of a paradox, beautifying all that is painful and humiliating here below. This was not the impression made on the hearers of Jesus: they were not shocked by His teaching, but won by it; the best in them responded to His doctrine. They doubtless felt themselves led beyond their familiar ideas, but it was towards an ideal which they had already thought of and loved: this poor and humble life, in which the soul is gentle and the heart at peace, was often praised in

[31] This Sermon is found in *Matt.* v-vii and *Luke* vi, 20-49. These two versions are notably different, and yet the identity of the two sermons seems beyond doubt. St. Matthew has inserted into it teaching given on other occasions by Jesus, such as the teaching of the Our Father (vi, 9) related by St. Luke (xi. 2-4) in quite different circumstances. We recognise here one of the characteristics of the method of the first evangelist, who deliberately groups together in one logical scheme sentences or incidents which explain one another, although they belong to different periods in the ministry of Christ. This editorial method must not make us lose sight of the fundamental unity of the sermon. Cf. *Life and Teaching of Jesus Christ*, Vol. I, p. 126.

[32] Here especially we find a difference in editing between Matthew and Luke: Matthew has eight beatitudes, and understands them plainly in the spiritual sense: "Blessed are the poor in spirit. . ." Luke has only four beatitudes, and seems at first sight to beatify a material condition: "Blessed are you poor . . ." These four beatitudes are followed by four anathemas, which are lacking in Matthew. Again, in the first evangelist, the form is sententious; in the other it is direct: the sermon, instead of addressing itself to the whole human race, directly affects the "little flock" of poor, hungry and persecuted disciples. These differences can be explained by the fact that Our Lord's discourses, before being inserted into the Gospel, had often been reproduced in the Christian catechesis, and in many forms. One of these recensions is reproduced by St. Matthew, another by St. Luke. Cf. *Life and Teaching of Jesus Christ*, Vol. I, p. 127.

the Psalms. Isaias had shown its ideal model in the Servant of
Jahveh. Now it is He Himself who comes, and in His life even
more than in His teaching they recognise and love the ideal long
since foreseen.

The New Law

Next we have the fundamental question of the Old Law and the
New. No case of conscience was graver or more pressing for the
hearers of Christ. Nothing was more sacred to them than the Law,
which was the Oracle of God. Nothing was dearer, for it was the
privilege of Israel. And yet this law was heavy to bear, and Jesus
more than once had given an example of a freer observance of the
Sabbath, and of the distinction between pure and impure. In the
presence of the scandalised Pharisees, he upheld this liberty, affirming that "the Sabbath was made for man, and not man for the
Sabbath" (Mark ii, 27). He had also said that "no man seweth a
piece of raw cloth to an old garment" or "putteth new wine into
old bottles" (ibid., 21-22). Soon afterwards he would say: "Not
that which goeth into the mouth defileth a man, but what cometh
out of the mouth" (Matt. xv, 11).

How strange this sounds when we remember that the distinction
between pure and impure food was so sacred for the Jews that in
order to uphold it the martyrs had laid down their lives in the days
of the Machabees (II Mach., vi-vii).

Of the principles laid down by Jesus the applications were to
appear only progressively, in the light of the Holy Spirit,[33] but
already the Sermon on the Mount quietened the uneasiness of the
Jews and showed them that the Gospel is not the abrogation but
the accomplishment of the Law:

"Do not think that I am come to destroy the law or the prophets. I
am not come to destroy, but to fulfil. For amen I say unto you, till
heaven and earth pass, one jot or one tittle shall not pass of the law,
till all be fulfilled. He therefore that shall break one of these least
commandments, and shall so teach men, shall be called the least in the
kingdom of heaven. But he that shall do and teach, he shall be called
great in the kingdom of heaven. For I tell you, that unless your justice

[33] The vision at Joppa was necessary to make St. Peter understand that he
was no longer to regard as impure what God had purified (Acts x, 15).

abound more than that of the scribes and Pharisees, you shall not enter into the kingdom of heaven" (*Matt.* v, 17-20).

We see already what the Gospel is going to give to the Law: a greater perfection, more intimate requirements. The part of the sermon that follows enables us the better to understand this. It is not only murder that is forbidden, but also anger in thought and word; not only adultery, but also evil desires. Divorce was tolerated by Moses, this toleration is suppressed; no more vain oaths, but the simplicity of a speech which is always sincere; no more vengeance or even resistance to evil: no more narrowness in charity, but the love of enemies after the example of the Heavenly Father, "who maketh his sun to shine upon the good and bad, and raineth upon the just and the unjust. . . . Be you therefore perfect, as also your heavenly Father is perfect."

Henceforth in the moral and religious life all is sincere, all is deep. This is indeed a new and more intimate requirement, but at the same time it is a deliverance. No more regulated attitude or correct appearance masking evil desires, or whited sepulchre concealing a corpse; virtue springs forth quite spontaneously from the depths of life; it is this living water that Jesus promises to those who believe in Him.[34] Hence as the soul becomes stronger, it can lay aside all those precepts which protected its infancy as a hedge protects a young crop; the Christian will be able to say with St. Paul: "Now that I have become a man, I have put away the things of a child." And if he gives himself up wholly and without reserve to the requirements of Christ, he will realise that the multiplicity of precepts are reduced to unity: the love of God and of one's neighbour is the whole law and the prophets (*Matt.* xxii, 36), and he will find that all the powers of his soul are carried along by the simplicity of the divine life which inspires it. Truly the yoke of Christ is easy, and his burden light (*Matt.* xi, 30).

It is above all when he promulgates this Christian moral teaching, so exigent and so beneficial, that Jesus speaks with full independence and authority: he recalls the imperfect laws which the Jews had received from Moses: "It was said to you"; and he adds: "But I say to you. . . ." All readers, even the most distant from

[34] "He that believeth in me, out of his belly shall flow rivers of living water" (*John vii,* 38).

our faith, have felt the force of these antitheses.[35] Certainly no one who was not the author of the Law could treat it with at once more independence and more respect; the legislator had been able to give to a difficult people only a sketchy law; upon Christians, whom the Spirit is going to teach and fortify, the Master imposes, with his sovereign authority, a perfect law.

Interior Religion

Then he carries on the religious formation of his disciples, leading them on towards a wholly internal righteousness, in the secret of a life which is witnessed only by the heavenly Father (*Matt.* vi, 1-18). Here above all the example of Jesus is even more pressing than his teaching: "He that sent me is with me and he hath not left me alone," "I do always the things that please him"; "my meat is to do the will of him that sent me, that I may perfect his work." There is, of course, in the Father and the Son a unity of nature to which we cannot attain, and even in the human nature of Jesus there is the beatific vision which raises him up irresistibly towards the Father and which we do not possess here below. But though all this surpasses us, it is, as it were, the ideal model to which we must unceasingly tend. The Master who has said to us: "Be ye perfect as your heavenly Father is perfect," has also said of us, addressing his Father: "That they may be one even as we are one, I in them and thou in me, that they may be made perfect in one."

In this teaching on internal religion and union with the heavenly Father, as in the preaching of the beatitudes, Jesus manifests Himself to us in and through His doctrine; more so than His first hearers, we who know Him better, realise that what He gives us here is the secret of His own life, and this life draws us more strongly still than His words. It is by this discreet revelation that He makes Himself henceforth known and loved. The imitation of Christ will be for all Christians from St. Paul onwards the supreme rule of morality; the Master, always anxious to efface Himself, will set forth this ideal model only towards the end of His life, and

[35] Thus Rabbi Klausner, *Jésus de Nazareth*, p. 545. Cf. W. Bousset, art. *Bergpredigt, Religion in Geschichte und Gegenwart*, 1st edn., Vol. I, p. 1038: "This new spirit is manifested with the greatest force in these powerful antitheses. . . . Here he boldly sweeps away all the barriers. . . ."

above all at the Last Supper,[36] but already from the beginning of His ministry, His most faithful and clear-sighted disciples will be able to contemplate it in the transparency of His teaching.

Above all, there is the authority of His words: "It was said to them of old. . . . But I say to you. . . ." This sovereign dignity appears perhaps even better in the blessings attached to persecution: "Blessed are ye when they shall speak all that is evil against you, for my sake" (*Matt.* v, 11), and in the description of the Last Judgment: "Then will I profess unto them, 'I never knew you, depart from me, you that work iniquity'" (*Matt.* vii, 23). To sacrifice one's life for Jesus is eternal bliss; not to be recognised by Him is damnation.

It is thus that Jesus revealed Himself to the multitude of His disciples;[37] the superhuman greatness of His mission and His nature is manifested discreetly but very efficaciously in the doctrine in which it is implied: whoever recognises in Jesus the supreme legislator, the unique revealer of the Father, the master whose cause deserves every sacrifice, and promises every reward, the judge who will decide the fate of all—such a one has only to confess, with St. Peter: "Thou art Christ, the Son of the living God."

But in order that this teaching may bear its fruit, it is not sufficient that the mind should understand it and be pleased with it: it is necessary that this doctrine should become the efficacious rule of our lives. That constitutes the concluding part of the sermon of Jesus:

"Everyone therefore that heareth these my words, and doth them, shall be likened to a wise man that built his house upon a rock. And the rain fell, and the floods came, and the winds blew, and they beat upon that house, and it fell not, for it was founded on a rock.

"And everyone that heareth these my words, and doth them not, shall be like a foolish man that built his house upon the sand. And the rain fell, and the floods came, and the winds blew, and they beat upon that house, and it fell, and great was the fall thereof" (*Matt.* vii, 24-27).

At the time of the great crisis, when, in presence of an almost universal defection, Jesus says to the Apostles: "Will you also go

---

[36] *Mark* x, 45; *John* xiii, 15; xiii, 34; xv, 10; xv, 20.

[37] We find, especially in St. John, many more explicit declarations, but usually these revelations are made to a few isolated listeners, such as the Samaritan woman (*John* iv, 26), to the man born blind (ix, 37), or again were called forth by discussions with opponents (x, 25, 30).

away?" Peter replies: "To whom shall we go? Thou hast the words of eternal life" (*John* vi, 68). Here we have the house built upon the rock, the rock against which the gates of hell shall not prevail, but what gives to this faith the firmness of a rock is the generous practice which has tested the words of Jesus and has recognised therein "the words of eternal life." Many admired the "words of grace" which proceeded from the mouth of Jesus (*Luke* iv, 22), many rejoiced in His light, but this admiration and joy were dissipated by the first storm. The most certain proof of the faith, and the one which gives it its unshakable firmness, is the fruits which it bears; but he only can taste these who has made his faith the rule of his life.

Jesus and the Pharisees

The Sermon on the Mount, the first preaching of Jesus, aims above all at the moral formation of its hearers. Jesus wanted to make disciples of them, to lead them from the Law to the Gospel, from a formalist religion to one which was internal, living, and wholly in spirit and in truth. The Jews who were before Him, and who had flocked together not only from Galilee but "from Judea and Jerusalem, and the sea coast both of Tyre and Sidon" (*Luke* vi, 17), were still very ignorant and very imperfect, but they listened eagerly to His words, they were not yet, for the most part, prejudiced against Him. Jesus was able to speak to them in all freedom and sympathy. But already at this time the Pharisees were alarmed: they followed Jesus in order to watch Him, and very soon in order to oppose Him.

This opposition is described by St. Mark above all and by St. Luke when relating incidents which were connected together, and which show an increasing hostility. On the occasion of the miraculous cure of a paralytic (*Mark* ii, 1-12), the Scribes who were sitting in front of Jesus, in a house full of people, were scandalised at the words of the Master to the sick man: "Son, thy sins are forgiven thee." Internally they were in a state of revolt, but they kept silent. A little later, there came the calling of the publican Levi, and the banquet to which the latter had invited many of his colleagues and friends. The Scribes and Pharisees intervened: they did not yet dare to attack Jesus directly, but they questioned His disciples: "Why doth your master eat with publicans and sinners?"

Jesus hearing it said: "They that are in health need not a physician, but they that are ill. . . . I am not come to call the just, but sinners" (*Matt.* ix, 16-17). Then on a day when the disciples of John the Baptist and the Pharisees were fasting, they went to Jesus and asked, "Why do not thy disciples fast?" Jesus answered: "Can the children of the bridegroom mourn as long as the bridegroom is with them? The days will come when the bridegroom shall be taken away from them, and then they shall fast" (*ibid.*, 14-15). Another day, Jesus and His disciples were walking through a field of wheat and the disciples plucked a few ears and ate them. The Pharisees came up: according to the Law it was forbidden to gather the harvest on the Sabbath day. The Pharisees interpreted this prohibition so strictly that they would not allow "a branch, or a leaf, or a fruit" to be picked on that day.[38]

Jesus protested against this casuistry, and added: "The Sabbath was made for man, and not man for the Sabbath" (*ibid.*, 28). On another Sabbath day Jesus was in a synagogue. Amongst those present there was a man with a withered hand; the Scribes and Pharisees were there, and they watched Jesus in order to accuse Him of violating the Sabbath if He should cure the infirm man. Jesus said to the latter: "Stand up in the midst," and then said to the Pharisees: "Is it lawful to do good on the Sabbath day, or to do evil? to save life or to destroy?" They kept silent. Then He looked round on them with anger, being grieved for the blindness of their hearts, and He said to the man: "Stretch forth thy hand." He did so, and the hand was restored. The Pharisees, going out of the synagogue, immediately held a consultation with the Herodians as to how they might destroy Jesus (*Mark* iii, 1-6).

We are able to trace in these incidents the boldness of the Pharisees growing with their anger. The cure of the sick man upset them completely. The miracle was brought about by a word, and Jesus had not even touched the man. It would be very difficult to see in this a violation of the Sabbath. But the exasperation of the enemies of the Master was only the greater: already they were planning His death, they sought for accomplices, and found them amongst the Herodians.

[38] Philo, *De vita Mosis*, II, 4. The disciples were not criticised for injuring the owner of the field, for then, as now in the East, custom authorised passers-by to pluck a few ears or a few fruits.

They also endeavoured to calm the excitement of the people. Amongst the opponents of Jesus the more moderate said: "He is mad," and this rumour became so strong that the brethren of the Lord [39] were upset by it, and they came from Nazareth to Capharnaum to take Jesus away (*Mark* iii, 21, *cf.* 31). But the crowd was so dense around Jesus that they could not get to Him.[40] This crowd had come "from Galilee, and Judea, and from Jerusalem, and from Idumea, and from beyond the Jordan, and from Tyre and Sidon" (*Mark* iii, 7-8). They were so eager to see and touch Jesus that the Master was obliged to go up into a boat to get a little distance from them (iii, 9), and when He returned to the house, they did not give Him time even to eat (iii, 20). But in the midst of this enthusiastic multitude there were enemies: Scribes who had come down from Jerusalem continued to repeat: "He is possessed; if he casts out devils, it is by Beelzebub, the prince of devils."

This odious and ridiculous calumny was repeated with such insistence that Jesus had to rebut it. He called together these Scribes, and said to them: "How can Satan cast out Satan? . . . If Satan be risen up against himself, he is divided, and cannot stand, but hath an end" (*ibid.*, 23, 26). The Scribes made no answer— what could they have said without withdrawing their opinion? But they remained obdurate. Later on, at Jerusalem, the Jews who were under Pharisaic influence persisted in regarding Jesus as possessed.[41] That was indeed the blasphemy against the Spirit: these people recognised in Jesus a supernatural power; they were capable of seeing that this power destroyed and expelled Satan, and yet they insisted on attributing it to Satan himself. Against such bad faith God Himself is powerless, and His grace helpless: "Amen I say to you, that all sins shall be forgiven unto the sons of men, and the

[39] Those whom the Gospel calls the "brethren of the Lord" were not children of Mary, who had decided to remain always a virgin (*Luke* i, 34), nor were they children of Joseph. In all the narratives of the infancy, we find with Mary and Joseph only one child, Jesus. The "brethren" were cousins. The Gospel names four of these: James, Joseph, Simon and Jude, and also mentions several sisters without naming them. Of these brethren two, James and Joseph, are described as sons of one of the holy women present at Calvary: "Mary, the mother of James and Joseph" (*Matt.* xxvii, 56; cf. *Mark* xv, 40). On this whole question of the relatives of Jesus, see *Life and Teaching of Jesus Christ*, Vol. I, pp. 32-7.

[40] On this action by the relatives of Jesus, see *Life and Teaching of Jesus Christ*, Vol. I, pp. 227 *et seq.*

[41] *John* vii, 20; viii, 48, 52, 20.

blasphemies wherewith they shall blaspheme. But he that shall blaspheme against the Holy Ghost, shall never have forgiveness, but shall be guilty of an everlasting sin" (*Mark* iii, 28-29).

The Parables of the Kingdom of Heaven

Jesus had already been preaching for some months. Now not only Galilee was moved by His words, but the whole land of Israel. To Him flocked the sick and the possessed, and souls eager for truth, but also, alas! some who were envious, and others who were enemies. The prophecy of Simeon was verified more and more: in respect of Jesus the contradiction became more and more violent; it divided into two contrary parties all the Jews, as it would later on divide all mankind. The calumnies of the scribes of Jerusalem were atrocious; doubtless people hesitated to give them full credence, but many minds were upset. Were not the Scribes the guides of the people, and the qualified interpreters of the Law? Instinctively people turned to them, and already we can say what the Pharisees were to say later to their agents troubled by the words of Jesus: "Hath any one of the rulers believed in him, or one of the Pharisees? But this multitude, that knoweth not the Law, are accursed" (*John* vii, 48-49). Already the timid ones, and these were as always numerous, were paralysed by this opposition on the part of the leaders. This will be seen later at Jerusalem, we feel it already in Galilee.

And yet to this divided and undecided crowd, Jesus must now preach the Kingdom of God and the Messias. Previous discourses, such as the Sermon on the Mount, should have prepared men's minds; it was now time to put before them the "mystery of the Kingdom of God." But this preaching ran the risk of being misunderstood: would not these Galilean crowds, so impatient to see the kingdom of Israel re-established, try to lead Him on to the great adventure, to force Him to put himself at their head, and to make Himself king?

These fears were only too well justified as the sequence of events show. Jesus, who "knew what was in man," recognised with clear certitude the dangers of such preaching, which nevertheless He could not delay any longer. To meet the danger, He presented the preaching of the Kingdom of God under the veil of parables. It was not the first time that He had spoken in parables: nothing was more familiar to His audience than these figurative addresses, and He Himself had had recourse to them many times.[42] But prior to the period with which we are dealing, these parables were only short figurative sentences, giving more point to the discourse, but not constituting the essence of the preaching. Now, on the contrary, they are developed at length, and cover the whole teaching of Jesus. This gives His preaching a new aspect: the Apostles are struck by it, and ask Him why He has recourse to this method: "Why speakest thou to them in parables?" Jesus replies: "Because to you it is given to know the mysteries of the kingdom of heaven, but to them it is not given" (*Matt.* xiii, 10).

Certainly we must not infer from this that Jesus did not wish to instruct the Jews, or that the parables had no other aim but to blind them. St. John Chrysostom says very rightly: "If He did not wish the Jews to be saved, He had only to be silent; He had no need to speak in parables; He wanted, on the contrary, to stimulate them by the very obscurity of His words."

But it is true that the obscurity of His words was due to the blindness of His hearers, their tenacious prejudices, and their slowness to believe; and that is why the Apostles, themselves better disposed, received from Jesus an interpretation of the parables which enabled them to understand them better, and which was not set forth to the crowd. Here is verified the providential law of the distribution of grace: "He that hath, to him shall be given, and he shall abound: but he that hath not, from him shall be taken away that also which he hath." [43] It is by fidelity to the first graces from God that we dispose ourselves to receive more precious gifts from Him. We must also note the care which the Apostles take to interrogate the Master: conscious that they have imperfectly understood the parables, they ask from Him the interpretation of them, and receive it. "The Jews also," remarks St. John Chrysostom, "could have gone to Him, and have interrogated Him, as the disciples did, but they did not wish to do so, because they were lazy, and because they cast themselves away."

[42] Thus: "They that are well have no need of a physician" (*Mark* ii, 17); "Can the children of the bridegroom fast, as long as the bridegroom is with them?" (19); "No man seweth a piece of raw cloth to an old garment, . . . and no man putteth new wine into old bottles" (21).

[43] This sentence of the Master, reported in this place by St. Matthew (xiii, 12), is found again later on in the parable of the talents: *Matt.* xxv, 29, cf. *Mark* iv. 25; *Luke* viii, 18.

Jesus made use of this culpable carelessness of the Jews in order to prepare for the constitution of His Church, and to train the Apostles for their office as teachers. The knowledge of the kingdom of Heaven which He gives them is to be communicated to all:

"Doth a candle come in to be put under a bushel, or under a bed? and not to set on a candlestick? For there is nothing hid, which shall not be made manifest; neither was it made secret but that it may come abroad" (*Mark* iv, 21-22).

There is no esoteric doctrine in the Church, there are no secret initiations; certainly there are some to whom are entrusted the secrets of God, but these confidants are witnesses whose mission it is to make known to all what has been said to them: "That which I tell you in the dark, speak ye in the light; and that which you hear in the ear, preach ye upon the housetops." [44]

This general law becomes more and more manifest as we proceed in our reading of the Gospel: the most decisive manifestations in the life of Jesus, Cæsarea Philippi, the Transfiguration, and above all the Resurrection and the Ascension, had but few witnesses, but these had a mission to make them known to all.

These parables, clarified by the interpretation given by Jesus to the Apostles, have been graven into the Christian conscience, and the Church unceasingly reminds her children of them. The word of God is the seed which the sower casts on the wayside, where the birds of the air come and eat it, or it falls on stony ground, where the sun scorches it, or amongst thorns, which choke it, or lastly upon good ground, where it brings forth fruit, thirty, or sixty, or even a hundredfold (*Mark* iv, 3-9). The Kingdom of God is like to a seed which a man cast into the earth; he sleeps and rises, and the seed springs and grows up, he knows not how, and then, when the harvest is ready, he puts in his sickle (*ibid.*, iv, 26-29). A man sowed good seed in his field, his enemy came and sowed cockle, when the cockle appeared amongst the wheat,

[44] This sentence, connected with that which precedes, is included by St. Matthew (x, 27) in the instructions given by Jesus to the Apostles when He sent them out on a mission. At the end of the interpretation of the parables, He gives them the same teaching in another form: "Have ye understood all these things? . . . Therefore, every scribe instructed in the kingdom of heaven is like to a householder who bringeth forth out of his treasure new things and old" (*Matt.* xiii, 51-2).

the servants wanted to gather it up, but the master said to them: Suffer the wheat and the cockle to grow until the harvest (*Matt.* xiii, 24-30). The Kingdom of Heaven is like to a grain of mustard seed, the least of all seeds, but from whence comes a great tree (*ibid.*, 31-32), or as leaven which a woman takes and hides in three measures of meal until the whole is leavened (*ibid.*, 33). It is like a treasure, or like a pearl of great price (*ibid.*, 44-45). Again it is like to a net cast into the sea and gathering good and evil fish (*ibid.*, 47-50).

What we notice first of all in this preaching is that it is a moral teaching which all its hearers were able to understand, and which was indeed necessary for all of them: the dispositions which the Kingdom of God requires in all those who aim at it are a boundless good will, determined to purchase the treasure, the pearl, at all costs; and the fruitfulness of a well-prepared soul—good ground, which is not the ordinary road, or stony ground, or a field of thorns. What is perhaps more important still is the description of the Kingdom of God and its growth: at the beginning, it is an imperceptible seed like a grain of mustard, or hidden like leaven in paste; its growth is not noticed, but it is strong like life itself; the man who has sown the seed on the land does not think of it again, but it germinates, the leaf appears, then the ear, then the formed grain, and we have the harvest. These parables bring home to us more than all affirmations the true nature of the kingdom of God and of its development: its growth and progress are noticed by no one; in the souls wherein God has planted it, it is as it were hidden, lowly, silent, and yet it ferments, germinates, and affects everything with its life; and the same law applies to Israel and to the whole human race. No lesson was more needed by those people who were always seeking for a sign from Heaven, and who awaited from one day to the next the dreadful advent of the Kingdom of God.

No less needed was the lesson of patience taught them by the cockle and the net: instinctively we all would say to the good man of the house: Wilt thou that we go and gather it up? No, he replies, lest perhaps gathering up the cockle you root up the wheat also together with it. Wait for the day of the harvest, the Last Day.

This teaching was suggested by the parables to all those who heard them, but Jesus set it forth with more emphasis in the interpretation He gave to the Apostles; and there were also other mysteries which He revealed to them, and which were not comprised in the parables: if we compare the parable of the wheat and the cockle with the interpretation given by Jesus we see the perspective extended to infinity: "The harvest is the end of the world; the reapers are the angels. . . . The Son of Man shall send his angels, and they shall gather out of his kingdom all scandals, and them that work iniquity, and shall cast them into the furnace of fire: there shall be weeping and gnashing of teeth. Then shall the just shine as the sun, in the kingdom of their Father. He that hath ears to hear, let him hear" (*Matt. xiii*, 39-43).

What is evident in this scene of the Last Judgment is not only the condemnation of the wicked and the bliss of the just, but also the superhuman majesty of the Son of Man who sends angels, his angels, to carry out His will and to purify His kingdom. This revelation of the office of Christ throws a new light on the parable and gives it a tremendous meaning which the interpretation alone makes known to us.

The Galilean Ministry

The parable of the cockle which we have just studied shows us, in the Lord's field, the growing wheat, and mingled with it, the cockle, which already appears everywhere. Such was the land of Israel towards the end of the first year of the ministry of Jesus, in the spring of the year 29. The crowds, above all in Galilee, had been roused by the preaching and miracles of the Lord, but their enthusiastic admiration, which at times seemed about to carry all before it, came up against a treacherous and violent opposition which, supported by the religious authority of the Scribes and the Pharisees, troubled men's consciences and intimidated their hesitating wills.

After the preaching of the parables, Jesus, wearied by the teaching given to the Jews and his Apostles, went to sleep in the stern of a boat. He had told the Apostles to cross over to the other side of the Lake. Suddenly a storm of wind arose, and the frightened Apostles awoke Jesus: "Master, doth it not concern thee that we perish?" Jesus at once commanded the wind and the sea, and there came a great calm. The Apostles feared exceedingly, and said one to another: "Who is this, then, that both wind and sea obey him?" (*Mark* iv, 35-41).

As soon as they had disembarked on the other side of the lake, in the night-time, there ran to him a nude and wounded man. He came before Jesus, crying: "What is to me and to thee, O Jesus, Son of the Most High God? I adjure thee by God that thou torment me not!" He was possessed, but Jesus freed him saying: "Go out of the man, thou unclean spirit!" And the devils—they were many—entered into a herd of swine, and cast these animals into the sea. The alarm was given by the men who were looking after the herd; the inhabitants came together; they found at the feet of Jesus, calm and decently clad, the man who had been possessed, and who was a few hours before the terror of the countryside (*Mark* v, 1-20).

Jesus crossed over the lake once more. At once a multitude ran to Him. One of the rulers of the synagogue, Jairus, fell at His feet, saying: "My daughter is at the point of death, but come, lay thy hands upon her, that she may be safe, and may live." As Jesus followed him and the crowd pressed upon Him, a woman who had suffered from an issue of blood for twelve years made her way through the crowd and touched His garment: she was cured. Jesus at once stopped: "Who has touched me?" he asked. Trembling all over with emotion and shame, the woman threw herself at his feet, and confessed all to him. "Daughter, thy faith hath made thee whole: go in peace, and be thou whole of thy disease." He was still speaking when some came and told Jairus: "Thy daughter is dead; why dost thou trouble the master any further?" Jesus heard this, and said: "Fear not, only believe." He sent away all the people, and took with him only Peter, James and John. They entered the house, where everyone was weeping and wailing. "Why make you this ado and weep?" he asked, "the damsel is not dead, but sleepeth." And they laughed him to scorn. He put them all out, and followed only by the father and mother of the girl and his three companions, He entered into the death chamber; He took the damsel by the hand, and said to her: "Talitha, koum—Damsel, arise," and the little one rose and walked. Jesus requested silence, and said to the parents: "Give her to eat" (*Mark* v, 21-43).

These miracles, recounted by St. Mark from the recollections of St. Peter with such simplicity and life, bring home to us the character of Our Lord's ministry in Galilee at this time. He preached, He cured, He cast out devils; pressed by the crowd wherever He went, He devoted Himself to them until He fell asleep at the end of His day. No master was so accessible, none so mighty: with a word He raised from the dead the daughter of Jairus, as He had raised the son of the widow at Nain and as He would later raise up Lazarus. With a word He calmed the wind and the sea; the Apostles in presence of this miracle were full of fear, and yet even before they had awaked Him, they knew well that the storm which terrified them did not threaten Him: "Master, doth it not concern thee that we perish?" In this way He passed through all dangers, and soon we shall see Him similarly pass through the midst of the people of Nazareth when they wanted to kill Him. God had long ago said, speaking of the children of Israel: "Touch not mine anointed!" These words apply above all to Him who is the Christ: the elements obey Him, and even those men who are His enemies do not dare to touch Him. If we wish to understand the extent of this divine protection, let the life of Jesus be compared with that of the Apostle St. Paul, for instance, five times scourged, thrice beaten with rods, once stoned, five times shipwrecked. Jesus aroused more hatred even than His Apostle, but He was never touched, until the day when God delivered Him up and He gave Himself up to the powers of darkness. Throughout all His luminous life, menaced by all but injured by none, we hear the echo of the Father's words: This is my beloved Son, in whom I am well pleased!"

And yet there were eyes whom this light hurt; there were souls who preferred darkness in its place. After the raising of the daughter of Jairus, Jesus went up to Nazareth; [45] He preached in the synagogue; He commented, as we have said already, on the prophecy of Isaias concerning the Servant of Jahveh. At first they were under the spell of His "words of grace," but very soon there were doubts and murmurs: this prophet was known at Nazareth, and also His family:

[45] *Mark* vi, 1-6; *Matt.* xiii, 53-8; *Luke* iv, 16-30. Several historians distinguish two visits of Jesus to Nazareth in the narrative of St. Luke: the first would be at the beginning of the Galilean ministry; the other, related also by Mark and Matthew, would be later on, at the time we are now discussing. This duplication does not seem to us to be likely.

"Is not this the carpenter, the son of Mary, the brother of James and Joseph and Jude and Simon? Are not also his sisters here with us?" [46]

Certainly they had heard talk of His miracles at Capharnaum, but the people of Nazareth displayed less admiration than jealousy. Jesus said to them:

"Doubtless you will say to me this similitude: Physician, heal thyself: as great things as we have heard done in Capharnaum, do also here in thy own country. Amen I say to you, that no prophet is accepted in his own country."

He then reminded them of Elias and Eliseus: it was for the benefit of strangers, and not of their fellow citizens, that these prophets worked their greatest miracles; it was to a woman of Sidon that Elias was sent; it was a Syrian, Naaman, that Eliseus cured of leprosy. That was equivalent to warning them of the reprobation of the Jews and the calling of the Gentiles. There was a burst of anger: they rose up and took Jesus out of the synagogue to the top of the hill, from which they intended to throw Him down. "But he, passing through the midst of them, went his way."

The Crisis in the Galilean Ministry

These episodes in the ministry of Jesus show us the state of mind of people in Galilee: in some it was one of enthusiastic admiration; in others it was a mistrustful and jealous reserve, quite ready to become violent opposition. It was then that Jesus sent out His twelve Apostles on a mission; He sent them without provision, "no scrip, no bread, nor money in their purse"; "be shod with sandals, and put not on two coats." He added: "Wheresoever you shall enter into a house, there abide till you depart from that place. And whosoever shall not receive you nor hear you: going forth from thence, shake off the dust from your feet for a testimony to them." And going forth they preached repentance, and cast out many devils, and anointed with oil many sick and healed them. (*Mark* vi, 10; 13).

This preaching and miracles, which extended through the

[46] *Mark* vi, 3. On these brethren and sisters of the Lord, cf. *supra*, p. 111, n. 39. What St. John says later on must here be borne in mind: "His brethren did not believe in him" (vii, 5). This unbelief amongst the nearest relatives of Jesus enables us to understand better the sentiments of the people of Nazareth.

whole country, created a great sensation. At home in his palace of Machaerus, where he had just killed St. John the Baptist, Herod was roused. He said to his servants: "This is John the Baptist, he is risen from the dead, and therefore mighty works show forth themselves in him" (*Matt.* xiv, 2).

The tyrant's alarum was a great danger for Jesus. Not long before, when John was cast into prison, the Master had had to leave Judea; the death of the Forerunner was a fresh warning to Him: Galilee, subject to Herod's rule, was no longer a safe retreat. He went into the desert (*Matt.* xiv, 13). An additional reason led Him there: the crowds which pressed round Him were so great that the Apostles had no longer time even to eat (*Mark.* vi, 31).

He entered a boat, and following the northern bank, reached Bethsaida Julias, beyond which was desolate hill country. Jesus was not to find solitude there: He had been seen to leave, and the crowd followed Him on land almost as quickly as He had crossed by sea. Jesus had compassion on them, "because they were as sheep not having a shepherd, and he began to teach them many things" (*Mark* vi, 34).

When the evening came, the disciples said to Jesus: "This is a desert place, and the hour is now far spent; send these people away, that going into the villages they may buy themselves food to eat." He replied: Give you them to eat." "Must we then go and buy two hundred pennyworth of bread and give them to eat?" "How many loaves have you?"—"Five, and two fishes" (*Mark* vi, 35-38). Jesus made them sit down in groups of hundreds and fifties; the loaves and fishes were distributed to them, as much as they wanted. All were satisfied; the remainder was gathered up, and twelve baskets were filled. Those who were thus fed were five thousand, not counting women and children. Then these men, seeing the miracle which had been worked, cried out: "This is of a truth the prophet that is to come into the world." Jesus, knowing that they would come to take Him by force and make Him king, fled again into the mountain Himself alone (*John* vi, 14-15).

And so this day, begun in such enthusiasm, and crowned with so striking a miracle, ended in the withdrawal of Jesus to escape from the people. On this decisive occasion, the wrong idea to which the Jews held so tenaciously was clearly manifested: what they desired from Jesus was the re-establishment of the kingdom of

Israel, over which He would be king. Jesus could not allow that: His kingdom is not of this world; in presence of their blind enthusiasm which threatened Him, He fled. The Jews were hard hit by this disillusionment. If He was not the king of Israel, who was He? Very soon, at Cæsarea Philippi, when Jesus asks the Apostles what people think of the Son of Man, He will receive these confused answers, in which we see vestiges of Jewish belief: "Some say: John the Baptist, others Elias, and others Jeremias, or one of the prophets." Moreover, after the great disappointment of that evening, the discourse at Capharnaum on the bread of life must have completed their disillusionment: they were too much attached to things of earth to follow Jesus when He spoke to them of the bread of heaven.

The Apostles, nevertheless, passed over the lake; Jesus, before sending the crowds away, had insisted on the disciples going.[47] While they were at sea, a violent wind arose from the west. They had started out at nightfall, and at three o'clock in the morning they had only gone a small part of the way, about thirty furlongs (*John* vi, 19). Jesus appeared to them, walking on the water; St. Peter, impatient to rejoin Him, said: "Lord, if it be thou, bid me come to thee upon the waters."—"Come." Peter went down out of the boat, and walked towards Jesus, but seeing the wind, he took fright, and began to sink. He cried: "Lord save me!" Jesus stretched forth his hand, and took hold of him, saying: "O thou of little faith, why didst thou doubt?" The two of them went into the boat, the wind ceased, and those who were in the boat threw themselves at His feet, crying: "Truly thou art the Son of God!" (*Matt.* xiv, 25-33).

This great miracle must have strengthened the faith of the Apostles, which had been disturbed by the events of the evening, and which was going to be tried by the sermon on the bread of life, with its mysterious subject-matter. If they are then tempted to regard this discourse as too hard, they will recall the apparition in the night, Jesus walking on the waters, and they will have less difficulty in believing that this divine body can, if the Lord wills, overrule the laws of nature.

[47] This fact, noted by *Matt.* xiv, 22, and *Mark* vi, 45, shows what difficulty the Twelve had to get away from the crowd, and how Jesus insisted on their departure. The contagion of this national enthusiasm, followed by disillusionment, might have constituted a great danger for the Apostles.

The Bread of Life

On the next day the crowd searches for Jesus, and not finding Him beyond the lake, they go back to Capharnaum and there meet Him. "You seek me," says Jesus to them, "not because you have seen miracles, but because you did eat of the loaves and were filled. Labour not for the meat which perisheth, but for that which endureth unto life everlasting, which the Son of Man will give you" (*John* vi, 26-27).

From the beginning of the sermon, we sense the opposition which is brewing and which is going to manifest itself: Jesus seeks to awake in the hearts of the Jews the desire of heavenly goods, but they instead, proud and suspicious, remind Jesus of the manna which Moses had given to their fathers, and say to Him: "What sign dost thou show that we may see and may believe thee? What dost thou work?" For a moment the Jews yield to the divine attraction. Jesus had said to them: "The bread of God is he who cometh down from heaven and giveth life to the world." "Lord," they reply, "give us always this bread." They did not yet know this bread; they began nevertheless to desire it. Jesus reveals Himself more clearly: "It is I who am the bread of life, he that cometh to me shall no more hunger, he that believeth in me shall never thirst." But already the Jews no longer followed Him; like the people of Nazareth, they recalled what they thought they knew of Him and His family: "Is not this Jesus the son of Joseph, whose father and mother we know? How then saith he, 'I came down from heaven?'" Jesus replies to them: "Murmur not among yourselves. No man can come to me except the Father, who hath sent me, draw him, and I will raise him up in the last day. . . . I am the living bread which came down from heaven. If any man eat of this bread, he shall live for ever, and the bread that I will give is my flesh, for the life of the world." In face of renewed murmurs, He is more emphatic still: "Amen, amen I say to you. Except you eat the flesh of the Son of man, and drink his blood, you shall not have life in you. He that eateth my flesh, and drinketh my blood, hath everlasting life, and I will raise him up in the last day. For my flesh is truly food, and my blood is truly drink. He that eateth my flesh and drinketh my blood, abideth in me and I in him. As the living Father hath sent me, and I live by the Father, so he that eateth me, the same also shall live by me. This is the bread that has come down from heaven; not as your fathers did eat manna and are dead; he that eateth this bread shall live for ever" (*John* vi, 43-59).

This discourse is one of the most important in the Gospels. St. John, who leaves aside almost the whole of the Galilean ministry, is careful to relate the multiplication of the loaves and the sermon at Capharnaum. Of the institution of the holy Eucharist, recounted by the three synoptists, he says nothing, but he is careful to give us the whole of this great discourse, which promises and explains it. Belief in the Real Presence finds therein a very sure foundation; theology discovers therein inexhaustible riches: the Incarnation, the coming into the world of the Son of God, the bread from heaven which gives life to the world, the gift of the life which, flowing wholly from the Father to the Son, is communicated by the Son to mankind, the indispensable necessity of communicating in the flesh and blood of Christ in order to receive this life, and lastly, the revelation and attraction by the Father, the unique source of our faith: "No man can come to me except the Father draw him."

The history of the life and ministry of Jesus also receives much light from this narrative. Of the five thousand men who had followed Jesus beyond the lake, only a small number were gathered here in the synagogue of Capharnaum, and even these were drawn only by the memory of the bread they had eaten. In vain did Jesus endeavour to make them desire the living bread which had come down from heaven; after a moment's attention they drew back, they murmured, and finally went away, and this departure signified a definite abandonment.

"After this many of his disciples went back and walked no more with him. Then Jesus said to the Twelve: 'Will you also go away?' And Simon Peter answered him: 'Lord, to whom shall we go? Thou hast the words of eternal life. And we have believed and have known that thou art the Holy One of God.' Jesus answered them: 'Is it not I who have chosen you twelve? And one of you is a devil.' Now he meant Judas Iscariot, for it was he who was to betray him, whereas he was one of the Twelve." (*John* vi, 66-71.)

And so this great effort of Jesus ended in the desertion of the greater part of the disciples, and the betrayal by one of the Twelve. He had worked, not merely for a few sick but for thousands of men, a miracle which had aroused the admiration of all of them, and this enthusiasm had only intensified in them the fever for national independence which caused them to forget the good things from heaven. As for those who had recovered themselves and had rejoined Him, Jesus endeavoured at Capharnaum to make these love and desire the bread of life which He promised them; they rebelled, and abandoned Him. Amongst the Apostles, Judas was already a traitor. We have reached the time of the Pasch in the year 29. Jesus is going to struggle on, preach, and heal for still another year, and during the whole of this year. He will remain on intimate terms with this traitor, and nothing—not His most touching words, nor His most divine works, will regain this heart which has abandoned Him for ever.

This crisis transformed the whole apostolate of Jesus. He had to renounce His Galilean preaching, so long and so eagerly listened to. The hostility of Herod prevented His long stays on the borders of the lake; He returned there on several occasions, but only in passing. His disciples themselves deserted Him in great numbers; Jesus would still see more than once compact crowds pressing around Him: in the desert, where there would be a second multiplication of the loaves,[48] in Jerusalem at the time of the great festivals. In these great assemblies of people, and, above all, on Palm Sunday, the flame of enthusiasm which had burnt so long in Galilee would be relit, but its light would quickly die down; Jesus would no longer find amongst His Galileans the faithful and constant docility of the early days. Even after Pentecost, when the Church was founded in Jerusalem, we do not see a church being organised in Galilee. The Apostles were, of course, Galileans, and around them in the Church of Jerusalem they must have had many people from Galilee, but though Galilee gave to Jesus some of its sons, and those the best, it did not give itself entirely to Him.

As for the towns round the Lake, in which Jesus had worked so many miracles, they were unfaithful to Him, and the last words He addressed to them were words of malediction:

"Woe to thee, Corozain, woe to thee, Bethsaida: for if in Tyre and Sidon had been wrought the miracles that have been wrought in you, they had long ago done penance in sackcloth and ashes. But I say unto you, it shall be more tolerable for Tyre and Sidon in the day of judgment, than for you. And thou, Capharnaum, shalt thou be exalted up to heaven? thou shalt go down even unto hell. For if in Sodom had

[48] Matt. xv, 32-9; Mark viii, 1-10. Cf. Life and Teaching of Jesus Christ, Vol. I, p. 344.

been wrought the miracles that have been wrought in thee, perhaps it had remained unto this day. But I say unto you, that it shall be more tolerable for the land of Sodom in the day of judgment, than for thee." [49]

The Great Revelations

Jesus had to withdraw from Galilee, just as the year before He had left Jerusalem and Judea: the Gospel was apparently uprooted and expelled from the land of Israel. But though the multitude of Jews had dispersed, the little flock of the Apostles grouped around Peter was faithful, except Judas. It was to this group of disciples that the most exalted revelations were reserved.

Leaving the lands of Herod Antipas, Jesus retired into the northern province subject to Philip. In this province, which was almost entirely pagan, Jesus did not address himself to the multitude; He found there scarcely any other disciples besides those who had come with Him, and especially the Twelve. It was on these that He concentrated his efforts; in one year when he would have left this earth, they would remain the depositories of His secrets, and would enrich the Church with them.

The Confession of St. Peter

Returning up the Valley of the Jordan, the little group arrived at the source of the river. It was there, on grassy terraces where water trickles everywhere, near to a cave dedicated to Pan, that Philip the Tetrarch had at his coming founded the town which he had called Cæsarea Philippi. Into his pagan town Jesus did not enter; he stopped amidst the orchards which surrounded it. He went aside to pray; it was the eve of a decisive day. The Apostles rejoined Him, conversation began, familiar as always, and with a trustful intimacy. But all at once Jesus puts the question which dominates everything: "Whom do men say that the Son of Man is?" and the replies multiply, reflecting the uncertitude of the Jews: some say John the Baptist, others Elias, others again Jeremias, or one of the prophets. The attention and faith of the Apostles being thus aroused, the Master asks them:

"But you: whom do you say that I am? Simon Peter answered and said: 'Thou art the Christ, the Son of the living God.' Jesus answering

[49] *Matt.* xi, 21-4; cf. *Luke* x, 13-15.

said to him: 'Blessed art thou, Simon Bar-Jona: because flesh and blood hath not revealed it to thee, but my Father who is in heaven. And I say to thee that thou art Peter, and upon this rock I will build my Church, and the gates of hell shall not prevail against it. And I will give to thee the keys of the kingdom of heaven. And whatsoever thou shalt bind upon earth, it shall be bound also in heaven: and whatsoever thou shalt loose on earth, it shall be loosed also in heaven" (*Matt.* xvi, 15-19).

In this solemn scene we find once more what was apparent already at Capharnaum: the indecision of the Jews, and, contrasted with it, the sure faith of the Apostles. Here once more it is Peter who speaks in the name of his brethren: but in the course of the two or three months which separate these two confessions, the opposition between the two groups has become more manifest. We are no longer at Capharnaum, but at Cæsarea Philippi; the Jews are far off, and amongst them the hesitation of the first days has increased; they recognise still in Jesus a man invested with a supernatural mission, but no longer the Messias; their faith, incapable of ascending higher, puts Him on a level with the great men of the past. In Peter, on the contrary, faith has never been so firm or so clear; he has received a revelation from the Father, and he believes it. Once more is verified the providential law: "To him who hath shall be given; from him who hath not there shall be taken even that which he hath."

The grace of faith calls forth as recompense the grace of a new vocation: Simon, son of Jona, shall be Peter, the Rock, and on this rock the Church will be built, and the gates of hell shall not prevail against it.[50] Peter will have the power to bind and to loose, and all the sentences he declares on earth will be confirmed in heaven; later on this power of binding and loosing will be conferred on all the Apostles.[51]

[50] The meaning of this text is beyond doubt. Protestants attempted for a long time to diminish the office of St. Peter; their interpretations are nowadays universally abandoned. Plummer, an Anglican exegete, writes: "All attempts to explain the 'rock' in any other way than as referring to Peter have ignominiously failed. Neither the confession of Peter nor the faith of Peter is an adequate explanation. But at the same time it is clear that the promise is made to Peter, *as confessing his faith,* and also as confessing it *on behalf of the Twelve.*" The objections which have been advanced against the complete authenticity of this text must be similarly set aside: no statement of Jesus has more manifestly retained its Aramaic colour. Cf. *Life and Teaching of Jesus Christ,* Vol. I, pp. 354-8.

[51] Cf. *supra,* p. 100.

"Then Jesus commanded his disciples that they should tell no one that he was the Christ" (*Matt.* xvi, 20). This is not the first time that we find in the Gospels these injunctions of silence; [52] but never had they greater cause. In the confusion which existed at that time in the opinions of the Jews concerning Jesus, the greatest prudence was called for, and this reserve was especially necessary in the half-pagan land then being traversed by the Master with the little group of his disciples.

The Prediction of the Passion

At least in the Apostles themselves the faith which Peter had just confessed ought to be sufficiently strong to bear the weight of the saddest confidences. And so for the first time Jesus tells them of the future which awaits Him: "He must go to Jerusalem, and suffer many things from the ancients and scribes and chief priests, and be put to death, and the third day rise again." (*Matt.* xvi, 21). Later on Jesus will explain in more precise detail the terrible sufferings of His passion, the scourging and the cross; but His death, which He already foretells, is for the Apostles a terrible and unforeseen revelation. Jesus adds at once, as He always does, the prophecy of His resurrection to that of His death, but the blow has been so painful that this glorious vision remains unperceived. Peter cannot contain himself, and taking Jesus aside, he says to Him: "Lord, be it far from thee, this shall not be unto thee." But He, turning, says to Peter: "Go behind me, Satan! Thou art a scandal unto me, because thou thinkest not according to the views of God, but according to those of men." Peter keeps silent, humbly and sadly, but does not as yet understand. But this lesson of suffering is so indispensable that Jesus desires to give it even to those whom He had not admitted on this occasion to the communication of the Messianic secret:

"And calling the multitude [53] together with His disciples, He said to them: 'If any man will follow me, let him deny himself, and take up his cross, and follow me. For whosoever will save his life, shall lose it; and whosoever shall lose his life for my sake and the gospel, shall save

[52] On the Messianic secret in the Gospels as a whole, and particularly on this occasion, cf. L. de Grandmaison, *Jesus Christ*, Engl. tr., Vol. II, p. 17 and n. 7.

[53] We see by this word that even in this half-pagan country the fame of Jesus attracted to him other witnesses besides the Twelve.

it. For what shall it profit a man, if he gain the whole world, and suffer the loss of his soul? Or what shall a man give in exchange for his soul? For he that shall be ashamed of me, and of my words, in this adulterous and sinful generation: the Son of Man also will be ashamed of him, when he shall come in the glory of his Father with the holy angels.' " (*Mark* viii, 34-38. *Cf.* Matt. xvi, 24-27; *Luke* ix, 23-26.)

Many times had Jesus repeated to His disciples the conditions which He required in all those who desired to follow Him.[54] On this occasion, coming after this first prediction of the Passion, this instruction was particularly important: we see now what it means to follow Jesus, whither the Master leads His disciples, and by what way. Six days after this conversation at Cæsarea Philippi, a still more solemn revelation was granted to three Apostles, and by them to the whole Church: the Transfiguration.[55]

The Transfiguration

Jesus had taken with Him Peter, James and John, and had withdrawn to the mountain to pray; "and whilst he prayed, the aspect of his countenance was transfigured, and his raiment became white and glittering"; close to Him were two men talking with Him: these were Moses and Elias. The Apostles were impressed by this vision; Peter cried out: "Master, it is good for us to be here, let us make three tents, one for thee, one for Moses, and one for Elias." He knew not what he said, adds St. Mark, for they were all afraid.

But Jesus was going to receive a testimony still more sacred than that of Moses and Elias: a luminous cloud overshadowed them, and the Apostles were frightened when they entered the cloud. From the cloud a voice was heard: "This is my beloved son, hear him." At Cæsarea Philippi Jesus had said to Peter: "Flesh and blood hath not revealed it to thee, but my Father who is in heaven"; now this revelation made itself heard; from the cloud where He dwelt, God repeated to the Apostles the supreme testimony which He had already given to His Son at His baptism; and this time the

[54] We find them in *Matt.* x, 34-9, in the instructions given to the Apostles; in *Luke* xiv, 26-7, addressed to all the disciples; in *Luke* xvii, 33, in an eschatological discourse; in *John* xii, 25-6, when Jesus entered Jerusalem.

[55] This scene is related by the three synoptists: *Matt.* xvii, 1-13; *Mark* ix, 2-13; *Luke* ix, 28-36. Contrary to their custom, all three give the date: six days (*Luke* says "about eight days") after Cæsarea Philippi; they mean thereby to bring out the close link which attaches these two revelations to each other.

testimony was better understood and more perfectly obeyed, finding hearts better prepared.

"And as they came down from the mountain, he charged them not to tell any man what things they had seen, till the Son of Man shall be risen again from the dead" (*Mark* ix, 8). Here once more we find the providential economy of the Christian revelation: this manifestation, the most striking in the whole life of the Lord, had only three witnesses, and its secret was to be kept until His Resurrection. Then the witnesses would speak, and the Church would believe on their word.[56]

The Disciples

After these great revelations, which mark the summer of the year 29, Jesus did not delay in leaving Galilee; he was going to ascend to Jerusalem for the great festivals, cross Samaria, preach in Perea, and withdraw to the desert. We cannot follow in detail all these episodes which filled the last year in the life of Christ. Two most important facts demand our attention: the choosing and training of the disciples, and the efforts made by Jesus at Jerusalem.

Already at the beginning of the public ministry we have seen how the Lord called to Him the Twelve; these Apostles were evidently the pastors and doctors of the Church that Jesus intended to found. They will remain such always; Judas will fall away, but he will be replaced in the apostolic college by St. Matthias. When there is question of adding this twelfth Apostle, Peter, the head of the apostolic college, will ask that he be chosen from "those men who have companied with us all the time that the Lord Jesus came in and went out among us, beginning from the baptism of John until the day when he was taken up from us" (*Acts* i, 21-22). There were, then, during the whole life of Jesus, a group of faithful disciples who followed Him closely like the Apostles themselves.

It is St. Luke above all who tells us of these disciples [57] in the second part of his Gospel, in the course of the accounts that he gives

---

[56] An echo of this preaching will be found in the Second letter of St. Peter (i, 16-19). Cf. *Life and Teaching of Jesus Christ*, Vol. I, pp. 367-8.

[57] It is very likely that in the course of the long stay which he made at Cæsarea near to St. Paul when a prisoner (60 to 62), St. Luke came to know personally some of these disciples, or persons connected with them, as for instance Philip the Deacon and his four daughters, or again Cleophas, one of the two disciples of Emmaus.

of the journeys of Jesus to Samaria, Judea, and Perea. He first narrates some incidents which show the conditions laid down by Jesus on whosoever wished to follow Him:

"As they walked in the way, a certain man said to him: 'I will follow thee whithersoever thou goest.' Jesus said to him: 'The foxes have holes, and the birds of the air nests; but the Son of Man hath not where to lay his head.' But he said to another: 'Follow me.' And he said: 'Lord, suffer me first to go and to bury my father.' And Jesus said to him: 'Let the dead bury their dead: but go thou, and preach the kingdom of God.' And another said: 'I will follow thee, Lord; but let me first take my leave of them that are at my house.' Jesus said to him: 'No man putting his hand to the plough, and looking back, is fit for the Kingdom of God.'" [58]

The Mission of the Disciples

We see that Jesus demanded first of all from those who desired to follow Him, detachment from family ties and the abandonment of earthly goods. That is what He set before the rich young man, and the poor fellow recoiled before the sacrifice: that is what He preached to the little group of faithful ones who followed Him:

"Fear not, little flock, for it hath pleased your Father to give you a kingdom. Sell what you possess and give alms. Make to yourselves bags which grow not old, a treasure in heaven which faileth not: where no thief approacheth, nor moth corrupteth. For where your treasure is, there will your heart be also" (Luke xii, 32-34).

In this whole chapter of St. Luke we find again many sayings included by St. Matthew in the Sermon on the Mount; but the requirements are here more urgent: Jesus is addressing himself to chosen ones, to the "little flock" which is following Him. This distinction between the multitude and the chosen few is very clear in the story of the rich young man related by the three synoptists. [59] This young man had faithfully carried out the Law, he sincerely desired eternal life, and when he came to kneel before Jesus, there

[58] Luke ix, 57-62. Cf. Matt. viii, 19-22. These incidents are placed by Luke in the journey across Samaria; Matthew narrates the first two and puts them in Galilee. The date matters little, what makes these incidents important is the lesson which follows from them.

[59] Matt. xix, 16-30; Mark x, 17-31; Luke xviii, 18-30.

was in him so much uprightness that Jesus looked on him and loved him; he lacked only one thing:

"If thou wilt be perfect, go sell what thou hast, and give to the poor, and thou shalt have treasure in heaven: and come, follow me."

There are, then, besides the commandments, some more exacting rules of conduct which are imposed on all those who "will be perfect." Jesus sums them up in one word: the abandonment of earthly goods. This distinction between commandments and counsels will be found again very clearly in the teaching of the Apostles at Jerusalem,[60] in St. Paul,[61] and in the Apostolic Fathers.[62] From the first it has characterised Christian morality.

In presence of the severe conditions which Jesus imposes on those who want to follow Him, one must reflect well:

"Which of you having a mind to build a tower, doth not first sit down, and reckon the charges that are necessary, whether he have the wherewithal to finish it; lest, after he hath laid the foundation, and is not able to finish it, all that see it begin to mock him, saying: 'This man began to build, and was not able to finish'? . . . So likewise every one of you that doth not renounce all that he possesseth, cannot be my disciple" (*Luke* xiv, 28-33).

These disciples gathered together by the Master are called not only to follow Him, but also to preach; at the beginning of the journeys in which Jesus was once more to undertake the evangelisation of Southern Palestine, He sent forth seventy disciples on a mission.[63]

"The Lord appointed also other seventy-two and he sent them two and two before his face into every city and place whither he himself was to come. And he said to them: 'The harvest indeed is great, but the labourers are few. Pray ye therefore the Lord of the harvest, that he send labourers into his harvest. Go: Behold I send you as lambs among wolves. Carry neither purse, nor scrip, nor shoes; and salute no man by the way. Into whatsoever house you enter, first say: Peace to this house. And if a son of peace be there, your peace shall rest upon him; but

[60] Ananias and Sapphira had the right either to keep their property or the price of it (*Acts* v, 4).

[61] In particular, in the question of virginity (*I Cor.* vii, 25-40).

[62] Above all in the *Pastor* of Hermas, fifth similitude.

[63] The manuscripts and Fathers give two readings: seventy and seventy-two. The variation is unimportant.

if not, it shall return to you. And in the same house remain, eating and drinking such things as they have: for the labourer is worthy of his hire. Remove not from house to house. And into what city soever you enter, and they receive you, eat such things as are set before you. And heal the sick that are therein, and say to them: The kingdom of God is come nigh unto you. But into whatsoever city you enter, and they receive you not, going forth into the streets thereof, say: Even the very dust of your city that cleaveth to us, we wipe off against you. Yet know this, that the Kingdom of God is at hand. I say to you, it shall be more tolerable at that day for Sodom, than for that city" (Luke x, 1-12).

These instructions given to the disciples recall those which the Master had given to the Twelve when sending them out on a mission.[64] The mission of the Apostles crowned the ministry of Jesus in Galilee and extended its influence; the mission of the disciples prepared for the evangelisation of the southern provinces. This second preaching, like the first, was eagerly welcomed: the disciples returned full of joy: "Lord," said they to Jesus, "the devils themselves are subject to us in Thy name!" (Luke x, 17). And Jesus answered: "I saw Satan like lightning fall from heaven." This was one of the most lively joys in the Gospel, it arose not only from the successes already obtained, but from those still greater ones which it heralded:

"In that same hour, Jesus rejoiced in the Holy Ghost, and said: 'I confess to thee, O Father, Lord of heaven and earth, because thou hast hidden these things from the wise and prudent, and hast revealed them to little ones. Yea, Father, for so it hath seemed good in thy sight. All things are delivered to me by my Father; and no one knoweth who the Father is, but the Son, and to whom the Son will reveal him.' And turning to his disciples, he said: 'Blessed are the eyes that see the things which you see. For I say to you, that many prophets and kings have desired to see the things that you see and have not seen them; and to hear the things that you hear and have not heard them.'"[65]

This statement of Jesus, one of the most luminous recorded by the synoptists, clarifies the whole Gospel history: it explains the

[64] The mission of the Apostles is related by Matt. x, 1-15, Mark vi, 7-13, and Luke ix, 1-6.
[65] These two statements of Jesus are reported by St. Matthew but in different circumstances: the first after the embassy from John the Baptist (xi, 25), the second after the parables (xiii, 16). We must add that the mission of the disciples is given only in St. Luke; it provides a better setting for these words and makes their bearing clearer.

infinite importance of this revelation, so ardently awaited by the prophets and so misunderstood by the majority of the Jews; it distinguishes between the humble folk who receive it and the wise who reject it; lastly, and above all, it introduces us into the secret of God: the ineffable union of the Father and the Son, who know each other fully, and are the only ones who do so, apart from those whom they deign to introduce by grace into this intimacy. In this sentence is reflected the whole theology of the speeches of Jesus at Jerusalem as reported to us by St. John.

The Preaching of Jesus at Jerusalem

From the commencement of his ministry, Jesus had directed his efforts towards Jerusalem. Driven out by the hostility of the leaders, and above all, of the Pharisees, he returned there only in the course of the last year of his ministry. The Master did not prolong his stay, but He went there and spoke on the occasion of the great festivals: Pentecost,[66] the Feast of Tabernacles, the Dedication of the Temple, and the Pasch; the concourse of pilgrims made this preaching more fruitful; in addition, the presence of Galileans at Jerusalem was a help to Jesus: even at the approach of the supreme crisis, His enemies did not want His arrest and trial to take place during the feast, "lest there should be a tumult among the people" (*Mark* xiv, 2; *Matt.* xxvi, 5).

These addresses are reported only by St. John, but the accounts of the synoptists (*Matt.* xxiii, 37, *Luke* xiii, 34) presuppose them. All these scenes, described in the fourth gospel, are of a dramatic and poignant truth. Here better than anywhere else are manifested the fluctuations of opinion. Thus, at the beginning of the Feast of Tabernacles (vii, ii), "the Jews sought him, and said: 'Where is he?' And there was much murmuring among the multitude concerning him. For some said: 'He is a good man.' And others said: 'No, but he seduceth the people.'" Jesus nevertheless showed Himself openly and spoke. Immediately there was a repetition of the odious calumny of the Pharisees: "Thou hast a devil" (vii, 20). Jesus silenced His calumniators; the people of Jerusalem cried out: 'Is not this he whom they seek to kill? And behold he speaketh openly, and they say nothing to him. Have the

---

[66] We may with probability put the miracle at the pool of Bezatha on the Feast of Pentecost. Cf. *Life and Teaching of Jesus Christ*, Vol. I, p. xxix.

rulers known for a truth that this is the Christ? Yet we know this man, whence he is: but when the Christ cometh, no man knoweth whence he is." (25-27).

But many hearing Him were touched, and said amongst themselves: "When the Christ cometh, shall he do more miracles than these which this man doth?" (31).

"On the last and great day of the festivity, Jesus stood and cried, saying: 'If any man thirst, let him come to me, and drink. He that believeth in me, as the scripture saith, Out of his belly shall flow rivers of living water.' . . . Of that multitude therefore . . . some said: 'This is the prophet indeed"; others said: 'This is the Christ.' But some said: 'Doth the Christ come out of Galilee?' . . . Some of them would have apprehended him: but no man laid hands upon him. Attendants sent by the high priests and the Pharisees returned without having arrested him. 'Why have you not brought him?' demanded the leaders. The men replied: 'Never did man speak like this man.' The Pharisees therefore answered them: 'Are you also seduced? Hath any one of the rulers believed in him, or of the Pharisees? But this multitude that knoweth not the law, are accursed.' Nicodemus tried to intervene: 'Doth our law judge any man unless it first hear him and know what he doth?' They tried to intimidate him like the others: 'Art thou also a Galilean? Search the scriptures and see that out of Galilee a prophet riseth not.' " (vii, 37-52).

And in the midst of this hesitant multitude, and of the Pharisees and high priests who wished to destroy Him, Jesus dominated all by the ascendancy of His words and His power. Here even more than in Galilee we realise His superhuman greatness, which His enemies could neither destroy nor even hurt. We have just seen Him on the occasion of the Feast of Tabernacles routing the emissaries sent to arrest Him by the authority of His speech. A few days later, Jesus said to the Jews who appealed to Abraham against Him: "Before Abraham was, I am." The exasperated Jews took up stones to cast at Him; Jesus withdrew and went out of the Temple (viii, 59). At the Feast of the Dedication the same scene was repeated: Jesus had just said: "That which my Father hath given me is greater than all. . . . I and the Father are one" (x, 29-30). The Jews once more took up stones to stone Him. Jesus said to them: "Many good works I have showed you from my Father; for which of those works do you stone me?" The Jews answered Him: "For a good work we stone thee not, but for blas-

phemy, and because that thou, being a man, makest thyself God."
Jesus thereupon reminded them of His works: [67] "If I do not the
works of my Father, believe me not; but if I do, though you will
not believe me, believe the works, that you may know and believe
that the Father is in me, and I in the Father." The Jews then
sought to take Him, but He escaped from their hands (x, 39). It
was, indeed, a struggle between light and darkness; darkness endeavoured in vain to seize the light: it escaped them.

Theological Character of these Discourses

In these discourses and the lively and sometimes violent discussions which they aroused, theological affirmations are more
frequent and more categorical than in the Galilean preaching. We
notice this already in the first incident, the healing of the paralytic
at the pool. This miracle was performed by Jesus on a Sabbath
day, and the reaction to which it led amongst the Pharisees was
the same as that which we have already found more than once:
"Therefore did the Jews persecute him," says St. John (v,16)
"because he did these things on the Sabbath." But in His reply,
Jesus no longer confined Himself to the motives to which He had
appealed in other circumstances, such as "the sabbath is made
for man, and not man for the sabbath." His reply is now on a
higher plane: "My Father worketh until now, and I work" (v, 17).
The Jews understood all the bearing of this statement, and their
hatred was redoubled because of it: "Hereupon therefore the Jews
sought the more to kill him, because he did not only break the
sabbath, but also said God was his Father, making himself equal
to God" (v, 18).

We have noticed in the other discourses of Jesus, on the Feast
of Tabernacles and the Feast of the Dedication, equally decisive
affirmations: in the Father and the Son there are the same action,
the same power, the same knowledge, the same doctrine, the same,
nature: "I and the Father are one"; and the Son is above all the
great men of the Old Testament, and before them, in a life which
knows neither beginning nor end: "Before Abraham was made,
I am."

[67] First of all, in verses 34-5, Jesus points out how in the Old Testament the
divine majesty was communicated to simple men, to judges, and how, *a fortiori*,
he could claim a much higher communication. Cf. *Life and Teaching of Jesus
Christ*, Vol. II, pp. 106-9.

Similar theological affirmations are found in the synoptic gospels: it suffices to recall what we have found in St. Luke and St. Matthew: "All things are delivered to me by my Father; and no one knoweth who the Son is, but the Father; and who the Father is, but the Son, and to whom the Son will reveal him." But it is manifest that such texts are much more numerous in St. John. The reason is to be found in the object of the evangelist, who wrote above all to support the belief of his readers in Jesus Christ, the Son of God (xx, 31). With this object in view, he dwells with predilection on these discourses at Jerusalem. If we ask further why this preaching at Jerusalem had a more theological character, the reply is simple: those whom Jesus had before Him were no longer, as in Galilee, timid and uneducated peasants, but people who had spent their lives in examining the Scriptures (v, 39). Their pressing argumentation called for categorical replies, and their knowledge was wide enough to enable them to grasp the bearing of these; if they were scandalised thereby, this arose not from a weakness which could be treated gently, but from a malice which was inexcusable.

Furthermore, by thus carrying on the discussion on the theological plane, Jesus cut short the dangerous misunderstandings called forth by Messianism. His enemies, at Jerusalem even more than in Galilee, endeavoured to draw Him on to political ground; if He had followed them there, He would certainly have had to inculcate either prudence, in which case the multitudes would have abandoned Him, or else revolt, and then He would have been denounced to the Romans. That is the significance of so many urgent interrogations: "How long dost thou hold our souls in suspense? If thou be the Christ, tell us plainly" (John x, 24). The same summons was repeated by the Sanhedrin: "If thou be the Christ, tell us" (Luke xxii, 66). And it was this also which prompted captious questions: "Is it lawful to give tribute to Cæsar?" (Mark xii, 14).

He escaped all these traps by ascending high above all these human ambitions: My kingdom is not of this world." To this also tends the question He put concerning the Messias: "David calleth him Lord, how then can he be his son?" (Mark xii, 35-37). Jesus did not mean to deny thereby His Davidic sonship; He wanted them to see that He had another origin, infinitely higher. The discourses at Jerusalem constantly bring before His hearers and even His adversaries these same perspectives, in which the prejudices of a nationalistic Messianism are no longer to be feared. True, His enemies will find even here subject-matter for accusation: in these affirmations they will see blasphemies, and they will seek to stone Him. But at least the controversy becomes purely religious. Thus at the decisive hour of His condemnation before the Sanhedrin and before Pilate, Jesus will set aside every other accusation and will leave only this one remaining: He will not, as they had desired, be condemned as a seditious person threatening the Roman power; but because He said that He was the Son of God.[68]

The Last Weeks

The preaching at Jerusalem already foreshadowed the Passion: the homicidal projects which the enemies of Jesus had formed already at the time of the Galilean ministry were now firmly fixed in their minds; on several occasions they tried to put them into execution, but the hour fixed by God had not yet arrived; Jesus escaped from their hands. He knew well that this protection which now saved Him would soon be withdrawn, and that that would be the hour of darkness; He went on towards this in full confidence: "I must work the works of him that sent me, whilst it is day; the night cometh, when no man can work. As long as I am in the world, I am the light of the world" (*John* ix, 4).

The Raising of Lazarus

One miracle of the Lord's, more striking than any that He had hitherto performed, was to precipitate the crisis. Lazarus died at Bethany; his sisters, Martha and Mary, hesitated for some time to summon Jesus, their friend. They knew that He had withdrawn to Perea in order to escape the intrigues of the Jews; to bring Him back to the gates of Jerusalem would be to expose Him to great danger. Nevertheless, seeing that the death of their brother was imminent, they sent a messenger charged to say to Him: "Lord, thy friend is sick." Jesus allowed two days to pass, and then set out for Bethany; the frightened Apostles endeavoured to dissuade Him from doing so: "Rabbi, the Jews but now sought to stone thee;

[68] Cf. *Life and Teaching of Jesus Christ*, Vol. II, pp. 105-6.

and goest thou thither again?" Jesus answered: "Are there not twelve hours of the day? If a man walk in the day, he stumbleth not, because he seeth the light of this world." Thomas said: "Let us also go, that we may die with him." At Bethany Jesus found the whole house in mourning: Martha and Mary were lamenting their brother, who was now dead four days; many friends had come from Jerusalem and were weeping with them. Martha went out to meet Jesus: "Lord, if thou hadst been here, my brother had not died." She hoped still, but with an imperfect faith. "But now also I know that whatsoever thou wilt ask of God, God will give it thee." Jesus calls her higher: "I am the resurrection and the life," and Martha then says: "Yea, Lord, I have believed that thou art Christ, the Son of the living God, who art come into this world." Mary came in her turn and wept. Jesus wept with her; he made them lead Him to the tomb. The Jews followed Him there; before all the multitude, Jesus cried with a loud voice: "Lazarus, come forth." And the dead man came forth, bound feet and hands with winding bands, and his face covered with a napkin. "Loose him," said Jesus, "and let him go" (John xi, 1-44).

Many Jews who had witnessed this miracle believed; but some went to the Pharisees and told them what Jesus had done. Then the high priests and the Pharisees called together the Sanhedrin, and on the motion of Caiphas, decided on the death of Jesus: "It is expedient that one man should die for the people, and that the whole nation perish not" (xi, 50). Jesus withdrew with His disciples to Ephrem, on the borders of the desert.

At the approach of Easter, He made the journey down to Jericho, where He cured a blind man, and from thence He went up to Jerusalem, leading His frightened disciples:

"They were in the way going up to Jerusalem, and Jesus went before them, and they were astonished, and following were afraid. And taking again the Twelve, he began to tell them the things that should befall him, saying, 'Behold, we go up to Jerusalem, and the Son of Man shall be betrayed to the chief priests, and to the scribes and ancients, and they shall condemn him to death, and shall deliver him to the Gentiles. And they shall mock him, and spit on him, and scourge him, and kill him; and the third day he shall rise again'" (Mark x, 32-34).

On the Sabbath day before the Pasch, Jesus, followed by His apostles, arrived at Bethany; the sisters of Lazarus welcomed Him, moved with gratitude, but moved still more by the danger that He was incurring. Was it not in order to raise up their brother that He had exposed Himself to death? Mary poured out a precious ointment on His head, and then on His feet; the whole house was full of its odour. Judas, who had charge of the common purse, and who had robbed His Master, was indignant at this prodigality, by which he thought himself a loser. Jesus defended Mary: "Let her alone: why do you molest her? She hath wrought a good work upon me. . . . She is come beforehand to anoint my body for the burial. Amen I say to you, wheresoever this gospel shall be preached in the whole world, that also which she hath done shall be told for a memorial of her" (*Mark* xiv, 6-9).

Palm Sunday

The Jews flocked to Bethany to see Jesus, and Lazarus, whom He had raised from the dead. The next day, as it was known that Jesus was going to enter Jerusalem, an immense crowd came to meet Him, carrying palm branches and shouting: "Hosanna! Blessed is he that cometh in the name of the Lord: the King of Israel!" As He went on, the crowd became larger and more enthusiastic. "When he was come into Jerusalem, the whole city was moved, saying 'Who is this?' And the people said: 'This is Jesus the prophet, from Nazareth of Galilee' " (*Matt.* xxi, 10-11). The Pharisees were alarmed: they said to each other: "You see that we prevail nothing; the whole world is gone after him" (*John* xii, 19). Being unable to silence the crowd, they called upon Jesus to intervene: "Master, rebuke thy disciples." To whom He said: "I say to you, that if these shall hold their peace, the stones will cry out" (*Luke* xix, 39). He entered into the Temple, cured the blind and the lame, and the shouts redoubled, and also at the same time the indignation of the chief priests and scribes: "Hearing the children crying 'Hosanna to the Son of David,' they were moved with indignation, and said to him: 'Hearest thou what these say?' And Jesus said to them: 'Yea; have ye never read: Out of the mouth of infants and sucklings thou hast perfected praise?' " (*Matt.* xxi, 14-16).

But in the very midst of His triumph, Jesus did not lose sight of His approaching Passion, and the ruin of his unfaithful people. When descending the Mount of Olives towards Jerusalem, he contemplated the city and wept: "If thou hadst known, and that in this thy day, the things that are to thy peace; but now they are hidden from thy eyes. For the days shall come upon thee, and thy enemies shall cast a trench about thee, and compass thee round, and straiten thee on every side, and beat thee flat to the ground, and thy children who are in thee, and they shall not leave in thee a stone upon a stone, because thou hast not known the time of thy visitation." [69]

At the close of this day Jesus withdrew and hid Himself (John xii, 36). And indeed, in spite of all these acclamations, the Jewish people, intimidated by its leaders, refused to believe. That is the last impression which St. John leaves with us of this day: "Whereas he had done so many miracles before them, they believed not in him" (xii, 37).

Holy Week

Thus began the last week, the most tragic in the life of the Master. Each evening He retired to Bethany, each morning He went to Jerusalem and taught in the Temple. Barely a few weeks previously, when Jesus, after raising Lazarus, had withdrawn to Ephrem, the chief priests and Pharisees had given orders that anyone who knew where He was should denounce Him so that they could arrest Him (John xi, 57). Now He was in the Temple, in their very presence, and no one dared to lay a hand on Him. Never had their hatred been so violent, but they were afraid of the crowd, and wished to wait for the end of the festival; Judas was to sell his Master to them, and thus enable them to seize Him without giving the alarm to the people.

During these last days, Jesus carried on His work, foiling the plots of His enemies, and setting before them with more force than ever the terrible responsibility which they were incurring and putting upon their people: like murderous husbandmen, these men, to whom God had allotted the task of looking after His well-beloved vineyard the land of Israel, had outraged, beaten, and put to death

[69] *Luke* xix, 41-4. It was also in the course of entering Jerusalem that Jesus experienced the first pangs of the agony: "Now is my soul troubled. And what shall I say? Father, save me from this hour. But for this cause came I unto this hour. Father, glorify thy name!" A voice then came from heaven: "I have both glorified it, and will glorify it again" (*John* xii, 27-8).

the servants whom God had sent them to gather in His name the fruits of the vineyard.

"Having yet one son, most dear to him; he sent him also unto them last of all, saying: 'They will reverence my Son.' But the husbandmen said one to another: 'This is the heir; come let us kill him, and the inheritance shall be ours.' And laying hold of him, they killed him, and cast him out of the vineyard. What, therefore, will the lord of the vineyard do? He will come and destroy those husbandmen, and will give the vineyard to others" (*Mark* xii, 1-9).

The parable was so transparent that the Pharisees could not help crying out: "God forbid!" (*Luke* xx, 16). And Jesus, "looking on them, said: 'What is this then that is written, the stone which the builders rejected, the same is become the head of the corner? Whosoever shall fall upon that stone, shall be bruised: and upon whomsoever it shall fall, it will grind him to powder" (*Luke* xx, 17-18).

This text makes this impressive and terrible scene live again before our eyes: Jesus, upon whom is already falling the shadow of the Cross, makes one supreme effort in order to stop the Pharisees and the people whom they are destroying. We see Him as St. Luke describes Him, fixing His eyes upon His adversaries and threatening them with this fall and destruction. The chief priests and the Pharisees would have seized Jesus, but they dared not do so, fearing the crowd.

Yet once again Jesus repeated these warnings, and this time it was not a parable, but maledictions which fell with all their force on the scribes and Pharisees:

"Woe to you, scribes and Pharisees, hypocrites: because you shut the Kingdom of Heaven against men, for you yourselves do not enter in; and those that are going in, you suffer not to enter. Woe to you, scribes and Pharisees, hypocrites; because you devour the houses of the widows, praying long prayers. For this you shall receive the greater judgment. Woe to you, scribes and Pharisees, hypocrites; because you go round about the sea and the land to make one proselyte; and when he is made, you make him the child of hell twofold more than yourselves.

". . . Woe to you, scribes and Pharisees, hypocrites, because you are like to whited sepulchres, which outwardly appear to men beautiful, but within are full of dead men's bones, and of all filthiness. So you also outwardly indeed appear to men just; but inwardly you are full of hypocrisy and iniquity. Woe to you, scribes and Pharisees, hypocrites; that build the sepulchres of the prophets, and adorn the monuments of the just, and say: 'If we had been in the days of our fathers, we would not have been partakers with them in the blood of the prophets.' Wherefore you are witnesses against yourselves, that you are the sons of them that killed the prophets.

"Fill ye up then the measure of your fathers. You serpents, generation of vipers, how will you flee from the judgment of hell? Therefore, behold I send to you prophets, and wise men, and scribes: and some of them you will put to death and crucify, and some you will scourge in your synagogues, and persecute from city to city: that upon you may come all the just blood that hath been shed upon the earth, from the blood of Abel the just even unto the blood of Zacharias the son of Barachias, whom you killed between the Temple and the altar. Amen I say to you, all these things shall come upon this generation" (Matt. xxiii, 13-36).

This invective, the most terrible in all the Gospel, reveals the sadness of the Master in face of His people whom perverse leaders were seducing and destroying. This discourse ended with a cry of anguish, and a supreme appeal to Jerusalem:

"Jerusalem, Jerusalem, thou that killest the prophets, and stonest them that are sent to thee, how often would I have gathered together thy children, as the hen doth gather her chickens under her wings, and thou wouldest not! Behold, your house shall be left to you, desolate. For I say to you, you shall not see me henceforth till you say: 'Blessed is he that cometh in the name of the Lord!' " (Ibid., 37-39).

Leaving Jerusalem, Jesus went up the Mount of Olives with His Apostles. It was there that, turning once more to gaze at the Temple and the Holy City, the Master predicted to His disciples that all would be destroyed: "Seest thou all these great buildings? There shall not be left a stone upon a stone that shall not be thrown down" (Mark xiii, 2). The Apostles were astounded; when Jesus had reached with them the top of the Mount, Peter, James, John and Andrew took Him aside and asked Him about the end of time. Jesus replied by describing the catastrophe in which Jerusalem and the Temple would disappear, and then the still more terrible cataclysm in which the whole world will disappear,[70] and all this ended in this moral exhortation:

[70] On this eschatological discourse, cf. Life and Teaching of Jesus Christ, Vol. II, pp. 185-212; L. de Grandmaison, Jesus Christ, Vol. III, pp. 61-97; Lagrange, The Gospel of Jesus Christ, Vol. II, pp. 170-85; Prat, Jésus Christ, Vol. II, pp. 239-56; K. Weiss, Exegetisches zur Irrtumslosigkeit und Eschatologie Jesu Christi, Münster, 1916.

"Take ye heed, watch and pray. For ye know not when the time is. Even as a man who going into a far country, left his house; and gave authority to his servants over every work, and commanded the porter to watch. Watch ye therefore, for you know not when the lord of the house cometh: at even, or at midnight, or at the cockcrowing, or in the morning. Lest coming on a sudden, he find you sleeping. And what I say to you, I say to all: Watch" (*Mark* xiii, 33-37).

The Last Supper

For a long time the leaders of the Jewish people, the chief priests and Pharisees, had been engaged in a fight to the finish against Jesus; now this struggle had reached its climax; in His last discourse, Christ had clearly revealed their homicidal projects and had foretold to them the punishment for these. These threats only angered them the more. Nothing but the fear of the people held them back; they decided, in order to avoid a rising, to wait for the end of the Paschal festivities.

Then Judas presented himself to them. For more than a year already this unhappy man had abandoned his Master in his heart; at Bethany he considered himself injured by the prodigality of Mary; he resolved to turn traitor: he would thereby gain some money, and he would shield himself from the measures which would doubtless threaten the Apostles as well as Jesus. Accordingly, he went to the chief priests: "What will you give me, and I will deliver him unto you?" They paid him thirty pieces of silver, and from thenceforth he sought opportunity to betray Him (*Matt.* xxvi, 14-16).

Nevertheless, the Pasch drew near, and Jesus desired to celebrate it with His disciples.[71] He therefore sent Peter and John to make the necessary preparations, and Himself followed them with the Apostles.

When the hour was come, He sat down at table, and the Apostles with Him, and He said to them: "With desire I have desired to eat

[71] It is clear from St. John that Jesus was killed on the 14th Nisan, the day when the Jews ate the Pasch: xviii, 28; cf. xiii, 1, xix, 31; *Life and Teaching of Jesus Christ*, Vol. I, p. xxxi. But on the other hand, the texts in the Synoptics give one to understand sufficiently clearly that Jesus had celebrated the Pasch with his disciples: *Luke* xxii, 15, and other texts quoted, *ibid.*, Vol. II, pp. 217-18. Various solutions have been advanced of this problem: the most likely one supposes a divergence in the computation of the days of the month; see *ibid.*, pp. 219 *et seq.*; Prat, *Jésus Christ*, Vol. II, pp. 518-20.

this pasch with you, before I suffer. For I say to you, that from this time I will not eat it, till it be fulfilled in the Kingdom of God" (*Luke* xxii, 14-15).

Seeing that His Apostles even in this solemn hour still quarreled about the first places (*ibid.*, 24-27), Jesus, not content with giving them a verbal lesson in humility, gave them one by His own example, in washing the feet of all of them (*John,* xiii, 1-20). Then, repeatedly and with great sorrow, the Master announced the betrayal which was about to take place; Judas, whom no warning could touch, went out suddenly to consummate his crime.

Jesus then accomplished what He had promised the preceding year at Capharnaum: He gave to His Apostles, and by them to the Church, the bread from heaven. This institution of the Holy Eucharist is attested to us by the three synoptics and by St. Paul. He must transcribe here the narrative of this fact which will govern the whole life of the Church and all its worship:

"Whilst they were at supper, Jesus took bread, and blessed, and broke, and gave to His disciples, and said, 'Take ye, and eat. This is my body.' And taking the chalice, He gave thanks, and gave to them, saying: 'Drink ye all of this. For this is my blood of the New Testament, which shall be shed for many unto the remission of sins. And I say to you, I will not drink from henceforth of this fruit of the vine, until that day when I shall drink it with you anew in the kingdom of my Father.'" [72]

The teaching of St. Paul to his converts sufficiently reveals to us the simple and docile faith with which from the first the Church has received these solemn affirmations of the Master:

"As often as you shall eat this bread, and drink the chalice, you shall show the death of the Lord, until he come. Therefore, whosoever shall eat this bread, or drink the chalice of the Lord unworthily, shall be guilty of the body and of the blood of the Lord. But let a man prove himself: and so let him eat of that bread, and drink of the chalice. For he that eateth and drinketh unworthily, eateth and drinketh judgment to himself, not discerning the body of the Lord" (I Cor. xi, 26-29).

The discourse at Capharnaum which we have given above, had prepared the Apostles for the understanding of this mystery, and

[72] *Matt.* xxvi, 26-9. Cf. *Mark* xiv, 22-5; *Luke* xxii, 14-20; *I Cor.* xi, 23-9. On the meaning of these four passages, cf. *Life and Teaching of Jesus Christ,* Vol. II, pp. 236 *et seq.*

has subsequently initiated all Christians into it. Thereby they have come to understand the intimate connection between the Incarnation and the Eucharist, and the indispensable necessity for every man to receive this bread from heaven, the life of the world:

"I am the bread of life. Your fathers did eat manna in the desert, and are dead. This is the bread which cometh down from heaven, that if any man eat of it, he may not die. I am the living bread which came down from heaven. If any man eat of this bread, he shall live for ever, and the bread that I will give is my flesh, for the life of the world" (*John* vi, 48-51).

These promises are now clarified and completed: this flesh is going to be given for the salvation of the world. It is already given at the Supper, as it will be in a few hours on the Cross, and that is what is signified by these words of the institution: 'This is my body, delivered for you," [73] "this is my blood, the blood of the testament, which is shed for many, for the remission of sins." [74] And when the faithful receive this body and blood, they communicate in the sacrifice of the Lord.[75] Until the last day, this sacrifice will be represented really before their eyes; Jesus will have left the earth, but the Apostles, and priests after them, will offer His sacrifice, obedient to the command He gave them: "Do this in memory of me." [76]

The Discourse After the Supper

The great discourse which followed the Supper, and which St. John reports,[77] constitutes an echo of the words of institution of the Eucharist: "Abide in me, and I in you. As the branch cannot bear fruit of itself unless it abide in the vine, so neither can you, unless you abide in me. I am the vine, you the branches: he that

[73] Text of St. Paul and St. Luke.
[74] Text of St. Matthew, and also of St. Mark ("this is my blood, the blood of the covenant which is shed for many"), of St. Paul ("this chalice is the new testament in my blood"), and of St. Luke ("this chalice is the new testament in my blood, shed for you").
[75] This is the express teaching of St. Paul, *I Cor.* x, 14-21.
[76] *Luke* xxii, 19; *I Cor.* xi, 24. Cf. *Life and Teaching of Jesus Christ*, Vol. II, pp. 247-50, and p. 242.
[77] Cf. *Life and Teaching of Jesus Christ*, Vol. II, pp. 255-88.

abideth in me, and I in him, the same beareth much fruit: for without me you can do nothing." [78]

And together with our union with Him, Jesus urges our own union with each other; this is the "new commandment" which Jesus repeats with emphasis in the discourse after the Supper.[79] As the ideal model of this union, He puts before us the unity of the divine persons: "That they may be one, as we also are one; I in them, and thou in me, that they may be made perfect in one." [80]

This union of all Christians in Himself is the supreme desire of the Lord, and is what He asks from His Father in His last prayer. In order to elevate Christians to this height, He reveals Himself and also the Father: "I have made known thy name to them, and will make it known, that the love wherewith thou hast loved me may be in them, and I in them" (xvii, 26). That is the last word in this prayer; in beginning it, Jesus had likewise said: "This is eternal life: That they may know thee, the only true God, and him whom thou hast sent" (xvii, 3).

This revelation is not yet completed: Jesus has hidden from the Apostles nothing that they could bear, but there are many mysteries which they cannot bear yet (John xvi, 12); the Holy Spirit, whom Jesus will send them, will reveal these to them. This will be the great divine gift and the fruit of the death of Christ: until his sacrifice is consummated, the Spirit is not given by God (vii, 39). Thus Jesus can say to the Apostles: "I tell you the truth: it is expedient to you that I go: for if I go not, the Paraclete will not come to you; but if I go, I will send him to you" (xvi, 7).

Thus these farewells of Jesus to the Apostles, while full of emo-

[78] John xv, 4-5. This great law governs all supernatural life. We can receive it only from Christ, but this communication is made chiefly by the Eucharist, and it is to this communication that all the other graces and all the other sacraments are orientated as to their end. Cf. De La Taille, Mysterium Fidei, pp. 557-88.

[79] "A new commandment I give unto you, that you love one another; as I have loved you, that you also love one another. By this shall all men know that you are my disciples, if you have love one for another" (John xiii, 34-5). "This is my commandment, that you love one another, as I have loved you. Greater love than this no man hath, that a man lay down his life for his friends" (xv, 12-13). "These things I command you, that you love one another" (xv. 17).

[80] John xvii, 22-3; cf. ibid., 21: "That they all may be one, as thou Father in me, and I in thee, that they also may be one in us." In the unity of this divine nature, Jesus in this discourse after the Supper shows us the Holy Spirit, together with the Son and the Father: xiv, 16-26; xv, 26; xvi, 7-14. Cf. Life and Teaching of Jesus Christ, Vol. II, pp. 263-74; History of the Dogma of the Trinity, Vol. I, pp. 400-4.

tion and tenderness, are full also of hope; He can say in all truth: "I will not leave you orphans" (xiv, 18): He remains with them, as He will repeat to them after His resurrection, "until the consummation of the world" (*Matt.* xxviii, 20), and He will give them the Holy Spirit.

The Passion and Death of Jesus

From the beginning of His ministry, Jesus appears to us as in conflict with the leaders of the Jewish people. It was to escape from their threats that He had had to leave Jerusalem after a few days, then, a few weeks later, abandon Judea, and finally, at the end of a year, Galilee. During the last year He could not stay long anywhere; He passed along the Phœnician coast, the region of Cæsarea Philippi, the borders of the Lake, Samaria, Judea, Perea, and returned to Jerusalem at the periods of the feasts. At the same time the hatred of His opponents became more threatening; it no longer confined itself, as during the Galilean ministry (*Mark* ii, 6), to hatching plots against Him; it now involved the Sanhedrin. On the motion of the high priest Caiaphas, it was decided to have Him put to death (*John* xi, 49-53), and as He had withdrawn into the desert, orders were given that any man who knew where He was should give information so that He might be arrested (*John* xi, 56).

In view of these extreme measures, it is not the arrest of the Master that astonishes us, but its tardy character. The long hesitation of the enemies of Jesus is explained by the fear of a popular tumult. But that is only a partial explanation: in many cases it cannot be appealed to, as above all in the case of the riots which more than once menaced Jesus at Nazareth (*Luke* iv, 30), or at Jerusalem (*John* viii, 59; x, 39). The ultimate explanation is to be sought in the divine protection which surrounded Him so long as His hour had not come. This is pointed out with emphasis by St. John: "No man laid hands on him, because his hour was not yet come" (vii, 30; viii, 20). And Jesus said the same to the chief priests and officers of the Temple who arrested Him: "I was daily with you in the Temple, and you did not stretch forth your hands against me: but this is your hour, and the power of darkness" (*Luke* xxii, 53).

If this protection now failed Jesus, it was because He Himself had deliberately renounced it. He knew that His hour had come, the hour which He had had constantly before His eyes, and for which He had come into this world (*John* xii, 27). He knew the will of His Father, and submitted to it: "That the world may know that I love the Father, and as the Father hath given me commandment, so do I" (xiv, 31). Saying this, He went forth to the garden, where He knew the traitor was to come to take Him. And even after His arrest, He knew that He had only to will it to escape from His enemies: "Thinkest thou," He said to Peter, "that I cannot ask my Father, and he will give me immediately more than twelve legions of angels? How then shall the scriptures be fulfilled, that so it must be done?" (*Matt.* xxvi, 53-54). Jesus, then, sees the divine will, freely accepts it, and gives Himself up: "Therefore doth the Father love me, because I lay down my life, that I may take it up again. No man taketh it away from me, but I lay it down of myself, and I have power to lay it down, and I have power to take it up again. This commandment have I received of my Father" (*John* x, 17-18).

The Agony in the Garden

This submission of the Son to the Father was not withheld for a moment, but it had to overcome temptations and terrible trials: not only the attacks of the prince of this world and of his minions, but also of terror and disgust amounting even to agony. The narrative of this intimate struggle that begins the story of the Passion; [81] it is, perhaps, the most moving and revealing page in it. In the scenes which follow, our attention tends to be fixed on the atrocious torture of the scourging and of the Cross, the cries of hatred of the Jews, the cruelty of Pilate, the obstinacy of Caiaphas and the Pharisees. But in the Garden we see neither torturers nor judges: Jesus is alone in presence of His Father, but He bears the weight of the sins of the world, He is crushed by it, and His suffering is such that it causes Him to sweat blood.

Going forth from Jerusalem, Jesus withdrew with His Apostles

[81] *Matt.* xxvi, 36-46; *Mark* xiv, 32-42; *Luke* xxii, 40-46. Cf. *Life and Teaching of Jesus Christ*, Vol. II, pp. 289-321. In this narrative, the two first Synoptics are strictly parallel to each other. Luke departs from them: he does not distinguish the three visits made by Jesus to His Apostles; he reports two things of which he is the only narrator: the visit of the angel, and the sweat of blood. The account of the agony is absent from St. John: on the other hand, he alone reports the first mental anguish of Jesus on the occasion of the entry into Jerusalem (xii, 24-7).

beyond the brook Cedron, to the foot of the Mount of Olives, into the Garden of Gethsemane. He said to His disciples: "While I go yonder, watch and pray." We have seen how Jesus passed the night in prayer on the eve of the great events in His life, but of all these none could be compared with what was to take place on the morrow. This time Jesus did not return alone: He took with Him His three intimate friends, Peter, James and John, so that they should be witnesses of His prayer, and above all to associate them in it: they also, in the course of this night, would be tempted, and to repulse this assault, they would need great strength, and they should pray for this.

"And when he was gone forward a little, he fell flat on the ground; and he prayed, that if it might be, the hour might pass from him. And he saith: 'Abba, Father, all things are possible to thee; remove this chalice from me; but not what I will, but what thou wilt.' And he cometh, and findeth them sleeping. And he saith to Peter: 'Simon, sleepest thou? Couldst thou not watch one hour? Watch ye, and pray, that you enter not into temptation. The spirit indeed is willing, but the flesh is weak.' And going away again, he prayed, saying the same words. And when he returned, he found them again asleep (for their eyes were heavy), and they knew not what to answer him. And he cometh the third time, and saith to them: 'Sleep ye now, and take your rest. It is enough; the hour is come: behold the Son of Man shall be betrayed into the hands of sinners. Rise up, let us go. Behold, he that will betray me is at hand" (*Mark* xiv, 35-41).

This account of the agony of the Lord was a scandal to the pagans. At the end of the second century, Celsus wrote: "If things happened as he willed, if he was stricken in obeying his Father, it is clear that nothing could have been hard or difficult for him, since he was God and willed all that. Why then did he lament? why groan? why did he seek to escape the death which he feared, saying: 'Father, if it be possible, let this chalice pass from me!" [82]

These objections concern us to-day only because of the attitude of mind they manifest: in this world which was hard and heartless (*Romans* i, 31) this agony, so bitterly felt, so simply described, must have seemed a weakness. The evangelists were aware of this state of mind, but they hid nothing. They narrate with the same transparent sincerity the whole Passion, the weakness of the Apos-

[82] *Apud Origen, Contra Celsum*, II, 21 (Migne, P.G., XI, 841); cf *ibid.*, 9 (808).

tles, and the torments and death of Jesus, just as they here recount His agony. This mystery of suffering and humiliation which had so dismayed the Apostles, and which they could scarcely believe, was to be for every Christian "the power and the wisdom of God" (*I Cor.* i, 24).

Judas arrived, guiding a large body of men armed with swords and staves. The "chief priests, officers of the Temple, and elders" had made up their minds to lead the group; a detachment of Roman soldiers accompanied them to lend them their strong arm. Jesus was before them, walking; Judas gave Him a kiss. Peter attempted to resist by force; Jesus stopped him, and healed Malchus; then He surrendered to His enemies: "The chalice which my Father hath given me, shall I not drink it?" (*John* xviii, 11). The disciples all abandoned Him and fled.

Jesus before Annas and Caiphas

Jesus was taken first to Annas. The old pontiff was no longer high priest, but he had occupied that office for a long time. His five sons succeeded him in it, and this year it was his son-in-law Caiphas who was the supreme pontiff. The head of the family was first given this mark of deference, and then Caiphas had Jesus brought before him, and took the matter of His trial in hand.[83]

He interrogated Jesus "concerning his disciples and his doctrine." As to His disciples, Jesus made no reply, not wishing to compromise anyone; on His doctrine He appealed to His public teaching: "I have spoken openly to the world; I have always taught in the synagogue and in the Temple, whither all the Jews resort; and in secret I have spoken nothing. Why askest thou me? Ask those who have heard what I have spoken unto them: behold, they know what things I have said." A servant struck Him. Jesus said: "If I have spoken evil, give testimony of the evil; but if well, why strikest thou me?"

This first interrogation made Caiphas realise that the trial was not going to be an easy one: would he be able to overcome the reserve of the accused man, and lead Him on to imprudent declarations, as he hoped? He did not know as yet whether he would

[83] On this succession of the facts, cf. *Life and Teaching of Jesus Christ,* Vol. II. p. 338 and n. 1. We assume here as probable an inversion in ch. xviii of St. John: verse 24 is to be read immediately after v. 13. The text is thus read in the Syriac Sinaiticus and in St. Cyril of Alexandria.

succeed. At least he realised that he would have to prepare with care for the morning session; the rest of the night should be devoted to this. Meanwhile, Jesus was taken to the prison, where He would be at the mercy of the Sanhedrin and their servants. In crossing the courtyard, Jesus turned round and looked at Peter, who had been taken inside by John and interrogated by servants and soldiers, had allowed himself to be intimidated, tried to extricate himself by equivocations, and ended finally in formal denials, oaths, and imprecations. The glance of Jesus aroused him and saved him: he went out weeping bitterly.

At daybreak, Caiphas resumed the interrogation of Jesus.[84] He had gathered together a great number of suborned witnesses; but their evidence did not agree. Two of them brought forward what Jesus had said about the Temple, misrepresenting it. Caiphas realising that all these charges were inconsistent, endeavoured to compromise Jesus by eliciting a reply: "Answerest thou nothing to the things which these witness against thee?" Jesus was silent. Then the high priest, dropping the false witnesses, went straight to the fundamental question, adjuring Jesus in the name of the living God[85] and asking Him: "Art thou the Christ, the Son of the Blessed One?" Jesus answered: "I am he. And you shall see the Son of Man sitting on the right hand of the Power, and coming on the clouds of heaven."[86]

This reply of Jesus was bound to lead to sentence of death: He knew this. He seemed to be the plaything of His enemies, constrained by them to this declaration which He had always refused to make. In reality, it was He who had chosen the ground on which He would fall. They wanted to make Him a rebel, a blasphemer against the Temple: all these accusations collapsed; they had to come to the decisive question. Did Jesus claim to be the Messias, the Son of God? The Jews had not wanted to be taken on to that ground: to condemn Jesus for calling Himself the Messias was a very dangerous thing: the Messianic claim was not in itself a blasphemy; it could only be so if the Messias claimed at the same time to be the Son of God; Jesus had implied this publicly, for instance, in the parable of the vineyard, but would He repeat it categorically before the Sanhedrin? Everything depended on Him,

[84] *Matt.* xxvi, 59; xxvii, 2; *Mark* xiv, 53; xv, 1; *Luke* xxii, 54; xxiii, 1.
[85] *Matt.* xxvi, 63.
[86] *Mark* xiv, 61-2; cf. *Matt.* xxvi, 63-4; *Luke* xxii, 66-71.

and He had always been so circumspect and so completely in control of His speech that His enemies might well fear that this time again He would refuse them the affirmation which would destroy Him. Another fear haunted them: was it not, with regard to the people, a terrible responsibility to condemn to death someone who had certainly said that He was the Messias and the Son of God, but who had, after all, upheld His claim by so many miracles? Might they not be reproached with having destroyed the hope of Israel? [87]

This last fear was only too well founded; but, determined on the death of Jesus, they set it aside. And they did not encounter the obstacle which they had feared: hitherto all their questions had failed in presence of the silence of Christ; now the time had come to speak: adjured in the name of the living God, by the high priest, before the sovereign council of His nation, Jesus gave the answer. He, the first of martyrs, willed to give the testimony which would cause His death, but would also found the faith of the Church.[88]

As soon as this reply of Jesus was heard, the high priest rent his garments, and said: "What further need have we of witnesses? You have heard the blasphemy. What think you?" And all answered: "He is worthy of death." [89]

Jesus before Pilate and Herod

After spitting in the face of Jesus and buffeting and striking Him, they led Him to Pilate.[90]

They themselves set forth quite clearly the motive of this step: "It is not lawful for us to put any man to death" (*John* xviii, 31). In their eyes the case was finished, but the sentence which they had passed was without legal force; it was necessary that Pilate should condemn Jesus; all their efforts were to be directed to this end.

[87] We may recall what St. Paul was to say to the Jews in Rome: "For the hope of Israel I am bound with this chain" (*Acts* xxviii, 20).

[88] On this supreme testimony, cf. L. de Grandmaison, *Jesus Christ*, Vol. II, pp. 167-73.

[89] *Matt.* xxvi, 65-6; *Mark* xiv, 63-4.

[90] The Jewish historian Juster (*Les Juifs dans l'empire romain*, Vol. II, p. 134) has endeavoured to free the Jewish nation from any responsibility for the condemnation of Jesus, and to put it on Pilate alone; he has been followed by Loisy, in his edition of the *Acts*, p. 309. Nothing justifies this distortion of the Gospel narrative. Cf. *Life and Teaching of Jesus Christ*, Vol. II, pp. 330-2, 359-60.

The Procurator had been in office for four years; he knew enough of Jerusalem and Judea to understand that the accusations which echoed before his tribunal arose from the jealousy of the Sanhedrin. Full of contempt for the Jews, he decided without hesitation to deal severely with them: he had given an example of this quite recently in the affair of the Galileans, whose blood he had mingled with their sacrifices; [91] but he did not intend to be an instrument of Jewish hatred. He would willingly have done what Gallio did at Corinth twenty years later (*Acts* xviii, 14-17), and have dismissed both accusers and accused. He attempted this, but the Sanhedrin, more insistent and more powerful than the Jews of Corinth, forced his hand.

They had condemned Jesus for blasphemy; they kept this religious point in the background at first, and accused Jesus of being a rebel, a pretender to the kingdom, who had upset all Judea from Galilee to Jerusalem. Pilate had a police force sufficiently vigilant to know what reliance was to be placed on this, but all the same he interrogated Jesus, convinced himself that the kingdom which He claimed was not of this world, and that Rome had nothing to fear from Him. Hearing Galilee mentioned, he took the occasion to send Jesus to Herod, who was then at Jerusalem.[92]

Herod had for a long time sought to see Jesus (*Luke* ix, 9). His frivolous curiosity, which had on some occasions taken pleasure in listening to John the Baptist, desired to see Jesus. The Master had always kept away from him, and but lately He had spoken severely of "that fox" (*Luke* xiii, 31). But now, in the extreme danger in which He was placed, the Galilean prophet would doubtless fall in with his wishes. Herod hoped this would be so, and rejoiced to see Him. But though he plied Jesus with questions, he received no answer at all. Herod felt hurt, and in derision gave to this king of the Jews a white robe, and sent Him back to Pilate.

The trial then recommenced, and in more unhappy circumstances for the Procurator, whose weakness was known to the Jews. In vain did he use the most miserable and cruel expedients; in vain he called upon the Jews to choose between Jesus and Barabbas, had Jesus scourged and then presented Him to the mob disfigured and

---

[91] *Luke* xiii, 1. Cf. *Life and Teaching of Jesus Christ,* Vol. II, pp. 355-8.
[92] This appearance of Jesus before Herod is related only by Luke (xxiii, 4-12); it has been called in question, but unreasonably. Cf. *Life and Teaching of Jesus Christ,* Vol. II, p. 365 and n. 1.

with a crown of thorns, saying to them: "Behold the man!" The shouts redoubled: "Crucify him! crucify him!" Pilate had wished to evoke pity; he had merely encouraged their hatred. Being weary, and hating the whole thing, he replied: "Take you him, and crucify him: I find no fault in him." "We have a law," replied the Jews, "and according to this law he ought to die, because he made himself the Son of God."

Before Pilate, as in the Sanhedrin, they had been led in spite of themselves on to that religious ground where Jesus stood and where they did not wish to follow. Later on St. Peter will say to the Christians: "Let none of you suffer as a murderer, or a thief, or a railer, or a coveter of other men's things. But if as a Christian, let him not be ashamed, but let him glorify God in that name" (*I Peter*, iv, 15-16). Similarly, Jesus Himself was not condemned for having caused a popular rising, or for preventing the payment of tribute to Cæsar. The decisive ground, before the Sanhedrin and before Pilate, was His divine Sonship.

Pilate became frightened. He resumed his questioning: "Whence art thou?" Jesus was silent. "Speakest thou not to me? Knowest thou not that I have power to crucify thee?" "Thou shouldst not have any power against me, unless it were given thee from above." Pilate, alarmed at the responsibility which he began to realise, sought from that time to stop the case; it was too late. "If thou release this man, thou art not Cæsar's friend. For whosoever maketh himself a king, speaketh against Cæsar."

In face of this threat Pilate ceased to struggle any longer. He took his seat on his tribunal, and had Jesus brought forth: "Behold your king!"—"Away with him, away with him, crucify him!"— "Shall I crucify your king?"—"We have no king but Cæsar!" Then he delivered Him to be crucified.[93]

The Death on the Cross

Together with Jesus, two thieves were sent to their death. Escorted by Roman soldiers headed by a centurion, the three con-

---

[93] *John* xix, 1-16. To this narrative of St. John's we may add a feature reported by *Matt.* xxvii, 24-25: Pilate, feeling overwhelmed by the growing tumult, and being no longer able to make himself heard, had water brought to him, and washed his hands in the presence of the people, saying: "I am innocent of the blood of this just man: look you to it." And the whole people answering, said: "His blood be upon us and upon our children."

demned men, carrying their crosses, made their way to Golgotha, a rocky mound outside the city, quite close to the ramparts.[94]

Slowly the funereal procession threaded its way through the narrow streets filled with the crowds of Paschal pilgrims. Jesus, exhausted by the scourging, collapsed under the weight of the cross; Simon of Cyrene was told to carry it, and they set out once more. "And there followed him a great multitude of people, and of women, who bewailed and lamented him. But Jesus turning to them said: 'Daughters of Jerusalem, weep not over me, but weep for yourselves and for your children. . . . If in the green wood they do these things, what shall be done in the dry?' " (*Luke* xxiii, 27-30). They arrived at Calvary, and Jesus and the two thieves were nailed to the crosses. During this torture, Jesus prayed: "Father, forgive them; they know not what they do" (*Luke* xxiii, 33).

Then the soldiers divided His vesture, and drew lots for His tunic. Jesus was dying; the crowd watched Him; passers by insulted Him; they knew Him only through the echoes of the trial, which they repeated: "Vah, thou that destroyest the temple of God and in three days buildest it up again; Save thyself, coming down from the cross" (*Mark* xv, 29-30). The leaders mockingly said to one another: "He saved others; himself he cannot save. Let Christ, the King of Israel, come down now from the cross that we may see and believe!" (*Ibid.*, 31-32). The soldiers joined in: "If thou be the King of the Jews, save thyself!" (*Luke* xxiii, 37). And similarly one of the thieves: "If thou be the Christ, save thyself and us." But the other reproved him: "Neither dost thou fear God, seeing that thou art under the same condemnation? And we indeed justly, for we receive the due reward of our deeds; but this man hath done no evil. Lord, remember me when thou shalt come into thy kingdom."—"To-day," replied Jesus, "thou shalt be with me in paradise" (*Luke* xxiii, 39-43).

Darkness covered the land, there was silence around the cross, and the little group of faithful souls drew closer:

"There stood by the cross of Jesus, his mother, and his mother's sister, Mary of Cleophas, and Mary Magdalen. When Jesus therefore had

[94] On the site of Calvary, see Vincent, *Jérusalem*, Vol. II, pp. 89 *et seq.*: "Leaving aside the proofs till later, we will remark here that the authenticity of Calvary and the Holy Sepulchre is vested with the best guarantees of certitude which could be desired in such a subject." Cf. Dalman, *Les itinéraires de Jésus*, ch. xxi, *Golgotha et le tombeau*, pp. 449-96.

seen his mother and the disciple standing whom he loved, he saith to his mother: 'Woman, behold thy son.' After that, he saith to the disciple: 'Behold thy mother.' And from that hour, the disciple took her to his own" (*John* xix, 25-27).

Then, in the silence a great cry resounded: "Eloi, eloi, lama sabachthani?" These are in Aramaic the first words of Psalm xxi: "My God, my God, why hast thou forsaken me?" On the threshold of His ministry, it was by the oracles of the Bible that Jesus had repulsed the temptations; in this hour of agony, it was from the Psalms that He borrowed His prayer; the Gospel has conserved only the first verse, but Jesus doubtless continued the recitation of this prophetic psalm, which described in advance the torments of Christ; it begins with a cry of anguish, but finishes with a song of hope and triumph: "Ye that fear Jahveh, praise him! . . . For he hath not slighted, nor despised the supplication of the poor man; neither hath he turned away his face from me, and when I cried to him he heard me."

Another cry was heard from Jesus: "I thirst." The soldiers put to His mouth a sponge filled with vinegar. Jesus said: "All is consummated," and with a loud cry He added: "Father, into thy hands I commend my spirit," and bowing His head He died.

After the death of Jesus, the veil of the Temple was rent, the earth quaked, the rocks were rent, the tombs were opened, and dead saints came forth and walked in the streets of Jerusalem. The centurion cried: "Truly this man was the Son of God," and the crowds who had been present at this spectacle returned to Jerusalem beating their breasts.

A little group of faithful ones remained near the cross: Mary, the mother of Jesus, John His disciple, the holy women who up till recently had served Him in Galilee and had followed Him to Calvary; Mary Magdalen, Mary the mother of James the Less and of Joseph, Salome, and many others who had ascended to Jerusalem with Him (*Mark* xv, 41). Soldiers, sent by Pilate at the request of the Jews, approached the crucified ones, broke the legs of the two thieves, and one of them, seeing that Jesus was already dead, pierced His heart with a lance, and there gushed forth blood and water (*John* xi, 31-37).

Joseph of Arimathea, a member of the Sanhedrin, had obtained from Pilate permission to bury Jesus; he wished to place the body in the tomb which he had prepared for himself in a garden quite close to Calvary. He came with Nicodemus, who brought a hundred pounds of aromatical spices. They took the body of Jesus, bound it in clothes with the spices, and laid it in the tomb hewn from the rock. The women saw the entombment; returning to Jerusalem they bought spices and perfumes; then they stayed in their homes, because nightfall had come, and the Sabbath had begun.

The next day, the Sabbath day, the chief priests and the Pharisees went to Pilate and said: "Sir, we have remembered that that seducer said while he was yet alive: 'After three days I will rise again.' Command therefore the sepulchre to be guarded until the third day, lest perhaps his disciples come and steal him away, and say to the people: 'He is risen from the dead,' and the last error shall be worse than the first." Pilate replied: "You have a guard, go, guard it as you know." They therefore made the sepulchre sure, sealing the stone, and setting guards (*Matt.* xxvii, 62-66).

The Resurrection

As day dawned, the holy women, no longer held back by the Sabbath rest, ran to the tomb, carrying the spices they had bought, in order to complete the burial of Jesus. They were unaware of the presence of the guards, but they remembered that there was a great stone rolled to the entrance of the tomb, and on the way they said to one another: "Who shall roll us back the stone from the door of the sepulchre?"

But looking, they saw that the stone, which was very great, had been rolled on one side. Entering into the sepulchre, they saw a young man seated on the right, clothed with a white robe, and they were astonished. But He said to them "Be not affrighted. You seek Jesus of Nazareth who was crucified: he is risen, he is not here. Behold the place where they laid him. But go, tell his disciples, and Peter, that he goeth before you into Galilee; there you shall see him, as he told you." Then, going out, they fled from the sepulchre, trembling and frightened. And they said nothing to any man, for they were afraid (*Mark* xvi, 1-8).

Mary Magdalen had not stayed with the other women: as soon as she saw that the stone was rolled away and the tomb open, she had but one thought: "They have taken away the Lord out of the sepulchre, and we know not where they have laid him" (*John* xx,

2). She ran first to tell this to Peter and John; the two Apostles, greatly impressed, ran to the sepulchre. Peter entered first: he examined everything: the winding sheet laid aside, the linen with which the head had been covered, folded on one side. John entered also: he saw, and believed (*ibid.*, 3-10).

Mary had also followed them, but without entering into the sepulchre. Once more she glanced within: she saw two angels seated on the tombstone, one at the head, the other at the feet. "Woman, why weepest thou?" She could only repeat the thought which obsessed her: "They have taken away my Lord, and I know not where they have laid him." She turned from the tomb, and saw a man standing close by her; she thought it was the gardener. "Sir, if thou hast taken him hence, tell me where thou hast laid him, and I will take him away." Jesus said to her: "Mary!" She turned to Him and said: "Rabboni!"—"Touch me not," said Jesus to her, "for I am not yet ascended to my Father. But go to my brethren, and say to them: I ascend to my Father and to your Father, to my God and to your God" (*ibid.*, 11-12).

These incidents, which succeeded one another so rapidly on this Paschal morning, reveal to us, through the transparence of the simple and sober narrative, the confusion of the most faithful disciples, whom the death of the Master had shocked, and their slowness to believe. Their love was as ardent as ever, but hope was extinct. The holy women, at the discovery of the displaced stone and of the empty tomb, felt it was just one more blow to discourage them: "They have taken away the Lord, and I know not where they have laid him." Mary Magdalen above all, overwhelmed with sorrow, paid no attention to the angels, and perceived without noticing the One who appeared to her. She was recalled from her sorrow only by the voice of Jesus: the Good Shepherd calls His sheep by their name, and the sheep follow Him, because they know His voice.

The Appearances to the Apostles

The Apostles and the other disciples were, like the holy women, slow to believe. In the course of this day, the disciples from Emmaus were still to say: "Certain women of our company affrighted us, who before it was light, were at the sepulchre, and not finding his body, came saying that they had also seen a vision of angels who say that he is alive. And some of our people went to the sepulchre, and found it so as the women had said, but him they found not" (*Luke* xxiv, 22-24).

The Apostles were convinced only by the testimony of Peter: "The Lord is risen indeed, and hath appeared to Simon"; [95] those were the words by which they welcomed the account of the two disciples from Emmaus when these, greatly excited by the appearance of the Lord, came to tell them about it at the Cenacle.[96] And while the two disciples narrated how Jesus had joined them on the road and had talked with them, and how finally they had recognised Him in the breaking of bread, Jesus Himself suddenly appeared in the midst of the Apostles in this upper room with closed doors: "Peace to you. It is I, be not afraid"; and so that they should recognise Him, He showed them His hands and His side. And then again:

"Peace be to you. As the Father hath sent me, I also send you. . . . And he breathed on them, and he said to them: 'Receive ye the Holy Ghost. Whose sins you shall forgive, they are forgiven them; and whose sins you shall retain, they are retained.'" [97]

Jesus had told His disciples to return into Galilee. It was there that He promised to meet them,[98] and it was there that several of the most important appearances were to take place. The Apostles did not know the date of the meeting, and meanwhile they gathered round St. Peter and accompanied him when he went fishing. After a night of fruitless labour, Jesus appeared on the bank, was recognised through a miraculous draught of fishes, and after the meal which He took with them, He addressed Himself individually to St. Peter: "Simon, son of John, lovest thou me more than these?" —"Yea, Lord, thou knowest that I love thee." Three times did Jesus repeat His question; the third time the Apostle, deeply moved by the Lord's insistence and the memory of his fall, replied: "Lord,

[95] This appearance to St. Peter is one of the most formally attested: by St. Paul (*I Cor.* xv, 5) and by St. Luke (xxiv, 34), but it is not recorded in detail.

[96] Cf. *Life and Teaching of Jesus Christ*, Vol. II, pp. 410-11.

[97] *John* xx, 19-25; *Luke* xxiv, 36-43. Eight days later, there was a new appearance in the presence of St. Thomas (*John* xx, 26-9).

[98] This appointment, recorded by *Matt.* xxviii, 7, and *Mark* xvi, 7, is explained by the important appearances which took place in Galilee; it does not efface the express mention of the appearances in Jerusalem. Cf. *Life and Teaching of Jesus Christ*, Vol. II, pp. 417-20. [See also article by E. C. Messenger in *Clergy Review* for April, 1941, "The Appearances of the Risen Jesus."]

thou knowest all things; thou knowest that I love thee." This triple confession was rewarded by a triple investiture: "Feed my lambs," said Jesus to him, and then twice: "Feed my sheep." And to the Apostle thus reinstated before all and confirmed in his office as shepherd and head, Christ foretold the martyrdom which awaited him: "Thou shalt stretch forth thy hands, and another shall gird thee and lead thee whither thou wouldst not" (*John* xxi, 10-24).

A little while, apparently, after this appearance there took place the most solemn manifestation of all, which is related by St. Matthew (xxviii, 16-20):

"The eleven disciples went into Galilee, unto the mountain where Jesus had appointed them. And seeing him they adored; but some doubted. And Jesus coming, spoke to them, saying: 'All power is given to me in heaven and in earth. Going therefore, teach ye all nations, baptizing them in the name of the Father, and of the Son, and of the Holy Ghost. Teaching them to observe all things whatsoever I have commanded you: and behold I am with you all days, even to the consummation of the world.'"

On the occasion of their first mission, Jesus had said to the Apostles: "Go ye not into the way of the Gentiles, and into the city of the Samaritans enter ye not, but go ye rather to the lost sheep of the house of Israel" (*Matt.* x, 5-6). Now all the barriers were removed: the Apostles were sent to all nations. This universal mission is given in virtue of a sovereign power: "All power is given to me in heaven and in earth." All this was the fruit of the Passion of Christ: "When I shall be lifted up from the earth, I will draw all things to myself." And in this tremendous task Jesus will be with His Apostles, with the Church, till the end of the world.

The Ascension

One last mystery consecrates and transfigures all this teaching of the Son of God here below: his Ascension. Quite recently He had said to the Jews: "You are from beneath, I am from above" (*John* viii, 23), and to Nicodemus He had said: "No man hath ascended into heaven but he that descended from heaven, the Son of Man" (iii, 13); and to His hearers at Capharnaum: "Does this scandalise you? If then you shall see the Son of Man ascend up where he was before?" (vi, 62). In these various ways Jesus directed towards heaven the dawning faith of those who were listening to Him. The same teaching was to be given to the Apostles, to the whole Church, and in so clear a light that they would never forget it.

The Apostles had returned to Jerusalem. Once more Jesus came amongst them; He shared their repast; He requested them to remain at Jerusalem and to await there the Holy Spirit whom He had promised them in the name of the Father. Even then the Apostles could not forget their dream of national restoration: "Lord, wilt thou at this time restore again the kingdom to Israel?"—"It is not for you," the Lord replied to them, "to know the times or moments, which the Father hath put in his own power. But you shall receive the power of the Holy Ghost coming upon you, and you shall be witnesses unto me in Jerusalem, and in all Judea, and Samaria, and even to the uttermost part of the earth" (*Acts* i, 4-8).

While this conversation was going on, they had arrived at the top of the Mount of Olives. Forty days earlier, Jesus and His Apostles had followed the same route; the Master was then going to the garden of the agony; the Apostles, to the supreme test which was to overcome them and disperse them. Now all was restored for ever, and Jesus ascended to heaven.

"And when he had said these things, while they looked on, he was raised up: and a cloud [99] received him out of their sight. And while they were beholding him going up to heaven, behold two men stood by them in white garments. Who also said: 'Ye men of Galilee, why stand you looking up to heaven? This Jesus who is taken from you into heaven, shall so come, as you have seen him going into heaven'" (*Acts* i, 9-11).

The Apostles returned joyfully to Jerusalem; but the memory of this vision did not depart from them. To their faithful disciples they would say with St. Paul: "Seek the things that are above, where Christ is sitting at the right hand of God, mind the things that are above, not the things that are upon the earth" (*Col.* iii, 1-2). The Holy Ghost was to come, revealing to them this wide horizon: henceforth there would be question not of the kingdom of Israel but of the kingdom from on high, where Jesus was enthroned and awaited them.

[99] The cloud is the mysterious veil which hides God from man. It was in the cloud that God appeared in the Old Testament; it is from a cloud that He spoke at the baptism and at the Transfiguration of the Master. The cloud of the Ascension gave the Apostles to understand that Jesus is henceforth entered into His glory, and that it is by faith, under a veil, that we can attain to Him here below.

CHAPTER II

THE PREACHING OF THE APOSTLES, AND THE BEGINNINGS OF THE CHURCH[1]

§I. PENTECOST

The Book of the Acts

THE public life of Christ was from the earliest years of the Church the subject of the apostolic catechesis, and our synoptic gospels are the echo of this preaching; they present themselves to us as the testimony which the Church gives to her Lord. The Book of the Acts has not the same character; it is the personal work of St. Luke. The sacred writer has brought to his task not only a conscientious probity, but a pious veneration. The history of the first years of the Church is dear to him and sacred. At the same time, he himself weaves the web; this history is truly his work.

It is moreover an outline rather than a complete history. We know very little of these first years of the Church, but we know enough to realise that St. Luke has not told us everything. The Epistle to the Romans and the narrative of the Acts itself (ch. xxviii) bear witness to the existence of a church at Rome. We would like to know about its origin and its development; the Acts tell us nothing. The Epistles of St. Paul show us many features in

[1] Bibilography.—C. Fouard, St. Peter and the First Years of Christianity; Mgr. Le Camus, L'œuvre des apôtres, Paris, 1905, 3 vols.; E. Jacquier, Les Actes des apôtres, Paris, 1926; A. Boudou, Actes des apôtres, Paris, 1933; A. Wikenhauser, Die Apostelgeschichte und ihr Geschichtswert, Münster, 1921. The preceding are Catholic works. The following are by non-Catholics: C. Weiszaecker, Das apostolische Zeitalter, Tübingen, 1886, 3rd edn., 1902; J. Weiss, Das Urchristentum, Göttingen, 1917; A. C. MacGiffert, History of Christianity in the Apostolic Age, Edinburgh, 1897; F. J. Foakes Jackson and Kirsopp Lake, Beginnings of Christianity, London, 1920-33, 5 vols., the first two contain prolegomena, the third an edition of the Acts, the last two, notes and studies on the Acts; E. Meyer, Ursprung und Anfänge des Christentums, Stuttgart, 1921-3, 3 vols., the first is devoted to the Gospels, the second to Judaism and to Jesus of Nazareth, the third to the Acts, and the history of Christian origins; W. Bousset, Kyrios Christos, Göttingen, 1913, 2nd edn., 1921.

the life of the Apostle that St. Luke has passed over in silence.[2]

The title itself of the book must not deceive us: it is not the acts of all the Apostles that are given therein; Peter fills the first chapters, Paul all the rest. The other Apostles hardly appear at all. In the first part of the book, the most active missionaries are persons in the second rank: Stephen, Philip, Barnabas. These lacunæ were later on greatly regretted, and some endeavoured to fill the gap by apocryphal Acts. In the choice made by the author of the Acts we must doubtless see a consequence of the conditions in which he found himself: Luke had been a companion of St. Paul and during his stay at Cæsarea, he had known Philip, and similarly at Antioch he had been close to Barnabas. Above all we must not forget that this book, like all those in the New Testament, is not designed to satisfy curiosity by the mere narration of facts, however interesting these may be, but it sets out to uphold and to illumine the faith. Luke pursues this end by describing first of all the origins of the Church at Jerusalem, and then its wonderful expansion, which he himself witnessed and helped to bring about.

The First Years: Their Character

Before entering into the details of this history, one is struck with certain features which are evident at first sight, and which characterise these first years of the infant Church immediately after the death of Jesus. The first is the immense void created by the departure of the Master. We shall never again find in the history of the Church a personality comparable to that of Christ. St. John says of the Baptist: "He was not the light, but was to give testimony of the light." The same applies here: the Apostles, even the greatest, were not the light; they reflected it, they propagated it, but they were not its source. Never again will be heard that sovereign voice of someone speaking in His own name, who commands by His own authority, who claims for Himself the complete surrender of men's souls. This fact is a very obvious one, but there is nevertheless none which has greater consequences.

Another characteristic also strikes us: the development of Christianity was a slow progress, without leaps and bounds, without haste, and even without a plan preconceived by men; the Apostles did not anticipate the action of the Holy Spirit; they waited for

[2] Cf. *infra*, ch. iii, "The Missions of St. Paul."

it, they accepted it, they submitted to it; they collaborated with it docilely. They retained from Judaism all that was not incompatible with the Christian faith; they were assiduous in attending the Temple and in public prayer, deferential to the authorities of their nation, while claiming the inalienable freedom of their ministry. Their preaching was prudent without being weak, and based itself on the Jewish faith in order to raise men's souls by degrees to Christ. They were indeed the disciples of the humble and gentle Messias, who did not break the bruised reed, and did not quench the smoking flax, and one is surprised to find men hitherto violent and impulsive, and all more or less "sons of thunder," so faithful to the spirit of the gospel. But while we admire in these facts the wisdom of Christ and the unction of the Spirit, we must at the same time notice the fidelity of the narrator, who sets forth a past so rapidly and so profoundly transformed, with such truthfulness.

The Apostles in Jerusalem

The prelude to this history is the account of the Ascension of the Lord [3] This manifestation of the glory of Christ is henceforth for the Apostles one of the high lights of their faith; it encouraged them to aspire to heaven, "where Christ is seated at the right hand of God"; it sustained their hope, for they knew that He would come again from heaven whither He had gone. This return which they awaited with an infallible certitude and with much impatience ought to find them watchful. They laboured accordingly as faithful servants whom the coming of the Master ought not to surprise, as friends who had now only one desire, to be with the Lord.

They returned to Jerusalem. This gathering and stay constitute one of the most indisputable facts in the history of Christian origins, and one of those which show most clearly a commandment by Christ. The Apostles were Galileans (i, 11; ii, 7); they were fishermen for the most part; nothing could keep them at Jerusalem except the order of Jesus; they had nothing to do there except to give testimony of Him. And yet it is certain that they were there, and that they remained there. The history of the infant Church unfolds itself far from Galilee, Capharnaum, the Lake, and from all that had provided the framework for the activity of Jesus. Everything took place at Jerusalem. This was due to a commandment of the

[3] We have commented on it above (p. 160).

Lord, reported by St. Luke (i, 4-8): Jerusalem was for the Apostles the scene of the death of Jesus and the centre of the power of His enemies; neither their memories nor their safety would lead them to remain there. But it was there that the Lord wanted them to be; they had to make a supreme effort to save the "city of the great King." Doubtless it would perish, but at least a good number of its children would escape from the catastrophe; the Church would be for them the ark of salvation. While the ark was being built, during the first years at any rate, the little community at Jerusalem enjoyed a certain toleration. The Apostles were ill-treated, and insulted, but not persecuted to death. When the persecution broke out, striking St. Stephen and the Hellenes, the Church had already been able to establish itself and to take root.

The first event which is reported to us, even before Pentecost, is the election of St. Matthias (i, 15-26). This fact is revealing in more than one way: it shows in the first place the importance attached to the apostolic college: the defection of Judas had left a vacancy in it; this had to be filled without delay. What were required in a candidate were doubtless moral qualities, but these were taken for granted and were probably to be found in all those who might have been chosen; above all was required the personal knowledge of Jesus, of whom every Apostle had to be a witness, and be content to be just that. The Apostles, in fact, were not independent masters; they had present before their minds the precept of the Lord: "You have but one master, Christ." Never would they put forth their authority as independent, never would they set up their own thrones. Their testimony was to deal with the whole public life of Christ "from the baptism of John until the Ascension." The rest, the years of His infancy and the hidden life, were at first outside the scope of the apostolic preaching. At the same time, this election not only shows us the indispensable function of an Apostle and the law which governed his office, but it also brings out the primacy of Peter: it was he who took the initiative in this matter and who directed it. In point of fact, the whole history of these early years shows quite clearly this primacy.[4] The disciples presented two candidates, Joseph and Matthias, but did not choose between them; the choice belonged to the Lord. He alone could appoint the Apostles; to find out His will prayer was made, and

---

[4] Cf. Weiszaecker, *op. cit.*, pp. 12-13; Wernle, *Die Anfänge unserer Religion*, p. 85, and *infra*, ch. vi. § 2.

recourse was had to the drawing of lots. This manner of election was motived by the exceptional character of the apostolate; we shall not find it again. Thus was St. Matthias designated, and given a place alongside the eleven Apostles.

This election took place in the "upper room" [5] where the Church was assembled; the Apostles dwelt there, and with them, persevering in prayer, were Mary the Mother of Jesus, and holy women, and the brethren of the Lord, numbering in all a hundred and twenty persons (i, 15). This was the first nucleus of the Church, the little flock which Jesus had gathered round Him, and which His memory kept united.[6]

Pentecost

On Pentecost Day, "suddenly there came a sound from heaven, as of a mighty wind coming, and it filled the whole house where they were sitting. And there appeared to them parted tongues as it were of fire, and it sat upon every one of them. And they were all filled with the Holy Ghost, and they began to speak with divers tongues, according as the Holy Ghost gave them to speak" (ii, 1-4).

On that day the Church was founded. Thirty years earlier the Holy Ghost had descended upon the Virgin Mary, and she had conceived the Son of God; to-day the Holy Ghost descended anew on Mary, on the Apostles, and on all the disciples gathered together in the cenacle, and of these people it formed the Church, the mystical body of Christ.

This out-pouring of the Spirit was to be one of the features of the Messianic age. On the Messias Himself the Spirit was to descend and to remain (*Isaias* xi, 2; xlii, 1 *et seq.*); but It was also to spread around Him: "I will give you a new heart, and put a new spirit within you: and I will take away the stony heart out of your

---

[5] Was this room, called "cenaculum" by the Vulgate, the cenacle in which Our Lord had celebrated the Last Supper? It may have been, but there is no proof of this. All that St. Luke says is that the room served as a dwelling for the Apostles. It has been suggested that it was in the house of Mary, the mother of John Mark, where later (xii, 12) we find the Apostles assembled; but this hypothesis is equally gratuitous.

[6] There were even at this time other disciples of the Lord; an appearance of Christ was witnessed by more than five hundred disciples (*I Cor.* xv, 6); the preaching of the Apostles was soon to strengthen these in the faith and to gather them together; but in these days of waiting, the majority were scattered in various places, and only a hundred and twenty were gathered together in the cenacle.

flesh, and will give you a heart of flesh, and I will put my spirit in the midst of you, and I will cause you to walk in my commandments, and to keep my judgments and do them"; "I will pour out upon the house of David, and upon the inhabitants of Jerusalem, the spirit of grace and of prayers." [7] Jesus had repeated these promises; [8] but His death alone could bring about this effect; until then, "as yet the Spirit was not given." [9] Now Jesus was dead, He had been glorified, He had left His own; and according to His promise He sends them the Holy Spirit.

This gift of the Holy Spirit will be constantly renewed in the Church: "If any man have not the Spirit of Christ, he is none of His" (*Romans* viii, 9). The effusion of the Spirit on the centurion Cornelius and the pagans around him was to be for St. Peter the decisive proof of the vocation of the Gentiles: "Can any man forbid water, that these should not be baptised, who have received the Holy Ghost, as well as we?" (*Acts* x, 47). Indeed, one could not be fully Christian if one had not received this gift: the people of Samaria, converted by St. Philip and baptised by him, had to receive the laying on of hands by the Apostles, and thereby received the Holy Spirit.[10]

Thus this most precious treasure is also the most common: it is not at all reserved to an élite in the Church, it belongs to all Christians. It is true that the Spirit conferred upon all does not impart to all the same gifts, but there is "one and the same Spirit, dividing to every one according as he will" (*I Cor.* xii, 11).

The Pentecostal effusion did not only bring about an inner transformation of souls; it had also a great external effect. This was felt already on this day at Jerusalem. The festival had attracted to the holy city people from "every nation under heaven." The great noise which had resounded in the cenacle caused them to come together; approaching the cenacle they were astonished, each one hearing the disciples speaking in his own tongue. Some marvelled, others were scornful: "these men are full of new wine." [11] In the

[7] *Ezechiel* xxxvi, 26; *Zacharias* xii, 10; cf. *Isaias* xxxii, 15; xliv, 1 *et seq.*
[8] *John* vii, 38; xiv, 16; xvi, 7.
[9] *John* vii, 39.
[10] *Acts* viii, 17; cf. xix, 2.
[11] These contradictory reactions show that in this first manifestation the gift of tongues was already obscure, as it would be later on at Corinth: "He that speaketh in a tongue, edifieth himself; but he that prophesieth, edifieth the church" (*I Cor.* xiv, 4). The hearers recognised their own tongues, but what they heard were exclamations, praises of God.

same way St. Paul will later on write to the Corinthians: "If all speak with tongues, and there come in unlearned persons or unbelievers, will they not say that you are mad?" (*I Cor.* xiv, 23).

St. Peter's Sermon

In presence of this astonishment and these accusations, St. Peter stands up: he is the prophet who interprets the exclamations of those who have spoken in tongues, but he is above all the head of the Church, defending his brethren and preaching Christ. These praises of God, which have caused wonderment in those who have heard them, are not at all signs of drunkenness; they are the result of the pouring out of the Holy Spirit, foretold by the prophet Joel for the last days. These last days, then, have come; it is the hour of salvation:

"Ye men of Israel, hear these words: Jesus of Nazareth, a man approved of God among you by miracles and wonders and signs . . . being delivered up by the determinate counsel and foreknowledge of God, you by the hands of wicked men have crucified and slain. Whom God hath raised up, having loosed the sorrows of hell, as it was impossible that he should be holden by it."

After showing that David (*Ps.* xv (xvi), 8-11) foretold the resurrection of Christ by God, Peter continues:

"This Jesus hath God raised again, whereof all we are witnesses. Being exalted therefore to the right hand of God, and having received of the Father the promise of the Holy Ghost, he hath poured forth this which you see and hear. For David ascended not into heaven, but he himself said: 'The Lord said to my Lord, sit thou on my right hand, until I make thy enemies thy footstool.' Therefore let all the house of Israel know most certainly, that God hath made both Lord and Christ, this same Jesus whom you have crucified" (*Acts* ii, 22-36).

This discourse of St. Peter is the earliest piece of apologetics and example of Christian preaching. Its archaic character is a guarantee of its authenticity: at the date when St. Luke wrote the Acts these prudent formulas had long since been left aside; they were already surpassed in this first day of the Church in the faith of St. Peter and the other Apostles. The solemn profession of faith at Cæsarea Philippi: "Thou art the Christ, the Son of the living God," is much more explicit than that which we read here: "Jesus of Nazareth, a man approved of God . . ."; but in these early days of Christian preaching, this is how Messianism was generally presented to the Jews. At the same time it must be noted that, whatever intentional reserve there may be in this preaching, the Messianism which it claims for Jesus, even in this very sermon, is much more transcendent than that of Jewish dreams: with all the precautions of language which were deemed necessary, St. Peter reminds the Jews that King David died and was buried, and that his tomb was in their midst, that he had not ascended to heaven. Jesus on the contrary had risen again and had ascended into heaven, and thus God had shown Him to be Lord and Christ.

Many Jews were impressed, and said to Peter and the Apostles: "What shall we do?" The same question had been put to John the Baptist by the penitents who pressed around him (*Luke* iii, 10 *et seq.*); the Forerunner preached to them justice, and recommended baptism, but only a baptism of water: "I indeed baptise you with water, that he that is mightier than I shall baptise you with the Holy Ghost and with fire (*ibid.*, iii, 16). The day of this baptism had come: "Do penance, and be baptised every one of you in the name of Jesus Christ, for the remission of your sins, and you shall receive the gift of the Holy Ghost" (*Acts* ii, 38).[12] That was how St. Peter answered the question.

The First Expansion of the Church

The converts were obedient to the word of Peter; they received baptism, and in that day about three thousand souls entered the Church.

This effusion of the Holy Spirit, and powerful expansion of the Christian faith, were the first stirrings of a movement of evangelisation which would never cease. St. Peter made this clear at the end of his discourse: "The promise is to you, and to your children, and

---

[12] The rite of baptism is not described in this text. We know from the *Didache,* vii, 3, that baptism was ordinarily administered by immersion, but that it could in exceptional circumstances be administered by aspersion; this latter rite was most likely used in the case of the baptism of St. Paul (*Acts* ix, 18; xxii, 16), the jailor of Philip, and his family (xvi, 33). Cf. A. d'Alès and J. Coppens, article *Baptême,* in *Supplément* to the *Dictionnaire de la Bible.* We may remark that St. Peter (*Acts* x, 48) and St. Paul (*I Cor.* i, 14, 17) had baptism administered by others rather than administer it themselves.

to all that are far off, whomsoever the Lord our God shall call" (ii, 39). Those who heard St. Peter were not only Jews of Jerusalem; there were there "Parthians and Medes and Elamites, and inhabitants of Mesopotamia, Judea, and Cappadocia, Pontus and Asia, Phrygia, and Pamphylia, Egypt and the parts of Lybia about Cyrene, and Romans residing at Jerusalem, Jews and proselytes, Cretes and Arabians" (ii, 9-11).

The majority of these people were not resident at Jerusalem; when the feast was ended they would return to their own lands; they would carry there the faith and the gifts of the Holy Spirit which they had just received. They would not be founders of churches, but missionaries; their action would spread abroad the evangelical seed throughout the whole Roman world. We find that, already at the time of the persecution begun at Jerusalem against St. Stephen, there was at Damascus a group of Christians; they were sufficiently well known for Saul to ask and obtain against them powers from the Sanhedrin. A little later we shall find that the Christian faith had been carried to Rome, and probably also to Alexandria. The first diffusion of Christianity was not the work of the Apostles, who remained at Jerusalem; it must be attributed in great measure to the individual action of the pilgrims who had come to Jerusalem, had found there the Christian faith, and had taken it back with them into their own cities and provinces. Thus from the first day of the Church the Gospel parables of the kingdom of God were realised; the grain of mustard seed already put forth its first shoots; the leaven was working not only in the Jewish world but also the Hellenic and Roman worlds, and making it to ferment.

At Jerusalem itself, the Church grew and spread:

"[The disciples] were persevering in the doctrine of the apostles, and in the communication of the breaking of bread, and in prayers. And fear came upon every soul: many wonders also and signs were done by the apostles. . . . All they that believed were together, and had all things common. Their possessions and goods they sold, and divided them to all, according as every one had need. And continuing daily with one accord in the Temple, and breaking bread from house to house, they took their meat with gladness and simplicity of heart, praising God, and having favour with all the people. And the Lord increased daily together such as should be saved" (ii, 42-47).

A little lower, after the account of the miracle in the Temple and of the first persecutions, St. Luke contemplates and describes once more this life of the first Christians:

"The multitude of believers had but one heart and one soul; neither did any one say that aught of the things which he possessed was his own, but all things were common unto them. And with great power did the apostles give testimony of the resurrection of Jesus Christ our Lord, and great grace was in them all. For neither was there any one needy among them. For as many as were owners of lands or houses, sold them, and brought the price of the things they sold, and laid it down before the feet of the apostles. And distribution was made to every one, according as he had need" (iv, 32-35).

Some historians have regarded these narratives of conversions and these descriptions of primitive Christian life, as idyllic pictures imagined by St. Luke; the figures, they say, are exaggerated; the sympathy of the people is incredible, as are the miracles of the Apostles.[13] Such criticism is not justified: the numerous conversions and the sympathy of the people can be accounted for by the first-fruits of grace so abundantly showered down, and also by the memory left by the Lord Jesus at Jerusalem; His discourses, His works, still lived in all men's minds; the miracles and the words of Peter revived the recollection, and those who a little while previously had been profoundly touched were once more affected by this preaching which was so simple and so effective, and above all by this life in which the faithful Israelites saw the ideal of the religious life to which they themselves aspired.

The Church of all time will venerate these admirable pictures as a model of Christian life; it will nevertheless recognise that even in this clearness of the early days there were shadows: what will be said soon about neglected widows and murmurings shows that even then human weakness made itself felt, and that it would be an exaggeration to take all the expressions literally, such as for instance this one: "there were no needy amongst them." In spite of these human failings which will soon be accentuated, we find in this life of the first Christians the most faithful realisation of the Gospel morality as the Lord had taught it in His Sermon on the Mount and particularly in the beatitudes; very likely the form

[13] Weiszaecker, *op. cit.*, pp. 21-3; Renan, *Les apôtres*, p. 48.

which the beatitudes take in Luke bear the trace of this voluntary and joyful poverty.

The Life of the Christians

We should like to penetrate beyond this outline into this life that we glimpse, at least to the extent of determining its chief features. In this assembly of the disciples, the Apostles are seen to be the leaders; they are above all witnesses to Christ, but they are also the spiritual guides and even the administrators of the Christian Church; they will soon have to give up this charge. Their external activity is shown in the discourse of St. Peter; every opportunity is seized to make known Jesus, His position as Messias, and His resurrection. The three discourses which are reported here arise from the effusion of the Holy Ghost at Pentecost (ii, 14-40), the healing of the lame man (iii, 12-26), and the summoning before the Sanhedrin (iii, 8-12). Such facts, however, were exceptional. The daily influence of the Apostles was doubtless more discreet, affecting each individual or at least each family in the intimacy of its domestic life, preaching to the ear more often than from the housetops.

Besides the great apologetical discourses, we must not forget the apostolic catechesis which is made known to us by the Gospels: the life of Jesus "from the baptism of John until the Ascension," His teaching and His miracles were the subject of the daily instructions by which the new disciples were initiated into the Gospel. How many words of Christ come back to our memories when we consider these first Christians? Before all, the Sermon on the Mount and the beatitudes, but also many other sentences such as: "Come to me, all you that labour, and are burdened, and I will refresh you; take my yoke upon you, and learn of me, because I am meek, and humble of heart, and you shall find rest to your souls, for my yoke is sweet, and my burden light" (*Matt.* xi, 28-30). "Fear not, little flock, for it hath pleased your Father to give you a kingdom. Sell what you possess and give alms. Make to yourselves bags which grow not old, a treasure in heaven which faileth not: where no thief approacheth, nor moth corrupteth. For where your treasure is, there will your heart be also." (*Luke* xii, 32-34).

The Christians were at first called "disciples," as they had been while Jesus was alive; then they were called "brethren" or "saints," as we see already in the narratives in the Acts, and constantly in the epistles of St. Paul. To the first term corresponds the collective appellation of the "community" (κοίνωνία); to the second, that of the "church." [14]

To people outside they still appear as a sect, αἵρεσ'ς (xxiv, 5, 14). They do not seem to have formed a separate synagogue; at the beginning they assembled in the cenacle, a little later we find them all together in the Temple, in Solomon's Porch (v. 12; iii, 11). This was a public place, but no others dared to join them; when Peter and John, after their appearance before the Sanhedrin, returned to their own people, they "prayed, and the place wherein they were assembled was moved" (iv, 31); this place is not otherwise specified. The breaking of bread takes place at home (ii, 46); already we notice, side by side with general assemblies, domestic meetings.

These repasts seem to have had a liturgical character; but they were also occasions for the organisation of mutual assistance: Christians "had but one heart and one soul," and "all things were common unto them" (iv, 32, cf. ii, 44). The Lord had established this rule for His Apostles; He had called upon them to leave all things in order to follow Him; similarly He had said to the rich young man: "Go, sell all that thou hast, and give to the poor . . ." This teaching was certainly recalled by the evangelical catechesis, and it bore its fruit: "As many as were owners of lands or houses, sold them, and brought the price of the things they sold, and laid it down before the feet of the Apostles" (iv, 34-35). The example of Barnabas is given as a model (iv, 37); the history of Ananias and Sapphira (v, 1-11) shows with what severity God punished deception, but, as we see from this account, this practice of poverty was spontaneous, and imposed by no law (v, 4); in these two guilty persons, what was punished was dissimulation and lying. It is likely that in the Church at Jerusalem those who made rich offerings were rare; more numerous were those who had to be assisted by the community. Very soon, even the community was not sufficient for its needs, and other Christians had to come to its assistance. Paul collected for the saints in Jerusalem and for its poor. [15]

[14] The name "saints" belongs rather to liturgical language. On the primitive sense of the term, see Delehaye, Sanctus, Brussels, 1927, pp. 28 et seq.; R. Asting, Die Heiligkeit im Urchristentum, Göttingen, 1930, pp. 133-51.

[15] I Cor. xvi, 1-3; II Cor. ix, 1; Gal. ii, 10; Rom. xv, 26.

This help was inspired not only by a spirit of solidarity, but above all by brotherly love,[16] and also by contempt for the goods of this world, this mammon of iniquity which could at least enable one to make sure of friends in heaven.

All this shows a very vigorous life. It was not individualistic, as some imagine; never was seen a church more intimately united, even as far as the fusing of personal interests; it was not anarchical; hierarchical authority was binding on all; Christians of good will ranked themselves around it; those who tried to deceive it were really lying to the Holy Ghost, and were struck dead. Everywhere we find an overflowing life; it is the fulfilling of the promise of Jesus: "He that believeth in me, out of his belly shall flow rivers of living water" (*John* vii, 38).

The Action of the Spirit

The whole Church was conscious of this constant direction by the Spirit and relied on it: the gravest decisions concerning the evangelisation of the pagans, or the observance or abandonment of the mosaic rites, were made from day to day under the evident pressure of circumstances according to the inspiration of the Spirit of Jesus, and there is no suggestion of a plan drawn up in advance. Jesus had said: "When they shall bring you into the synagogues, and to magistrates and powers . . . the Holy Ghost shall teach you in the same hour what you must say" (*Luke* xii, 11-12). This promise was fulfilled in the letter when the Apostles were taken before the Sanhedrin, but it was realised also every day in the life of the Church. This plasticity and suppleness gave to the infant Church a facility for adaptation and in consequence a triumphant power and an assurance of permanence which might well reveal even to outsiders the living treasure which it possessed; and those who lived thereby knew well that it arose not from a fragile enthusiasm, and still less from an eschatological frenzy, but from the living union of the Church with Christ its Head and with the Holy Spirit.

In describing this intimate life, we have left on one side the account of miracles: one only is related in detail, but many others are mentioned in passing (v, 12, 15-16). This profusion of miracles is

---

[16] *John* xiii, 35; Weiszaecker, *op. cit.*, p. 47, remarks that this love was foreign to official Judaism; he finds some traces of it in Essenism. Certainly one finds a communal life there, but not this tenderness and intimacy of brotherly love.

not astonishing in the beginning of a work the development of which was so wonderful and so manifestly divine. The healing of the lame man is narrated at length (iii, 1-10); it attracts the attention of the writer mainly because of the consequences to which it led, the excitement of the crowd, Peter's exhortation, and the measures taken by the Sanhedrin. The fact, in its general character and in its details, is very similar to many of the miracles reported by St. John, for instance the healing of the paralytic in the pool of Bezatha or that of the man born blind. In all these cases the initiative in the miracle comes not from the sick man, who does not dream of asking for it, but from the Lord, and in this case from St. Peter; and the faith is the fruit of the miracle: here the lame man when healed joins the Apostles and glorifies God; the whole crowd is astonished; Peter takes the opportunity of preaching to them.

The First Persecutions

The chief priests and the Sadducees were alarmed, and had the Apostles arrested. The scribes and the Pharisees did not intervene here, as they did against Jesus. In these early years the enemies of the Church of Jerusalem were mainly the Sadducees.[17] It was they who had played the decisive part in the trial of Christ; the preaching of the Apostles was therefore particularly unwelcome to them: it revived the political difficulties which they thought they had escaped by putting Jesus to death, it incriminated the judgment which they had passed, and lastly it affirmed in a concrete case, well known to all, the doctrine of the resurrection which they obstinately rejected.

Thus, in the interrogation and in the sentence (iv, 7, 18), they brought up none of the accusations constantly made against Jesus by the Pharisees concerning the Sabbath and the Law; they fastened only on the name of Jesus: they absolutely forbade the Apostles to speak and teach in this name.

After this sentence and the bold reply of the Apostles, preaching began again, and with it the diffusion of Christianity. The Apostles were thrown into prison; an angel delivered them and instructed them to preach once more in the Temple; at once they were arrested but without violence, for fear of the people (v, 26). In the Sanhe-

[17] The Pharisees nevertheless very soon supported them, as we shall see in the history of Saul.

drin, the high priest questioned them: "We commanded you that you should not teach in this name, and behold, you have filled Jerusalem with your doctrine, and you have a mind to bring the blood of this man upon us." The reply of Peter and the Apostles was: "We ought to obey God rather than men." The Sanhedrin, very angry, wanted to put them to death. On the intervention of Gamaliel they abandoned the idea; they had the Apostles scourged, and forbade them once more to speak in the name of Jesus. The Apostles withdrew, rejoicing that they had been considered worthy to suffer reproach for the name of Jesus.

These first conflicts were but a foretaste of the persecution which was soon to break out; but already we perceive in the Apostles the power of the Holy Spirit promised by Jesus a little while before; the priests were surprised to find such assurance in unlettered men whom they thought they could easily intimidate (iv, 13); after the scourging it was still more astonishing to find such a joy in men recently so weak.

Another point which clearly appears in this struggle is that the one object with which it was concerned was Jesus, his person and His name.[1] The Jews regarded the Church merely as the party of the old disciples of Jesus; the Christians themselves were conscious of being only His witnesses, and when soon afterwards Saul persecuted them, it was Jesus whom he persecuted, and who intervened to defend them.

§2. THE MARTYRDOM OF ST. STEPHEN AND THE CONVERSION OF ST. PAUL

The Hellenists

"In those days, the number of the disciples increasing, there arose a murmuring of the Greeks against the Hebrews, for that their widows were neglected in the daily ministration" (vi, 1). This incident is reported by St. Luke only in order to explain the institution of deacons, and the office of St. Stephen, but it is of great interest in itself, and it would be desirable to know more about it. The first nucleus of the faithful had been formed of Galileans; the preaching at Pentecost had led into the Church Jews from all lands, and amongst them, Hellenists. Since then, the influence of these

[1] Cf. Bousset, Kyrios Christos, pp. 224 et seq.

first converts had made itself felt round about; conversions had multiplied amongst the Hellenists, and yet the heads of the Church were all Hebrews. This led to the fact that in the organisation of assistance, mentioned here for the first time, the widows of the Hellenists were neglected; bonds of relationship and of language favoured the Judeans and tended to isolate the Hellenists.

We understand these difficulties better when we remember how the Jews grouped themselves in their synagogues according to their origin. This custom is clearly attested for Jerusalem in the Book of the Acts [2]; it seems also to have existed in Rome.[3] Accustomed to these ethnic groupings, Judeans and Hellenists remained on friendly terms. But it is also easy to understand how dangerous these national distinctions were within the Christian community whose unity they threatened. Very soon St. Paul would have to remind Christians that there is no longer amongst them "Greek nor Jew . . . nor Barbarian nor Scythian, nor slave nor free, but Christ all in all" (*Coloss.*, iii, 11, *Galat.*, iii, 26). From the first this was clear, and this affirmation of the Christian conscience triumphed over nationalist and provincial separatism.

The Deacons

But it was necessary to take from the Hellenists all grounds of complaints. The Apostles could not devote all their time to ministering at tables, to the detriment of their essential duties, prayer and preaching (vi, 2-4). They saw to the matter by having seven deacons chosen by the Christian community. Those chosen all bore Greek names. The majority and perhaps all belonged to the Hellenist group [4]; we notice amongst them a "proselyte of Antioch, Nicholas." This election of a circumcised pagan shows that already at this date the Church numbered amongst her members men born

[2] vi, 9; synagogues of the freedmen, the Cyrenæans, the Alexandrians, and of those from Cilicia and Asia. Cf. Schuerer, *op. cit.*, II, p. 87.

[3] Cf. Frey, *Les communautés juives à Rome*, in *Recherches de science religieuse*, 1930, especially pp. 289 *et seq.*

[4] This origin is seen in the history of St. Stephen and St. Philip: their names would not indeed be in themselves a certain proof, for many Hebrews bore Greek names. A western reading found in the *Codex Bezae* and above all in the *Floriacensis* seems to say that the Hebrews already had their deacons: "Facta est contentio Græcorum adversus Ebreos, eo quod in cotidiano ministerio viduae Græcorum a ministris Hebraeorum despicerentur" (*Flor.*, cf. Jacquier, *in hoc loco*). If this was the case, it would be still clearer why the seven chosen ones all belonged to the Hellenist group.

amongst the Gentiles, and that these could be selected for hierarchical functions.

The diaconate had nothing in common except the name with the ministry of the *hazan* in the Jewish synagogues. The seven were to be charged with the distribution of alms, but also with the ministry of preaching. The importance of their office is already shown by the ordination they received; after their election by the people, the deacons were presented to the Apostles, who prayed and laid their hands on them.[5]

This ordination was to give a new impulse to the preaching of the Gospel; the Hellenists had already been converted in fairly large numbers (the complaints of their widows show this), but though there were many believers amongst them, hitherto they had had no preacher, no leader; henceforth those they had chosen were charged with an important mission and with a great responsibility. Two of them above all, Stephen and Philip, were in the front rank. Their authority of course remained subordinate to that of the Apostles; they were not like them witnesses to Jesus, chosen personally by Him; they were not heads of the Church. But they were the preachers of the Gospel; they devoted to this ministry admirable natural gifts, supplemented by miraculous charisms.

Immediately after the account of this election and ordination of the seven, St. Luke continues:

"And the word of the Lord increased, and the number of the disciples was multiplied in Jerusalem exceedingly: a great multitude also of the priests obeyed the faith. And Stephen, full of grace and fortitude, did great wonders and signs among the people" (vi, 7-8).

St. Stephen

These few words show the fruits of the new preaching. A Hellenist, and possibly of Alexandrian origin,[6] Stephen could approach his fellow citizens more easily than could the Hebrews. He met with a violent fanaticism on the part of some of them—his martyrdom shows this—but in others he found more independence towards the

[5] vi, 6. On this ordination, and on the character of the diaconate of the seven, cf. Coppens, *L'imposition des mains,* pp. 120-3.

[6] This supposition is rather a weak one; endeavours have been made to support it by comparisons between the discourse of Stephen and Philonian exegesis, and also by the mention of "wisdom," which is found four times in the narrative and discourse: vi, 3, 10; vii, 10, 22 (Jacquier, *op. cit.,* p. 104).

rabbinical traditions than was commonly found in Palestine. He himself developed his preaching more boldly than the Apostles had hitherto done. The discourses of St. Peter in the cenacle and in the Temple aimed at showing that Jesus had been raised by God from the dead, and that He had been made both Lord and Christ; they left in obscurity many themes of the evangelical preaching which were to be brought out little by little as hearers were able to bear them: the Temple would be destroyed; the Law, which the patriarchs had not known, was only a temporary dispensation which would have to give place to the Gospel.

All this began to appear in the preaching of St. Stephen, and met at once with a passionate opposition. At first it was merely a controversy which broke out amongst the Hellenists at Jerusalem; they tried to argue with Stephen, but "they were not able to resist the wisdom and the spirit that spoke." Then they suborned witnesses: "This man," they said, "has blasphemed Moses and God." The people were aroused, and the elders and scribes.

Until then the favour of the populace had protected the Apostles (v, 26); now public sentiment changed; people were roused as they had been against Jesus at His Passion. The scribes joined forces with the chief priests; all Judaism made a common front. Stephen's enemies took him before the Sanhedrin, and produced against him false witnesses: "This man ceaseth not to speak words against the holy place, and the Law. For we have heard him say that this Jesus of Nazareth shall destroy this place, and shall change the traditions which Moses delivered unto us."

This was a new accusation; even if we separate it from the calumnies added by the false witnesses, that Stephen had blasphemed against the Temple and the Law, it remains not only that Jesus is the expected Messias—as St. Peter had already preached— but also that this Messias would substitute a new order of things for that which Moses had established. This theme appears more clearly in the great speech which St. Stephen made in his own defence.

St. Stephen's Discourse

This speech is one of the most valuable documents of early Christian literature.[7] It is less a plea than an instruction, and

[7] The authenticity of this speech has often been attacked, e.g., by Weiszaecker, op. cit., pp. 55 et seq.; and often defended, e.g. by Jacquier, op. cit., p. 201; Wikenhauser, op. cit., p. 149; Schumacher, Der Diakon Stephanus, p. 101.

thereby St. Stephen appears as the first "martyr" or witness; the constant preoccupation of Christians taken before judges will be less to save themselves than to expound and defend their faith. That was the great aim of Stephen. He sacrificed his life for his Master; he did not seek to rescue it from his accusers; but since he was able to make himself heard by the great Council of his nation, he wished to defend Christ there, as he had so often done before his Hellenist opponents. Careless of his own fate, he set forth once more the demonstration so familiar to him, of the divine plan which had prepared the ways of the Messias with wisdom and power, and the infidelity of the Jews who had revolted against God and repulsed his envoys.

First he gives the history of Abraham, Isaac, Jacob, and Joseph (vii, 2-19); St. Paul will also delight to find his starting point before Moses in the patriarchs; [8] Christ had done the same.[9] Then we have the story of Moses; God wanted to make him the saviour of his people, but the Jews refused him (vii, 35). It was Moses who said to the children of Israel: "A prophet shall God raise up to you of your own brethren, him shall you hear as myself." [10] This Moses, who conversed on Sinai with the Angel of the Lord, and received the words of life in order to give them to you, was not obeyed by our fathers; they turned back towards Egypt, and adored the golden calf. God punished them by giving them up to the worship of the host of heaven (vii, 42). Then, in the last portion, Stephen comes to the Temple, which he was accused of blaspheming (vii, 44-50): in the desert, and afterwards in the Holy Land until the time of Solomon, our fathers had the Ark of the Covenant; Solomon built God a temple; but the Most High dwelleth not in temples made with hands: he said so by his prophet (*Isaias* lxvi, 1-2).

This long speech, brimful of accusations, ends in a terrible conclusion:

"You stiffnecked and uncircumcised in heart and ears, you always resist the Holy Ghost: as your fathers did, so do you also. Which of the prophets have not your fathers persecuted? And they have slain them who foretold of the coming of the Just One; of whom you have been

[8] In particular, in the Epistle to the Galatians, especially ch. iii.

[9] He went even beyond the patriarchs to the origin of the human race to establish that the concession of divorce by Moses was neither primitive nor definitive; *Matt.* xix, 3-6.

[10] This text of *Deut.* xviii, 15, was already classic in Christian apologetics; we find it in a discourse of St. Peter (iii, 22).

now the betrayers and murderers; who have received the law by the disposition of angels, and have not kept it."

Stephen's speech, the bearing of which has often been exaggerated and sometimes even entirely misrepresented,[11] is certainly very different from the discourses of St. Peter which we have described above. These differences are a confirmation of its authenticity, but they immediately present a problem: to what extent does the preaching of St. Stephen represent Christian preaching as a whole? It is difficult to give a precise and certain reply to this question. We must certainly reject the oft-made attempts to set up chair against chair in the Church and make Stephen a sectary [12]; but we might allow that the Holy Spirit made use of Stephen to direct the Christian Church towards a greater independence in regard to Judaism, its rites and its laws.

The final peroration of Stephen angered the Jews, especially the last accusation, the gravest of all of them, of disobedience to the Law. They trembled with rage and gnashed their teeth. And before this exasperated audience, Stephen suddenly affirmed that he saw the heavens opened, and the Son of Man standing on the right hand of God. Immediately there was an uproar: he was dragged out and stoned, while Saul took care of the garments of the witnesses. Stephen cried: "Lord Jesus, receive my spirit!" and then "Lord, lay not this sin to their charge!" This martyrdom, the first in the history of the Church, was the faithful echo of the Passion of Christ, and in it we hear this prayer which at the supreme moment goes up to

[11] The bearing of the discourse of St. Stephen has often been misrepresented, as for instance in the otherwise not unworthy book by W. L. Knox, St. Paul and the Church of Jerusalem, Cambridge, 1925, p. 54, n. 24: "The whole implication of St. Stephen's speech is that the historical development of Judaism has been entirely false. This view is, of course, contrary to St. Paul's belief in the Law as the necessary preliminary to the Gospel; the attitude of St. Stephen in primitive Christian literature can only be paralleled in the Epistle of Barnabas. . . . The whole method involves, of course, a completely arbitrary selection of certain passages in the Old Testament, and a radically false interpretation of them; it can only be made logical and consistent by the Marcionite doctrine that the God of the Old Testament is a different being from the God of the New Testament." There is a great difference between Barnabas and Stephen: for Barnabas, all Judaism has gone astray; a material interpretation has been given to what God intended to be taken symbolically. Stephen does not go so far as that: his strongest statements concerning the Temple do not go beyond what Solomon himself said when the Temple was dedicated: "If heaven, and the heavens of heavens cannot contain thee, how much less this house which I have built?" (I Kings viii, 27; cf. II Paralipom. vi, 18). Cf. Jacquier, op. cit., p. 231.

[12] Cf. infra, p. 188.

the Lord Jesus, just as that of Jesus had gone up to His Father.[13]

The question has been asked how it was that the Jews, who did not possess the right of life and death, and who had not dared to take upon themselves the responsibility for the death of Jesus, were so bold on this occasion. Certain historians have thought to explain everything by a popular rising. That is an inadequate explanation. The Sanhedrin certainly displayed at this time more independent initiative than in other circumstances: this is shown again by the sending of Saul to Damascus. It is likely that the Jews had profited by the recall of Pilate and the vacancy in the Roman magistracy, and this would enable us to put these events as most probably belonging to the year 36. The period of relative peace which marked the beginnings of the Church would then have lasted six years.[14]

The persecution which broke out at this time, and of which Stephen was the first victim, continued more or less violently until the death of Agrippa (A.D. 44). It affected above all the Hellenists but it threatened also the Apostles. Incidentally, it contributed to the development of the Church; the hostility of the Jews detached the Christians from the Law, and led them to a clearer consciousness of their independence with regard to Judaism; the forced dispersion of the faithful, and above all of the Hellenists, spread the good news everywhere; and lastly, it was the persecution that turned Saul into St. Paul.

Conversion of St. Paul

It is in the account of the martyrdom of St. Stephen that St. Paul appears for the first time in the history of the Church. A "young man named Saul" (vii, 58) consented to Stephen's death, and took part in it by guarding the clothing of the witnesses who stoned him (xxi, 20). Saul was in fact a bitter enemy of the Christians. By birth he belonged to the Hellenistic group; he was born at Tarsus (ix, 11; xxi, 30; xxi, 3; cf. ix, 30; xi, 25), and he had inherited from his family the freedom of the city of Tarsus (xxi, 39), as well as the rights of a Roman citizen (xvi, 37; xxii, 25, et. seq., xxv, 10). But he had also received from them a still more precious

---

[13] The belief implied by this prayer helps us to interpret the speech itself, and completes its Christology, which was deliberately elementary. Cf. History of the Doctrine of the Trinity, Vol. I, pp. 263-4.

[14] Cf. infra, p. 185 n. 24.

heritage: he was "of the stock of Israel, of the tribe of Benjamin, an Hebrew of the Hebrews" (*Philippians* iii, 5). In this family, established on Greek territory but faithful to the Jewish and Pharisaic traditions, "Saul, also called Paul" (xiii, 9) had learnt from infancy both Greek and Aramaic. It was in the Aramaic tongue that Jesus spoke to him on the road to Damascus (xxvi, 14), it was in Aramaic that he himself harangued the people of Jerusalem on the day of his arrest (xxi, 40). Aramaic was to him the religious and national language, but Greek was the language of daily use, and Greek was to be the language of his apostolate.

His Jewish formation, begun at Tarsus, was continued at Jerusalem; Saul received it "at the feet of Gamaliel" (xxii, 3). There he was "taught according to the truth of the law of the fathers, zealous for the law, as also all you are this day" (*ibid.*); "according to the law, a Pharisee; according to zeal, persecuting the Church of God; according to the justice that is in the Law, conversing without blame" (*Philipp.* iii, 5-6). In the Hellenist groups at Jerusalem so disturbed by the preaching of Stephen, he stood out by the violence of his anger: "You have heard," he said later on to the Galatians (i, 13-14), "of my conversation in time past in the Jews' religion: how that, beyond measure, I persecuted the Church of God, and wasted it, and I made progress in the Jews' religion above many of my equals in my own nation, being more abundantly zealous for the traditions of my fathers." To the Jews of Jerusalem he could recall the same memories with more precision: "I persecuted this way unto death, bending and delivering into prisons both men and women, as the high priest doth bear me witness, and all the ancients" (xxii, 4-5).

The martyrdom of Stephen was not enough for him; he asked and obtained a mission to Damascus: "also receiving letters to the brethren, I went to Damascus, that I might bring them bound from thence to Jerusalem to be punished" (xxii, 5).

It was there that God awaited him. People have wondered what might have prepared the conversion of St. Paul. Mgr. Le Camus wrote: [15] "Paul regarded Stephen as the adversary of the law and the enemy of his people. His hatred went so far as to desire his death. But in vain did he harden himself against the triumphant truth; in spite of himself, and unknown to himself, the living and altogether new words of the holy deacon penetrated within him.

[15] *L'œuvre des apôtres*, Vol. I, p. 113.

Like a ruthless goad, it was to work upon him until the time when he was to fall vanquished and to declare himself the convert and determined representative of the ideas and the faith of the One he had anathematised." But all this is a fragile hypothesis. The same author writes with more justice [16]: "The apostle himself, so careful to study himself and to make himself known in the various phases of his religious life, sees no other cause for his conversion than the heavenly manifestation by which he was thrown down. But if he has never said anything of that inner working which would have prepared for his sudden adhesion to Christanity, it is because in his recollections he found nothing."

What we can say of his past is that his good faith partly excused his rancour. What he did, he did "in ignorance"; moreover, his tenacious attachment to the Law was a more favourable disposition for Christianity than would have been the indifference of the Sadducees. We see from other texts how seriously he regarded the obligation of the Law: "I testify again to every man circumcising himself that he is a debtor to do the whole Law" (*Galat.* v, 3), and how this crushing obligation was a torment to his upright and sincere soul.[17] From this torment Christ was to deliver him; he would feel first of all the pain of being torn away from his past, but speedily, and sooner than any others, he would understand the value of this deliverance.

This event, which was to have such a decisive importance for the history of the Church, is narrated three times in the Book of Acts,[18] and recalled by St. Paul himself in his epistles.[19] As he approached Damascus, a great light shone round about him; he fell to the ground, and he heard a voice which said to him in the Hebrew language: "Saul, Saul, why persecutest thou me?"

"Who art thou, Lord?"—"I am Jesus whom thou persecutest. Arise, go into the city, and it shall be told thee what thou must do."

[16] *Op. cit.*, Vol. I, p. 177.

[17] Cf. *Rom.* vii.

[18] The first of these accounts is written by St. Luke (ix, 3-8); the two others are given in the discourses of St. Paul to the Jews of Jerusalem after his arrest (xxii, 6-11), and to King Agrippa (xxvi, 12-16). These three narratives are given together in a comparative table by M. Tricot, *Saint Paul*, pp. 46-7. These differ only by insignificant details. Cf. Tricot, *op. cit.*, p. 43.

[19] The most explicit mention is in *I Cor.* xv, 7-8: ". . . After that, he was seen by James, then by all the apostles, and last of all, he was seen also by me, as by one born out of due time. For I am the least of the apostles, who am not worthy to be called an apostle, because I persecuted the church of God."

In the course of the thirty years of his life as a Christian, St. Paul will hear words from the Lord many times and he will have many visions. But none of these graces will be comparable to this appearance of Jesus on the way to Damascus. He had seen the Lord [20]; it was because of this that he was an Apostle, a witness of the Resurrection of Christ, like the other Apostles.[21] And Jesus, who appeared to him, revealed His Gospel to him,[22] and gave to him the apostolate of the Gentiles.[23]

Baptism and First Preaching of St. Paul

Blinded, Paul was led into Damascus, and there healed and baptised by Ananias: "Brother Saul, the Lord Jesus hath sent me, he that appeared to thee in the way as thou camest, that thou mayest receive thy sight, and be filled with the Holy Ghost." As soon as he had received baptism the Apostle began his work, "preaching Jesus in the synagogues, that he is the Son of God. And all that heard him, were astonished, and said: 'Is not this he who persecuted in Jerusalem those that called upon this name; and came hither for that intent, that he might carry them bound to the chief priests?' " (ix, 20-21). The Acts continue: "But Saul increased much more in strength, and confounded the Jews who dwelt in Damascus, affirming that this is the Christ. And when many days were passed, the Jews consulted together to kill him. . . ." (22-23), and Paul had to evade them.[24]

[20] I Cor. ix, 1: "Am I not an apostle? Have not I seen Christ Jesus our Lord?"

[21] I Cor. xv, 8: In this appearance, Jesus was seen only by Saul; the others "heard indeed a voice, but saw no man" (Acts ix, 7). This appearance of Jesus to Paul is also attested by Ananias (ix, 17; xxii, 14), and by Jesus Himself (xxvi, 16). Cf. Wikenhauser, op. cit., p. 179.

[22] Gal. i, 11-12: "I give you to understand, brethren, that the gospel which was preached by me is not according to man. For neither did I receive it of man, nor did I learn it but by the revelation of Jesus Christ."

[23] Acts xxvi, 15-18: "I am Jesus whom thou persecutest. But rise up, and stand upon thy feet, for to this end have I appeared to thee, that I may make thee a minister, and a witness of those things which thou hast seen and of those things wherein I will appear to thee, delivering thee from the people and from the nations, unto which now I send thee, to open their eyes, that they may be converted from darkness to light, and from the power of Satan to God, that they may receive forgiveness of sins, and a lot among the saints." In this speech made by Paul to King Agrippa, the instructions which Ananias had given him (xxii, 14) are attributed directly to the Lord Jesus; this is merely the suppression of an intermediary, in whom Agrippa would not be interested.

[24] II Cor. xi, 32; cf. Acts ix, 23-5, Gal. i, 17. When Paul had to leave Damascus

Between these two series of events which Luke connects, suppressing, as he often does, all that happened in between, we must insert a long stay in Arabia, mentioned in the Epistle to the Galatians.[25] We have no further information concerning this journey and stay. Many think that Paul wished to spend some time in retreat before beginning a life so different from that which he had hitherto led; Lightfoot and Cornely think that he withdrew to Sinai; Lagrange, on the contrary, thinks that "the revelations granted to Paul were always mingled with his active life as their immediate principle" [26] and that if he went to Arabia it was to preach there. This conjecture is a likely one, but it must be added that this preaching, if it took place, had little echo and perhaps small success; [27] the Christians of Jerusalem had not heard of it.

St. Paul in Jerusalem

After his second stay at Damascus and his escape, he arrived in the holy city; he essayed to join himself to the disciples, "but they were all afraid of him, not believing that he was a disciple" (ix, 26).

---

the city was under the rule of Aretas. Aretas, King of the Arabians, was at war with Antipas, who had dismissed his sister. Antipas had been upheld by Tiberius, who ordered Vitellius, governor of Syria, to proceed against the King of the Arabians; this expedition was stopped by the death of Tiberius (March 16th, 37). At Damascus there have been found coins of Tiberius dated 33-34. Aretas was accordingly not the master of Damascus at this date, nor probably until the death of Tiberius; he must have been invested by Caius, who ascended the throne on March 18th, 37, and who in this matter, as in all others, took an opposite course to that of Tiberius. The escape of Paul therefore could not have been anterior to 37, nor his conversion, three years before the journey to Jerusalem (Gal. i, 18), before 34. We may date the conversion in the year 36; the first stay at Damascus, the journey to Arabia, and the second stay at Damascus from 36 to 38; the escape from Damascus, the first journey to Jerusalem, in 38-39. In this hypothesis there will be only fourteen years from the conversion of St. Paul to the Council of Jerusalem; the three years (Gal. i, 18) will not be added to the fourteen (Gal. ii, 1), but the two periods will begin from the same point, i.e. from his conversion. Cf. Prat, Recherches de science religieuse, 1912, pp. 372-92; art. Chronologie, in Supplément to the Dict. de la Bible, 1283-4.

[25] Gal. i, 15-19: "When it pleased him, who separated me from my mother's womb and called me by his grace, to reveal his Son in me, that I might preach him among the Gentiles, immediately I condescended not to flesh and blood, neither went I to Jerusalem to the apostles who were before me; but I went into Arabia, and again I returned to Damascus. Then, after three years, I went to Jerusalem to see Peter, and I tarried with him fifteen days. But other of the apostles I saw none, saving James the brother of the Lord." On the silence of the Acts, cf. Wikenhauser, op. cit., p. 184.

[26] Epître aux Galates, p. 17 (on i, 17).   [27] This is the opinion of St. Jerome.

Then Barnabas became his surety; [28] he "took him and brought him to the Apostles, and told them how he had seen the Lord, and that he had spoken to him, and how in Damascus he had dealt confidently in the name of Jesus." Thus suspicions were dissipated; Paul was able to see Peter, as he had desired, and to discuss matters for fifteen days with him; he also saw James the brother of the Lord. From that time he shared in Jerusalem the life of the disciples, speaking with full assurance in the name of Christ.

It was doubtless during this first stay at Jerusalem that Paul had in the Temple the vision which he narrated later on to the Jews (xxii, 17 *et seq.*):

"When I was come again to Jerusalem, and was praying in the Temple, I was in a trance, and saw him saying unto me: 'Make haste, and get thee quickly out of Jerusalem, because they will not receive thy testimony concerning me.' And I said, 'Lord, they know that I cast into prison and beat in every synagogue them that believed in thee. And when the blood of Stephen thy witness was shed I stood by and consented, and kept the garments of them that killed him.' And he said to me, 'Go, for unto the Gentiles afar off will I send thee.'"

This notification by Divine Providence was shortly afterwards realised in effect: Paul argued with the Hellenists; very soon he was, like Stephen, threatened with death. "Which when the brethren had known, they brought him down to Cæsarea, and sent him away to Tarsus." He remained in Cilicia until Barnabas sought him there to take him to Antioch (in 42 or 43).

Philip the Deacon

The conversion of St. Paul, closely connected with the death of St. Stephen, has led us to omit the events which had immediately followed that death.

"At that time there was raised a great persecution against the church which was at Jerusalem; and they were all dispersed through the countries of Judea and Samaria, except the Apostles. And devout men took order for Stephen's funeral, and made great mourning over him. But Saul made havock of the church, entering in from house to house, and dragging away men and women, committed them to prison" (vii, 1-3).

[28] Barnabas was of great repute in the Christian community. He was a Levite, a Cypriot by origin; he possessed a field, sold it, and laid the price at the feet of the Apostles (iv, 36-7). Barnabas was a Hellenist, and may have known Paul before his conversion.

These verses are of interest in more than one way: the Apostles remained at Jerusalem, while all the rest were scattered. Protestant historians see in this a new proof of the opposition which they think they find between the Hellenists, who had fallen out with official Judaism, and the Apostles, who respected it.[29] Without going so far as that, Le Camus writes: "The Apostles seem to have been less affected by it, either because they felt they had the protection of the people, or else because being apparently more visibly attached to Mosaism than Stephen and his followers, they were not directly aimed at by the persecution. They remained peaceably at Jerusalem, while the Hellenists . . . left the holy city *en masse.*" [30] It certainly seems that the two groups were not equally menaced; we see this again on Paul's return to Jerusalem. Nevertheless, we cannot speak of a "peaceable stay"; the Apostles themselves were obliged to scatter and to hide themselves; Paul returning from Damascus could see only Peter and James; less directly concerned than the Hellenists, they were nevertheless suspect, and could no longer pursue their free action of the first years.

Reuss writes as follows on the subject of the burial of Stephen: [31] "We must above all stress what is said here of the last honours rendered to Stephen. This man, the victim of religious fanaticism, and put to death as a criminal, found friends who dared to mourn him publicly. These courageous friends were not the Apostles, they were . . . converts from paganism, uncircumcised proselytes. . . . All this shows us that we have here the symptoms of a first transformation of the Church, a transformation which, like all the similar phases of its history, is at once a progress and an occasion of schism. The Apostles remain at Jerusalem, in the shadow of the Temple; the persecuted Hellenists go to carry the word of God to the Samaritans and the pagans. Providence carried on its work by confiding it to other hands." This account disfigures the facts, and the historian is projecting back into the primitive church the shadow of the schisms which were to lacerate it later on. In reality there was no trace of schism at all: the conversion of the Samaritans, begun by a Hellenist, was concluded by two Apostles; and if Philip introduced into the Church a proselyte, the Ethiopian

[29] Reuss, *op. cit.,* p. 102; Monnier, *La notion de l'apostolat,* pp. 168 *et seq.*
[30] Le Camus, *op. cit.,* p. 147.
[31] Reuss, *op. cit.,* p. 102.

eunuch, it was Peter who was to give admission to the first pagan, Cornelius.

The persecution, by scattering the Hellenists, helped to propagate Christianity. Philip, who was, it seems, of Cæsarea, went to Samaria, "and the people with one accord were attentive to those things which were said by Philip, hearing and seeing the miracles which he did." [32]

This rousing of the city recalls the excitement caused at Sichem by the first preaching of Jesus. Many were baptised, and amongst them a certain Simon Magus. The Apostles, learning of the success of this evangelisation, sent Peter and John, who laid ·hands on the newly baptised and gave them the Holy Spirit. [33]

Simon Magus, seeing the wonderful effects produced by the laying on of hands by the Apostles, offered them money if they would give him the same power. Peter repelled him with indignation, and Simon seems to have been inclined to repent: "Pray you for me to the Lord, that none of these things which you have spoken may come upon me" (viii, 24). The New Testament says nothing further of Simon; later literature attributes to him a great role, it makes him the god of the Samaritans, and later on, the constant opponent of Peter. [34]

At an angel's orders, Philip went to the Gaza road; there he met a eunuch, a servant of Candace, Queen of the Ethiopians; he joined his chariot, offered to explain to him the passage of Isaias which

[32] viii, 6. The text of viii, 5, is not certain: we may read either "the town of Samaria" or "a town of Samaria." If it is Samaria or Sebaste which is referred to, this was then a town more Hellenist than Jewish or Samaritan: Pompey had rebuilt it, and had made it a free city (*Antiquities of the Jews*, XIV, 4, 4; *Wars of the Jews*, I, 7, 7; Gabinius had restored it and fortified it (*Antiquities of the Jews*. XIV, 5, 3; *Wars of the Jews*, I, 8, 4); Herod had embellished it and named it Sebaste; it was there he had had his wife Marianne and her sons put to death; during the Jewish War, Sebaste passed to the Romans (*Antiquities of the Jews*, XVII, 10, 3, 9; *Wars of the Jews*, II, 3, 4; 4, 3; 2, 5).

[33] Reuss writes (*op. cit.*, p. 105): "It is not that these gave a teaching superior to that of Philip, or that their pre-eminent dignity had greater claim on the grace of God (although this latter explanation is not excluded by the text), but their presence was able to provoke a more intense movement, more energetic transports, and consequently, psychical phenomena analogous to those which had already been noticed elsewhere." This interpretation only too well betrays a disbelief in any sacramental grace conferred by the Apostles; the text says nothing of these intense transports, it affirms only the action of the Apostles, and the results which it produced.

[34] Cf. Bk. II, ch. vi, § 3.

he was reading, preached Jesus to him, and baptised him (viii, 26-40). This new triumph was, like the evangelisation of Samaria, an act of expansion and liberation, but a still bolder one.[35] After baptising the eunuch, Philip was taken away from him to Azotus; thence he went to Cæsarea, evangelising all the cities *en route*.

§3. MISSIONS OF ST. PETER

The Evangelisation of the Sharon

Just as Peter and John had gone through Samaria after Philip, Peter now decided to visit Sharon, which Philip had just evangelised. The Church was then enjoying peace, but it was a temporary calm rather than a permanent state. At Lydda Peter stayed with "the saints"; there he found a paralytic. "Eneas," he said, "the Lord Jesus Christ healeth thee: arise and make thy bed." Eneas was cured; Lydda and Sharon were converted by this miracle.

The presence of Peter became known at Joppa; he was asked to go to the house of a pious lady named Tabitha, who had just died. When he was taken into the upper chamber where the body lay all ready for burial, he found there widows who wept and showed him the garments which the charitable Tabitha had woven for them. Peter knelt and prayed, and then turning to the body, said: "Tabitha, arise!" She opened her eyes, saw Peter, and sat up. Many people were converted at Joppa in consequence of this miracle.

In this evangelising expedition, Peter had in the first place gone to the Jewish cities, Lydda and Joppa. He had not gone to the pagan city of Cæsarea, but God was to summon him there.

The Conversion of Cornelius

The conversion of the centurion Cornelius is narrated in full detail; it was in fact an event of capital importance in the history of the development of Christianity.

---

[35] The eunuchs were excluded from the community of Israel (*Deut.* xxiii, 1); the *Book of Wisdom* (iii, 14) was less severe in their regard. Was the eunuch a Jew? St. Irenæus thought so, and his opinion is regarded as certain, or at least as probable, by a good number of commentators and historians such as Tillemont, *Mémoires*, Vol. II, p. 67; Foakes-Jackson, *The Acts*, London, 1931, p. 76; Boudou, *Actes*, p. 174. But his attitude, his understanding of Isaias, his desire for instruction, should lead us to regard him rather as a proselyte, not belonging to the Jewish community, but fearing God and adoring Him.

In the *cohors italica* which held the garrison at Cæsarea [1] there
was a centurion, Cornelius by name, "a religious man, and fearing
God" [2] together with all his household. About the ninth hour of
the day, an angel appeared to him and commanded him to send to
Joppa for a certain Simon surnamed Peter, who was lodging with
Simon the tanner, near the sea. Cornelius called to him one of his
soldiers, inclined like himself towards the religion of Israel, told
him of the vision, and despatched him to Joppa together with two
servants.

On the morrow, about midday, as these men were approaching
Joppa, Peter went up to the roof of the house to pray. He fell
into an ecstasy: he saw the heavens opened, and there came down
from thence something like a great sheet held at its four corners
and hanging from heaven to earth. In it were to be seen all the
four-footed beasts and creeping things of the earth, and all the birds
of the air. At the same time a voice was heard: "Arise, Peter, kill
and eat." "Far be it from me, Lord," replied Peter, "I never did
eat anything that is common or unclean." "That which God hath
cleansed, do not thou call common." Three times the same vision
appeared, with the same invitation, and the same replies. And
while Peter was asking himself what all this might signify, the men
from Cæsarea arrived, and the Spirit commanded Peter to follow
them.

The next day they set out together for Cæsarea. A few of the
faithful from Joppa accompanied Peter: in so delicate a situation,
the Apostles wanted to make sure of their witness. When they
arrived on the day following at Cæsarea, they found Cornelius
surrounded by his relatives and friends. Cornelius came forward
towards Peter, and knelt before him. Peter lifted him up: "Arise,
I myself also am a man." He entered into the house, and said to
all those there present: "You know that it is forbidden to a Jew to
have relations with a stranger, or to enter into his house; [3] but as
for myself, God has instructed me to regard no man as common

---

[1] There was no legion in Judea, which was a Procuratorial province, but there
were cohorts. The presence of a *cohors italica* is mentioned in 69; it could have
been there already about the year 40 (Ramsay, *Was Christ born at Bethlehem?*,
pp. 260-9, and Jacquier, *op. cit.*, p. 312).

[2] These expressions are those by which Luke designates uncircumcised proselytes. Cf. Ramsay, *St. Paul*, p. 43.

[3] The Jews could enter into a pagan house without scruple, but not to eat or
receive hospitality there. Cf. Jacquier, *op. cit.*, p. 324.

or unclean; that is why I have had no objection to coming here as you requested. Tell me, therefore, for what cause you have sent for me?"

Cornelius then related his vision. Peter, hearing this, praised the universality of God's mercy: "In very deed I perceive that God is not a respecter of persons, but in every nation, he that feareth him and worketh justice is acceptable to him." He then went on to preach the Gospel of peace which God had sent to the children of Israel by Jesus Christ, who is the "Lord of all" (x, 36). The life of Jesus was apparently already known to Cornelius: "You know the word which hath been published through all Judea. . . ." Peter recalled the death of Jesus, and stressed His resurrection. This was witnessed not by the whole people, but by witnesses whom God had chosen, "we who did eat and drink with him after he rose again from the dead"; God has made Him judge of the living and the dead; whosoever believes in Him receives through His name the pardon of sins.

"While Peter was yet speaking these words, the Holy Ghost fell on all them that heard the word." The Jews who had accompanied Peter were astonished, hearing these pagans speaking in tongues. Peter immediately went on: "Can we refuse the water of baptism to those who have received the Holy Ghost as well as us?" And he had them baptised in the name of the Lord. Then they prayed him to stay for a few days.

This decisive step, narrated with such detail, reveals to us what obstacles existed to the preaching of the Gospel, and how they were removed. The distinction between pure and impure foods may appear to us now to be unimportant; it was not at all such for the Jews. Every faithful Jew was ready to say again like the seven martyred brethren: "We are ready to die rather than to transgress the laws of God, received from our fathers" (II Mach. vii, 2). It might be urged that Christ had revoked these Jewish laws: "There is nothing from without a man that entering into him can defile him, but the things which come from a man, those are they that defile a man." [4] But this bold word had even then alarmed the disciples, and they hesitated to put it into practice. Here it was above all necessary that the Holy Spirit should remind the Apostles of what Jesus had said to them, and help them to understand it.

The social laws made them hesitate even more than the food laws:

[4] Mark vii, 14. Cf. supra, p. 105.

were they obliged to admit pagans into the Church, and not only circumcised pagans like Nicholas the proselyte of Antioch, but religious men and those fearing God who had not received circumcision? The Holy Spirit himself decided the matter by pouring forth upon Cornelius and his household the gifts of Pentecost, and Peter, the head of the Church, allowed himself to be led patiently and with docility into this new way by the Spirit, not anticipating its action but not resisting it, though all his moral and religious formation was alarmed.

Peter in Jerusalem

This alarm is made more evident by the reaction of the Christians at Jerusalem. When they learnt of the happenings at Cæsarea, they were astounded. As soon as Peter arrived, they took him aside, and said to him: "Thou didst go in to men uncircumcised, and didst eat with them!" (xi, 3).

Peter had brought with him the six men who had accompanied him from Joppa. In their presence he gave to the faithful an account of all that had taken place: the vision at Joppa, the command from heaven, the visit to Cornelius, and, above all, the descent of the Holy Ghost while he was yet speaking:

"When I had begun to speak, the Holy Ghost fell upon them, as upon us also in the beginning. And I remembered the word of the Lord, how that he said: 'John indeed baptized with water, but you shall be baptized with the Holy Ghost.' If, then, God gave them the same grace, as to us also who believed in the Lord Jesus Christ; who was I, that could withstand God? Having heard these things, they held their peace, and glorified God, saying: God then hath also to the Gentiles given repentance unto life" (xi, 15-18).

As we see, the basis of the discussion had been altered and widened. At first complaint was made that Peter had gone amongst pagans; at the end, he had won not only on this point, but also on the much more serious question of the baptism of a pagan. Several historians hesitate to accept this account literally: the resistance which we find later on this question of the baptism of the uncircumcised seems to them to be irreconcilable with an agreement arrived at in this way on the occasion of the baptism of Cornelius. They think that the Apostles alone were convinced, and that the mass of the faithful still resisted, or else that the case of Cornelius was regarded, like that of the Ethiopian eunuch, as only an exceptional one, justified by a miraculous divine intervention.[5] We do not maintain that this particular decision sufficed to convince the whole community at Jerusalem; but there is no indication that the case was dealt with as an exceptional one, which was not to form a precedent. On this occasion, as in many another, we must not be surprised that several Divine messages were required to change habits of mind which were so deeply rooted and which appeared so sacred.

In Judean territory, and above all at Jerusalem, the case of the centurion Cornelius was to remain an exception for a long time, but already Christianity was spreading outside Judea, at Antioch. It was there that the evangelisation of the pagans was going to give the Apostles the joy of new and immense harvests, but also the anxiety of very serious problems.

§4. ANTIOCH AND JERUSALEM

The Evangelisation of Antioch

The persecution which had expelled the Hellenist Christians from Jerusalem dispersed them as far as Phœnicia, the island of Cyprus, and the city of Antioch. They preached, but there were some of them who announced the Gospel only to the Jews. Others, on the contrary, Cypriots or Cyreneans, after their arrival at Antioch, preached also to the Greeks, "and the hand of the Lord was with them, and a great number believing, were converted to the Lord" (xi, 19-21). Here again God intervened, and by the very abundant blessings which He bestowed upon the Greek missionaries, showed the Church the path she was to tread.

The Church obeyed with joy: as soon as those at Jerusalem learned of the success of the mission at Antioch, they sent there

[5] Reuss writes (*op. cit.,* pp. 131-2): "The account ends with these words: 'They calmed down, and showed themselves convinced.' These words say far too much, if we bear in mind the rest of the history. We must greatly modify them. Either Luke has in mind here only the Twelve, the masses showing themselves always hostile to the admission of pagans, or else the agreement related only to this special case of the household of Cornelius, and there was no intention of making it a general rule." A similar interpretation will be found in Renan, *Les apôtres,* p. 166.

Barnabas, just as a little earlier Peter and John had been sent to Samaria to crown the work of Philip there. The Hellenic mission at Antioch had been inaugurated by Cypriots and Cyreneans, and perhaps for this reason another Cypriot, Barnabas, was chosen to direct it. The Church at Jerusalem was aware of his disinterestedness and his zeal, and it set before him a magnificent field for his apostolic labours.

Barnabas was, in fact, "a good man, and full of the Holy Ghost and of faith" (xi, 24). When he arrived at Antioch and had seen the grace of God, he rejoiced. In order to gather in such an abundant harvest, he decided to appeal to the powerful preacher whom he had a little previously introduced to the Apostles at Jerusalem; he therefore went to Tarsus to seek Paul. He found him there, conducted him to Antioch, and for a whole year they worked there together, teaching a great multitude. It was at Antioch that the disciples were for the first time called Christians. This fact, recorded by St. Luke (*Acts* xi, 26) reveals the success of the Christian preaching. Henceforth the disciples of Jesus were no longer regarded as a Jewish sect similar to so many others; the pagans themselves distinguished the Christians from the Jews.

The strong position which Christianity won at Antioch naturally provided a better centre for the propagation of Christianity than Jerusalem. The missions mentioned up to the present, in Samaria and Sharon, were restricted to Palestine; Jerusalem provided a sufficient centre for them. But now the Greek and Roman world was being penetrated, and Antioch, the great eastern metropolis, was to be the starting point of this effort. It was from there that Saul and Barnabas would soon set forth for the conquest of Asia Minor, and thither they were to return after their mission as to their centre of action.

Thus during these years Antioch appears as the centre of the universal Church. Jerusalem had occupied this position until about the year 40; Rome will hold it later. This translation of the centre of Christian unity is marked in an ancient tradition by the setting up of the chair of St. Peter at Antioch.[1]

[1] Tillemont writes on this subject (*Mémoires*, Vol. I, *Saint Pierre*, art. 27, pp. 159-60): "According to the Fathers, he (St. Peter) founded the Church at Antioch before going to Rome, and there lived, and it was quite fitting that the city which first received the name 'Christian' should also have had as its master and pastor the first apostle. Antioch was his first see, and he was its first bishop. . . . Nevertheless, it is not necessary to suppose that he remained there through-

The sojourns that Peter certainly made at Antioch confirm this tradition, without making it necessary to hold to a solemn translation of the chair of Peter, or to determine the time during which he was the Bishop of Antioch.[2]

Famine and Persecution in Jerusalem

"In these days, there came prophets from Jerusalem to Antioch. And one of them named Agabus, rising up, signified by the Spirit that there should be a great famine over the whole world, which came to pass under Claudius. And the disciples, every man according to his ability, purposed to send relief to the brethren who dwelt in Judea. Which also they did, sending it to the ancients, by the hands of Barnabas and Saul" (xi, 27-30).

This incident, narrated thus in passing by St. Luke, is interesting for more than one reason: it shows us the office held in the primitive community by the prophets,[3] it also manifests to us the close bonds of charity which united the different churches to each other. From this date begin the collections for the poor of Jerusalem; they will not cease until the ruin of the holy city. Lastly, and above all, we see here for the first time the presbyters or ancients of the Christian church. This fact proves that St. Luke did not set

out this period, as we see from what followed. Thus it seems that he was the bishop of Antioch only because he took a particular care of that church, and not because he always resided there. For it seems that no apostle, other than St. James at Jerusalem, was at first completely attached to a particular church." The feast of the chair of St. Peter at Antioch is of Gallican origin. Cf. Duchesne, *Origines du culte chrétien*, p. 296; Kirsch, *Der Stadrömische Festkalender*, Münster, 1924, p. 18; Lietzmann, *Petrus und Paulus in Rom*, Berlin, 1927, p. 96. Tillemont adds in note 25: "Baronius thinks that St. Peter could have founded the church of Antioch and established his see there without going there, because all this signifies only that by his authority he erected it as a patriarchal see. But I do not know if many people would follow him in this."

[2] Fouard (*op. cit.*, p. 189) thinks that Peter went to Antioch in 40, before the vision at Joppa, and translated his see there; two years later on he transferred it to Rome. Belzer (*Die Apostelgeschichte*, 150, quoted by Jacquier, *op. cit.*, p. 357) distinguishes two successive evangelisations of Antioch: the first, begun about 33, was addressed only to the Jews; it ended in the establishing of a Judeo-Christian community, of which Peter was the head, from 34 or 35 until 39. About 39 or 40, when news came of the baptism of Cornelius, Hellenists came and preached to the Greeks. These hypotheses seem gratuitous; the suggestion of Tillemont seems better founded.

[3] The Christian prophets were above all preachers inspired by God: *I Cor.* xiv, 29-32; but they could also foretell the future, as Agabus did on this occasion and later on (xxi, 10).

out to give us an exact account of the origin of all ecclesiastical institutions; it reveals the development of the Christian church and its character. Already at this date the Church had constituted its hierarchy and its local organisation. This manifests its independence with regard to the synagogue; it is equally a sign of the hierarchical spirit, which was strong from the first.

It was also at this time that there broke out the persecution provoked by Agrippa. This prince was the son of Aristobulus and Berenice. His father, a son of Herod and Mariamne, was put to death by Herod in the year 7; brought up at the court of Tiberius, he had led there a disordered life. A few months before his death in 37, Tiberius had thrown him into prison; Caius, his companion in debauchery, set him free when he ascended the throne (A.D. 37), and gave him the tetrarchy of Philip, then that of Lysinias, with the title of king, and then in 40, after the deposition of Antipas, Galilee and Perea. In 41, Claudius added to these Samaria and Judea; the kingdom of Herod was thus reconstituted.

As soon as he arrived in Jerusalem, the king displayed a great zeal for the Law.[4] Taking the opposite course to that of Herod, his predecessor, he manifested a particular sympathy for the Jews and a great veneration towards the Law; "he loved to live continually at Jerusalem, and retained in their completeness the institutions of the forefathers. He kept himself in a continual state of purity, and never allowed a day to pass without offering the prescribed sacrifices."[5] The Mishna narrates that one day, when celebrating in the Temple the Feast of Tabernacles, he was reading the Book of Deuteronomy in accordance with the custom of sabbatic years.[6] When he arrived at the text: "Thou shalt not have to reign over thee a stranger who is not thy brother," he felt that this applied to himself, and burst into tears, but all the people then cried out: "Do not be dismayed! Thou art our brother; thou art our brother."[7]

[4] Josephus, *Antiquities of the Jews*, XIX, 6, 1, 293: "Arriving at Jerusalem, he immolated sacrifices in thanksgiving, without forgetting any prescription of the Law. For this reason he commanded that a great number of Nazarites should have their heads shorn. The golden chain which Caius had given him, and which weighed as much as the iron one which had been attached to his royal hands . . . was hung inside the sacred precincts . . ."

[5] *Ibid.*, XIX, 7, 3, 328-31.

[6] The year 40-41 was a sabbatic year. Cf. Schuerer, *op. cit.*, Vol. I, p. 555.

[7] M. Sota, vii, p. 8; Schuerer, *op. cit.*, Vol. I, p. 555.

Martyrdom of St. James the Great

Anxious to gain the goodwill of the people by his religious zeal, Agrippa actively revived the persecution of the Christians. "He killed James, the brother of John, with the sword; [8] and seeing that it pleased the Jews, he proceeded to take up Peter also" (xii, 2-3). It was the time of the Azymes; as on the occasion of the trial of Jesus, it was thought prudent to wait for the end of the feast of the Pasch. Peter was kept in prison, and surrounded by all possible precautions: a double chain, keepers at his sides, keepers at the door of the prison.

The Deliverance of St. Peter

During the night which preceded the day fixed for his trial, Peter was miraculously delivered. A great light shone in his cell; the Apostle was roused by an angel; his chains fell from his hands, he dressed and followed the angel, thinking it was a dream. He passed the guards, saw the great door open, and went out into the street. The angel then left him, and Peter, coming to himself, said: "Now I know in very deed, that the Lord hath sent his angel, and hath delivered me out of the hand of Herod, and from all the expectation of the people of the Jews." He went to the house of Mary, the mother of John surnamed Mark, and knocked at the door. The servant, Rhoda, ran to open it. Recognising the voice of Peter, she was overcome with joy, forgot to open the door, but ran to announce that Peter was there. They said to her: "Thou art mad." She insisted that it was indeed he. Then they said to her: "It is his angel." Peter meanwhile continued to knock. They opened the door, and recognised him with astonishment. He told them how he had come out of the prison, and

[8] On this martyrdom, related in a word, Eusebius, *Ecclesiastical History*, II, 9, 2-3, adds this fact, found by him in Clement of Alexandria (*Hypot.*, vii): "The one who had taken him before the tribunal, seeing the testimony which he had given, was moved thereby, and confessed that he also was a Christian. Both of them were led out to death. On the way, this man prayed James to forgive him. The Apostle reflected for a moment, and then said to him: 'Peace be with thee,' and embraced him. And so both were beheaded at the same time." A certain number of historians, following Wellhausen, *Evangelium Marci*, p. 90, and above all E. Schwartz, *Ueber Tod der Sohne Zebedaei*, 1904, have endeavoured to associate together the deaths of the two sons of Zebedee. This hypothesis of the early death of St. John has been thoroughly refuted, and in particular by L. de Grandmaison, *Jesus Christ*, Vol. I, pp. 147-55.

said to them: "Tell these things to James, and to the brethren."
Then he left them and went into another place.

This account of St. Luke, so full of life, brings home to us all
the emotion of this miraculous deliverance. It also reveals to us
more than one feature of the life of the Christians in Jerusalem,
of which we know so little. They were gathered together in a
great number in the house of Mary, mother of Mark, and prayed
for Peter (xii, 5-12); the evangelist of prayer has taken care to
show us how the whole Church had obtained this miracle from
the Lord. Mark appears here for the first time. He is still young,
his cousin Barnabas will very soon take him on his apostolic
mission; he will work first of all with St. Paul, then with Barnabas
alone. Later on we shall find him again at Rome, near to St.
Peter, whose interpreter he was, and near to St. Paul, of whom
he was once more the companion and friend.[9] Amongst the numerous disciples gathered together in the house of Mary we see
no Apostle, but St. Peter, before leaving, asks that the account of
his deliverance should be communicated "to James and to the
brethren." This is the first time that James, the brother of the
Lord, appears as the head of the church of Jerusalem; he will
occupy this office until his death. As for St. Peter himself, he
left the holy city, and went "into another place." It is easy to
understand that after this escape he could not remain in Jerusalem.
It is certain that this departure was not a farewell for ever; he will
be once more in Jerusalem at the time of the Council (xv, 7).
Where did he go in the interval? We do not know for certain;
Jacquier thinks it "probable" that he went to Antioch, "possible"
that he went to Rome. His later sojourns in these two cities can
be indeed affirmed as certain, but their dates are not certain.

The persecution which led to Peter's departure was soon to come
to an end by the death of Agrippa. This painful and sudden
death, which struck the king at a moment of great triumph in 44,
shortly after the Pasch, seemed to be a punishment by Providence:
"An angel of the Lord struck him, because he had not given the
honour to God." [10] And Christianity continued to grow: "The
word of the Lord increased and multiplied" (xii, 24).

[9] On all this, cf. Lagrange, *Saint Marc*, pp. xvi-xix; *Huby, Saint Marc,* pp. ix-
xiv.
[10] xii, 23. The account in Josephus (*Antiquities of the Jews,* XIX, 8, 2,
343-50) is longer and less vigorous than that of St. Luke, but it confirms its

Persecutions and Growth of the Church

These last words of St. Luke sum up all this first period of the history of the Church. Fourteen years had elapsed since the death of Jesus; during this very short period of time the work had grown. It was no longer the grain of mustard seed, but already a great tree which covered the whole of Palestine and was extending its branches over Damascus, Cyprus, Antioch; everywhere this expansion was opposed; we can affirm in all truth what the Jews were to say fifteen years later to St. Paul in Rome: "This sect is everywhere contradicted"; and nevertheless everywhere the Church was taking root and growing. In Jerusalem, the stronghold of Judaism, Christianity had won many disciples, even among the priests (vi, 7); when Paul returned there in 58, James could say to him: "Thou seest, brother, how many thousands of Jews have received the faith." Doubtless these thousands would never be more than a minority in Jerusalem, and an oppressed minority; we have told of the martyrdom of St. Stephen and that of St. James the Great; very soon there will be the captivity of St. Paul and the martyrdom of the Bishop of Jerusalem, St. James the Less, and then all through this period there will be the expulsion of the Hellenists, the imprisonment of St. Peter, the persecution, now gentle, now violent, which unceasingly threatens the Church. And in face of this opposition, which slackens sometimes, but never ceases completely, the Church continues to grow.

What happened during these fifteen years at Jerusalem is a forecast of the history of the propagation of Christianity through the missions of St. Paul: everywhere, after a first contact, and often numerous conversions, the Church encounters the insidious, obstinate and violent opposition of the Jews; everywhere there is verified the prophetic words of Jesus to Ananias: "I will show to Paul how great things he must suffer for my name's sake" (ix, 16). It is through these persecutions, and at the price of these sufferings, that the Church develops.

---

essential features: the king appearing in the theatre covered with a robe of silver which sparkles in the light of the setting sun; the flatterers crying out that he is not a man but a god, and the immediate seizure of the king by intestinal pains which led to his death at the end of five days.

CHAPTER III

THE MISSIONS OF ST. PAUL[1]

The Sources: The Epistles and the Acts

THE history of the infant Church is hardly known to us other than by the Acts; at most we have been able to complete the account on a few matters by the letter of St. Paul to the Galatians. The history of the missions of St. Paul, on the other hand, is clarified not only by the Acts, but also and above all by the Epistles of St. Paul. Doubtless there is a great difference between the account of St. Luke, drawn up twenty or thirty years after the events with a view to describing the progressive expansion of the Church, and the letters of St. Paul, written from day to day to settle practical and urgent questions. This difference in character and date must guide the historian in the use of his sources, but he must not neglect any of them. The Acts will provide the main framework for this history, but we must look to the Epistles for an intimate knowledge of the Apostle, his Christians, and his doctrine.[2]

[1] Bibliography.—Consult in the first place the general works on Christian origins mentioned in the Bibliography of the preceding chapter. See also: C. Fouard, *Saint Paul*, Paris, 1908-10, 2 vols; F. Prat, *The Theology of St. Paul*, Eng. tr., 1926, 2 vols.; F. Prat, *Saint Paul*, in collection *Les Saints*, Paris, 1922; K. Pieper, *Paulus, Seine missionarische Persönlichkeit und Wirksamkeit*, Münster, 1929; H. Deissmann, *Paulus*, Tübingen, 1925; J. Gresham Machen, *The Origin of St. Paul's Religion*, New York, 1921; W. L. Knox, *St. Paul and the Church of Jerusalem*, Cambridge, 1925; A. Schweitzer, *Die Mystik des Apostels Paulus*, Tübingen, 1930; *Geschichte der paulinischen Forschung*, Tübingen, 1911.

[2] In this matter we differ in the first place from the radical critics of the Dutch school, who reject not only the Acts, but the totality of the Epistles of St. Paul. This school is represented by Van Manen, one of the two authors (the other is E. Hatch) of the article *Paul* in the *Encyclopædia Biblica*. This concludes: "All the representations formerly current—alike in Roman Catholic and Protestant circles—particularly during the nineteenth century—regarding the life and work of Paul the Apostle of Jesus Christ, of the Lord, and the Gentiles, must be set aside, in so far as they rest on the illusory belief that we can implicitly rely on what we read in the Acts and the 13 (14) epistles of Paul." Similarly, all the expositions of Paul's theology based on the same sources have "irrevocably passed away" (col. 3630). This extreme thesis is still maintained to-day by Van den Bergh van Eysinga, *La littérature chrétienne primitive* (Collection *Christianisme*), 1926. This polemic has at any rate the interest of showing that there are just as many—or as few—intrinsic and extrinsic reasons for rejecting the Epistle to the

§1. FIRST MISSION OF ST. PAUL. CYPRUS, PISIDIA, LYCAONIA[3]

There were some prophets in the Church at Antioch. One day, when they were performing the liturgy and fasting, the Holy Spirit said: "Separate me Barnabas and Saul, for the work whereunto I have taken them." The prophets fasted, prayed, laid hands on them, and sent them away.

Cyprus

Barnabas is mentioned here before Saul, and it seems that it was he who decided the direction to be taken: they went to Cyprus, Barnabas's birthplace, and they took as assistant his cousin, John Mark.[4] The missionaries disembarked at Salamina, and preached in the synagogues. Custom demanded that notable strangers should be invited to speak; the Apostles profited by this, as Jesus had done;[5] the discourse at Antioch in Pisidia, which we will summarise from St. Luke, tells us the nature of this preaching.

At Paphos, Barnabas and Saul found with the proconsul Sergius Paulus a magician named Barjesus, who called himself Elymas ("learned doctor"). Saul, whose preaching he endeavoured to hinder, struck him wih a temporary blindness; the proconsul, a witness of this, became a believer, "admiring at the doctrine of the Lord." From that moment, Saul was called Paul.[6]

Romans or that to the Galatians as the Epistles to the Colossians or the Philippians (col. 3626). The disciples of the Tübingen school are more moderate: they retain, at least in part, the Pauline Epistles, but reject the Acts. Thus Weiszaecker accepts (*op. cit.*, p. 184) as authentic the following Epistles: *Galatians, I* and *II Corinthians, I Thessalonians, Philippians, Romans;* but he constantly tries to find contradictions between the *Acts* and the *Epistles.* This critique of the *Acts* is the weakest part in a book which is very solid in other respects. We may point out, moreover, that it is solely from *Acts* xiii-xiv that Weiszaecker himself endeavours to describe the apostolate of Paul amongst the Galatians (pp. 230-2). Nowadays the Tübingen school has lost its prestige, and the account in the *Acts* of St. Paul's activity is judged more fairly. Thus Bultmann, art. *Paulus*, in *Religion in Geschichte und Gegenwart,* 1023 *et seq.*; Juelicher, *Einleitung* (1931), p. 35.

[3] This mission is known to us only by Acts xiii and xiv.

[4] On Mark, see above, p. 199.

[5] Cf. *supra*, p. 102.

[6] xiii, 9. Not that Saul took the name of the proconsul as freed slaves did, but probably because the Apostle had a double name (cf. "John Mark," "Simon Niger," etc.), and also because, going into a pagan land, he now uses more ordinarily his Roman name.

Anatolia

Cyprus offered to the two missionaries only a very restricted field of action; accordingly they took ship for Pamphylia and went to Perge. St. Paul, henceforward the head of the expedition, undertook the conquest of Anatolia. There he was to find, mingled with the Hellenes whom the Seleucids had implanted in these provinces, indigenous peoples: the Lycaonians, whom he was to evangelise at Lystra, and later on, in the northern provinces, the Galatians, and then, in the whole of the ancient kingdom of the Seleucids, the Jews, who enjoyed a privileged position. Seleucus Nicator had granted them civic rights in his capital (Antioch in Syria) and in all the cities founded by him; Antiochus the Great had continued the same policy; thus these Seleucids, hated in Palestine as persecutors, acted in Syria and Anatolia as protectors of the Jews, and could count upon their support.[7]

The mission which the two Apostles now commenced was to be extremely laborious: they had to cross the chain of the Taurus Mountains, redoubtable for its height, and more still because of the brigands who infested it, before they could reach the high plateaux in the interior, at a mean altitude of more than 3,200 feet.[8] These obstacles were not the worst: they still had to encounter the contempt of the Greeks, the grosser and more violent idolatry of the natives, and above all the powerful and bitter opposition of the Jews. Faced with this difficult expedition, which he had not expected at the beginning, the young John Mark withdrew and returned to Jerusalem.

Antioch in Pisidia

After the difficult crossing of the Taurus, Paul and Barnabas reached Antioch in Pisidia. On the Sabbath day, they went to the synagogue. After the reading of the Law and the prophets, the heads of the synagogue invited the strangers to address them. St. Paul spoke: his discourse, analysed at length by St. Luke (xiii,

[7] Cf. Ramsay, *Historical Commentary on the Galatians*, pp. 189-92. This book contains (pp. 180-232) a good description of the towns visited by St. Paul in this first mission. A shorter description is given in another book of the same author, *The Church in the Roman Empire*, ch. ii, "Localities of the First Journey" (pp. 16-58).

[8] Antioch in Pisidia is at a height of 3,900 feet, Iconium 3,600 feet, Lystra 3,900 feet, Derbe about the same.

204 THE HISTORY OF THE PRIMITIVE CHURCH

16-41, makes known to us better than any other document the preaching of the Apostle in the synagogues. A first part [9] reminds the Jews and proselytes of the mercies of God towards Israel. Its theme is very similar to that of the discourse of Stephen, but whereas the latter wanted to bring out Israel's obstinacy, Paul sets out to bring into prominence the providential activity of God, leading up to the Christ. The second part explains the mission of Jesus; He was rejected and crucified by His people, and yet He is the Messias: God has manifestly proved this by raising Him from the dead; this resurrection is established by the testimony of the Apostles, "who are his witnesses to the people"; the Scriptures, and especially the Psalms, confirm this testimony.[10] Paul concludes by an exhortation to conversion and justification by faith.[11]

The impression made by this preaching seems to have been very great; Paul was asked to return to the same subject on the following Sabbath, and at the end, many Jews and proselytes accompanied the Apostle home in order to receive from him further instruction. "The next sabbath day, the whole city almost came together, to hear the word of God. But the Jews, seeing the multitudes, were filled with envy, and contradicted those things which were said by Paul, blaspheming." It was thus the very success of the preaching to the Gentiles which aroused the jealousy of the Jews; it is, moreover, possible that Paul, encouraged by the numbers of the proselytes, may have announced more openly the calling of the nations. In face of Jewish opposition, Paul and Barnabas declare courageously: "To you it behoved us first to speak the word of God, but because you reject it, and judge yourselves unworthy of eternal life, behold we turn to the Gentiles." The Gentiles were glad; the Jews became more violently angry, and stirring up the ladies of the city who attended the synagogue, and the chief men of the place, they had the two Apostles expelled. Paul and Barnabas shook off the dust of their feet against them, and went on to Iconium.

[9] The three parts of the discourse are clearly marked by the threefold apostrophe, "my brethren," with which each fresh section begins: 16, 26, 38. Cf. Prat, *Theology of St. Paul*, Vol. I, pp. 54-7.

[10] This argument resembles that of St. Peter in more than one feature (*Acts* ii, 25-32).

[11] This feature anticipates the theology of St. Paul as it will be developed in the Epistle to the Romans, and particularly in ch. x.

Iconium

Here their preaching was welcomed, as it had been at Antioch (xiv, 1-7): a fairly large number of Jews and Greeks were converted; the Apostles remained a long time in the city, witnessing there to the Lord, and performing many miracles. But opposition broke out, and here once more it came from the Jews; those who remained unbelievers stirred up the pagans against Paul and Barnabas; there was a riot, in which the pagans and Jews, with their *archontes* at their head, endeavoured to ill-treat and stone the missionaries. The latter fled into Lycaonia, evangelising Lystra, Derbe, and the whole region.

Lystra

At Lystra (xiv, 7-20) a man lame from birth listened to Paul's preaching. Paul said to him: "Stand upright on thy feet." He at once rose, and the crowd, stupefied, cried out in Lycaonian: "The gods have come down to us in the likeness of men." They called Barnabas Zeus, and Paul Hermes; [12] the priest of Zeus, whom they sought out, saw nothing impossible in this apparition, and hoped to utilise it for his cult; he arrived with oxen and garlands to offer sacrifice. The Apostles, preoccupied with their preaching, had not noticed the gross misunderstanding by the people; they realised it when they saw the priest and the oxen. Full of horror, they rent their garments, and rushed into the crowd, crying: "What are you doing? We are but men like you; we are come to convert you from all these vanities to the living God, who made heaven and earth and the sea and all things that are in them: who in times past suffered all nations to walk in their own ways. Nevertheless, he left not himself without testimony, doing good from heaven, giving rains and fruitful seasons, filling hearts with food and gladness."

Here we are no longer in the synagogue; Paul's hearers are no longer Jews or proselytes, but credulous pagans who think their gods have come down to earth; it is interesting to see how the Apostle's preaching is adapted to this audience. We learn already

[12] As Ramsay remarks (*The Church in the Roman Empire*, p. 57 n.), it is quite an oriental idea to see a secondary deity in the one who acts and speaks, and the supreme deity in the one who remains silent.

what the Epistle to the Romans later on will develop further: God has punished the pagans, abandoning them to their perverse ways, and yet He has left them light in the creation in which He reveals Himself.

The superstitious enthusiam of the people of Lystra was so great that the Apostles were hard put to it to prevent them offering the sacrifice which they had prepared. But these poor pagans were easy to sway: Jews came in from Antioch and Iconium, aroused the crowd, and stoned Paul, dragging him out of the city and leaving him for dead. This was doubtless the stoning which the Apostle recalled later on (*II Cor.* xi. 25), and which fixed in his flesh the wounds of Christ (*Gal.* vi, 17). But the disciples stood around Paul; he arose, and the next day he went to Derbe with Barnabas. We may see in this very rapid cure a new miracle.

Derbe

At Derbe the two missionaries gained many followers; then they retraced their steps, to Lystra, Iconium, and Antioch, to strengthen the faith of the disciples, reminding them that "through many tribulations we must enter into the kingdom of God." They installed presbyters in these different churches, and by prayer and fasting commended them to the Lord in whom they had believed. They thus went through Pisidia and Pamphylia, preaching once more at Perge, and took ship at Attalia for Antioch in Syria. There they "assembled the church, and related what great things God had done with them, and how he had opened the door of faith to the Gentiles."

The work accomplished during these two or three years of the mission [13] was wonderful; Christ said that the missionaries of Judaism compass sea and land to make one proselyte; their propaganda, though fruitful, could not be compared to this: Paul had won for Christ not only a great number of the children of Israel, and still more numerous proselytes, but idolators who had never yet been touched by any Jewish preaching. This was a great glory for the infant Church; but to many Christians, coming from Judaism and still timid, it was the occasion of a most difficult case of conscience. Were these newly converted pagans, such as these Lycaonians for instance, who only yesterday were still sacrificing to Zeus and

[13] This first apostolic journey of St. Paul took place between A.D. 45 and 48.

Hermes, to enter openly into the Church, without first submitting themselves to initiation into Judaism, and without even being circumcised? The case was going to be discussed and decided at Jerusalem.

§2. ST. PAUL AND THE JUDAISERS[1]

St. Paul's Narrative

The controversy begun by the Judaisers and settled at Jerusalem is made known to us by two documents: the *Epistle to the Galatians* (ii, 1-10) and the *Acts* (xv, 1-35). St. Paul narrates the facts thus: fourteen years after his first voyage to Jerusalem he went up there again, urged by "a revelation." He took with him Barnabas and Titus: Barnabas was of great repute at Jerusalem; Titus, being uncircumcised, would by his very presence raise the problem which had to be solved; it was his apostolate and its fruits that Paul presented to the Church at Jerusalem.

He set forth his gospel to the Church, and then in private to the prominent men, who, as we see from what follows, were Peter, James and John, "lest perhaps I should run, or had run in vain." Certainly Paul did not doubt the divine origin of his teaching, or its truth.[2] But he had to make sure of the attitude of the Church at Jerusalem: if they did not approve of the freedom of his preaching, was not everything compromised?

What might well have led to these fears were the suspicions of "false brethren unawares brought in, who came in privately to

---

[1] Cf. the commentaries on the *Acts* (Jacquier, Boudou) and the *Galatians* (Lightfoot, Lagrange); W. L. Knox, *St. Paul and the Church of Jerusalem* (Cambridge, 1925); Thomas, *L'Eglise et les Judaïsants à l'âge apostolique*, in *Mélanges d'Histoire et de Littérature*, Paris, 1899; Lemonnyer, *Concile de Jérusalem*, in *Supplément* to Dict. de la Bible, 113-20.

[2] "The moderns," writes Lagrange, "are unanimous in rejecting the opinion of Tertullian (*Adv. Marcion*, I, 20; IV, 2; V, 3) thus set forth by St. Jerome: Paul would not have felt himself secure in his preaching of the gospel if he had not been confirmed by the authority of Peter and the other apostles. . . . Paul was certain as to the revelation he had received, and the authority it had conferred on him. . . . He had no doubt at all on the truthfulness of his gospel which he received from God." Lagrange accordingly sees here merely a question put to the Apostles: "Paul loyally put the question, the whole question with its difficulties. But he was certain in advance of the reply. It could only be in the negative." This interpretation is correct, but we may complete it, and see here a real anxiety, not as to the veracity of Paul's gospel, but as to the future of his work.

spy our liberty which we have in Christ Jesus, that they might bring us into servitude." [3]

These false brethren were not able to gain anything. Titus was uncircumcised, and so he remained.[4] What was the attitude of the Apostles on this occasion? Paul does not tell us; the historians who try to find in every incident a trace of division between the Apostles suggest that the leaders of the church of Jerusalem brought pressure on Paul to persuade him to give way; this weakening on their part irritated the Apostle, and prepared the way for future conflicts.[5] The Epistle does not suggest such opposition; in face of the partisans of a rigid Judaism, Paul and Barnabas defend their cause without giving way; and the Apostles, who play the part of judges, side with them:

"Of them who seemed to be something—what they once were is nothing to me, God accepteth not the person of man—to me they that seemed to be something added nothing. But contrariwise, when they had seen that to me was committed the gospel of the uncircumcision, as to Peter was that of the circumcision . . . James and Cephas and John, who seemed to be pillars, gave to me and Barnabas the right hands of fellowship, that we should go unto the Gentiles, and they unto the circumcision: only that we should be mindful of the poor, which same thing also I was careful to do" (ii, 6-10).

We find in this passage the clear statement of an agreement; we also sense a certain impatience in its expression. We must not infer that Paul regarded as "nothing" the basis of the authority of the "notables"; [6] if Paul had regarded their authority as negligible he would not have gone to Jerusalem. He must have regarded it

[3] Where were these false brethren? Weiszaecker (*op. cit.*, p. 140) thinks they were in the Church of Jerusalem, the only one in question here, but the expression used by St. Paul suggests that they had insinuated themselves into a community of converted pagans, upon whom they wished to spy.

[4] At least this is the most likely and most generally received interpretation of ii, 3: "Neither Titus, who was with me, being a Gentile, was compelled to be circumcised." On the different Latin readings, "quibus neque ad horam cessimus" and "ad horam cessimus," see Lagrange, *op. cit.*, pp. 28-30; Lightfoot, *op. cit.*, p. 120.

[5] Thus Weiszaecker (*op. cit.*, p. 155), who thinks that there is a trace of this disagreement in the awkward form of verse 4. Lightfoot is more reserved, but writes that the question "is not easily answered. On the whole it seems probable that they recommended St. Paul to yield the point, as a charitable concession to the prejudices of the Jewish converts; but convinced at length by his representations, that such a concession at such a time would be fatal, they withdrew their counsel and gave him their support."

[6] This is the interpretation of Loisy, rebutted by Lagrange, *op. cit.*, p. 34.

as worthy of respect, but he thought that the esteem in which
the Apostles at Jerusalem were regarded did not justify the contempt which some had for himself; the Lord alone was the judge
of them all; moreover, these leaders, whose authority was being
extolled, had sanctioned the freedom which he was claiming.[7]

The Account in the Acts

So far we have followed St. Paul step by step; but after the
Epistle to the Galatians we ·must read the Acts; the meeting at
Jerusalem which is narrated in ch. xv is the same as that mentioned
in the Epistle to the Galatians.[8] But whereas the Epistle to the

[7] Of these three Apostles, who are "pillars," James is named the first, not because he possessed the greatest authority, but because he was regarded by the
Judaisers as their leader, and consequently, in this controversy, his consent carried
more weight. Between Peter and Paul there was a division, not of territory, but of
race; the mission of the Apostles was universal, and especially that of Peter.

[8] This identity is fairly generally held, and seems to us certain. At the same
time we must allow that there are difficulties at first sight. They are thus set
forth by Weiszaecker, *op. cit.*, pp. 167-75: the tone and character of the two
accounts are very different; the facts themselves differ; the Acts say nothing about
Titus nor of the conflict at Antioch; the difference between Paul and Barnabas
is mentioned later on, and attributed to another cause; the Acts paulinise Peter; if
he had spoken in that way at Jerusalem, his attitude at Antioch would have been
a veritable *volte face;* above all, the decree itself is irreconcilable with the Epistle
to the Galatians: it quotes Talmudic regulations quite probable in themselves,
but which cannot be reconciled with the narrative or the conduct of Paul: he
affirms that the Apostles imposed nothing on him; he speaks differently (*I Cor.*
viii, 1-13; x, 14-30) of food offered to idols; the care he takes to observe the recommendation made to him concerning alms shows by contrast his independence
towards these supposed regulations. Nevertheless the decree is probably a
historic fact; it left some traces in the history of the Church, but it is later
than the conflict at Antioch. Hence Paul does not speak of it. Harnack (*Lukas der
Arzt,* p. 91) accepts the substantial identity of the facts in the two accounts, but
he thinks that the decree has been pre-dated. Lietzmann (*Geschichte der alten
Kirche,* Vol. I, p. 107) suggests that the decree was made after Paul and Barnabas
had left the holy city; Paul, according to him, deliberately ignored it throughout,
and received official knowledge of it only at his last visit to Jerusalem (*Acts* xxi,
25). Cf. E. Hirsch, *Petrus und Paulus,* in *Zeitschrift f. N. T. Wissenschaft,*
1930, pp. 64 *et seq.* Of all the difficulties thus put forward, only one is really
serious, and that is the one concerning the decree itself: we give the answer below. At the same time we must add that several exegetes consider that the two
accounts cannot be harmonised: consequently they think that the visit narrated
in the Epistle to the Galatians is the one mentioned in *Acts* xi; thus Le Camus,
op. cit., Vol. II, p. 118; Levesque, in *Revue pratique d'Apologétique,* 1 février,
1920, p. 531; Emmett, in *The Beginnings of Christianity,* Vol. II, p. 277. This
identification is not very likely. Cf. Lemonnyer, *op. cit.,* pp. 115-16; Wikenhauser,
Die Apostelgeschichte und ihr Geschichtswert, Münster, 1921, pp. 202-25.

Galatians was written in the midst of the fight against the Judaisers in Galatia, the work of Luke was written when the controversy had died down; we no longer feel the excitement of the combat, and the sadness of the disciples who have been torn away from the Apostle and are being lost; instead we have a calm contemplation of something which happened some time ago, and which we can now understand better.[9] Of this whole history, which moreover is already known to his correspondents, Paul recalls only certain points which concern the controversy in which he is once more engaged, above all the decisive question of circumcision, and the agreement arrived at on this matter between the great Apostles and himself. In the narrative in the Acts, we get the whole succession of events. The Church at Antioch was disturbed by the intervention of certain people coming from Judea who maintained that those who were not circumcised according to the Mosaic rite could not be saved. Paul, Barnabas and a few others were sent to Jerusalem to see the Apostles and presbyters. On their journey through Phœnicia and Samaria they told of the conversion of the pagans, and all the brethren heard of this with great joy. At Jerusalem they were received by the Apostles and presbyters, and related to them all that God had done through them. But some Christians, converted Pharisees, rose up to maintain the thesis that the Gentiles must be circumcised and observe the law of Moses. The question thus raised was not decided in a general session, but the discussion was begun in a private conference of the Apostles and presbyters (xv, 6). After a long discussion, a new meeting was called. Peter spoke first:

"Men, brethren, you know, that in former days God made choice among us, that by my mouth the Gentiles should hear the word of the gospel and believe. And God who knoweth the hearts, gave testimony, giving unto them the Holy Ghost as well as to us; and put no difference between us and them, purifying their hearts by faith. Now therefore, why tempt you God to put a yoke upon the necks of the disciples which neither our fathers nor we have been able to bear? But we believe that we are saved by the grace of the Lord Jesus Christ, as they also" (xv, 7-1).

This grave and authoritative declaration was received with silence; Barnabas and Paul then recounted the signs and prodigies

[9] On the character of these two sources (*Galatians* and *Acts*), see the remarks of J. Weiss, *Urchristentum,* pp. 193-5.

which God had worked through them amongst the Gentiles. Then James arose in his turn: this conversion of the Gentiles of which Simon had just spoken had been foretold by the prophets. He concluded: "For this cause I judge that they who from among the Gentiles are converted to God, are not to be disquieted, but that we write unto them that they refrain themselves from the pollutions of idols, and from fornication, and from things strangled, and from blood. . . ."

Then the Apostles and presbyters, together with the whole Church, decided to send to Antioch Judas and Silas with Paul and Barnabas. They charged them with a message which ought to put an end to all anxiety:

"The Apostles and ancients, brethren, to the brethren of the Gentiles that are at Antioch, and in Syria and Cilicia, greeting. Forasmuch as we have heard that some going out from us have troubled you with words, subverting your souls, to whom we gave no commandment: It hath seemed good to us, being assembled together, to choose out men and to send them unto you with our well beloved Barnabas and Paul, men that have given their lives for the name of our Lord Jesus Christ. We have sent therefore Judas and Silas, who themselves also will, by word of mouth, tell you the same things. For it hath seemed good to the Holy Ghost and to us to lay no further burden upon you than these necessary things: that you abstain from things sacrificed to idols, and from blood, and from things strangled, and from fornication; from which things keeping yourselves, you shall do well. Fare ye well" (xv, 23-29).

The Decree

The decree comprised two parts, of very different import: the first, the part of most weight, was the charter of liberty accorded to the new converts: "It has seemed good to the Holy Ghost and to us to lay no further burden upon you than these necessary things" (xv, 28). This decision corresponds directly to the question which had been put: can one be saved without receiving circumcision? (xv, 1). That was in fact the chief point in the controversy, as we see not only from the Epistle to the Galatians, but by the two speeches of Peter and James narrated in the Acts. This vital question was decided in the sense requested by Paul, and he could say that he had won his point, and that nothing had been imposed upon him.

But this decision is followed by four precepts, the text and meaning of which must be determined.[10] The text is found in a double form, Eastern and Western. The former contains four prohibitions of a legal character: "It hath seemed good to the Holy Ghost and to us to lay no further burden upon you than what is necessary, namely: that you abstain from things sacrificed to idols, and from blood, and from things strangled, and from fornication; from which things keeping yourselves you shall do well. Fare ye well." The Western form contains only three prohibitions, but it usually adds the golden rule; all these regulations have the character of moral precepts rather than of ritual observances: ". . . that you abstain from things sacrificed to idols, and from blood, and from fornication, and that you do not to others what you would not have them do to you. From which things keeping yourselves you shall do well. Walk in the Holy Ghost. Amen."

Of these two redactions, it is the former which is authentic; the manuscript tradition shows this, and also the text itself; the Western text is clearly an interpretation, arising from a desire to give to the decree a perpetual value, and to this end it effaces the ritual and Jewish character of the observances. This tendency is still more manifest in the variants which forbid "idolatry, homicide, impurity." [11]

The ritual precepts, set forth in the Eastern form of the decree, are aimed at teaching the converted pagans to respect what the Jews regarded as precepts of the natural law: to abstain from food offered to idols, from fornication,[12] and also from the eating of blood.[13]

This decree applied directly only to Christian converts from among the Gentiles; on the occasion of the dispute at Antioch, St. Paul very soon drew the inferences it implied for the faithful from Judaism, and St. Peter accepted his view. The decisions given later to the Corinthians (I Cor. x, 25) on food offered to idols do not contradict the prescriptions of Jerusalem; they required respect for the conscience of others, which was the very principle of James (Acts xv, 21); but they were communicated to a community in

[10] This decree is quoted or referred to three times: Acts xv, 19-20; xv, 28-9; xxi, 25. In these three passages it is found in the double form, Eastern and Western.

[11] Coppieters, op. cit., pp. 50-8; Lemonnyer, op. cit., p. 116.

[12] Instead of "illicit marriages." Cf. Coppieters, op. cit., pp. 47-8.

[13] Cf. Lagrange, Epître aux Galates, p. xlvii.

THE MISSIONS OF ST. PAUL

which the Judæo-Christians no longer occupied the position which they held at Jerusalem, or even at Antioch, ten years earlier.[14] The condemnation of the practices of the Gnostic Judaisers (*Col.* ii, 21; *I Tim.* iv, 1) is concerned with things quite different from the observances imposed by the decree.

The prohibitions passed by the Council of Jerusalem were long observed in the Church; towards the end of the second century, the apologists and the martyrs of Lyons invoke this custom in order to make the pagans realise the horror Christians had for blood and for the worship of idols.[15] Later on, and down to the Middle Ages, canonists, especially in the East, will regard this legislation as still binding.[16] Nevertheless, the example of St. Paul shows sufficiently that these interdictions were meant to be only temporary; what was definitive was the principle of freedom: circumcision is not necessary for salvation. The solemn affirmation of this principle gives a decisive importance to the Council of Jerusalem, and that is why St. Luke has brought it out so prominently; this account is one of the chief parts of the Book of Acts. God there elevates souls by degrees, by the vision at Joppa, by the conversion of Cornelius, as Peter recalls in his discourse; and we may look back even further into the past, and see in the oracles of the prophets the promise of this calling of the Gentiles. That is what St. James contemplates and admires: "To the Lord was his own work known from the beginning of the world."

This divine light does not dissipate all the shadows; Christian freedom does not dispense from the consideration which the Jews claimed, and to which St. Paul will adapt himself: he who did not circumcise Titus will circumcise Timothy, he will submit himself at Cenchrae, and later at Jerusalem, to the practices of the Nazarites. But this condescension must never compromise either the

---

[14] Cf. Coppieters, *op. cit.*, pp. 227-8. Lietzmann in his edition of *I Cor.* (note on ch. v, p. 25) remarks that Paul alludes to a letter written to the Corinthians (v, 9); the two points he discusses, offerings to idols and fornication (v, 9-13; vi, 12-20, and viii, 1-13) bear on the two prohibitions which were likely to cause most difficulties; these new explanations would be a reply to the latter which the Corinthians wrote to the Apostle on the reception of his first letter. These hypotheses are not unlikely. Much less likely is the suggestion that the decree was made known to the Corinthians by St. Peter when passing through their city.

[15] Tertullian, *Apolog.*, 9; Minucius Felix, *Octav.*, 30; Eusebius, *Hist. Eccles.*, V, 1, 26; Origen, *Contra Celsum*, viii, 30.

[16] Texts cited by Boudou, *Acts*, pp. 342-3; the most recent is that of Theodore Balsamon (12th cent.), and in the West, Pope St. Gregory III (731-41).

freedom of the Christian or the unity of the Church. It will be understood that these opposite preoccupations will give rise to more than one case of conscience which will be difficult to solve.

The Dispute at Antioch

This incident is known to us only by the Epistle to the Galatians (ii, 11 et seq.). This passage sets forth sufficiently clearly the succession of events. It was after the Council of Jerusalem that Peter went to Antioch. It is certain that the dispute was not a scene arranged beforehand by Peter and Paul, as has sometimes been supposed,[17] and that it was really the Apostle Peter who was concerned, and not another disciple named Cephas.[18] These flimsy hypotheses have been invented in order to efface a difference between the two Apostles from the history: an excusable desire, but one to which, here as always, we must prefer respect for the text and for facts. Moreover, if carefully read, there is nothing in the narrative which should embarrass us: on the contrary, it gives us valuable information on the life of the Church.

We note, in the first place, the presence of Peter at Antioch. We do not know when or why he went there, but we find him there. The Acts do not mention his journey; this fact, amongst others, shows that Peter's activity extended beyond Palestine, and we cannot confine it to what the Acts mention explicitly.

On his arrival there, Peter did the same as Paul and Barnabas, living and eating with converted pagans. In this he went beyond the letter of the decree of Jerusalem: he was a Jew by birth, and he adopted without fear the freedom accorded to those coming from paganism. But some people came from James's circle,[19] and Peter, in order not to shock them, changed his attitude:

"When they were come, he withdrew and separated himself, fearing them who were of the circumcision. And to his dissimulation, the rest

[17] On this interpretation and its history, cf. Lightfoot, *Galatians*, pp. 130 *et seq.*
[18] Hypothesis of Clement of Alexandria, mentioned by Eusebius, *Hist. Eccles.*, I, 12 (Lightfoot, *ibid.*, p. 129).
[19] Lagrange thinks that "these were probably people sent by James." The text does not say this expressly, and several exegetes and historians translate: "people from the entourage of James" (Cornely, Zahn, Thomas). Lightfoot, without coming to a definite decision, leans towards the former interpretation; this interpretation is admissible, but I do not think it imperative, or even the most likely one.

of the Jews consented, so that Barnabas also was led by them into that dissimulation. But when I saw that they walked not uprightly unto the truth of the gospel, I said to Cephas before them all: If thou, being a Jew, livest after the manner of the Gentiles, and not as the Jews do, how dost thou compel the Gentiles to live as do the Jews? (*Gal.* ii, 12-14).

This false step by Peter has been very rightly described by Tertullian as "an error of attitude and not of doctrine" (*Praescr.*, 23). Peter doubtless regarded these observances as indifferent, and in order to avoid scandalising the Jews, he adapted himself to their ideas, as Paul himself did on other occasions; [20] but here this accommodation led to very serious consequences; the other Judæo-Christians, including Barnabas himself, imitated Peter and withdrew from the Gentiles. This shows how great was the authority of the head of the Church even at Antioch, and in the presence of Paul; but the more powerful his ascendency, the more prudent had to be its exercise. St. Peter's complacency threatened to rend the Church asunder, or to compel the pagans to become Jews. This latter consequence was directly contrary to the statements which Peter himself had made at Jerusalem. It was therefore to this point that Paul at once brought him back; and putting the question higher, he repeated the principle of salvation by Christ which both admitted equally:

"We by nature are Jews, and not of the Gentiles, sinners. But knowing that man is not justified by the works of the law, but by the faith of Jesus Christ, we also believe in Christ Jesus, that we may be justified by the faith of Christ, and not by the works of the law. . . ." [21]

Paul, intent on his controversy with his opponents in Galatia, does not relate the result of the incident, but there is no question that he gained his point: otherwise he would not have derived from this dispute an argument against the judaisers. [22]

Thus by degrees the Church freed herself: at Jerusalem the

[20] *Acts* xvi, 3; xviii, 18; xxi, 26.
[21] *Gal.* ii, 15-16. Paul's discourse is here addressed to the Galatians, to whom he preaches salvation by faith.
[22] If Paul convinced Peter, he must also have convinced Barnabas, and hence we must not look to this incident for the origin of the separation of the two Apostles (*Acts* xv, 36-9). Luke explains it by a disagreement about Mark, and there is no reason to doubt his testimony.

liberty of pagan converts was recognised, but nothing was decided in the case of Christians coming from Judaism itself. This latter point, however, was decided implicitly; it was impossible to maintain the unity of the Church without granting to Jews the liberty accorded to the pagans. This inference was explicitly drawn at Antioch. The solution of these matters had a tremendous importance for the further development of Christianity; at the beginning it could be regarded as a Jewish sect, at a time when Judaism could appear as a comprehensive system which included within itself the Nazarenes, side by side with the Pharisees, Essenes, Sadducees, and others. But henceforth there could be no mistake: it was Christianity which revealed itself as the great system comprising Jews and pagans, and which united both together by faith in Christ.

This liberty, however, which was essential in mixed communities, naturally took longer to penetrate the church at Jerusalem itself, composed as it was almost entirely of converted Jews. They rejoiced at the propagation of Christianity amongst the pagans, they refused to impose upon them the yoke of the law, but they did not wish to abandon it themselves. This was the attitude of St. James (*Acts* xxi, 20 *et seq.*); and St. Paul respected it, since he accommodated himself at James's request to the practice of the Nazarites (*ibid.* 26). The martyrdom of James, the exodus of Christians to Pella, the fall of Jerusalem, were little by little to loosen the bonds which linked these Christian faithful to the Temple and the Law.[23]

The Church and the Judaisers

In all this the Church was patient, and reverent towards the past: she did nothing to precipitate the rupture; as long as God allowed it, she did not condemn the pious regard which the Jerusalem Christians retained for the Law which they had so revered and loved; these, moreover, like Paul and Peter, did not in any way seek in the works of the Law the source of salvation, but found this in faith in Christ;[24] and if out of piety they continued to carry

[23] Cf. *infra.* ch. v, § 1.
[24] Cf. Lagrange, *Epître aux Galates*, p. liv: "James's group, and James its head, recognised once for all that the Gentiles could be saved without the observance of the Law of Moses. Hence they must, according to the most elementary logic, have believed that salvation, even for the Jews, did not depend on the Law as its prin-

the burden of the Law, they abstained from imposing it on the Gentiles.[25]

Other observers of the Law were less tolerant; not content with submitting to it themselves, they tried to impose it on all, even on Christian converts from the Gentiles; such were the preachers of a perverted gospel whom Paul had to combat in his Epistle to the Galatians.[26] Others, again, began to mingle gnostic practices with their Jewish traditions; these were denounced already in the Epistle to the Romans, and still more in the letter to the Colossians, the letter of St. Jude, and the Second Epistle of St. Peter.[27]

These combats already foreshadow the great crisis which in the second century will set Christianity and Gnosticism one against the other.

The struggles of the Apostolic Church against the Judeo-Christians and against the Gnostic Jews were destined to be bitter, but even for observers from outside, the issue could not be doubtful. The Church was conscious that she was free, and the mistress of her destiny. Agar might continue to serve, but Sara was free with the freedom wherewith Christ had made her free.

§3. THE SECOND MISSION OF ST. PAUL (AUTUMN OF A.D. 49 TO AUTUMN OF A.D. 52)

Paul and Barnabas

In the course of his first mission, St. Paul had made contact with that pagan world the conquest of which God had reserved for him. His rapid journey beyond the Taurus chain across the high plateaux of Anatolia had brought home to him the distress of men's souls and their immense religious needs, and the power of the Gospel to meet them. He knew at what price these conquests would have to be purchased; the wounds of Christ impressed on his flesh at Lystra reminded him of it, but he also knew that these sufferings would be fruitful, and that if death acted in him, it was in order

---

ciple. Peter said so expressly: James, if he was consistent, must have thought so, and if he had not thought so, Paul would not have been on terms of ecclesiastical communion with him."

[25] Cf. *infra*, ch. v, § 1, and Lagrange, *Galates*, lvi *et seq.*
[26] Cf. *infra*, pp. 257-9.
[27] Cf. Bk. II.

to produce life in the souls of others. His apostolic experience had been consecrated by the Council of Jerusalem with a fresh guarantee: Peter was to have the apostolate of the circumcision, Paul that of the Gentiles. The conflict provoked by the Judaisers was, if not ended for ever, at least settled in principle; Paul could set out again, strong in a new assurance, for the immense field of the apostolate which he had seen on his first journey.

He therefore said to Barnabas: "Let us return and visit our brethren in all the cities wherein we have preached the word of the Lord" (*Acts* xv, 36). Barnabas accepted without hesitation, but he wanted to have with him his cousin Mark. Paul, who remembered the defection of this young man in the preceding expedition, did not want to take him this time. Neither Barnabas nor Paul felt it possible to give way; they therefore parted. Paul went to Cilicia; Barnabas, accompanied by Mark, left for Cyprus, his native land. The Acts henceforth tell us nothing about his apostolic career; we are unable to make up for this silence; [1] but we ought not to forget all that the infant Church owed to Barnabas. In the earliest days he had sold his possessions and laid the price at the feet of the Apostles; he had brought to them a still more precious gift when he presented Saul to them, though mistrusted by the faithful, and became surety for his conversion, and also when later on he went to seek him at Tarsus and conducted him to Antioch, thereby giving a decisive impulse to the evangelising of that great city. Now, after many years of close collaboration, the two friends separated; but this brief disagreement was to help still further the expansion of the Gospel: Barnabas and Mark [2] were going to preach in Cyprus, while a much wider horizon was opening before Paul.

In place of his former companion, Paul took Silas. He was one of the prophets of the Church at Jerusalem, sent by the latter to Antioch (xv, 32); this fact heightened his repute amongst the converted Jews, and in the official world, Hellenic and Roman, his privilege as a Roman citizen would be a safeguard for him. [3]

---

[1] We shall refer later (Bk. II) to the so-called Epistle of Barnabas; but this work, written about the year 130, is not by the Apostle, and does not even claim to have been written by him.

[2] Mark, after having been the companion of Barnabas, became that of Peter, and once more the friend of Paul: *Philem.* 24; *Col.* iv, 10; *II Tim.* iv, 11.

[3] Much later (*I Pet.* v, 12) Silas appears as Peter's secretary; Silas and Mark were thus two links between Paul and Peter, and between the communities consisting of Christians coming from Judaism and the pagan mission.

Timothy

Paul, who never abandoned the communities he had founded, commenced his new expedition by visiting those in Lycaonia. "He came to Derbe and Lystra. And behold there was a certain disciple there named Timothy, the son of a Jewish woman that believed, but his father was a Gentile. To this man the brethren that were in Lystra and Iconium gave a good testimony. Paul decided to take him with him" (xvi, 1-3). Towards the end of his life, the Apostle reminded Timothy, now his inseparable companion, of these things: "I have a remembrance of thee in my prayers night and day, desiring to see thee, being mindful of thy tears, that I may be filled with joy; calling to mind that faith which is in thee unfeigned, which also dwelt first in thy grandmother Lois, and in thy mother Eunice, and I am certain that in thee also" (*II Tim.*, i, 4-5).

"He therefore took Timothy and circumcised him, because of the Jews who were in those places, for they all knew that his father was a Gentile." This step has astonished many historians; [4] Paul, however, was not changing his attitude; at Jerusalem he had refused to circumcise Titus in order to affirm the liberty of converted pagans; in the case of Timothy, there was no longer any question of principle, but one of prudence: born of a Jewish mother, the child ought, according to the legislation of Israel, to have been circumcised; in the eyes of the Jews, so long as he had not been subjected to this rite, he would be regarded as a renegade, and could not accompany Paul into the synagogues.[5] In this matter, as in so many others, Paul became a Jew to the Jews.

Galatia

So now, with his two companions, Paul began the conquest of the world. Already in the course of his first mission, the Apostle had had a hard task; he had crossed the high chain of the Taurus by bad roads infested by brigands; he had gone through the plateaux of the interior from Antioch in Pisidia to Derbe; beyond the

[4] "In the case of Timothy, Paul did precisely the contrary of what he had done at Jerusalem in the case of Titus. . . . The contradiction is so clear that we must either give up the narrative of the Acts or that of Paul: the choice is not doubtful" (Weiszaecker, *op. cit.*, p. 179. On the other hand, J. Weiss thinks that Paul gave way in both cases: he circumcised Titus at Jerusalem, just as he circumcised Timothy at Lystra (*Urchristentum*, p. 203 and n. 1).

[5] Cf. Boudou, *Actes*, p. 349.

Hellenic zone dotted with Jewish colonies he had made contact with the Lycaonian peoples; but he had stopped there, without penetrating into that immense Anatolia which extended before him towards the north, as far as the eye could see, with the high and sunburnt plateaux of Phrygia, and beyond them the deep valleys and rocky gorges of Galatia. It was in that direction that he now went, and when he had gone through Phrygia and Galatia, he wanted to descend by the wide valley of the Hermus towards Sardis, Smyrna, and the coast of Asia Minor, from whence for a thousand years Hellenism had spread throughout the East. But the Holy Spirit willed otherwise. Then he wanted to go through Mysia, Bithynia, Brusa, Nicea and Nicomedia, but once again the Spirit of Jesus opposed this journey. Accordingly, he turned once more towards the West, and finally arrived at Troas. Since their departure from Syria, the three travellers had walked on foot for over nine hundred miles; [6] they had traversed from north to south and from east to west the whole of Anatolia. There many races were mingled together; the Greeks had colonised all the coast, and the Jews had established their settlements. Going inland, there were new peoples to encounter: those enthusiastic Phrygians who at that time were zealous worshippers of the Great Mother, and who, after being converted to Christianity, were in the second century to be led astray by the prophecies of Montanus. When Paul arrived at Pessinonte to the north of the Phrygian plateau, he was already in the land of the Galatians. [7]

[6] In his study on *Roads and Travel in the New Testament* (Hastings' *Dictionary of the Bible*, Extra Vol., col. 385), Ramsay estimates the distance from Troas to Antioch by Philadelphia at 880 Roman miles, and by Laodicea 930. The route which the Apostle followed was much longer.

[7] Until the last century, the Galatia of which there is mention here (*Acts* xvi, 6) had always been regarded as the region inhabited by the Galatians with Ancyra as its capitol, and it was thought that it was to these Galatians that Paul wrote. But another view finds these Galatians in the southern region evangelised by St. Paul in the course of his first mission: Antioch in Pisidia, Iconium, Lystra, Derbe. This opinion, set forth in 1825 by a Dane, Mynster, was defended in 1867 by G. Perrot in his thesis *De Galatia provincia Romana*. Renan accepted it. Ramsay gave much weight and favor to this opinion; during some thirty years many exegetes and historians adopted it, e.g. Cornely, Le Camus, MacGiffert, Lemonnyer, J. Weiss. Nowadays it is more commonly abandoned. We cannot discuss the matter here: the materials will be found in Lightfoot, *Galatians*, pp. 18-21; Lagrange, *Epître aux Galates*, pp. xiii-xxvii; Lietzmann, *Galater*, pp. 3-4; Wikenhauser, *Apostelgeschichte*, pp. 227-9; Boudou, *Actes*, pp. 352-3. The establishment of the Galatians in Eastern Phrygia took place about 278 B.C. Cf. Jullian, *Histoire de la Gaule*, Vol. I, pp. 303-5, 367-9, 514-5. The three

Of the evangelisation of Galatia the Acts tell us nothing; but the Epistle of St. Paul reveals to us the great welcome which the sick Apostle had received from the Galatians, and the close relations, full of gratitude and of paternal confidence, which existed between him and them:

"Be ye as I, because I also am as you: brethren, I beseech you: you have not injured me at all. And you know how through infirmity of the flesh, I preached the gospel to you heretofore: and your temptation in my flesh. You despised not, nor rejected: but received me as an angel of God, even as Christ Jesus. Where is then your blessedness? For I bear you witness that, if it could be done, you would have plucked out your own eyes and would have given them to me" (*Gal.* iv, 12-15).

To these disciples who had received him with such open hearts, the Apostle had presented Christ crucified; his preaching had been so vivid that it set Christ [8] forth before their very eyes (iii, 1); and together with the faith, the Holy Spirit had been poured out into their hearts. But then this spiritual movement, begun so energetically, had been stopped, or rather diverted towards an illusory end. Already when passing through, Paul had feared this perversion and had endeavoured to forestall it; he had warned the Galatians: "If any one preach to you a gospel besides that which you have received, let him be anathema." The warning had been received submissively, but the Galatians, impressionable and fickle, must have forgotten it very quickly.[9]

It was necessary that Paul should, towards the year 56, rescue his former disciples from the seduction of Judaism, by his epistle written to them from Macedonia.

This evangelisation of Galatia is mentioned in the Acts only by

---

Gallic tribes which settled there kept, according to St. Jerome, *In Gal.*, ii, praef. (*P.L.*, xxvi, 357), the use of the Gallic tongue; nevertheless Greek was the official language of the nation, and as in all the East, was also the language of commercial relations.

[8] The Greek means literally to placard.

[9] The Galatians showed themselves more than once excessively submissive; they had undergone not only Hellenic but also Phrygian influences: "The Asiatic Artemis received the homage of the barbarians, and the wives of their leaders agreed to look after its altars and to appear in its processions. When the territory of Pessinonte had been attached to the Tolistoboians, the Great Mother who reigned there became the object of their devotion, and the priest-king was soon taken from amongst the Celts themselves" (Jullian, *Histoire de la Gaule*, Vol. I, p. 367). The Galatians were established at Pessinonte after 189; a Galatian was high priest in 163 and 159 (Dittenberger, *Or. inscr.*, n. 315, I, p. 484, quoted by Jullian, *ibid.*, n. 12).

a word; evidently Luke hastens on towards Macedonia. For the rest, the Spirit urged Paul there. In these few lines, three decisive spiritual directions are mentioned: the first, turning the Apostle away from Asia, directs him towards Phrygia and Galatia; the second turns him away from Bithynia and leads him to Troas; the third is the most solemn of all:

"A vision was shewed to Paul in the night, which was a man of Macedonia standing and beseeching him and saying: 'Pass over into Macedonia, and help us.' " (*Acts* xvi, 9).

At once the decision was taken: "Immediately we sought to go into Macedonia, being assured that God had called us to preach the Gospel to them."[10]

Macedonia

The Macedonian mission which began through this divine call was to give St. Paul some of the greatest joys in his apostolate; these joys would indeed be accompanied by many sufferings and persecutions; all his conquests, here as everywhere else, were dearly bought; nevertheless, in Macedonia the Apostle was less contradicted and less opposed in his churches; he met at Philippi and at Thessalonica with an attachment to his person which was nowhere so devoted or so faithful. Of these two churches, the former remained the dearest and the closest to the Apostle; Thessalonica came first in the number of its members and by reason of its situation as chief town in the province.

Philippi

From Troas to Neapolis by Samothracia, the sea journey was quick and took only two days;[11] from Neapolis the missionaries at

[10] It is here at Troas that the account of the journey written in the first person commences; the "we" appears here (xvi, 10); it disappears at Philippi (xvi, 17); it reappears later in Macedonia, perhaps in this same town of Philippi, and on the arrival of St. Paul in Jerusalem (xx, 5-15; xvi, 1-18); lastly, we find it again in the account of the sea-crossing until the arrival at Rome (xxvii, 1-xxviii, 16). From this it is reasonable to infer that Luke joined the Apostle at Troas, was left by him at Philippi, rejoined him there later on, and followed him to Jerusalem, and then to Rome.

[11] Later on Luke allows six days for the passage from Neapolis to Troas (xx, 6).

once went on about seven miles to Philippi, "the chief city of the province of Macedonia, a colony." [12] The city was governed by a duumvirate of two prætors, assisted by lictors; it was proud of being ruled according to Roman law; [13] the Jews seem to have been very few in number there, and to have had no synagogue. On the Sabbath Paul and his companions went to the *proseuche*, on the banks of the river; there they found some women and preached to them. The Lord "opened the heart" of a certain Lydia, a seller of purple, of the city of Thyatira. She was baptised with her household, and said to the Apostle: "If you have judged me to be faithful to the Lord, come into my house and abide there." The hospitality offered with open heart was gratefully accepted, and thus was formed the first nucleus of the Church of Philippi.

The Apostle nevertheless continued to frequent the *proseuche*; on the way there with his companions he was importuned by the cries of a girl with a pythonical spirit.[14] Several days in succession she repeated as they passed by: "These men are the servants of the most high God, who preach unto you the way of salvation." In the end, Paul said to the spirit, "I command thee, in the name of Jesus Christ, to go out from her." The exorcism was at once effective; but the masters of this woman, having thus lost all the profit they had been making by her, brought the missionaries before the magistrates. They did not accuse them of having exorcised their slave, but they said: "These men disturb our city; they are Jews, who preach a fashion which it is not lawful for us to receive nor observe, being Romans." The people were aroused against them; the magistrates had them scourged and put in prison; the jailor shut them up in the interior dungeon, and made their feet

[12] The town of Philippi had been founded by Philip of Macedon on the site of the ancient Crenides ("the Springs"). It overlooked the rich plain of the Gangites, a tributary of the Strymon; Cæsar had established a Roman colony there; Augustus, in memory of his victory over Brutus and Cassius, had named it Colonia Augusta Julia Philippensis, and had given it the *jus italicum;* according to Dio Cassius (II, 4) he had transported there the inhabitants of the Italian cities which had supported Antony. On Philippi, cf. Lightfoot, *Philippians,* pp. 46-64.

[13] Paul alludes to this in his Epistle, i, 27; iii, 20.

[14] Macedonia was well known for its serpents. Lucian relates that it was there that Alexander of Abonouteichos had purchased for a few obols the python which he then used to give his pretended oracles (*Alexander, 7*). In such a matter it was easy to pass on from imposture to sorcery; the Philippian slave had taken the step.

fast in the stocks. During the night there was an earthquake, and the gates of the prison were opened. Thinking that his prisoners were escaping, the desperate jailor was going to kill himself; Paul and Silas reassured him, and preached to him, and that very night he and all his family were baptised. At daybreak the magistrates sent the lictors to release the prisoners; the jailor transmitted the message, but Paul replied: "They have beaten us publicly, uncondemned, men that are Romans, and have cast us into prison, and now do they thrust us out privately? Not so, but let them come and let us out themselves" (xvi, 37).

The magistrates were alarmed, and came to present their apologies, and begged the missionaries to leave the city. Paul and his friends returned to the house of Lydia, exhorted the brethren, and departed.

This scene, like the evangelisation of Philippi, has been reported by St. Luke in much detail; [15] contrary to what had happened and would happen everywhere else, the Jews were in no way responsible for the expulsion of the Apostle; the pagans alone had carried out the affair, and we see from this fact what their reactions to the Gospel, their anger, or their fear could become. In addition—and this is of still greater interest to us—this narrative shows us in Paul that apostolic zeal which no assaults could overcome, and also the Roman and Christian dignity which defends honour and demands reparation.

Paul left Philippi, but he ever retained a special tenderness towards this church. He never had to reproach the Philippians for dissensions such as those which divided the church of Corinth, nor for the weaknesses which the Galatians manifested in face of Judaising threats. In his epistle, Paul will utter hard words against dogs, and the false circumcision (iii, 2), but though he thinks it prudent to warn the faithful against these, there is no indication that the church had been already affected by this contagion. The Philippians were the "joy and crown" of the Apostle (iv, 1); they alone had ministered to his needs (iv, 15), and they were still doing so. They had also suffered: "Unto you it is given for Christ, not only to believe in him, but also to suffer for him" (i, 29).

---

[15] As we have pointed out above (p. 178, n. 2), Luke seems to have remained six years at Philippi; and so he takes a particular interest in the history of the origins of this church.

Thessalonica

"And when they had passed through Amphipolis and Apollonia, they came to Thessalonica, where there was a synagogue of the Jews" (xvii, 1). Paul must then have found there an important centre of Jewish life, and hence a starting point for the preaching of the Gospel. He established himself in the capital of Macedonia; [16] when Christianity had taken root there, it would expand thence all through the province.

According to his custom, Paul went to the synagogue, and on three sabbaths in succession he preached out of the Scriptures, "that the Christ was to suffer and to rise again from the dead, and that this Christ is Jesus, whom I preach to you" (xvii, 3). Some Jews were converted, a great number of Greek proselytes and many women of the best families. Here particularly we see that the converts of the Apostles were made above all from among the proselytes; prejudices were less tenacious in them than in the Jews, and good will was greater. We shall find also at Thessalonica, as at Philippi and at Berea, that from the first, women played an important part in the work of evangelisation. [17]

After these three sabbaths, Paul probably left the synagogue and carried on his work outside. His stay at Thessalonica was fairly long; on two occasions he received help from the Philippians (Phil., iv, 16). Moreover, all the time he was preaching he gained his own livelihood by working. A few months after his departure, in his first letter to the Thessalonians, he put before their eyes a living and touching picture of the life which he had led amongst them:

[16] Founded on the site of the ancient Therma by Cassander, the son-in-law of Philip of Macedonia, about 315 B.C., and called by him Thessalonica in honour of his wife, Thessalonica had speedily become a flourishing city. In 168 Macedonia had been conquered by the Romans; Thessalonica then became the capital of Macedonia secunda. In 146 the different districts were reunited and the town became in fact the capital of the whole province. In 49 it was Pompey's headquarters; in the second civil war it was on the side of Octavius and Antony, and received in reward the rights of a free city; its magistrates were politarchs, numbering five or six. Cf. Milligan, Thessalonians, pp. xxi et seq.; Dict. of the Bible, Vol. IV, 315.

[17] Lightfoot, Philippians, pp. 54-6, points out this fact, and links it up with the social part which women seem to have played in Macedonia, more than in the rest of Greece. Cf. also Ramsay, St. Paul the Traveller, p. 227: "In Macedonia, as in Asia Minor, women occupied a much freer and more influential position than in Athens, and it is in conformity with the known facts that such prominence is assigned to them in the three Macedonian cities."

"Never have we used, at any time, the speech of flattery, as you know, nor taken an occasion of covetousness, God is witness: Nor sought we glory of men, neither of you, nor of others, whereas we might have been burdensome to you, as the apostles of Christ: but we became little ones in the midst of you. As a nurse should cherish her children: so desirous of you, we would gladly impart unto you not only the gospel of God, but also our own souls, because you were become most dear unto us. For you remember, brethren, our labour and toil, working night and day, lest we should be chargeable to any of you, we preached among you the gospel of God" (I Thess. ii, 5-9).

Such care bestowed on the whole community and on each of its members (ii, 11) bore its fruit: the Christians of Thessalonica became models for Macedonia and Achaia (i, 6-10); the faith was so widespread that the attacks of the Jews put the city in an uproar (Acts xvii, 5). For the rest, Paul did not work alone; Silas and Timothy supported him; and in his two letters he associates them with himself as he had associated them in his work. Also in Thessalonica itself he had found helpers in his apostolate (I Thess., v, 12).

This apostolic activity and its success irritated those Jews who had remained unbelievers; they stirred up a band of rogues on the market place, and led them to the house of Jason, where Paul was staying. They wanted to take him before the assembly of the people, but the Apostle was not to be found. And so instead, Jason and a few of the brethren were taken before the politarchs:

"These people," cried the Jews, "have already turned the whole world upside down, and now they have come here: Jason has harboured them. They all act against the laws of Cæsar, saying that there is another king, Jesus" (Acts xvii, 6-7).

We recognise here the accusations brought forward by the Jews at Jerusalem before Pilate. They will be constantly made against Christians, and there could not be more dangerous ones.[18] The crowd and the magistrates felt that the least they could do was to require bail from Jason and the others.

---

[18] We find them again in the Apocalypse (infra, ch. v, § 2) and often in the Acts of the martyrs, e.g. the Scillitan martyrs. On this subject, see the discussion in Tertullian's Apology, 34.

Berea

The persecution which broke out must have been patiently borne by the church of Thessalonica (*I Thess*. ii, 14; iii, 8), but the Apostle could not remain there longer without seriously compromising his host and his disciples. He therefore left that night for Berea, fifty miles to the south-west of Thessalonica. There he found Jews who were better disposed, and received the word gladly, "daily searching the scriptures, whether these things were so." Many of them were converted, as well as many Greek ladies of rank, and a good number of men (*Acts* xvii, 11-12). But as soon as the Jews in Thessalonica heard of this, they came to Berea to rouse the people. The brethren then sent Paul away; a number of them took him as far as Athens and then returned, taking to Silas and Timothy, who were still at Berea, instructions to rejoin him as soon as possible.[19]

The Macedonian Churches

This brief outline of the beginnings of the Macedonian churches can be supplemented by a few facts mentioned in the epistles. In spite of their generous fidelity, the Thessalonians seem to have required warnings against impurity and injustice (*I Thess*. iv, 1-12). These two vices were particularly rampant in the pagan circles in which they lived [20] and they had to react vigorously against them. Above all, they were perplexed concerning the Second Coming: were the dead to be without their part therein? [21] St. Paul tells them in reply that the dead will rise again first, and precede

[19] We gather from this fact that in the little apostolic band it was Paul who was aimed at: once he had gone, his two companions could remain and carry on the work without molestation. Amongst the associates of Paul we shall find later on (*Acts* xx, 4) Sopater of Berea. Tradition makes Onesimus the first Bishop of Berea (*Constitut. Apost.*, vii, 46).

[20] Fornication (*I Thess*. iv, 3) had been expressly forbidden by the decree of Jerusalem; at Corinth as at Thessalonica Christians had to be deterred from it (*I Cor.* vi, 15; vii, 2). Dishonest dealing (*I Thess*. iv, 6) was no less prevalent: the Christians of Bithynia, interrogated by Pliny, told him that one of the promises they made when they became Christians was to return the deposits they had received.

[21] Milligan compares *II (IV) Esdras* v, 41: "Et dixi: Sed ecce Domine, tu praees his qui in fine sunt, et quid facient qui ante nos sunt aut nos aut hi qui post nos? Et dixit ad me: Coronae adsimilabo judicium meum; sicut non novissimorum tarditas, sic non priorum velocitas."

the living in the triumph of Christ (iv, 13-18); he also reminds them that the Day of the Lord will come unexpectedly, and that they must therefore live watchfully (v, 1-11).

The second letter followed soon after the first.[22] It reveals the same state of fervour in the church of Thessalonica (i, 3), but it undeceives the faithful, who thought, on the strength of communications from the Spirit, or of a pretended letter from Paul, that the Day had already come. The Apostle reminds them of what he had taught them concerning the signs which would precede the great event. In the interval, they must work, as he himself has given them an example. These two letters reveal to us a lively interest in eschatology, degenerating sometimes into a feverish expectation of the great day. This state of mind of the Thessalonians enables us to understand better the incidents in their evangelisation, and in particular, the calumnies of the Jews concerning the king Jesus.

The excitement which had been so great seems to have been quietened by the exhortations of St. Paul. Docile and faithful, these Macedonian churches appear to us as true types of Pauline churches, neither Judaising nor Gnostic, after the manner of the pagans. The influence of the Apostle seems to have spread gradually there from house to house, and he seems to have based himself directly on the words of the Lord, rather than upon texts of Scripture, which he recalls more frequently elsewhere in centres of Jewish thought.

Athens

From Macedonia St. Paul went to Athens. He wrote to the Thessalonians (I Thess. iii, 1) saying that, being unable himself to return to them, he was sending them Timothy, and was himself staying alone at Athens. The Acts alone make known to us his activity during this stay.[23] According to his custom, Paul spoke with the Jews and proselytes in the synagogue, and in the market place with all whom he met (Acts xvii, 17). He was full of indignation and sorrow at the sight of the idols of which Athens was full.

[22] The two letters were written from Corinth in 50-51.
[23] This account is rejected by those historians who regard the Acts with suspicion, e.g. Weiszaecker, op. cit., p. 255; J. Weiss, op. cit., pp. 181 et seq., and 219. The discourse on the Areopagus has been especially attacked: cf. infra, p. 230, n. 29.

No doubt the Athenians of this time, influenced by their philoso-phers, possessed, not more religion, but more scepticism than other people: their roads, squares, and temples were full of statues. These were splendid works of art, but they were idols. It was of Athens that Petronius wrote: "Our land is so full of divinities that it is easier to meet a god than a man" [24] and Josephus, like Paul, calls the Athenians "the most devout of men." [25] On the great road called Hamaxitos, which linked the Piræus to Athens, there were at intervals altars "to the unknown gods" [26] and when, having gone through this long avenue, the Apostle entered Athens, he saw all around him or up on the Acropolis those monuments breathing beauty, the ruins of which still win our admiration, the Temple of Theseus, the Ceramicus, the Parthenon, and the Erechtheion. It is easy nowadays to see only the artistic splendour of these temples, which have long since ceased to be used for worship; but the Apostle saw in them idolatry, which is an abomination. "The idol is nothing," he himself will say to the Corinthians, "but the worship given to it is offered to devils, and not to God" (I Cor. viii, 4; x, 19-20). And his whole effort at Athens will be to turn the pagans away from idolatry and to lead them to Christ, and by Christ to God.

Amongst those whom he tried to convert, Luke mentions some Epicureans and Stoics (xvii, 18). These were, in fact, representa-tives of the two most widespread sects; always ready for something new (xvii, 21), they listened to this stranger. Some said contemptu-ously, "What is it that this word-sower would say?" Others, hearing him speak of Jesus and of the resurrection, said: "He is setting forth strange gods." [27] Drawn by this attraction of exotism, and find-ing the market place too noisy, they took him to the Areopagus. [28]

[24] Satir., 17.
[25] C. Ap., II, 12.
[26] On these dedications, cf. Deissmann, Paulus, pp. 226-9. It has often been remarked that this formula had a polytheistic sense, although the Apostle makes it the occasion of a monotheistic sermon. As Deissmann notes, he does not inter-pret it as a modern epigraphist would do, but tries to find in it a profound religious meaning, suggested to him by the line of the poet: "We are of his race."
[27] They saw in Jesus and the Anastasis, either seriously or in mockery, a new divine pair.
[28] St. John Chrysostom thinks that Paul was taken to a Court of Justice. Ramsay also sees a tribunal in the Areopagus (The Bearing of Recent Discovery on the Trustworthiness of the New Testament, London, 1915, pp. 103 et seq.) Many historians regard it as a local indication, and not the name of a tribunal. Cf. Wilkenhauser, op. cit., pp. 351-3.

The Speech at the Areopagus

Paul at once seized the opportunity given him. Standing in the midst of the Areopagus, he said:

"Ye men of Athens, I perceive that you are in all respects most religious. For passing through your city and noticing your sacred monuments, I saw an altar with this inscription: To an unknown god. What you adore without knowing, I come to preach to you.

"God, who made the world and all things therein, being Lord of heaven and earth, dwelleth not in temples made with hands. Neither is he served with men's hands as though he needed anything, seeing it is he who giveth to all life and breath and all things, and hath made of one, all mankind, to dwell upon the whole face of the earth, determining appointed times, and the limits of their habitation, that they should seek God, if happily they may feel after him or find him, although he be not far from every one of us. For in him we live, and move, and are, as some of your own poets have said: 'For we are also his offspring.' Being therefore the offspring of God, we must not suppose the divinity to be like unto gold, or silver, or stone, the graving of art and device of man. And God, indeed, having winked at the times of this ignorance, now declareth unto men, that all should everywhere do penance. Because he hath appointed a day wherein he will judge the world in equity, by the man whom he hath appointed, giving faith to all by raising him up from the dead" (Acts xvii, 22-31).[29]

[29] The discourse of St. Paul at Athens is one of those which still to-day makes a very great impression on its readers. The remark is made by the historian who has most strongly attacked it: Norden, Agnostos Theos, Leipzig, 1913, p. 125. This impression, he thinks, is not justified by the personality of the orator, but by the force of the tradition expressed in this discourse. Norden, in fact, tries to show that this discourse is an artificial composition dominated by two influences: that of Jewish and Christian apologetic, nourished on recollections of the Old Testament, and that of the Stoic philosophy. All this is not only not Pauline, but is profoundly opposed to Paul's thought. To prove this, Norden (p. 130) contrasts with this discourse, Romans i, 18, and Wisdom xii, 27 et seq. Norden's thesis has been thoroughly refuted by Lagrange in Review Biblique, 1914, pp. 442, 448; Harnack, Ist die Rede des Paulus in Athen ein ursprünglicher Bestandteil der Apostelgeschichte? Leipzig, 1913, T.U., XXXIX, 1, and Mission und Ausbreitung, pp. 391 et seq.; Jacquier, op. cit., pp. 271-81; Boudou, op. cit., pp. 391-4. In particular, it must be pointed out that the chief themes of this discourse are not contradicted but confirmed by St. Paul (Mission, l.c.): Jesus and Anastasis, cf. I Cor. i; the natural knowledge of God, cf. Rom. i, 19; ii, 14. On the Judgment linked with the mention of God naturally known or unknown, cf. Rom. ii, 14, 16; on salvation by faith: iii, 31; this faith has as its object the resurrection of Christ. The only difference is in the responsibility for ignorance, strongly set forth in Romans, but implied also in the exhortation to the Athenians to come

When he spoke to the Jews, as at Antioch in Pisidia, for instance,[30] St. Paul dwelt on the memories of Israel, which were dear to them as to himself, at the same time stressing their Messianic import. Here similarly, after discreetly extolling the religion of the Athenians, he reminds them of the religious principles which their own philosophers and poets had recognised. Just as the Jews were happy in their traditions, so the Greeks delighted in their thinkers and artists. They willingly followed the Apostle as far as the threshold of Christianity, but there they halted, as generally did the Jews. The Judgment, and, above all, the resurrection of the dead, repelled them, or made them smile: some mocked, and others said: "We will hear thee again concerning this matter." "Some, adhering to him, did believe, among whom was Dionysius the Areopagite, and a woman named Damaris, and others with them."

Nowhere had the fruits of Paul's apostolic labours been so small: not only in the great cities, Antioch in Syria, Antioch in Pisidia, Iconium, Thessalonica, but in the humble townships, Lystra, Derbe, Philippi, Berea, numbers of believers had been grouped by Paul and organised into churches. At Athens there was nothing like that: a few generous souls gave themselves to him, but there was no question of founding a church. All this brilliant and sonorous group of orators and philosophers had seen him pass by, had heard him preach, and had dismissed him with an ironic smile. Paul himself has written a commentary on this scene in ineffaceable words:

"The word of the cross, to them indeed that perish, is foolishness, but to them that are saved, that is, to us, it is the power of God. For it is written: 'I will destroy the wisdom of the wise, and the prudence of the prudent I will reject.' Where is the wise? Where is the scribe? Where is the disputed of this world? Hath not God made foolish the wisdom of this world? For seeing that in the wisdom of God the world, by wisdom, knew not God, it hath pleased God, by the foolishness of our preaching, to save them that believe" (I Cor. i, 18-21).

In these few words we find the condemnation of the proud and blind wisdom of the Athenians, and the whole programme of the preaching of Paul at Corinth.

---

out of this ignorance. On this point, moreover, Lagrange rightly says (op. cit., p. 447): "One does not speak to people one wants to convert in the same way as to believers one wants to preserve from evil."

[30] Cf. supra, p. 203.

Corinth

In the time of St. Paul, a traveller who went from Athens to Corinth had somewhat the impression which we have nowadays in going from Oxford to London. Instead of the university city in which life is wholly concentrated in its colleges, we find ourselves thrown into the feverish agitation of the city and its port. Athens was scarcely more than a university city, but it certainly retained all its ornamentation and all its pride; it had rejected the preaching of Paul, and for a long time it was to remain one of the most dangerous centres of pagan opposition to Christianity. Corinth was a cosmopolitan city; destroyed in 146 by Mummius, the town had been raised to a colony by Cæsar in 46 B.C. It was one of the chief centres of Mediterranean commerce.[31] But it was no longer a Greek town; the Italian colonists and their descendants were very numerous there, and the Orientals still more so; the inhabitants of Hellenic origin formed only a part of the population, and certainly were not the most numerous portion. At the same time, here, as in the rest of the Mediterranean world, Greek was the language of social relations and of business, and Hellenism covered all this variegated population with the mantle of its brilliant civilisation and of its easy life. The easy morality which was to be found in the whole of Hellenic paganism degenerated at Corinth into a licentiousness which had become proverbial, and which shocked the pagans themselves; it opposed to the preaching of the Gospel an obstacle which might well appear insurmountable, and which only the grace of God could conquer. The consultations by the first Christians of Corinth, and the replies of St. Paul, reveal the slough from which he had had to rescue them.[32]

When he entered this great city, so pagan, so busy, and so dissolute, the Apostle was without the help of his usual collaborators,

[31] The western port, Lechaeum, linked to the city by long walls, was 12 stadia away from it; the eastern port, Cenchrae, was 70 stadia away. The citadel, Acrocorinthos, nearly 2,000 feet above the level of the sea, commanded the whole passage. In spite of a few attempts to pierce it, the isthmus always divided the two seas, but cargoes were transported, and light boats were drawn from one side to the other. This could not be done with big boats (*Acts* xxvii, 6, 37).

[32] Thus St. Paul had written to his faithful: "Do not keep company with fornicators." The Corinthians replied to him: "In that case we must leave this world." The Apostle had to explain to them that he was not forbidding all relations with these sinners, but that he forbade them to tolerate them in the church (*I Cor.* v, 9-11).

THE MISSIONS OF ST. PAUL

Silas and Timothy, who had remained in Macedonia. He was still feeling sad at the resistance shown by the Athenians towards the Gospel, and though not fearing for himself, he felt the weight of the responsibility which he was bearing. Later on he revived these memories when writing to the Corinthians:

"I, brethren, when I came to you, came not in loftiness of speech or of wisdom to declare unto you the testimony of Christ. For I decided myself not to know anything among you but Jesus Christ and him crucified. And I was with you in weakness, and in fear, and in much trembling. And my speech and my preaching was not in the persuasive words of human wisdom, but in shewing of the Spirit and in power, that your faith might not stand on the wisdom of men, but on the power of God" (*I Cor.* ii, 1-5).

Certainly we have here the statement of a thesis dear to the Apostle, but there is also a memory of his past experience. When he made contact alone with these men of Corinth, so far removed from the Gospel, he realised the prestige exerted on them by rhetoric, human wisdom, and all those arts which he had decided not to employ there; his recent experience at Athens made this impression a very vivid one. The Corinthians for their part noticed his timidity, and later Paul's opponents brought it up against him.[33]

No one had ministered to his needs, and he owed his subsistence to the brethren of Macedonia (*II Cor.* xi, 8-9). True, he had regarded this independence as a point of honour, but at Philippi and Thessalonica he had not acted in that way; at Corinth itself he affirmed the right of the Apostles to be kept by the faithful (*I Cor.* ix, 6-27). But when he arrived in this great city, he could not vindicate this right in regard to people who were quite ignorant of Christianity, without rendering his preaching suspect in advance. Moreover, the sectional spirit which divided the church of Corinth imposed on him a special reserve in this matter; later he resolved not to encourage by his own example the pretensions of some interested preachers (*II Cor.* xi, 12).

When he arrived at Corinth, he joined himself to Aquila and Priscilla, who had come from Rome, which they had been obliged to leave in consequence of the edict of Claudius; they worked at the same trade as himself; he lodged with them, and worked with them. On the Sabbath, "he reasoned in the synagogue, and he

[33] *II Cor.* x, 1, 10; xi, 6; xiii, 3.

persuaded the Jews and the Greeks." When Silas and Timothy arrived from Macedonia, he redoubled his apostolic activity; the alms he received doubtless gave him more leisure, and the assistance of his two helpers enabled him to extend his efforts. The Jews could not bear this success: they opposed him, and reviled him. Then he shook his garments, and said: "Your blood be upon your own heads; I am innocent, and from henceforth I will go unto the Gentiles." He was received in the house of a proselyte, Titius Justus, who lived near the synagogue; Crispus, the ruler of the synagogue, believed in the Lord, with all his house, and many Corinthians received baptism. One night the Lord said to Paul in a vision: "Do not fear, but speak, and hold not thy peace, for I am with thee, and no man shall set upon thee to hurt thee, for I have much people in this city." And he remained there a year and six months, continuing his preaching (*Acts* xviii, 2-11).

Preaching and Charisms

Concerning this preaching, we have some brief but very valuable information in the letters to the Corinthians, whom St. Paul reminds, as we have said, that he had determined to know nothing amongst them but "Jesus Christ and him crucified." His Christians came for the most part from paganism (*I Cor.* xii, 2); they lived in surroundings thoroughly impregnated with pagan superstitions. To take them away from their past, and to safeguard them from contamination, he relied only on the preaching of Christ crucified:

"Seeing that . . . the world by wisdom knew not God, it pleased God by the foolishness of our preaching, to save them that believe. For both the Jews require signs, and the Greeks seek after wisdom. But we preach Christ crucified, unto the Jews indeed a stumbling block, and unto the Gentiles foolishness, but unto them that are called, both Jews and Greeks, Christ, the power of God and the wisdom of God. For the foolishness of God is wiser than men, and the weakness of God is stronger than men" (*I Cor.* i, 21-25).

Later on (*I Cor.* xv) Paul reminds his converts of the tradition which he has transmitted to them: its chief articles are the death and resurrection of Christ; elsewhere (xi, 23) he repeats the account of the Last Supper which he had taught them; elsewhere again, he gives various words of the Lord concerning the union of husband and wife (*vii*, 10), the stipend of the teachers of the

Gospel (ix, 14). These are his weapons, by which he overthrows all reasoning against the knowledge of God, and subjects all minds to the obedience of Christ (*II Cor.* x, 4-6).

This preaching was upheld by the power of the Spirit, and it was this power that provided the foundation for the belief of the faithful (*II Cor.* ii, 4). The most evident work of this power was the transformation of men's souls:

"Do we need, as some do, epistles of commendation to you, or from you? You are our epistle, written in our hearts, which is known and read by all men. It is manifest that you are the epistle of Christ, ministered by us, and written not with ink, but with the Spirit of the living God, not in tables of stone, but in the fleshly tables of the heart" (*II Cor.* iii, 1-3).

In addition to this moral transformation, the charisms were still more evident: supernatural gifts, bestowed by the Holy Spirit upon Christians for the general edification, these had been poured out upon the church of Corinth with a truly divine profusion. These gifts should be a glory and a power for the whole Church, and they would be, if those who received them, remembering that they were members of Christ, made them serve only for the good of the body. That is the lesson which the Apostle gives them when he enumerates these charisms and determines their relative values:

"You are the body of Christ, and member of member. And God indeed hath set some in the church; first apostles, secondly prophets, thirdly doctors, after that miracles, then the graces of healing, helps, governments, kinds of tongues, interpretations of speeches. Are all apostles? Are all prophets? Are all doctors? Are all workers of miracles? Have all the grace of healing? Do all speak with tongues? Do all interpret? But be zealous for the better gifts. And I shew unto you yet a more excellent way. If I speak with the tongues of men, and of angels, and have not charity, I am become as sounding brass or a tinkling cymbal. . . ." (*I Cor.* xii, 27-xiii, 1).[34]

[34] This teaching of St. Paul on the gradation of the charisms and the esteem in which one ought to hold them is completed by the rules given later on (ch. xiv) concerning their use. These chapters are of very great interest for the historian: they reveal the spiritual life of the Church of Corinth, filled with divine graces, but at the same time torn by divisions and saddened by scandals; they show above all the wisdom of the Apostle: the weaknesses of the Corinthians who were exalted by their charisms did not make him despise these gifts of God, but made him more anxious to verify their divine origin, regulate their use, and prevent their abuse. The above list can be completed by the other lists given by St. Paul: *I Cor.* xii, 8-10; *Rom.* xii, 6-8; *Ephes.* iv, 11. Cf. Prat, *Theology of St. Paul,* Vol. I, pp. 127-33.

Conversions and Persecutions

This preaching and these graces had borne their fruits: "Many of the Corinthians hearing, believed, and were baptised." [35] A small number alone are known to us; [36] the majority were of servile or lowly origin (*I Cor.* vi, 9-11); many had led before their conversion a very lax moral life (*I Cor.* vi, 9-11), and these vices would not be all abolished in one day; we find traces of them still in the church of Corinth. At the same time, these disappointments and even these scandals ought not to conceal from us the transformation of the majority of souls; the Corinthians became "rich in Christ" (*I Cor.* i, 5), and even when factions were ravaging it, the church of Corinth still remained the letter written by the hand of God.

St. Paul's success aroused the envy and hatred of the Jews. When Gallio arrived as proconsul for Achaia, [37] the Jews with one accord denounced Paul before his tribunal; the Apostle prepared to defend himself; Gallio stopped the argument:

"If it were some matter of injustice, or an heinous deed, O Jews, I should with reason bear with you. But if they be questions of word and names, and of your Law, look you to it: I will not be judge of such things" (*Acts* xviii, 14-15).

And he drove them from the judgment seat. They then laid hold of Sosthenes, the ruler of the synagogue, and beat him before the tribunal, but Gallio cared for none of these things (*ibid.,* 16-17).

[35] *Acts* xviii, 8. St. Paul himself baptised only a small number of them: Crispus, Gaius, and the house of Stephanus (*I Cor.,* i, 14-16).

[36] Besides those who are named in the preceding note, we may mention Aquila and Priscilla, Chloe and her household (*I Cor.* i, 11), Phœbe who took the letter to the Romans (*Rom.* xvi, 1-2), Erastes (*ibid.,* 23), Tertius, Quartus, Fortunatus, and Achaicus.

[37] The date of this proconsulate has been fixed definitely by the inscription found at Delphi and published by E. Bourguet in his thesis *De rebus Delphicis imperatoriae aetatis capita duo,* Montepessulano, 1905, pp. 63 *et seq.* This inscription, much mutilated, contains a letter from the Emperor Claudius to the town of Delphi; this letter is dated by the tribunal power and the imperial acclamation; the figure of the tribunal power has disappeared, but the figure of the acclamation is extant, 26. This enables us to determine the date of the letter: between the end of 51 or more probably the beginning of 52, and August 1st, 52. Now according to the inscription, Gallio was already proconsul in Achaia; in all probability he remained in charge only a short while, a year at most, and perhaps only a few months. We infer that he took charge in the spring of 52. At that date Paul had spent eighteen months at Corinth (*Acts* xviii, 11); he had therefore arrived there in the last months of the year 50, and left there at the end of 52. Cf. Deissmann, *Paulus,* 1925, pp. 203-25; Hennequin, *Inscription de Delphes,* in *Supplément* to *Dict. de la Bible,* 355-73. These give bibliographies on the subject.

Paul remained a fairly long time at Corinth after this; then, accompanied by Priscilla and Aquila, he left for Syria. At Cenchræ he shaved his head, because he had made a vow. At Ephesus, where his companions had decided to stop, he made only a short halt; he preached in the synagogue; the Jews pressed him to stay; he promised them to return, and left for Cæsarea; he went up from there to Jerusalem, saluted the church there, and went down once more to Antioch. There he spent some time, and then set out for a new voyage.[38]

Before we follow the Apostle into Anatolia and Asia Minor, we can pause a few moments with him at Antioch and consider the work already accomplished. The first mission had penetrated into the Hellenic and pagan world. How much·had happened since the day when, at Cæsarea, in the house of Cornelius, Peter had cried: "In very deed I perceive that God is not a respecter of persons, but in every nation he that feareth him and worketh justice is acceptable to him!" At that time a few men, chosen by God, entered into the Church; very soon the crowds of Antioch hastened in, and then, in the course of Paul's mission, the Church won not only Jews and proselytes, but also pagans whom no missionary had hitherto reached. The grain of mustard seed was becoming a great tree, and those who considered its rapid and strong growth were full of admiration and joy. And now, what Paul, Silas and Timothy had to relate was still more wonderful: the Gospel had penetrated amongst the Galatian tribes, and above all into that Hellenic world which Jewish propaganda had attacked but had never conquered. This was truly "the salvation which God had prepared before the face of all peoples, a light to the revelation of the gentiles, and the glory of Israel." But this canticle of Simeon was no longer a *Nunc dimittis,* but a hymn of victory.

§4. THIRD MISSION (SPRING, A.D. 53 TO SUMMER, A.D. 57)

In the Spring, Paul set out once more, crossed again the steep and dangerous passes of the Taurus, then reached Galatia in the

[38] If it is desired to make more precise these indications in the Acts, we can say that Paul left Corinth in the autumn of 52. His mission had lasted three years; he visited Ephesus, Cæsarea and Jerusalem, then he stayed "some time" at Antioch. He probably passed the winter there, and in the spring of 53 set out for a third mission.

north-east, and went anew through the Galatian and Phrygian country, strengthening all the disciples in the faith. It was from there that, three years earlier, he had wanted to pass over into Asia; then the Spirit had turned him away towards Macedonia; now everything called him there, and following the path that so many conquerors had trod, he descended from the high plateaux of the interior, through Philadelphia and Sardis, towards the wealthy coasts of Asia. The Ephesians had extracted from him a promise to return to them; he kept his promise.

Ephesus

Ephesus, the most opulent of the cities of Asia Minor, is now the most decayed; for many centuries its port has been silted up, and its ruined temples and houses have served as a quarry for the neighbouring Turks. But the excavations of the last twenty years have at last brought to light once more the plan of the double church, the library, the market place, the theatre, and the sacred way. From the little hill of Ayasolouk, we may contemplate this mass of ruins, and perceive in the marshy plain the sites of the old ports which mark the successive displacements of the shore receding towards the west. When St. Paul arrived there in 53, all this splendour, now in ruins, was at its highest.

Strong in the imperial protection, the old city surpassed its ancient rivals, Smyrna and Pergamus, and stood out as a capital city. It appeared then to Seneca as the great city of the Orient, similar to Alexandria.[1]

In this great metropolis, the oriental worship of Artemis was sovereign; but in the imperial epoch, the Roman cults, and above all those of Rome and of Augustus, were associated everywhere with the worship of the local divinities.

In the year 5 B.C., "Augustus installed right in the *temenos* a temple to Rome and the Emperor, destined for the meetings of the Κοινὸν'Ασίας."[2] It was against these apparently all-powerful forces that St. Paul's preaching was going to be directed. It would also

---

[1] *Ep.* cii, 25: "Humanum animus . . . humilem non accipit patriam Ephesum aut Alexandriam, aut si quod est etiam nunc frequentius incolis, laetius tectis solum."

[2] C. Picard, *Éphèse*, p. 664.

encounter other obstacles: the jealousy of the Jews, and the sorcery which affected both Jews and pagans.[3]

Apollos

When he went from Corinth to Cæsarea, Paul, as we have said, called at Ephesus and spoke to the Jews in the synagogue. This first contact had aroused a sympathetic curiosity; the Apostle had promised to return. Meanwhile, he had left at Ephesus his former Corinthian hosts, Aquila and Priscilla. In the course of the winter of the year 52-53, an eloquent and clever Alexandrian named Apollos preached in the synagogue. This man was full of zeal, but badly instructed, and knew only the baptism of John; nevertheless "he taught diligently the things that are of Jesus" (*Acts* xviii, 25), that is, no doubt, he set out to prove that Jesus was the Messias. Aquila and Priscilla took him aside, taught him Christian doctrine, and as he wished to return to Achaia, they recommended him to the brethren. While Apollos was thus at Corinth, Paul arrived at Ephesus. There he found a group of about a dozen faithful. He conversed with them, and asked them whether they had received the Holy Ghost. They replied: "We have not so much as heard whether there be a Holy Ghost." Paul asked: "What baptism have you received, then?" "The baptism of John," was the reply. Paul thereupon instructed them, and as soon as they were baptised, they spoke in tongues and prophesied.

Preaching of St. Paul

Paul then began the evangelisation of Ephesus. According to his custom, he frequented the synagogue; he preached there during three months; the Jews of Ephesus seem to have been less intolerant than those of Thessalonica. But many refused to believe, and in presence of the assembly, uttered imprecations against the Apostle's

[3] On the cults of Ephesus, and above all the cult of Artemis, the chief work is that of C. Picard, *Ephèse et Claros* (Paris, 1922). We do not follow him in the interpretation he gives of the narrative of the *Acts*, dating the arrival of St. Paul in 56 (p. 668), etc. The article by P. Antoine on *Ephèse* in the *Supplément* to the *Dict. de la Bible* may usefully be consulted. Cf. R. Tonneau, *Ephèse au temps de S. Paul*, in *Revue Biblique*, 1929, pp. 5-34 and 321-63.

doctrine. Paul thereupon left the synagogue, taking with him his disciples; each day he taught in the school of Tyrannus.[4] This daily teaching continued for two years, "so that all they who dwelt in Asia heard the word of the Lord, both Jews and Gentiles" (*Acts* xix, 10). In the first letter to the Corinthians, written during this evangelisation of Ephesus, Paul wrote: "I see a great door opened before me, and many adversaries" (xvi, 9). That is certainly the picture presented to us by the reading of the account in the Acts. In this great city, the gateway of Asia, during these two years it was not only the citizens of Ephesus who were able to hear each day the teaching of Paul, but all the strangers who passed through the city or stayed there, coming from Rome, Egypt, Syria or Asia, heard the doctrine in their turn. Several doubtless opposed it, but many accepted it, as the riot of the silversmiths soon showed.

Miracles

God, moreover, confirmed this activity of the Apostle by miracles: "There were brought from his body to the sick, handkerchiefs and aprons, and the diseases departed from them, and the wicked spirits went out of them" (*Acts* xix, 12). This domination over devils became so well known that Jewish exorcists had recourse to it: the seven sons of a Jewish chief priest named Skeuas exorcised thus: "I conjure you by Jesus, whom Paul preacheth." "Jesus I know," replied the spirit, "and Paul I know, but who are you?" And the possessed man throwing himself upon them knocked down two, who had to take flight, naked and covered with wounds. All the inhabitants of Ephesus, Jews and Greeks, heard of this; all were in consequence in great fear, and the name of the Lord Jesus was glorified. Many believers abandoned their superstitious practices; they brought their books and burnt them. Their value was estimated at fifty thousand pieces of silver. This last fact shows the attraction exercised on the Ephesians by magical books and practices. When the Spirit breathed, all these poisonous mists were

---

[4] The Western text adds: "from the fifth to the tenth hour," that is, at the equinox, from 11 o'clock to 4 o'clock; in the summer later, in the winter earlier. This timing is quite probable: teaching was given late in the morning (Lake recalls Martial, IX, 68; XII, 57; Juvenal, VII, 222 *et seq.*). The fifth hour marked the end of work (Martial, IV, 8). Paul could then make use of the place, and having spent the morning in working at his trade, pass the warm hours of the afternoon in teaching doctrine.

dissipated; but we must not be surprised to find them later on infecting Asia anew, and spreading Gnosticism there.

Apostolic Labours

This daily preaching, these miracles, and these great victories do not completely reveal to us the apostolate of St. Paul, or the secret of his power; he won disciples, attached them to Christ, brought them forth, by the Spirit, to a new life, and this less by his general activity than by his conversations, his visits, and his truly fatherly affection. Later, when passing through Miletus, he will remind the Ephesians of this period, so full of devotion:

"You know from the first day that I came into Asia, in what manner I have been with you, for all the time, serving the Lord with all humility and with tears, and temptations which befell me by the conspiracies of the Jews; how I have kept back nothing that was profitable to you, and taught you publicly and from house to house, testifying both to Jews and Gentiles penance towards God, and faith in our Lord Jesus Christ. . . . Therefore watch, keeping in memory that for three years I ceased not, with tears to admonish every one of you night and day (*Acts* xx, 18-21, 31).

And while he was still at Ephesus he wrote thus to the Corinthians:

"Even unto this hour we both hunger and thirst, and are naked, and are buffeted, and have no fixed abode, and we labour, working with our own hands; we are reviled, and we bless; we are persecuted, and we suffer it; we are blasphemed, and we entreat; we are made as the refuse of this world, the offscourings of all, even until now" (*I Cor.* iv, 11-13).

These warm words make us feel still the heat of these years of combat and of suffering; they bring home to us what were his days of labour; the mornings, devoted to work of. his trade; the warm hours of the afternoon to preaching, the evenings to personal interviews, and all the while, so many snares, insults, persecutions, and amongst even the converts, such weakness and inconstancy.

The Ephesians were not the only ones that he had to uphold and correct: the Apostle felt himself weighed down by "the care of all the churches" (*II Cor.* xii, 28). It was during and after his stay at Ephesus that Paul wrote his two letters to the Corinthians; no other document reveals to us more the weight of this solicitude, and the pain which sometimes accompanied it.

First Letter to the Corinthians

Paul had received bad news from Corinth through the household of Chloe.[5] Not being able to leave Asia, he had sent Timothy to Corinth (I Cor. iv, 17; xvi, 10). Later there arrived Stephanus, Fortunatus, and Achaicus, bearers of better news, which relieved the Apostle's mind (xvi, 17). Thereupon he wrote the first letter to the Corinthians. We find in it an authority certain of itself, but anxious to correct the abuses which had been reported.

The Divisions in Corinth

The first of these abuses was the division of the Corinthians into parties: "It hath been signified unto me of you, by them that are of the house of Chloe, that there are contentions among you . . . that every one of you saith: 'I indeed am of Paul,' and 'I am of Apollo,' and 'I of Cephas,' and 'I of Christ.' Is Christ divided?" (i, 11-13).

These divisions were doubtless not absolute schisms: all the faithful celebrated the Eucharist together; all recognised the authority of the Apostle; but they were so many parties, after the manner of the Greeks, who delighted to claim to belong to one particular master, and to set him up against others. That these oppositions and preferences were the origin of disagreements which imperilled the charity and union of hearts was evident in the commencement of the Church, and how often shall we find the same in its subsequent history![6]

[5] I Cor. i, 11. Before this first Epistle Paul had written to the Corinthians a letter which we do not possess; therein he had recommended them not to keep company with evil doers (I Cor. v, 9). His instructions had not been properly understood, and he had to return to this question of immorality and also to that of offerings made to idols; these two points were the ones in the Apostolic decree which could give rise to most difficulties. Lietzmann, in his commentary (note on v, 9), thinks that the decree had been taken to Corinth by St. Peter: this is a mere hypothesis: Paul might himself have communicated this decree to the Corinthians.

[6] Without seeking for other examples, it will suffice to mention the dissensions which forty years later divided once more the Church of Corinth, and which the Bishop of Rome, St. Clement, had to pacify. Cf. Bk. II.

On this occasion, the weakness of the disciples was all the more manifest inasmuch as the masters whom they thus set one against the other had not desired any such opposition. We know how Apollos, then a catechumen, had come to Ephesus, had there been more completely instructed by Aquila and Priscilla, and recommended by them to the faithful at Corinth. He had preached in that city with much fruit, then he had gone to rejoin St. Paul at Ephesus, and he was there when the Apostle wrote his Epistle (xvi, 12). He had done nothing to form a party: Paul himself wanted to send him again to Corinth, but he could not persuade him to go (*ibid.*). The Apostle, moreover, willingly acknowledged the good work which this preacher had accomplished: "I have planted, Apollo watered, but God gave the increase . . ." (iii, 6). But his preaching, more cultured and more elegant than that of Paul, had fascinated some fashionable listeners, who delighted in the speculations of Apollos and in his interpretations of Scripture, and thus in spite of himself he found himself the head of a school. Others invoked the authority of Cephas. To explain this it would suffice to recall the fact that Peter was recognised as the head of the Apostles, and that those who contested the apostolic authority of St. Paul delighted to set St. Peter against him; but it would seem also that St. Peter had personally visited Corinth; [7] those who had come under his influence may have exploited it against St. Paul, just as others made similar use of Apollos.

These three groups, which appealed to Paul, Cephas, Apollos, are recalled later on by St. Clement (xlvii, 3). To them must be added the fourth party, those who said: "I am of Christ." [8] This group was doubtless analogous to that of the Judaisers, who went from Jerusalem to Antioch and intimidated Peter himself, boasting of James, the brother of the Lord, as of the holder of a purer tradition. For the rest, there is no trace here of any propaganda in favour of circumcision or of Jewish observances, but merely a rivalry

---

[7] Dionysius of Corinth attests this visit: "Rome and Corinth are the two trees planted by Peter and Paul, for both planted in our Corinth, and instructed us; and after teaching together in Italy, they suffered martyrdom at the same time" (Eusebius, *Hist. eccles.*, II, 25, 8).

[8] Some exegetes think that "I am of Christ" is a comment by Paul, and that there was no fourth party. The construction of the phrase suggests the contrary interpretation: the four members are parallel, and depend equally on "one saith . . ." Cf. the note by Lietzmann on l. 12; this interpretation is confirmed by *II. Cor.* x, 7. Cf. Prat, *op. cit.*, Vol. I, pp. 89-91.

directed against Paul, and attempts to lessen his authority.[9]

All these parties divided and weakened the Corinthian church; yet they did not shake the authority of St. Paul, or the attachment of the Corinthians to him. We feel this in the assurance of his reply, and also in the affection which he expresses and which he expects: "I write not these things to confound you, but I admonish you as my dearest children. For if you have ten thousand instructors in Christ, yet not many fathers. For in Christ Jesus, by the gospel I have begotten you" (iv, 14-15). What he urges upon them over and over again is the superiority of the power of the Spirit over the words of human wisdom, and in this he is not attacking Apollos, but the weaknesses of the Greek mentality, and its empty infatuation. A last word affirms the authority of the Apostle and sums up his teaching:

"Some among you are puffed up. But I will come to you shortly, if the Lord will, and will know, not the speech of them that are puffed up, but the power. For the kingdom of God is not in speech, but in power. What will you? Shall I come to you with a rod; or in charity, and in the spirit of meekness?" (iv., 18-21).

Immorality and Injustice

While pride exalts the Corinthians, immorality stains them, and yet they tolerate this:

"It is absolutely heard, that there is fornication among you, and such fornication as the like is not among the heathens, that one should have his father's wife. And you are puffed up; and have not rather mourned, that he might be taken away from among you that hath done this deed. I indeed, absent in body, but present in spirit, have already judged, as though I were present, him that hath so done, in the name of our Lord Jesus Christ, you being gathered together with my spirit, by the power of our Lord Jesus, to deliver such a one to Satan for the destruction of the flesh, that the spirit may be saved in the day of our Lord Jesus Christ." [10]

Already the Apostle had instructed the Corinthians to avoid all

[9] Juelicher, *Einleitung*, p. 82, sees in those "of Christ" some Christians who claimed to be taught immediately by Christ and not by men. The words of Paul (xi, 1), "Be ye imitators of me, as I am of Christ," would be aimed at these. This is not very likely. Lietzmann nevertheless follows Juelicher in this interpretation of i. 12 (p. 7).

[10] v, 1-5. On this scandal, and the Apostle's condemnation of it, cf. Prat, *Theology of St. Paul*, Vol. I, pp. 99-102.

contact with impure people. They had not understood this, or pretended not to understand it: "we should have to leave this world," they said. St. Paul pointed out that he had not meant that: we are not the judges of sinners outside the Church; God will judge them. But the sinner within the Church must not be tolerated: "put away the evil one from among yourselves." He therefore excommunicates the incestuous man, and is ready to deliver him to Satan, as he will do later with Hymeneus and Alexander, "that they may learn not to blaspheme" (*I Tim.* 1, 20). Then St. Paul deals with those who, on the basis of contempt for the body, think that all things are permissible: "The body is not for fornication," he says, "but for the Lord" (vi, 13).

These grave warnings enable us to judge how dangerous the old leaven of immorality, so prevalent in Corinth, still was to the new converts; but we must call attention above all to the high and noble thoughts which Paul suggests to men's minds to counter the danger: "Shall I take the members of Christ and make them the members of an harlot? . . . Know you not that your members are the temple of the Holy Ghost? . . . and that you are not your own?" (vi, 15, 19). These exhortations presuppose and nourish a truly Christian faith.

Another abuse is denounced and condemned: "Dare any of you, having a matter against another, go to be judged before the unjust, and not before the saints? . . . Is it so that there is not among you any one wise man that is able to judge between his brethren? But brother goeth to law with brother, and that before unbelievers!" And recalling the Gospel morality, he insists: "Why do you not rather suffer wrong? Why do you not rather allow yourselves to be defrauded?" (vi, 1-7).

After these rebukes, inspired by such absolute faith and expressed so strongly, St. Paul deals with questions which had been submitted to him. This second part of the letter is, like the first, of the highest interest, for it makes known to us the life of the Corinthian community in all its aspects, and the direction which the Apostle wishes it to take.

Marriage and Virginity

Is it good to marry? That is the first question put to the Apostle. In this city, stained by so much immorality, there were also teachers who forbade marriage. These two exaggerated moral tendencies will manifest themselves also amongst the Gnostics. St. Paul rejects both. He has condemned fornication, he defends the sanctity of marriage; but he shows, to those souls who desire to seek God only, an ideal which is higher than marriage, namely, that of virginity:

"He that is without a wife, is solicitous for the things that belong to the Lord, how he may please God. But he that is with a wife, is solicitous for the things of the world, how he may please his wife, and he is divided. And the unmarried woman and the virgin thinketh on the things of the Lord, that she may be holy in body and in spirit. But she that is married thinketh on the things of the world, how she may please her husband. And this I speak for your profit, not to cast a snare upon you, but for that which is decent, and which may give you power to attend upon the Lord without impediment." [11]

Idol Offerings

St. Paul next settles the cases of conscience which arose in a pagan city from the custom of offering food to idols, and participating in religious repasts. The idol is nothing, but one must avoid scandal. In the market one can eat food without anxiety as to its origin; one can eat if invited to a meal by an unbeliever; but "if any man say: 'This has been sacrificed to idols,' do not eat of it, for his sake that told it, and for conscience' sake" (x, 28). In the case of the religious repasts of the pagans, a greater strictness is necessary; to take part therein would be to participate in an idolatrous worship, and that could not be allowed: "You cannot drink the chalice of the Lord, and the chalice of devils: you cannot be partakers of the table of the Lord, and of the table of devils" (x, 21).

The Eucharist

Christians have themselves their own sacrificial banquet, the Supper of the Lord: "The chalice of benediction which we bless, is it not the communion of the blood of Christ? And the bread which we break, is it not the partaking of the body of the Lord?" (x, 16). Christians cannot take part in any other sacred meal;

[11] vii, 32-5. This great preoccupation, to serve God without impediment, is still more urgent if we remember that "the time is short," and that "the fashion of this world passeth away" (vii, 29, 31).

their worship is exclusive, like their faith; they have but one God and one Lord. To the celebration of this Supper, the Corinthians did not always bring the respect which they ought, or proper preparation; the meal was taken not all together, but in little groups, without waiting, and without putting together what each had brought, and this had led to excesses: "One is hungry, and another is drunk." It is likely that in this matter again, pagan and Jewish customs [12] had made their influence felt; people naturally copied the religious repasts to which they had been accustomed. In addition, some did not hesitate to communicate in the body and blood of the Lord though unworthy of it; the Apostle points out to them the gravity of this fault:

Whosoever shall eat this bread, or drink the chalice of the Lord unworthily, shall be guilty of the body and of the blood of the Lord. But let a man prove himself, and so let him eat of that bread, and drink of the chalice. For he that eateth and drinketh unworthily, eateth and drinketh judgment to himself, not discerning the body of the Lord" (xi, 27-29).

To explain the significance of such grave warnings, Paul repeats to his Christians the account of the Supper and its meaning. We shall have occasion later on [13] to quote these texts, which throw so strong a light on the faith of the Apostolic Church in the eucharistic mystery. St. Paul goes on to speak of charisms, of which he regulates the esteem and the use, [14] then he speaks of the resurrection of the body, which some Christians at Corinth rejected; [15] against this negation the Apostle protests with all his authority:

"If there be no resurrection of the dead, then Christ is not risen again. And if Christ be not risen again, then is our preaching vain, and your faith is also vain, Yea, and we are found false witnesses of God" (xv, 13-15).

[12] Cf. the description of the Paschal meal in the *Mishna, Pesachim,* X (ed. Beer, pp. 186 *et seq.*): ". . . After the paschal meal there is the *aphiqomen*. If some have fallen asleep, the others can still eat; if all are asleep, they cannot." Beer notes: "This sleep may be caused by wine. If some are asleep, the others at least save the honour of the evening." Cf. *Life and Teaching of Jesus Christ,* Vol. II, p. 217.

[13] Bk. II.

[14] Cf. above, p. 234.

[15] This reluctance to admit the resurrection is much more understandable in Gentile converts than in Christians coming from Judaism. This feature thus confirms what we gather from others, the origin of the neophytes.

On this occasion Paul repeats all the traditional catechesis concerning the death of Christ, his burial, resurrection, and appearances (xv, 1-11). This witness is of the greatest value to us; once more the early disciples, by their resistance to the faith, have called forth attestations which enlighten us in turn.

Christian Life in Corinth

This Epistle is valuable to us not only because of the doctrines which it affirms, but also because of the Christian life which it reveals. We learn a great deal about these Corinthians, upon whom God has showered such gifts, who are so beloved by the Apostle, and yet are still so carnal (iii, 2), and so unmanageable. The charisms have been communicated abundantly to the church of Corinth: people speak there in tongues, perform miracles, and prophesy, and yet they get drunk at the Supper: it seems more difficult for God to make saints than to make wonder-workers.

This enables us to understand better, and to judge more fairly, the suspicions which could arise amongst the Judeo-Christians in respect to these first Gentile churches;[16] accustomed from infancy to a severe morality, and also to despise pagans, the Hebrews would be tempted to judge severely these "sinners coming from paganism" (*Gal.* ii, 15). This infirmity of the flesh, so manifest still amongst the Corinthians in the year 55, should become less; these stains must be purified; the Corinthians are still only children in Christ, and carnal; the Apostle cannot give them meat, but only milk (iii, 1-3). This Epistle has often been compared with the letter to the Ephesians[17] or again with the first Epistle of St. Peter,[18] in order to show the progress in the moral training of Christians, and consequently, in the preaching of Christianity.

The more we consider the weakness of these little children in Christ, the more we admire the Apostle's educational method. He is patient and knows how to forgive, but from the first day he is intransigent. Christian morality is inflexible, just as the rule of

[16] Cf. W. L. Knox, *St. Paul and the Church of Jerusalem*, Cambridge, 1925, p. 286 and n. 14; p. 312 and n. 12 *et seq.*

[17] This comparison was especially familiar to Origen, who delights to see in the Corinthians carnal Christians, and in the Ephesians, the perfect. Cf. *Recherches de Science Religieuse*, 1922, p. 279, n. 1.

[18] Cf. Knox, *op. cit.*, p. 293, n. 14.

faith: to those who allow themselves still to be led by their pagan relatives to participate in the religious repasts which they previously attended, Paul opposes a categorical "No." "You cannot be partakers of the table of the Lord and of the table of devils." Similarly, in the case of those who deny the resurrection: if this is denied, "our preaching is vain, and your faith is vain." And again: "If Christ be not risen again, your faith is vain, for you are yet in your sins." And together with its intransigence, we note the absolute authority of this faith: it is sovereign, and judges everything. Whatever be the question which is submitted to him, Paul in order to settle it invokes the highest principles of Christianity. To the degrading vices which the Corinthians have before their eyes and which they know from experience, he opposes, not indeed the care of health, nor even respect for human dignity, but the Christian faith: "You are the members of Christ, and the temples of the Holy Ghost."

It is also by the same principles of faith that he decides all the other questions put to him, whether these are concerned with offerings to idols, or legal proceedings, or marriage, or the Supper, or the resurrection. All this brings home to us the exalted level of the Apostle's thought, to which he would lift up by the grace of the Holy Spirit even such children in the faith, such carnal people as the Corinthians. It was in this way that he made Christians of all his disciples.

Yet this great effort did not immediately win all hearts: Timothy, returning from Corinth to Ephesus, brought back bad news; the Epistle had not succeeded in ending the oppositions of the parties or in reforming morals, and Timothy had also failed. Paul then decided, doubtless about the summer of 55, to return personally to Corinth; he himself encountered a resistance which he could not overcome. He went back to Ephesus, grievously hurt by this check. He at once wrote to the Corinthians a letter which is severe, and full of sadness (II Cor. ii, 4); then he sent Titus to Corinth, either as bearer of the letter, or more probably to ascertain the effect which it produced.[19]

---

[19] The succession of events as set forth here is only a probable conjecture; the journey of Paul from Ephesus to Corinth seems to be attested by II Cor. xiii, 1-2; cf. xii, 14; the letter between I Cor. and II Cor. is similarly referred to (II Cor. ii, 4; vii, 12). Cf. Juelicher, Einleitung zum N.T., pp. 89-95; Leitzmann, note on II Cor. ii, 4; Meinertz in Theol. Revue, 1923, pp. 266-8. In a contrary sense, see E. Golla, Zwischenreise und Zwischenbrief, 1922.

The Riot at Ephesus

This letter was written most likely in the autumn of 55. Paul then thought he would continue his work at Ephesus until the Pentecost of the year 56. In April and May [20] the great festivals of Artemis would bring to the city crowds of pilgrims and sightseers; the preaching of the Gospel might reach them, and spread by their means through the whole of Asia.

The festival was held, but it was the occasion of a riot which imperilled Paul's life. A silversmith named Demetrius complained that his trade was being injured by the Apostle; the little votive temples in honour of Artemis had brought him and his workmen great profit, but "this Paul by persuasion hath drawn away a great multitude, not only of Ephesus, but almost of all Asia, saying 'They are not gods which are made by hands.' So that not only this our craft is in danger to be set at nought, but also the temple of great Diana shall be reputed for nothing; yea, and her majesty shall begin to be destroyed, whom all Asia and the world worshippeth" (*Acts* xix, 25-27). Demetrius aroused the jewellers by thus haranguing them; they went round the city crying: "Great is Diana of the Ephesians!" The whole city was moved; they rushed into the theatre, taking with them two companions of Paul, Gaius and Aristarchus. Paul wanted to go there, but he was prevented. A Jew named Alexander tried to speak, probably in order to clear his race, but as soon as it was known that a Jew was speaking, the tumult redoubled. Eventually the town clerk made himself heard: for private matters there are the tribunals; for public matters a lawful assembly could be convoked; but this tumultuous meeting must be dissolved: "we are in danger of being accused of sedition."

"The scene described here," says Reuss in his Commentary on this passage, "is perhaps the most picturesque in the whole book; it has in such a high degree the *cachet* of psychological truth that it is clearly in each line the writing of an eye-witness." But if it merits attention, it is above all because it reveals to us the apostolic activity of Paul and its fruitfulness; when the Apostle had passed

[20] In the time of St. Paul, the most solemn feast, that of the birthday of the goddess, was celebrated on the 6 Thargelion (roughly, May). In 160 it was put back to the month of Artemision, in which the Panegyrics were already celebrated. Cf. Picard, *Ephèse et Claros*, pp. 323 *et seq.* This inscription of 160 will be found in the *Sylloge* of Dittenberger, p. 867. Cf. *Beginnings,* Vol. V, p. 255.

through Ephesus the first time in 52, he had found no Christians there (*Romans* xvi, 5); when he returned there the following year, he had met, besides Aquila and Priscilla, a dozen half-converted people; at the end of two or three years the progress of Christianity had been so rapid that the makers of idols felt their business threatened.[21] The friendly intervention of the Asiarchs (xix, 31) shows that Paul had won some of these high officials of Ephesus,[22] if not as believers, at least as friends.

So rapid and so extensive a penetration of Christianity was bound to lead to opposition; at Ephesus, as elsewhere, the Jews were against the Apostle, and had laid traps for him (*Acts* xx, 29); they found in the pagan multitude, with its interests, and above all with its passions, accomplices quite ready for a fight. From the year 55 Paul felt himself so endangered that he wrote to the Corinthians in his first letter: "If the dead rise not, why are we in danger every hour? Yea, by that glorifying in you, brethren, which is mine in Christ Jesus our Lord, day by day am I meeting death. If according to man I have fought with wild beasts at Ephesus, what doth it profit me? If the dead rise not again, 'let us eat and drink, for to-morrow we die.' "[23]

We have no further information about this first crisis: most probably it was not then dispelled, but merely lessened; the commotion made by Demetrius once more aroused men's hate, and put the Apostle in great danger. A few weeks later, he wrote thus to the Corinthians:

[21] Some sixty years later, the letter of Pliny to Trajan will display a similar anxiety: Christian propaganda was so effective in Bithynia that those who sold animals destined for the sacrifices found it difficult to meet with purchasers: *Epist.* x, 97. The Ephesian decree of the year 160 shows that the cult of Artemis was much endangered.

[22] The Asiarch was the high priest of the worship of Rome and Augustus, and the President of the Provincial Assembly; he was elected for one year, but retained his title during his lifetime. Cf. Chapot, *op. cit.*, pp. 468-89; Guiraud, *Les assemblées provinciales*, pp. 97-106.

[23] *I Cor.* xv, 30-2. Starting from this text, the *Acts of Paul* relate that the Apostle had been condemned to the beasts at Ephesus. This account was published in 1936 from a papyrus. The tradition is reproduced in a Marcionite prologue to *Colossians*, Hippolytus *In Danielem*, iii, 29, and afterwards in Nicephorus Callistus, *H.E.*, II, 25 (*P.G.*, CXLV, 821); cf. Vouaux, *Actes de Paul*, p. 25. This literal interpretation is generally and rightly abandoned: if Paul had been condemned to the beasts, he would thereby have lost his freedom and his rights as a Roman citizen (*Digeste*, XXVIII, 1, 8, 4). On all this, cf. in *Revue Biblique*, 1919, pp. 404-18; J. Lebreton, in *Recherches de Science religieuse*, 1937, pp. 468-70.

"We would not have you ignorant, brethren, of our tribulation which came to us in Asia, that we were pressed out of measure above our strength, so that we were weary even of life. We had in ourselves the sentence of death, that we should not trust in ourselves, but in God who raiseth the dead" (*II Cor.* i, 8-9).

The Departure from Ephesus

Once more St. Paul had to bow to the storm: he left Ephesus,[24] as he had left Philippi, Thessalonica, Berea, Corinth; in the eyes of his foes he appeared to be a fugitive, but he was rather an indefatigable missionary who, leaving behind him established churches, went forth to found new ones. At the same time, it must be said that this church of Ephesus in which the Apostle had made the longest stay of all, disappeared henceforth from his history; the epistles to the Thessalonians, Philippians, and Corinthians bear witness to the vigilant authority which St. Paul continued to exercise over his disciples; but there is no epistle extant which reveals the same relations towards the Ephesians.[25] A few months after

[24] Several historians have thought that Paul was imprisoned at Ephesus, and that it was from there that he wrote the Epistles of the Captivity; see in this sense W. Michaelis, *Pastoralbriefe und Gefangenschaftsbriefe,* Gütersloh, 1930; Michaelis thinks that this hypothesis enables him to group together all the Epistles of Paul except the Pastorals, and that the former were all written in 54-5, so that there is no reason to speak of a development in Pauline thought. On the other hand, there would be a long interval between *Philippians* and the Pastoral Epistles, which would make their Pauline authorship more likely. These arguments are not convincing: there is no reason why we should not admit a progressive evolution of Paul's thought; and as to the Pastoral Epistles, the difference in circumstances suffices to explain the development of institutions. Finally, it would be very difficult to understand why the Apostle should have written so much during the years 54-5, and then remained silent during the whole of the remainder of his life. Cf. Juelicher, *Einleitung,* pp. 43-4, and the monograph of J. Schmid quoted above. The study of the Epistles of the Captivity provides no solid argument for this hypothesis, and many considerations are against it: Paul's silence in his discourse at Miletus, in *II Cor.,* and the silence of Luke: he was at Philippi, apparently, when Paul was at Ephesus, and when it is supposed that he wrote to the Philippians.

[25] We have a letter of Paul "to the Ephesians," but this ascription is not primitive: cf. J. Schmid, *Der Epheserbrief des Apostels Paulus,* Freiburg, 1928, pp. 37-129: "The community of the metropolis of Asia cannot in any case be the (sole) destination of the letter" (p. 46); and there is nothing in the letter itself which particularly concerns the Ephesians. Several exegetes have thought that there is in the Epistle to the Romans (*Rom.* xvi, 3-16) a note addressed to the Christians of Ephesus: thus Renan, *op. cit.,* pp. lxv-lxix; Reuss, *Romains,* pp. 19-20; Weiszaecker, *op. cit.,* pp. 331 *et seq.;* Feine, *Die Abfassung des Philip-*

his departure from Ephesus, when Paul went up to Jerusalem, he summoned the presbyters of Ephesus to Miletus; the discourse which he made to them manifests the deep affection which he had for them and they for him; [26] but it was a discourse of farewell. Very soon John was to come to Ephesus, and the churches of Asia would pass to his sphere of action. At the end of the first century, and also in the next, the Corinthians were still the disciples of Paul, whereas Ephesus was, above all, the city of John. [27]

§5. THE JOURNEY TOWARDS JERUSALEM

Paul in Macedonia

"When we were come into Macedonia, our flesh had no rest, but we suffered all tribulation; combats without, fears within" (*II Cor.* vii, 5).

The days which followed the departure from Ephesus were for St. Paul days of great anxiety: he was obliged to abandon, after many combats and trials, this church which he had founded with such difficulty, and to which he had devoted himself night and day for three years; also he was troubled about the Church of Corinth, which was also so dear to him, and which had caused him so much pain. Had it been won back by his letter? He did not know yet. He went first of all to Troas to preach; there also, as just before at Ephesus, a promising prospect opened out before him; but Titus, whom he had hoped to find with a message from Corinth,

---

perbriefes in Ephesus mit einer Anlage über Rom., xvi, 3-20, *als Epheserbrief*, Gütersloh. As an argument in favour, there is brought forward the personal relations which this note shows between Paul and twenty-six named Christians: how, it is asked, would he know so many in a church which he had never visited? It is added that Aquila, Priscilla, Epenetes are names of Christians in Ephesus. Sanday (*Romans*, pp. xcii-xcv and 421) replies that it is not surprising that Paul should know twenty-six people in Rome, and that he names them the more willingly because he was unknown to the Church of Rome as a whole. As for the three "Ephesians," it must be remembered that Aquila and Priscilla had previously lived in Rome. There remains Epenetes, "the first-fruits of Asia"; but that is certainly too slender a basis upon which to build the hypothesis of a note to the Ephesians.

[26] From the fact that Paul did not go to Ephesus in the course of this journey one must not infer (with Weiszaecker, *op. cit.*, p. 310) that the Church of Ephesus was estranged from him. The explanation of Luke (*Acts* xx, 16) is sufficient: Paul was anxious to get to Jerusalem.

[27] To-day the neighbouring hill still bears the name Ayasoluk. Cf. *infra*, ch. V, § 2.

was not there. He could not rest, and set out to meet him in Macedonia (*ibid.* ii, 12-13). There at last God comforted him: "God, who comforteth the humble, comforted us by the coming of Titus, and not by his coming only, but also by the consolation wherewith he was comforted in you, relating to us your desire, your mourning, your zeal for me" (vii, 6-7).

Never had Paul felt so deeply the "care of all the churches," his sorrows and his joys; and it is this poignant emotion which gives to this second letter to the Corinthians its pathetic tone; we do not find there the great doctrinal controversies which fill, for example, the epistle to the Romans; but nowhere else does the personality of the Apostle appear in so warm a light.

The Second Letter to the Corinthians

To understand the nature and bearing of the conflict, we must realise the opposition which had for so long been raised against him at Corinth. If we compare the opponents whom St. Paul combats in his letters to the Corinthians with those whom he refutes in the Epistle to the Galatians, the difference is manifest: we have here no anti-Judaising doctrinal polemics; the attacks which Paul has to repel seem to concern less his doctrine than his person. At the same time, it is clear that these attacks originated in Judaising circles. The replies of the Apostle are directed there: "They are Hebrews? So am I. They are Israelites? So am I. They are the seed of Abraham? So am I. They are the ministers of Christ? . . . I am more" (xi, 22-23). These last words give us to understand that these people boasted of Christ. Again, we read: "If any man trust to himself that he is Christ's, let him think this again with himself, that as he is Christ's, so are we also" (x, 7; *of.* v, 16). In all this we recognise most probably these "of Christ" mentioned in the first letter. In the interval they had, apparently, been supported and encouraged by an agitator from elsewhere; mention is made of this individual (x, 10); and of others also (x, 12; xi, 4). These intruders had produced letters of recommendation (iii, 1). From whom were these letters? We cannot answer this with certainty, but it is likely that these intruders had sought to claim authority from the "great Apostles," [1] as had been done by the Judaisers of Antioch and Galatia. They were false apostles, deceitful workmen, ministers of

[1] Ch. xi, 5; xii, 11.

Satan (xi, 13-15). Such grave accusations show certainly that it was not a matter of rival personalities, but indeed, as Paul says (xi, 4), of another Christ, another Holy Ghost, another Gospel.[2]

To press home their attacks more effectively, these intriguers did their best to discredit the Apostle: he was inconstant, and irresolute (i, 17), domineering,[3] a liar (xi, 31); he was accused of writing threatening letters, while weak in bodily presence, and not knowing what to say (x, 10); he was foolish (xi, 16), a deceiver (xii, 16-18); if he declined the support of his faithful, it was because he knew he had no right to it.[4]

The Apostle's Defence

This bitter opposition compelled Paul to defend himself; it called forth some of the strongest passages in the New Testament; and inasmuch as the Apostle's person was most directly involved, he appears in full relief in the brilliant light of the combat: the whole Paul is there, with his labours, his sufferings, and also his revelations. It is with reluctance that he makes known these secrets; this reserve itself shows us that they were for him the most precious treasures, but also graces which it was dangerous to publish, and which the soul ought to guard jealously as a secret between itself and God:

"If I must glory (it is not expedient indeed), I will come to visions and revelations of the Lord. I know a man in Christ who about fourteen years ago (whether in the body I know not or out of the body I know not, God knoweth), was caught up to the third heaven, and I know

[2] When Paul was faced by jealousies and personal animosities, his attitude was quite different; thus *Phil.* i, 15-21, speaking of those who preach Christ through envy and in a spirit of contention: "Whether by occasion, or by truth, Christ is preached, in this I rejoice, yea, and will rejoice."

[3] i, 23; cf. x, 8; xiii, 10.

[4] xii, 11-18; cf. vii, 2. All this polemic is set forth in the first seven chapters of the letter and the four last (x-xiii), chapters viii-ix being devoted to the question of the collection. Between the first part and the last we notice a difference in tone: in chapters i-vii, Paul displays a trustful affection towards the Corinthians, even when he is complaining of them, e.g. vi, 11-13; vii, 2-11; on the contrary, in chapters x-xiii we have a painful struggle against bitter opponents. It has sometimes been inferred that these four last chapters form a letter distinct from the nine earlier ones, and that this was written either before or after the other. This conclusion is not necessary. Cf. Juelicher, *Einleitung*, pp. 96-101, and Lietzmann, *op. cit.*, n. on x, 1.

such a man (whether in the body, or out of the body, I know not, God knoweth), that he was caught up into paradise, and heard secret words which it is not granted to man to utter. For such an one I will glory; but for myself I will glory nothing but in my infirmities. For if I should have a mind to glory, I shall not be foolish, for I will say the truth. But I forbear, lest any man should think of me above that which he seeth in me, or any thing he heareth from me. And lest the greatness of the revelations should exalt me, there was given me a sting of my flesh, an angel of Satan, to buffet me. For which thing thrice I besought the Lord, that it might depart from me. And he said to me: My grace is sufficient for thee: for power is made perfect in infirmity. Gladly therefore will I glory in my infirmities, that the power of Christ may dwell in me. For which cause I take pleasure in my infirmities, in reproaches, in necessities, in persecutions, in distresses, for Christ. For when I am weak, then am I powerful" (xii, 1-10).

These last words introduce us to the deepest aspect in the Apostle's doctrine. On the day of his conversion at Damascus, Jesus said to Ananias when sending him to Paul: "I will shew him how great things he must suffer for my name's sake" (Acts ix, 16). Twenty years had passed since then, charged for Paul with more painful trials and heavy burdens than he could have foreseen, but all these blows wounded him only in order to make Christ live in him and to enable him to communicate this life to other souls:

"We bear always about in our body the dying of Jesus, that the life also of Jesus may be made manifest in our bodies. For we who live are always delivered unto death for Jesus' sake, that the life also of Jesus may be made manifest in our mortal flesh. So then death worketh in us, but life in you" (iv, 10-12).

"For which cause we faint not, but though our outward man is decaying, yet the inward man is renewed from day to day. For our present momentary and light tribulation worketh for us above measure exceedingly an eternal weight of glory, while we look not at the things which are seen, but at the things which are not seen. For the things which are seen are temporal, but the things which are not seen are eternal. For we know that if our earthly house of this habitation be dissolved, we have a building of God, a house not made with hands, eternal in heaven. For in this also we groan, desiring to be clothed upon with our habitation that is from heaven, yet so that we be found clothed, not naked. For we who are in this tabernacle do groan, being burthened because we would not be unclothed, but clothed upon, that that which is mortal may be swallowed up by life" (iv, 16—v, 4).

The Letter to the Galatians

At the same time that this painful crisis was becoming less acute at Corinth, Paul had to face up to other opponents, also of Judaising origin, who had invaded the church founded by him in Galatia,[5] and had endeavoured, not without success, to entangle the new Christians in the practices of Judaism.[6]

To his disciples, once so devoted, Paul recalls the welcome which they ·had given him: afflicted by illness, the Apostle had been received by them as an angel of God, as Jesus Christ (iv, 13-14); till then they knew only gods who are not God; now they knew God (iii, 8-9); they had become his children and heirs (iii, 7); they had received the Spirit, they had suffered, miracles had been worked amongst them (iii, 3-5); they had run well (v, 7); now however all was upset; how speedy this change had been! "I wonder that you are so soon removed from him that called you into the grace of Christ, unto another Gospel" (i, 6).

To lead the Galatians astray Paul's opponents had attacked him personally, saying that he was not an immediate disciple of Christ. He replies by telling how he had received his Gospel, not of men, but by revelation of Jesus Christ (i, 11 et seq.). They had said that he was disowned by the great Apostles; he vindicates his agreement with them by giving an account of the meeting at Jerusalem (ii,

[5] We think that this letter was addressed, not to the churches of Lycaonia, but to the Galatians (cf. *supra*, p. 220, n. 7). Accordingly we cannot put this letter before the second journey to Galatia (*Acts* xviii, 23), or before the stay at Ephesus. Many exegetes think that this letter was written at Ephesus before the two Epistles to the Corinthians; Lightfoot prefers to put it between *II Corinthians* and *Romans*; in this case the letter would have been written from Macedonia or Achaia. Cf. Prat, *Theology of St. Paul*, Vol. I, p. 163; Lagrange (*op. cit.*, p. xxviii) leaves the question undecided between Ephesus and Corinth. It is certain that *Galatians* is prior to *Romans*; it seems to us most likely that it was written after the two letters to the Corinthians.

[6] Many exegetes think that the opponents of St. Paul were endeavouring to spread in Galatia a mitigated Judaism, holding that the Law was not indispensable for salvation but that it was a source of moral perfection. This interpretation would harmonise with the Decree of Jerusalem, but not easily with the Epistle: the Judaism preached in Galatia appears therein as an extreme and virulent Judaism; there is question not of privileges or of perfection, but of salvation. Cf. Lagrange, *op. cit.*, pp. xxxviii-xlv.

1-10). Lastly, he was reproached for inconsistency; alluding perhaps to his circumcision of Timothy, he was accused of preaching circumcision when with the Jews: "If I yet preach circumcision, why do I yet suffer persecution?" (v, 11; cf. i, 10).

After thus upsetting the Galatians by these attacks against St. Paul, the false apostles had endeavoured to seduce them: the yoke of the Law might attract them because it imposed on them material observances similar to those which they had previously practised, "days and months, and times and years" (iv, 10); they were told that circumcision alone would ensure for them the inheritance of the promises, they had been made to fall from grace inasmuch as they had been taught to seek for justification in the Law (v, 4). One can understand that this teaching could win a good number of these ardent new Christians who were as yet not properly instructed; they were persuaded that they were as yet only half children of God, and that these new masters were leading them beyond Paul to Jesus, and beyond Jesus to Moses and Abraham. Besides the prestige of ancient doctrine and the attraction of Jewish rites, they were subjected to the fear of persecution: circumcision would keep them from this by giving them the safeguard of Jewish privileges (vi, 12).

To rescue them from this propaganda, Paul preaches to them the Cross of Christ; this had been his first preaching: he had set before their eyes Jesus Christ crucified (iii, 1). He returns to this in his epistle with passionate insistence:

"I am dead to the Law that I may live to God: with Christ I am nailed to the Cross. And I live, now not I, but Christ liveth in me. And if I live now in the flesh: I live in the faith of the Son of God, who loved me and delivered himself for me (ii, 19-20).

"They that are Christ's have crucified their flesh, with the vices and concupiscences" (v, 2).

After dictating his letter, he adds to it these last words:

"See what large letters I am writing to you with my own hand. As many as desire to please in the flesh, they constrain you to be circumcised, only that they may not suffer persecution for the cross of Christ. For neither they themselves who are circumcised keep the law, but they will have you to be circumcised that they may glory in your flesh. But God forbid that I should glory, save in the cross of our Lord Jesus Christ, by whom the world is crucified to me, and I to the world. For in Christ Jesus neither circumcision availeth anything, nor uncircumcision, but a new creature. And whosoever shall follow this rule, peace on them, and mercy, and upon the Israel of God. From henceforth let no man be troublesome to me, for I bear the marks of the Lord Jesus in my body" (vi, 11-17).

The Christian liberty which Christ consecrated by his Cross is the whole theme of this epistle. In his letter to the Romans, St. Paul takes it up again and enlarges upon it: there he will reveal the great perspectives of the salvation of the world and of the Christian life, but addressing himself to a church which he had neither founded nor visited, he will not write his letter in the tone of paternal tenderness which makes the Epistle to the Galatians so moving: "My little children, of whom I am in labour again, until Christ be formed in you" (iv, 19). Of all the letters of St. Paul there is none which makes us understand better the first years of Christianity, or that makes more vivid and actual the preaching of the Apostle.[7]

The Letter to the Romans

The letter to the Romans,[8] much richer than the Epistle to the Galatians in dogmatic teaching, is poorer in historical information, and this is easy to understand, for the church to which Paul addresses his letter had neither been founded nor visited by him.[9] Several times Paul had wanted to go to Rome;[10] his apostolate covered all the Gentiles, and the Romans in consequence; but he had abstained from treading in the footsteps of others; hence he could not go to preach in Rome.[11] In order to keep to this rule and yet not to fail in what he owed to the Romans, Paul thought of going to Spain, seeing the Romans *en route* (*Rom.* xv, 23). For he

[7] Loisy (*Lettre aux Galates*, Paris, 1916) thus ends his introduction: "The critical analysis of our epistle will help us to penetrate not only the secret of primitive Christian history, but also that of the very special ferment from which sprang the ideas which were destined to constitute eventually the substance of Christian dogma." This impression is correct, provided one recognises in this "ferment" the divine inspiration which revealed Christian dogma.

[8] This letter was written from Corinth in the course of the winter of 56-7.

[9] On the origin of the Roman Church, cf. *infra*, ch. iv.

[10] *Acts* xix, 21; *Rom.* i, 11-15; xv, 23.

[11] *Rom.* xv, 20-22; cf. *II Cor.* x, 15-16. At Ephesus Paul had had no scruple at preaching after Apollos, or even after Aquila and Priscilla; these preachers had made Christ known, but had not founded a church; at Rome the situation was different.

considered that he had "no more place" in the East, inasmuch as he had spread abroad the Gospel from Jerusalem as far as Illyricum (xv, 19). The communities thus founded would grow, and the West was calling him. God had in reserve for him an opportunity of evangelising Rome which he could not yet foresee: He would say to him later on: "As thou hast testified of me in Jerusalem, so must thou bear witness also at Rome" (*Acts* xxiii, 11).

Meanwhile it was useful to remove the misunderstandings which might arise in Rome, either concerning this journey always desired and always put off, or above all as to the gospel of Paul. There was no urgent danger, but the enemies of the Apostle, active everywhere, might extend their intrigues to Rome, and it was important to forestall them (*Rom.* xvi, 17-20). Paul did this by taking up once more the theme of the letter to the Galatians, and developing its dogmatic teaching for its own sake, without direct reference to opponents who had not yet shown themselves. The circumstances were momentous: Paul was at Corinth, in land won by him; behind him the whole Greek world had been evangelised; before him was Rome and the distant West, and between the two, Jerusalem, where he went not without apprehension (xv, 30-33). He felt that this letter would perhaps be his testament; at least it closed a period in his life. It is the most fully developed exposition of the Gospel of freedom and adoption for which he had laboured so hard and suffered so much.

The Reign of Sin

The religious truth which he saw illumined the whole world for him: from the beginning, sin had entered into the world through the act of just one man, and death had entered as well (v, 12), and in the whole world sin reigns over the pagans and the Jews: "All are under sin, as it is written: 'There is not any man just' " (iii, 9). The pagans could have known God by his works; they had not recognised Him, they had not glorified Him, they had not thanked Him; and God, to punish them, had given them up to their shameful passions and to unnatural vices (i, 18-27); "and as they liked not to have God in their knowledge, God delivered them up to a reprobate sense, to do those things which are not convenient; being filled with all iniquity, malice, fornication, avarice, wickedness, full of envy, murder, contention, deceit, malignity, whisperers, detractors, hateful to God, contumelious, proud, haughty, inventors of evil things, disobedient to parents, foolish, dissolute, without affection, without fidelity, without mercy. Who, having known the justice of God, did not understand that they who do such things, are worthy of death; and not only they that do them, but they also that consent to them that do them" (i, 28-32).

Such is the pagan world, with its inexcusable impiety and its shameful impurity; will the Jew turn out to be more religious and more holy? He boasts that he is, but St. Paul continues the relentless examination:

"Thou art called a Jew, and restest in the Law, and makest thy boast of God, and knowest his will, and approvest the more profitable things, being instructed in the Law, and art confident that thou thyself art a guide of the blind, a light of them that are in darkness, an instructor of the foolish, a teacher of infants, having the form of knowledge and of truth in the Law. Thou therefore that teachest another, teachest not thyself: thou that preachest that men should not steal, stealest: thou that sayest men should not commit adultery, committest adultery: thou that abhorrest idols, committest sacrilege: thou that makest thy boast of the Law, by transgression of the Law dishonourest God. For the name of God through you is blasphemed among the Gentiles, as it is written" (ii, 17-23).

This terrible indictment does not make the Apostle forget the privileges of the Jews or the utility of circumcision (iii, 1); he proclaims it, and he will later on (ix, 4) recall that to the Jews belong "the adoption as of children, and the glory, and the testament, and the giving of the Law, and the service of God, and the promises, whose are the fathers, and of whom is Christ according to the flesh" (ix, 4-5). But just as the pagans who could have known God through his works did not recognise Him, so also the Jews, with whom God had made this alliance, were unfaithful to Him. Thus "every mouth is stopped, and all the world is shown to be guilty before God" (iii, 19). "There is no distinction, for all have sinned, and do lack the glory of God, and must be justified freely, by his grace, through the redemption that is in Christ Jesus" (iii, 22-24).

God's Mercy

Thus God's plan begins to be revealed: if He has allowed the whole human race to be involved in this catastrophe, it is that He may save it all. "God hath concluded all in unbelief, that He may have mercy on all. O the depth of the riches of the wisdom and of the knowledge of God! How incomprehensible are his judgments, and how unsearchable his ways!" (xi, 32-33).

These tremendous perspectives, in face of which man is confounded with fear and wonder, prepare the Christian to understand the mystery of his death and his life. Such is the centre of St. Paul's mysticism; these profound intuitions appear in several epistles, but it is in the letter to the Romans that they are most powerfully set forth.[12]

"All we who are baptized in Christ Jesus, are baptized in his death. For we are buried together with him by baptism unto death, that as Christ is risen from the dead by the glory of the Father, so we also may walk in newness of life. For if we have been planted together in the likeness of his death, we should be also in the likeness of his resurrection. Knowing this, that our old man is crucified with him, that the body of sin may be destroyed, to the end that we may serve sin no longer. For he that is dead is justified from sin. Now if we be dead with Christ, we believe that we shall live also together with Christ. Knowing that Christ rising again from the dead, dieth now no more, death shall no more have dominion over him. For in that he died to sin, he died once; but in that he liveth, he liveth unto God. So do you also reckon, that you are dead to sin, but alive unto God, in Christ Jesus our Lord" (vi, 3-11).

In this important passage we have the thought of the Apostle in all its force: Christ has died and risen; by baptism he unites us to his death and resurrection; under several different images St. Paul tries to bring out the great mystery of the destiny of the Christian: he was a slave of sin; he is going to become a child of God; he can do so only by being incorporated into the only begotten Son of God; Christ, in taking hold of him, unites him to His death and resurrection; He buries him together with Himself in death, in order to make him rise again with Himself to a new life.

This transformation of the Christian by baptism is in other passages described as a new birth;[13] elsewhere again as a purification, an ablution.[14] St. Paul prefers to regard it as a passing from death to

[12] On the mysticism of St. Paul, cf. A. Wikenhauser, *Die Christusmystik des hl. Paulus*, Münster, 1928, and A. Schweitzer, *Die Mystik des Apostels Paulus*, Tübingen, 1930.

[13] Above all in the discourse of Jesus to Nicodemus (*John* iii, 5-7) and in St. Paul's Epistle to Titus (iii, 5).

[14] *I Cor.* vi, 11; *Eph.* v, 26; *Titus* iii, 5.

life, and what he means thereby is not only a symbol, but a profound reality, which is seen by us first of all in Jesus Himself, "delivered up for our sins, and raised again for our justification" (iv, 25) [15] and is reproduced in every Christian: united to Christ in baptism, he is dead to sin and lives to God. Doubtless so long as he is here below, neither this death nor this life is perfect. While the inner man, the new man, delights in the law of God, he feels still in his members another law which captivates him in the law of sin. "Unhappy man that I am, who shall deliver me from the body of this death?" (vii, 22-24). He is saved only in hope (vii, 24), but "hope confoundeth not, because the charity of God is poured forth in our hearts by the Holy Ghost who is given to us" (v, 5).

This gift of the Spirit is what makes a Christian, and gives him life: "If any man have not the Spirit of Christ, he is none of his. And if Christ be in you, the body indeed is dead because of sin, but the spirit liveth because of justification. And if the Spirit of him that raised up Jesus from the dead, dwell in you, he that raised up Jesus Christ from the dead shall quicken also your mortal bodies, because of his Spirit that dwelleth in you" (vii, 9-11).

All this deep mysticism has its immediate echo in the moral life of the Christian: "Therefore brethren we are debtors, not to the flesh, to live according to the flesh. For if you live according to the flesh you shall die, but if by the Spirit you mortify the deeds of the flesh, you shall live" (vii, 12-13).

In this constant and intimate effort, our weakness is supported by the Spirit; we do not even know what to ask for, but the Spirit asks for us with unspeakable groanings, and God who searcheth hearts knows what the Spirit desires, for the Spirit pleads before God for the saints (viii, 26-27).

Lastly, we are not alone: the whole creation groans, it is in travail (viii, 22), aroused by the expectation of a new life. Thus is revealed to us the unity of humanity and the world: everything in it was wounded and blighted by sin, everything is restored under the action of Christ and leads towards God.

God as Beginning and End

God is the beginning and end of all things. Certainly, in the mysticism of St. Paul Christ is in the foreground, but that is as

[15] Cf. Prat. *op. cit.*, Vol. II, pp. 256-60.

coming from the Father and leading us to the Father. "God commendeth his charity towards us, because when as yet we were sinners, Christ died for us" (v; 8).

This infinite gift is applied to each Christian. by a special predestination:

"Those whom we foreknew, he also predestinated to be made conformable to the image of his Son, that he might be the firstborn amongst many brethren. And whom he predestinated, them he also called. And whom he called, them he also justified. And whom he justified, them he also glorified. What shall we then say to these things? If God 'be for us, who is against us? He that spared not even his own Son, but delivered him up for us all, how hath he not also, with him, given us all things? Who shall accuse against the elect of God? God justifieth: who shall condemn? Christ Jesus? He who died, yea is risen also again, who is at the right hand of God, who also maketh intercession for us. Who shall separate us from the love of Christ? . . . I am sure that neither death, nor life, nor angels, nor principalities, nor powers, nor things present, nor things to come, nor might, nor height, nor depth, nor any other creature, shall be able to separate us from the love of God which is in Christ Jesus our Lord" (vii, 29-39).

All the mysticism of St. Paul appears in this glowing passage, and not only, as it has been said,[16] Christological mysticism, but also Divine mysticism. Indeed, the two are inseparable, it is in Christ our Lord that we attain to God, but we really attain to Him, and the terminus of this gradual transformation which the life of Christ brings about in the Christian is God all in all (I Cor. xv, 28).

Paul Leaves for Jerusalem

Leaving Corinth, where he had written this letter,[17] Paul went to Jerusalem to hand in the alms he had gathered. For a long time

---

[16] Schweitzer, op. cit., p. 3: "In Paul there is no Divine mysticism, but only the mysticism of Christ by which man enters into relation with God."

[17] Of these few months, spent by Paul in Macedonia and Achaia, we know hardly anything: "Paul set forward to go into Macedonia. And when he had gone over those parts, and had exhorted them with many words, he came into Greece. There he spent three months. The Jews laid wait for him as he was about to sail into Syria, so he took a resolution to return through Macedonia" (Acts xx, 1-3). In his Epistle to Titus (i, 5), Paul mentions a stay he made in Crete; it has been conjectured that this belongs to this time, after the departure from Macedonia and before the arrival in Corinth (MacGiffert, Christianity in the Apostolic Age, p. 411); but we can also put it in the last years of the Apostle, after his captivity

he had prepared this collection.[18] There is nothing more moving than these efforts of the Apostle on behalf of the church of Jerusalem from which so many opponents had come in the past; he hoped that such a display of charity would touch the brethren, and at the same time he regarded it as a work of justice in favour of the saints who had been the first-fruits of the Gospel.[19] Such generous efforts were not sterile: Paul set forth for Jerusalem laden with the offerings of his Christians, and accompanied by representatives of the churches (*Acts* xx, 4).

Nevertheless he was anxious: he wondered how the unconverted would receive him at Jerusalem, and whether the saints themselves would accept his offerings; he begged the prayers of the Romans to this end (xv, 31). These fears were not groundless; from the start he met with traps laid by the Jews; in order to avoid them he had to abandon the projected route, and enter Syria by Macedonia (*Acts* xx, 3).

Paul and the Church at Jerusalem

Before we follow Paul to Jerusalem, we should like to know the history of this church during the years which preceded this journey. Unfortunately this history is very obscure: Luke follows Paul, and speaks of Jerusalem only when the Apostle returns there. Nevertheless, a few facts are known to us: from the persecution under

(Prat, *Saint Paul*, p. 186). The extended stay which Paul made at Corinth and the tone of his letter to the Romans show that he no longer felt around him the opposition which he had encountered previously: the cause was won. Later, when St. Clement wrote to the Corinthians, he bears witness to the veneration which their church kept for its founder (xlvii).

[18] "Concerning the collections that are made for the saints, as I have given order to the churches of Galatia, so do ye also. On the first day of the week let every one of you put apart with himself, laying up what it shall well please him" (*I Cor.* xvi, 1). In his second letter he returns to this subject with more insistence, rousing the emulation of the different churches, promising that, if the offering should be worth it, he would go himself to take it: he put before the Corinthians the example of the churches of Macedonia (viii, 1-5); and on the other hand he wrote to them: "I know your forward mind, for which I boast of you to the Macedonians, that Achaia also is ready from the year past, and your emulation hath provoked very many" (*II Cor.* ix, 2).

[19] "Now I shall go to Jerusalem, to minister unto the saints. For it hath pleased them of Macedonia and Achaia to make a contribution for the poor of the saints that are in Jerusalem. For it hath pleased them, and they are their debtors. For if the Gentiles have been made partakers of their spiritual things, they ought also in carnal things to minister to them" (*Rom.* xv, 25-7; cf. *Gal.* vi, 6; *II Cor.* ix, 12-14).

Agrippa until the death of James, the Lord's brother, the Church was at peace. This truce of twenty years (42-62) was doubtless ensured by the Roman administration, which had once more taken in hand the government of Judea; it was due also to the respect which the Christians of Jerusalem had for the Law. When Paul arrived at Jerusalem, James said to him: "Thou seest, brother, how many thousands there are among the Jews that have believed, and they are all zealous for the Law" (*Acts* xxi, 20). The portrait of James given by Hegesippus [20] presents him as the ideal of fidelity to the Law. It is possible that the liberties granted to the Gentiles by the Decree of Jerusalem led converted Jews to a more exact observance; they were also aware of Paul's action amongst the pagans; the best amongst them rejoiced at it; others did not oppose it; all at least decided to show, in the holy city, the alliance between the Gospel and the Law.

Amongst the Christians at Jerusalem, all could not share the sympathetic trust which the Apostles and the elders had displayed for St. Paul; there were even some who were not able to maintain the reserve which they should at least have shown: it was members of this Church who went to Antioch, upset the converted pagans, and sought to intimidate Paul and Barnabas (*Acts* xv, 1 *et seq.*). It was also probably from thence that the false brethren came who threatened the work of Paul in Galatia, and those "of Christ" who fostered the divisions at Corinth. They do not seem to have undertaken any mission of evangelisation, but they followed the Apostle and countered his activity. The fact that they appealed directly to Christ and above all the distinction between those "of Christ" and those "of Cephas" shows that they could not claim the support of the Apostles; nevertheless they did not fail to oppose these to Paul.

Faced with these intrigues, Paul had to vindicate his independence, and his immediate mission from Our Lord (*Gal.* i, 1, 11-12).[21] He recognised that he was one born out of due time, unworthy to be called an apostle because he had persecuted the Church of God, but he added with humble pride: "By the grace of God I am what I am, and his grace in me hath not been void, but I have laboured more abundantly than all they: yet not I, but the grace of God with me: for whether I, or they, so we preach, and so you have believed"

[20] Cf. *infra*, ch. v, § 1.
[21] Hence also the impatience with which he speaks of these "pillars" (*Gal.* ii, 9), these "great apostles" (*II Cor.* xi, 5; xii, 11).

(*I Cor.* xv, 9-11). At the same time we find in this same chapter the faithful mention of the appearances of the Lord to the eleven, the first witnesses (xv, 5 and 7), and in the first place to Cephas, the chief of them all (xv, 5). Indeed, in all this epistle, the high place occupied by Cephas is clear: even those who exaggerate the weight of the Judaising opposition, and who see here, as in the Epistle to the Galatians, coldness and reserve on the part of Paul towards Peter, cannot deny the respect and the esteem which he displays for him.[22]

What we must insist on before all else—and it is a point of great importance—is that though divergences of opinion were displayed at Antioch, Jerusalem, or elsewhere, these discussions may indeed have raised the question of ritual observances, or again the admission of the Gentiles to salvation and the conditions which ought to be imposed upon them, but never were the Christological or theological dogmas the subject of debate: the preaching of the Gospel was everywhere the same, no matter who might be the apostle who set it forth. That is affirmed by St. Paul in the text we have just recalled: "Whether I, or they: so we preach, and so you have believed." [23]

What precisely these Apostles, and Peter in particular, were doing at this time remains very obscure.[24] It is certain that they also were engaged in missionary work (*I Cor.* ix, 5). Like Paul himself, they took care not to intrude on the fields of other men's labours; from Antioch to Rome we never see any of them with Paul. Certain historians accuse them of not supporting him against the Judaisers at Corinth or in Galatia; [25] that is to decide without proof a question which the texts do not enable us to answer. Moreover, it must be pointed out that Paul, who was so jealous of his apostolic independence, could not deliberately appeal to those whose authority was quoted against him, nor adduce in his own defence the steps

[22] Cf. Weiszaecker, *op. cit.,* p. 350.
[23] Cf. *History of the Doctrine of the Trinity,* Vol. I, pp. 288-9.
[24] Cf. *infra,* ch. iv.
[25] Two points seem certain to Weiszaecker (*op. cit.,* p. 349); "the apostles did not take part in the hostility towards Paul," and "Paul was not openly upheld by them." Lietzmann goes much further; he admits that in the Epistles there is no word against James or against Peter, but he thinks that "if we can read between the lines, we see behind the 'ministers of Satan' and the 'lying apostles' and the 'false brethren' the shadow of the great apostles of Jerusalem; Paul was isolated in his new Christian world, and he felt the worst of oppositions behind him" (*Geschichte,* pp. 108-9). It is dangerous to try to read between the lines.

which these might make on his behalf. On the other hand, we willingly admit that in the midst of so many conflicts, the attitude of the Apostle was admirable: the more he found himself opposed in the Judeo-Christian groups, the more jealous he was to maintain the unity of the Church, and to ensure his union with the saints in Jerusalem; and together with this care for union he shows the veneration, which he retained in spite of everything, for the community which had been the source of Christianity, and to which all the others were debtors. Thus the collection which he was carrying to them was not only a mark of fraternal charity, but a veritable act of homage.

In these circumstances we can understand Paul's fears. Going up to Jerusalem, he no longer asks as previously whether he had "run in vain"; his work was too evidently prosperous and blessed; but he did not know how he would be received by the Jews, and even by the brethren; he could not forget that his life had been often threatened by the ambushes of the Jews; but neither could he forget that the unity of the Church involved consideration for the saints of Jerusalem. And so he set out, and like Christ, he did so with a firm countenance, towards the fate that was in store for him.

The Journey

His companions went on ahead; he rejoined them at Troas.[26] On the Sunday, during Paul's sermon after the breaking of bread, a young man named Eutychus went to sleep, fell from the first floor, and was picked up dead; the Apostle went down and raised him up, and then returned to his preaching. They continued the voyage by coasting vessels from port to port, in order to arrive at Jerusalem for Pentecost. At Miletus Paul summoned the presbyters from Ephesus; after recalling his labours amongst them, he continued:

"And now, behold, being bound in the spirit, I go to Jerusalem; not knowing the things which shall befall me there: save that the Holy Ghost in every city witnesseth to me, saying that bands and afflictions wait for me at Jerusalem. But I fear none of these things, neither do I count my life more precious than myself, so that I may consummate my course, and the ministry of the word which I received from the Lord Jesus, to testify the gospel of the grace of God" (Acts xx, 22-24).

[26] It is here that Luke in his narrative returns to the "we" interrupted at Philippi (xvi, 16): "We sailed from Philippi after the days of the Azymes, and came to them of Troas in five days, where we abode seven days" (Acts xx, 6).

He thought that he would see them no more; he therefore gave them his final counsels: wolves would enter in amongst the flock, they were to be watchful. He commended them to God; for the last time he reminded them that he had asked nothing for his labours besides his upkeep and that of his companions: "It is more blessed to give than to receive." When he had ended, they all knelt down, prayed, and wept, embracing him, and saddened above all at the thought that they would see him no more. A moving scene which shows the close union amongst Christians, and the tenderness of Paul's heart.[27]

Paul and his companions thus continued their journey stage by stage. At Patara they found a vessel bound for Phœnicia; they arrived in Syria, then at Tyre, where they waited seven days. There the scenes at Miletus were repeated; the faithful begged Paul not to go to Jerusalem; being unable to dissuade him, they accompanied him to the shore, and all knelt for a common prayer. After passing a day at Ptolemais, Paul arrived at Cæsarea, where he stayed for some days with Philip the Deacon, whose four daughters were prophetesses. The warnings given previously were renewed still more urgently: Agabus, taking Paul's girdle, bound himself hand and foot, saying: "Thus saith the Holy Ghost: The man whose girdle this is, the Jews shall bind in this manner in Jerusalem, and shall deliver him into the hands of the Gentiles." All the Christians of Cæsarea and Paul's own companions begged him not to go on to Jerusalem. "What do you mean, weeping and afflicting my heart?" said he to them; "I am ready not only to be bound, but to die also in Jerusalem for the name of the Lord Jesus." They gave way, saying: "The will of the Lord be done!" (*Acts* xxi, 11-14).

§6. THE CAPTIVITY

St. Paul in Jerusalem

Going up to Jerusalem, Paul had a twofold fear: the refusal of his alms by the saints, and persecution by the Jews. The latter fear was to be realised; the former was not. Paul arrived at

[27] In his Commentary, Reuss has stressed the historic value of this discourse: "the most beautiful of all the discourses included in our book, and which, even in the abridged form in which it is given to us, reveals a depth of feeling and a conception of apostolic duty such that it admits of comparison with the most touching pages in the epistles. Everything makes us feel that we have here a summary made by an immediate listener."

Jerusalem, escorted by his two fellow travellers, a few Christians from Cæsarea, and a Cypriot named Mnason, who gave them hospitality. They were also cordially received by the brethren. The next day they went to the house of James, where all the elders were assembled together. Paul gave a detailed account of the success of his ministry amongst the Gentiles; they glorified God and said to the Apostle: "Thou seest, brother, how many thousands there are among the Jews that have believed: and they are all zealous for the Law. Now they have heard of thee that thou teachest those Jews who are among the Gentiles to depart from Moses, saying that they ought not to circumcise their children, nor walk according to the custom." What was to be done? There were in the community at Jerusalem four men bound by a vow: let Paul join them, and defray the expenses of all. The presbyters add: "As touching the Gentiles that believe, we have written decreeing that they should only refrain themselves from that which has been offered to idols, and from blood, and from things strangled, and from fornication." Paul agreed to what was asked.[1]

The Apostle, as he had recommended to the Corinthians (*I Cor.* viii, 9) took care that his liberty should not become a stumbling block to the weak; he seems to have attained his object; the violent opposition which he was to encounter came not from the Judaising Christians, but from the Jews. The seven days of purification were almost at an end when the Jews from Asia noticed him in the Temple. Thinking that he had introduced there an uncircumcised man, Trophimus of Ephesus, they stirred up the populace against him, and there was an attempt to put him to death. The Romans came up and took him away in chains; they thought at first that he was an Egyptian leader of brigands who had fled after the failure of his enterprise.[2] Paul explained who he was, and obtained permission to address the crowd; as he spoke in Hebrew [3] they listened

---

[1] Some exegetes reject the narrative in the Acts; thus Weiszaecker, *op. cit.*, p. 354. Others accept it, but regard it as a weakness in Paul: Reuss, *op. cit.*, pp. 208 *et seq.* What the Apostle was asked to do here he had done of his own accord at Corinth (*Acts* xviii, 18), and he had written to the Corinthians: "I became to the Jews a Jew, that I might gain the Jews; to them that are under the Law, as if I were under the Law, whereas myself was not under the Law, that I might gain them that were under the Law" (*I Cor.* ix, 20). On this condescension in Paul, cf. J. Lebreton, *Saint Paul*, in *L'Histoire générale comparée des Missions*, pp. 79 *et seq.*

[2] Cf. Josephus, *Antiquities of the Jews*, XX, 8, 6; *Wars of the Jews*, II, 13, 5.

[3] I.e. in Aramaic. Cf. Cadbury, *Beginnings of Christianity*, Vol. V, pp. 59-74.

to him. In this long discourse he gave an account of his Jewish education,[4] his opposition in earlier days to Christianity, his conversion, and finally the vision which determined his vocation as Apostles of the Gentiles: "When I was come again to Jerusalem, and was praying in the Temple, I was in a trance, and saw the Lord saying unto me: Make haste, and get thee quickly out of Jerusalem, because they will not receive thy testimony concerning me." Paul hesitated, it seemed to him that his past gave him a right to protest, and also he was moved by his love for his people; but the Lord insisted: "Go, for unto the Gentiles afar off will I send thee."[5]

These last words resulted in an explosion of anger amongst the audience; men shouted out, threw off their garments, cast dust into the air. The tribune, who did not know Aramaic, failed to understand what was happening. He ordered Paul to be scourged, but the latter said to the centurion charged with the order: "Is it lawful for you to scourge a man that is a Roman, and uncondemned?" The tribune, alarmed, had Paul brought in; the next day he put him before the Sanhedrin. Profiting by the hatred between the Pharisees and Sadducees, the Apostles set them against one another; the argument became so violent that the sitting had to be suspended. The next day more than forty Jews informed the chief priests that they had taken an oath not to eat until they had slain Paul. A nephew of the Apostle learnt this; he warned Paul, and, on his advice, informed the tribune Lysias also, who decided to send the accused well guarded to Cæsarea. Thus what the Lord had revealed to St. Paul the night before began to be realised: "Be constant, for as thou hast testified of me in Jerusalem, so must thou bear witness also at Rome."[6]

[4] We notice in all this speech the Judaic elements stressed by Paul, not only his education (xxii, 3) and his intolerance (4-5), but in the account of his conversion, the picture he gives of Ananias: "a man according to the Law, having testimony of all the Jews of Damascus" (12); the discourse of Ananias: "The God of our fathers hath preordained thee that thou shouldst know his will, and see the Just One, and shouldst hear the voice from his mouth"; and lastly the circumstances of the decisive vision at Jerusalem in the Temple.

[5] This mention made by the Apostle of his vision in the Temple reveals to us an unknown fact in his life (how many others there must be!), one of the visions summarily mentioned in II Cor. xii; it also shows us the inmost dispositions of Paul in the first days of his apostolate. This stay at Jerusalem is doubtless the one mentioned in Acts ix, 26.

[6] xxiii, 11. The coup aimed at Paul did not affect the Christians at Jerusalem; it was an explosion of anger against the Apostle of the Gentiles, not a general persecution.

St. Paul at Cæsarea

The procurator Felix, into whose hands the Apostle now came, was one of the worst governors Judea ever had. A freedman, brother of Pallas, he had been called to the government thanks to his protection, and as Tacitus says, "cruel and debauched, he exercised the royal power with the soul of a slave." [7]

The Jews did not abandon the struggle; five days later, the high priest Ananias arrived at Cæsarea with the elders and a lawyer, Tertullus. After a flattering address, they all demanded that Paul should be given up to them, since the crime of which they accused him came within the competence of the Sanhedrin. Paul replied that he had been guilty neither of sedition nor of disorder; he had been arrested in the Temple while carrying out the sacred rites of his religion; he demanded that his accusers, the Jews from Asia, should come forward themselves. Felix must have known about Christians, since there were some at Cæsarea. He adjourned the case. A few days later he summoned Paul in the presence of his wife Drusilla, and desired him to speak about faith in Christ. Paul did not satisfy his curiosity any more than Jesus had done before Herod, and his debauched court; Paul spoke "of justice, and chastity, and of the judgment to come"; Felix broke off the conversation, and sent Paul away. He kept the Apostle in prison for two years, calling him to him from time to time in the hope of receiving money.

Concerning these two years, the Acts tell us nothing further; [8] it is certain, nevertheless, that the prolonged stay of St. Paul in Palestine was not without fruit; it put the Apostle in personal and close touch with the Palestinian circles which were outside his domain and which he had scarcely touched hitherto; it also enabled St. Luke, the faithful companion of St. Paul, to gather at Cæsarea and Judea in general the tradition of the early disciples of Jesus. This was to constitute a source of inestimable value for his Gospel and for the whole Church. [9]

In 59 Felix was replaced by Portius Festus. The new procurator

[7] *Hist.*, V, 9; cf. *Annals*, xii, 54. Josephus judges him as severely as Tacitus (cf. *Wars of the Jews*, II, 13, 7; *Antiquities of the Jews*, XX, 8, 5, 162; XX, 8, 7, 177). He had married Drusilla, the sister of Agrippa II, daughter of Agrippa I.

[8] Some historians, e.g. Sabatier (*L'apôtre Paul*, 1896, p. 233), date the letters to the Ephesians, Colossians, and Philemon from Cæsarea; there is nothing to be said in favour of this hypothesis.

[9] Cf. *supra*, p. 222.

seems to have been an upright but weak magistrate. The Jews requested him to transfer Paul to Jerusalem; Felix consulted the prisoner; the latter, fearing the favour which the governor was showing for his opponents, and tired of the interminable delays in the case, appealed to Cæsar.[10]

The prisoner, under the guard of an escort commanded by the centurion Julius, set out for Italy. It was already autumn; the crossing was dangerous; when Crete was reached, Paul advised his companions to winter there; but they disagreed, and set forth. Hardly had they gone outside the port when the storm broke; for fourteen days the vessel, with all sails reefed, was driven before it, and ended by being wrecked on the coast of Malta. All this is narrated with an abundance and precision of detail in which we recognise Paul's companion. The Apostle is seen, although a prisoner, as dominating the rest not only by his supernatural gifts, revelations (xxvii, 23), and miracles (xxviii, 5), but also by his human qualities of prudence, decision, and firmness.[11]

St. Paul in Rome

Disembarking at Puteoli, Paul found some Christians there, and spent seven days with them, and then he left for Rome. Some brethren from Rome came to meet him at the Forum of Appius and the Three Taverns; "whom when Paul saw, he gave thanks to God, and took courage"; this was his first contact with the Roman community. Three days after his arrival, he called together the principal Jews and set forth his case, dissipating with his usual tact the suspicions which his appeal to Rome might have caused; he had done nothing against his people, or against the traditions of

[10] A few days later, Agrippa II arrived with his sister Berenice; Festus consulted him about the case; Agrippa was curious to hear Paul himself; Paul gave an account of his conversion, and his calling to the apostolate (xxvi, 1-23); Festus, not understanding anything of this, said impatiently: "Paul, thou art beside thyself: much learning doth make thee mad." Paul then appealed to Agrippa as a witness, and said to him: "Believest thou the prophets, O king Agrippa? I know that thou believest." The king, worried by the presence of Festus and the Jews, gave the reply: "In a little, thou persuadest me to become a Christian!" After a courteous and clever retort by Paul, they all stood up, and said he was innocent.

[11] xxvii, 10, 21, 31, 33. We may compare this journey to that which Josephus made three or four years afterwards (Life, 3): in 63-4 he went to Rome to take aid to some Jewish priests taking part in a trial before Cæsar; he was shipwrecked, arrived at Puteoli, had himself presented to Poppea by a Jew, Aliturus, and obtained not only the liberation of his friends, but also presents.

the fathers; he had not come to Rome to plead against his nation; lastly, "for the hope of Israel I am bound with this chain." These last words led to questionings, the more because the Romans knew that "this sect is everywhere contradicted." On the day they had fixed, they came in greater numbers, and from morning till evening Paul preached to them Jesus, basing himself on Moses and the prophets. Some were touched; others did not believe. To this resistance Paul opposed only this:

"Well did the Holy Ghost speak to our fathers by Isaias the prophet, saying 'Go to this people, and say to them: With the ear you shall hear, and shall not understand; and seeing you shall see, and shall not perceive. For the heart of this people is grown gross, and with their ears have they heard heavily, and their eyes they have shut; lest perhaps they should see with their eyes, and hear with their ears, and understand with their heart, and should be converted, and I should heal them.'

"Be it known therefore to you, that this salvation of God is sent to the Gentiles, and they will hear it" (xxviii, 25-28).

This prophetic warning brings to a close the book of the Acts.[12] This oracle of Isaias had been quoted by Jesus to the crowds in Galilee when He preached to them the kingdom of God in parables; St. John will soon recall it towards the end of his gospel (xii, 39-41); but this hardening of the Jews will not be without compensation; God will not be deprived of His glory; the message refused by Israel will be received by the Gentiles.[13]

The Prisoner of Christ

The captivity of St. Paul at Rome continued for two years. He was not shut up in the public prison; he was allowed to stay in a

[12] St. Luke adds only a word or two to say that Paul thus spent two years in Rome, preaching the Lord Jesus without prohibition. This abrupt ending has caused much comment. We may say with Père Boudou (*op. cit.*, p. 567): "The best explanation would seem to be that Luke knew nothing further. He arrived at the same time at the end of his roll, and the close of the events which had been going on before his eyes." He adds: "He had aimed at showing the expansion of Christianity as far as the ends of the earth." Lake emphasises this last point: "It was enough for the author to have conducted Paul to Rome to bear witness to the Gospel. His last sentence is a song of triumph in his chains. It is not a sentence written by chance. It was rather the conclusion deliberately chosen by the author." Cf. *infra*, p. 278, n. 1.

[13] These last words likewise constitute an echo of the gospel and the apostolic preaching (*Acts* xiii, 46-8).

house which he had hired (*Acts* xxviii, 30), but he was loaded with chains; [14] he was linked to a soldier who left him neither day nor night; he could no longer go about; when he wished to give explanations to the Jews he had to call them to him. All this was obviously not only a great trial but also a great hindrance; there was no more preaching in the synagogues, no more of those visits to houses which he had so often made. On the other hand, this "prisoner of Christ" acquired a new authority; his mission was no longer discussed or countered as it had been; at the price of his liberty he had purchased the liberation of the pagans. [15] Moreover, at Rome his captivity proved to be to the advantage of the Gospel. All the soldiers who successively were appointed to guard him, and were witnesses of his conversations and of his whole manner of life, came to know Christ: "throughout the whole prætorian guard and everywhere else it is known that it is for Christ that I am in bonds" (*Philippians*, i, 13). The Roman Christians were encouraged by his bonds, and spoke with more assurance in consequence (*ibid.* 14); certainly there were some who preached out of envy; but this did not matter, so long as Christ was preached (15-18). We see by this that opposition displayed itself even at Rome (*cf.* iii, 2); but it showed itself in an emulation in preaching rather than in direct attacks.

There were some faithful friends grouped around the prisoner: Luke, his fellow traveller, his "beloved physician," soon to become his historian; [16] Timothy, his most dear disciple, already intimately associated with his labours, [17] soon to be charged with heavy pastoral responsibilities; "Mark, cousin to Barnabas," who had once been separated from Paul by a slight disagreement, but now was again his "helper"; [18] then some representatives of the churches of Macedonia and Asia: Aristarchus of Thessalonica, who but lately had shared the danger of Paul at Ephesus [19] and now shared his captivity in Rome; [20] from Colossa had come Epaphras, himself also

[14] As at Cæsarea (xxvi, 29) so at Rome (xxviii, 17, 20); *Philemon*, i, 9, 10, 13; *Phil.* i, 7, 13, 14, 17; *Coloss.* iv, 3, 18; *Ephes.* vi, 20.

[15] Cf. A. Robinson, *Ephesians*, p. 10, and on this captivity at Rome, Lightfoot, *Philippians*, pp. 1-29.

[16] *Coloss.* iv, 14; *Philem.*, 24.

[17] Thus he appears together with Paul in the salutations addressed to the Colossians and the Philippians.

[18] *Coloss.* iv, 10; *Philem.*, 24.

[19] *Acts* xix, 29.

[20] *Coloss.* iv, 10.

a companion in Paul's captivity; [21] from Ephesus Tychicus; [22] from Philippi, Epaphroditus. The latter had come to Rome, bringing to Paul the aid sent to him by his faithful Philippians; he would have liked to devote himself to the service of the Apostle, but his strength was not equal to his devotion; he fell gravely ill, and his life was in danger; "but God had mercy on him, and not only on him, but on me also, lest I should have sorrow upon sorrow; therefore I sent him the more speedily, that seeing him again you may rejoice, and I may be without sorrow." [23]

Thus this lengthy trial had not loosened the bonds which united the Apostle to the churches he had founded; Paul saw hastening to him from the far-off provinces of Greece and Asia disciples whose filial tenderness was now penetrated with a new veneration for the prisoner of Christ. It was thus that the disciples of John the Baptist had gathered round him in his prison at Machaerus; in the same way during the three next centuries the confessors will see their brethren in the faith hastening to their dungeons to serve and venerate them.

The Epistles of the Captivity

To this veneration and these services Paul replies by letters. To the Philippians he sends his thanks and his counsels. [24] To the Colossians, threatened by a Judaising gnosis, he gives urgent warnings. [25] To the Christians of the churches of Asia he sends doctrinal instructions bearing chiefly on the mystery of Christ and the Church. [26] These letters, and especially the two last, do not put before us the Apostle and his churches in vivid descriptions such as those which we read in the epistles to the Corinthians or the Galatians but they set forth a theology, the wide perspectives of which shine with a peaceful and warm light. Thus, to encourage the Philippians to cultivate Christian humility, Paul puts before them the example of Christ:

"Being in the form of God, he thought it not robbery to be equal with God, but emptied himself, taking the form of a servant, being made in

[21] *Philem.*, 23.
[22] *Coloss.* iv, 7; *Ephes.* vi, 21.
[23] *Philipp.* ii, 25-30; iv, 14-18.
[24] *Supra*, p. 222.
[25] *Bk. II.*, ch. vi, § 3.
[26] This is the epistle which was later on given the name of Epistle to the Ephesians; cf. *supra*, p. 252, n. 25.

the likeness of men, and in habit found as a man. He humbled himself, becoming obedient unto death, even to the death of the cross. For which cause God also hath exalted him, and hath given him a name which is above all names, that in the name of Jesus every knee should bow, of those that are in heaven, on earth, and under the earth, and that every tongue should confess that Jesus Christ is Lord, to the glory of God the Father." [27]

In order to turn away the Colossians from the ambitious and perverse speculations which were threatening their faith, the Apostle sets before them the dogma of the universal mediation of Christ, and His transcendence:

"God hath delivered us from the power of darkness, and hath translated us into the kingdom of the Son of his love, in whom we have redemption through his blood, the remission of sins; who is the image of the invisible God, the firstborn before every creature. For in him were all things created in heaven and on earth, visible and invisible, whether thrones, or dominations, or principalities, or powers: all things were created by him and in him, and he is before all, and by him all things consist. And he is the head of the body, the Church, who is the beginning, the firstborn from the dead, that in all things he may hold the primacy; because in him it hath well pleased the Father that all fullness should dwell, and through him to reconcile all things unto himself, making peace through the blood of his cross, both as to the things that are on earth, and the things that are in heaven." [28]

In the Epistle to the Ephesians he sets forth as a whole the theology of the Church, the body of Christ, which he had already sketched out in strong lines in the Epistle to the Corinthians (I, xii, 12-27):

"Christ gave some Apostles, and some prophets, and other some evangelists, and other some pastors and doctors, for the perfecting of the saints, for the work of the ministry, for the edifying of the body of Christ, until we all meet into the unity of faith, and of the knowledge of the Son of God, unto a perfect man, unto the measure of the age of the fullness of Christ, that henceforth we be no more children tossed to and fro, and carried about with every wind of doctrine by the wickedness of men, by cunning craftiness, by which they lie in wait to deceive, but doing the truth in charity, we may in all things grow up in him who

[27] *Philipp.* ii, 5-11. Cf. *History of the Doctrine of the Trinity*, Vol. I, pp. 311-14.
[28] *Coloss.* i, 13-20. Cf. *History of the Doctrine of the Trinity*, Vol. I., pp. 297-302.

is the head, even Christ, from whom the whole body, being compacted and fitly joined together, by what every joint supplieth, according to the operation in the measure of every part, maketh increase of the body, unto the edifying of itself in charity." [29]

These splendid pages do not set forth a new revelation, but in them the Christian theology unfolds itself in light; it is all there: in the forefront we have the redemptive plan which saves all humanity, which calls the nations to share the inheritance, and which makes them into members of the body of Christ:

"It is by revelation that the mystery has been made known to me, such as I have written above in a few words. As you read, you may understand my knowledge of the mystery of Christ, which in other generations was not known to the sons of men as clearly as it is now revealed to his holy Apostles and prophets: it is that the Gentiles should be fellow heirs and of the same body, and co-partners of his promise in Christ Jesus, by the gospel" (*ibid.*, iii, 3-6).

Then above all we have Christ Himself and His "unsearchable riches": that is the Gospel which has been entrusted to Paul, "the least of all the saints" (*ibid.*, iii, 8).

At the same time that he sets forth these high doctrines, the prisoner of Christ intercedes for a fugitive and thieving slave: that is the subject of the note to Philemon, one of the most charming pages written by the Apostle's pen:

"If therefore thou count me a partner, receive him as myself. And if he hath wronged thee in any thing, or is in thy debt, put that to my account. I Paul write this with my own hand: I will repay it. . . ."

And then he expresses his hope of a speedy deliverance:

"Prepare me also a lodging. For I hope that through your prayers I shall soon be given unto you" (*Philemon*, 17-22).

§7. THE LAST YEARS

The hope which St. Paul expressed to Philemon was at last to be realised: after his long imprisonment which, at Cæsarea and Rome, had lasted four or five years, the Apostle was set at liberty.[1]

[29] *Ephes.* iv, 11-16. Cf. E. Mersch, *Le Corps mystique du Christ*, Louvain, 1933, Vol. I, pp. 119-23 (pp. 184-5 in 1936 edn.).
[1] Was the case terminated by a judgment of the Emperor? Or was the prosecu-

St. Paul in Asia

This deliverance, certainly anterior to the summer of 64,[2] was to enable St. Paul to make a last effort. We can hardly get a glimpse of it; now that the Acts no longer help us, we have to guide us nothing but a few scattered indications, combined with conjectures. For a long time the Apostle had wished to go to Spain (*Rom.* xv, 24); he seems indeed to have gone there.[3] Then he made a tour amongst his Christian communities in Asia and Greece. We can follow his path in the Pastorals: he left Timothy at Ephesus when returning to Macedonia (*I Tim.*, i, 3); he passed into Crete, where Titus remained (*Titus* i, 5); at Miletus he had to part from Trophimus, who was ill (*II Tim.* iv, 20); he went on to Corinth, where Erastes stopped (*ibid.*). He went to Nicopolis in Epirus, where he intended to spend the winter (*Tit.* i, 5). From thence he seems to have gone back to Asia, and to have been made a prisoner there.[4]

The succession of these steps is very uncertain. What we gather at any rate is the Apostle's intention. Time presses, his life is ebbing away; when a prisoner at Rome, he wrote to the Philippians: "If I be made a victim upon the sacrifice and service of your faith, I rejoice, and congratulate with you all" (ii, 17). Now the hour has

---

tion abandoned, in the absence of his accusers? We do not know at all. In favour of the second hypothesis may be mentioned an edict of Nero which has come down to us in a papyrus (BG-U, 628 recto, reproduced by H. J. Cadbury, *Beginnings*, Vol. V, pp. 333-4): in capital causes which are passed on from the provinces to Rome, the Emperor determines the lapse of time within which the accused and the accusers must present themselves: "et accusatoribus et reis in Italia quidem novem menses dabuntur transalpinis autem et transmarinis annus et sex menses." On this edict, cf. E. Cuq, in *Nouvelle Revue historique de droit français et étranger*, Vol. XXIII, 1899, pp. 111 *et seq.* The text, which is incomplete, does not say what will happen in case of default; we may believe that the accused would be sent away free. If this happened in the case of Paul, we understand why Luke did not mention a final judgment which did not take place. Cf. Cadbury, *op. cit.*, p. 335. We are thus led back to the hypothesis suggested by Lake (quoted *ibid.*, p. 328) to explain the abrupt ending of the book: "The result of the case was favourable to Paul, but such that it added nothing to Luke's argument, and was from this point of view a disappointment."

[2] Date of the burning of Rome and of Nero's persecution: if at this date Paul had still been at Rome he would have been one of the first victims.

[3] Thirty-five years later, Clement will write: "He went to the extremities of the West" (*I Clem.*, V).

[4] Perhaps at Troas, which would explain how he came to leave his cloak with Carpus, and his books also, which he asks for later on (*II Tim.* iv. 13). Cf. Prat, *Saint Paul*, p. 190.

come (II Tim. iv, 6). In presence of the imminence of the separation, his anxiety for the future becomes more urgent: all these Churches of which he was the father were going to be deprived of his support; it was necessary to see that they were taken in hand by faithful leaders who would maintain the work of the Apostle and of Christ.

For the rest, this care for organisation was not a new thing in Paul: he was eminently a founder. We have seen how at the end of his first mission he returned the same way, passing once more through Lystra, Iconium and Antioch to strengthen the courage of the brethren and to give them presbyters (Acts xiv, 20-22). When he left again three years later, his first desire was to "visit our brethren in all the cities wherein we have preached the word of the Lord, to see how they do" (xv, 36). We find the same preoccupation at the end of this journey, when, on passing by Miletus, he called there the elders from Ephesus, and urged them to watch over the flock under their charge, and to defend it against wolves (xx, 29). Now the departure he contemplates is definitive, and the wolves threaten. Thus the letters to Timothy and to Titus are as it were a testament: to his disciples, whom he had made his collaborators, and to whom he is going to leave a part of his heavy charge, the Apostle hands on the deposit which he had received, that they might guard it by the Holy Ghost, "who dwelleth in us." [5] Thus once more we find in the teaching of St. Paul these two essential and inseparable characteristics: authority, and the Spirit. There is a tradition, a deposit, received with obedience and faithfully handed on; and this deposit is living, animated by the Holy Spirit who through it communicates light and life to each believer and to the whole Church.

Prisoner in Rome

The second letter to Timothy was written from Rome. Paul was once more a prisoner there, but this new captivity was not like the first. The persecution which broke over the church of Rome in 64 dealt it a terrible blow. Those who were taken formed, in Tacitus's words, "an immense multitude"; the tortures which the criminal

---

[5] II Tim. i, 14; cf. I Tim. vi, 20. We shall return later to the Pastoral epistles, when studying the primitive hierarchy and the struggle against Gnosticism (Bk. II).

ingenuity of Nero invented for them terrified and revolted even their enemies. Stricken down by this barbarous assault, the Roman Church was silent; but it was not dead, as we shall see very soon. In the words of Hermas, it will become green again like the willow; but its life was dormant, as it were, for a few years; many Christians doubtless left Rome, and the others hid themselves.

This oppression and terror weighed heavily on those around St. Paul; he who was so prodigal in his devotion, and surrounded hitherto with such faithful friends, felt himself alone for the first time: "All they who are in Asia, are turned away from me, of whom are Phigellus and Hermogenes"; Onesiphorus at least had consoled him and had not been ashamed of his chains; at Rome he had carefully sought him and had found him; [6] "The Lord give mercy to his house!" (i, 15-18).

Towards the end of the letter we get the same impression, but its tone is even more sad:

"Demas hath left me, loving this world, and is gone to Thessalonica; Crescens into Galatia, Titus into Dalmatia. Only Luke is with me. . . . Alexander the coppersmith hath done me much evil; the Lord will reward him according to his works: whom do thou also avoid, for he hath greatly withstood our words. At my first answer, no man stood with me but all forsook me: may it not be laid to their charge. But the Lord stood by me and strengthened me, that by me the preaching may be accomplished, and that all the Gentiles may hear; and I was delivered out of the mouth of the lion. The Lord hath delivered me from every evil work, and will preserve me unto his heavenly kingdom" (iv, 10-18).

These eternal hopes are the only ones which henceforth support the Apostle; here below he expects nothing but death:

"I am even now ready to be sacrificed, and the time of my dissolution is at hand. I have fought a good fight, I have finished my course, I have kept faith. As to the rest, there is laid up for me a crown of justice, which the Lord the just judge will render to me in that day, and not only to me, but to them also that love his coming. Make haste to come to me quickly" (iv, 6-9).

[6] This feature reveals the great difference between the first captivity and the second: in the first, not only the whole Church, but all the prætorian guard knew Paul; now his most devoted helpers had difficulty in discovering his prison and joining him there.

Paul's Death

This letter, so full of sadness, hope, and affection, is the last which we have of St. Paul; the death which he awaited followed soon after, uniting him at Rome in the glory of martyrdom to him who had been at Jerusalem the first witness of his apostolate, St. Peter.[7]

The Epistle to the Hebrews

We cannot end this chapter without recalling a last echo of the Pauline theology in the Epistle to the Hebrews. This letter comes in our Bibles at the end of the Epistles of St. Paul, and certainly one cannot fail to recognise in it the thought of the Apostle. But on the other hand it displays a vocabulary and a style so different from his that it does not seem possible that Paul could have written it himself. Who was the actual writer? The early Fathers were unable to identify him;[8] we will make no attempt to do so ourselves.

For the rest, this literary problem is of only secondary importance; what is important is to recognise that this writing, inspired by God and received as such by the Church, reveals to us the thought of St. Paul.[9] To the speculations of an empty Gnosticism which dreamed of the glory of angels and failed to recognise the far

---

[7] It is impossible to determine exactly the date of the martyrdom of St. Paul. The succession of the facts as we have set them forth takes us to the end of the reign of Nero; Eusebius dates the death of St. Paul in the last year but one of Nero, i.e. in 67. This date is a very probable one, and is fairly generally accepted. Cf. Prat, *Saint Paul*, p. 194.

[8] Origen already wrote: "If I may give my own opinion, I would say that the thoughts are the thoughts of the Apostle, but the phraseology and the composition are of someone who is giving the teaching of the Apostle and, as it were, a scholar who is writing down the things said by the master. If therefore some church regards this epistle as Paul's, it is to be congratulated for this, for it is not by chance that the ancients have handed it down as being Paul's. But who drew up the letter? God knows the truth" (quoted by Eusebius, *Ecclesiastical History*, VI, 25, 13-14). More than one exegete has identified this redactor with Barnabas, and this hypothesis is preferred by Prat (*Theology of St. Paul*, Vol. I, p. 360), but he gives it only as a hypothesis.

[9] This Pauline character of the epistle was strongly affirmed by the Greek Fathers, who were nevertheless aware of the differences of language and of expression between this letter and all the others. Cf. Prat, *op. cit.*, Vol. I, p. 357. The Pauline character of Hebrews has been often established; let it suffice to mention the treatment in Prat, *op. cit.*, Vol. I, pp. 355-63, and our *History of the Doctrine of the Trinity*, Vol. I, pp. 332-43. It is certainly wrong to seek in Philonian thought the source of the theology of the epistle. Cf. *History of the Doctrine of the Trinity*, n. v, pp. 440 *et seq.*

higher glory of the Son of God, the Epistle to the Hebrews opposes the affirmation of His transcendental and truly divine glory:

"God, who at sundry times and in divers manners, spoke in times past to the fathers by the prophets, last of all, in these days, hath spoken to us by his Son, whom he hath appointed heir of all things, by whom also he made the world. Who being the brightness of his glory, and the figure of his substance, and upholding all things by the word of his power, making purgation of sins, sitteth on the right hand of the majesty on high. Being made so much better than the angels, as he hath inherited a more excellent name than they. For to which of the angels hath he said at any time, 'Thou art my Son, to-day have I begotten thee?'" (i, 1-5).

This transcendence of the Son above all creatures, and above the angels themselves, was the teaching which St. Paul had given to the Colossians, themselves menaced by Gnosticism; [10] and the Apostle showed them the Son "making peace through the blood of His cross, both as to the things that are on earth, and the things that are in heaven" (i, 20). Similarly in the Epistle to the Hebrews we have the "great high priest that hath passed into the heavens, Jesus the Son of God" (iv, 14). As high priest of eternal things, He has entered into the heavenly sanctuary, not with the blood of goats or of oxen, but with His own blood, assuring thus an eternal redemption (ix, 10-11); He is "the great pastor of the sheep, whom God raised again, covered with the blood of the eternal testament, our Lord Jesus Christ" (xiii, 20).[11] This new and eternal testament, which St. Paul delights to extol,[12] is described here with magnificence; it is indeed the theology of St. Paul; it no longer dazzles us by its brilliance, but it unfolds before us in wide paths of light.

Already at the end of the first century this high teaching was enshrined in Christian tradition; we shall find echoes of it in the letter of St. Clement.[13]

[10] Cf. *supra*, p. 276.

[11] We are reminded of the words of the Lord at the Supper: "This chalice is the new testament in my blood" (*I Cor.* xi, 25).

[12] *Rom.* xi, 27. Cf. Prat, *op. cit.*, Vol. I, pp. 385-7.

[13] Cf. Bk. II.

CHAPTER IV

ST. PETER AND THE BEGINNINGS OF THE ROMAN CHURCH[1]

ST. PAUL was the great converter of the Gentiles to the new Christian faith: Asia Minor, Thrace, Macedonia, Greece, and as far as the boundaries of Illyricum were won to Christ through his efforts; he had also made the Gospel heard in Rome and doubtless even as far as Spain. But the Apostle to whose name his own is constantly joined because quite early they appeared together as the two heads of the infant Church, St. Peter, the leader of the apostolic college, played in the original development of the Christian Society a part which, although not so brilliant, was nevertheless of the first importance: it ended in the founding of the Roman See, which was to become the visible centre of the Church.

§ I. FROM JERUSALEM TO ROME

The history of Peter after his departure from Jerusalem is little known. Only a few episodes emerge into the light; here and there we have some likely hypotheses; but we arrive at certainty again at the end, which was undoubtedly in Rome.

St. Peter at Antioch

The stay of St. Peter at Antioch after the Council of Jerusalem is beyond question. It was marked by an incident of great importance and consequence for the future of the relations between Judaism

[1] Bibliography.—We shall indicate in the course of the chapter, as they are utilised, the early Scriptural or Patristic sources, and the archæological data which give us information on the apostolic life of St. Peter and his final arrival in Rome. On this matter, the literature is abundant. The last upholder of the thesis, now almost universally abandoned, which rejects the Roman apostolate of St. Peter, is M. Charles Guignebert, whose works are also mentioned in the notes. The most important work in the contrary sense is that of Lietzmann, also mentioned in the course of the chapter. An excellent setting forth of the question, with illustrations from archæological monuments, will be found in Mgr. M. Besson's *Saint Pierre et les origines de la primauté romaine*, Geneva, 1928. (To the above may be added the works of the late Mgr. A. S. Barnes, and especially *St. Peter in Rome.*—Tr.)

and Christianity, but of less importance, apparently, for the history of the relations between Peter and Paul, who then met and were momentarily in opposition, than some have been tempted to suggest. St. Paul had not felt it possible to accept the kind of inferior place to which the attitude of the one who possessed the highest authority in the apostolic college seemed to relegate the Gentiles, and he had resisted Peter to the face. He had evidently won his point, for the passage in the Epistle to the Galatians [2] in which Paul gives an account of the incident does not allow one to suppose that it ended otherwise than in the acceptance by St. Peter of his point of view. But it has for us the great interest of showing at once the very special place held by Peter in the Christian community, since his attitude was of such importance in the eyes of Paul, and also the spirit which animated Peter at this period in the history of the infant Church, in which were being manifested tendencies which were distinct, if not divergent, and which time alone could bring together. The Jewish Christians, who had at least some difficulty in agreeing to the complete emancipation of Christianity from Judaism, and for whom the external observances still retained their ancient value, invoked James, the brother of the Lord; Paul represented the opposite tendency, resolutely in favour of emancipation. Peter, who, as is shown by the part he took in the admission of the first Gentiles to baptism and by the very reproaches of Paul set forth in the Epistle to the Galatians, was fundamentally of the same opinion, endeavoured to bring about a conciliation which was sometimes very difficult: the affair at Antioch showed that a moment had to come when it would be necessary to take sides. The spread of Christianity throughout the whole Roman world, and the progressive effacement of the element of Jewish origin in the Church, brought about very soon the success of the movement for freedom.

St. Peter in the Provinces of Asia Minor and in Macedonia

But it has been asked [3] whether the Epistle to the Galatians bears witness, not only to the coming of Peter to Antioch, but also to the existence there of a party inclined to strictness which boasted of Peter, and which the epistle aimed at combating. That the epistle

[2] Cf. above, pp. 214-16.
[3] Cf. H. Lietzmann, *Zwei Notizen zu Paulus*, in *Sitzungsberichte der preussischen Akademie der Wissenschaften*, Vols. VI-VIII, 1930, pp. 151-6.

attacks those holding a less broad solution of the question which had arisen between Judaisers and Christians of Gentile origin is quite evident; but that there was in Galatia a "party of Peter" is a conjecture which finds no support elsewhere. On the other hand, an indication, at least, that Peter went into Pontus, Bithynia, Cappadocia and Macedonia, as stated by Origen in words transmitted to us by Eusebius,[4] may be found in the fact that the first epistle of the Apostle was addressed to the faithful in these provinces. Even if this address was not his own work, it would bear witness to a very ancient tradition linking Peter with these lands.

St. Peter in Corinth

Still more sure is the presence of Peter at Corinth. The well-known phrase in the first Epistle of Paul to the Corinthians (i, 12): "I am of Paul; and I am of Apollo; and I of Cephas; and I of Christ," reveals that in the church in this city there were divisions, superficial perhaps rather than deep, which owed their beginning to the influence on the spot of the persons who are named, though they themselves may not have been responsible. Thus Paul himself is the first to protest against those who thus boast of himself. Hence we have good reason to think that, at the date when this epistle was written, about A.D. 57, Peter had already visited Corinth. In any case it would be difficult to doubt his visit, seeing that the legitimate inference suggested by the Epistle of St. Paul is corroborated by Dionysius, Bishop of Corinth, who towards the middle of the second century writes formally that his church owes its foundation to the Apostles Peter and Paul.[5] Further, Corinth was on one of the routes which Peter must have taken from Antioch to Rome, though we do not know any other stages. In any case we do not know what Peter did at Corinth. To infer from the passage of St. Paul just quoted that he had favoured a party of Judaisers there would be to derive from the text much more than would be allowable.

§ 2. THE COMING OF ST. PETER TO ROME

Hypotheses and Certainties

The same must be said of the hypothesis according to which the Epistle of Paul to the Romans, belonging to the same period as

---

[4] *Historica ecclesiastica*, III, 1.

[5] *Epist. ad Roman.*, quoted by Eusebius, *Hist. Eccles.*, II, 25, 8.

the first to the Corinthians, indicates a warning by Paul to the Romans against a Judaising activity on the part of Peter.[1] The actions and doings of Peter at Rome remain unknown to us. Two things only are certain: he went there, and after governing the Roman church he ended his apostolic life by being martyred there under Nero. As to the time of his arrival, we are reduced to conjectures. Still, the fact itself of the coming of Peter to Rome must be thoroughly established, seeing that it has been contested; these denials arose at the time of the Reformation through Protestant controversy against the Roman primacy, and have never since ceased; but we must at once add that the number of critics, even amongst those most opposed to Catholicism, who uphold this view grows ever less.[2]

Literary Testimonies

One of their main arguments consists in the affirmation that the tradition concerning the Roman stay of Peter depends on apocryphal works put in circulation in the second and third centuries, beginning with the legend of Simon Magus. But the mention of the presence of St. Peter in Rome in a certain number of apocryphal writings does not necessarily make this presence itself legendary; it proves merely that this sojourn of Peter was believed in at the time when these writings were composed. Besides, and this is the essential point, are there not other texts besides the apocryphal ones, or those which depend on them, which witness to Peter? Certainly there are such texts; they are numerous, and several go back to a time incontestably earlier than that of the apocryphal works.

Before quoting them, we must also point out that when in the second or third centuries there were conflicts affecting the Roman authority, no one ever put forth any doubt as to the apostolate, martyrdom, and burial of Peter at Rome. At that time it was the

---

[1] Cf. H. Lietzmann, art. mentioned above, p. 285, n. 3.

[2] Cf. H. Lietzmann, *Petrus und Paulus in Rom. Liturgische und archäologische Studien*, Berlin and Leipzig, 2nd edn., 1927. The latest denial worth mentioning of the coming of St. Peter to Rome is, in France, Ch. Guignebert, *La primauté de Pierre et la venue de Pierre à Rome*, Paris, 1909. P. Monceaux, *L'apostolat de Pierre à Rome*, in *Revue d'histoire et de littérature religieuses,* 1910, pp. 216-40, has written a critique of this work which has remained without serious reply. The *War Petrus in Rom.*, by K. Heussi (Gotha, 1936), is categorical rather than convincing in its negations.

general belief that Peter and Paul had their tombs at Rome, Peter on the Vatican Hill, Paul on the Ostian Way: this is stated, in terms hardly capable of a different interpretation, by the Roman cleric Gaius, a contemporary of Pope Zephyrinus (199-217), for he says that in these two places there are the "trophies" of the apostles. Eusebius, to whom we are indebted for this quotation,[3] does not seem to have thought for a moment that the "trophies" could mean anything other than their relics, or *memoriæ*.[4]

This belief is echoed by the episcopal lists of the Roman Church, which give the names of the first Roman bishops: the list called Liberian because it dates back to Pope Liberius in the fourth century but which is based on annals drawn up in 235 by the Roman priest Hippolytus; and the catalogue of Hegesippus, belonging to the second half of the second century.

In this same second half of the second century, about 180, the Bishop of Lyons, St. Irenæus,[5] one of the men of the time who was best acquainted with ecclesiastical traditions, is quite as definite in affirming the foundation of the Roman Church by the blessed Apostles Peter and Paul. In 170, Bishop Dionysius of Corinth, in the passage already quoted on the beginnings of his own church,[6] does not fail when addressing the Romans to remind them that they had the same founders.

We can go back further still, to the first half of the second century. The *Explanation of the Words of the Lord* made by the Asiatic bishop Papias of Hierapolis who had known personally some direct disciples of the Apostles, says that St. Mark summarised, in his gospel composed at Rome, the preaching of St. Peter in that city.[7]

We go a step further back, to St. Ignatius, Bishop of Antioch,

[3] *Historia Ecclesiastica*, II, 25, 5-7.

[4] Cf. P. Monceaux, *loc. cit.*, M. Guignebert (*La sepulture de Pierre*, in *Revue historique*, 1931) still tries to set aside this interpretation. But he does not seem to bring forward any positive argument in favour of his wholly personal view, which is on the contrary clearly weakened by an African inscription, that of the virgin martyrs of Thabarka, where the word "tropæa" undeniably means the relics of the saints, and by extension, their tombs; cf. P. Monceaux, *Enquête sur l'épigraphie chrétienne d'Afrique*, in *Mémoires presentés par divers savants étrangers à l'Académie des inscriptions*, Vol. LXXXVIII, part I, 1908, pp. 161-339, no. 260.

[5] *Contra hæreses*, III, 3, 3.

[6] Cf. p. 286, n. 5.

[7] Quoted by Eusebius, *Historia Ecclesiastica*, III, 39, 15.

martyred at Rome under Trajan A.D. 107. Writing to the Christians of the capital of the Empire, he says that it is not for him to give them orders like Peter and Paul (*Rom.* iv, 3). Certainly the affirmation of the Roman sojourn of the Apostles is not so explicit here, but the phrase would have little meaning if it did not presuppose it. The stay of Paul, established by the Acts, cannot be called into question; does not the association of Peter with him in all the preceding texts give to the argument the crowning force which might otherwise possibly be lacking to critical minds?

Lastly, going back before the year 100, and returning to Rome itself after having gone round the Christian world, we come about the year 95 to the testimony of St. Clement, the third successor of Peter, who must have known him personally. In a celebrated letter addressed to the Christians of Corinth in the name of the Church of Rome, which appears there already as a church whose word has a special authority, Clement recalls the martyrdom of Peter and Paul, and adds: "To these men, whose life was holy, there is joined a great multitude of elect ones who, in the midst of numerous tortures inflicted for their zeal, gave *amongst us* a magnificent example." [8] Would it be possible to state much more explicitly that Peter and Paul were martyred at Rome?

There is just one earlier statement [9] in favour of the Roman sojourn of Peter: his own, in his first epistle, written from Babylon, the symbolical name for Pagan Rome which we find also in the Apocalypse [10] and again elsewhere. [11] We need not give serious consideration here to the hypothesis, set forth by some writers nevertheless, [12] that Babylon here means the town of that name in Chaldæa, for this was then depopulated and decayed, and scarcely

[8] St. Clement, *Epistle to the Corinthians,* 5-6.

[9] We might also add to that of St. Clement the evidence furnished by the apocryphal work known as the *Ascension of Isaias,* which is anterior to the end of the first century. This speaks of a certain Beliar, who seized one of the Twelve. If Beliar is none other than Nero, as commentators agree, we do not see what Apostle other than Peter could be referred to, and his presence at Rome at the time to the Neronian persecution thus receives a supplementary confirmation. Cf. *Ascensio Isaiae,* IV, 3, edited by Tisserant, in *Documents pour servir à l'histoire de la Bible,* published under the direction of F. Martin, Paris, 1909, pp. 116-17.

[10] xvi-xviii.

[11] Cf. St. Augustine, *De civitate Dei,* XVIII, 2, n. 29.

[12] Cf. C. Guignebert, *La primauté de Pierre* (mentioned above, p. 287, n. 2), p. 182.

likely to attract St. Peter, whose name, in point of fact, is completely absent from the Christian traditions of those parts.[13] The Babylon in Egypt is equally unlikely.[14] Moreover, tradition, which is echoed by Eusebius,[15] places the composition of the epistle at Rome. But was it really written by Peter himself? Some critics like Harnack [16] have denied this, because they find in it a Pauline tone. But is not this suspicion inspired after all by the systematic conception of the permanent opposition between the two Apostles? The recollection, mentioned by Eusebius,[17] of the utilisation of the epistle by Papias, on the other hand, makes the ascription to Peter very probable. Some who have denied the Petrine authorship have put forward the name of Barnabas, which would again support the Roman sojourn of Peter by an apostolic witness of the first order. In any case, the critics in determining the date of this letter scarcely go beyond the period between the year 43 and the commencement of the second century.[18] Were it not Peter's, either directly or indirectly, the fact that its redactor in presenting it as Peter's puts it forth as written at Rome would retain its great weight.

Archæological Testimony

All written tradition, going back to the Apostolic period or its immediate neighbourhood, testifies therefore in favour of the historic reality of the presence in Rome of St. Peter, whose name is at the head of all the Roman episcopal lists, while no claim advanced by any other see opposes it.

[13] When Persia claims an Apostle as founder of its churches it is Thaddæus, or Bartholomew, or Thomas, but never Peter. Cf. Cosmas Indicopleustes (Migne, P.G., LXXXVIII, 113), and Vol. II.

[14] Cf. E. Smothers, A Letter from Babylon, in Classical Journal, Vol. XXII, 1926, pp. 202-9.

[15] Historia Ecclesiastica, II, 15, 2.

[16] Die Chronologie der altchristlichten Litteratur, Vol. I, Leipzig, 1897, p. 164, and Vol. II, Leipzig, 1904, pp. 455 et seq.

[17] Historia Ecclesiastica, III, 39, 17.

[18] The allusions in the epistle (iv, 12 et seq.) to the sufferings undergone by the faithful, and the threats against them, may refer to the persecution of 64. On this has been based an argument against the Petrine authenticity of the letter, for this persecution ended the Apostle's life. But there is no proof that between the first manifestation of the danger and the execution of Peter there was not time sufficient to enable him to write to far-off churches still dear to his heart. We must add, moreover, that the allusion to persecution is fairly general, and has not necessarily a precise historic signification.

Archæology confirms this testimony. An inscription called that of the *Platonia*,[19] composed by Pope St. Damasus towards the end of the fourth century in the catacomb of St. Sebastian on the Appian Way a short distance from the walls of Rome, recalls that St. Peter and St. Paul "dwelt" there,[20] and a *graffita,* an inscription written by hand by a visitor in the fourth or fifth century, also mentions in this place the *Domus Petri.*[21] Thus we have two local references, either to a sojourn of Peter himself during his life, or else of his body after his death.

The second hypothesis is supported by the indication in ancient itineraries,[22] which say that the burial places of the Apostles were for a time at the catacomb, and by *graffiti* which show that the faithful gathered often at St. Sebastian's to celebrate the *refrigerium* or funeral *agape* in their honour.[23] A feast of the Apostles Peter and Paul mentioned in two martyrological documents, the *Depositio martyrum* of the *Chronograph* of 354 and the *Hieronymian Martyrology*, which, indeed, seems to connect the institution with the year 258,[24] suggests an explanation of this transference to St. Sebastian of the body of Peter, who, according to the testimony—later, it is true—of the *Liber Pontificalis*,[25] had been first buried at the Vatican, where it was then replaced permanently.

This year 258 was that of one of the most terrible persecutions which ever ravaged the Church, that of Valerian. Would not the Roman Christians have decided to put beyond the reach of possible profanation or destruction the remains of their first bishop, and those of St. Paul, by giving them a home which they thought safer, in another cemetery far from the city, which seemed to them to be better protected?[26] Or, more simply, if these profanations were

[19] Corruption of *platona,* or rather *platonum,* a marble plaque.

[20] St. Damasus, *Epigrammata,* 26 (Edit. Leipzig, 1895; p. 26; Migne, *P.L.,* XIII, 382).

[21] Cf. J. Wilpert, *Domus Petri,* in *Römische Quartalschrift,* 1912, pp. 117-22; A. de Waal, *Zur Wilpert's Domus Petri,* in *ibid.,* pp. 123-32.

[22] *Notitia ecclesiarum,* in J. B. de Rossi, *Roma Soterranea,* Vol. I, pp. 139 and 141.

[23] At the *triclinia,* a meeting-place close to the tomb.

[24] III *Kal (endas) jul (ias)* . . . *Tusco et Basso consulibus.* The feast in question is therefore that of June 29th.

[25] Duchesne's edn., Vol. I, p. 118.

[26] Cf. the account by Mgr. L. Duchesne, *La Memoria Apostolorum de la via Appia,* in *Atti della Pontificia Academia romana di archeologia, Memorie,* I, 1, 1913 (*Miscellana de Rossi*), p. 7. To this dating and explanation of the sojourn of the relics of SS. Peter and Paul in the catacomb of St. Sebastian it has been

not really to be feared, would they not at least want to make certain thereby that it would still be possible to visit bodies of saints, which otherwise they could no longer honour, because of the guard placed by the Imperial authority at the burial places known as Christian? [27] In any case, this provisional transportation seems

objected that such a transportation of the bodies, above all at the precise period of hostilities against the Christians, would not have been able to escape the notice of the authorities, and would moreover have been useless, inasmuch as the catacombs and the Christian use of them was in no wise unknown to them. Thus P. Delehaye (*Le sanctuaire des apôtres sur la voie Appienne*, in *Analecta Bollandiana*, XLV, 1927, pp. 297-306) thinks that the *domus Petri* designates the residence of Peter when alive, and not his tomb, and he has no difficulty in showing that the martyrs were honoured more than once by religious monuments erected in places which were not their tombs, and notably in the places where they lived. But in this case how could we explain the celebration of the *refrigerium*, a funeral rite, at St. Sebastian? Perhaps it will be said that St. Sebastian's may have been the first burial-place of the Apostles. This has been maintained by, amongst others, K. Erbes, *Die geschichtlichen Verhältnisse der Apostelgräber in Rom*, in *Zeitschrift für Kirchengeschichte*, Vol. XLIII, 1934, pp. 38-92. The reference in the Liber *pontificalis* to the Vatican burial would not be decisive in a contrary sense, in view of its late date. But it is the condition of the places which causes difficulty, for the monuments of the first two centuries found in the cemetery of St. Sebastian are solely pagan. But if we accept the remarkably ingenious conclusions of M. Carcopino, *Lezingen en Voordrachten*, in *Bulletin van de Vereeniging tot Bevordering der Kennis van de Antieke Beschaving*, 1932, pp. 33-4, we may find the solution of the mystery: the second century tombs are those of followers of Gnostic sects, and the inscriptions mention amongst them numerous slaves and freedmen of the emperor. Now, though the Church warmly opposed Gnosticism, which was a complete deformation of the Christian religion rather than a heresy, the common threat to both in the form of the renewal of the Imperial strictures may have brought together Christians and Gnostics in measures of common defence, and it is not impossible that the Christians may have accepted, not indeed Gnostic hospitality, even momentarily, but their proximity, in order to safeguard their precious relics in land which seemed to be more likely to be free from police investigation because its owners or users were men well known at court.

[27] The explanation given above of the cult of the Apostles at the catacomb of St. Sebastian has indeed been opposed by other arguments: the respect of the Romans for burial places, and the severity of their laws in this matter, a new example of which has recently been found in the famous Nazareth inscription (F. Cumont, *Un rescrit impérial sur la violation de sépulture*, in *Revue historique*, Vol. CLXIII, 1930, pp. 241-66), was so great that the remains of the Apostles cannot have appeared to be in danger in their original tombs. This severity would on the contrary make it very dangerous to attempt to transfer them elsewhere, and the attempt would scarcely have escaped the notice of the police. In any case, the transfer would have been useless, as it would soon have become known. But to this we can reply that the Roman police, like that of most modern countries, were not incorruptible—the acts of the martyrs give many proofs of the contrary—and further, bodies interred already for two centuries must have been reduced to very little, and the transfer, not of heavy sarcophagi, but of two little boxes containing a few bones, could have taken place without attracting attention.

certain. The two bodies remained *ad Catacumbas* until the day when, after the definitive peace given to the Church by the Emperor Constantine, the latter had them taken back to their original tombs, in the Vatican for the one, and on the Ostian Way for the other, and over them were soon built great basilicas.

In any case, the discoveries made in the catacomb of St. Sebastian have, so to speak, given palpable proof of the reality of the presence in Rome of the bodies of St. Peter and St. Paul. And as there exists not even the shadow of an indication that they had been brought there from elsewhere, this presence, authenticated in this way by irrefragable material witnesses, is yet another proof that both Apostles ended their lives there.[28]

§3. ST. PETER'S RESIDENCE IN ROME

Duration of Peter's Stay in Rome

How long had St. Peter lived in Rome before his martyrdom? Here we must confess an almost complete ignorance. The so-called tradition of the twenty-five years of Peter's Roman episcopate rests on no historic data.[1] In any case, the Apostle could not have dwelt in the capital of the Empire continuously for twenty-five years, since his presence at the Council at Jerusalem which dis-

[28] One of the most recent historians of the commencement of the Roman Church, inspired certainly by no religious prejudice, H. Lietzmann, ends his study on the coming of St. Peter to Rome (*Petrus und Paulus in Rom,* p. 238), by these words: "To sum up, all the early sources about the year 100, become clear and easily understandable, agree with their historic context, and with each other, if we accept what they clearly suggest to us, namely, that Peter sojourned in Rome and died a martyr there. Any other hypothesis on Peter's death heaps difficulty upon difficulty, and cannot be supported by a single document. I cannot understand how, in face of this state of things, there can be any hesitation in accepting the conclusion."

[1] This tradition may have originated in a confusion. One of the earliest ecclesiastical chronologies, that of Hippolytus, sets forth the two persons generally regarded as the first two successors of St. Peter, St. Linus and St. Anacletus, as having already governed the Roman Church during Peter's lifetime and under his authority, and on the other hand it attributes to each an episcopate of twelve years; St. Clement, who comes next, is called the successor of St. Peter in this chronology, and thus we get the twenty-five years of Peter's episcopate. Cf. *Liber Pontificalis,* I, p. 118 (Duchesne's edn.), which adopts the tradition of the episcopates of Linus and Anacletus as having been contemporary with that of St. Peter. E. Caspar, *Die älteste römische Bischofliste,* in *Schriften der Königsberger gelehrten Gesellschaft, Geistesgewissenschaftliche Klasse, 2 Jahr, Heft 4,* 1926, has defended this explanation.

cussed the case of Gentile converts to the Christian faith [2] coincided with the year 49, and shortly afterwards, on the occasion of his disagreement with St. Paul, he was at Antioch, and lastly, neither the letter written by Paul to the Romans in 58, or the account in the Acts of the captivity in Rome (61-62) contain the slightest allusion to the presence of Peter there. On the other hand, the supposed meeting between the Apostle and Simon Magus in Rome at the beginning of the reign of Claudius (41-54) is related only by late authors whose historical accuracy is not beyond question.[3]

If, on the other side, we note that "when St. Paul wrote to the Romans, their Church was strong and flourishing," that in his eyes it must have had "a particular importance, since it was to her that he addressed his great doctrinal manifesto on predestination," we are constrained to ask if a Christian community which had already those characteristics could have been constituted, if not originated, "apart from the influence of an apostle." [4] As the Apostle could certainly not be St. Paul, who says expressly in his Epistle in the year 58 that he had not been able till then to go to Rome, it would seem admissible that Peter may have made a previous journey to Rome, before definitely fixing his residence there. But the proof of this point is lacking, and still less could we affirm that this first visit, which remains conjectural, took place twenty-five years before his death.

Moreover, the manner of reckoning the twenty-five years varies with the writers who have transmitted this estimate to us. The Liberian Catalogue makes Peter go already in the year 30, under

[2] Cf. above, p. 207 *et seq.*

[3] It is the historian Eusebius who, in the fourth century, relates in his *Historia ecclesiastica*, I, 14, not indeed expressly that Peter met Simon Magus in Rome, but that his preaching there put an end to the success of the magician. He refers here to the second century apologist, Justin, according to whom (*Apology*, 26) Simon was honoured at Rome as a god: he adds that a statue was erected to him in the island in the Tiber, with the inscription *Simoni Deo sancto* (*C.I.L.*, VI, 567-8). In point of fact, in this island of the Tiber there has been discovered a vase bearing the words *Semoni Sanco Deo*, i.e. "To the god Simo Sancus," an Etruscan divinity. The confusion is evident, and the whole story of the visit of Simon Magus to Rome may be baseless. True, there is also an allusion to it in the *Acts of Peter,* but this third-century work is a romance which is, if not of Gnostic origin, at least open to suspicion, and while it may have retained the trace of exact facts, it certainly could not itself guarantee their reality.

[4] M. Besson, *Saint Pierre et les origines de la primauté romaine*, Geneva, 1928, p. 66.

Tiberius, to Rome, and die there in 55. The impossibility of this chronology is evident: it is equivalent to saying that Peter went to Rome the day after the Passion, and that he perished there some time before the persecution started by Nero. Eusebius more reasonably puts the arrival of Peter in Rome in 42 and his martyrdom in 67. But the year 67 seems late, for the wholesale slaughter of Christians in Rome under Nero's orders took place in 64. Perhaps the poet Lactantius, who wrote at the beginning of the fourth century, is echoing a tradition more in harmony with the truth when he writes thus of the Apostles in *De mortibus persecutorum*: [5] "They scattered through the earth to preach the Gospel, and during twenty-five years, until the beginning of the reign of Nero, they laid the foundations of the Church throughout the provinces and cities. Nero was already in power when Peter came to Rome." Here the twenty-five years of Peter's Apostolic activity no longer refer to the time of his Roman residence, but only mark its end.

The Beginnings of the Roman Church

In any case, when Peter arrived at Rome for this last visit, he undoubtedly found a Church there. Even if we accept the hypothesis of a very early visit by St. Peter to Rome, and that he then organised the Church there, it would still be natural to trace the origin of the Roman Church to the "Romans" who were at Jerusalem for Pentecost, and thus the Church there would have originated before St. Peter's arrival. It would seem to have begun, doubtless very humbly, under Tiberius, and to have acquired a little more importance in the reigns of Caligula and Claudius.

Under the latter, about 49, it experienced a first crisis, which already gives us some idea of its progress: the Christians were sufficiently numerous or strong to bring about in the Jewish colony in Rome, as in so many other places, disturbances which led to the intervention of authority; the Jews, or, at any rate, some Jews, and, of course, with them, the Christians, who were not yet distinguished from them, were expelled from the capital. Such is the sense, impossible to call in doubt, of the well-known passage in Suetonius: *Judaeos impulsore Chresto assidue tumultuantes Roma*

[5] *De mortibus persecutorum*, II.

expulit.[6] *Chrestus* [7] is Christ, whom Suetonius, whose information is rather vague, regards as the head of one of the opposing parties. Another pagan witness long neglected, namely Thallus,[8] confirms the penetration of Christian ideas in Roman circles at this time.

The Acts of the Apostles, which tell (xviii, 2) of Christians, Aquila and Priscilla, obliged to leave Rome, and in consequence, being found at Corinth when St. Paul went there about 51 or 52, agrees perfectly with the statement in Suetonius. Dio Cassius [9] certainly says—and with great likelihood—that the general expulsion of the Jews turned out to be difficult to carry through, and that it ended in a prohibition of assemblies. But the example of Aquila and Priscilla shows that there were at least a certain number of expulsions. The truth would seem to be that the measures taken affected those Jews who had become Christians.[10] If Peter was already then in Rome, he must have been amongst those expelled.

These measures did not prevent the little group from being reconstituted and increasing, and when St. Paul a few years later, in 57 at the latest, wrote his Epistle to them,[11] the primitive

[6] Suetonius, *Claudius*, XXV, 4.

[7] A common confusion of Χρηστός with Χριστός. The Roman populace called the Christians *chrestiani*, as is shown also by the passage in Tacitus concerning the Neronian persecution, *Annales*, XV, 44. On the evolution of the name, cf. P. de Labriolle, *Christianus*, in *Bulletin Du Cange*, Vol. V, 1929-30, pp. 69-88.

[8] Transmitted in a fragment of Julius Africanus conserved by the Byzantine chronicler George Syncellus (*Fragmenta historicorum graecorum*, ed. Carl Muller, Vol. III, p. 519). Cf. M. Goguel, *Un nouveau témoignage non chrétien sur la tradition évangélique*, in *Revue de l'histoire des religions*, Vol. XCVIII, 1928, pp. 1-12.

[9] LX, 6.

[10] This, moreover, may be the precise sense of the phrase of Suetonius: "He expelled from Rome the Jews who (i.e. those of the Jews who), led by Christ, were the cause of continual agitations." It has been suggested that a letter of Claudius to the Alexandrians, known by a papyrus threatening in 41 severe penalties against the Jews who invited or received in the Egyptian capital co-religionists from the remainder of the province or from Syria, mentions Christians, describing them as "an evil which is spreading through the whole world." But in spite of the ingenious comparisons of H. Janne (*Un passage controversé de la lettre de Claude aux Alexandrins*, in *Revue archéologique*, series 5, Vol. XXXV, 1932, pp. 268-82), the terms used are too vague to justify such a conclusion, the weakness of which has been well set forth by W. Seston (*L'empereur Claude et les chrétiens*, in *Revue d'histoire et de philosophie religieuses*, May-June, 1931, pp. 275-304). He also gives a copious bibliography on the question. The text of the letter is given in H. Idriss Bell, *Jews and Christians in Egypt, the Jewish Troubles in Alexandria and the Athanasian Controversy*, London and Oxford, 1922. A French commentary on the letter by P. Jouguet is in *Journal des Savants*, 1925, pp. 5-19.

[11] On this date, cf. above, p. 259.

Roman Church was already "numerous, well known, and celebrated for its faith and its works." [12] We can also gather from this
same letter of Paul the nature of the elements which composed it:
as in most other cities, there had been added to the original Jewish
nucleus an already fairly large number of converted pagans; these
represented the future. But for a fairly long time the oriental
element must have prevailed over the strictly Roman element;
Greek remained, in fact, the official language of the Roman Church
down to the end of the second century, doubtless because it was
the language of the majority of its members.

Shortly afterwards, Paul, accused before the Imperial tribunal,
himself landed in Italy: Christians welcomed him at Puteoli, a
fact which constitutes a valuable testimony to at least a beginning
of the spread of Christianity in the old *Magna Græcia*, and Christians from Rome came to meet him on the Appian Way (*Acts*
xxviii, 15).

When he arrived in Rome as a prisoner enjoying a certain
amount of freedom,[13] Paul conferred with the leaders of the Jewish
colony, and put his case before them. They replied, as he had
evidently hoped, by questioning him on the subject of his preaching, and he proceeded to explain this. His audience was divided.
Some were against him, and these would seem to have formed the
majority, in view of the words on the hardness of heart of the
Jewish people which come almost at the end of the Book of Acts
(xxviii *in fine*). Nevertheless, the Roman Church was enriched
by a new contingent of converts from Judaism. Perhaps these
increased still more during the two years of captivity, which Paul's
zeal could not allow to be fruitless. But his Judaising opponents
also came, as we gather from his letter to the Philippians, and the
young Church experienced some disturbances in consequence;
nevertheless, they do not seem to have been very serious, as we
gather from Paul's own words.[14]

Released or declared not guilty, and set at liberty, Paul, who
seems then to have gone on to Spain,[15] disappears from the Roman
scene. But he was replaced there by St. Peter, who arrived perhaps

[12] L. Duchesne, *Histoire ancienne de l'Eglise,* Vol. I, p. 56.

[13] Cf. p. 274.

[14] "So that by all means, whether by occasion or by truth, Christ be preached;
in this also I rejoice, yea, and will rejoice" (*Phil.* i, 18).

[15] According to the letter of St. Clement, on which see Bk. II, and above,
p. 235.

before his departure. But the obscurity which surrounds the history of the prince of the Apostles during the previous years continues still, for we know nothing of his Roman sojourn except the martyrdom which crowned it. Vague traditions concerning the place where he baptised *ad nymphas sancti Petri, umi Petrus baptizabat*,[16] which would seem to have been the Ostrian cemetery on the Via Nomentana just outside Rome, do not go sufficiently far back (fourth century) to inspire full confidence. They are not to be set aside altogether.[17] But of Peter's life in Rome we know for certain only the last act, his martyrdom. But this, combined with that of St. Paul, suffices to make the Roman Church the Apostolic Church *par excellence*.

[16] Cf. A. Profumo, *La memoria di san Pietro nella regione Salaria-Nomentana*, in *Römische Quartalschrift*, 1916, supplement 21.

[17] The *Acta Marcelli*, which contain them, are fourth century. This tradition concerning the Ostrian cemetery would be against that of the Catacomb of St. Sebastian, if the *Domus Petri* designates the residence of St. Peter during his lifetime. Cf. above, p. 291, n. 26.

CHAPTER V

ST. JAMES AND ST. JOHN [1]

§1. ST. JAMES AND THE CHURCH AT JERUSALEM

St. James

THE story of the beginnings of the Church of Jerusalem and of the missions of St. Paul has already brought before us the figure of St. James, the Lord's brother. In St. Paul's enumeration of the appearances of the risen Christ, he mentions, after those to Cephas, the eleven, and the five hundred, an appearance to James (*I Cor.* xv, 7). Recalling to the Galatians the memories of his first years of Christian life, he tells them that three years after his conversion he went up to Jerusalem to see Peter; he adds: "Other of the apostles I saw none, saving James the brother of the Lord" (*Gal.* i, 19). These are only brief references, but they show the prominent place which James occupied in the Church from the first.[2]

[1] Bibliography.—J. Chaine, *L'epître de saint Jacques,* Paris, 1927; M. J. Lagrange, *Evangile selon saint Jean,* Paris, 1925; E. B. Allo, *Saint Jean, L'Apocalypse,* Paris, 1933; C. Fouard, *St. John and the End of the Apostolic Age;* L. Pirot, *Saint Jean,* Paris, 1923; G. H. Rendall, *The Epistle of St. James and Judaic Christianity,* Cambridge, 1927; V. H. Stanton, *The Gospels as historical documents,* Part III, *The Fourth Gospel,* Cambridge, 1920; B. F. Westcott, *The Epistles of St. John,* London, 1905.

[2] Was James one of the Twelve? The question has been discussed for centuries. As Tillemont points out, the Greeks distinguish James of Alphæus, who was one of the Twelve, from James, the brother of the Lord; their liturgy has two feasts, and two legends; the Latins, on the contrary, have followed the opinion of St. Jerome and identify the two. In favour of the identification, see Lagrange, *Saint Marc,* pp. 78 et seq.; *Epître aux Galates,* p. 18; Chaine, *Epître de saint Jacques,* pp. xxx-xxxiii; in favour of the distinction, see Malvy, in *Recherches de Science Religieuse,* 1918, pp. 122-32; Mader, in *Biblische Zeitschrift,* Vol. VI, 4, pp. 393-406. What *John* vii, 5 (cf. *Mark* iii, 21) says of the incredulity of the brethren of the Lord six months only before the Passion is a difficulty for those exegetes who count amongst the Twelve not only James, but also two other brethren of the Lord, Simon and Jude (Chaine, *op. cit.,* p. xxxii). On the other hand, the text in *Gal.* i, 19, quoted above, is explained more naturally if we regard James as one of the Apostles. To harmonise these data, various hypotheses have been suggested: the appearance of Jesus to James made an Apostle of him, like the appearance to Paul; or else, in order to replace James the son of Zebedee, who was martyred in 42, James the Lord's brother was called into the apostolic college; in this way the group of three, Peter, James and John,

From the time of the persecution by Agrippa, his authority increased; James, the brother of John, died a martyr; Peter was thrown into prison, delivered by an angel, and then left Jerusalem. James, the brother of the Lord, appears from that time on as the head of the community; it was he, indeed, that Peter informed of his deliverance (*Acts* xii, 17). He played a decisive part in the Council of Jerusalem: those who, according to Paul's story, were regarded as "pillars," were James, Cephas and John (*Gal.* ii, 9); at the general assembly described in the Acts, two speeches were made, one by Peter, and the other by James (xv, 13). When Paul arrived at Jerusalem, he went to see James, who was surrounded by presbyters (*Acts* xxi, 18).

All these facts, and, above all, the last mentioned, indicate that James was the head of the Church of Jerusalem; whereas the other Apostles were missionaries carrying the Gospel beyond Judea and founding churches, James resided at Jerusalem, and was bishop there.[3]

The Bishop of Jerusalem

This exceptional position of St. James must not be lost sight of. It shows the attachment of the Apostles to the holy city, and the efforts they made for its conversion: the greater metropolises of the East, Antioch, Thessalonica, Corinth, Ephesus, did not keep St. Paul for more than two or three years; Peter must similarly have passed through Antioch, Corinth, and apparently Bithynia and Pontus; at Rome he probably made several stays, leaving it for some far-off mission before returning and dying there.[4] James remained always at Jerusalem; no mission could draw him from the holy city; he knew that the great catastrophe was nigh; he saw how conversions were increasing, and he redoubled his efforts to bring back Israel to the Messias it had despised and crucified. He rejoiced to hear the account of the victories of Paul (*Acts* xxi, 20); his own successes were the "many thousands among the Jews that have believed, all zealous for the Law" (*ibid.*). These fateful cir-

---

may have been reconstituted with a new James. But it must be admitted that all this is merely conjectural.

[3] The Judeo-Christians, anxious to magnify the office of James, attributed to Jesus Himself his designation as Bishop of Jerusalem: *Recognitiones*, I, 43 (Migne, *P.G.*, I, 1232). Cf. Chaine, *op. cit.*, pp. xxxiii-xxxiv.

[4] Cf. *supra*, p. 294.

cumstances and the Apostolic ardour which they inspired explain the attitude of St. James during these twenty years. Some have pictured him as an obstinate Jew, "who had understood nothing of the profound thought of Jesus"; [5] such a view is unjust, and misrepresents the Christian character of the martyr-bishop; if we study more closely the position he took in the two decisive events in the Council of Jerusalem and the visit of Paul to the holy city, we see that in both instances he was influenced by concern for charity rather than for a doctrinal scruple; if he formulated the restrictions in the decree of Jerusalem, this was to enable the disciples of Moses to live without scandal with the pagan converts (*Acts* xv, 21); if he asked St. Paul to give a proof of his respect for the Law, this was because of the multitude of converts faithful to the Law, whom one should not offend (xxi, 20). And it was because the request was made for this reason that Paul agreed to it: what James was advocating was not a theology of law and grace, but respect for the conscience of converted Jews; he could make his own the words of Paul to the Corinthians (*I Cor.* viii, 11); "Through thy knowledge, shall the weak brother perish, for whom Christ hath died?"

These two incidents fall naturally into their place in the religious life of James and of his church as we know it: he and his church aimed at giving to the Jews amongst whom they lived the picture of an exemplary fidelity to the Law. Paul, writing to the Corinthians, spoke thus of his opponents: "They are Hebrews? So am I. They are Israelites? So am I. They are the seed of Abraham? So am I" (*II Cor.* xi, 22). The Christians of Jerusalem had the same pride of race, but Judaism was not for them merely a privilege of birth but also a rule of life, and they desired to follow this rule in all strictness. They hoped to gain thereby the esteem, and, with God's help, the conversion if not of all their compatriots at Jerusalem, at least of the most fervent of them; and once the élite were won, would not the whole populace follow them? In the first days of the Church, the first believers, thanks to the wonderful vigour of their religious life, were regarded with favour by all the people (Acts ii, 47). That is what James and his followers had in view, and was this not applying to the Jews of Jerusalem Paul's principle of becoming all things to all men, in order to gain all to Jesus Christ?

[5] Meyer, *Ursprung*, Vol. III, p. 227.

St. James and the Judaisers

This attitude was quite legitimate, and it was doubtless the most suitable for Jerusalem;[6] but it was not without danger: did not this scrupulous fidelity to the Law practised by Christians born in Judaism run the risk of being regarded not as counselled by charity and prudence, but as required by religion itself? And was not the liberty of other Christians, and particularly those who came from the Gentiles, calculated to disturb them? Amongst the followers of James several succumbed to this temptation (*Acts* xv, 5, 24; *Gal.* ii, 12). James himself disavowed them (xv, 24) and recognised the liberty of the Gentiles (*Gal.* ii, 9; *Acts* xv, 13 *et seq.*, xxi, 25). As regards Christians coming from Judaism, James could scarcely imagine any possible conduct differing from that which he and his followed at Jerusalem (xxi, 21). He does not seem to have thought it possible for others to refuse to the Law the docile veneration with which he himself regarded it. Does that mean that he regarded this practice of the Law as the source of salvation? Certainly not.[7] Did he at any rate regard it as a condition for salvation or perfection? Good judges have thought so;[8] but it seems to us difficult

[6] Paul himself adopted it, not only in the practice of the Nazarite vow—that might be regarded merely as a concession to the wish of James—but in his defence before the Sanhedrin, in which he describes himself as a Pharisee, and the son of Pharisees (xxiii, 6).

[7] Cf. Lagrange, *Galates*, pp. liv *et seq.*: "The group of James, with James at its head, recognised once for all that the Gentiles can be saved without the observance of the Law of Moses. They must, therefore, in accordance with the most elementary logic, have believed that salvation, even for the Jews, did not depend on the Law as a principle. Peter said so very explicitly; James, if he was consistent, must have thought so, and if he had not thought so, Paul would not have kept relations of ecclesiastical communion with him. . . . Did James regard the Law as obligatory for the Jews, not as a principle but as an essential condition of salvation? We are less in a position to answer in the affirmative here. This was evidently the opinion of a very great number of converted Jews. James and his presbyters did not controvert this opinion. Perhaps they respected it without sharing it. However, without making a categorical statement, in the absence of decisive proofs, it certainly seems that James regarded the Law as salutary, since he practised it so faithfully, and did not allow Paul to be reproached with declaring it to be abrogated for the Jews."

[8] Chaine, *Saint Jacques*, pp. xxxiv *et seq.*: "Did he regard legal works as necessary for the Jews as a condition of salvation or of perfection? The narrative of the Acts concerning the last visit of Paul to Jerusalem would lead us to think so. . . . If in these circumstances the discourse (xxi, 20-5) was made by James or approved by him, as we may well think, we are led to conclude that the latter really regarded the Law as obligatory for the Jews from the standpoint of perfection or as a condition of salvation." Cf. Lagrange, passage quoted above, n. 7.

to seek in our documents so precise a theological answer; as to the conduct which one should adopt, James's preferences are easy to perceive; but everything suggested such conduct to him, not only his Jewish surroundings which he wanted to win for Christ, but equally the assiduous and fervent practice of these rites which had left its imprint on his soul. Peter, whom God destined to a wider apostolate, felt that Judaism was an intolerable burden (xv, 10); James, whom God reserved exclusively for the apostolate in Jerusalem, does not seem to have felt its weight. That a converted Jew, and especially an Apostle, should carry this yoke until his death, and should exhort his brethren born in Judaism to the same fidelity, was quite a natural attitude for James to take, and does not call for discussion.

The Epistle of St. James

The Epistle of St. James does not deal with the question of legal observances; this silence is all the more noteworthy because, in all probability, the Epistle belongs to the last years of the Apostle's life.[9] If, after the Council of Jerusalem, and so many controversies which had troubled Syria, Galatia and Achaia, the Bishop of Jerusalem put aside a question so keenly discussed, it is because he was not the head of a party, seeking to impose his own view, but an Apostle of Christ anxious to maintain concord everywhere.[10]

He does indeed discuss the question of faith and works (ii, 14-26); but this discussion itself leaves entirely on one side the controversy concerning legal observances; the works of which St. James speaks are not the works of the Law, in which some Judaisers were seeking the source of justification, but the works of religion, and above all works of well-doing arising out of faith, of which they were at once the sign and the fruits.[11]

---

[9] It seems certainly later than the Epistle to the Romans, and must therefore be dated in the years 57-62.

[10] Cf. Chaine, *op. cit.*, p. lxxxviii: "It is better to explain the silence of James by a reason other than the date. Prudence . . . explains it well. Since the Jews could be sanctified in Christ without being obliged to renounce the Law, James thought it superfluous to consider the difficulties of those who thought themselves dispensed from it. He desired peace, and deliberately avoided all thorny questions."

[11] Hence there is no difference here between St. James and St. Paul. St. Augustine remarks: "Paul speaks of the words which precede faith; James, of works which follow faith" (*De diversis quaestionibus*, q. 76; Migne, P.L., XL, 89).

"What shall it profit, my brethren, if a man say he hath faith, but hath not works? Shall faith be able to save him? And if a brother or sister be naked, and want daily food, and one of you say to them: Go in peace, be ye warmed and filled; yet give them not those things that are necessary for the body, what shall it profit? So faith also, if it have not works, is dead in itself" (ii, 14-17).

St. James here merely repeats what he has taught earlier in the same Epistle: "Be ye doers of the word, and not hearers only, deceiving your own selves. For if a man be a hearer of the word, and not a doer, he shall be compared to a man beholding his own countenance in a glass; for he beheld himself, and went his way, and presently forgot what manner of man he was . . ." (i, 22-24, cf. iv, 17). And all this brings us back to the conclusion of the sermon of Jesus on the Mount: "Everyone that heareth these My words, and doth them, shall be likened to a wise man that built his house upon a rock . . ." (Matt. vii, 24).

For the rest, it is not only by this feature that the Epistle of St. James recalls the Sermon on the Mount; no other writing in the New Testament so faithfully echoes it: in the condemnation of oaths and of vain words,[12] the prohibition of cursing and judging,[13] the example of the prophets,[14] the beatitudes, and particularly the praise of mercy [15] and of poverty. In the Gospel of St. Luke the beatifying of poverty is, by contrast, associated with the malediction of riches (vi, 20-27); so James, after having extolled the privilege of the poor, whom God has chosen as "heirs of the kingdom" (ii, 4), pronounces against the rich anathemas which have the same tones as the maledictions pronounced by the Lord:

"Go to now, ye rich men, weep and howl in your miseries which shall come upon you. Your riches are corrupted, and your garments are moth eaten. Your gold and silver is cankered, and the rust of them shall be

---

Doubtless it is not by chance that James (ii, 2) takes up also the example of Abraham, in order to draw from it a doctrine which is seemingly opposed to that of Paul (Rom. iv, 2). We may reasonably think that James is here correcting the error of some Christians who had wrongly interpreted Paul's thought (cf. Augustine, ibid.). In these matters such errors were not rare, and more than one had to be dealt with by St. Paul himself (Rom. iii, 8; vi, 1; I Cor. v, 10). On this whole question, cf. Chaine, op. cit., pp. lxix-lxxv.

[12] v, 12; cf. Matt. v, 34-7.

[13] iii, 9; cf. Matt. v, 44; Luke vi, 28; James iv, 11; v, 9; cf. Matt. vii, 1-2; Luke vi, 37.

[14] v, 10; cf. Matt. v, 44; Luke vi, 23.

[15] ii, 13; cf. Matt. v, 7; Luke vi, 37. Cf. Chaine, op. cit., pp. lxvi-lxvii.

for a testimony against you, and shall eat your flesh like fire. You have stored up to yourselves wrath against the last days. Behold the hire of the labourers, who have reaped down your fields, which by fraud has been kept back by you, crieth, and the cry of them hath entered into the ears of the Lord of sabaoth. You have feasted upon earth, and in riotousness you have nourished your hearts in the day of slaughter. You have condemned and put to death the Just One, and he resisted you not. Be patient, therefore, brethren, until the coming of the Lord." [16]

The Martyrdom of St. James

"You have condemned and put to death the Just One, and he resisted you not." The martyrdom of St. James, which followed so soon after his Epistle, gave to these words a tragic grandeur. The Church of Jerusalem was truly a "little flock" of poor, whom the Christians of the whole world had to help; numerous, fervent, punctual in the observance of the Law, it compelled the veneration of the best amongst the Jews. But the rich, the Sadducean chief priests and their party opposed it as at the beginning with all the violence of their jealousy and their bitterness. As they had killed Jesus and slain Stephen and James the son of Zebedee, as they had tried to kill Paul, so also they now set upon James the Lord's brother.

In 61 or 62, the high priest Hanan the Young, "profiting by the fact that Festus was dead and Albinus his successor had not yet arrived, summoned the Sanhedrin, and caused to be brought before it the brother of the Lord called James, and some others, as guilty of having violated the Law; he had them stoned." [17]

This execution, adds Josephus, angered the moderate men, who denounced it to Albinus; Hanan was deposed from his position,

---

[16] v, 1-7; cf. *Life and Teaching of Jesus Christ*, Vol. I, p. 137.
[17] *Antiquities of the Jews*, XX, 9, 1, 199; *Ecclesiastical History*, II, 23, 21. This text of Josephus, who was in Jerusalem that year, is that of an eye-witness. (Cf. Meyer, *Ursprung*, Vol. III, p. 74.) This martyrdom is narrated in quite a different way by Hegesippus, quoted by Eusebius, *Historia Ecclesiastica*, II, 23, 4-18; this very detailed passage has long been regarded by historians with mistrust (Tillemont's *Mémoires* contain in an appendix a long dissertation by Arnaud, *Difficultés sur ce que conte Hégésippe de saint Jacques évêque de Jérusalem*); the life of James, like his death, is there transformed by Ebionite legends; this passage tells us nothing about the historic personality of James; but it shows us how his memory was venerated, and exploited, by the Judeo-Christians. The Clementine apocrypha manifest the same tendentious transformation. Cf. Chaine, *op. cit.*, pp. xxxvii-xl.

and replaced by Jesus, son of Damoeas. Very soon a more terrible chastisement was to fall on "the city which killed the prophets."

The Fall of Jerusalem

In 64, Gessius Florus became Procurator of Judea; in 66 his tyrannical administration brought to a head the rebellion which had long been contemplated. After terrible civil dissensions which increased still more the calamities of the Roman invasion, the city of Jerusalem was invested in the spring of 70; it was taken and destroyed in September.[18] Josephus narrates that, when Titus entered into the city, he cried out: "God has indeed fought with us; it is God who has expelled the Jews from these fortresses, for what could human hands or machines do against these towers?" (Wars of the Jews, VI, 9, 1, 411). Every Christian will feel the force of this statement still more when, after reading in Josephus the details of this appalling catastrophe, he remembers the death of Jesus and his prophecies.

Before the siege, the Christians left the city: "By a prophecy which had been revealed to the leaders of the Church of Jerusalem, the faithful were admonished to leave the city before the war, and to go and live in a town in Perea named Pella; they accordingly withdrew there, and thus the metropolis of the Jews and all the land of Judea was completely abandoned by the saints."[19]

This exodus had decisive consequences for the Church of Jerusalem: the last link was broken which bound the faithful to Judaism and to the Temple; down to the end they had loved its magnificent construction, its ceremonies, and its memories; now there remained of it not a stone upon a stone; God had weaned them from it. And this exodus finally alienated Jewish opinion from them; they had abandoned Jerusalem at the hour of its great tribulation; their faith was, then, not that of their nation, and they were seeking their salvation elsewhere. From the year 70, the rabbinical literature becomes more violently hostile to Christianity;[20] later on, when the revolt of Bar-Kokhba broke out, and the Jews were, for

[18] The upper city, the last refuge of the besieged, was taken by assault "the eighth day of the month of Gorpieus" (September 26th, 70), (Wars of the Jews, VI, 8, 5, 407).
[19] Ecclesiastical History, III, 5, 3. Harnack, Texte und Untersuchungen, Vol. I, p. 124, conjectures that this narrative of Eusebius depends on Ariston of Pella.
[20] Cf. Klausner, Jésus de Nazareth, pp. 54 et seq.

two or three years (133-135) the masters of Judea, the Christians were tortured by the adherents of the false Messias; [21] and in the whole Empire the synagogues became the centres of persecution.

St. Simeon and the Church of Jerusalem

Nevertheless, the Church of Jerusalem, exiled at Pella, organised itself: Simeon, son of Clopas, uncle of Christ, was chosen to succeed St. James. "All preferred him because he was a cousin of the Lord's." [22] This new election emphasised what is already evident from the choice of the first bishop of Jerusalem, who was the Lord's brother: in this church, great importance was attached to blood relationship; the relatives of Christ held a position there which they did not hold elsewhere. [23]

St. Simeon was a worthy successor of St. James, and died a martyr about the year 107. Of his long episcopate we know very little; we learn, however, that the church returned from Pella into Judea; the city of Jerusalem was then scarcely more than a Roman garrison, and the great rebellion which was to break out in 130 would lead to a destruction still more complete than that of 70.

What Eusebius, guided by Hegesippus, narrates concerning these obscure years, affects above all the history of the Lord's relatives: Vespasian had a search made for all the descendants of David, which gave rise to a great persecution (III, 12); Domitian adopted the same measures; the grandsons of Jude, the Lord' brother, were denounced and taken before the emperor; they were modest agriculturalists, and showed their horny hands; Domitian questioned them on the reign of Christ and His coming; then he sent them away with disdain; "when they were set free, they governed the churches, both as martyrs and as relatives of the Lord, and, peace being restored to the church, they lived until the time of Trajan." [24]

[21] Justin, *Apology*, I, 31.

[22] Hegesippus, quoted by Eusebius, *Ecclesiastical History*, IV, 22, 4. Eusebius mentions again this election (*Ecclesiastical History*, III, 11), dating it "after the martyrdom of James and the destruction of Jerusalem"; he adds: "is is said that those of the Apostles and disciples of the Lord who were still in this world came together from everywhere and gathered in the same place with the relatives of the Lord according to the flesh."

[23] In the text quoted above (*Ecclesiastical History*, III, 11), we notice the part played in the election by the relatives of the Lord, with the Apostles and the disciples; doubtless this account is legendary; but this legend arose in the Church of Jerusalem, and reveals its preferences.

[24] *Ecclesiastical History*, III, 20, 1-6. Cf. III, 32, 6.

Hegesippus also narrates that, in the reign of Trajan and the government of consul Atticus, Simeon, when a hundred and twenty years old, was denounced by heretics, and after long days of torments died on a cross; the constancy of this old man in undergoing such tortures aroused great wonder in the assistants and the consul himself.[25]

After the two long episcopates of James and Simeon, the bishops of Jerusalem succeeded one another very rapidly: from the death of Simeon (A.D. 107) to the rebellion which broke out in the twelfth year of Hadrian (A.D. 128-129), there were thirteen bishops. Eusebius knows practically nothing of them except their names; all that he can add—but this information is interesting—is that "they all belonged to the circumcision;"[26] and he gives this explanation: "The church of Jerusalem was at that time composed solely of Hebrew believers; it was so from the time of the apostles until the siege undergone by the Jews who had once more rebelled against Rome, in which they were destroyed in terrible battles."[27]

After this supreme catastrophe, the old Jerusalem disappeared; the new city which gradually and slowly arose on its ruins was a Hellenic city; its bishops were to play a prominent part in the history of the Church already in the time of Clement and Origen, and still more in the struggle against Arianism, but they were all Greeks, far removed from the Judaism of the bishops of the days before Hadrian.

Thus about 130 there disappeared the only church that we know of composed entirely of Jews who were faithful to the Law. Some thirty years later, St. Justin [28] distinguishes between two groups of Jewish Christians: some observe the Law but do not try to impose it on others; he does not refuse to communicate with these, although some Christians are more severe in their regard; other Jews, on the contrary, who are repelled by all, want to compel the Gentiles to observe the Law. This indulgence on the part of Justin towards the tolerant Jewish Christians is the last vestige of a state of mind which is disappearing; the Christians remain respectful towards the Law, but unanimously regard it as an institution of the past.[29]

[25] *Ibid.*, III, 32, 3 and 6.
[26] *Ibid.*, IV, 5, 4; cf. *ibid.*, 2.
[27] *Ecclesiastical History*, IV, 5, 2.
[28] Justin Martyr, *Dialogue*, xlvii.
[29] Cf. above, p. 174.

§2. ST. JOHN AND THE CHURCHES OF ASIA

St. John in Jerusalem

The life of the Apostle St. John after the Ascension and Pentecost appears at first in full light in the early history of the Church of Jerusalem. The son of Zebedee had, before his call by Jesus, been a fellow fisherman with Peter at Bethsaida (*Luke* v, 10). These links had not been broken, but confirmed by the Master,[1] and we find John closely associated with Peter in the first evangelisation of Jerusalem (*Acts* iii, 1 *et seq.*), and of Samaria (viii, 14 *et seq.*). On the occasion of the Council of Jerusalem, John is named by St. Paul with Peter and James as one of the "pillars" of the Church (*Gal.* ii, 9). But that is the last time we find him at Jerusalem: when Paul returned there in 57, he found there James and the elders, but neither Peter nor John, nor any other Apostle, was there at that time. From that moment John carried on his apostolic mission outside Jerusalem; the details of this mission are unknown to us, as are those of the other Apostles, but St. Paul mentions their existence (*I Cor.* ix, 5).[2]

[1] We find the two Apostles thus associated already in the Gospels: *Luke* xxii, 8; *John* xviii, 15; xx, 3; xxi, 20.

[2] Some historians have thought that St. John died a martyr. They base themselves above all on the reply of Jesus to the sons of Zebedee: "You shall indeed drink of the chalice that I drink of" (*Mark* x, 39); they infer from this that the two brothers were martyred together: thus E. Schwartz, *Ueber den Tod der Söhne Zebedaei*, Göttingen, 1904, and several articles in the *Zeitschrift für N.T. Wissenschaft*, Vol. XI, 1, 10, pp. 89-102; Vol. XV, 1914, pp. 210-21; W. Heitmueller, *ibid.*, Vol. XV, pp. 189-90. This hypothesis cannot be maintained: James the Great died in 42, or at the latest in 44, martyred by Herod Agrippa (*Acts* xii, 2), but many years later John took part in the Council of Jerusalem (*Gal.* ii, 9). Other historians separate the two martyrdoms, but hold that John was killed by the Jews at some date unknown. Thus Lietzmann, *Geschichte*, Vol. I, p. 247. This hypothesis respects the testimony of St. Paul, but takes away from Schwartz's argument its main force: if we separate the end of the two sons of Zebedee there is no more reason for saying that in both cases the "chalice" necessarily signifies a violent death. We must also remember the words of Jesus to Peter in the last chapter of the fourth Gospel, and the commentary which they called forth (*John* xxi, 21-3): the obvious sense of the text is that the "disciple whom Jesus loved" survived Peter for a long time, and that this prolonged survival which astonished Christians is explained by a special will of the Lord. On all this question, see L. de Grandmaison, *Jesus Christ*, Vol. I, pp. 147-55. Here will also be found a refutation of the very flimsy arguments based on a text in Papias, and the statements of a few early martyrologies.

St. John in Asia

After long years of obscurity, John appears once more, not at Jerusalem but in Asia. When did he go there? That is impossible to determine. The latest references to Ephesus and Asia which we can find in St. Paul, in the two letters to Timothy, give no indication of the presence at or even of the visits to these churches by St. John; there is the same silence in the first letter of St. Peter, addressed about this time "to the strangers dispersed through Pontus, Galatia, Cappadocia, Asia and Bithynia." On the other hand, the Apocalypse, the Gospel, and the Johannine Epistles show that the writer of these was in Asia and enjoyed great authority there. In this prophet and this evangelist we recognise the Apostle John, and the testimony of the books themselves is clarified and upheld by a very early and well-founded tradition.[3]

The Church and the Empire

From this Johannine literature we have to cull here only that which gives us information concerning the history of the Church, and in particular of the churches of Asia towards the end of the first century. What we note to begin with is the war waged against the Church by the powers of this world, and in particular by the Roman Empire. This feature did not appear in the Pauline literature; on the other hand, it shows itself already in the first letter of St. Peter: the pagans adopt an attitude of distrust and even of hostility towards the Christians, who are calumniated (ii, 12), persecuted (iii, 13), and reproached for the name of Christ (iv, 14). Christians must be prepared for everything, and endure all things, as Christ suffered (iii, 18 et seq.); they must be ready to give a reason for their hope (iii, 16). In all this we see the hostile treatment of individuals rather than an administrative persecution. Even so, Christians are henceforth liable to suffer for the name of Christ (iv, 16), and in the midst of all these dangers, in face of a hostile power, Peter advises them to submit to all legitimate authority, including that of the king (ii, 13 et seq.), who at that time was Nero.

[3] We cannot repeat here a demonstration which has often been given: For the Apocalypse, see P. Allo, *Apocalypse*, ch. 13 of the Introduction, pp. clxxxviii-ccxxxii; for the Gospel, see P. Lagrange, *Saint Jean*, ch. i, pp. xii-lxvi, and on the whole question, L. de Grandmaison, *Jesus Christ*, Vol. I, pp. 125-90.

The Apocalypse reveals a still graver situation: the Church has to meet not only the hostility of the pagan world, but also a bloody persecution: it is a fight between Christ and Antichrist, the saints and the beast.[4]

John himself shared in these tribulations: he was exiled to Patmos because of the word of God and the testimony of Jesus (i, 9). Antipas at Pergamus had been slain for the faith (ii, 13); others had suffered the same penalty, and the prophet beheld them impatient for the triumph of God:

"I saw under the altar the souls of them that were slain for the word of God and for the testimony which they held. And they cried with a loud voice saying: How long, O Lord, holy and true, dost thou not judge and revenge our blood . . .? (vi, 9-10).

In another vision he saw the great multitude of the elect; amongst them he noticed some who were clothed in white robes. Who were they?

"These are they who are come out of great tribulation, and have washed their robes, and have made them white in the blood of the Lamb. Therefore they are before the throne of God, and they serve him day and night in his temple, and he that sitteth on the throne shall dwell over them. . . . God shall wipe away all tears from their eyes" (vii, 14-17; cf. xii, 11; xx, 4).

This "great tribulation" was the persecution begun by Nero with a barbarous ferocity, and continued by Domitian with a tenacious hatred.[5] Rome is the Beast which has on its forehead: "Babylon the Great, the mother of the fornications and the abominations of the earth"; it is the "woman drunk with the blood of the saints and with the blood of the martyrs of Jesus" (xvii, 5-7). These maledictions are easy to understand if we remember that Rome at that time was set forth as an object of worship for all the subjects of the Empire. Above all from the time of Domitian,

---

[4] We cannot go into details here concerning the interpretation of the Apocalypse (cf. Allo, especially pp. 200-10; Charles, especially pp. xciii-cxvii); we are only concerned with what the book tells us about Christianity in Asia.

[5] The Apocalypse was very probably written towards the end of the reign of Domitian; cf. Allo, op cit., pp. cciii-ccx; Charles, op. cit., pp. xvi-xcvii. At the same time it makes known to us the situation of the Church under Domitian, and the still bleeding wounds of the Neronian persecution.

and especially in the province of Asia,[6] the imperial worship of Rome and of Augustus was accepted with enthusiasm by the whole pagan population of the Empire; it was at once a religious worship, and a sign of loyalty, and anyone who refused it was suspect; "no man might buy or sell but he that hath the character, or the name of the beast" (xiii, 17). This suspicion was especially dangerous under Domitian, who was so jealous of divine honours.[7] To this day, when we visit the ruins of Pergamus, and contemplate on the top of the great Acropolis the remains of the altar of Rome and Augustus, we have a lively impression of the "throne of Satan" which dominated Asia and the world.

Thus broke out the antagonism between the two Empires which were to dispute the ownership of the world,[8] and the leaders of the two camps: on the one hand the Lamb, and on the other the Beast. Already the prophet could hear the heavenly canticles which celebrated the triumph of the Lamb[9] and the death of the Beast.[10]

The Letters to the Seven Churches

This struggle of the Church against the Empire shows its attachment to its Master, the firmness of its hope, and also its impatience; but the Johannine writings, and in particular the Apocalyse, enable us to penetrate into its inmost life, and to attain to the centre of faith and life from which sprang the strength of the martyrs. The

[6] Cf. Chapot, *La province romaine proconsulaire d'Asie,* Paris, 1904, pp. 419-53. From 725-9, Pergamus had obtained permission to erect a temple to Rome and Augustus. Tacitus (*Annales,* IV, 55-6) relates at length the sending of embassies to Tiberius in 780/26 by the cities of Asia who were quarrelling about the honour of erecting a temple to Tiberius: these were Tralles, Hypaepa, Laodicea, Magnesia, Ilium, Halicarnasse, Pergamus, Ephesus, Miletus, Sardis, Smyrna; the last-mentioned city was chosen (p. 440).

[7] Cf. Gsell, *Essai sur le règne de l'empereur Domitien,* Paris, 1893, p. 312: "Outside Rome there was one god who was adored everywhere, the reigning Emperor. He had to be worshipped, above all under Domitian, who required belief in his divinity even in Rome itself. But those who were converted to Judaism or to Christianity did not recognise this deity any more than the others. And this was, in the eyes of Domitian, the greatest possible crime."

[8] On the struggle, cf. Allo, *op. cit.,* pp. 200-10; Westcott, *The Two Empires,* in his edition of the Johannine epistles, pp. 250-82.

[9] v, 9-13. We may see in these canticles some echoes of the liturgical hymns of the Church. Cf. *History of the Doctrine of the Trinity,* Vol. I, p. 264.

[10] xiv, 8; cf. xvii, 8.

letters to the seven churches are, from this point of view, a very valuable document.[11]

Viewing them as a whole, we note in the first place that nothing in them directly recalls the memory of St. Paul; ten or fifteen years afterwards, St. Ignatius, writing to the Ephesians, will remind them that they were formed in the Christian life by St. Paul; St. John, however, does not mention it. There is nothing strange about that: he was a prophet, and an Apostle; he spoke in his own name, in the fulness of his own authority, without mentioning anyone, except the Lord Jesus and the Spirit.[12]

The seven letters make known to us communities which are numerous and full of life, but are being attacked. Some of them have fallen off from their first fervour. At Ephesus there is watch-fulness and perseverance, but no longer as in the beginning (ii, 2 et seq.). Smyrna, with Philadelphia, is the only one which is not reproached; but it is poor and persecuted. Pergamus resists Satan valiantly, though he has his throne there; Antipas was a faithful witness, and suffered death; but there are some Nicolaites there, and they are tolerated. Thyatira is faithful and growing, but it also tolerates the Nicolaites and their prophetess Jezabel. Sardis is enfeebled and dying, although it seems to be alive. Philadelphia is also weak, but faithful; it seems to be destined to develop: the door is open, and God will give it some of those who are of the synagogue of Satan, those who say they are Jews and are not. Laodicea is rich, but lukewarm.

These brief descriptions bring home to us the dangers which threatened these Asiatic churches: they were being ravaged not so much by a persecuting paganism as by an undermining paganism, the moral corruption and perverse gnosis of which were penetrating everywhere. The danger for these churches was the doctrine of

[11] The churches to which these letters were addressed were not the only ones then existing in Asia, and not the only ones with which St. John was concerned; their number was chosen because of its symbolical value, and the choice of the particular seven seems to have been determined, at least in part, by geographical considerations: these churches were seven centers whence the message would spread to the surrounding Christian communities. Cf. W. R. Ramsay, *Letters to the Seven Churches* (London, 1904); Swete, *Apocalypse*, p. lxxii; Allo, *op cit.*, p. xvi.

[12] Renan (*Saint Paul*, pp. 303 et seq., 367 et seq.; *L'Antichrist*, pp. 363 et seq.) tries to find in these letters "a cry of hatred against Paul and his friends," who are the Nicolaites, and the synagogue of Satan. Jezabel is the "symbolical designa-tion of Paul." This exegesis is absurd, and it is now universally abandoned. Cf. Swete, *op. cit.*, p. lxii.

Balaam, "who taught the children of Israel to eat and to commit fornication"; this was the "doctrine of the Nicolaites." [13]

The Christian Church

The Christian church which the Apostle was addressing had to keep itself from contamination by these sects. But she herself was in no way a sect: she comprised amongst her elect some from all the twelve tribes of Israel, but these Jews were not alone: they formed part of an immense multitude that no man could number, of every nation, tribe, people and tongue (vii, 4-9). The worship which they gave to God was truly that which God desired. It was not at all confined to Jerusalem or Mount Garizim, but it was worship in spirit and in truth (John iv, 21-23). This worship was addressed to God and the Lamb (v, 8; 12-14), and to these was offered one and the same adoration in one religious act. Here below the saints are the "servants of Jesus" (i, 1; ii, 20, etc.), as well as the servants of God (vii, 3; x, 7, etc.); those who will have "part in the first resurrection" [14] will be "priests of God and of Christ" (xx, 6). This divine worship given to Christ is based on belief in His divinity: He is the "beginning of the creation of God"; [15] He is, like God, the beginning and the end, the first and the last, the alpha and omega; [16] like God, He is "alive"; [17] like God, He is

[13] ii, 14-15. These "Nicolaites" mentioned in the letter to Pergamus and in that to Thyatira are not otherwise known to us. It is difficult to gather from these two brief references any precise knowledge concerning this sect. Allo devotes an excursus to them (op. cit., pp. 46-8); he sees in them disciples of a "syncretistic mysticism," who considered themselves at liberty to fornicate, to eat idol offerings in pagan temples, and who indulged in speculations which John calls "the depths of Satan."

[14] What is said here of the "first resurrection" and of the thousand years which follow it, has led within the Christian Church to very different interpretations. We shall mention these later on when we give the history of Millenarianism. As to the mind of St. John himself, we must recognise that the Second Coming of the Lord is not prior but posterior to the Millennium, that this reign of a thousand years does not apply to the whole of humanity, and that it coexists with the empire of Antichrist. From all this we infer with Allo: "The prophecy of the Millennium, which perfectly coheres with the other prophecies in the book, is simply a figure of the spiritual domination of the Church Militant, united to the Church Triumphant, from the glorification of Jesus down to the end of the world." Cf. Allo, op. cit., excursus 37 (pp. 317-29); Swete, op. cit., pp. 264-6.

[15] iii, 14; cf. Col. i, 15-18.
[16] i, 17; ii, 8; xxii, 13. Cf., referring to God, i, 8; xxi, 6.
[17] i, 18. Cf. iv, 9-10; x, 6.

holy and true; [18] like God, He searches the reins and the hearts, He has the keys of death and of hell.[19]

What brings out best the significance of this belief and this worship is its intransigence: on two occasions (xix, 10; xxii, 9) John tries to prostrate himself at the feet of the revealing angel, but he was at once prevented; "See thou do it not; I am thy fellow servant and of thy brethren the prophets. Adore God." In the Epistle to the Colossians and that to the Hebrews we find a condemnation of the divine worship which certain Gnostics, under colour of humility, rendered to the angels, compromising the transcendence of the Son of God and the jealous worship which they owed to Him. Here we find the same intransigence of the Christian belief: "We have but one God and one Lord."

The Gospel of St. John

This faith in the Son of God which we find in the Apocalypse already prepares us for the fourth Gospel. At the end of the latter book John will write: "these miracles have been related that you may believe that Jesus is the Christ, the Son of God, and that believing, you may have life in his name" (xx, 31). When John was at Patmos seeing the visions which he communicated to the churches in the Apocalypse, he had not yet written his gospel; but for many years he had already been preaching it; [20] and already the whole of Asia was penetrated with the reflection of this teaching which was so soon to become a book; is it not this reflection which we already perceive in the eucharistic prayers of the *Didache?* [21]

When studying the life of the infant church at Jerusalem, we endeavoured to recognise there the echo of these daily repeated Gospel texts: the beatitudes, the blessedness of the "little flock," and the trust which it ought to have in the Heavenly Father. Similarly, we shall best understand the Christian life at Ephesus and the churches under the influence of St. John if we re-read his Gospel, the discourse on the bread of life, the Good Shepherd, and the discourse after the Last Supper.

---

[18] iii, 7. Cf. vi, 10.
[19] i, 18; ii, 23. On all this, see *History of the Doctrine of the Trinity,* Vol. I, pp. 349-52.
[20] Cf. Stanton, *The Gospels as Historical Documents,* Vol. III, pp. 50 *et seq.*
[21] *Infra,* Bk. II.

We cannot give here a detailed study of this book;[22] but it is indispensable to point out its distinctive features; these will reveal to us the personality of the Apostle John, and the churches which he penetrated with his spirit.

Clement of Alexandria already at the end of the second century set forth with much force the peculiar character of the Gospel of St. John: it is a "spiritual gospel." After mentioning the origin of the three synoptics, he goes on: "John then, the last, seeing that the external features (of the life of Christ) had been set forth in the gospels, being pressed by the disciples, and divinely moved by the Spirit, composed a spiritual gospel."[23] And Origen, at the beginning of his commentary, writes: "I think that, as the four gospels are the foundations of the faith of the Church[24]—and on these foundations rests the whole world reconciled to God in Christ—the first fruits of the gospels are to be found in that which you have asked us to interpret according to our power, the Gospel according to St. John. . . . We will make bold to say that, if the gospels are the first fruits of all the Scriptures, we have in this book the first fruits of the gospels, and no one can grasp its meaning if he has not rested on Jesus' breast and received from Jesus Mary as his own mother also."

These two venerable texts draw our attention to the most salient characteristics of this book. It is a spiritual book, and it owes this excellence to the inspiration of the Holy Spirit, but also to the intimacy which united the well-beloved disciple to Jesus and His Mother. Sometimes attempts have been made to find the source of this high theology in the Christian tradition prior to St. John, and in particular in Paulinism,[25] and we must certainly recognise the profound agreement of thought here, but also at the same time the individual characteristics which distinguish them so clearly from one another.[26] Above all, we must abstain from regarding this book, with its deep and living unity, as an artificial synthesis of the evangelical tradition with Pauline theology; John could say

---

[22] It is unnecessary, as commentaries are plentiful. It will suffice to mention here those of P. Lagrange and of P. Durand. For a theological study, see the chapter in *History of the Doctrine of the Trinity,* Vol. I.

[23] *Hypotyposes,* fragment quoted by Eusebius, *Ecclesiastical History,* VI, 14, 7.

[24] We have here the thought and the very expression of Irenæus, III, 11, 8.

[25] We do not mention Philo: thirty years ago many thought to find in Philo the key to the fourth Gospel; nowadays this illusion deceives far fewer historians. So much the better. Cf. *History of the Doctrine of the Trinity,* Vol. I, pp. 447-50.

[26] Cf. *infra,* p. 320.

with St. Paul: "The gospel which I preach is not according to man, for neither did I receive it of man, nor did I learn it, but by the revelation of Jesus Christ."

And when we speak here of "the revelation of Jesus Christ," we must think, not exclusively indeed but primarily, of the revelation which the beloved disciple received from his Master when he was living with Him. This revelation was clarified by the Spirit from the first; after the death of Jesus, and after Pentecost, this illumination became more penetrating, more intimate, more complete, bringing out into full consciousness many a point previously seen for a moment and then lost sight of, interpreting many words of the Master hardly heard and scarcely understood. In all this the evangelist recognises the effect of the promise of Jesus: "The Holy Ghost . . . will teach you all things, and bring all things to your mind, whatsoever I shall have said to you." [27]

It is that that gives to this gospel the character of quiet confidence which distinguishes it from the others. Doubtless the synoptics also put before us the "mystery of the kingdom of God" entrusted only to disciples (*Mark* vi, ii), these words "whispered in the ear" (*Matt.* x, 27). But these words themselves have not the note of discreet, moving and intimate utterance which characterises the discourse after the Last Supper and the great prayer with which it concludes. Neither shall we find in the synoptics these personal recollections so soberly worded but so full of emotion, such as the account of the first meeting with Jesus [28] or the confidential whisper by Christ concerning the treason of Judas; [29] or the last testament of Jesus bequeathing Mary to John: "He saith to His mother: Woman, behold thy Son. . . . And from that hour the disciple took her to his own" (xix, 26-27).

Thence also comes the great place given in this gospel to the private conversations of Jesus with Nicodemus, the Samaritan woman, and the man born blind. The dramatic form of these accounts has rightly been admired, but what gives them their value

[27] xiv, 26; cf. ii, 22; xii, 16; xvi, 4.
[28] i, 38-9: " 'Rabbi, where dwellest thou?' He saith to them: 'Come and see.' They came, and saw where he abode, and they stayed with him that day: now it was about the tenth hour."
[29] xiii, 23-6: "There was leaning on Jesus' bosom one of his disciples, whom Jesus loved. Simon Peter therefore beckoned to him, and said to him: Who is it of whom he speaketh? He therefore, leaning on the breast of Jesus, saith to him: Lord, who is it? Jesus answered: He it is to whom I shall reach bread dipped . . ."

most of all is their depth of religious intuition: nowhere else do we find, in face of the revelation by Christ, the hesitation of the master in Israel who is touched by the truth but embarrassed by its knowledge, or the courageous desire of a sinful woman who allows herself to be won by the attraction of the living water and sacrifices all to it, or the quite simple loyalty of the man who is healed, who recognises the work of God and believes in it whatever the risk. And Jesus, who did not trust Himself to man "because he knew what was in man," immediately entrusts Himself to a generous and loyal soul, no matter whose it may be. To the Samaritan woman He says: "I am the Messias, who am speaking with thee" (iv, 26); to the man born blind: "Dost thou believe in the Son of God?"— "Who is he, Lord, that I may believe in him?"—"Thou hast both seen him, and it is he that talketh with thee" (ix, 36-37).

The Son of God

In addition to these individual conversations, there are also in this gospel some great theological discourses, and these in turn are no less characteristic. We recognise in them the aim of the evangelist to which the whole work converges: it is to lead Christians to faith in the Son of God. Such is the discourse on the bread of life; such above all are the discourses pronounced by Jesus at Jerusalem on the Feast of Tabernacles, or again at the Feast of the Dedication.[30] The insistence of the evangelist on these discourses omitted by the synoptics has been noticed by all exegetes; to explain it, some have tried to see in the author of the fourth gospel an inhabitant of Jerusalem who knew Jesus only in that city on the occasions of the feasts [31]—an hypothesis which nothing suggests and nothing requires. Instead of attributing to an unknown disciple, or to St. Mark, this glorious heritage, it is infinitely wiser to leave it to St. John the beloved disciple, whom the Gospel itself sufficiently makes known and whom tradition explicitly identifies. It is not difficult to understand why, in his plan of bringing out into full light the Son of God, John gives so great a place to this preach-

[30] Cf. above, p. 135.
[31] This hypothesis is developed, for instance, in the book of J. Weiss on *Christian Origins*, p. 612. The author even adds: "It is possible that this author is John Mark, the one who is commonly regarded as the author of the second gospel." This chapter was composed after the death of Weiss by R. Knopf, but from notes and other works by Weiss.

ing at Jerusalem: to the Galilean crowds, timid, wavering, but well disposed, Jesus manifested Himself only with a prudent reserve, and first of all it was His Heavenly Father whom He made known and His kingdom, then, little by little, the Messianic King. In the case of the Jews of Jerusalem Jesus did not have to take the same steps, and even could not do so. After two years of public ministry, in presence of opponents or disciples accustomed to theological discussions, and who went straight to the divine mystery which they suspected or feared, Jesus could not stop half way, and did not attempt to do so. And then, if Christ felt that the opposition against Him was becoming exasperated, and saw the Cross appearing at the end of this last stage, He determined to choose Himself the ground of the combat, and to be condemned, not for sedition, but as the Son of God. Accordingly, He set aside all the captious questions concerning the Messias, the Son of David, and the tribute due to Cæsar, and brought back the discussion to His great religious affirmation, to His divine filiation. This it is that, in the synoptic gospels, dominates all the controversies of the last week, the only time which in their accounts was spent in Jerusalem and the Temple. It is this also that appears in the preaching on the great feasts of the autumn and winter which St. John has transmitted to us.

Now, are not these dispositions of the crowds at Jerusalem at the end of the ministry of Jesus somewhat similar to the dispositions of the crowds in Asia at the end of the apostolic age? The hearers, docile or mistrustful, whom John wants to reach, are indeed no longer those he had known at Jerusalem when Peter began his preaching: only a few weeks had elapsed since the death of Jesus, and they were still moved by His preaching and His miracles, and cast down by the terrible crisis of the Passion: for these, what was required was to recall the immediate past, so many touching and revealing words, so many good deeds, and then to show that this death had been foretold by the prophets, and that God had permitted it only to glorify Christ by raising Him up. More than sixty years had passed since then; Judea was now only a desert, Jerusalem a heap of ruins. But already the Church had grown, spreading throughout the Roman empire and even beyond its boundaries, and Jesus appears in a majesty truly divine. The death on the Cross is a glorious exaltation: Jesus had foretold it; from this height He draws all to Himself (xii, 32; cf. iii, 14; viii, 28; xii, 27). Those who were won by Him contemplate not only His passion, but His whole life, in the splendour of this glory: "we saw his glory, the glory as it were of the only begotten of the Father, full of grace and truth" (i, 14). Hence their preferences, like those of the evangelist, draw them to the theological discourses; they like to hear Him saying again: "Before Abraham was made, I am" (viii, 58); "I and the Father are one" (x, 30); "He that seeth me, seeth the Father also" (xiv, 9); "I came forth from the Father, and am come into the world, again I leave the world and I go to the Father" (xvi, 28).

All these texts bring no new revelation, nothing which goes beyond the belief of St. Paul or that of the first evangelists and the first Apostles; [32] and yet it is certainly true that this spiritual gospel is distinct from the others: in the synoptics, the divinity of the Son of God underlies all the evangelical message and alone makes it intelligible, but it is only in a few incidents of the life of Jesus or a few of His words that this divinity appears in full light. In St. John it is quite different: the great mystery is already clearly set forth to the reader in the prologue: "In the beginning was the Word, and the Word was with God, and the Word was God"; [33] at the end of the Gospel the cry of St. Thomas constitutes an echo to the prologue: "My Lord and my God!" (xx, 28), and in the whole Gospel the actions and words of Jesus set forth to us the same revelation.

The Word Made Flesh

This spiritual gospel, this revelation of the glory of the only begotten Son, is not an Apocalypse; what John describes to us here are not the visions of Patmos; it is the life of the "Word made flesh," who "dwelt amongst us." "That which was from the beginning," affirms St. John, [34] "which we have heard, which we have seen with our eyes, which we have looked upon, and our hands have handled, of the Word of life . . . we declare unto you." And

[32] See *Origins of the Doctrine of the Trinity: the Son of God in the Synoptic Gospels* Vol. I, pp. 198-251), in the early Church (pp. 259-80), and in St. Paul (pp. 286-314).

[33] On the "Word," cf. *Origins of the Doctrine of the Trinity*, Vol. I, pp. 367-80.

[34] I *John* i, 1 *et seq.*; The identity of the author of this Epistle and the gospel is manifest, and is generally accepted. Cf. Westcott, *The Epistles of St. John*, London, 1909, pp. xxx and xliii *et seq.*; Stanton, *op. cit.*, Vol. III, pp. 83-103.

at the end of the account of the Passion: "One of the soldiers with a spear opened his side, and immediately there came out blood and water. And he that saw it, hath given testimony, and his testimony is true. And he knoweth that he saith true: that you also may believe" (xix, 34-35).

This historic reality of the words and actions of Jesus reported by John is the indispensable foundation of the gospel: it was written "that you may believe that Jesus is the Christ, the Son of God, and that believing you may have life in his name" (xx, 31). If the miracles of Jesus are merely symbols, and his discourses are but the meditations of John himself, the faith of the disciples is vain, and the preaching of the Apostle is but a false witness.[35]

This consideration, already very strong, becomes still more evident and more powerful if we bear in mind the controversies which the author of the fourth gospel has to refute: the most dangerous opponents he denounces are the Docetic Gnostics, who deny the reality of the Incarnation: according to these heretics, Jesus is not the Christ; the Son of God has not come in the flesh. This is to deny the essential doctrine of Christianity: "By this is the spirit of God known. Every spirit which confesseth that Jesus Christ is come in the flesh, is of God. And every spirit that dissolveth Jesus, is not of God" (I John iv, 2-3). To these negations the Apostle replies by a categorical affirmation of the doctrines contested: Jesus is the Messias; the Son of God has truly become incarnate. This controversy is carried on explicitly in the Epistle; the Gospel, written about the same date, in the same surroundings, by the same Apostle, is inspired by the same preoccupations. Certainly it is not a book of controversy, but it is a testimony and a teaching, and as such, it aims at establishing the faith and clarifying it. That is why, at the very beginning of the book, the reality of the Incarnation is so strongly affirmed: "The Word was made flesh." If in reading this gospel we bear in mind the doctrinal war waged by the Apostle, we shall see in it the solemn affirmation of a witness who maintains, against the heretical denials, the reality of that humanity which he had seen, heard, and touched. But in this case one could not give to this book a symbolical interpretation

[35] This is what St. Paul said to the Corinthians, with an irresistible force: "If Christ be not risen again, then is our preaching vain, and your faith is also vain. Yea, and we are found false witnesses of God, because we have given testimony against God that he hath raised up Christ whom he hath not raised up" (I Cor. xv, 14-15).

without ruining the very faith which it was intended to establish.[36]

This historic reality of the actions and discourses of Jesus as they are reported by St. John is of the greatest importance. If it is not accepted, then we have in this gospel no more than a beautiful theological speculation, or, if one prefers, an exalted mystical contemplation. We might still admire it, and even allow ourselves to be uplifted by it, but it would be St. John who was attracting us, not Jesus. The merit of the gospel is precisely that it presents to the Christian Jesus Himself: in the closing days of this apostolic age wholly illumined by the light of the Incarnate Word, the beloved disciple makes Him known in the reality of His flesh and in the splendour of His glory. It is towards Him that the Epistles of St. Paul were drawing the faithful soul, and never will a Christian weary of reading his moving appeals; but in this gospel it is no longer the Apostle who is heard, but the Master. His voice is not, like that of St. Paul, trembling with emotion, but discreet, profound, recollected; his discourses, especially the most intimate ones, are pronounced in a whisper; their tranquillity is so pronounced that a distracted reader hears them without understanding them, and lets their smooth flow glide over his soul. But those whose hearts God opens listen greedily; these discourses are Spirit and Life.

The Influence of St. John

On the churches of Asia, and on the entire Church, the influence of St. John has been incalculable. In his lifetime he, like St. Paul, met with resistance. His Epistles bear the trace of them: witness the jealous and quarrelsome Diotrephes (*III John* 9). These human imperfections, and the more grave dangers of Gnosticism and Docetism saddened the Apostle; but all that has passed away like clouds which leave no trace, while the teaching of St. John is graven on the hearts of Christians. We recognise its influence in

---

[36] This controversy carried on by St. John is clarified by a comparison with the letters of St. Ignatius and St. Polycarp, written a dozen years later, and in the same Asiatic circles: "Whosoever does not confess that Jesus Christ is come in the flesh, is an antichrist, and whoever does not confess the witness of the cross, is of the devil (Polycarp, *Phil.* vii). "It is in truth that he was born, ate and drank, it is in truth that he was persecuted under Pontius Pilate, it is in truth that he suffered and died . . . and it is in truth that he rose from the dead" (Ignatius, *Trall.*, IX, X; cf. *Smyrn.*, II; *Ephes.*, VII). Cf. *infra*, ch. x, 2 and 3, and *History of the Doctrine of the Trinity*, Vol. I, pp. 361-4.

St. Ignatius, St. Polycarp, and above all in the latter's disciple, St. Irenæus. It was not only the theology of St. John, but also his liturgical tradition, which left its impress on the churches of Asia. In 154, the two great bishops of Rome and Smyrna, Anicetus and Polycarp, will endeavour in vain to unify their paschal customs, and though not succeeding, will at least keep unity of communion; thirty years afterwards, Pope St. Victor will impose uniformity: the resistance of Polycrates of Ephesus will reveal the attachment of the Asiatics to their special tradition, authorised, in their eyes, by the gospel and the memory of "John who rested on the bosom of the Saviour" (*Ecclesiastical History*, V, 24, 3, 6). Another disciple of John, Irenæus, will make the love of peace prevail over this too jealous fidelity.[37]

The Dispersion of the Apostles

In our study of the writings of the apostolic age, we have been able to follow, at least in their main outlines, the apostolic careers of St. Peter, St. Paul, St. John and the two St. James. Of the other Apostles, these documents tell us nothing. Towards the end of the second century and the commencement of the third, the Church will see the appearance of new Acts of Apostles, apocryphal works which are not without interest: they make known to us the legends and romances which could then charm and sometimes deceive the Christian people. The Church was severe in their regard; it is prudent to imitate her reserve, and not to transform into historical documents these works of imagination.[38]

But while we put on one side these legends or these romances, we can retain a few traditional facts. A very early tradition puts the dispersion of the Apostles in the twelfth year after the Resurrection;[39] this date coincides in fact with the persecution by Herod Agrippa I; in the years which follow we never see the Twelve

[37] On this conflict, cf. *infra*. Bk. II.

[38] That these apocryphal Acts are of no historic value is a point on which all their editors agree. Cf. Hennecke, *N.T. Apocryphen*, Tübingen, 1933, p. 169; Amann, art. *Apocryphes du N.T.*, in *Supplément* to *Dict. de la Bible*, Vol. I, p. 488.

[39] This tradition is found in the *Kerygma Petri*, *apud* Clement of Alexandria, *Strom.*, VI, 5, 43, 3; Apollonius, *apud* Eusebius, *Eccles. Hist.*, V. 18, 14; *Actes de Pierre avec Simon*, 5, Voaux's edn., p. 253; cf. Harnack, *Chronologie*, pp. 243 et seq. He regards this tradition as "very ancient and well attested." Duchesne is more reserved (*Histoire ancienne de l'église*, Vol. I, p. 20, n. 1).

gathered together again in Jerusalem. But though we can determine the starting point of the mission of the Apostles, the destination of most of them escapes us. In a chapter of Eusebius's *Ecclesiastical History*,[40] in which he claims to reproduce textually a passage from Origen, we read that "Thomas, according to tradition, was allotted the land of the Parthians; Andrew, Scythia; John, Asia." Then he mentions the apostolate of SS. Peter and Paul. In his translation of this passage, Rufinus adds: "Matthew was given Ethiopia; Bartholomew, Further India."[41] These are only vague indications, but they are not without value; what we know of the primitive evangelisation of the countries thus mentioned gives to these statements a confirmation which is not decisive, but is not to be disregarded.

[40] *Ecclesiastical History*, III, 1.
[41] On this text, cf. Harnack, *Mission und Ausbreitung*, pp. 109 *et seq.*

GENERAL BIBLIOGRAPHY

We here indicate a certain number of sources which will be constantly utilised, or collections of ancient texts which should be known. This bibliography holds good also for the next few books.

The first name to be mentioned is that of *Eusebius*, Bishop of Cæsarea in Palestine at the beginning of the fourth century, and author of an *Ecclesiastical History* in ten books, from the beginnings of the Church to 324, and also of a *Chronicle*. St. Jerome translated the second book of the latter work, revised it, and continued it until the year 378. The best edition of the Greek text of the *Ecclesiastical History* is that of E. Schwartz in the Berlin *Corpus: Eusebius Werke*, II, *Kirchengeschichte*, Leipzig, 1903, 1908, 1909, 3 vols.

The *Chronicle* is likewise edited in the Berlin *Corpus*, by R. Helm (*Eusebius Werke*, VII: *Die Chronik des Hieronymus*, Leipzig, 1913, 1926, 2 vols.) and by J. Karst (*Eusebius Werke*, V: *Die Chronik des Eusebius aus dem armenischen übersetzt*, Leipzig, 1911).

The *Ecclesiastical History* was translated into Latin by Rufinus, who added two books to it. (Edited by Schwartz and T. Mommsen, 2 vols., in Berlin *Corpus*, Leipzig, 1909. An English translation by Kirsopp Lake and J. Oulton is included in Loeb's Classical Library.)

A Latin historian, the Gallo-Roman Sulpicius Severus, wrote two books of *Chronicles* embracing universal history as far as he knew it, from the creation to the end of the fourth century (edited by Halm in Vienna (*Corpus scriptorum ecclesiasticorum latinorum*, 1866). Another Latin writer, the Spanish priest Paul Orosius, a disciple of St. Augustine, also wrote a universal history which, like that of Sulpicius Severus, was independent of that of Eusebius of Cæsarea: *Adversus paganos historiarum libri VII*. This stopped at the year 416 (edited by Langemeister in Vienna *Corpus*, 1882).

The *Liber Pontificalis* is a chronicle of the Popes begun by an unknown author of the sixth century, and of very unequal value.

The best edition is that of Duchesne, Paris, 1886-1892, 2 vols.

In order not to make this bibliography too long, we confine our-selves here to historians properly so called. A list of other Christian writers in Latin and Greek in the first three centuries, who will be referred to on several occasions in the notes to this work, will be found in O. Bardenhewer's *Patrologie,* 3rd edn., Freiburg in Bresgau, 1910 (English translation by Shahan, Herder, 1908), and *Geschichte der altkirchlichen Literatur,* 5 vols., 2nd edn., Freiburg in Bresgau, 1913-1924, with supplement to vol. III, 1923. Their works will be found in Migne's *Patrologia Græca* and *Patrologia Latina,* and also a great number of them in the two new collections in course of publication, the Berlin *Corpus* for Greek writers (*Die griechischen christlichen Schriftsteller der ersten Jahrhunderte*) and the Vienna *Corpus* for the Latins (*Corpus scriptorum ecclesi-asticorum latinorum*).

Christian inscriptions must be looked for in the *Corpus inscrip-tionum græcarum* and the *Corpus inscriptionum latinarum,* both published by the Berlin Academy, the former from 1856 to 1877, the latter from 1863 and still in course of publication. The Chris-tian inscriptions in Rome have been published by J. B. de Rossi, *Inscriptiones christianæ Urbis Romæ,* I, Rome, 1857-1861; II, Rome, 1888. A third volume with the title *Nova series I* was pub-lished by A. Silvagni, Rome, 1922.

On Christian writers in Greek, one should consult A. Puech, *Histoire de la littérature grecque chrétienne depuis les origines jusqu' à la fin du IVe siècle,* Paris, 1928-1930, 3 vols., and on those of Latin language, P. de Labriolle, *Histoire de la littérature latine chrétienne,* 2nd edn., Paris, 1924. See also: P. Batiffol, *Anciennes littératures chrétiennes: I. La littérature grecque,* 2nd edn., Paris, 1898; H. R. Duval, *La littérature syriaque,* Paris, 1899; M. Mo-ricca, *Storia della Letteratura latina cristiana,* Turin, I, 1925; II, 1st part 1928, III, 1st part, 1932.

The *Acts of the Martyrs* are catalogued in the *Bibliotheca hagio-graphica orientalis,* edited by the Bollandists, Brussels, 1909, the *Bibliotheca hagiographica græca,* edited by the same, Brussels, 1909, and the *Bibliotheca hagiographica latina,* edited by the same, Brussels, 1898-1911, and utilised, with critique and commentaries, in the *Acta Sanctorum,* published likewise by the Bollandists, Ant-werp, 1643-Brussels, 1931 (date of the first volume, the work is still in course of publication). The second volume of the month of

November of the *Acta Sanctorum*, Brussels, 1894, concludes the systematic edition of J. B. de Rossi and L. Duchesne, of the *Martyrologium Hieronymianum*, the most important martyrological document of antiquity; critical re-edition by Père H. Delehaye and Dom H. Quentin, under the title *Acta Sanctorum novembris tomi II pars posterior qua continetur H. Delehaye commentarius perpetuus in Martyrologium Hieronymianum ad recensionem H. Quentin*, Brussels, 1931.

One of the best known collections of the *Acts of the Martyrs* was made in the seventeenth century by Dom Ruinart: *Acta primorum martyrum sincera*, Paris, 1889. Others are mentioned in the bibliography to Chapter IX.

Numerous texts of Eastern writers are published in the *Patrologia orientalis*, edited by R. Graffin and F. Nau, in course of publication, Paris, 1908—, and in the *Corpus scriptorum christianorum orientalium* of J. B. Chabot, I. Guidi, H. Hyvernat, B. Carra de Vaux, also in course of publication, Paris, 1903.

The *Acts of the Councils* are gathered together in the great collections by Labbe and Cossart (ed. Coleti, Venice, 1728), Mansi (*Conciliorum amplissima collectio*, 31 vols. Florence and Venice, 1759—), and general councils only, in E. Schwartz, *Acta Conciliorum œcumenicorum*, in course of publication, Strasburg, Berlin and Leipzig, 1914—. The history of councils has been written by Hefelè, translated and completed and corrected by Dom H. Leclercq: J. Hefelè, *Histoire des Conciles*, in course of publication, Paris, 1907—.

The great juridical collections constitute complementary sources for early ecclesiastical history: *Codex Theodosianus*, ed. J. Godefroy, with commentaries, 6 vols. in 4, Lyons, 1665, republished by J. D. Bitter, 6 vols., Leipzig, 1739-1743; ed. T. Mommsen and P. Meyer, *Theodosiani libri XVI*, Berlin, 1903, and *Corpus Juris civilis*, I. *Institutiones et Digesta*, ed. P. Krüger and T. Mommsen, Berlin, 1889; II. *Codex Justinianus*, ed. P. Krüger, Berlin, 1888; III, *Novellæ*, ed. K. Schoell and G. Kroll, Berlin, 1895.

Now we come to a number of general works on the early history of the Church. We must mention in the first place a great monument of erudition, somewhat out of date, especially in the last chapters, but still of the greatest value on the whole because of its fullness, the richness of its documentation, and the soundness of its criticisms: the sixteen volumes of the *Mémoires pour servir à l'his-*

toire ecclésiastique des six premiers siècles, by the learned and upright Lenain de Tillemont, Paris, 1693-1712.

We must also mention his *Histoire des Empereurs,* Vol. I, 2nd edn., revised by the author, Paris, 1700, Vol. II, Paris, 1691-1738, which contains some valuable material for the early history of the Church.

Here are other works:

Achelis, H. *Das Christentum in den ersten drei Jahrhunderten,* 2 vols. Leipzig, 1912; 2nd edn. of 1st vol., Leipzig, 1924.

Allard, P. *Histoire des persécutions pendant les deux premiers siècles,* 3rd edn., 2 vols. Paris, 1903, 1905.

— *Les persécutions du IIIe siècle,* 2nd edn., Paris, 1898.

— *La persécution de Dioclétien,* 2nd edn., 2 vols., Paris, 1903.

— *Le christianisme et l'Empire romain,* 6th edn., Paris, 1903.

Aube, B. *Histoire des persécutions de l'Eglise,* 2nd edn., 4 vols. Paris, 1875-1886.

Batiffol, P. *Le catholicisme des origines à saint Léon,* I. *L'église naissante et le catholicisme,* 12th edn. Paris, 1927.

Bihlmeyer, K. *Kirchengeschichte, auf Grund des Lehrbuches von F. X. Funk, I: Das christliche Altertum,* 9th edn. Paderborn, 1931. French translation, or rather an adaptation of the 1st edn. of Funk was published by the Abbé H. Hemmer, 2 vols., Paris, 3rd edn., 1891.

Boulanger, A. *Histoire générale de l'Eglise,* I: *L'antiquité chrétienne,* Vol. I: *Les temps apostoliques,* Paris, 1931; Vol. II: *Le temps des persécutions,* Paris, 1931.

Duchesne, L. *Histoire ancienne de l'Eglise,* 3 vols., Paris, 1906, 1907, 1910, English translation: *Early History of the Christian Church,* 1909—.

— *Les origines du culte chrétien,* 5th edn., Paris, 1920. English translation: *Christian Worship,* 5th edn., 1919.

Dufourcq, A. *Histoire ancienne de l'Eglise:*
   I. *Les religions païennes et la religion juive comparée,* 6th edn. Paris, 1924.
   II. *La révolution religieuse, Jésus,* 6th edn. Paris, 1927.
   III. *Le christianisme primitif. Saint Paul, Saint Jean, Saint Irénée,* 6th edn. Paris, 1929.
   IV. *Le christianisme et l'Empire romain,* Paris, 1930.

Ehrhard, A. *Die Kirche der Märtyrer*, Munich, 1932.

Gwatkin, H. M. *Early Church History to A.D.* 313, 2 vols., London, 1909.

Harnack, A. *Geschichte der altchristlichen Literatur*:
  I *Die Ueberlieferung und der Bestand*, Leipzig, 1893.
  II *Die Chronologie*, Leipzig, 1897-1904, 2 vols.

— *Die Mission und Ausbreitung des Christentums*, 4th edn., Leipzig, 1924, 2 vols. English translation: *Expansion of Christianity in the first three centuries*, 2 vols., 1904-1905.

Jacquin, A. M. *Histoire de l'Eglise*, I: *L'Antiquité chrétienne*, Paris, 1929.

Kidd, A. *History of the Church to A.D.* 461, Oxford, 1922, 3 vols.

Kirsch, J.P. *Kirchengeschichte*, I: *Kirchengeschichte in der antiken griechisch-römischen Kulturwelt*, Freiburg in Bresgau, 1930.

Krüger, G. *Handbuch der Kirchengeschichte*, I: *Das Altertum*, Tübingen, 1923.

Lietzmann, H. *Geschichte der alten Kirche*, I: *Die Anfänge*, Berlin and Leipzig, 1932.

Mourret, F. *Histoire de l'Eglise*, new edn., Paris, 1921, 9 vols.

Müller, K. *Kirchengeschichte, I Band, i Lieferung* 1924, ii *Lieferung* 1927, iii *Lieferung* 1929, Tübingen.

Poulet, C. *Histoire du Christianisme*, fasc. I-VI, Paris, 1932-1934.

Renan, E. *Histoire des origines du christianisme* (Paris, 1861—), 8 vols.

Rosenstock, E. and Wittig, J. *Das Alter der Kirche*, Berlin, 1908, 3 vols.

Zellier, J. *L'Empire romain et l'Eglise*, Vol. VI of the *Histoire du monde*, published under the direction of E. Cavaignac, Paris, 1928.

We must add to this list the *Dictionnaire d'Archéologie chrétienne et de Liturgie*, by Dom F. Cabrol and Dom H. Leclercq (Dom Cabrol alone for the four first volumes), in course of publication, Paris, 1907—; the *Dictionnaire d'Histoire et de Géographie ecclésiastiques*, published under the direction of A. Baudrillart, A. Vogt and M. Rouzies, continued by A. de Meyer and E. van Cauwenbergh, in course of publication, Paris, 1912—; the *Dictionnaire de théologie catholique*, begun under the direction of A. Vacant and continued under that of E. Mangenot and E. Amann, in course of publication, Paris, 1909—; the *Dictionnaire apologétique de la foi catholique*, 4th edn., under the direction of

A. d'Alès, 4 vols. and Tables, Paris, 1911-1931; the *Lexicon für Theologie und Kirche* under the direction of Buchberger, in course of publication, Freiburg in Bresgau, 1930—; the *Realencyclopädie für protestantische Theologie und Kirche,* 3rd edn., under the direction of A. Hauck, 24 vols., Leipzig, 1896-1913; *Die Religion in Geschichte und Gegenwart,* 2nd edn. by H. Gunkel and L. Zscharnack, 5 vols., Tübingen, 1927-1932; *Encyclopædia of Religion and Ethics,* under the direction of J. Hastings, 13 vols., Edinburgh, 1908-1926.

On the history of dogma, see: J. Tixeront, *Histoire des dogmas,* I, *La théologie antenicéenne,* 11th edn., Paris, 1930; II, *De saint Athanase à saint Augustin,* 9th edn., Paris, 1931; III, *La fin de l'âge patristique,* 8th edn., Paris, 1928; Harnack, A., *Lehrbuch der Dogmengeschichte,* I. *Entstehung des kirchlichen Dogmas,* 4th edn., Tübingen, 1909; English translation: *History of Dogma,* 1894—. Loofs, F. *Leitfaden zum Studium der Dogmengeschichte,* 4th edn., Halle, 1906.

BOOK II

*From the Death of St. John
to the End of the
Second Century*

NIHIL OBSTAT:

REGINALDUS PHILLIPS, S.T.L.
Censor deputatus

IMPRIMATUR

E. MORROGH BERNARD
Vic. Gen.

WESTMONASTERII
die 28a Juli, 1944

TRANSLATOR'S PREFACE

The welcome extended to the first book of this History has encouraged the continuation of the work. It will be completed in four books, and an Index to the whole will be given at the end of the fourth book.

The present book carries on the story from the death of St. John to the end of the second century.

The principles governing citations from the Scriptures, and from ecclesiastical writers, are the same as those adopted for the first book. Notes within brackets have been added by me on my own responsibility.

ERNEST C. MESSENGER

CHAPTER VI

CHRISTIAN LIFE AT THE END OF THE FIRST CENTURY [1]

§1. CHRISTIAN LIFE AND WORSHIP

REJECTED by the synagogue and persecuted by the Roman Empire, the Church nevertheless developed an intense interior life. From the first, this life calls for the admiration of the historian by reason of its overflowing plenitude, but precisely because of its richness it seems to defy all description. Attempts have been made to grasp this exuberance by describing successively the various aspects of the new-born Christianity. In this way, Harnack, in his *Mission and Expansion of Christianity*, has studied, in a series of chapters, the Gospel of Love and Charity, the religion of the Spirit and of Power, of Moral Earnestness and Holiness, the Religion of Authority and of Reason, of the Mysteries and of Transcendentalism, the Tidings of the New People, the Religion of a Book and a Historical Realisation, the Conflict with Polytheism and Idolatry.[2] All these developments are of interest, and bring into the light some characteristics of primitive Christianity. However, as we are not able here to enter into detail, we would prefer to study the principle of unity from which all the rest proceeds. We know that Harnack, in his *Essence of Christianity*, thought he could trace everything back to the religion of God the Father. It seems to us that, during the apostolic period, Christianity is above all the religion of the Christ.[3] This may seem a truism, but nevertheless it deserves to be considered attentively: it is indeed the distinctive character of this religion, and the secret of its power.

[1] Bibliography—P. Batiffol, *L'Eglise naissante et le catholicisme*, 9th edn., Paris 1927 (English tr.: *Primitive Catholicism*, London, 1911); J. Lebreton, *La vie chrétienne au premier siècle de l'Eglise*, Paris, 1927; E. Amann, *L'Eglise des premiers siècles*, Paris, 1927; Dom Cabrol, *La prière des premiers chrétiens*, Paris, 1929; G. Bardy, *L'Eglise à la fin du premier siècle*, Paris, 1932.

[2] All these chapters form Book II of *Mission und Ausbreitung*, pp. 111-331.

[3] This does not mean that the emphasis on Christ caused the Father to be forgotten; quite the contrary. Hence we are entirely opposed to the extreme thesis of A. C. MacGiffert, *The God of the Early Christians*, New York, 1924.

The Religion of the Christ

Already in the early days at Jerusalem, the conflict centred round this point. The Sanhedrin forbade the apostles to preach in the name of Jesus; Peter replied that there was no other saving name. Later on, when the procurator Festus wished to inform King Agrippa as to the case against St. Paul, he told him that it concerned "one Jesus deceased, whom Paul affirmed to be alive" (*Acts* xxv, 19). Tacitus himself, whose information is limited, nevertheless speaks correctly when he thus defines Christianity: "He who gave His name to this sect, the Christ, was put to death. . . ."; and Suetonius in turn, speaking of the Edict of Claudius, expresses himself thus: "The Jews caused disturbances, under the impulse of a certain Chrestus."

And what the earliest adversaries perceived appears clearly in the first Christian preaching: "God has made him Lord and Christ"; "He raised him up": that is what Peter affirmed from the first days at Jerusalem, Paul at Antioch in Pisidia, at Athens and everywhere else. Doubtless, when he was preaching to pagans, the apostle had first of all to preach to them the One God and to draw them away from their idols; but he at once went on to Christ, to His resurrection, and to His second coming, even at the risk of being abandoned by his sceptical hearers.

At the same time that Christ is the central object of faith, He is also the Saviour in whom every man must hope. The prize which the apostles set forth constantly to those they wish to win is the forgiveness of sins and salvation through Christ. Such is the theme of St. Peter's sermon on Pentecost day (*Acts* ii, 38), and in his speeches on his two appearances before the Sanhedrin (*ibid.*, iv, 12; v, 31); it is also the theme of St. Paul's homily at Antioch in Pisidia (xiii, 38). This is the echo of the appeal which Jesus himself made to his hearers, and through them, to all men: "Come to me, all you that labour, and are burdened, and I will refresh you" (*Matt.* xi, 28). Later on Celsus will write with indignation: "Those who endeavour to win followers for the other mysteries, say: 'Let him whose hands are pure . . . enter here!' . . . But we hear these people on the contrary cry: 'Whosoever is a sinner, foolish, simple or miserable, will receive the kingdom of God.' " [4]

[4] Quoted by Origen, III, 59.

Those who have thus been won and redeemed belong no longer to themselves; they belong to the Lord:

"None of us liveth to himself, and no man dieth to himself. For whether we live, we live unto the Lord; or whether we die, we die unto the Lord. Therefore, whether we live or whether we die, we are the Lord's. For to this end Christ died and rose again; that he might be Lord both of the dead and of the living" (*Rom.* xiv, 7-9).

"You are not your own, for you are bought with a great price" (I *Cor.* vi, 19-20).[5]

Christianity is not only a new condition of life: it is a new life. By baptism, Christians are buried with Christ in death, and raised again with him to life.[6] And they do not rise again as isolated individuals, but as members of the body of Christ, the Church: "We were all baptised into one body, whether Jews or Gentiles, whether bond or free."[7] And this life-giving primacy of Christ extends not only to the Church which He sanctifies, but also to the whole world of which He is the Ruler and the Head:

"All things were created by him and in him. And he is before all, and by him all things consist. And he is the head of the body, the Church, who is the beginning, the first-born from the dead; that in all things he may hold the primacy, because in him, it hath well pleased the Father that all fulness should dwell, and through him to reconcile all things unto himself, making peace through the blood of his cross, both as to the things that are on earth, and the things that are in heaven" (*Col.* i, 16-20).

All this is not mere speculation, for it governs the whole of the Christian life. The Church is the body of Christ; all its functions are produced in it by the action of the Head who dispenses its life (*Ephes.* iv, 11-16). The sacraments are set forth only in this light: baptism is the burial and resurrection with Christ; marriage is a union representing that of Christ and the Church (*Ephes.* v, 25 32); the Eucharist above all, which is the centre of all worship and

[5] To make his thought better understood, St. Paul employs the very terms used to signify sacred manumissions: just as the slaves who wished to put their newly acquired liberty under the patronage of a god had to be purchased by him by a fictitious sale, so also, but this time in reality, the Christian has been redeemed by Christ to be free: I *Cor.* vii, 23; *Gal.* v, 1-19. Cf. *Histoire du Dogme de la Trinité*, I, p. 406.

[6] *Rom.* vi, 3-11; *Col.* ii, 12; iii, 4.

[7] I *Cor.* xii, 13; cf. xii, 27; *Rom.* xii, 5; *Col.* i, 18; iii, 15; *Ephes.* iv, 4.

the indispensable food of the Christian, is the representation of the death of the Lord, the participation of his body, the communion in his blood.[8]

Moral exhortations are inspired by this ever-present thought: we must flee fornication because our bodies are the members of Christ (*I Cor.* vi, 15); we must be generous, after the example of Christ, who being rich became poor (*II Cor.* viii, 9); we must forget ourselves in order to imitate Jesus Christ, who being in the form of God humbled himself and took the form of a slave (*Phil.* ii, 6-7); husbands must love their wives as Christ loved the Church (*Ephes.* v, 25); servants must be obedient to their masters as to Christ (*ibid.,* vi, 5). This constant reference to the highest mysteries in order to inculcate upon Christians fidelity to their duties, even the most humble ones, fills the whole of life with the memory of Christ and of his love.

These are a few of the very numerous features in which St. Paul's theology reveals the ineffaceable impress with which Christ ·had marked the apostle's life: "for me, to live is Christ" (*Phil.* i, 21).

The same impress is found in the other apostles, as for instance in this text of St. Peter, quoted already in the early years of the second century by St. Polycarp: [9] "Jesus Christ, whom having not seen, you love; in whom also now, though you see him not, you believe: and believing shall rejoice with joy unspeakable and glorified, receiving the end of your faith, even the salvation of your souls" (*I Pet.* i, 8-9). And further on: "Desire the rational milk without guile, that thereby you may grow unto salvation: if so be you have tasted that the Lord is sweet. Unto whom coming, as to a living stone, rejected indeed by men, but chosen and made honourable by God" (ii, 2-4). And yet again: "Christ suffered for us, leaving you an example that you should follow his steps." [10]

We find the same note in the Johannine literature, the epistles [11] and the *Apocalypse;* Christians are the servants of Jesus (i, 1; xii, 20); the martyrs are the witnesses of Jesus (ii, 13); the closing sentence is the suppliant cry of the Church: "Amen. Come, Lord Jesus!" (xxii, 20).

This last prayer brings home to us what it was that the Christians

---

[8] *I Cor.* x, 16-17; xi, 26-27.
[9] Letter to the Philippians, i, 3.
[10] ii 21; cf. iii 18; iv 1, 13, 14.
[11] It is sufficient to recall the commencement of the first epistle, i, 1-4.

desired when they awaited the Second Coming with such impatience: admittedly it was the triumph and coming of the Kingdom, but above all it was the coming and the definitive presence of the Son of God. Thus we read in the first letter to the Thessalonians (iv, 16): "So shall we be always with the Lord." Later on, when this perspective of the Second Coming was less prominent in the apostle's mind, the desire to be with Christ remained as active as ever (*Phil.* i, 23).

All this is clear, and yet too often it is overlooked. Thus, in the question of virginity, the apostle's counsels are manifestly inspired by the desire to belong wholly to the Lord without other cares: "He that is without a wife, is solicitous for the things that belong to the Lord, how he may please God. But he that is with a wife, is solicitous for the things of the world, how he may please his wife, and he is divided" (*I Cor.* vii, 32-33). Accordingly numerous Protestant critics are wrong when they explain this counsel of the apostle as due solely to the expectation of an imminent Second Coming.[12]

The Sacraments

The spiritual life is not purely individual; it is the life of members of the Body of Christ which is the Church. The latter is likewise not purely spiritual: it is maintained and expressed by material symbols. The old Protestant thesis which rejected the sacraments as late corruptions has been definitively condemned by history.[13]

---

[12] Thus Sabatier, *L'apôtre Paul*, p. 160: "On one single point the judgment of the apostle seems still narrow: I refer to celibacy. This narrowness, for which he has been so much reproached, does not at all arise from a dualistic asceticism. . . . What narrows and confines the apostle's judgment here are his eschatological opinions, The Second Coming is imminent; the time is short; all other interests disappear before this immediate future. But very soon there is a progress in this respect in Paul's thought. He succeeds in freeing himself from the narrow bonds of Jewish eschatology; in the epistles of the Captivity we shall see that he arrives at a wider and juster view of marriage and of domestic life." Certainly "the time is short," "the figure of this world passes away," and it is foolish to be too much attached to it; but the decisive motive is the desire to belong exclusively to the Lord.

[13] Let us recall, for instance, what Harnack wrote in *Mission und Ausbreitung*, p. 247: "To regard water, bread, and wine, as holy elements, to plunge into water in order that the soul may be washed and purified, to regard bread and wine as the Body and Blood of Christ, and as a food which confers immortality upon men's souls—this is a language which was well understood at that time. The dull-minded realist understood it, but the most sublime spiritualist did so equally.

It is true that sacramental theology has escaped the attacks of the
Reformed theologians only to be a prey to the hypotheses of the
historians of Comparative Religion. These new opponents recognise that the apostolic theology is wholly penetrated with the
sacramental idea, but they see in this penetration a pagan influence which·in their view dominated the Church from the beginning.

Catholic historians have continued the fight on this new ground,
and nowadays scientific opinion agrees with them, even that of
those who do not accept the Catholic faith: these recognise that
the sacraments, and in particular, baptism and the Eucharist, which
have been specially attacked, cannot, as was supposed, be explained
by the influence of the pagan mysteries, and still less by the
Mandæan liturgy.[14]

The two most sublime spiritualists in the Church, John and Origen, became the
most powerful exponents of the mysteries, and the great Gnostic theologians
linked their most abstract theological theorems to realist mysteries; they were all
theologians of sacraments. . . . The phrase of the later scholastics, 'sacramenta
continent gratiam,' is as old as the Church of the Gentiles; it is even older than
that; it existed long before her." Again, p. 252: "Read the stories concerning the
Supper told by Dionysius of Alexandria, a disciple of Origen, or what Cyprian
narrates concerning the miracles of the Host. . . . It is objected *Ab initio sic non
erat.* That may be so, but one would have to go back very far—so far, in fact, that
this very brief period cannot be discovered by us."

[14] On this question, consult L. de Granmaison, *Les mystères paiens et le
Mystère chrétien; Jésus Christ,* Vol. II, pp. 535-561; E. Jacquier, *Les mystères
paiens et saint Paul,* in *Dictionnaire apologétique,* Vol. III, col. 964-1014; on
baptism, col. 1004-1008; on the Eucharist, col. 1008-1010); F. Prat, *Saint Paul et
le paulinisme,* Vol. III, *Le paulinisme et les religions orientales hellénisées, ibid.,*
Vol. III, col. 1047-1051.

The question of baptism has been specially dealt with from this point of view
by J. Coppens' article, *Baptême,* in *Supplement* to *Dictionnaire de la Bible, Le
baptême et les religions à mystères,* Vol. I, p. 883-886; *Mystères paiens et baptême
chrétien,* p. 903-924. This question of the Eucharist is dealt with by W. Goossens in *Les Origines de l'Eucharistie,* Gembloux, 1931, pp. 252-323.

The Mandæan hypothesis has been specially pressed by R. Reitzenstein, *Die
Vorgeschichte der christlichen Taufe,* Leipzig, 1929, especially pp. 152-292. This
hypothesis has been generally rejected, even by the independent critics; cf. H.
Lietzmann, *Ein Beitrag zur Mandäerfrage,* in *Sitzungsberichte der Akad. Berlin,*
1930, pp. 596-608; A. Loisy, *Le Mandéisme et les origines chrétiennes,* 1934,
especially pp. 104-141; Erich Fascher, art. *Taufe,* in Pauly-Wissowa, *Real-
Encyclopädie,* Vol. IV, A², 1932, p. 2507; the influence of the pagan mysteries
is similarly rejected, *ibid.,* pp. 2511-2512. On this last question see also A. von
Stromberg, *Studienzur Theorie und Praxis der Taufe in der christlichen Kirche
der ersten zwei Jahr hunderte,* Berlin, 1913, pp. 36-45, cf. pp. 125-126, and A.
Schweitzer, *Die Mystik des Apostels Paulus,* Tübingen, 1930, pp. 27-41.

Baptism

What we have said above concerning the life and teaching of Christ has enabled us to attain to the real origin of the sacraments, and in particular, of baptism and the Eucharist.[15] We saw how Jesus received the baptism of John (*Matt.* iii, 13-17), and that, when He began His public life, baptism was administered by His own disciples,[16] and that after the Resurrection He commanded his apostles to baptise all nations in the name of the Father, Son, and Holy Spirit (*Matt.* xxviii, 19). This baptism was not a ritual ablution, like those to which the Jews were accustomed,[17] nor a baptism of penitence, like the baptism of John;[18] it was a new birth, by which the person baptised was regenerated "by water and the Holy Ghost."[19] It was thus that Jesus explained to Nicodemus the nature and effect of baptism, and this conception will remain familiar to the apostles and to the Church.[20] The mysteries of the death and resurrection of Christ put this transformation in a new light: by baptism the neophytes were incorporated into Christ, died with Him and rose again with Him; they died to the flesh, they rose again in the spirit; being members of Christ, living with His life, they were freed from the servitude of the old Adam. Doubtless the old man still lived in them, but he had been mortally wounded by

[15] The other sacraments appear already in the apostolic period, but we cannot give them a special treatment here; what we have to say later on concerning the primitive hierarchy will deal with Order and its chief degrees, the episcopate, priesthood and diaconate; Confirmation appears in the laying on of hands which completes the graces of baptism (*Acts* vii, 24); cf. J. Coppens, *L'imposition des mains*, pp. 174-248.

[16] *John* iii, 22; iv, 2. On the nature of this baptism, two different opinions have been held by the Fathers and theologians: some see in it only the baptism of John the Baptist; others regard it as Christian baptism. This second view is the more common. Cf. A. d'Alès, *De Baptismo*, Paris, 1927, p. 19, and art. *Baptême* in *Supplement to Dictionnaire de la Bible*, Vol. I, p. 858.

[17] On the baptism of proselytes and the other Jewish ablutions, cf. J. Coppens, art. *Baptême*, col. 892-894.

[18] John himself expressly recognised this: "I have baptized you with water; but he shall baptize you with the Holy Ghost" (*Mark* i, 8); "I indeed baptize you in water unto penance . . . he shall baptize you in the Holy Ghost and fire" (*Matt.* iii, 11); cf. *Luke* iii, 16.

[19] *John* iii, 5; cf. iii, 3, 7-8.

[20] *Tit.* iii, 5; *I Pet.* i, 3. Often again the new birth is set forth as a divine adoption; *John* i, 12-13; *Rom.* viii, 15-16; *Gal.* iii, 26-27; *I John* iii, 1-2; v. 18; or as a new creation: *Gal.* vi, 15; *Ephes.* ii, 10. On all these ideas cf. A. d'Alès, art. *Baptême*, col. 863-866.

baptism, and would be constantly mortified by faithful christians until death was swallowed up in life, and Christ was all in all.[21]

Baptism was indispensable for salvation. On Pentecost Day, the Jews, touched by the preaching of Peter, asked him: "What must we do?" "Do penance, and be baptised every one of you in the name of Jesus Christ" replied the apostle, and at the same time he promised them the fruits of baptism: the forgiveness of sins, and the gift of the Holy Spirit (Acts ii, 38). The converts of Samaria were baptised in the same way (viii, 12), also the Ethiopian eunuch (viii, 38), Saul (ix, 18), Cornelius the centurion and his household (x, 48), and indeed all the neophytes who appear in the apostolic history.

All were called to baptism: it was the Lord's command (Matt. xxviii, 19), and in the case of the centurion Cornelius, the Holy Ghost himself dispelled all hesitation. This principle was never questioned, even by the Judaisers.[22] In all candidates for baptism, faith was required; hence the custom, witnessed to already in apostolic times, of requiring from the candidates for baptism a profession of faith; this was the origin of the baptismal creed.[23] Every Christian, in order to be saved, had to confess with his mouth that Jesus was Lord, and believe with his heart that God had raised him from amongst the dead (Rom. x, 9); this profession of faith showed the adhesion of the neophyte to the traditional catechesis, such as that we find referred to, for instance, in the epistle to the Corinthians (I Cor. xv, 3 et seq.).

As to the rite of baptism in the apostolic age, the most explicit account we possess is the sixth chapter in the Didache:

"Baptize in the following manner: After saying all which precedes, baptize into the name of the Father, and of the Son, and of the Holy Ghost, in running water. If you have not running water, baptize in other water; and if you cannot baptize in cold water, baptize in warm. If both are lacking, pour some water thrice upon the head, in the name of the Father and of the Son and of the Holy Ghost. Before baptism,

[21] Cf. Bk. I, p. 262; D'Alès, art. Baptême, col. 866-868; Schweitzer, Die Mystik des Apostels Paulus, pp. 119-158; in this book this idea is developed with great force, but the author wrongly contrasts it with the conception of regeneration, which he thinks foreign to St. Paul, pp. 13-15 and 120-211.

[22] What they desired was not to keep the pagans from baptism, but to impose circumcision on them.

[23] Cf. Histoire du dogme de la Trinité, Vol. II, pp. 146 et seq.; P. Feine, Die Gestalt des apost. Glaubensbekenntnisses in der Zeit des N.T., Leipzig, 1925. We return to the baptismal creed later.

let the baptizer and the baptized fast, and other persons who are able; enjoin the baptized person to fast one or two days before." [24]

The Eucharist

The origin of the Eucharist is already known to us.[25] We know that Christ instituted at the Last Supper this living representation of His sacrifice, and commanded his apostles to "do this in memory of him." Jesus was obeyed: the apostolic writings bear witness to the celebration of the Eucharist at Jerusalem and in the Pauline churches.[26]

This celebration is called in the accounts in the *Acts* (ii, 41-42; 46-47; xx, 7-11) the "breaking of bread." [27] In the first days of

[24] Jacquier remarks on this passage: "This is the earliest mention we have of baptism by infusion; nevertheless it is likely that this was the most usual mode of baptism in apostolic times: the three thousand Jews who were converted by Peter's sermon on Pentecost Day and were baptised (*Acts* ii, 41) must have been baptized thus. The same applies to the five thousand converts mentioned in *Acts* iv, 4, and to the Philippian jailor and his family baptized by St. Paul in the prison (*ibid.*, xvi, 33). It would also appear that the baptism of the Ethiopian eunuch could not have been by complete immersion (*ibid.*, viii, 38)" (p. 194). This mention of baptism by infusion was suppressed when this text passed into the *Apostolic Constitutions*, vii, 22. Cf. St. Cyprian, ep. 69, 12-16, who had to defend the validity of baptism administered by infusion to the sick; and Cornelius, letter to Fabius of Antioch (*Hist. Eccles.*, vi, 43, 17), which says that those who had been thus baptized could not be admitted into the ranks of the clergy. At the date of these various documents, the construction of the baptismal piscinas had caused baptism by infusion to fall into desuetude for a time, and it was practised only in the case of the sick.

On baptism for the dead mentioned in *I Cor.* xv, 29, cf. Prat, *Theology of St. Paul*, Vol. I, p. 136: "A curious usage existed in Corinth and probably also in other Christian communities. When a catechumen died before being far enough advanced as to be baptized, one of his relatives or friends received for him the ceremonies of the sacrament. What precise signification was attached to this act? It is difficult to say. St. Paul neither approves nor condemns it; he treats it only as a profession of faith in the resurrection of the dead." See also Père Allo,O.P., I *Ep. aux Corinthiens*, Paris, 1934, pp. 411-13.

[25] Cf. Bk. I, pp. 143-5.

[26] The apostolic texts relating to the Eucharist have been conveniently collected together by W. B. Frankland in *The Early Eucharist*, London, 1902, pp. 3-11, and less completely by G. Rauschen, *Florilegium Patristicum*, Vol. VII, *Monumenta Eucharistica et Liturgica vetustissima*, Bonn, 1909. A detailed and exact interpretation of the texts will be found in W. Goossens, *Les origines de l'Eucharistie*, Gembloux, 1931, especially pp. 147-174.

[27] Cf. Goossen, *op. cit.*, pp. 172-173. Jacquier, in his commentary, recognises the eucharistic reference in the first and third texts, but not in the second; Goossens writes, apparently more correctly: "The breaking of bread in two passages so close to one another and having the same subject must have the same meaning in the two cases."

the Church at Jerusalem, the faithful were "persevering in the doctrine of the apostles, and in the communication of the breaking of bread and in prayers" (ii, 42); "continuing daily with one accord in the Temple, and breaking bread from house to house, they took their meat with gladness and simplicity of heart" (ii, 46). This brief description indicates, side by side with the Eucharist, a common meal which probably took place at the same time.[28] This meal was certainly the custom at Corinth; but there it had led to abuses which St. Paul corrected:

"When you come therefore together into one place, it is not now to eat the Lord's supper. For every one taketh before his own supper to eat. And one indeed is hungry and another is drunk." [29]

The apostle, in order to put an end to these abuses, writes:

"Wherefore, my brethren, when you come together to eat, wait for one another. If any man be hungry, let him eat at home; that you come not together unto judgment." [30]

Again, we have the Supper celebrated at Troas by St. Paul: it was the first day of the week (Sunday); the faithful were gathered together for the breaking of bread. Paul, who was to depart the next day, was speaking to the brethren; he continued his discourse until midnight. In the upper room in which the meeting was taking place, many lamps were lit; in the course of the apostle's long discourse, a young man named Eutychius went to sleep; he fell from the third floor to the ground, and was picked up dead. Paul went down, took him in his arms, and brought him to life again; then he went back, broke bread, ate, and conversed with the brethren until daybreak (*Acts* xx, 7-11).

The vigil was exceptionally prolonged on that occasion because of the imminent departure of the apostle, but this fact did not make any change in the character of this liturgical assembly: the breaking of bread was its central feature; it took place on the Sunday, the day especially assigned for the celebration of the Eucharist.[31]

[28] It seems to me that this is wrongly contested by Goossens, *op. cit.*, p. 134; but it does not follow that this meal was the agape. The agape is certainly attested for the end of the second century; nothing justifies us in affirming its use in the first century. Cf. Goossens, pp. 127-146.

[29] 1 *Cor.* xi, 20-21. Cf. Bk. I, p. 246.

[30] *Ibid.*, 33-34. It seems to follow from this text that the Christian assembly ought to be exclusively eucharistic, and that all other meals were to be banished from it (Goossens, *op. cit.*, pp. 138-141).

[31] Cf. I *Cor.* xvi, 2; *Didache* xiv, 1; Goossens, *op. cit.*, p. 172, n. 6.

These few texts enable us to see how from the time of the apostles the command of the Lord: "Do this in memory of me" was carried out; and already we recognise here the outline of the liturgy which was very shortly to develop. Some have endeavoured to distinguish between two different types of apostolic Eucharist: they suggest that in the accounts in the Acts concerning Jerusalem and Troas, we have a brotherly meal, a symbol of the union of Christians with each other and with Jesus; in the epistle to the Corinthians we have a sacrificial meal, wholly penetrated with the memory of the death of the Lord.[32] This hypothesis is an arbitrary one, and is contradicted by the texts of St. Paul; the apostle, far from being aware of innovating in any way in this matter, appeals expressly to the tradition which he has received and transmitted;[33] he himself moreover sets forth the double aspect of the eucharistic mystery, the sacrifice (*I Cor.* x, 16-21) and the mystery of union (*ibid.*, 17; cf. *Rom.* xii, 5).

But though from the first we see only one Eucharist, we can distinguish already in the eucharistic doctrine the trace of the two great dogmas of the Incarnation and the Redemption. The Son of God present in us, uniting us to himself and to our brethren, is what St. John brings out above all in the two discourses of Christ at Capernaum and after the Last Supper; the Son of God who died for us and unites us to His sacrifice is what St. Paul chiefly dwells upon. And from that time onwards in the whole history of eucharistic theology, we can follow these two doctrinal currents; they will never be isolated from each other, but they will lead theologians to contemplate by preference either our life-giving union with the "bread which has come down from heaven," or else our participation in his death, in the communion of the "blood of the testament."[34]

[32] This thesis has been maintained by H. Lietzmann, *Messe und Herrenmahl,* Bonn, 1926, pp. 238-263. Cf. *Recherches de science religieuse,* 1927, pp. 330-333.

[33] *I Cor.* xi, 23. On this text, cf. the article *Eucharistie* in the *Dictionnaire apologétique,* col. 1552 *et seq.* Also Allo, *op. cit.,* pp. 302-16.

[34] Already in the *Didache* we can recognise, in the eucharistic prayers, this double influence, Pauline and (above all) Johannine.

§ 2. THE PRIMITIVE HIERARCHY[1]

Peter and the Twelve

In our account of the life of Jesus, we found around him a group of twelve apostles.[2] These were chosen by Him, formed by Him, sent by Him, and invested with the powers of teaching and government which constituted them the heads of the Church here below,[3] and in heaven the judges of mankind.[4] After His Resurrection, the Lord confirmed these privileges to the apostles, gave them the Holy Spirit, and sent them forth to convert and baptize all nations.[5]

Amongst these twelve apostles, we saw that Peter was the first (*Matt.* x, 2). It was on him in the first place that the Church rested as on an unshakable rock; it was he who, before the other apostles, received the power of binding and loosing (*Matt.* xvi, 16-19); it was he who, after the Resurrection, was once more singled out by Jesus from the apostolic group, and charged with the feeding of the lambs and the sheep (*John* xxi, 15-19).

Thus, even before founding the Church by His death and the outpouring of the Holy Spirit, Jesus revealed the plan of the building He intended to construct: the Christian Church was to be a hierarchical society, taught and governed by the apostles, with Peter at their head.

In point of fact, that is how the Church appears, from the first day, in the Upper Room. The Twelve formed a privileged group, in which the defection of Judas left a gap; this gap had to be filled; Peter took the initiative in the election of Matthias and directed it (*Acts* i, 15-26). On Pentecost Day it was Peter who, assisted by the eleven, explained to the people the mystery of the Spirit (ii, 14), and told the converts what they had to do (ii, 37); three thousand people were converted, and "were persevering in the doctrine of the apostles, and in the communication of the breaking of bread, and in prayers" (ii, 42). It was at the feet of the apostles that the Christians laid down the price of the possessions which they gave up (iv, 35-37; v, 2). Thus, all power was committed to their hands; their manifold cares became too absorbing, and the apostles, in order to devote themselves to the ministry of prayer and the word

---

[1] Cf. Batiffol, *Primitive Catholicism*; Michiels, *L'origine de l'Episcopat*, Louvain, 1900; Harnack, *Entschung und Entwicklung der Kirchenwerfassung und des Kirchenrechts in den zwei ersten Jahrhunderten*, Leipzig, 1910.
[2] Cf. Bk. I, pp. 98-100.   [3] *Matt.* xvi, 16-19; xviii, 17-18.
[4] *Matt.* xix, 27-30; *Luke* xxii, 28-30.   [5] *John* xx, 21-22; *Matt.* xxviii, 18-20.

of God, caused seven deacons to be chosen for the ministry of tables (vi, 2 *et seq.*). These deacons also assisted the apostles in preaching, whether at Jerusalem (as Stephen) or elsewhere (as Philip).

In this group of apostles which so clearly asserted its authority from these first years, there was one leader who dominated all the rest by his supreme authority: Peter. We have seen this in the election of Matthias and in the great manifestations on Pentecost day; we shall find it again in all the events which follow: in the Temple, where he goes with John, it is he who addresses the word to the lame man, heals him, and speaks to the people (iii, 14, *et seq.*); before the Sanhedrin, it is he who speaks (iv, 7; v, 29); when Ananias and Sapphira try to conceal the price of their field, it is he who rebukes and condemns them (v, 1 *et seq.*). The Apostles, says Luke, performed great miracles; then he becomes more explicit: the sick were placed in Peter's path, so that at least his shadow might fall on them (v, 15). Peter and John are sent to Samaria; it is Peter who addresses the people (viii, 20). The decisive step in missions to the pagans, the baptism of the centurion Cornelius, is the work of Peter (x). When in the Council of Jerusalem the conditions of admission of pagans into the Church are being discussed, it is Peter who speaks first, and his opinion prevails (xv, 7).

This prominent situation of St. Peter, so manifest in the first chapters of the Acts, is less apparent in the rest of the narrative, because St. Paul is the chief centre of interest; but even there, the unparalleled authority of the head of the apostles is shown in the steps taken by St. Paul; in the care he takes to put himself in touch with Peter (*Gal.* i, 18), in the rank he assigns to Peter amongst the witnesses of the Resurrection of Jesus (*I Cor.* xv, 5), in the way, even, in which a small group of Corinthians try to abuse the respected name of Peter (*I Cor.,* i, 12).[6]

Authority and the Spirit

These powers of jurisdiction and teaching conferred upon St. Peter and the other apostles, are gifts of the Holy Spirit, charisms, ordained for the good of the Church. Of all the functions of the

[6] All this is not contradicted or even obscured by the incident at Antioch; cf. Bk. I, p. 195. But from this incontestable primacy of St. Peter, one must not infer that his relations towards the other apostles were the same as those of the Pope towards other bishops. The Apostles received from Christ the power of universal jurisdiction, and the assurance of a personal infallibility in doctrine, privileges which they did not transmit to the bishops who succeeded them.

members of the body of Christ, the apostolate is the highest, but like the others, it derives its origin from a divine grace, and it has as its object the well-being of the body:

"Christ gave some apostles, and some prophets, and other some evangelists, and other some pastors and doctors, for the perfecting of the saints, for the work of the ministry, for the edifying of the body of Christ" (*Ephes.* iv, 11-12).

This double character, spiritual and hierarchical, is essential to the Church; this indissoluble union of authority and charism is manifest not only in the doctrine of St. Paul, but also in the facts, and that from the first day of the Church, and even before Pentecost. When the risen Jesus appears to His apostles and gives them power to bind and to loose, He says to them at the same time: "Receive the Holy Spirit" (*John* xx, 22). The highest exercise of the apostolic ministry is the gift of the Spirit; it appears at Pentecost (ii, 6-13) and later at Samaria (viii, 14), Cæsarea (x, 44), and Ephesus (xix, 6). To those who ask Paul for a letter of recommendation in proof of his apostolate, he replies: "You are our epistle, written in our hearts, which is known and read by all men: being manifested, that you are the epistle of Christ, ministered by us, and written not with ink, but with the Spirit of the living God, not in tables of stone, but in the fleshly tablets of the heart" (*II Cor.*, iii, 2-3).

Protestant writers may endeavour to oppose the Church of authority to the Church of the Spirit;[7] this opposition does violence to the history of Christian origins, and especially to the conception of the apostolate as this appears in the Gospels, Acts, and above all in the epistles of St. Paul.[8]

---

[7] This is the thesis of the posthumous work of Auguste Sabatier, *Les religions d'autorité et la religion de l'esprit,* Paris, 1904.

[8] The apostolate is a charism: the apostle must have seen the Lord (*I Cor.* ix, 1-2) and have received a direct call from Christ (*Gal.* i, 1; *Acts* xiii, 2; cf. i, 26); his ministry is proved by its fruitfulness in grace and charisms (*I Cor.* ix, 2; *II Cor.* iii, 3; xii, 12). But this charism of the apostolate confers an authority which the apostle exercises; even the spiritual gifts, the most divine and most independent element seemingly in Christianity, are regulated by the apostle (*I Cor.* xii). He also regulates the celebration of the Supper, and corrects abuses in it (*ibid.,* xi, 34); by his own authority he defines the duties of married people (*ibid.,* vii, 12); he excommunicates the incestuous man (ix, 3); he sends Timothy, who will make known to the Corinthians what the apostle teaches in all the churches, and he adds: "What will you? Shall I come to you with a rod; or in charity, and in the spirit of meekness?" (iv, 17-21).

But if it be true that Jesus decided to found a Church which would endure as long as the world itself, and if He promised to His apostles to be with them, even "till the consummation of the world," it must surely be true that these essential characters of the Church, spiritual and hierarchical, will not disappear at the death of the apostles, and that these first leaders will have successors.

The Deacons

Besides the apostolic office, we see appearing from the first years of the Church others which, like the apostolate, have their origin in a divine call, and whose object is the building up of the body of Christ; in these also we find the union of charism and authority. Such are in the first place the deacons: we have seen that the apostles instituted these in order to hand on to them the ministry of tables which had become too absorbing;[9] the people chose the seven, and the apostles ordained them by prayer and the laying on of hands.

In addition to the humble serving of tables, the apostles entrusted to the deacons the ministry of preaching; and St. Stephen, the first and best known of the seven, showed himself to be a man "full of grace and power"; the Holy Ghost spoke and acted in him with an irresistible force; his opponents could silence him only by slaying him.

The Presbyters

A little later (*Acts* xi, 30) we find in the Church of Jerusalem some "presbyters," but we do not know when or in what way they were instituted in the community. On the occasion of the famine foretold by the prophet Agabus, the Church of Antioch sent help to the church of Jerusalem; it sent alms by Barnabas and Saul to the presbyters. In an earlier episode (iv, 35) we saw that those who yielded up their possessions to the community laid the price of them at the feet of the apostles; thus we find here again the passing on to new officials of a ministry of which the apostles at first were in charge. And for the presbyters as for the deacons, the administrative charge went hand in hand with a spiritual ministry: at the Council of Jerusalem they deliberated and decided with the

[9] Cf. Bk. I, p. 177; and *Acts* vi.

apostles;[10] in 57, when St. Paul arrived at Jerusalem with the alms of his churches, he presented himself to James, who was surrounded by all the presbyters (xxi, 18).

These various incidents show us the important part played by the presbyters in the church of Jerusalem. To them we must add this precept which St. James gives in his epistle (v, 14):

"Is any man sick among you? Let him bring in the presbyters of the Church, and let them pray over him, anointing him with oil in the name of the Lord. And the prayer of faith shall save the sick man: and the Lord shall raise him up: and if he be in sins, they shall be forgiven him."

The presbyters referred to here are not merely notable and influential members of the community; they are ministers charged with a liturgical function and capable of conferring thereby spiritual graces.

Paul and Barnabas, when returning from their mission, instituted presbyters in every church (xiv, 23).[11] The same institution had taken place at Ephesus; the exhortation which Paul at Miletus gave to the presbyters of Ephesus brings out in full evidence their pastoral functions:

"Take heed to yourselves, and to the whole flock, wherein the Holy Ghost have placed you bishops, to rule the church of God, which he hath purchased with his own blood. I know that, after my departure, ravening wolves will enter in among you, not sparing the flock. And of your own selves shall arise men speaking perverse things, to draw away disciples after them. Therefore watch, keeping in memory that for three years I ceased not with tears to admonish every one of you night and day" (Acts xx, 28-31).

The office of a presbyter, as set forth in this account and discourse, is the office of a pastor and a doctor. Moreover, here as in

---

[10] Acts xv, 2: the brethren of Antioch depute "Paul and Barnabas and certain others of the other side, to go up to the apostles and presbyters at Jerusalem"; when they arrive at Jerusalem, they are received "by the church, and by the apostles and presbyters (4); after the report of the two envoys, "the apostles and presbyters assembled to consider this matter" (6). Peter speaks, then Barnabas and Paul, then James. "Then it pleased the apostles and presbyters, with the whole Church, to send to Antioch . . . Judas and Silas" (22). These messengers took with them a decision which began thus: "The apostles and presbyters, brethren, to the brethren that are at Antioch . . ." (23). This decree was promulgated everywhere as "the decrees decreed by the apostles and presbyters who were at Jerusalem" (xvi, 4).

[11] Cf. Bk. I, p. 206.

Pisidia, but more explicitly, the presbyters have as their mission the continuance of the work of the apostle, and they are to take his place.

Lastly we must note that the same men whom St. Luke calls presbyters in his narrative (*Acts* xx, 17) are called bishops by St. Paul in his discourse (Acts xx, 28).[12]

In the first epistle of St. Peter, we find exhortations to presbyters very similar to those in the discourse of Paul at Miletus:

"The presbyters therefore that are among you I beseech, who am myself also a presbyter, and a witness of the sufferings of Christ. . . . Feed the flock of God which is among you, taking care of it, not by constraint, but willingly, according to God, not for filthy lucre's sake, but voluntarily; neither as lording it over your charges, but being made a pattern of the flock from the heart. And when the Prince of Pastors shall appear, you shall receive a never fading crown of glory. In like manner, ye young men, be subject to the presbyters" (v, 1-5).

In the pastoral epistles, St. Paul sets forth the virtues which he requires in presbyter-bishops (*I Tim.* iii, 2; *Tit.* i, 6); they must be irreproachable, sober, prudent, able to instruct others, husbands of one wife, and ruling well their own households; not brutal, arrogant, quarrelsome, or covetous.[13] These presbyters are to be established everywhere; their appointment belongs to the delegates of the apostle, Titus and Timothy, who are to lay hands on them (*I Tim.* iv, 14; II *Tim.* i, 6; cf. *Acts* xiv, 23). Nowhere is there any mention of an election by the people.

What is to be noted above all in these letters is the object of this institution, which is, as St. Clement will very soon define it, the continuation of the apostolic succession, the preservation and defence of the deposit.[14]

We have just collected from the apostolic writings the indications

---

[12] In his epistles, except the pastorals and the epistle to the Hebrews, Paul does not speak of "presbyters"; but he mentions some who preside (*I Thess.* v, 12; *Rom.* xii, 8); pastors and teachers (*Ephes.* iv, 11); bishops and deacons (*Phil.* i, 1). In three places in the Epistle to the Hebrews (xiii, 7, 17, 24) there are references to superiors. Note what is said in *I Tim.* v, 17 of presbyters who rule well. These προεστῶτες, identified with the presbyters, seem identical also with the προϊστάμενοι of the epistles to the Thessalonians and Romans.

[13] In his letter to Timothy, he lays it down that the candidate must not be a neophyte (iii, 6); this condition is not found in the letter to Titus; we may infer that the church of Crete was too recent a foundation to make this condition feasible.

[14] *I Tim.* vi, 10; II *Tim.* i, 14; cf. *Tit.* iii, 10.

we find there concerning the primitive hierarchy, and especially concerning presbyters and bishops; we must now discuss the interpretation of these texts.

The presbyterate in the primitive Church was not merely a title of honour attributed to old age or for services rendered.[15] A presbyter became such by apostolic institution (*Acts* xiv, 23); and when one became a presbyter, he was invested with hierarchical and liturgical functions.[16] The "leaders," "presiding ones," "superiors" mentioned in the epistles of St. Paul are not distinguished from the presbyters; must they be distinguished from the bishops?

A distinction between bishops and presbyters in the apostolic Church is accepted by two groups of writers: some theologians, but only a small number,[17] and at the other extreme, a fair number of radical critics.[18] This thesis does not fit in at all well with the apostolic texts; presbyters and bishops there appear to be identical,[19] and they are understood in that sense by the best representatives of patristic exegesis, St. John Chrysostom[20] and St. Jerome.[21]

[15] Cf. Michiels, *op. cit.,* p. 134.

[16] *Acts* xx; *James* v, 14; and texts in pastoral epistles indicated above.

[17] Thus Franzelin, *De Ecclesia,* thesis 17.

[18] When Hatch gave his conferences in 1880, the identity of the two terms was universally accepted, as he pointed out (*The Organisation of the Early Church,* 1881, p. 39 and n. 1); his book was destined to reopen the question: by reason of the theory therein defended, he tended to separate the bishops (financial administrators) from the presbyters (members of the council or senate). Sohm (*Kirchenrecht,* p. 92) gives credit to Hatch for the differentiation introduced between these two terms, and he is right. Cf. Michiels, *op. cit.,* p. 134. J. Reville (*Origines de l'épiscopat,* p. 179) similarly writes: "All that we hope to have established is that the episcopate and presbyterate have distinct origins." This distinction will be found also in Harnack, *Entstehung und Entwicklung der Kirchenverfassung,* p. 44.

[19] *Acts* xx, 17-28; cf. *I Pet.* v, 5 (doubtful text); *Tit.* i, 5-7; *I Tim.* iii, 2; cf. v, 17.

[20] *Hom. I,* in *Phil.* Commenting on *Phil.* i, 1, he says: "What does this mean? Were there several bishops in one city? Not at all, but Paul gives this name to the priests, for until then the denomination was common." Cf. Michaels, *op. cit.,* p. 122.

[21] *In Tit.* i, 5 (Migne, P.L., XXVI, p. 562): "The same person is priest and also bishop, and before the time when, under the instigation of the devil, there arose parties in the Church, and it was said: 'I am of Paul, I am of Apollos, I am of Cephas,' the churches were governed by the council of priests. But when each one wanted those baptized by him to belong to him and not to Christ, it was decreed in the whole world that one of the priests should by election be set over the others, and that he should have the care of the whole Church and suppress the seeds of schism"; and he quotes in support of his view *Phil.* i, 1; *Acts* xx, 28; *Heb.* xiii, 17; *I Pet.* v, 1-2. In this passage of St. Jerome and in other texts in his works we find traces of his animosity against abuses of episcopal

Accepting this identification of presbyters and bishops, one last question presents itself: were the dignitaries designed by these two names bishops or simple priests? The second alternative seems the most likely;[22] so long as St. Paul was alive, he was "the sole pastor of the immense diocese which he had won to faith in Christ. Neither in Greece or Macedonia, Galatia, Crete or Ephesus was there during his lifetime any bishop other than himself and his delegates. . . . The churches in the jurisdiction of Paul were served by deacons and governed by a council of dignitaries named indifferently presbyters or bishops, under the ever watchful surveillance and the ever active guardianship of the founder or his substitutes."[23]

These "delegates" or "substitutes" of the Apostle were the recipients of the pastoral epistles, Titus and Timothy; they were associated by St. Paul in the government of the churches, and received from him the power to ordain deacons and priests; they were therefore certainly bishops; and thus we find in the Pauline Churches, as at Jerusalem, the three distinct orders of bishops, priests and deacons.[24]

We also grasp the motive and object of this institution: Paul feels that he is at the end of his course; he is very soon going to be poured out as a libation; he wants to ensure the perpetuity of his work; he entrusts it, with a full authority, to those whom he has long associated in his work.

This apostolic succession, already attested in the letters of St.

---

power; we can leave aside these features, and also what he says about the schism of Corinth, in which he finds the occasion for the distinction between bishops and priests. In his letter to Evangelus, *P.L.* XXII, 1193, he sets aside the hypothesis of a college of bishops distinct from the priests and superior to them: "Ac ne quis contentione in una Ecclesia plures episcopos fuisse contendat, audi et aliud testimonium, in quo manifestissime comprobatur eumdem esse episcopum et presbyterum: *Tit.* i, 5." On the authority of St. Jerome, cf. Petavius, *Hier.*, II, c. 4 and 5. In this work, Petavius adopts the opinion of St. Jerome; in his *Dissertations sur la dignité des evêques,* he had thought that the presbyter-bishops who governed the churches were true bishops; here he prefers to regard them as simple priests, amongst whom the apostles chose a president who became the bishop.

[22] The former alternative is chosen by Boudinhon, *Canoniste Contemporain,* 1901, pp. 390-392, and by Batiffol, *Etudes d'histoire et de théologie positive,* Vol. I, pp. 268-269; the latter by Michiels, *op. cit.,* pp. 218-230, and by Prat, *Theology of St. Paul,* Vol. I, p. 345, Vol. II, p. 306.

[23] Prat, *Theology of St. Paul,* Vol. II, p. 306, cf. Vol. I, p. 345: "These two terms are used indifferently to denote the same persons, and are applied to members of the second rank of the hierarchy—in other words, to priests."

[24] Cf. Medebielle, art. *Eglise* in *Supplement* to *Dict. de la Bible,* col. 658.

Paul, is expressly confirmed by the witness of St. Clement at the end of the first century:

"Christ comes from God, and the apostles come from Christ. . . . Having received the instructions of Our Lord Jesus Christ, and being fully convinced by his resurrection, the apostles . . . set out to announce the good news of the coming of the Kingdom of God. Preaching in country and cities, they tested in the Spirit their first fruits, and instituted them as bishops and deacons of the future believers" (xlii, 2-3).

"They appointed those of whom we have spoken, and then they laid down this rule, that when the latter should die, other approved men should succeed to their ministry. We do not think it right to reject from the ministry those who have been thus instituted by the apostles, or later by other eminent men [25] with the approbation of the whole Church" (xliv, 3).

This letter was written at the end of the reign of Domitian or at the beginning of that of Nerva (95-96). At that date St. John was returning from exile and taking up once more this apostolic ministry at Ephesus: "After the death of the tyrant," says Eusebius (*Ecclesiastical History*, III, 23, 6), "the apostle John left the island of Patmos and came to Ephesus: from thence he went whither he was called to the Gentiles in the neighbourhood, either in order thoroughly to establish churches there, or else to choose as clerics those who were designated by the Spirit."

We could wish to make these indications more precise by referring to the *Apocalypse*, and interpreting what is said there of the angels of the seven churches (i, 20 *et seq.*), but the symbolism of these chapters makes them difficult to interpret.[26] In the epistles of St. John (II and III) there seem to be traces of a conflict between the local authorities and the apostle, but from these fugitive allusions it would be dangerous to try to draw exact conclusions.[27]

---

[25] These "eminent men" are the disciples, such as Titus or Timothy, upon whom the apostles conferred, together with the episcopate, the power to institute and ordain bishops.

[26] Père Allo (*Apocalypse*, p. lxv) sees in them the collective council rather than the prelates who preside over them; cf. p. 18. This is also the interpretation of Swete (p. 28), who sees in them the angel guardians of the churches, and hence a personification of the churches.

[27] Westcott writes in his Commentary (p. lvi): "Diotrephes . . . is able for a time to withstand an Apostle in the administration of his particular Church. On the other side, the calm confidence of St. John seems to rest on himself more than on his official power. His presence will vindicate his authority. Once more

§3. THE ORIGINS OF GNOSTICISM

The great Christian Gnostic systems appear only in the course of the second century; the writers of the Great Church who opposed these heretics regarded their theses as late deformations of Christian ideas,[1] and they were right. But Basilides and Valentinus had fore-runners, the Gnostics combatted by St. Ignatius of Antioch, St. Jude, St. Peter, St. John and St. Paul. Even before the preaching of Christianity, Gnosticism was already prevalent in Syria, Palestine, and Egypt; the episode of Simon Magus narrated in the *Acts of the Apostles* shows the remarkable diffusion of the Gnostic fancies.

Pagan Gnosticism

Gnosticism, in point of fact, was a great religious movement before Christianity, to which it was opposed in its most profound tendencies. In the first centuries of our era, it invaded the whole Greco-Roman world, coming into collision with the Hellenic and Jewish religions before attacking Christianity.[1a] Its origin must be sought in the religious syncretism which, from the time of the conquests of Alexander, and still more since the Roman conquest, had mingled and fused together the Oriental cults. The name "gnosis" indicates the object aimed at: the knowledge, or rather the vision of God; it is a divine revelation which almost always

---

the growth of the Churches is as plainly marked as their independence." Streeter (*Primitive Church*, London, 1929, pp. 84-89) thinks that the local episcopate, represented by Diotrephes, was held in check by the quasi metropolitan authority of the writer of the letters, who was Bishop of Ephesus. To attribute to metropolitans at this date so great an influence is an anachronism.

[1] Thus Clement of Alexandria, *Stromat.* VII, 17, 106: "The teaching of Our Lord during his life began with Augustus and finished towards the middle of the reign of Tiberius; the preaching of the Apostles, as far as the end of the ministry of Paul, finished under Nero; the heresiarchs, on the contrary, began very much later, in the time of the king Hadrian, and lasted until the epoch of Antoninus the Elder. For instance, Basilides. . . ." Similarly Hegesippus, quoted by Eusebius, *Hist. Eccles.*, III, 32, 7: "In the time of the apostles, the Church remained, as it were, a pure virgin without spot; but after the death of the apostles, wicked error found the beginning of its organisation through the deceits of those who taught another doctrine."

[1a] I here summarize the chapter dealing with the origin of Gnosticism in *Histoire du Dogme de la Trinité*, Vol. II, pp. 81-93, completing this at the same time by means of the works which have since 1928 thrown light on this obscure subject.

claims to be based upon some ancient message transmitted secretly by a chain of initiates; through this mysterious tradition, one is linked up with primitive peoples such as the ancient Egyptians, and through them, to the gods. Thus the hermetic books present themselves as revelations made to Hermes or received by him; others appeal to Asclepios. Similarly the Christian Gnostics place their revelations under the patronage of some apostle, or, often, of Mary Magdalene, who is supposed to have received them from the risen Christ before the Ascension.

Gnosticism claimed to be a doctrine of salvation as well as a revelation; it taught the soul how to free itself from the material world in which it is imprisoned, and to ascend once more towards the spiritual and luminous world from which it has fallen. This liberation is brought about by the communication of a heavenly revelation, accompanied often by magical formulas and rites. Participation in this gnosis is not accorded or even offered to all men; like the Mysteries, Gnosis is reserved for initiates, and this was one of its most powerful attractions.

The religious doctrine thus transmitted was characterised by a very marked dualism; matter is to be despised and hated. The supreme Deity is removed as far as possible from all contact with matter; the creation of the material world is ascribed either to an inferior deity or demiurge, or else to angels or *archontes*. Between the visible world and this god there are more or less numerous intermediaries; it is by these that the divine action is extended and abased as far as the material world, and it is also through them that the soul is able to elevate itself step by step up to the supreme deity.

These ideas admit of being adapted to many different religions or mythologies: thus in the hermetic books, the same office of the revealing and saving deity is attributed to the Logos (Book I), to the Eon (Book XI), to Agathodæmon (Book XII), and to the Sun (Book XVI). The ascent of the soul, which passes successively through the seven planetary spheres, giving the password to the *archontes* and becoming transformed into the image of the angels it meets, is a common theme which is found, with more or less marked variants, in pagan, Jewish and Christian Gnostics. The Naassene Gnostics spoken of by Hippolytus [2] laid claim to a secret revelation which James, the Lord's brother, is supposed to have en-

[2] *Philos.*, V, 6-11.

trusted to Mariamne; but at the same time they were initiated into the mysteries of the Great Mother (v, 9-10), and they repeated two hymns to Attis which they had learnt there.

Simon Magus

This elasticity which is capable of adaptation to all religions appears already in the Gnosticism of Simon Magus, which preceded Christianity and became its rival, and later on endeavoured more and more to assimilate its theology.[3]

When Philip the Deacon arrived at Samaria, he found the town led away by Simon:

"There was a certain man named Simon, who before had been a magician in that city, seducing the people of Samaria, giving out that he was some great one; to whom they all gave ear, from the least to the greatest, saying: 'This man is the power of God which is called Great.' And they were attentive to him, because for a long time he had bewitched them with his magical practices" (*Acts* viii, 9-11).

Simon nevertheless had himself baptized by Philip. When Peter and John arrived, he tried to buy with silver the power of conferring the Holy Spirit. Peter rebuked him severely; Simon seemed to be penitent and humble. The New Testament says no more about him, but later works enable us to follow the development of the sect. St. Justin, who came from Nablus and knew well his compatriots, relates that "almost all the Samaritans, and a few men in the other nations, acknowledged Simon and adored him as the supreme God." [4]

This Gnosticism thus progressively exalted its hero: first of all it saw in him only an intermediate divinity, the great Power of God; then it adored him as the supreme deity. At the end of the second century, Irenæus showed this Gnosticism endeavouring to adapt itself to the Trinitarian dogma: "Simon claims to have descended amongst the Jews as the Son, in Samaria as the Father, and in the other nations as the Holy Spirit." [5]

[3] On Simon Magus, cf. the studies of Hans Waite, *Simon Magus in der altchristlichen Literatur*, in *Zeitschrift für N.T.W.*, Vol. V, 1904, pp. 121-148, and Lucien Cerfaux, in *Recherches de Science religieuse* Vol. XV, 1925, pp. 489-511; Vol. XVI, 1926, pp. 5-20, pp. 265-285, and pp. 481-503.

[4] *Apol.*, I, XXVI, 3; cf. LVI, 1-2. Justin was mistaken concerning the supposed statue to Simon in Rome, but we can accept his witness concerning the religion of the Samaritans and the cult which they gave to Simon.

[5] *Haer.*, I, 23.

Besides this supreme deity, a goddess named Helena was also honoured. This cult seems to have arisen at Tyre, where the Moon (Selena or Helena) was associated with the worship of the Sun; the Simonian Gnostics identified this goddess with Wisdom, while the Alexandrian Gnostics regarded her as Isis.

The Clementines and the *Acts of Peter* describe a struggle between St. Peter and Simon Magus, first in Syria and then at Rome.[6] In these creations of the imagination we can discern the memory of the bitter opposition of Gnosticism to Christianity, from Syria to Rome.

Gnosticism in the Apostolic Churches

Between the Simonian Gnosticism and Christianity there could only be an ineluctible opposition. The danger of contamination could be greater when the Gnosticism which attacked Christianity was less openly pagan, and when it took the appearance of a Christian or Judaising sect. Such was more generally the Gnosticism against which the apostolic writings reacted.

At the beginning, St. Paul had to defend himself above all against attacks from without; the opponents he had in view were usually Jews or Judaisers, as for instance, in the Epistle to the Galatians. But very soon there arose heretics from the very bosom of the Church; the earliest epistles hardly mention them, but from the time of the captivity, the controversy occupies a much larger place in the theology of the apostle. "The letters to the Colossians and Ephesians—the latter, more especially, exhibit an advanced stage in the development of the Church. The heresies, which the Apostle here combats, are no longer the crude, materialistic errors of the early childhood of Christianity, but the more subtle speculations of its maturer age. The doctrine which he preaches is not now the 'milk for babes' but the 'strong meat' for grown men. . . . These epistles bridge the gulf which separates the Pastoral letters from the Apostle's earlier writings. The heresies of the Pastoral letters are the heresies of the Colossians and Ephesians grown rank and corrupt." [7]

[6] On this combat in the *Acts of Peter*, cf. Vouaux, *Les Actes de Pierre*, 1902, pp. 100-109, and on the Clementine romance, C. Schmidt, *Studien zu den Pseudo-Clementinen*, 1929, pp. 47-66, and Chapman in *Catholic Encyclopædia*, Vol. IV. An English translation of the *Acts of Peter* will be found in M. R. James, *Apocryphal New Testament*, Oxford, 1924, pp. 300-36.

[7] Lightfoot, *Philippians*, p. 45.

If we endeavour to trace from the apostolic writings an outline of the kind of Gnosticism which then threatened Christianity, we can perceive the following features:

(*a*) *Dualism,* which showed itself by contempt for the flesh; this led to a denial of the resurrection (*I Cor.* xv, 12), or to its being understood in a figurative sense, probably of baptism (*II Tim.* v, 18). From this principle divergent moral inferences were drawn: sometimes in a libertine sense: everything is allowed, because all that is fleshly is to be despised (*I Cor.* vi and x; *Apoc.* ii, 14; *II Pet.* ii, 10; *Jude* 8); sometimes, on the contrary, in the sense of a rigid asceticism, forbidding contacts deemed impure, also certain foods, and marriage (*Col.* ii, 16-21; *I Tim.* iv, 3).

(*b*) *Ambitious speculations,* including supposed visions or imaginations concerning the angels;[8] delighting in genealogies (*Tit.* iii, 9), and in "cunningly devised fables" (*II Pet.* i, 16).

(*c*) These resulted in *putting Christ below the angels* (*Col.* xxx), or even denying him altogether (*I John* ii, 29; *II Pet.* ii, 1; *Jude* 4). Many who did not go so far as this radical denial rejected the reality of the Incarnation: Jesus Christ had not come in the flesh. This Docetism was combatted above all by St. John, and soon afterwards by St. Ignatius.

(*d*) These heretics were *mainly Jews,* who claim to be doctors of the law (*Tit.* i, 10; *I Tim.* i, 7; *Apoc.* ii, 9). In the second letter of St. Peter, we find them appealing also to the authority of St. Paul (*II Pet.* i, 20; iii, 16). Some[9] have at times tried to reduce all this Gnosticism to a radical Paulinism; this is an insufficient explanation: Gnosticism arose above all from the speculations which were at that time widespread in Judaism and Hellenism; these attacked Christianity as they attacked every living religion; they were eliminated by it after a long struggle. This struggle was, however, not fruitless; it gave to church authority more vigour, and to dogma greater precision. The study of the apostolic Fathers, and particularly of St. Ignatius, will soon show this.

[8] These errors are above all combatted in *Col.* ii. Cf. A. L. Williams, *The Cult of the Angels at Colossæ,* in *Journal of Theol. Studies,* Vol. XI, 1909, pp. 413-438.

[9] E.g., MacGiffert, *History of Christianity in the Apostolic Age,* 1897, pp. 502 *et seq.*

CHAPTER VII

THE PROPAGATION OF CHRISTIANITY[1]

WHILE Christianity was developing its interior life, it was continuing its territorial expansion. The persecution which broke out suddenly and cost SS. Peter and Paul their lives, did not arrest and indeed scarcely hindered the diffusion of the Christian Faith.

§1. THE EVANGELISATION OF THE ROMAN WORLD

The First Propagation of Christianity in Italy

When persecution broke out under Nero, only to die down, and then to be revived for a first time some thirty years later under Domitian, Christianity had already secured a strong footing in the capital of the Empire. St. Paul when landing in Italy had, before arriving in Rome, found Christians at Puteoli.[2] Possibly there were also some Christians at Pompeii before 77, the year of the destruction of the city.[3]

Illyria, Spain and Gaul

Earlier still (for he speaks of it in his Epistle to the Romans written in 57 or 58) Paul had, apparently in the course of his travels

---

[1] Bibliography.—Cf. the various Histories of the Church mentioned in the General Bibliography. But the essential work to consult here is Harnack's *Die Mission und Ausbreitung des Christentums in den ersten drei Jahrhunderten,* 2 vols., 4th edn., Leipzig, 1924. The sources and special works concerning the various regions in which Christian propaganda progressed in early times are indicated in the notes to this chapter.

[2] *Acts* xxviii, 14.

[3] *Graffiti* published in *C.I.L.,* IV, pl. xvi, nos. 3 and 813. The words "audi christianos" at first seems conclusive, but those which follow are still puzzling. Cf. *Bolletino di archeologia cristiana,* 1864, p. 71, where de Rossi sets forth an explanation which is not a necessary one. On the other hand, there have been discovered at Pompeii examples of a kind of word square, called a magic square, the Christian character of which seems fairly certain, though it has not yet won complete acceptance, and their discovery *in situ* is still a matter of discussion. Cf. Jalabert, *A propos des nouveaux exemplaires trouvés à Pompei du carré magique "sator"* (C. R. Acad. Inscr., 1937, pp. 84 *et seq.*). Cf. also D. Mallarde, *La question dei cristiani a Pompei* (extract from *Rivista di Studi pompeiani,* 1934-1935, Vol. I), which concludes that there are not sufficient proofs of the existence of Christianity in Pompeii.

the preceding year in Macedonia, gone as far as the confines of the Illyrian region,[4] and his disciple Titus visited Dalmatia while the Apostle himself was in Rome.[5] The preaching of Paul doubtless also made itself heard in Spain.[6]

In the course of the stops which his boat must have made,[7] in accordance with the sailing custom of that time, along the Mediterranean coasts of Gaul, Paul's voice very likely sounded in some synagogue or public place of Marseilles or Narbonne. One of his disciples, Crescentius, seems, according to the second epistle to Timothy, to have preached in Gaul,[8] but the towns he may have evangelised are unknown: the church of Vienne claimed him only later, and cannot make good its claim.[9]

As to the apostolic claims of so many other churches of the Gauls, their number and assurance do not suffice to justify them; they are too late in time, and are too manifestly inspired by the sentiments of an ill-informed piety and an intemperate local patriotism to call for a place in a history of the Church.

Some have fancied that Lazarus, the friend of Jesus, came into Provence, that he was the first bishop of Marseilles, and that he was accompanied by his sisters Martha and Mary, whom tradition associates with the town of Tarascon and the caves of Sainte-Baume. Again, the most prominent episcopal sees in France have been generously given as founders direct disciples of St. Peter, such as Trophimus, first bishop at Arles, or disciples of St. Paul, such as Dionysius, the illustrious convert of the Areopagus at Athens, awarded the bishopric of Paris; or again of Jesus Himself, as Martial of Limoges, who is supposed to have been none other than the boy

---

[4] *Rom.* xv *et seq.*

[5] *II Tim.* iv, 11.

[6] Cf. Bk. I, p. 279.

[7] St. Jerome says that Paul made the voyage by sea.

[8] Some good manuscripts have Κρήσκης εἰς Γαλλίαν while others give εἰς Γαλατίαν. The two words can equally signify Gaul or Galatia in Asia Minor. But the latter seems more likely, from the fact that the same passage mentions together with the mission of Crescentius that of Titus to Dalmatia, i.e., to a country which was evidently still to be evangelized, whereas Galatia had already heard the Gospel. [R. St. J. Parry in his *Pastoral Epistles*, Cambridge, 1920, *in loc.*, says, "There is nothing to decide which district is meant, even if we could be certain that the point of departure was Rome."—Tr.]

[9] That the apostolic travels of Crescentius should have led him to go up the Rhone Valley is itself very plausible. But if the church of Vienne had really had such an early origin, it would not have failed to oppose this to the claims of Arles when there was rivalry for the primacy of jurisdiction in the fifth century.

with the loaves and fishes on the occasion of the Gospel miracle of the multiplication of the loaves! These are naive legends, which edify or amuse, but have their basis only in the imagination and local pride of particular districts.

These stories are for the most part very late: the belief in the coming of SS. Mary and Martha to Provence cannot count a thousand years of existence, and the best proof of its inexactitude is the fact that it was preceded by another, the Burgundian tradition, which placed the bodies of these saints at Vezelay, whither they were supposed to have been brought from the East. There certainly was a bishop of Aix in Provence named Lazarus, but he was a contemporary of St. Augustine. The legend of the apostolic if not Athenian origin of St. Dionysius is somewhat earlier than the provençal legends: we can trace it back to the sixth century,[10] when he begins to be set forth as having been sent by Pope Clement I, the third successor of St. Peter. But what credit can we give to an account so far removed from the actual events?

The oldest apostolic claim in Gaul is that of the church of Arles, which already in the beginning of the fifth century regarded Trophimus its founder as a disciple of St. Peter. But this is unfortunately closely linked with the ambition of Arles at that time to be recognised as the first of the episcopal sees in Gaul, merely because, having become the administrative capital, Pope Zosimus momentarily invested its bishop with the title of Papal Vicar.[11]

The Spanish "traditions" of the evangelisation of the country by St. James the Great have as little foundation and are almost more unlikely than the apostolic legends of Gaul, seeing that St. James was martyred at Jerusalem before the dispersion of the apostles.[12]

Putting legends aside, it remains that some privileged regions of

[10] Cf. L. Levillain, Etude sur l'Abbaye de Saint-Denis à l'époque mérovingienne, I. Les sources narratives, in Bibliothèque de l'Ecole de Chartes, Vol. LXXXII, 1921, p. 528, and Le crise des années 507-508 et les rivalités d'influence en Gaule (Mélanges Jorga, Paris, 1933, pp. 537-567).

[11] On the apostolic legends in general concerning the churches in Gaul, see J. Zeiller, Les origines chrétiennes en Gaule, in Revue d'Histoire de l'Eglise de France, 1926, pp. 16-33, which contains a bibliography on the subject. The only monograph of the present day on Christian origins in Gaul is that of T. Scott Holmes, The Origin and Development of the Christian Church in Gaul during the First Six Centuries of the Christian Era, London, 1911.

[12] On Christian origins in Spain, cf. Z. Garcia Villada, Historia ecclesiastica de Espana, Vol. I, El cristianismo durante la dominacion romana, Madrid, 1929, 2 vols.

the West, Rome and southern Italy, the Illyrian littoral and also, apparently, the coasts of Provence and Spain, received the first announcement of the Gospel in the apostolic period. We may conjecture that the same was the case with Africa, since there were inhabitants of Cyrene amongst those who heard the sermon at Pentecost, and a great metropolis like Carthage was in constant relation with the East.[13] The relatively numerous Oriental elements in several Western cities, especially in seaports such as Puteoli, Marseilles, and Carthage, must have provided at the beginning very active agents of Christian propaganda.

Christianity in Asia

But in this second half of the first century, the East from which they came was much more thoroughly penetrated by the Christian Faith than was the West. Palestine was its original focus, and Syria, through its metropolis Antioch, was the second centre from which it spread. Asia Minor, in which so many cities had received the word from St. Paul, and perhaps from St. John, was by the end of the first century one of the parts of the Empire in which the religion of Christ had been most widely preached. The Church of Ephesus owed its foundation to St. Paul, and the apostle John, according to the generally received tradition, governed it subsequently for many years.[14] The churches of Alexandria, Troas, Laodicea and Hierapolis, the dwelling place of Philip the deacon (later confused with the apostle of the same name) and his daughters known as prophetesses, are mentioned in the Pauline epistles. The Churches of Smyrna, Pergamus, Sardis, Philadelphia and Thyatira were, together with those of Ephesus and Laodicea, the recipients of the *Apocalypse* of John. The Christian communities of Tralles in Lydia and Magnesia in Caria appear about the year 100 in the letters of St. Ignatius of Antioch, the successor of Evodius, left in that city by St. Peter when his own apostolate called him elsewhere.

[13] A vague memory was conserved in the church of Carthage that its first preachers of Christianity originally came from the East. The idea that it had received Christianity from Rome seems to have originated only later on. Cf. P. Monceaux, *Histoire littéraire de l'Afrique chrétienne*, Vol. I, Paris, 1901, ch. 1, pp. 3-11, and A. Audollent, *Carthage romaine*, Paris, 1901, L. V, part I, ch. I, pp. 435-441.
[14] Cf. Bk. I, pp. 238, 310.

Further away from the coastal region of Asia Minor, Christianity penetrated into Pisidia with St. Paul. Iconium, Antioch in Pisidia, Lystra and Derbe possessed very early their Christian communities, and the rest of the country became Christianised rapidly. The Christian churches in Galatia were also among the fruits of the apostolate of St. Paul, who addressed to them one of his best known letters. He wrote also to the Christians of Colossæ in Phrygia, though he seems not to have evangelised them.

Bithynia on the Black Sea was evidently reached before the end of the first century, since already in the dawn of the second Christianity was, according to the letters of Pliny the Younger, invading "not only the cities but also the towns and the country-side, emptying the precincts of the temples." [15]

Shortly afterwards, the town of Sinope had a bishop, who was the father of the heretic Marcion.[16]

Christianity also spread into the islands of the Archipelago. Paul and Barnabas had preached in 44 or 45 at Cyprus, and Paul there brought about the striking conversion of the proconsul, Sergius Paulus.

Christianity in the Hellenic Peninsula

The various countries in the hellenic peninsula, Macedonia, Greece, and at least some of the neighbouring islands, had been evangelised at the very beginning of Christian preaching by St. Paul himself or his disciples such as Titus, who was the apostle of Crete. At any rate, the epistle which Paul addressed to Titus tells us that the apostle had placed him at the head of the Christian community constituted in the island, in which he had perhaps himself preached after his imprisonment in Rome and his voyage to Spain.

Philippi in Macedonia, Thessalonica, Berea, Nicopolis in Epirus, Athens, Corinth and Cenchrae near Corinth, had their churches towards the latter part of the first century. Those of Develtum and Anchialo in Thrace, Larissa in Thessaly, Lacedæmon and Cephalonia are mentioned in the second century. The church of Byzantium, which was to have so striking a future, cannot bring forward any proof of its existence at this time other than that of

---

[15] Cf. *infra*, p. 386.
[16] Eusebius, *Hist. Eccles.*, V, 13, 3.

having produced the heretic Theodotus, who went to Rome about 190.[17]

True, later on its claimants to pre-eminence in the East were able to appeal to the "tradition" of a Thracian apostolate of St. Andrew, whose Acts make him die a martyr in Achaia. But these Acts are not earlier than the end of the third century, and are clearly legendary in some respects.[18] They may indeed convey to us an echo of memories which are earlier and less unworthy of belief, and the fact that Eusebius, relying perhaps on Origen, mentions the tradition [19] of a mission of Andrew in Scythia (that is, apparently, on the Roman shores of the Black Sea south of the Danube, inhabited by ancient Greek colonies) would support the hypothesis that Andrew was in touch with the Hellenic world, whose patron saint he became. But this remains wholly conjectural.

Christianity in Egypt

To the south-east of Palestine there is Egypt, destined to play a prominent part in the history of early Christendom. Did this country receive the Christian seed in apostolic times? That is, in itself, quite likely. A passage in the *Acts* (xviii, 24-25) perhaps confirms it when it speaks of the Alexandrian Jew, Apollos, "who had been instructed (in his own country) in the way of the Lord"; unfortunately the parenthesis is not found in all the manuscripts. In any case it must be admitted that nothing is known of this primitive evangelisation. A tradition which came to be accepted, and is found in Eusebius,[20] attributes the foundation of the great ecclesiastical see of Egypt, that of Alexandria, to St. Mark the evangelist, the disciple of St. Peter, and we have a list of bishops which begins with him. We are not in a position to estimate the value of the first names on this list, but equally we must not dismiss them entirely.[21] If the letter of Claudius to the Alexandrians,

---

[17] Hippolytus, *Philosophumena*, VII, 35.
[18] Cf. J. Flamion, *Les Actes apocryphes de l'apôtre André*, Louvain-Paris, 1911. The *Acts of Andrew* have been published by Lipsius and Bonnet in *Acta Apostolorum apocrypha*, Vol. II, Leipzig, 1898, Vol. I. English translation in James, *Apocryphal New Testament*, pp. 337-363.
[19] Eusebius, *Hist. Eccles.*, III, i, 1. The text is given in the works of Origen, Migne, *P.G.*, Vol. XII, 92, but it does not follow clearly from the text of Eusebius that the statement about Andrew was already in Origen.
[20] *Hist. Eccles.*, II, 16, 1.
[21] Cf. Eusebius, *Hist. Eccles.*, II, 24; III, 14; IV, 19.

which has aroused such interest and controversy, could be accepted as a witness to the reality of Christian activity at Alexandria in the year 41, this would decidedly strengthen the information given in Eusebius for this very same year. But the testimony seems ever less satisfactory,[22] and we must resign ourselves to an ignorance as to the origin of the Egyptian church which does not lessen the probability of its very great antiquity. Already in the second century the bishops of Alexandria appear in history,[23] and this great city had then a large Christian population, which implies a much earlier evangelisation.

Progress of the Evangelisation of the West in the Second Century. Gaul

In the course of this century, Christianity made good progress in the West, which hitherto had not been much affected. The churches of Gaul and Africa, in fact, figure gloriously in history well before the year 200.

The well known story of the martyrdom of Christians at Lyons in 177 shows us a church which was already of some importance in the Gallic metropolis in the reign of the Emperor Marcus Aurelius.[24] At its head was Bishop Pothinus, who came originally from Asia, where he had been a disciple of St. Polycarp of Smyrna; in Lyons he was assisted by clerics of various ranks.

We find also amongst the martyrs of Lyons a deacon of Vienne, which accordingly reveals the existence of a Christian community in that city. All this implies an evangelisation which had taken place some time before, and probably we shall not go far wrong if we think that the beginnings of Christianity at Lyons were not later than the reign of Hadrian, in the first half of the second century. An inscription, preserved at Marseilles,[25] and coming doubtless from that neighbourhood, which seems to refer to two martyrs Volusianus and Fortunatus, burnt to death, may well be at least as ancient.

[22] Cf. Bk. I, p. 296, n. 10.

[23] At least beginning with Demetrius (180). The earlier names, again, are not summarily to be rejected, but the constant ascription of exactly twelve years of episcopate by the list in Eusebius to each one of the predecessors of Demetrius after Annianus, the successor of Mark, barely conceals a chronological ignorance which must be taken into consideration.

[24] Cf. infra, p. 399.

[25] Corpus inscriptionum Latinorum, Vol. XII, 489.

Africa

The martyrological documents of Africa are concerned with events very close in time to those of Lyons, and lead to a similar conclusion. African Christianity, which gave to the church several martyrs towards the end of the second century, certainly began many years earlier. An archæological testimony confirms this in a very remarkable way: at Susa, the ancient Hadrumetum, Christian catacombs have been found in one of which there is an inscription of the Severian epoch, belonging to a tomb which is chronologically one of the last of a series numbering more than five thousand. The catacomb therefore must have come into use at least half a century previously, which would put the first evangelisation in the first half of the second century.[26] It is likely that Christian preaching reached Carthage before secondary towns like Hadrumetum.

Spain

May we think that Christianity developed in a similar way in Spain in the second century? Here there are no traces perpetuated in stone such as can be appealed to by the churches of Gaul and Africa.[27] The darkness which envelopes the Christian origins in Spain after the preaching of St. Paul, the immediate consequences of which escape us entirely, is at most interrupted by one glimmer of light.

An entry in the Martyrology of Adon[28] states that a mission consisting of seven bishops was sent into Spain by St. Peter: the absence of this information in the Hieronymian Martyrology is not calculated to add to its credibility; the number seven and the sending by St. Peter increase our mistrust. Yet there is one point which inclines us to a more favourable judgment: the head of the mission is said to have founded the church of the *Civitas Accitana* (Guadix). Now when about the year 300 there was held at Illiberi (Elvira) a council famous in the religious annals of Spain, the Bishop of Acci presided over it: it is allowable to infer from this

[26] Mgr. Leynaud, *Les catacombes africaines. Sousse-Hadrumète,* 2nd edn., Algiers, 1922, pp. 9-16. The inscription in question is dated in the consulate of Lupus, who may be L. Virius Lupus, consul in 232.

[27] A Tarragonian inscription (*C.I.L.,* II, p. 25,* no. 231 *) alluding to the penetration of Christianity in this province under Nero is obviously a forgery.

[28] Under date May 15th.

that the church of Acci was regarded then as the mother church of Spain, or at least of the province of Tarragona. But the inference is not a peremptory one.

In any case, the date of the mission which gave birth to the church of Acci and to those of the surrounding region is impossible to determine even approximately.

§2. EVANGELISATION BEYOND THE EMPIRE

Christianity in Persia

There are good grounds for believing in a very early preaching of Christianity outside the Empire, in the great kingdom which extended beyond the eastern frontiers of the Roman world, the Parthian kingdom, which at the beginning of the third century became once more the Persian realm. The "traditions" of a threefold apostolate of Bartholomew, Thaddæus and Thomas in Persia are without solid foundation.[1] But the text in the Acts of the Apostles (ii, 9) which mentions among those present on Pentecost Day "Parthians and Medes, and Elamites, and inhabitants of Mesopotamia" supports the view that "towards the year 80, the churches of the greco-roman world knew of the existence of Christian communities in the far away lands of the East."[2]

It is likely that the missionary activity of these first propagators of Christianity in Persia was confined to the Jewish colonies of Babylonia. But it would seem that it met with little success, seeing that it left no trace, and on the contrary a passage in the Talmud speaks of the Babylonian region as at that time entirely outside Christian influence.[3]

Was Christian preaching rejected by the synagogues, and addressed instead, as elsewhere, to the pagans? This is possible, if it be true that, as the documents which give us some knowledge, though imperfect, of Mandæism (a transformation of the old Iranian religion combined with semitic elements) state, relations were established between the Mandæans and the Christians of early times. But in reality, what we know of Mandæism—in spite of

[1] Cf. Bk. I, pp. 323-4, and J. Labourt, Le christianisme dans l'Empire perse sous la dynastie sassanide, Paris, 1904, pp. 11-15.

[2] Labourt, op. cit., p. 16.

[3] Ibid., p. 17.

recent attempts which have gone so far as to endeavour to find in it one of the religious currents from whence Christianity itself arose [4]—remains too uncertain to enable us to specify, or even to establish a relation between Christianity and the oriental movement of religious syncretism of which the Babylonian Gnosticism shown in Mandæism constituted a phase.

In short, what had been and was again to become the Persian kingdom was touched by Christian propaganda already in apostolic times; but the results, such as they were, are so little apparent to us that we may well wonder whether the seed sown by these first evangelists was not almost completely choked. In any case we cannot number Persia amongst the countries in which we find at the end of the first, or even in the first half of the second century, a properly constituted Church.

Christianity in Osroene

Between the Roman Empire and the Parthian kingdom, which became Persia once more later, there existed until the third century a little independent state, that of Edessa or Osroene, in which Christianity was planted quite early. The tradition recorded by Eusebius which puts King Abgar in correspondence with Jesus Himself, and says that his country was evangelized by the apostle Thomas and the disciple Thaddeus (Addai), has all the appearances of a legend; the fourth century veneration of the tomb of St. Thomas at Edessa and the reading there of supposed letters from Jesus to Abgar certainly do not suffice to make it authentic.[5] It is not even certain that the legend of Thaddeus may not be merely an embellishment of the acts and deeds of an historic personage

[4] Cf. R. Reitzenstein, *Das mandäische Buch des Herrn des Grosse und die Evangelienüberlieferung*, Heidelberg, 1919. Critique by M. J. Lagrange, *La gnose mandéenne et la tradition évangelique*, in *Revue biblique*, 1927, pp. 321-349 and 481-515, and 1928, pp. 5-32. A. Loisy, *Le mandéisme et les origines chrétiennes* (Paris, 1934) also declines to accept the thesis of Reitzenstein. H. Lietzmann, *Ein Beitrag zur Mandäerfrage* (*Sitzungsberichte Akad. Berlin, phil.-hist. Klasse*, 1930, pp. 596-608) has set forth the reasons for thinking that the Mandæans were an oriental Gnostic sect, of a relatively late date, and that it had nothing to do with Christian origins. [A useful summary of recent Mandæan studies is given in F. C. Burkitt's *Church and Gnosis*, Cambridge, 1932.]

[5] Cf. J. Tixeront, *Les origines de l'Eglise d'Edesse*, Paris, 1888. The text of Abgar's letter and our Lord's reply is given in translation in M. R. James, *Apocryphal New Testament*, pp. 476-77.

named Addai. Doubtless we may think that Eusebius, who was fairly well informed as to the local traditions of the countries near Syria, would not trouble to include a recently formed legend concerning the planting of Christianity in Osroene. But how are we to explain the fact that the apostle of Edessa, who is supposed to have died a martyr, is not even mentioned in the Syrian martyrology of the year 412? It is best to admit that the circumstances of the evangelisation of Osroene escape us. But the great number of the Christians in the region of Edessa at the end of the second century compels us to allow that its evangelization had begun long before.

From Edessa, the Gospel must have been very soon carried beyond the Tigris, into Adiabene, if we may believe the Chronicle of the Church of Arbela [6] which attributes this apostolate across the Tigris to the supposed founder of the church of Edessa. But the re-appearance at the commencement of the church of Adiabene of this doubtful founder of that of Edessa, together with more than one anachronism and contradiction in various martyrological testimonies, are not calculated to win [7] for the Chronicle of Arbella a credit which critics such as Harnack [8] have nevertheless not refused to give it.

As to an apostolic preaching of the Gospel on the African or Arabian shores of the Red Sea and as far as the Indies, we have already remarked that its historic reality remains uncertain, and that in any case its immediate results, if there were any, are entirely hidden from us.

[6] Edited by P. Zorell, *Orientalia christiana*, VIII, 4, no. 31 (1927).

[7] Cf. Paul Peeters, *La Passionaire d'Adiabène* in *Analecta Bollandiana*, Vol. XLIII, 1925, pp, 261-325.

[8] In his last edition (4th) of *Mission und Ausbreitung des Christentums*, Leipzig, 1924.

CHAPTER VIII

THE FIRST PERSECUTIONS, AND IMPERIAL LEGISLATION CONCERNING THE CHRISTIANS[1]

§1. THE NERONIAN PERSECUTION

WHILE the expansion of Christianity was taking place in the Roman world and beyond, the Empire, well before the end of the second century, had declared war upon the Church, beginning by putting its first head to death.

The Martyrdom of St. Peter

The martyrdom of St. Peter is, with that of St. Paul, the most important event in the first bloody persecution ordered by the imperial authority, which struck at Christians in the Empire and began in the reign of Nero.

The Burning of Rome and the Accusing of the Christians

This persecution, which might have burst forth some day or other on other excuses, since an occasion would probably have been sought sooner or later to proscribe Christianity, had an accidental immediate cause. In July, 64, a terrible fire devastated several parts of Rome; an almost unanimous and possibly well-informed opinion regarded Nero as having caused the fire, or at any rate of having helped its spread, in the desire to clear a place for the extension of his palace. To turn aside the current of hostile opinion, the emperor conceived the idea of putting the blame on the

---

[1] Bibliography.—The general bibliography for this chapter is the same as that of the preceding one.

Particular works to be referred to for the study of the character of the persecutions are, together with the ancient sources which give information on this subject, indicated in the notes to the chapter.

To the above may be added: A. Bouché-Leclercq, *L'intolérance religieuse et la politique,* Paris, 1911; A. Manaresi, *L'impera romano e il cristianesimo,* Turin, 1914; L. Homo, *Les empereurs romains et le christianisme,* Paris, 1931.

Christians, now named as such for the first time by Tacitus [2] and described as men "hated for their infamies" and "convicted of hatred of the human race." [3] Whether because of the hatred which they inspired, or more probably because of that of which they were thought to be guilty because they had not the spirit of the world, the hostility of public opinion towards them is beyond doubt. Was this spontaneous? Probably it was, in great measure: the mass of the people, perhaps because they still confused Christians with the Jews, who were always and everywhere disliked for their sectarianism, was certainly not favourable. They came to impute to them the crimes of atheism, magic, cannibalism, and other abominations. Nevertheless there may have been other factors in 64.

In the Emperor's entourage, the influence of the Judaism which was loyal to the Empire and which would play a prominent part a little later under the Flavian dynasty, was already fairly strong: the Judaising sympathies of the favourite Poppea are known. [4] And the hatred of the followers of the Old Law for those of the New did not diminish. Did protégés of Poppea admitted into the circle immediately surrounding the emperor, think that they would serve Nero as well as themselves "by pointing out as the authors of the crime the Christians" [5] who took pleasure, it was said—and the sentiments of which the *Apocalypse* of St. John is a vehement though late echo, might seem to give an appearance of justification to such sayings—"in the ideas of heavenly vengeance, a universal conflagration, and the destruction of the world"? [6] The conjecture is a plausible one; positive arguments to support it are lacking. Nevertheless, a passage in the celebrated letter addressed to the Corinthians by St. Clement, one of the first successors of St. Peter, saying that SS. Peter and Paul perished as victims of jealousy, [7]

---

[2] *Annales*, XV, 44.

[3] The manuscript of Tacitus long regarded as the best, the *Mediceus*, has instead of the word *convicti*, that of *conjuncti*, which would mean that the Christians were involved in one and the same persecution both for having caused the fire, and because of their *odium generis humani*. Cf. E. Coq, *De la nature des crimes imputés aux chrétiens d'après Tacite*, in *Mélanges d'archéologie et d'histoire* published by the *Ecole française* in Rome, Vol. VI, 1886, pp. 115-139. The general nature of events is more or less the same in either interpretation.

[4] Josephus, *Life*, 3; *Antiquities of the Jews*, XVIII-XX. Cf. Tacitus, *Hist.*, i, 22.

[5] Cf. E. Renan, *L'Antichrist*, pp. 159-161.

[6] Duruy, *Histoire des Romains*, Vol. IV, p. 507 (edn. 1882, Paris).

[7] *First Epistle to Corinthians*, V.

may be a reference to this hostile intervention of the Jewish element. In any case, from that day the Christians began to be distinguished by the Roman authorities from the Jews, who remained in possession of their privileges, while Christians were arrested, judged and condemned.

Possibly internal discords played some part in the denunciations which sent some of the Christian community of Rome to their deaths, together with their leaders: the letter of St. Clement is equally capable of being interpreted in this sense. One may infer that the disagreements, due very likely to the action of Judeochristians, led to imprudences which helped to cause the intervention of the Roman police, if they did not go as far as positive acts of denunciation—a hypothesis which may be supported by a phrase in Tacitus concerning indications given to the authorities by some Christians—*indicio eorum*.[8]

The Martyrs

First were arrested, according to Tacitus,[9] those who admitted (*fatebantur*) perhaps the crime of arson [10]—the untrue confession may have been extorted by torture—or more probably their Christianity, which from this moment became a crime. Then, *indicio eorum* (this may just as well mean formal denunciations obtained from these first prisoners, or else simple indications drawn from their talk, their very silences, their relations, and from all that was known of their life), the arrests increased rapidly, and a great number of Christians—*multitudo ingens*, writes Tacitus, who would not wish to exaggerate greatly the number of those he regarded as enemies of Roman society,[11] were eventually given over to the torments which Nero's cruelty had invented for them. He

---

[8] Cf. O. Cullmann, *Les causes de la mort de Pierre et de Paul d'après le témoignage de Clément Romain*, in *Revue d'histoire et de philosophie religieuse*, 1930, pp. 294-300.

[9] *Loc. cit.*

[10] The hypothesis of the guilt of the Christians has found a few defenders in our days: cf. Pascal, *L'incendio di Roma e i primi cristiani*, 2nd edn., Turin, 1901; it has no support in early writers: not one of those who have spoken of the burning of Rome after Tacitus imputes it to the Christians. Cf. A. Profumo, *Le fonti ed i tempi dell' incendio neroniano*, Rome, 1905.

[11] The Hieronymian Martyrology gives 979 as the number of martyrs who perished with SS. Peter and Paul. It is difficult to estimate the value of this figure, but it is worth mentioning.

conceived the idea of "transforming their torture into a spectacle, and in his gardens on the Vatican he gave nightly festivals, in which the unfortunate Christians, covered in pitch and devoured by the flames, cast a sinister light on the circus performances." [12]

Peter was one of the martyrs. [13]

Eusebius, in his *Ecclesiastical History*, [14] gives the date 67 or 68, instead of 64 or 65 for this, probably merely because he attributes to Peter the famous twenty-five years as Bishop of Rome, beginning in 42. But the persecution once begun may have continued after 64, and it is not at all impossible that Paul, arrested after his return to Rome, may have suffered the capital penalty [15] just one or two years after St. Peter. But the same immemorial cult which unites them together attests the at least relative chronological proximity of their death.

§2. THE PROHIBITION OF CHRISTIANITY

Possible Extension of the Persecution to the Provinces

Did the persecution extend to the provinces? We do not possess any positive statement to this effect, but there may be an allusion to it in the Epistle to the Hebrews, [1] and it may also be urged that after the measures ordered by Nero the profession of Christianity was prohibited in the Empire. But the reality of this prohibition by Nero, or of an *institutum neronianum* expressly forbidding the Christian religion, has not met with universal acceptance. In point

[12] L. Duchesne, *Histoire de l'Eglise*, Vol. I, p. 63.

[13] According to a tradition of which Tertullian, *De Præscriptione* 36, *Scorpiacus* 15, is our first witness, he was condemned to be crucified. This is quite in harmony with the account of Tacitus, which speaks of Christians as crucified in the Vatican gardens, and it may also be alluded to by St. John's Gospel (xxi, 18, 19): "When thou shalt be old, thou shalt stretch forth thy hands, and another shall gird thee, and lead thee whither thou wouldst not. And this he said, signifying by what death he should glorify God."

[14] Eusebius, *Eccles. Hist.*, II, XIV, 6, where he makes Peter arrive in Rome in the year 42, and attributes to him a Roman episcopate of 25 years.

[15] Clement, the successor of Peter (*Epistle to the Corinthians*), Tertullian, and the priest Caius agree in saying that St. Paul was beheaded on the Ostian Way, and buried there.

[1] In x, 32-38 there is a reference to tribulations endured by believers for their faith. But it is not certain that this can be understood of the persecution under Domitian, inasmuch as the Epistle to the Hebrews written in the name of St. Paul was somewhat later in appearance.

of fact, it is known only indirectly,[2] but its existence can scarcely be questioned.

The Neronian Legislation against Christianity

The questions put about half a century later by Pliny the Younger, Governor of Bithynia, to the Emperor Trajan as to the attitude to be adopted towards the Christians of his province, and the imperial rescript [3] which sent him the instructions asked for, prove the existence of an earlier legislation, the application of which had only to be clarified. Tertullian asserts, moreover,[4] in the most formal manner that Nero was the first to promulgate a law against Christians, and it cannot be doubted that the proscription of Christianity as such dates back to him: the Christians, first of all persecuted as incendiaries through the dishonest expedient of the frightened Nero, were evidently subsequently outlawed after police enquiries which ascertained their religious profession.[5]

Until then they had continued to be confused with the Jews in the eyes of the Roman authority; they were regarded doubtless as a particular sect, and thus enjoyed the privileges which enabled the Jews to retain their national religion in the Empire without performing acts of obedience in respect of the official cults. But henceforth a discrimination was made; possibly the Jews themselves were partly responsible for this, and this may be the most exact element in the thesis which regards the Jewish element as in some measure the cause of the outbreak of the first persecution. Henceforth Christianity was no longer regarded as a dissident form of Judaism, and had no longer any right to the favours enjoyed by the latter.[6] Consequently, the Christians were now bound, as

[2] Cf. the full bibliography of the question in Cabrol-Leclercq, *Dictionnaire d'archéologie chrétienne*, article *Loi persecutrice*.

[3] Cf. *infra*, pp. 378-9.

[4] *Ad nationes* 7; *Apologeticus*, 5.

[5] The Neronian origin of the prohibition of Christianity is indirectly confirmed by the text of *I Peter* iv, 16, which opposes the glory of suffering *ut christianus* to the opprobrium involved in a condemnation for a crime against common law. The Epistle reflects the events in the primitive community.

[6] Cf. above, Bk. I, pp. 33-34, 68 *et seq.*; also G. Costa, *Religione e politica nell impero romano*, Turin, 1923, pp. 97-108. According to him, Jews and Christians were still confused together for a much longer time. He suggests that the text in Tacitus concerning the first persecution was modified, and that the *ingens multitudo* referred to included also a great number of Jews. But he brings forward no proof. Still, it is feasible that Christianity was not from this very moment

citizens of the Empire, to comply with the minimum of religious conformity called for by the idea of the ancient State [7] or else disappear. Their faith, which allowed no concession, internal or external, to polytheism, excluded such conformity, and so there remained only outlawry, and this is undoubtedly the basis of the legislation made in their regard by Nero, and which may be summed up in one short phrase: *non licet esse christianos,* it is not lawful for Christians to exist.

§3. JURIDICAL CHARACTER OF THE PERSECUTIONS

The persecutions were not the effect merely of the application of laws previously existing.

The existence of a special legislative act explicitly prohibiting Christianity has nevertheless been much discussed. It has been said that it was sufficient to apply to Christians existing laws specifying penalties for the crime of sacrilege or of *lèse majesté,* as this would involve them in punishments.[1] But sacrilege properly so called supposes a positive criminal act, which could not be found in the case of Christians; as for the crime of *lèse majesté,* closely connected, in point of fact, with that of sacrilege, committed in refusing to take part in the cult of the Emperor's divinity, we do not see Christians explicitly accused of this in the first two centuries: it is only in the third that the magistrates tried regularly to force Christians to sacrifice to the divinity of the emperor in consequence of new edicts of persecution, and condemned them if they refused to do so.

Doubtless one may say that the crime existed implicitly from the

---

regarded as a religion absolutely distinct from Judaism, but rather as a dissident form of it. The Emperor Domitian who, as we shall see, had a certain number of Christians put to death, was equally hostile to the Jews, as may be seen from the development of the *fiscus judaicus* in his reign. Cf. S. Gsell, *Essai sur le règne de l'emperor Domitien,* Paris, 1893, pp. 287-316. The enquiry which he caused to be made (cf. *infra,* p. 387) as to the descendants of the family of Jesus seems to show that he busied himself politically about Christianity regarded at least up to a certain point as a branch of Judaism.

[7] Cf. Fustel de Coulanges, *La cité antique.*

[1] Thesis of K. J. Neumann, *Der römische Staat und die allgemeine Kirche bis auf Diocletian,* Leipzig, 1890, pp. 12 *et seq.*

beginning, inasmuch as Christians did not recognise the Emperor as a god, and hence adopted an attitude which was bound to lead to their being regarded as defective citizens or subjects. But before the third century no text proves that the proper motive of the persecution of the Christians was a refusal which made them guilty of *lèse majesté*. They were accused rather, at first, of failing to reverence the gods of the Empire in general, and even this did not make them officially atheists, as they were judged to be by popular ignorance.

The same is true of the accusation of other especially serious crimes against common law, such as magic, incest, or infanticide: it was never more than popular rumour which imputed these to the Christians, and official justice did not take up these accusations.[2] Hence we shall not find in previous penal law the precise juridical basis of the persecutions.

Nor were they due merely to the coercive power of the magistrates.

Others have sought for this basis in the power of *coercitio*,[3] i.e., police powers which belonged to all the Roman magistrates. In order to maintain public order, these had a very extensive authority which went as far as putting to death anyone who disturbed the peace. Hence it is suggested that it was as public disturbers that the Christians, disobeying the injunction to abandon a profession of faith which was in itself a public disorder, were condemned by the decision of the magistrates, without any need of applying to them a more express law.

But if the magistrates merely had to exercise towards the Christians their power of *coercitio*, why did they more than once think it necessary to consult the prince as to the way to treat them, as we see Pliny the Younger writing to Trajan, and other governors under Antoninus or Marcus Aurelius? Moreover, Pliny speaks formally of the steps taken against the Christians as resulting from the exercise of criminal jurisdiction, *cognitio*, and accordingly, not as a result of *coercitio*. Lastly, the *coercitio* extending to the capital penalty could not be exercised in the case of a Roman citizen.

[2] Contrary to what is maintained by E. Le Blant, *Sur les bases des poursuites dirigées contre les chrétiens*, in *Comptes-rendus de l'Académie des Inscriptions et de Belles-Lettres*, 1866, pp. 358 *et seq.*, according to whom Christians were condemned as guilty of homicide or of magic, as well as of sacrilege or *lèse majesté*.

[3] Theory of T. Mommsen, *Der Religionsfrevel nach römischen Recht*, in *Historische Zeitschrift, Neue Folge*, XXVIII, 1890, pp. 389-429.

Special Legislation against the Christians

Thus we are compelled to accept [4] the reality of special legislative measures against the Christians, of which the Emperor Nero was the author, as in fact affirmed by Tertullian.[5] From his reign to that of Septimius Severus, who introduced a new regime, the juridical situation of Christians in the Roman Empire remained the same: they were proscribed, not as guilty of crimes against the common law such as incest, cannibalism or magic, as imputed to them so often by popular hostility, itself caused by difference of beliefs and customs, nor of the crimes of sacrilege or *lèse majesté*, but as guilty of professing a religion which had been forbidden: *christianos esse non licet.* Thus it is the very name of Christian, the *nomen christianum*, that was forbidden and condemned, as Christian apologists more than once contended.

The Clarifications in Trajan's Rescript

The rescript of Trajan added to the principle of Nero about half a century later some necessary clarifications, the need of which had been shown in practice.[6] This imperial reply to the questions from a governor consisted of three points. The first two were modifications of a rule which the progress of a propaganda that could in no wise be stopped made it difficult to apply in all strictness, as is

---

[4] As C. Callewaert well brought out over thirty years ago, in a series of works: *Les premiers chrétiens fuerint-ils persécutés par édits généraux ou par mesures de police?* in *Revue d'histoire ecclésiastique*, 1910, pp. 771-797; 1902, pp. 5-15, 324-348, 607-615; *Le délit de christianisme dans les deux premiers siècles*, in *Revue des questions historiques*, 1903, Vol. LXXIV, pp. 28-55; *Les premiers chrétiens et l'accusation de lèse-majesté*, in *ibid.*, 1904, Vol. LXXVI, pp. 5-28; *Les persécutions contre les chrétiens dans la politique religieuse de l'Empire romain*, in *ibid.*, 1907, Vol. LXXXII, pp. 5-19; *La méthode dans la recherche de la base juridique des premières persécutions*, in *Revue d'histoire ecclés.*, 1911, pp. 5-16, 633-651.

[5] "Institutum Neronianum" is how he describes the law of persecution in *Apolog.*, 5.

[6] Pliny the Younger, *Epistolæ* X, 97 and 98. Doubts have sometimes been raised as to the authenticity of this correspondence, especially in view of the improbability of the picture which Pliny gives of his province, as already so strongly affected by Christian propaganda that the temples were deserted, and the sacrifices abandoned. We may reply with E. Babut, *Remarques sur les deux lettres de Pline et de Trajan relatives aux chrétiens de Bithynie*, in *Revue d'histoire et de Littérature religieuses*, new series Vol. I, 1910, pp. 289-305, that Pliny, who manifestly desired not to pronounce too many condemnations, may have been led to magnify the number of Christians in order to discourage repression by the very perspective of its extent.

shown well by Pliny's hesitation before the prospect of too numerous condemnations.

The Emperor accordingly declared in substance: 1. Governmental authority is not to take the initiative in the processes: it is not to seek out Christians, *christiani conquirendi non sunt.* 2. Those who are accused and who declare that they are not Christians, or are such no longer, that is to say, those who have committed the legal crime of being Christians but have effaced it by apostasy, manifested by an external act of adhesion to paganism, are to be dismissed. 3. Those who confess to being Christians are to be condemned.

The letter of Pliny, and the sequence of events, show that this condemnation could only be the capital penalty, i.e., death, or one of the penalties which, like exile or forced labour in the mines involved civil death. But on the other hand, and in virtue of the second point in the rescript, we shall no more see governors before whom Christians are taken doing their utmost to obtain from them a word, or sometimes just a simple act, such as offering a few grains of incense to the statue of the Emperor, which could be interpreted as a disavowal, even if only a temporary one, of the Christian faith.

Tortures were in many instances less a punishment than a means attempted in order to extract this denial from the accused. As for the Emperors themselves, the best of them, as we shall see in detail in the case of Hadrian and Antoninus, if not Marcus Aurelius, who regarded Christians with contempt rather than pity, added new precautions which mitigated the application of a legal system the principle of which they were nevertheless careful to maintain in all its strictness.

Main Idea of the Legislation against the Christians

What, then, was the underlying idea which alone explains the transformation of an expedient of the frightened Nero into a rule of the State? It was that Christianity, a strictly monotheistic religion, whose God would not divide his honour with other divinities or with the world, could not be reconciled with the fundamental conceptions upon which the Roman State rested. For this was closely associated with a number of religious traditions, if not also of habits of life, which were incompatible with the new faith; the mere fact that the Christians did not worship the gods of Rome made them rebels, or at least suspect, even before the time when the worship or refusal of worship of the Emperor's statue became the touchstone of their Roman conformity.

The religious position of the Jews was similar; but they had before the year 70 formed a national body which had received privileges and retained them after their final dispersion. Even when the obligation to sacrifice to the Emperor could be imposed upon every citizen, they obtained legal dispensations which safeguarded them from persecution.[7] Doubtless the Roman authority only gradually learnt to make a distinction between Christians and Jews. But the day came when all confusion ceased. Christians did not, like the Jews, form a compact national body, but a religious society scattered abroad from its origin, the members of which were all equally subjects who could not claim any special favour. This explains the imperial legislation against Christianity.

Juridical Origin and Form of this Legislation

The juridical origin was probably an ancient law of the republican epoch which forbade *superstitio illicita*,[8] and its form an imperial edict. Like the edicts of the prætors of the Republic, this particular edict was theoretically in force only during the reign of the Emperor who had published it. Thus it had to be renewed, and adopted, so to speak, by his successor.

This gives us, perhaps, a first reason for the intermittent character the persecutions at first displayed. Trajan decided at the beginning of the second century that there were to be no measures against Christians without previous accusation. But in the first place, these measures had to be in conformity with the imperial will. This was expressed for the first time by Nero. But then there was no severity towards Christians under the two first Flavians. The anti-Christian laws were renewed, in circumstances which we shall explain later, under Domitian; and this commencement of persecuting legislation by the two first century rulers who had left the worst reputations enabled the Christian apologists of the second

[7] Instead of offering a sacrifice to the divine emperor, they offered one to God for the emperor (cf. Josephus, *Contra Apionem*, II, 6, 77). See an account of the various privileges of the Jews in the matter of the imperial cult, in J. Juster, *Les Juifs dans l'Empire romain*, Paris, 1914, Vol. I, pp. 339-354.

[8] Cf. Tertullian, *Apologeticus*, 6.

century to set forth the idea that hostility towards Christianity emanated from bad emperors, and those whom every Roman had cause to hate.

But Trajan, the *optimus princeps* as he was called in his own lifetime, and whose reputation for goodness survived the Middle Ages, when faced with the question put to him by Pliny, who was worried by the prospect of the great number of capital sentences which would have to be pronounced against people who did not seem to be great criminals—Trajan could not avoid the issue, and it is by his reply that we know the principle of the laws directed against the Christians. True, the precise instructions emanating from him constitute already a modification, since he forbids the authorities to take the initiative—an interdiction so radical that the emperors themselves, when Christians boldly declared themselves by addressing to them their apologies for their faith, never answered what might seem to us to be challenges—if they ever know of these—by juridical measures. Nothing shows better the singular and exceptional character of this legislation against the Christians than this disposition, by which the State seemed to take no cognisance of a legal crime so long as the guilty were not specifically pointed out, though it nevertheless punished with death those denounced in the appointed way. It is like a tacit confession of regret at having to punish in virtue of old ordinances, which nevertheless the State did not wish to revoke.

CHAPTER IX

THE PERSECUTION UNDER THE FLAVIANS AND THE ANTONINES[1]

THE Church had come into collision with the traditions which the Empire represented, and the authorities which embodied them, in a first tragic encounter in the reign of Nero, and from that moment persecution, or more precisely, the constant danger of persecution, the effective realisation of which depended on circumstances, became its lot.

§ I. THE CHURCH UNDER THE FLAVIANS

The Roman Church under the Flavian Emperors

But just at first, being little known in spite of all, even after the bloody outburst of the year 64, and benefiting perhaps by the fact that the Emperors who followed Nero did not set out to imitate their predecessor who had left so deplorable a memory, the Church enjoyed a brief period of unquestionable tranquillity. There is

[1] Bibliography.—The general bibliography is the same as that for chapter VII. In addition, there are good monographs dealing with the various Roman emperors of the end of the first and the second century: S. Gsell, *Essai sur le règne de Domitien*, Paris, 1893; R. Paribeni, *Optimus princeps. Saggio sulla storia e sui tempi dell' Imperatore Traiano*, Messina, 1926-1927, 2 vols.; G. Lacour-Gayet, *Antonin le Pieux et son temps*, Paris, 1888.

For the authentic texts of Acts of the Martyrs, see the *Acta Sanctorum* of the Bollandists, the publication of which began in Antwerp in 1643 and is being continued in Brussels; it is a collection undertaken from the first in a scientific spirit which won for it much hostility: a more searching criticism has been made in our own days. A selection of Acts of the Martyrs will be found in Ruinart, *Acta Sincera*, Paris, 1689; Dom H. Leclercq, *Les martyrs*, Paris, 1902-1911, 11 vols.; Knopf, *Ausgewählte Märtyreracten*, in *Sammlung ausgewählter kirchen-und dogmengeschichtlicher Quellenschriften*, 2 Reihe, 2 Heft, Tübingen and Leipzig, 1901; P. Monceaux, *La véritable légende dorée*, Paris, 1928. We must also mention, for the Roman martyrological accounts, A. Dufourcq, *Etude sur les Gesta martyrum romains*, Paris, 1900-1910, 4 vols. The conclusions as to the very low historical value of most of the Roman *Gesta martyrum* has been generally accepted, but the same is not the case with those which attempt to explain their progressive elaboration.

On the Christian martyrs of Lyons in 177, it will be profitable to read C. Jullian, *Histoire de la Gaule*, Vol. IV: *Le gouvernement de Rome*, Paris, 1914, pp. 484-498.

absolutely no indication that in the ephemeral reigns of Galba, Otho and Vitellius, or under the two first Flavian emperors, Vespasian and Titus, Christians were attacked as such. In point of fact, it was then that at Rome, in the very heart of the Empire, Christianity, which there as elsewhere attracted mostly the humble, made also some of its most notable conquests in the highest circles of imperial society.

These conquests had moreover begun even before the first persecution. Already under Nero a great lady, Pomponia Græcina, married to a certain Plautius, a consul whose cousin espoused the emperor Claudius, had become suspect because she led a life which was too austere in the eyes of those of her circle, and had been accused of foreign superstition;[2] it is all the more probable that she had been converted to the Christian faith because subsequently we find the name of the Pomponii fairly well represented in the inscriptions in the Roman catacombs.[3] Á. Plautius, her husband, claimed as head of the family the right to judge her according to ancient domestic custom, and declared her innocent. She lived until the reign of Domitian.

Converts to Christianity from the Aristocracy

The Flavians doubtless had no preconceived hostility against a religion which had issued from Judaism. Though they had brought about the ruin of Jerusalem, the siege of which had been begun by Vespasian before he came to the throne, and which had finally collapsed under the blows of Titus in 70, they had admitted into their entourage the representatives of a revived Judaism, including the princess Berenice, of the house of Herod, and the historian Flavius Josephus.

Jewish ideas, which under Nero had possessed a temporary protector in Poppea, enjoyed then a return of favour in Rome, and the tendency towards religious monotheism profited thereby. The situation in Flavian Rome must thus have helped the progress of Christian propaganda even amongst the families of the senatorial aristocracy: after the Pomponii, it made converts amongst the

[2] Tacitus, *Annals*, XIII, 32.
[3] There are Christian inscriptions of a Pomponius Græcinus of the end of the second or beginning of the third century, and of several Pomponii Bassi. Cf. De Rossi, *Roma sotterranea*, Vol. II, p. 281, 362 *et seq.*

Acilii: M. Acilius Glabrio, consul in the year 91, was very probably a Christian, and the oldest Christian cemetery, consecrated to the exclusive and collective use of those belonging to Roman Christianity, was a property of the Acilii on the Via Salaria.[4]

The Imperial house itself provided some converts. Flavius Sabinus, elder brother of Vespasian, was perhaps already a Christian[5] and his son, Flavius Clemens, a cousin german of Titus and Domitian, consul in 95, adopted the Christian faith. His wife Flavia Domitilla followed him, and made to the Roman Church a bequest similar to that of the Acilii, which became the cemetery on the Via Ardeatina still known to-day by their name; their two sons, pupils of Quintilian, who should have succeeded Titus and Domitian, themselves without male issue, also professed Christianity. If the tragic and premature end of Domitian, a natural epilogue to a tyrannical reign, had not annihilated the imperial hopes of these two young men, the Empire would have had at its head Christian princes two hundred years before Constantine.[6]

Another princess of the imperial house, a second Flavia Domitilla, niece of the first, would also have to be counted amongst the illustrious recruits to Christianity in Rome before the end of the first century, if her existence were more certain.[7]

The Persecution in Rome under Domitian

It was upon this flourishing Roman Christianity that, in spite of the bonds which linked some of its members to the throne itself, persecution broke out a second time in the year 95, under Domitian.

This ruler has left the memory of being a fickle tyrant; the philosophers, and all others who had the air of retaining some independence, were or became suspect to him. Moreover, he wanted to react against the spread of Jewish customs which had taken place under the rule of his father and brother. His antipathy towards the Jews was in harmony with his financial necessities, for his

---

[4] Cf. *infra*, p. 524.

[5] According to the description of his character given by Tacitus, *Hist.*, III, 65 and 75.

[6] The Christianity of Flavius Clemens and his wife Flavia Domitilla is attested by the accusation of atheism made against them by Domitian (Dio Cassius, LXVII, 14; cf. Suetonius, *Domitianus*, 15), and by the fact that the Christian cemetery named after Domitilla, was developed in land belonging to the latter.

[7] Cf. *infra*, p. 386.

Treasury was exhausted after the excessive expenses he had in-curred in the embellishment of Rome. Accordingly he caused to be levied with great strictness the tax of the didrachma, which the Jews, when independent, had paid to the Temple at Jerusalem, and the right to which had afterwards been claimed by Rome.[8] There were many recalcitrants amongst the proselytes who had adopted the faith of Israel but did not regard themselves as Jews.

Were the Christians who, though distinct from the Jews, were none the less still regarded as a Jewish sect, also called upon to pay the didrachma, and did their very natural resistance call for severe measures? There is, in point of fact, nothing which indicates this: it seems rather that only circumcised people were dealt with as refractory to the tax, and that if punishment was applied, it con-sisted only of pecuniary penalties. But on the other hand, the measures taken to compel the payment of the didrachma by all the circumcised may quite well have led indirectly to the persecution, by enabling the imperial power to take note of the number of citizens who led what was regarded as a Jewish life, whether they were proselytes of the faith of Moses or followers of that of Jesus.

Thus, so far as Christians were concerned, there was nothing to prevent the penal effect from being applied immediately; all that was required was to set once more in motion the Neronian inter-dict which had remained in abeyance for thirty years, but of which the murderous capabilities could be activated again at any moment. And this time also, in contrast to what the relative moderation of Trajan will prescribe a little later in requiring a previous accusa-tion, authority took the initiative in the repressive measures. This doubtless explains why Tertullian (*Apologeticus*) says that only the emperors Nero and Domitian were the enemies of the Chris-tians.[9] At this time there were put to death, as guilty of atheism,[10] Flavius Clemens, cousin of the emperor, and the consul, M. Acilius Glabrio, and also on this head, says Dio Cassius,[11] there were con-demned "many other citizens who had adopted Jewish customs."

The double accusation of atheism and of Jewish customs seems to us not very coherent, but it is a fact that Christians were often

[8] Suetonius, *Domitianus*, 12.

[9] Similarly Melito of Sardis (about 172), in a passage of his *Apology* quoted by Eusebius, *Hist. Eccles.*, IV, 26, 7, says that only Nero and Domitian made the Christian faith a matter of accusation.

[10] Dio Cassius, LXVII, 13.

[11] *Ibid.*

treated as atheists, either because they did not worship the gods of the Empire, or else because, precisely as Jews, they did not render worship, at least at first, to material representations of the Deity. The sentences passed were death or the confiscation of goods. The wife of Flavius Clemens, niece herself of Domitian, Flavia Domitilla, was, according to Dio Cassius, exiled to the island of Pandataria. To another island of the Tyrrhenian sea, Pontia, the second Flavia Domitilla, niece to Flavius Clemens, was apparently likewise exiled because of her Christian faith. But this second Flavia is known only by the somewhat late testimonies of Eusebius,[12] who, it is true, cites an unknown pagan of uncertain period, Bruttius, and of St. Jerome.[13] The Acts of Saints Nereus and Achilleus, also brought forward in favour of the historic reality of the second Flavia Domitilla, do not deserve any credence.[14] It is thus possible that there may have been a legendary doubling in the tradition, and that there was only one Flavia Domitilla who was a victim of the persecution under Domitian, the wife of Clemens, exiled in one of the two islands in the Mediterranean assigned as residence for the imperial personages condemned to deportation.[15]

The Persecution in the Provinces: Bithynia

The persecution extended at least to some provinces: in Asia, Bithynia and the province of Asia proper were affected. The passage in Pliny the Younger which gives us information of the persecution under Trajan in Bithynia speaks of apostasies which had followed from threats some twenty years earlier: Christians were thus affected about the year 95.

Asia Minor

In Asia Minor the persecution made, according to tradition, if not a martyr, at least the most glorious of confessors in the person of St. John. A story which we find for the first time in Tertullian [16] says that John was taken from Ephesus to Rome, that he was there

[12] Hist. Eccles., III, 18, 4.
[13] Epist., 108, ad Eustochium.
[14] Cf. A. Dufourcq, Etude sur les Gesta martyrum romains, Vol. I, Paris, 1900, pp. 251-255.
[15] Dio Cassius, LXVII, 13.
[16] De præscriptione, 36.

plunged into a vessel of boiling oil, and that he was then deported to the island of Patmos. The legendary character of the first part of this late narrative prevents us from discerning the exact memories which it may retain, if it be not a complete invention.[17] The exile to Patmos, on the other hand, has in the *Apocalypse* (i, 9) a testimony the value of which is rendered less unfavourable than many critics allow by the previous discussion on the authenticity of the Johannine writings. The *Apocalypse* is also filled on every page with the memory of those who have recently shed their blood for Jesus, and it names two of the great cities of Asia, Pergamum and Smyrna, whose churches have suffered.[18]

Palestine

Lastly, according to the historian Hegesippus, a converted Jew of the second century particularly well informed on Judeo-Christian matters, whose account is transmitted to us by Eusebius,[19] the emperor concerned himself, for reasons other than those which had motived the persecution, about Palestine, where descendants of the family of Jesus were still living.

But these attracted attention rather as descendants of David. Hegesippus asserts what may be an exaggeration of a less cruel fact, that Domitian had given orders for the destruction of all the survivors of a royal race which worried him. Some descendants of Jude, one of the "brethren of the Lord," were denounced as belonging to it. They were taken to the emperor, who after finding by interrogation that they were of modest condition, and free from any pretention to an earthly kingdom, dismissed them as inoffensive folk. The account adds that they were "respected as martyrs, they governed churches when peace was re-established, and lived until the time of Trajan."[20]

The reference here is to Judeo-Christian churches in the Palestinian region: the family of Jesus remained long in possession of the

[17] The trial of John at Rome would be not at all unlikely in itself, seeing that the emperor insisted on himself interrogating the representatives of the family of Jesus: cf. *infra*.

[18] II, 9, 10, 13. On the legitimate attribution of the martyrs of Pergamum and Smyrna to the persecution under Domitian, cf. E. B. Allo, *Saint Jean, L'Apocalypse*, Paris, 1921, pp. xcvi-ccx, 3rd edn., 1933, pp. ccxxv-ccxxviii.

[19] *Hist. Eccles.*, III, 19 and 20.

[20] Cf. Bk. I, p. 307.

honours which the sentiment of these communities, wholly imbued with the Semitic spirit, thought it natural to give to the family which seemed to continue the earthly life of the Master Himself. We gather from this account in the oldest of Christian historians, which there is no serious reason to doubt, that Palestine like all Asia Minor was affected under Domitian by the persecution, since it mentions the "re-establishment of peace."

Peace did return very soon throughout the Empire. Domitian, assassinated in 96, was succeeded by Nerva, who adopted a policy opposite to that of his predecessor, and did not worry about Christians. Then it was, writes Eusebius,[21] that "Nerva having allowed those unjustly exiled to return to their own places, the apostle John was able to leave the island to which he had been sent, and established himself once more at Ephesus, as is stated by a tradition of our elders."

§2. THE PERSECUTION UNDER TRAJAN

Reign of Nerva

The reign of Nerva was short—scarcely two years—and so was the peace of the Church. The persecution was renewed under his successor Trajan. But it was sporadic and intermittent in character, and this is explained by the legislation against the Christians; Trajan confined himself to making this more precise by limiting its effects in the way we have already explained.

Trajan and the Christians

Trajan has left the reputation of being one of the greatest and best of the Roman Emperors. The *optimus princeps* [1] was at once a legislator and a conqueror. But he had a very lively sense of the prerogatives of the State, and no leaning towards consideration for particular groups. From the second year of his reign, the year 99, he revived the old law forbidding unauthorised associations. This measure alone would have been sufficient to arouse once more judicial activity against the Christians.

[21] *Hist. Eccles.*, III, 20, 8.
[1] Cf. above, p. 380-1.

The Question of the Martyrdom of St. Clement

Did one first and great victim pay his tribute about the year 100 in the person of the then head of Roman Christianity, St. Clement, the third successor of St. Peter after Linus and Anacletus?

Clement is known by a letter to the Church of Corinth which will be dealt with later on, and which shows the head of the Roman Church already busy with the care of other churches. But apart from that, we know nothing positive about him. Was he related to the household of Flavius Clemens in any way? It is possible that he may have been one of his freedmen, and again that he is the same as the Clement mentioned by St. Paul in his epistle to the Philippians (iv, 3). But all this is merely conjectural.

Some Greek *Acts* [2] which are not earlier than the fourth century say, on the other hand, that he was exiled by the government's orders to the Crimean peninsula in the Black Sea, where he continued his apostolate amongst those condemned to the mines, and that as a punishment for this activity he was thrown into the sea with an anchor round his neck. Neither St. Irenæus nor Eusebius nor St. Jerome, who mention Clement, say a single word which suggests this legend; we only know that the tradition of the martyrdom of Clement away from Rome was accepted in the fourth century; but this does not carry much weight in favour of the reality and still less concerning the circumstances of this martyrdom.

Martyrdom of St. Simeon of Jerusalem

It is quite otherwise in the case of another illustrious personage of the primitive Church who perished about the same time, Simeon, Bishop of Jerusalem. He was a member of the little group of "brethren of the Lord," and had succeeded James as the head of the Church of Jerusalem, which as we have said seems to have done its best to retain authority in the family of Jesus.

Simeon was of a very advanced age in the year 107, which Eusebius gives for his martyrdom, the account of which he borrows from Hegesippus. But the figure of 120 years transmitted by him, apart from its little intrinsic likelihood, would make Simeon born before Christ. Hence there is probably some error here—such numerical errors are frequent in the texts—but this does not destroy the historical value of the narrative.

[2] Funk, *Patrum apostolorum opera*, Tübingen, 1901, Vol. II, pp. 28-45.

According to Hegesippus, some popular commotions against the Christians had taken place in various cities, and hostile Judeo-Christian heretics, Ebionites or others, had joined forces with them; Simeon was denounced by one of them both as a Christian and as a descendant of David. It would seem that the Roman authority was still uneasy concerning the representatives of the ancient royal race of Israel. In any case the old head of Christianity in Jerusalem was doubly accused before the imperial legate, T. Claudius Atticus, and after long torments, was crucified. The account of Hegesippus adds that his accusers were then convicted of belonging themselves to the family of David and condemned in their turn.[3]

Martyrdom of St. Ignatius of Antioch

But the chief figure in the persecution of Trajan, and the one who has left the most brilliant memory, was Ignatius, Bishop of Antioch. Like Clement of Rome, he was very closely connected with the apostolic generation of which Simeon was perhaps the last survivor, and his letters, like that of Clement to the Church of Corinth, were regarded by the early Church as almost canonical documents.

The Acts of his martyrdom merit little credence, but we know the first stages by his own letters, the authenticity of which has often been attacked, but never, as we shall see, by conclusive arguments.[4]

He was arrested in circumstances unknown to us, perhaps in consequence of some popular commotion, perhaps through a formal denunciation, and was condemned early in 107,[5] evidently by the governor of the province. He was sent to Rome with two companions, Rufus and Zosimus, to be thrown to the beasts, probably on the occasion of the great feasts given by the Emperor after his victories in Dacia, when a certain number of human victims had to lose their lives.

The bishop set out, full of a supernatural joy, certain, as he wrote to the Smyrnians [6] that "under the edge of the sword, as in the midst of wild beasts, he would be always near to God." On

---

[3] Eusebius, *Chronicle*, ann. 10 of Trajan, *Hist. Eccles.*, III, 32.
[4] Cf. *infra*, pp. 419 *et seq*.
[5] Date given in the *Chronicle* of Eusebius.
[6] *Ad Smyrn.*, 4.

his journey from Smyrna, where he made a fairly long stay and met Polycarp the bishop, to Philippi in Macedonia, he wrote seven letters for which he is for ever famous, to the churches of Ephesus, Magnesia, Tralles, Rome, Troas, Philadelphia, and Smyrna.

The letter to the Romans is the best known of all. After heaping praise on Roman Christianity, which leads him to evoke the memory of Peter and Paul, he adjures the faithful of Rome, whom he cannot, he says, command like those apostles, to do nothing to oppose his martyrdom. Any such opposition was not very likely, for its success would have been very doubtful, as a pardon was almost out of the question, and a withdrawal from torture *in extremis* would not have been much use. But some protestations of devotion towards his person had probably reached the bishop, and had led him to fear that he might be saved from death. And so he protests vehemently against any such action. "Allow me," he writes, "to be immolated while the altar is ready. . . . Let me be the prey of wild beasts; by them I shall attain to God. I am God's grain: let me be ground by the teeth of wild beasts, so that I may become the pure bread of Christ." So it came to pass, and Ignatius was "ground" by the wild beasts, perhaps in the Colosseum, if this building, begun under Domitian, was then sufficiently advanced.

The Persecution in Bithynia and Pontus

Lastly there was one more province, or rather a group of provinces, in the Asiatic domain of Rome, in which, as we are informed by one of the most precious testimonies we possess, the persecution raged under Trajan's rule. This was Bithynia and Pontus, placed in 111 under the government of Pliny the Younger. He wrote a letter to the Emperor and received from him a reply, which are both famous, and of which we have already spoken.[7]

We learn from this correspondence that, less than a hundred years after the death of Christ, Christianity had made marvellous progress in the northern portion of Asia Minor, and this not only in the towns but also in the country parts. Pliny may have exaggerated a situation which had disturbed him, but would he have wholly invented the statement that the temples were being abandoned and that some of the ceremonies could not take place for lack of participants?

[7] Cf. above, pp. 375, 378.

The former governors, annual proconsuls drawn by lot from among the senators, had remained inactive. But the two provinces had just changed their regime by coming under the direct administration of the Emperor: Pliny arrived there as imperial legate, *legatus Augusti propraetore*. This fact apparently emboldened the opponents of the innovators, and the denunciations began. The number of accusations, and consequently of those who should be victims, naturally worried Pliny, who was not a bloodthirsty man. Hence his questions to his prince. We know the latter's reply.

The reply is merely a simple application of an established legislation, but by the more precise instructions rendered necessary by the questions of an embarrassed magistrate it fixes a jurisprudence still vague in its details, and by limiting the initiative of the authorities it somewhat softens the rigour of principles which nevertheless remain inflexible. Trajan also rejects anonymous accusations—a very important restriction. But we cannot doubt that many Christians had already perished in Bithynia, for Pliny, whose moderation multiplied the interrogatories in the hope of obtaining an abjuration, expressly says that he had sent to death all those who persisted in their "disobedience and their invincible obstinacy." [8] He asserts nevertheless that the deserted temples are once more frequented, and that the sacrifices have begun again—official optimism, doubtless, to a large extent, but there may well have been a certain number of apostates as well as martyrs.

The Persecution in Macedonia

One European province of the Empire seems also to have experienced the rigorous measures of Trajan against the Christians: Macedonia. A letter from one of the best known bishops of the Eastern Church, Polycarp of Smyrna, written in the first half of the second century, mentions some martyrs in the city of Philippi, and also commemorates St. Ignatius, who passed by that city on his way to Rome. "Practise," Polycarp writes to the Philippians, "the patience of which you have seen models with your eyes not only in the blessed Ignatius, Zosimus and Rufus, but also in others from amongst yourselves." [9] These words do not make it absolutely certain that the Philippian martyrs were chronologically near to St. Ignatius, but they make it at least very probable.

[8] *Epist. cit., supra,* p. 378 n. 6.
[9] Polycarp, *Ad Philippenses.* On this letter, cf. p. 378, n. 6.

§3. THE PERSECUTION UNDER HADRIAN

The Emperor Hadrian and the Christians

The reign of Hadrian brought no marked change in the condition of the Christians; but it somewhat diminished the danger which constantly threatened them. This voluptuous *græculus* [1] could have no sympathy for Christianity, but this great administrator, who would never dream of weakening a law calculated to promote public security, had an intense dislike for disorders, and he could only condemn energetically the tumultuous conditions in which the accusations against the Christians were so often made. Particularly in the East, where religious passions were more excitable and superstitions more active, the popular sentiment towards the Christians more than once culminated in violence which reached as far as public authority itself.

The second century was the period when Christianity had come forth from its original obscurity, but was not yet as well known as it would be in the next century, and it was a prey to all kinds of calumnies arising out of ignorance and misapprehension. What did the crowds not imagine about it! Ritual murders, bloody communions, sacred banquets culminating in shameful orgies, magic, ideas compared with which that of the supposed adoration of a god with an ass's head appears a mere inoffensive pleasantry—such were the rumours current about the Christians amongst the simple folk, always ready to believe the worst, and echoed sometimes even by the learned. [2] They were increased by the great complaint in which government and people joined, that Christians withdrew themselves from their fellow citizens by not worshipping the gods, and the rulers who were themselves divine. It is not surprising that such ideas caused trouble and disturbances. Accusations against the Christians were sometimes accompanied by veritable riots. An emperor like Hadrian was not the man to favour such things.

On the other hand, there were magistrates whom the cold rigour of the official doctrine did not free perhaps from all scruples as to what was to be done in presence of passionate denunciations, and were not always disposed to give way blindly to popular clamour.

---

[1] This nickname had been given him because of his delight in all hellenic things.

[2] Cf. *infra*, p. 514.

Some there were who asked the Emperor for fresh elucidations. The proconsul of Asia, Licinius Granianus, amongst others, wrote to Hadrian setting forth his doubts. The imperial reply reached Granianus's successor, Minicius Fundanus, about the year 124.[3] It maintained the existing law, but clarified the formalities of procedure, in order to safeguard public order and to stop abuses, by forbidding the introduction of tumultuous processes, and requiring an individual and regular act of accusation, and a list of proved juridical crimes, and also by ordering the punishment of calumniators. By thus restricting the facility of denunciation and making accusers run the risk of being themselves accused of calumny should their victims suddenly apostatise, it somewhat lessened the danger which constantly threatened the Christians, though it did not remove it entirely.

Martyrs in Italy

Even so, there were certainly fairly numerous martyrdoms in the reign of Hadrian; but several of those explicitly attributed to him are known only by Acts of no value, while in the case of other persons, whose names come to us from sources better than that of Passions subject to caution, the chronological localisation is not more than probable. Such is the case with Pope Telesphorus, who seems to have been put to death under Hadrian, as his pontificate apparently ended in 136, though it may have lasted till 138 or even later, which would bring his end to the reign of Antoninus.[4] A

---

[3] Text in St. Justin, Apology, I, 68; Eusebius, Hist. Eccles., IV, 9; Rufinus, Hist. Eccles., IV, 9. The authentic text is partly given in a Greek translation by Eusebius. This writer speaks of the letter of Granianus also in his Chronicle, Olymp. 226, thinking that the very principle of Trajan's legislation was involved, and that the rescript modified it. But that is unlikely. Dom Capelle, Le rescrit d'Hadrien et saint Justin, in Revue Benedictine, 1927, p. 365, has again endeavoured to defend this interpretation of the rescript, which is that of St. Justin, by showing that the text annexed to his Apology was really written by him. The comparison between the language of the Apology and the introduction to the rescript seems conclusive on the matter of authenticity. But it does not at all follow that Justin correctly interpreted the rescript itself: his very benign interpretation might favour his apologetic thesis, but all the known facts contradict the thesis of a substantial modification of previous legislation. Cf. Callewaert, Le rescrit d'Hadrien, in Revue d'histoire et de littérature religieuses, Vol. VIII, 1903, pp. 152 et seq., who also shows that the doubts sometimes entertained on the authenticity of the rescript, mainly because of the defective interpretation given to it, are without foundation.

[4] Martyrs known by St. Irenæus (Eusebius, Hist. Eccles., V, 6).

certain Alexander, sometimes wrongly identified with the first pope of this name, was also probably a Roman martyr in the time of Hadrian, together with his companions Hermes, Quirinus, Eventius and Theodulus. Getulus, his wife Symphorosa, and their seven sons, perished in Sabina.

Other martyred saints are honoured in Umbria. Local traditional cults and inclusion in the martyrologies guarantee the historic reality and death for the Faith of some, but their *Acts* appear subject to such doubt that it is best merely to register their names.

The Jewish Rebellion of Bar Kokhba and the Christians

We also lack details concerning a local but violent persecution which in Hadrian's reign caused Christians to suffer for another reason. The bloody Jewish revolt of Bar Kokhba had fearful results for them: Justin in his first *Apology*[5] writes that Bar Kokhba "caused Christians, and Christians only, to suffer the last torments if they would not deny and blaspheme Jesus Christ."

§4. THE PERSECUTION UNDER ANTONINUS

The Emperor Antoninus and the Christians

The Emperor Antoninus, who succeeded his adoptive father Hadrian in 138, undoubtedly tended by nature to be more benevolent in regard to the Christians. He did not indeed modify the rigorous legislation under which they still remained, but like Hadrian, and perhaps with greater willingness and desire to avoid the shedding of blood, he forbade any giving way to popular commotions against them, as is shown by four rescripts addressed by him to the cities of Larissa, Thessalonica, Athens, and the provincial assembly of Achaia.[1] He has also been credited with a much more favourable rescript addressed to the provincial assembly of Asia, forbidding denunciations; but although Eusebius has preserved this document in his *Ecclesiastical History* (IV, 13), attributing it, however, to Marcus Aurelius, its apocryphal character is plain. The principles of the legislation itself were not changed. The Christians did indeed make at this time a great effort to persuade

[5] XXXI, 6.
[1] Eusebius, *Hist. Eccles.*, IV, 26, 10.

people to recognise the harmlessness, if not the beneficial character, of their religion. But these apologetic endeavours, the first of which in date was that of Marcianus Aristides, a contemporary of Hadrian, and which are dealt with in detail in a later chapter, did not have the wished-for result.

Martyrdom of St. Polycarp of Smyrna

The imperial orders themselves were not always obeyed. The most illustrious martyr who suffered under Antoninus,[2] Polycarp Bishop of Smyrna, was a victim of a veritable popular uprising, to which Quadratus, the proconsul of Asia, gave way. We know of this event, so glorious for the church of Smyrna, through a letter it sent to the church of Philomelium and all the communities "belonging to the holy universal Church." [3] Twelve Christians were denounced, condemned, and thrown to the beasts in 155; one of them, however, named Quintus, weakened at the last moment, sacrificed to the gods, and swore by the genius of the emperor. But the crowd was not satisfied, and called for the bishop.

The request was out of order, but the proconsul allowed it nevertheless. Polycarp was dragged to the amphitheatre, and in the governor's box was called on to shout, "Down with the atheists." Polycarp consented to do so, having no difficulty in agreeing with the populace in a declaration which he nevertheless made in an altogether different sense. But when he was ordered to curse Christ, he replied: "For eighty-six years now I have served him; he has never done me evil. How could I blaspheme my king and my

---

[2] The martyrdom of St. Polycarp was long put in the reign of Marcus Aurelius, on the strength of a statement in Eusebius. Waddington, *Fastes des provinces asiatiques,* Vol. I, Paris, 1872, pp. 219 *et seq.,* and also in *Mémoires de l'Academie des Inscriptions et Belles-Lettres,* Vol. XVI, 1867, p. 219, showed, by the list of governors of the province of Asia, that the martyrdom took place under Antoninus. Although the ancient chronology has still been defended by J. Reville, *La date du martyre de saint Polycarpe,* in *Revue de l'histoire des religions,* III, 1881, p. 369, it must be abandoned. The confusion between Antoninus and Marcus Aurelius, who was also known by the name of his adoptive father, Antoninus, is not at all surprising. Cf. also F. X. Funk, *Patres apostolici,* Vol. I, 3rd edn., Tübingen, 1913, pp. xciv *et seq.*

The more exact dating of Polycarp's death was the work of C. H. Turner's paper in *Studia Biblica,* Vol. II, 1887, pp. 105-55. Turner showed that the only date which accounts for all the data is February 22nd, 156. There is an annotated translation of the *Martyrdom* in Owen, *Some Authentic Acts of the Early Martyrs,* Oxford, 1927, pp. 31 *et seq.*

[3] Eusebius, *Hist. Eccles.,* V, 18, 9.

saviour?" He was finally burnt alive on a fire of wood made ready by a crowd consisting alike of Jews and pagans.

There were also under Antoninus other victims of pagan hatred: at Jerusalem, Mark the Bishop; in Rome, Popes Hyginus and Pius I, and about 160, a Christian priest or catechist called Ptolemy, and two laymen one of whom bore the name of Lucius. Their condemnation is narrated at the beginning of the second *Apology* of Justin: a husband, angry at the conversion of his wife, accused Ptolemy of having perverted her, and as the accused confessed to being a Christian, he was immediately condemned to death by Lollius Urbicus, the prefect of the city; the two other Christians, who were present in the crowd, manifested their belief and shared the same fate.

§5. THE PERSECUTION UNDER
MARCUS AURELIUS

Marcus Aurelius and the Christians

The reign of Marcus Aurelius witnessed more martyrdoms, and some of them are amongst the most famous in all the history of the persecutions. It was not that Marcus Aurelius in any way added to the legislation concerning the Christians: he maintained it, like his predecessors, but perhaps with more contemptuous inflexibility. He was humane as a philosopher, but had nothing but a haughty disdain for a sect which seemed to him to set little store by intelligence, and welcomed sufferings with a readiness which he regarded as an undignified affectation. Moreover, as a ruler he was fully conscious of his duties towards the Empire, and could not suffer rebels. Hence his severity.

But the much greater frequency in his reign of the applications of a principle always in force is not to be imputed to him alone. It has its explanation in the circumstances, the growth of popular animosity, due perhaps itself to public misfortunes, war, epidemics, or cataclysms the responsibility for which was laid by superstition on the Christians. Perhaps also the progress of Christian propaganda had something to do with it, for popular ignorance continued to regard Christians as enemies of the gods, of morality, and of the Empire. And this animosity more than once forced the hands of the magistrates.

Martyrs in Rome

This was the case, in the last years of the reign, in the trial of the martyrs of Lyons. But some fifteen years earlier, possibly in 162, there were put to death at Rome, after a regular denunciation, St. Felicitas and seven other martyrs regarded by tradition as her sons, and in any case related to her.[1]

Between 163 and 167, a legal accusation made by the Cynic philosopher Crescens similarly brought about the appearance before the prefect of Rome, Junius Rusticus, confidant of Marcus Aurelius, of the Christian philosopher and apologist Justin. He was arrested with some other believers, probably his disciples, amongst them being a woman, Charity, and a slave of Caesar's household, Evelpistus. The essential question, "Are you a Christian?" brought the reply: "Yes, I am." Then followed the sentence: "Those who have refused to sacrifice to the gods and obey the orders of the Emperor are to be scourged and taken away to suffer the penalty of death, in conformity with the laws." The execution took place immediately.[2]

Martyrs in Greece

The Churches in Greece also suffered, for a letter from Dionysius, Bishop of Corinth, to Pope Soter about 170, thanks the latter for sending help to the Christians condemned to the mines, and another letter of the same Dionysius mentions the martyrdom of Publius, Bishop of Athens.[3]

Martyrs in Asia Minor

Sagaris, apparently bishop of Laodicea in Asia Minor, where he was buried, perished in the proconsulate of Sergius Paulus, i.e., be-

[1] On the historical value of the *Passion* of St. Felicitas, see a summary of the various views in P. Allard, *Histoire des persécutions pendant les deux premiers siècles*, Paris, 1909, 3rd edn., p. 378, n. 2. It is worthy of note that the base of a small column coming from a ciborium and found in the ancient Catacomb of Priscilla bears the names of the martyrs Felix, Philip, Vitalis and Martial, mentioned in the *Passion* as sons of Felicitas. [English tr. of the *Passion* in Owen, *op. cit.*, pp. 74 *et seq.* Another by W. H. Sheering, London, 1931.—Tr.]

[2] *Acta Sancti Justini*, in Otto, *Corpus Apologetarum Christianorum sæculi secundi*, Vol. III, Jena, 1879, pp. 266-278. Engl. tr. in Owen, *op. cit.*, pp. 47 *et seq.*

[3] Eusebius, *Hist. Eccles.*, IV, 23.

tween 164 and 166; another Asiatic, Thraseas, Bishop of Eumenia, suffered probably at the same time.[4]

Other Christians in Italy and Greece were condemned to forced labour in the mines. Doubtless the denunciations multiplied, and the hostility of the populace increased. Theophilus, Bishop of Antioch under Marcus Aurelius, says that "the Christians were constantly persecuted. The most pious were continually stoned, and sometimes even put to death." [5] This doubtless refers to popular violence. But the events of 177 at Lyons shows that this could always lead to action by the magistrates.

The Martyrs at Lyons in 177

The martyrs of Lyons have, so to speak, told their own story in an ever-famous document, the letter of the church of Lyons to the churches of Asia, Phrygia and Rome,[7] one of the most beautiful documents of Christian antiquity, in which an account of the cruellest sufferings is given in a very simple manner; nevertheless it breathes all the ardour of the combat entered into for the love of Christ, and in it we find men threatened with the worst torments still anxious about all that concerned the universal church in their time. In particular they concerned themselves with the Montanist prophetic movement then troubling Asia Minor, and endeavoured to bring back to unity those who were going astray.

The church of Lyons was indeed, as far as we can judge from the information in the letter, partly of Asiatic origin and composition. Its head, Bishop Pothinus, over 90 years of age in 177, had been a disciple of St. Polycarp of Smyrna, and the names of several of its members show them to be Orientals, such as the Phrygian doctor Alexander, "long established," nevertheless, "amongst the Gauls."

The indigenous element was also represented; [7] and there were in this young Christian community some notable Gallo-Romans such as Vettius Epagathus, a Roman citizen, described in the letter as a Christian wholly filled with the Holy Spirit. There was also amongst the faithful summoned before the Roman magistrate at Lyons at least one representative of the church of Vienne, the

[4] Eusebius, *Hist. Eccles.*, V, 24.
[5] *Ad Autolychum*, III.
[6] In Eusebius, *Hist. Eccles.*, V, 24, English tr. in Owen, *op cit.*, pp. 53 *et seq.*
[7] In the list in the *Hieronymian Martyrology*, about half the names are Greek, and the other half Latin.

deacon Sanctus. Were the two churches really one community, under one head, in spite of the fact that they were in two different civil provinces, that of Lyons and Narbonne? Possibly so, and perhaps this is the most natural explanation of the one common measure taken against them. But there is nothing which formally excludes the hypothesis of two distinct churches, or that members of the one, that of Vienne, were involved in consequence of their momentary presence in Lyons in the process against their brethren.

From the point of view of public law, however, a common trial before one governor of people belonging to two different provinces might cause some surprise. But this admits of explanation: the Christians of Vienne—and it must be borne in mind that we know only one, the deacon Sanctus, who definitely came from there—may have been arrested at Lyons where they happened to be at the moment; or if the two churches had only one head, they may have been proceeded against as accomplices of their brethren at Lyons.

These latter found a more aggressive attitude taken up towards them by the pagans in the last years of the reign of Marcus Aurelius. The most ridiculous calumnies were re-echoed, and vexations multiplied: exclusion from the baths, markets, and even from the "houses" (which doubtless means that people refused to let houses to Christians, or expelled them from private meeting places),[8] and ill treatment of every kind: "They were insulted, beaten, dragged about, robbed, stoned, and confined together."[9]

The agitation increased at the beginning of August, on the eve of the feasts of Rome and Augustus, the annual manifestation of imperial loyalty which the Christians were bitterly accused of not observing. Did the movement become so hostile that the local authorities decided that they must intervene by taking the initiative in arrests though this was excluded by the imperial rescripts? Or were the Christians taken before them? We know that the governor was absent, and that the municipal magistrates and the tribune of the urban cohort stationed at Lyons took them, tortured them, and kept them in prison awaiting the return of the imperial legate. About ten of those tortured gave way, but most of these repented afterwards. But one serious feature was that some pagan slaves employed by the Christians, some of whom were of sufficient social

---

[8] Thus Owen, *op. cit.*, p. 138 n. He adds, however, that the word is thought by some to refer to public buildings.—Tr.

[9] Eusebius, *loc. cit.*, 6.

rank to have servants, when put to the question, consented to confess to having witnessed scenes of incest and anthropophagy. Nothing further was necessary to persuade more than ever people already
disposed to believe wholly in the reality of these crimes.

The tortures were repeated for several days, in the course of
which the aged bishop Pothinus, "who could scarcely breathe because of the exhaustion of his body, but who was upheld by the
ardour of the Spirit," [10] died in prison, and the apostates, ashamed
of their weakness, proclaimed once more their faith in Christ. The
legate when he returned pronounced the inevitable sentence of
death: Sanctus the deacon of Vienne, Maternus the neophyte, the
very young slave Blandina, and the Asiatic Attalus of Pergamum,
one of the most prominent members of the community in Lyons,
were condemned to the wild beasts.

But before Attalus died, it was discovered that he was a Roman
citizen: troubled, it seems, by this discovery, and by the number
of executions still awaiting, the legate wrote to the Emperor. The
reply was as it was bound to be: the confessors of the faith were
to die, but renegades were to be set at liberty. [11] Very few of these
latter remained, for almost all, at their last appearance, returned to
the side where death awaited them, to the astonishment of the
pagans and the joy of the other Christians.

Those of the condemned who were Roman citizens were beheaded, except Attalus who, in spite of his status, was thrown to the
beasts with the general body. Alexander, the Phrygian doctor, perished in the same manner. The last to suffer, whose apostasy was
doubtless hoped for right to the end, were Ponticus, a lad of fifteen
years, and Blandina, the young slave, who constantly animated her
companions by the example of her courage and by her words. She
suffered at the last alone: "Like a noble mother who had just
exhorted her children and sent them to their King, she repeated
herself the whole series of their combats, and hastened to them,
full of joy and exulting in her end." [12] By the heroism with which

---

[10] Loc. cit., 29.

[11] If the governor had not himself proceeded to this relaxation, called for by
the legislation of Trajan, it may have been because he had submitted to pressure
from the hostile populace, or else, as Babut remarks (art. cit. above, p. 378, n. 6
of the article) because he regarded the Christians as guilty of crimes against
common law, as attributed to them by popular hostility, and that this seemed to
justify their proscription.

[12] Loc. cit., 55.

she bore the tortures, she won the admiration of the pagans themselves, for these "confessed that never amongst them had a woman endured such manifold and cruel tortures." [13]

The Christian community in Lyons, almost fifty brethren of which [14] thus died, seemed to be decimated. But it was to be reconstituted almost at once under the direction of the priest Irenæus, who, having escaped the persecution, was charged to carry to Pope Eleutherus a letter similar to that addressed to the churches of Asia and Phrygia. Shortly afterwards Irenæus became bishop of Lyons.

More Martyrs at Rome

Finally, towards the end of the reign of Marcus Aurelius, between June 177 and March 180, a time suggested by a note in the martyrology of Ado, there were new martyrs in Rome: St. Cecilia, of the illustrious Roman family of the Cæcilii, and the three companions joined with her in the earliest martyrological tradition, Valerian, Tibertius and Maximus. The *Passion* which represents Cecilia as the virgin spouse of Valerian, brother to Tiburtius, is only a late romance; but the account it gives of the death of Cecilia, condemned to be suffocated in the bath of her own house, and finally decapitated, has been at least partially confirmed by remarkable archæological discoveries. Cecilia was buried near to the papal crypt in the cemetery afterwards named after Pope Callistus, in a piece of land belonging to her family; the latter subsequently presented it to the Church, and this explains the proximity of the saint's burial place to that of the Popes of later times. [15]

The Episode of the "Thundering Legion"

In contrast with all these quite certain facts of the persecution, a legendary account, which was once regarded with some favour though it merits none, attributes to the Emperor Marcus Aurelius a change of attitude towards the Christians, which came about in a very unexpected manner. This is the story of the famous prodigy

[13] Eusebius, *loc. cit.*, 56.
[14] The *Hieronymian Martyrology* (ed. Rossi-Duchesne, n. 73), gives forty-eight names.
[15] On the value of the *Acts* of St. Cecilia, cf. A. Dufourcq, *Etude sur les Gesta martyrum romains,* Vol. I, Paris, 1900.

of the "Thundering Legion," narrated in Tertullian's *Apologeticus* [16] and Eusebius's *Ecclesiastical History* [17] as follows: During a campaign against the Quadri in 174, the Roman army, on the point of perishing by thirst, and attacked by the enemy, was saved by a providential storm due to the prayers of the Christian soldiers of the *Legio XII Fulminata.* Thereupon Marcus Aurelius sent a message to the Senate, informing them of this miraculous event, and in gratitude published a kind of edict of toleration which even enacted penalties "against the accusers of the Christians." This is an invention the improbability of which is evident, especially in view of the fact that a pagan tradition attributing the army's salvation to Jupiter coexists with the Christian tradition, and that the latter is again at fault in supposing that the name of *Fulminata* was given to the Twelfth Legion in consequence of the prodigy, whereas it possessed it previously.

That does not mean that everything is to be rejected in a tradition found immediately after the events: the danger in which the imperial troops were, and the rain which descended in a named place, the memory of which is recalled by the Antonine column in Rome, are not to be called in question. And why should we refuse to allow that this salutary rain may have been asked for from heaven not only by pagan soldiers but also by their Christian comrades who may have been very numerous in a detachment of the legion coming from Syria, where the Twelfth Legion was stationed at that time? But whether Marcus Aurelius knew of it or not, he did not in any way deviate from the principles put in force by his predecessors and recalled by himself in regard to Christians.

§6. PERSECUTION AND PEACE UNDER COMMODUS

The Emperor Commodus and the Christians

But better times came to the Church with the reign of the son and successor of Marcus Aurelius, Commodus. There might have been a tendency among early Christian apologists to represent as persecutors only those emperors who had left the worst memories, and Nero and Domitian filled this office well. The quite relative

[16] 5.
[17] V, 5, 2-6.

moderation of the Antonines suggested a very tempting contrast; these great Antonines, conscientious rulers deeply imbued with the Roman tradition, were none the less and even because of that, fundamentally intractable towards Christianity.

Commodus, on the contrary, though son by blood of Marcus Aurelius, was not in the same moral line: he was careless of his real duties as sovereign, in contrast to Domitian, and much prone to violence, and the Roman Senate in condemning his memory could call him more impure than Nero and more cruel than Domitian.[1] But his political indifference itself explains why he showed himself to be less inflexible than his immediate predecessors in regard to a religion these had looked on as a danger to the State. Certainly his rule marks an incontestable change in the relations between the Church and the Empire.

African Martyrs

But this did not take place all at once. In the beginning of the reign of Commodus, we find the first Christian martyrs in Africa whose memory has come down to us.

Twelve Christians in the little town of Scillium, in the part of Numidia dependent on the proconsular province, were delated in 180 to the proconsul, Vigellius Saturninus, who resided at Carthage. They boldly professed their faith and refused to sacrifice to the gods or to swear by the genius of the emperor, and accordingly they were condemned to die by the sword, and were executed on the spot.[2] It is quite likely that the martyrs of Scillium were indeed the first martyrs in the African Church, for Tertullian asserts that Vigellius Saturninus began the measures of bloody repression in this province.[3] We might infer from this that this church was then at least relatively young, which would not exclude the possibility that there was a previous period in which a small number of faithful may have lived obscurely without being disturbed.

Many have put before the martyrs of Scillium, who appeared

[1] "Sævior Domitiano, impurior Nerone" (*Historia Augusta, Vita Commodi*, 19, 21).

[2] Passion of the Scillitan martyrs in Ruinat, *Acta Sincera*, pp. 77-81; Aube, *Etude sur un nouveau texte des Actes des Martyrs Scillitains*, Paris, 1881. Cf. De Smedt in *Analecta Bollandiana*, Vol. VIII, 1889, pp. 6-8. English tr. in Owen, *op. cit.*, pp. 71 et seq.

[3] *Ad Scapulam*, 3: "primus hic gladium in nos egit."

before the governor of Africa on July 16th, a group of martyrs of Madaura put to death on July 4th of the same year, 180. Unfortunately these latter martyrs, who bear native names, and the leader of which, Namphamo, has been called *archimartyr,* i.e., doubtless protomartyr of Africa, were most probably not witnesses to the Christian faith who became victims of the imperial persecutions, but fanatical followers of the Donatist schism, executed probably in the fourth century for having taken part in the crimes committed by the most extreme members of the sect known as the Circumcellians.[4]

Martyrs in Asia Minor

A few years later, about 184 or 185, the province of Asia was once more the scene of persecutions. The proconsul Arrius Antoninus, who was himself to be accused of aspiring to the Empire and was put to death in 188, acted according to Tertullian[5] in an especially cruel way.

Did he favour denunciations? Did he use torture more rigorously to obtain confessions or apostasies? Did he condemn his victims to more exquisite tortures? We know that as a kind of protest, the Christians of a town in Asia, where he was holding his assizes, presented themselves one day in a body at his tribunal to be dealt with by him. Their great number made him afraid: he arrested a few and sent the others away, saying to them: "Miserable people, if you wish to die, have you not sufficient ropes and precipices?"[6]

Martyrdom of Apollonius at Rome

Rome had an illustrious martyr under Commodus in the person of the senator Apollonius, a new example of the penetration of Christianity into the highest ranks of Roman aristocracy. Denounced as a Christian by one of his slaves, whose reward was merely to be executed himself, in accordance with the stipulations of an ancient law which forbade slaves to delate their masters, Apollonius read before a full meeting of the Senate an Apology for

[4] Cf. J. Baxter, *The Martyrs of Madaura,* A.D. 180, in *Journal of Theological Studies,* Vol. XXIV, 1924, pp. 21-37.

[5] *Ad Scapulam,* 5.

[6] *Ibid.*

the Christian Faith, but he was none the less finally beheaded, in virtue of the existing legislation, still in force, as is shown by his Acts.[7]

The Peace of the Church under Commodus

Nevertheless, the political situation underwent a change. Commodus had a favourite, Marcia, who had entered his palace as a slave and finished by becoming his wife, though without the title of Augusta. Now Marcia was a Christian by faith if not by baptism; her conduct had not perhaps been always in conformity with the Gospel ideal, but she was doubtless well disposed, and in any case she did what she could to ameliorate the lot of her brethren.

And so from this moment, in spite of the evident paradox in such a situation, there were Christians in the Imperial court. One of them, the freedman Proxenes, even became Commodus's chamberlain.[8] This favour accorded to Christians by a prince indifferent to a political tradition more than a century old evidently did not pass unnoticed, and the magistrates took account of this change of atmosphere. An African proconsul, for instance, made no secret of the excuses he accepted in order to absolve the Christians deferred to his tribunal.[9] Marcia herself obtained from Commodus the pardon of confessors condemned to forced labour, juridically a capital penalty, in the mines of Sardinia. Pope Victor (189-197) gave a list of these confessors, and the priest Hyacinth, foster-father and friend of Marcia, went to free the prisoners, amongst whom was a future Pope, Callistus.[10]

For the first time, a pardon was granted to Christians condemned for their religion, without any denial, even feigned, of their Faith; and the two powers, ecclesiastical and imperial, agreed in the appli-

---

[7] The martyrdom of Apollonius, known through Eusebius (*Hist. Eccles.*, V 21) and various redactions of his *Passion*, presents some difficulties. But the torture of the *delator*, if he was indeed the slave of the accused, is understandable, as is also the reading of the Apology, if Apollonius did indeed belong to the Senate. More embarrassing is the attributing of the introduction of the process before the Senate to the prefect of the prætorium, whereas the competent authority was the prefect of the city. But the prætorian prefect may have acted by delegation from the emperor. The literature of the subject is given in Duchesne, *Histoire ancienne de l'Eglise*, Vol. I, p, 251, n. 3.

[8] J. B. de Rossi, *Inscriptiones christianæ Urbis Romæ*, 5.

[9] Tertullian, *Ad Scapulam*, 4.

[10] St. Hippolytus, *Philosophoumena*, IX, 11.

cation of the decision made. An unexpected *modus vivendi* seems to have been established between the Church and the Empire. It was due doubtless to a relaxing of the rigid principles from which none of the Antonines had previously thought himself able to deviate. But the increase in the number of the Christians, shown by the very multiplicity of the condemnations, their penetration even into the interior of the palace,[11] and the ease with which the provincial authorities adapted themselves to the new situation might well have signified that the previous system would not work. The one bad emperor in the second century became, doubtless without knowing it, more just than all his glorious predecessors by performing the first act of benevolence towards the Church that she had as yet enjoyed.

Henceforth, in order that rigours should once more be applied, at least with some fulness and some duration, new imperial initiatives would be required, although the preceding legislation had not been abrogated.

[11] Cf. Irenæus, *Adversus hæreses*, IV, 30, 1 (1065).

CHAPTER X

THE APOSTOLIC FATHERS AND
THEIR TIMES [1]

WHEN passing from the history of Jesus to that of the apostles, we noted the infinite distance separating the Master from the disciples. "One is your master, Christ": these words of Jesus come home with an irresistible force to anyone who compares the discourses of the Lord reported in the Gospels with the letters of the Apostles. In turning from the apostolic writings to study the early documents of the history of the Church, we have a similar feeling—less keenly, no doubt, but still strongly. Coming out of the Holy of Holies, we were still in the Sanctuary; now we are in the Temple precincts. The apostles, guided by the Holy Spirit, spoke in its name with an infallible authority. Now they are all dead, and their successors, even the greatest and holiest, realise that they are beneath those whom they replace. St. Clement writes to the Corinthians: "Let us have before our eyes the excellent apostles," and he celebrates the glory of Peter and Paul (*Clem., V*); St. Ignatius, similarly, writes in his letter to the Romans (*Rom.* iv, 3): "I do not give you orders, as did Peter and Paul: they were apostles, I am only a condemned man." The years which follow in the course of the second century do not lessen this distance but increase it; they magnify the incomparable authority of the apostles. Very soon apocryphal works will circulate under their venerated names: *Preaching of Peter, Apocalypse of Peter, Letters* of the Apostles, *Acts* of Paul, John, Peter, or Thomas; all these pious frauds manifest the unequalled prestige of the apostles themselves.

This will be confirmed by Catholic theology: it recognises that down to the death of the last apostle, the deposit of revelation was progressively enriched, that, as St. Paul writes, "the mystery of Christ was not in other generations known to the sons of men as it is now revealed to his holy apostles and prophets" (*Ephes.* iii, 4-5). After the death of the apostles, there will be no new addition: "As soon as we believe," Tertullian will say, "we have no more

[1] Bibliography.—See the notes at the beginning of the treatment of each of the Apostolic Fathers.

need to believe anything further. For the first article of our belief is that there is nothing further which we ought to believe." [2]

At the same time, this deposit is not lifeless or inert; as St. Irenæus will shortly say, "It is as a precious deposit contained in an excellent vessel; the Spirit ever renews its youth and communicates its youthfulness to the vessel containing it." [3] Hence when studying the history of the Church, our effort will be to reach towards this deep life which the documents reveal to those who understand them. When leaving His apostles after the appearance in Galilee, the Lord promised to remain with them until the consummation of the world. The whole development of history since then manifests the realisation of this promise; if our exposition is faithful to its subject, it will bring out this divine life which rejuvenates the pagan world and reveals itself by its fruits of truth and grace.

§ 1.   ST. CLEMENT OF ROME [4]

We are fortunate to find at the outset of this history some documents of undeniable authenticity, which give us through the

[2] De præscriptione, VII, 13.

[3] St. Irenæus, IV, 24, 1.

[4] The letter of St. Clement has been transmitted to us in Greek in two manuscripts. The Alexandrinus, in fifth century uncials, is, as everyone knows, one of the chief authorities for the New Testament: cf. F. C. Kenyon, Handbook to the Textual Criticism of the New Testament, London, 1912, pp. 72-77; Lightfoot, The Apostolic Fathers, I, 1, London, 1890, pp. 116-121; but there is a great gap in this manuscript (LVII, 6—LXIII, 4). In 1875 a second manuscript was discovered, to which we owe the Didache: the Hierosolymitanus, written in 1056; its contents enable us to fill up the gaps in the Alexandrinus. With the Greek texts we can compare the early Latin, Syriac and Coptic versions.

There are numerous editions: Lightfoot, The Apostolic Fathers, Part I, St. Clement of Rome, 2nd edn., London, 1890, 2 vols.; O. von Gebhardt and A. Harnack. Clementis Romani Epistulæ, Lipsiæ, 1876, 2nd edn., 1900; Funk, Patres Apostolici, Tübingen, 1901. The text was published once more in 1924 by Bihlmeyer; also by H. Hemmer in Clément de Rome, Paris, 1909. Excellent English version, with notes by W. K. Lowther Clarke, published by the S.P.C.K. in 1937. Another by Lightfoot.

Abundant bibliography in O. Bardenhewer, Geschichte der altkirchlichen Literatur, Vol. I, pp, 110-113; cf. Rauschen-Altaner, Patrologie, pp. 56 and 58. Recent studies by Harnack, Das Schreiben der Römischen Kirche an die Korinthische aus der Zeit Domitians, Leipzig, 1929, and by Fr. Gercke, Die Stellung des ersten Clemensbriefes innerhalb der Entwicklung der altchristl. Gemeindeverfassung, Leipzig, 1931.

mouths of the two illustrious bishops Clement and Ignatius the witness of the two great churches of Rome and Antioch. We could not desire a better "introduction to the early history of the Church."[5]

St. Clement and his Letter

The first of these documents does not name its author, but presents itself as a letter from the church of Rome to that of Corinth. But this anonymity is dispelled by a very firm and very early tradition, almost contemporary with the letter itself.[6]

Clement, the author of the letter, was Bishop of Rome, as is stated by the majority of those who quote his letter.[7] Moreover, this is clear from the letter itself: only the bishop could thus speak in the name of his Church. His place in the episcopal succession at Rome is less easy to determine: the best attested tradition puts him third, after Linus and Anacletus.[8]

[5] The title of Harnack's last work, a translation and commentary of the letter of Clement (see preceding note).

[6] "The original manuscripts and the Latin and Syriac versions put at the head of the epistle the name of St. Clement: *Epistle of Clement to the Corinthians.* In view of the character of the Alexandrine manuscript and the early date of the versions, we may infer that already in the second century and even in the first half of that century the tradition was fixed in this respect" (Hemmer, *op. cit.,* p. xxiii). About 170, Dionysius of Corinth writes (*apud* Eusebius, *Eccles. Hist.,* IV, 23): "To-day we have kept the holy day of Sunday, during which we have read your letter; we shall continue to read it always as a warning, together with the first which Clement wrote to us." Cf. on the bearing of this testimony, W. J. Ferrar, in *Theology,* Aug., 1928, p. 282; Hermas, *Vis.* ii, 4, 3: "Thou shalt write two little books and thou shalt send one to Clement and the other to Grapte; and Clement will send it round to the other cities, for it is to him that this belongs"; cf. Harnack, *op. cit.,* p. 50. Irenæus (about 180), III, 3, 3: "In the time of this Clement there were very serious divisions amongst the brethren who were at Corinth, and the Church which is in Rome wrote to the Corinthians a very strong letter exhorting them to peace, renewing their faith, and the tradition which they had recently received from the apostles." Numerous other citations are collected in Lightfoot, *op. cit.,* Vol. I, pp. 148-200, beginning with the significant comparisons of the letter of Clement with that of Polycarp (in 110), pp. 149-152.

[7] The citation of Dionysius of Corinth here is especially interesting: writing in 170 to Soter, Bishop of Rome, he assures him of the public reading given to his letter, as of "the first written by Clement."

[8] Irenæus, *Hær.,* III, 3, 3; *Hist. Eccles.,* III, 4, 9, after Hegesippus (Hemmer II). A second tradition, coming no doubt from the Clementine romances, makes him the immediate successor of Peter: Tertullian, *De præscr.,* 32 (Lightfoot, *op. cit.,* p. 174). A third puts him immediately after Linus: Liberian catalogue. This transposition doubtless arises from a confusion with Cletus (Light-

Of the man himself, his origin, and religious formation, we know only what we can gather from the reading of his letter. Eusebius and St. Jerome [9] have rightly stressed the close contact between the letter of Clement and the Epistle to the Hebrews; it is also related to the Book of Wisdom. It reveals a very deep Christian faith in its author, yet he is one who delights to base himself on Jewish tradition and to feed himself thereby; hence it is not without reason that Clement has been regarded as a Christian convert from Judaism.[10] On the other hand, as regards the surrounding paganism, he shows a sympathetic understanding of all that is noble and good; he allows and admires the heroism of the great pagans Codrus, Lycurgus, Decius and others (ch. liv). Still more does he praise the world, the work of God (ch. xx-xxii); his Christianity is not at all that of which the pagans will make a bugbear, as the religion of a *gens lucifuga;* he is a man of the widest and most truly human sympathies.[11]

This humanism, discreetly revealed in the letter, has been transformed and elevated by the Christian faith; the language, accustomed to prayer, takes a liturgical tone. The great prayer (LIX-

foot, *op. cit.,* p. 170; cf. Augustine, *Epist.,* 53, 2; Lightfoot, *op. cit.,* p. 174). Attempts at harmonisation: (1) Rufinus, *Præf. in Recogn.* (Lightfoot, p. 174): Clement succeeded Peter as apostle, Linus and Cletus succeeded him as bishops. (2) *Apost. Constitut.,* VII, 46 (Lightfoot, *op. cit.,* p. 344); Linus was appointed by Paul, Clement by Peter. (3) Epiphanius, *Hær.,* XXVII, 6; Clement, with a view to peace, yielded his rank to Linus, and resumed it only after the death of Cletus, cf. *Epist.,* LIV, 2: it is better to yield one's place than to give rise to a schism. This is an ingenious comparison—doubtless too ingenious.

[9] *Hist. Eccles.,* III, 37-38; *De viris illustribus,* 15.

[10] Cf. Hoennicke, *Judenchristentum,* pp. 291 *et seq.;* Lightfoot, *op. cit.,* pp. 58-60; Tillemont, *op. cit.,* Vol. II, p. 149; Hemmer, *op. cit.,* p. xi. On the opposite side: Harnack, *op. cit.,* p. 51. The author of the letter cannot be identified with the Clement of *Phil.,* iv, 3 (cf. Lightfoot, *op. cit.,* p. 4, 52-58, and *Philippians,* p. 168).

Lightfoot, *op. cit.,* p. 60, and Harnack, p. 51, conjecture that Clement was a freedman of the imperial household; this is only a conjecture, but it is ingenious; the deputies sent by Clement would also be of Cæsar's household; Claudius Ephebus, Valerius Bito, and Fortunatus; Claudius and Nero were of the gens Claudia, and Messalina of the gens Valeria. On the death of Clement we have no certain information; the only indication in favour of a death away from Rome is the absence of any tomb, or of any indication of the burial of the saint at Rome; cf. Tillemont, *op. cit.,* pp. 159-160; Allard, *op. cit.,* Vol. I, pp. 173-180; Lightfoot, *op. cit.,* Vol. I, pp. 86 *et seq.*

[11] Many thoughts and turns of phrase show a Stoic influence. Bardy, *Expressions stoiciennes dans la Ia Clementis,* in *Recherches de Science Religieuse,* Vol. XIII, 1922, pp. 73-85; commentary by Knopf, ch. xix, xx, xxviii, xxxiii; cf. *Histoire du Dogme de la Trinité,* Vol. II, p. 254.

LXI) is one of the most revealing documents for early liturgy; we hear therein the voice of a bishop who, at the close of the exhortation he has just addressed to the community at Corinth, turns towards God, as he is accustomed to do at the end of his homilies, and invites his Christian hearers to pray and praise together with him.[12]

It is indeed a homily that we have in this document. Clement knows that it will be read at Corinth in his name in the assembly of the brethren, and he addresses these absent Christians, as he would address his own in Rome, exhorting them, rebuking them, but also persuading them to pray to God with him.

This exhortation already displays the characteristics the Roman Church's documents will always have: a wise and paternal gravity, a conscious responsibility; a firm insistence but at the same time mildness in reproaches, and in the exposition of doctrine, care to preserve in its integrity the heritage of the traditional deposit.[13]

The Roman Primacy

The date and occasion of the letter are fixed definitely by the document itself: a discord had broken out within the church of Corinth, and had resulted in the deposition of the presbyters (ch. xlvii); these facts had come to the knowledge of the Church of Rome, which had decided to intervene; it had nevertheless delayed to do so, because of the persecution to which it had been subjected (ch. 1.) "The letter must have been written during a pause in the persecution, or immediately after its end, in the last days of Domitian or the beginning of the reign of Nerva, i.e. in 95 or 96." [14]

[12] This great prayer does not stand alone in Clement's letter; we find therein, especially in ch. xx and xxxiii other portions of a very marked liturgical character; and we find a very manifest echo of it in the formulas of prayer in the *Apostolic Constitutions.* Cf. *Hist. du Dogme de la Trinité,* Vol. II, p. 251.

[13] This faithfulness in transmitting the deposit received from the apostles is recognised already by St. Irenæus (III, 3, 3) as one of the characteristics of this "very strong letter." Lightfoot (*op. cit.,* pp. 396-397) has repeated and confirmed this praise: "It was the special privilege of the early Roman Church that it had felt the personal influence of both the leading Apostles, St. Paul and St. Peter— who approached Christianity from opposite sides—the Apostle of the Gentiles and the Apostle of the Circumcision. Comprehensiveness therefore was its heritage. . . . Comprehensiveness was especially impersonated in Clement, its earliest and chief representative." This "comprehensiveness" does not wholly efface the personal character of this letter, and Harnack is mistaken (*op. cit.,* p. 50) in regarding this view of Lightfoot as failing to recognise the personal merits of Clement.

[14] Knopf, *op. cit.,* p. 43. This conclusion is generally accepted.

Was the intervention of the Church of Rome spontaneous, or had it been requested by the Corinthians? We cannot say; [15] what is certain is that Rome was conscious of its authority, and the responsibility which this involved; Corinth also recognised it and bowed to it.[16] Batiffol has described this intervention as "the Epiphany of the Roman Primacy," [17] and he is right.[18]

The Ecclesiastical Hierarchy

This is not the only lesson that may be learnt from this document: we find in it also a strong affirmation of the ecclesiastical constitution of the Church:

"The Master commanded us to perform the offerings and the divine service not haphazardly or without order, but at fixed times and hours. He himself determined where and by what ministers

[15] Batiffol, L'Eglise naissante, p. 154: "Had the Roman Church been asked by Corinth to intervene? The epistle does not say so; if the presbyters deposed by the sedition of the Corinthians had had recourse to Rome, it was perhaps better for Clement not to say so. In this hypothesis we should have here a noteworthy appeal to Rome, the very first in the history of the Church. But it is also possible that Rome derived its knowledge of the scandal at Corinth by public report, and that its intervention was spontaneous (XLVII, 7). In this hypothesis we should understand better that the intestine revolution at Corinth was most unusual, but also that Rome already felt itself in possession of that superior and exceptional authority which it never ceased to claim subsequently, and which was religiously obeyed at Corinth on the occasion of this first intervention." We may remark that the apostle John was still alive; it was not John, however, who intervened at Corinth, but the Bishop of Rome.

[16] This is clear from the letter of Dionysius of Corinth, quoted above, p. 410, n. 6.

[17] Batiffol, op. cit., p. 146.

[18] In an article published since the above was written, L'intervention de l'Eglise de Rome à Corinthe vers l'an 96, in Revue d'Histoire ecclésiastique, Vol. XXXI, 1935, pp. 267 et seq., Père R. Van Cauwelaert has recently called again into question the value of the letter of Clement as a support for the Roman primacy. He explains the Roman intervention at Corinth by the very special relations which existed between the two cities arising from the fact that Corinth was a Roman colony. But there is no proof that these relations involved a specially close intimacy between the two churches. Civic relations were essentially relations between Latins, as Père R. Van Cauwelaert himself expressly recognises. But the early Christian community in Rome was more than half Greek: Greek remained its official language until nearly 200, and the Letter of Clement is in Greek. Had it been in Latin, this point might have favoured the new thesis. Cf. J. Zeiller, A propos de l'intervention de l'église de Rome à Corinthe, in Revue d'histoire ecclésiastique, ibid., pp. 762 et seq. Père Van Cauwelaert nevertheless upholds his point of view (Réponse aux remarques de M. J. Zeiller, in Revue d'histoire ecclésiatique, ibid., pp. 765 et seq.).

these ought to be carried out . . . . To the high priest, special functions have been entrusted; to priests their own places have been assigned; the Levites have their own duties; layfolk are bound by precepts peculiar to layfolk" (XL).

In these Biblical recollections, it is the ecclesiastical hierarchy that Clement has in view.[19] The origin of this hierarchy, and in particular of the powers of government, is more clearly set forth in chapters XLII and XLIV:

"The apostles were sent to us as messengers of good news by the Lord Jesus Christ; Jesus Christ was sent by God. Christ, then, comes from God, and the apostles from Christ; these two missions come harmoniously from God's will. Having received the instructions of our Lord Jesus Christ, and being fully convinced by his Resurrection, the Apostles, strengthened by the word of God, went forth, with the assurance of the Holy Spirit, to announce the good news of the coming of the Kingdom of God. Preaching therefore through country and cities, and having tested their firstfruits by the Holy Spirit, they appointed these as bishops and deacons of the future believers." (XLII).

"Our Apostles knew by Our Lord Jesus Christ that there would be strife concerning the episcopal office. For this reason, in their perfect foreknowledge, they instituted those of whom we have spoken, and then laid down the rule that after their death, other approved men should succeed to their ministry. Those who have been thus instituted by the apostles, or later on by other eminent men, with the approbation of the whole Church, and who have served blamelessly the flock of Christ with humility, tranquillity and charity, and who have had good testimony borne to them for a long time—such men, we consider, cannot justly be deposed from their ministry" (XLIV).

Already we see here how deeply rooted is the assurance of the succession which links the whole ecclesiastical hierarchy through the apostles to Christ, and through Christ to God; here we have the foundation for the traditional thesis set forth by Irenæus and Tertullian: "Quod ecclesiæ ab apostolis, apostoli a Christo, Christus a Deo accepit." [20]

[19] Batiffol, op. cit., p. 152. "It is controverted whether the high priest here figures the bishop, or Christ: it is clear, at any rate, that the priests stand for the presbyters, and the levites for the deacons. In any case, Christian services belong to a hierarchy distinct from the laity: there are clerics, and layfolk."

[20] De præser, XXI, 4. In his History of the Papacy (Geschichte des Papstums, Tübingen, 1930, Vol. I, pp. 10 et seq.), Caspar recognises an apostolical succession here, but tries to make it a purely spiritual succession such as that which links up the teachers in a philosophical school to its founders. But this is to mis-

These two prominent features of the ecclesiastical constitution, the Roman primacy and the divine origin of the hierarchy, are not demonstrated here as theses which opponents deny and which have to be proved; they are truths generally admitted by Christians; Clement can bring them forward with full assurance against the seditious persons at Corinth.

The Christian Faith and the Christian Life

The aim of the letter, the summoning back of the divided and rebellious Christians to concord and obedience, had led Clement to bring out into full light the constitution of the Church. It was desirable that we should first of all stress the great importance of his teaching here, but it must not lead us to overlook all that surrounds this central thesis, for in a hortatory[21] form we have a picture of the Christian life and Christian faith which is of the greatest value to the historian. The Church is seen to be directed towards an ideal of peace, submission to God and to earthly rulers, and of fraternal concord, which even persecution does not disturb. The duty of obedience and union is recalled without weakness, but the strongest counsels or precepts are set forth in a benevolent, peaceable and truly paternal tone; the praise with which the letter begins is not a mere *captatio benevolentiæ* but is above all the sincere expression of esteem and affection for the Church of Corinth. There is only one severe feature: the advice given to the authors of the sedition to leave Corinth; even this is presented not as a condemnation inflicted upon them, but as an act of charity asked from them:

"Is there among you some one who is noble, compassionate, and filled with charity? Let him say: 'If I am the cause of the sedition, I will leave, and go wherever you wish. I will carry out the decisions of the people, only let the flock of Christ live in peace with the appointed presbyters!' He who will act thus will gain for himself great glory in Christ, and every place will welcome him. . . ." (LIV).

---

take the character of the Christian Church, which is not a philosophical school, but the Body of Christ, a visible society, governed by hierarchical heads.

[21] It is difficult to summarise this letter; but here are the chief developments: I-III, prologue; IV-XXXVI, moral considerations in order to prepare for the return to peace; XXXVII-XXXVIII, transition: the Body of Christ; XXXIX-LXI, teaching directly aiming at remedying the division amongst the Corinthians; LXII-LXV, conclusion.

Then, in order to give encouragement, Clement mentions examples of devotion given by pagans and Jews, and in these examples again we note with Hemmer the "breath of humanity which inspires Clement, and leads him to do justice to the devotion of Codros, Lycurgus, Decius, and other pagan heroes."

Not men alone, but also inanimate creatures teach us peace, concord, and harmony (ch. XX-XXI).

Still, it is true that the usual sphere of Clement's thought is sacred history; it is there he seeks by preference for his models and also for examples of God's punishments, as we see from the beginning (ch. IV) and throughout the epistle. These recollections of the Old Testament are moreover a common possession, and doubtless Clement utilises many developments which are already traditional.

What is more personal are the properly Christian features; these are not so numerous, but they are set forth very prominently. This is the case with the example of the excellent apostles Peter and Paul (ch. V) and of the Roman martyrs (ch. VI); and above all with the examples and lessons of Christ himself:

"Let us fix our gaze on the blood of Christ, and know how precious it is to God his Father, because having been poured out of our salvation, it has brought to the whole world the grace of repentance" (VII, 4).

"Above all let us remember the words which the Lord Jesus spoke to us to teach us fairness: . . . 'Be ye merciful, that ye may obtain mercy. . . .'" (XIII, 1).

"Christ belongs to those who are humble, and not to those who exalt themselves above the flock. The sceptre of the majesty of God, the Lord Jesus Christ, did not come with the pomp of pride or boastfulness, though He might have done, but in humility, as the Holy Spirit spake concerning him" (XVI, 1-2).

"The sovereign Creator and Master of the universe willed that all these things should remain in peace and concord, for He is good towards all, but especially towards us who have recourse to his mercy through Jesus Christ our Lord, to whom be glory and majesty for ever and ever, Amen" (XX, 11-12).

"Such is the way, my beloved, in which we find our salvation, Jesus Christ, the high priest of our offerings, the protector and help of our weakness. Through him we fix our gaze on the heights of heaven; through him we see as in a mirror the spotless and sublime countenance of God; through him the eyes of our heart are opened; through him our mind, hitherto closed and darkened, opens to the light; through him the Master has willed that we should taste the immortal knowledge, who, being the effulgence of God's majesty, is so much higher than the angels as he hath received a more excellent name. . . ." (XXXVI, 1-2).

We recognise in the last sentence an echo of the epistle to the Hebrews: Christ is our high priest, the mirror in which we contemplate the splendour of God; He is infinitely above the angels, and this transcendence is then proved by Clement by the Biblical texts already quoted in the Epistle to the Hebrews.[22]

A little further, we have a eulogy of charity which recalls the teaching of St. Paul (I Cor., xiii), and which concludes in the contemplation of the charity of Jesus Christ:

"Let him who has the charity of Christ fulfil the commandments of Christ. Who can describe the bond of the divine charity? Who is able to express its sublime beauty? The height to which charity raises us is ineffable. Charity unites us closely to God; charity covers a multitude of sins, charity suffers all things, bears all things; there is nothing low in charity, nothing proud; charity does not make a schism, charity does not create sedition, charity does all things in concord; in charity the perfection of all the elect of God is consummated; without charity nothing is pleasing to God. By charity the Master has raised us up to Him; because of the charity He had for us, Jesus Christ our Lord, by the will of God, gave His blood for us, and His flesh for our flesh, and His soul for our souls" (XLIX).

This is indeed a Christian sermon.[23] Doubtless the thought of Christ is not so constantly present to the mind of Clement as it was to Paul, but when He does appear He dominates everything: He is the "sceptre of the majesty of God" and the radiation of His glory; to mankind He is the Redeemer and Saviour. This exalted Christology will be more concealed in the apologists: desirous above all to demonstrate to catechumens or even to pagans the preliminaries of the faith, they will postpone the great theological theses to a later teaching; but the witness of the apostolic Fathers, and in particular of Clement and Ignatius, warns the historian not to think

[22] On all this cf. *Histoire du Dogme de la Trinité*, Vol. II, p. 270.
[23] Bousset, *Kyrios Christos*, 1921, p. 291, is mistaken in seeing in the primitive Roman Church as it appears in Clement, the religion of the Jewish Dispersion. So also Lietzmann, *Geschichte der alten Kirche*, Vol. I, p. 209: "This community did not spring from Paulinism, but received from it only a very superficial impress. It developed directly out of the Greek synagogue, and it sets forth a conception of Christianity such as we should expect to find amongst the proselytes." Against this, cf. *Hist. du Dogme de la Trinité*, Vol. II, p. 280.

that silence comes from forgetfulness, or that the second Christian century, before Irenæus, lost sight of the theology of the apostles.

The dogma of the Trinity is equally attested in this letter. We note particularly this solemn declaration in which Clement confirms his moral teaching:

"Accept our counsel, and you will not regret doing so. For as truly as God lives, and the Lord Jesus Christ and the Holy Spirit, the faith and hope of the elect, he who humbly carries out . . . the commandments given by God, will be included and counted among the number of those saved by Jesus Christ. . . ." (LVIII, 2).[24]

The Jews swore by the life of Jahveh; Clement swears by the life of the three divine Persons, in whom he sees "the faith and hope of the elect"; we feel here the energy of the Christian soul which, pressed by grace, professes by faith the Trinity of divine Persons, and by hope tends towards them; it is the same energy that we shall find at the end of the second century in Athenagoras; "We are moved by the sole desire to know the true God and His Word . . ., to know the community between Father and Son, and the union and distinction of these united terms, the Spirit, the Son, and the Father." [25]

Two other texts [26] also remind the Christians of their Trinitarian faith. As Harnack puts it: "The author sets forth the profession of the Trinitarian faith; he does not comment on it, evidently because he felt no difficulty in this formula, any more than St. Paul had done." [27] And certainly there is no indication of any hesitation here in Clement or the Corinthians. They believe in God, Father, Son and Holy Spirit; they aspire to know Him; this is the faith and hope of the elect.

The Christian life which these texts reveal to us expands into

[24] This important text was already quoted by St. Basil, *De Spiritu Sancto,* XXIX, 72 (Migne, P.G., XXIX, p. 201). As this chapter and the following ones are lacking in the *Alexandrinus,* the authenticity of this text was long questioned, but the discovery of the Jerusalem M.S. and the Syriac version has removed all doubts. Cf. on the doctrinal importance of this text, *Hist. du Dogme de la Trinité,* Vol. II, pp. 277-279.

[25] *Legatio,* c. XII.

[26] "The apostles, fully convinced by the resurrection of our Lord Jesus Christ, and strengthened by the word of God, with the assurance of the Holy Spirit" (XLII, 3); "Have we not one only God, and one only Christ, and one only Spirit (of Grace) poured out upon us, and is there not one only calling in Christ?" (XLVI, 6).

[27] *Der Erste Klemensbrief,* in *Sitzungsberichte der kon. Preuss. Akad.,* 1909, III, p. 51, n. 4.

the great prayer (ch. LIX-LXI); we shall study this later on, when
we deal with prayer and the liturgy.

§2. ST. IGNATIUS OF ANTIOCH[1]

Of all the witnesses of the Christian Church at the beginning of
the second century, there is none more qualified than the illustrious
Bishop and martyr, St. Ignatius of Antioch; and no testimony is
more explicit than his. For a long time this testimony was suspect;
Renan could still write: "The question of the epistles of St. Ignatius
is, after that of the Johannine writings, the most difficult of those
connected with primitive Christian literature," [2] and he answered
the question negatively.[3] But thanks above all to the work of Lightfoot, the critical problem has been studied more closely, and
definitively settled, and this has assured definite progress in the
early history of the Church.[4]

The confusion which so long paralysed the efforts of critics arose
in great part from the state of the manuscript tradition.[5]

[1] Editions: Lightfoot, *Apostolic Fathers*, Part II, 3 vols., 1889; Gebhardt-
Harnack, Funk-Bihlmeyer (*supra*, p. 409, n. 4); Lelong (1910); Bauer (1920).
English translation by Dr. Srawley, published by S.P.C.K., 1919. Historical and
theological studies: T. Zahn, *Ignatius von Antiochien*, Gotha, 1873; E. von der
Goltz, *Ignatius von Antiochen als Christ und Theologe*, Leipzig, 1894; H. de
Genouillac, *Le Christianisme en Asie-Mineure au début du IIe siècle*, 1907;
Rackl, *Die Christologie des hl. Ignatius v. Antiochien*, Freiburg, 1914; Lebreton,
Histoire du Dogme de la Trinité, Vol. II, pp. 282-331.

[2] *Les Evangiles*, p. x.

[3] *Ibid.*, p. xvii; cf. p. 492.

[4] In one of his last works, Loofs wrote: "There was a period of new biblical,
theological and historical researches in which one seemed to be retrograde if one
did not set out to interpret in the light of Philo and the literature deriving from
him, all the references to the Logos met with in the christological texts of early
Christian literature. That has changed now that the authenticity of the letters
of Ignatius has been definitively established" (*Paulus von Samosata*, Leipzig, 1924,
p. 312).

[5] The manuscript tradition presents three different forms:

The *short* recension, containing three letters, Polycarp, Ephesians and Romans,
in a very abridged form.

The *mean, mixed* or *long* recension, containing in a longer form the three
letters mentioned above, and in addition, Magnesians, Trallians, Philadelphians,
and Smyrnians.

The *long* or *longer* recension contained in a still longer form the seven preceding
letters, and in addition: Mary of Cassobola to Ignatius, Ignatius to Mary of
Cassobola, Ignatius to the Tarsians, to the Antiochenes, to Hero, and to the
Philippians.

But it is evident that the decisive reason for this opposition lay in the desire to defend a theological thesis threatened by these documents.[6]

St. Ignatius and his Letters

The circumstances in which these letters were written are very clearly determined: in the course of a persecution of which we know nothing otherwise, and which speedily died down,[7] Ignatius, Bishop of Antioch, was arrested; he was taken to Rome to be condemned to wild beasts. He made a first stop at Philadelphia,[8] a second at Smyrna, where he was received by Polycarp, the bishop, and met also by representatives of the churches of Ephesus, Magnesia and Tralles. When he was there he wrote to these three churches and to the church of Rome. Next he was taken on to Troas, from whence he wrote to the churches of Philadelphia and Smyrna, and also to Polycarp. He passed by Philippi on the way to Dyrrachium, and lastly reached Rome. At his request, the

---

This last form, obviously interpolated, was the first to be published, in 1498, by Lefèvre d'Etaples; the mean form, the only authentic one, in 1644 by Ussher; the short form in 1845 by Cureton.

To Lightfoot (in 1885 and 1889) belongs the merit of having elucidated the critical problem and bringing forward the decisive testimonies which established the authenticity of the seven letters (op. cit., Vol. I, pp. 135-232). O. Pfleiderer, in the first edition of his Urchristentum, 1887, pp. 825-835, had declared the letters of Ignatius to be "as certainly unauthentic as the pastoral epistles"; in his second edition (1902), pp. 226-232, he recognises them as authentic. Lightfoot (op. cit., Vol. I, p. 423) thus concludes his study of the question: "While external and internal evidence combine to assert the genuineness of these writings, no satisfactory account has been or apparently can be given of them as a forgery of a later date than Ignatius."

There is another grouping of the epistles, adopted by T. W. Manson in A Companion to the Bible (Edinburgh, 1939, p. 127): The Long Recension (13 epistles), the Short (the genuine 7), and the Syriac (3 only).

[6] J. Reville admitted this in his Origines de l'Episcopat: "The real reason, and the only really strong one, which from the beginning of modern historical criticism to our own day, has caused the disqualification of the epistles of Ignatius in their first recension is the ardent episcopalianism which inspires them from one end to the other" (p. 478). He himself accepts the authenticity but rejects the testimony: "To take literally the information furnished by the epistles on the ecclesiastical state of their time is about as reasonable as to represent the state of our modern society from the violent diatribes against the Republic of Freemasons by a militant clerical, or against the bourgeois by a revolutionary socialist" (p. 480). The clerical would at least know what was going on in his Church, and the Socialist in his party: that is all we ask from Ignatius.

[7] Ignatius to Polycarp, VII, 1.

[8] Philad., III, 1; VII, 1; VIII, 1.

Christians of Philippi wrote to Antioch to congratulate the Christians there on the return of peace; they sent their letter to Polycarp, who replied to them, and at the same time sent them at their request the letters of Ignatius which he possessed; in this way there was constituted the first *Corpus Ignatianum*.[9]

These letters, which are about fifteen years later than that of Clement,[10] are like that, and even more so, occasional papers; they were not written after long preparation, but in haste, by a prisoner condemned to wild beasts and closely guarded: "chained to ten leopards, that is, ten soldiers who show themselves to be the more wicked as one does them more good" (*Rom.* v, 1) We must not expect to find in them an elaborate exposition of the Christian doctrine, nor a complete description of ecclesiastical organisation, but we shall find there a most sincere and clear testimony concerning the Christian life and faith, that of a martyr who is already suffering for Christ, and desires only to die for him, who dearly loves the Church, and who warns it with the farsightedness of a man inspired by God, and with the authority of a bishop.

The Church and the Churches

We find many common features between these letters and that of Clement: there is the same desire for order and peace in the Church by submission to the hierarchy, and the same love of unity. But there is also a great difference between the two bishops: Clement does not confine himself to exhorting: he gives authoritative

[9] Harnack recalls these facts in his studies on early collections of letters: *Die Briefsammlung des Apostels Paulus und die anderen vorkonstantinischen Christlichen Briefsammlungen*, Leipzig, 1926, pp. 28-35. Polycarp to the Philippians, 13: "You and Ignatius have written asking that if anyone is going to Syria he may also take your letter. . . . The letters of Ignatius, both those he has addressed to us and the others which we possess, are being sent to you at your request; they are included with this letter. . . . If you on your side have certain news of Ignatius and his companions, please communicate it to me." This text is quoted by Eusebius, *Hist. Eccles.*, III, 14-15. On this letter of Polycarp we have also the testimony of Irenæus (III, 3, 4), and of Eusebius (*Hist. Eccles.*, IV, 14, 8). Now Irenæus was a disciple of Polycarp, as he reminds Florimus (*Hist. Eccles.*, V, 20). The letter of Ignatius to the Romans is quoted by Irenæus (V, 28, 4) without mention of the author's name, and also by Origen (*De Orat.*, 20, *In Canticum, Prol.*). In *Hom. VI in Luc.*, Origen quotes *Ephes.*, XIX. These two last citations are expressly attributed to Ignatius. The seven letters are enumerated by Eusebius, *Hist. Eccles.*, III, 36, 2.

[10] The date of these letters is that of Ignatius's martyrdom; this date belongs to the reign of Trajan (98-117), but it is difficult to be more precise. Cf. Lightfoot, *op. cit.*, Vol. II, p. 472.

advice which is to be followed. Ignatius's attitude is not the same: in spite of the prestige of his situation as a confessor, he adopts always a great reserve so far as he himself is concerned. Thus he writes to the Trallians (III, 3): "In my love for you, I refrain from more severe remarks which I might address to you concerning your bishop; I will not presume to command you like an apostle, being only a condemned man." Even these counsels, which he multiplies to other churches, disappear from the letter to the Romans; here we find only prayers, supplications, and veneration for the Roman Church. We may infer from this that in the mind of Ignatius, the various churches are mutually independent, and that a bishop, even of Antioch, and a confessor of the faith, can give only counsel to other churches, while the Roman Church alone has a rank apart, an authority which is over all the others, which justified the step taken by Clement, and calls for submission and deference from Ignatius.

If we pass from the churches as a whole to the local organisation of each church, we find everywhere a definitely constituted hierarchy. Ignatius requests that it shall be respected; he does not need to promote its establishment: it already exists.

A few texts, chosen from a great number, will give the sense and force of the directions of Ignatius:

"The youthfulness of your bishop ought not to lead you to treat him with too much familiarity, in him you must reverence the very power of God the Father. In this way act, as I know, your holy presbyters; they do not presume upon his youth, but being inspired by the wisdom of God, they are subject to him, or rather it is not to him they are subject, but to the Father of Jesus Christ, to the universal bishop" (*Magn.*, III, 1).

"All must reverence the deacons as Jesus Christ, the bishop as the image of the Father, the presbyters as the Council of God and the college of the apostles. Without them there is no church" (*Trall.*, III, 1).[11]

We learn from Clement and the *Didache* that the episcopate is not only a ruling authority but also a priesthood;[12] it has the same character in Ignatius; hence the indispensable place of the bishop in the administration of the sacraments:

[11] Cf. *Ephes.*, IV, 1; VI, 1; *Philad.*, III, 1; *Smyrn.*, VIII, 1; *Polyc.*, VI, 1.
[12] *Clement.*, XLIV, 4; *Didache*, XV.

"Do nothing without the bishop in what concerns the Church. Regard as valid only that Eucharist which is celebrated under the presidency of the bishop or of his delegate. Wherever the bishop is, there let also the community be, just as wherever Christ Jesus is, there is the Catholic Church. It is not permitted to baptize or to celebrate the agape apart from the bishop; but all that he approves is pleasing to God, and all that you do is secure and valid" (*Smyrn.*, VIII, 1-2).[13]

Authority and the Charisms

Lastly, we note the no less important fact of the union between the charisms and the hierarchy. Ignatius, the bishop who everywhere preaches obedience, is at the same time the enthusiastic confessor, full of desire for martyrdom; he is also a seer, whose vision has penetrated the heavens: "Though I am a prisoner of Jesus Christ, I am able to know heavenly things, and the hierarchy of angels, and the ranks of principalities, and things visible and invisible, but I am not thereby a true disciple" (*Trall.*, V, 2).[14]

At the end of his book on the idea of the apostolate, the Protestant historian H. Monnier wrote: "There came to pass this strange thing: the Spirit, in the second century, went over to the side of the bishops, deserting the cause of those inspired by profession. Ignatius and Polycarp, the known founders of the monarchical episcopate in Asia, are full of the fire of the Spirit: they prophesy, and have visions, while the free missionaries of their time are doubtful personages, whose vocation derives from their own caprice. And in the rest of this struggle between growing Catholicism and

[13] Cf. *Philad.*, IV. Amongst all the churches made known to us in these documents, there is one where the monarchical episcopate does not appear, namely, that of Philippi. Cf. Michiels, p. 367: "There is (in the letter of Polycarp) no mention of a bishop, but there is of priests and deacons. It seems to us that certain reasons compel us to infer from this silence the non-existence of a bishop at Philippi. No other satisfactory explanation has been advanced." Cf. H. de Genouillac, *op. cit.*, p. 143; Duchesne, *Histoire ancienne de l'Eglise*, Vol. I, pp. 88 et seq.

[14] Cf. *Philad.*, VII, 2: "They suspected that I spoke thus because I knew already of the schism which was to break out; but I take to witness him for whom I bear these bonds, that I had learnt nought from man. It was the Spirit which said aloud: 'Do nothing without the bishop. . . .'" *Polyc.* II, 2: "If you are both flesh and spirit, you ought to treat gently the things that come before you; as for things invisible, pray that they may be revealed to you, so that you may lack nothing, but possess the spiritual gifts in abundance." Cf. *ibid.*, I, 3: "Devote yourself to constant prayers, ask to grow in understanding, watch, and let your spirit never sleep."

free Inspiration it is evident to us that Catholicism represents the true interests of the Church. . . . Free Inspiration had created the Church, but at this moment it was becoming a danger; it had either to discipline itself or disappear. That is why the best among the Spirituals put their gifts at the service of the Church, and ended by being absorbed into its hierarchy." [15] The study of the apostolic times. and in particular of St. Paul, has shown what we are to think of this supposed sovereignty of Inspiration at the beginning of the Church; but it is interesting to note that at the period to which we have come, namely, the early years of the second century, the Catholic organisation of the Church is evident even to observers the least predisposed in its favour.

Ignatius found already some opponents who wished to refer only to Scripture: "I have heard some people saying: 'If I do not find (this point of belief) in the records, in the Gospel, I will not believe it!' And when I say to them: 'It is written,' they reply to me: 'That is precisely the question.' For me, the records are Jesus Christ, the inviolable records are his Cross, his death, his resurrection, and the faith which is by Him; it is by these things that I desire, thanks to your prayer, to be justified" (Philad., VIII). [16]

This Church is not a friendly group of scattered communities with no bond between them: it is truly a unity created by Jesus Christ: "Where the bishop is, there ought also to be the people, just as where Jesus Christ is, there is the Catholic Church" [17] (Smyrn., VIII, 2). "Jesus Christ is the Mind of the Father, just as the bishops established in the confines (of the world) are the Mind of Jesus Christ" (Ephes., III, 2).

The Roman Primacy

Moreover, this unity rests upon the special dignity of the Roman Church; in this matter the witness of Ignatius is of great weight. [18]

[15] La notion de l'apostolat des origines à Irénée, 1903, p. 374. Cf. ibid., p. 245.
[16] Batiffol, l'Eglise naissante, pp. 162 et seq.; on the following text, ibid., p. 166.
[17] This is the first occurrence of this expression; it signifies the "universal Church" in contrast to particular churches; so in Mart. Pol., inscr. VIII, 1; XIX, 2. Very soon it will signify the Great Church in contrast to the heretics; thus Muratorian Canon, 66, 69 (ed. Lietzmann); Clement of Alexandria, Strom., VII, 106, 107; cf. Mart. Pol., XV^r 2 (doubtful text). Cf. note by Bauer on Smyrn.; VIII, 2.
[18] It has often been studied: Funk, Der Primat der römischen Kirche nach Ignatius und Irenæus, in Kirchengeschichtliche Abhandlungen, Paderborn, 1897,

It is evident in the first place in the initial address of the letter, which is of a solemnity and high tone which distinguishes it from all the others:

"Ignatius, also called Theophorus, to the Church which has obtained mercy in the bounteous power of the Father most High and Jesus Christ his only son, to the Church which is beloved and illuminated by the will of Him who willed everything that exists, according to the love of Jesus Christ our God, to that Church which presides in the region of the Romans, worthy of God, worthy of honour, worthy of blessing, worthy of praise, worthy to be heard, worthy in purity, presiding in love, which has received the law of Christ, which bears the name of the Father, and which I salute in the name of Jesus Christ, the Son of the Father, to those who are attached in body and soul to all His commandments, filled for ever with the grace of God, and purified from every foreign dye, I wish a full and holy joy in Jesus Christ our God."

The impression we get from the reading of this address is confirmed by the letter as a whole: all the other epistles are full of recommendations and counsels; we find none such here, but only respectful requests; this complete change of attitude can only be explained by the singular veneration which the bishop of Antioch has for the Roman Church. Lastly, we must quote: "You have never envied anyone; you have given instructions to others. What I desire is that what you counsel and ordain may be always practised" (*Rom.*, III, 1); and still more this final recommendation: "Remember in your prayers the church of Syria which, having me no longer, has only God as its pastor. It will have no other bishop besides Jesus Christ and your charity" (*Rom.*, IX, 1). We will not exaggerate the importance of these words, but we must remark that Ignatius addresses them only to the Romans: from the other churches he asks only prayers.[19]

After re-reading these texts, we can without imprudence sub-

Vol. 1, pp. 2-12; Chapman, *Saint Ignace d'Antioche et l'Eglise romaine*, in *Revue bénédictine*, Vol. XIII, 1896, pp. 385-400; Batiffol, *Eglise naissante*, pp. 167-170; H. Scott, *The Eastern Churches and the Papacy*, London, 1928, pp. 25-34. Interpreted differently by Harnack, *Das Zeugnis des Ignatius über das Ansehen der römischen Gemeinde*, in *Sitzungsber. der Akademie*, Berlin, 1896, pp. 111-131; H. Koch, *Cathedra Petri*, Giessen, 1930, p. 175; E. Caspar, *Geschichte des Papstums*, Vol. 1, Tübingen, 1930, pp. 16-17.
[19] On all these texts we can accept the commentaries of Duchesne, *Eglises séparées*, pp. 127-129, recalled by Batiffol, *op. cit.*, p. 170.

scribe to this conclusion of an Anglican writer, S. H. Scott: "The Roman Church had a primacy, and that primacy was owing to its connection with St. Peter." [20]

Circumstances had led St. Ignatius to multiply his recommendations of unity between Christians, and of submission to the hierarchy, and thus no testimony is more explicit than his, or more valuable to us concerning the life and organisation of the Church at the beginning of the second century. But as we have already seen, this great bishop was at the same time a spiritual man and a prophet. As he himself recommends to St. Polycarp (*Polyc.*, II, 2), if he is flesh as well as spirit, this is in order to govern with gentleness those amongst whom he lives, while also contemplating invisible things. This contemplation is for him both a much desired grace and an imperious need. His whole theology is illuminated by it.

The Flesh of Christ

This theology naturally has traces of the controversies which then loomed large. In Asia as a whole, and above all in the churches of Tralles and Smyrna, Ignatius felt the menace of Gnosticism, and reacted against it with all his might. Deceived by their dreams, these people had gone so far as to deny the real life and real flesh of Jesus Christ; the Bishop of Antioch, like his master St. John,[21] sees in these denials the complete opposite of Christianity: [22]

"Refuse to listen to the speech of those who do not speak to you of Jesus Christ the descendant of David and the Son of Mary, who was really born, who really ate and drank, who really suffered persecution under Pontius Pilate, who was really crucified and died before the eyes of heaven, earth, and the lower regions; who really rose from the dead. . . . If He suffered only in appearance, as is said by certain atheists, that is, certain unbelievers, who themselves are only an appearance, why am I in bonds? Why am I impatient to fight against the wild beasts? Then I die in vain, and what I say of the Lord is a lie!" (*Trall.*, IX).

"He really suffered, just as He really rose again, although some unbelievers, who are themselves only an appearance, say that He suffered only in appearance. . . . As for me, I know and believe that, even after his resurrection, He had a body. . . . After His resurrection, He ate and

[20] *The Eastern Churches and the Papacy*, p. 34.
[21] Cf. *Histoire du Dogme de la Trinité*, Vol. I, pp. 482-485.
[22] *Ibid.*, Vol. II, pp. 80-81.

drank with His disciples like a corporeal being, although by the spirit He was united to His Father. . . . If it was only in appearance that Our Lord did all that, it is only in appearance that I am in bonds. Then why am I surrendered and given over to death by fire, sword and wild beasts?" (*Smyrn.*, II).

The Eucharist

These Christological errors had their immediate effect on the doctrine of the Eucharist, and Ignatius follows the controversy into this domain:

"They abstain from the Eucharist and from prayer, because they do not admit that the Eucharist is the flesh of our Lord Jesus Christ, which flesh suffered for our sins, and which the Father in His goodness raised up again. So those who deny the gift of God find death in their disputations. It were better for them rather to love, in order to rise again" (*Smyrn.*, VI).

In St. Ignatius as in St. John, these uncompromising affirmations of the reality of the flesh of Christ, in His life here below as also in the Eucharist, are penetrated with a belief in the vivifying activity of this flesh:

". . . You all break one bread, which is the medicine of immortality, an antidote which preserves us from death, and assures us of life for ever in Jesus Christ" (*Ephes.*, XX, 2).

Life in Christ

This belief unceasingly affirmed by Ignatius [23] is the deep source of his own life: if he repels Docetism with such energy, it is because the real flesh of Christ, denied by this heresy, is the indispensable principle of life: "Without him we do not possess true life" (*Trall.*, IX, 2): "The only thing necessary is to be found in Christ Jesus, for eternal life" (*Ephes.*, XI, 1).

Once more we find in the theology of Ignatius, as in that of Paul

[23] *Ephes.*, III, 2: "Jesus Christ, our inseparable life"; VII, 2: "in death, true life"; Magn., I, 2: "I desire for the churches union with the flesh and spirit of Jesus Christ, our eternal life"; *Trall.*, IX, 2: "We who believe in him will be raised up by the Father in Christ Jesus, without whom we do not possess true life"; *Smyrn.* IV, 1: "Jesus Christ, our true life." Cf. *Ephes.*, XI, 1; XIX, 3; Magn., V, 2; IX, 2; *Trall.*, II, 1, etc.

and John, and indeed in all Christianity, the indissoluble union of flesh and spirit: this defender of the hierarchy is, as we have said, a spiritual man; similarly, this defender of orthodoxy is also the great mystic who writes to the Romans (III, 3): "Nothing that is visible is beautiful. Even our God Jesus Christ is manifested better now that He has returned to the bosom of the Father." And there is in him a desire, deep as life itself, to disappear and to hide in the divine silence where God alone is heard; then he will be a "word of God," but as long as he lives in the flesh he is but a "voice" (*Rom.*, II, 1); or as he says further on: "It is when I shall have disappeared from this world that I shall be able to be called truly faithful" (III, 2). The dreadful death in store for him attracted him irresistibly: "Let me become the food of the beasts; by them I shall attain to God. I am the bread of God, I must be ground by the death of the beasts in order to become the stainless bread of Christ. . . . Then shall I be truly a disciple of Jesus Christ, when the world sees no longer my body. Entreat Christ for me, that by the beasts I may become a victim offered to God" (*Rom.*, IV, 1-2).

Christ and Martyrdom

In this impatient thirst for death, silence, and complete disappearance, we must not suspect the influence of the perverse mysticism spread everywhere by Gnosticism: God is not for Ignatius an abyss in which he is to lose himself, He is the Father who is calling him in Christ and who is waiting for him; his faith is radiant with light: this Christ, whose real human nature he defends with such vigour, is He who takes hold of him by his life and by his resurrection; it is He who, present in his faithful one, leads him on towards God:

"Let naught of things visible or invisible seek to deprive me of the possession of Jesus Christ! Come fire, and cross, and bodily combat with wild beasts, lacerations, tearings, dislocation of bones, mutilation of members, crushing of the whole body, come the worst torments of the devil upon me, provided only I possess Jesus Christ! . . . Him I seek, Him who died for us; Him I want, who rose again for our sakes! The hour draws near for my birth. Forgive me, brethren; hinder me not from living, do not desire my death; bestow not upon the world or the seductions of matter him who desires to be God's. Let me grasp the pure light; when I shall attain to it I shall be truly a man. Let me imitate the suffering of my God. If anyone has Him in his heart, let him understand my desires, let him be compassionate in my pain, since he himself knows it. . . . My love has been crucified, and there is not within me any fire for matter, but a living water, which murmurs within me and says to me: 'Come to the Father.' I have no more pleasure in corruptible food, nor in the joys of this life. I desire the bread of God, which is the flesh of Jesus Christ, the son of David, and for drink I desire his blood, which is love incorruptible" (*ibid.*, V-VII).

These flaming words of the great martyr were read over and over again in the early Christian church in the times of the martyrs; [24] there is none more vehement or more poignant, but what gives them superhuman beauty is the faith which inspires them; the man who speaks thus has directed all the activities of his life towards union with Christ; if he hears the murmur of living water which comes from Christ's bosom [25] and calls him to the Father, it is because all other love has been crucified in him. And Christ was not only passionately loved as a Master, but also as God: "Let me imitate the passion of my God!" And the faith which shines out so clearly in the face of death sheds a warm light on all the others letters. It is this that we must now briefly study.[26]

What we find here is what we have already found in Clement, "the faith and hope of the elect"; but these Christian mysteries appear in Ignatius in a more vivid light. The difference arises doubtless from the character of these letters: they are not, like the epistle of Clement, official documents or liturgical in style; they are short notes, written in haste by one condemned to death, with all the unconstrained zest of a martyr exhorting his brethren in the faith. Moreover, and this is very important, the fifteen years which separate Ignatius from Clement were marked by a noteworthy progress in the history of the Christian revelation, for during them there appeared the Gospel of St. John, which had a great influence on St. Ignatius. Lastly, in these churches of Syria and Asia where the holy martyr lived and wrote, theological problems were

[24] Irenæus, V, 28, 4; Acts of Perpetua and Felicitas, XIV; Origen, *De Orat.*, XX; *In Cant. Prolog.*

[25] Compare with this text that in the letter of the Martyrs of Lyons, speaking of the deacon Sanctus: "The heavenly spring of living water which comes from the bosom of Christ refreshed and fortified him" (*Hist. Eccles.*, V, 1, 22).

[26] A more detailed study will be found in *Histoire du Dogme de la Trinité*, Vol. II, pp. 282-331.

more keenly discussed than they were at Rome, and in a more technical form. Ignatius, full of impatience to be united to Christ by an imminent death, does not stay to discuss these problems, but he is aware of the danger, and is anxious to preserve the faith of Christians.

God the Father and Jesus Christ

What strikes the reader of these letters in a vivid way from the first is the ever-present mention of "God the Father and the Lord Jesus Christ." [27] Towards one and the other the faith and love of the holy martyr go out with the same force; life here below is life "in Christ" or "in God"; the end he aims at is to "attain to God," or to "attain to Christ." [28] Christians are the temples of God, and the temples of Christ; God dwells in them, and so does Christ. [29]

Thus in the Christian life we already find the inseparable union of Father and Son; both are our life here below, both are the goal at which we aim, the object of our hope in heaven. And yet they are not confused together: Jesus Christ, the Son of God, is the one Mediator who unites us to his Father: "Be subject to the bishop, and to one another, as Jesus Christ was to his Father according to the flesh." [30] By reason of his Incarnation, the Son of God appears to us indeed in a state of subjection and suffering which is due to his human nature: "He who is above all seasons, outside time, and invisible, became for us visible; being impalpable and impassible,

[27] These two terms are frequently united in this form (*Philad., inscr.* I, 1; *Polyc., inscr.*) or in equivalent forms: "God the Father and Jesus Christ" (*Ephes.,* XXI, 2; *Magn. inscr.; Trall.,* I, 1; XII, 2; *Philad.,* III, 2; *Smyrn., inscr.*); "God the Father and Jesus Christ our God" (*Ephes., inscr.*) or "our Saviour" (*Magn. inscr.*).

[28] Life "in Christ": *Ephes., inscr.,* I, 1; III, 1; VIII, 2; X, 3; XI, 1; XI, 2; XII, 2; XX, 2; XXI, 2; "in God," *Ephes.,* VI, 2; *Magn.,* III, 3; XIV; *Trall.,* IV, 1; VIII, 2; *Pot.,* I, 1; VI, 1. "Attain to God," *Ephes.,* XII, 2; *Magn.,* XIV, 21; *Trall.,* XII, 2; XIII, 3; *Rom.,* I, 1; II, 1; IV, 1; IX, 2; *Smyrn.,* XII, 1; *Pol.,* II, 3; VII, 1. "Attain to Christ," *Rom.,* V, 3; VI, 1.

[29] "Temples of God," *Philad.,* VII, 2. "God present in us," *Ephes.,* XV, 3. Christians are "Godbearers and Christbearers," *Ephes.,* IX, 2. "You have in you Jesus Christ," *Magn.,* XII. Cf. what we have said above concerning Jesus Christ as our life, p. 427.

[30] *Magn.,* XIII, 2. These last words, "according to the flesh," are lacking in the Armenian version and are suppressed by Lightfoot; but they are found in the Greek text, and the ancient Latin version, and are retained by the other editors: Bauer, Krueger, Funk-Bihlmeyer.

He became for us passible, and endured for us all kinds of sufferings" [31]

This distinction between the Father and the Son is not a consequence of the Incarnation: in His eternal pre-existence [32] the Son is distinct from the Father and is generated by Him: [33] "Before the ages, He was with the Father, and has appeared at the end" (*Magn.*, VI, 1); "there is only one God, who has manifested himself by Jesus Christ His Son, who is His Word, coming forth from silence, who in all things pleased Him who sent him." [34]

As we see from this last text, the Son of God is also His Word; God is the infinite and peaceful silence; [35] the Word has come forth by the Incarnation and has come to us to speak to us; He is "the true mouth through which the Father has truly spoken" (*Rom.*, VIII, 2). Now He has returned to the bosom of the Father; He has disappeared from this world, but more than ever He is active and is calling us (*Rom.*, III, 3); He enlightens us by His Spirit [36] and leads us towards the Father.

In this theology of Ignatius we can recognise the influence of St. Paul and above all of St. John; and this Christian tradition is

[31] *Pol.*, III, 2. We find the same idea in *Ephes.*, VII, 2: inasmuch as He is flesh, Jesus Christ had a beginning, He is in the flesh, in death, born of Mary, passible; inasmuch as He is spirit He is without beginning, God, true life, born of God, impassible. Cf. *Hist. du Dogme de la Trinité*, Vol. II, p. 294, n. 2.

[32] *Pol.*, III, 2. Cf. *Histoire du Dogme de la Trinité*, Vol. II, pp. 302-304.

[33] Attempts have sometimes been made to interpret the theology of St. Ignatius in a Modalist sense, thus G. Krueger, Kroymann, Bethune-Baker, and above all Loofs, *Paulus von Samosata*, pp. 293-322. This interpretation does not do justice to Ignatius's thought: cf. *Histoire du Dogme de la Trinité*, Vol. II, pp. 305-312. It is still more often said that in Ignatius filiation affects Christ only as man; this again is inexact; it is manifest that, considered in his "spirit," that is, in his divine nature, Christ is ἀγέννητος (*Ephes.*, VII, 2); but this term had not in the time of Ignatius the precise sense of "ungenerated" which it took on after the Arian controversy; it signifies "unproduced," and applies to all three divine Persons. Cf. *ibid.*, pp. 312-319 and 635-647.

[34] *Magn.*, VIII, 2. Cf. *ibid.*, VII, 2 (in an exhortation to unity): ". . . the one Jesus Christ who has come forth from the One Father, though remaining united to Him, and who has returned to Him."

[35] Cf. *Ephes.*, XIX, 1, speaking of the great mysteries of the life of Christ, the virginity of Mary, her child-bearing, and the death of the Lord: "These are resounding mysteries, which have been wrought in the peaceful silence of God." Cf. *Histoire du Dogme de la Trinité*, Vol. II, p. 321.

[36] On the Holy Spirit, the most explicit text is *Philad.*, VII, 1-2: "Some have wished to deceive me according to the flesh, but the Spirit is not deceived, it comes from God, it knows whence it comes and whither it goes, and it penetrates hidden secrets. . . ." Cf. above p. 423, n. 14, and *Histoire du Dogme de la Trinité*, Vol. II, pp. 326-331.

vivified by the intimate action of the Holy Spirit; the imminence of martyrdom brings out the depth of this life, the ardour of desire, and the assurance of faith. This fruitful tradition will be transmitted to heirs worthy of it, St. Polycarp and St. Irenæus.

§3. ST. POLYCARP[1]

The Witness of Tradition

St. Polycarp is of exceptional interest to us: he appears early in the second century, in touch with St. Ignatius; we follow him to Smyrna and Rome through the recollections of St. Irenæus, and lastly, the letter of the Church of Smyrna tells us of his martyrdom in 155. Thus he is for us, in this second century of which we know so little, the embodiment of tradition, as he was for his contemporaries.

When Ignatius stopped at Smyrna, Polycarp received him with such veneration that the martyr afterwards sent him from Troas a special letter; in the praises he gives him, and the advice he tenders him, we see already the bishop of Smyrna as he henceforth appears:

"I honour thy piety, solidly established as on an unshakable rock. . . . Take care of unity, the greatest of goods; assist all others, as the Lord assists thyself. . . . Pray without ceasing . . . watch, and let thy spirit never sleep. . . . Bear the infirmities of all, like a perfect athlete. . . ." (I, 1).

"As for invisible things, pray that they may be revealed to thee. . . ." (II, 2).

"Do not be dismayed by those who, in spite of a trustworthy appearance, teach error. Stand firm as an anvil under the hammer. A great athlete triumphs in spite of the blows which fall upon him. We ought all the more to endure all things for God, so that He may support us. . . ." (III, 1).

That is how Polycarp appeared throughout his life, and when he faced death forty years later. He was the perfect athlete, firm as an anvil, firm as a rock, upon whom rested the churches of Asia;

---

[1] The editions of St. Polycarp are the same as those of St. Ignatius; we may add to them the historical studies on the saint's martyrdom: H. Delehaye, *Les Passions des martyrs et les genres littéraires*, Brussels, 1921, pp. 11-59.

he was the irreconcilable enemy of error; [2] he was also a man of prayer, "whose spirit never slept," one whom the Church of Smyrna celebrated after his death as "an apostolic and prophetic doctor" (*Mart.*, XVI, 2).

Letter to the Philippians

The letter of Polycarp to the Philippians is especially valuable to us because of the guarantee it gives to the letters of St. Ignatius. But it is also interesting in itself, inasmuch as it shows us Christian morals and preaching at the beginning of the second century. The bishop of Smyrna is full of veneration for "the blessed Ignatius, Zosimus and Rufus" (IX, 1), still more for "the blessed and glorious apostle Paul" (III, 2); if he writes to the Philippians, it is to grant their desire (III, 1). He exhorts them to rectitude in the faith (VII, 1), to the memory of the death and resurrection of the Lord (I, 2; II, 2); he particularly urges them to follow the example of Christ:

"Let us have our eyes constantly fixed on our hope, and the pledge of our justice, Jesus Christ: He it is who bore our sins in His own body on the wood, who committed no sin, and in whose mouth was found no guile (*I Pet.* ii, 24, 22), but He suffered all things for our sakes, that we may have life in Him. Let us therefore imitate His patience, and if we suffer for His name, let us give glory to Him. For that is the example He has set forth to us in His own person, and we have believed therein." [3]

When he sets forth to the Philippians the imitation of Jesus Christ, Polycarp also reminds them of His teaching, especially according to the Sermon on the Mount: "Judge not, that you be not judged; forgive, and it will be forgiven you; be merciful, in order to obtain mercy; you will be served according to the measure you mete out to others. Blessed are the poor, and those who suffer persecution for justice, for the kingdom of heaven is theirs" (II, 3).

The Church of Philippi had been saddened by the scandal of the

[2] Thus he writes in his letter, VII, 1: "Whosoever interprets in the sense of his personal desires the words of the Lord, and denies the resurrection and the judgment, is the first born of Satan." Many years afterwards, he will reply to Marcion in the same terms: "Dost thou recognise me?—I recognise the first born of Satan" (Irenæus, III, 3, 4; Migne, *P.G.*, VII, p. 853).

[3] Cf. V, 2: "Let them walk in the way of truth marked out by the Lord, who became the servant of all. . . ."

presbyter Valens and his wife; Polycarp seizes the occasion in order to condemn avarice, and to recommend chastity and sincerity. And once more he urges his correspondents, in face of the threatened persecution and of heresy, to persevere in faith and patience.

Witness of Irenæus

This letter is the only writing we possess of Polycarp's; but his disciple Irenæus gives us a glimpse of his glorious career during the forty or forty-five years separating the martyrdom of Ignatius from that of Polycarp. In order to bring back to the faith one of the friends of his childhood, Florinus, who had fallen into the Gnostic heresy, Irenæus wrote to him thus:

"These doctrines, Florinus, to say nothing more, are not sound in thought; these doctrines do not agree with the Church; they involve those who believe in them in the greatest impiety; the heretics, even those outside the Church, have never dared to bring these doctrines into the light of day; these doctrines have never been transmitted to you by the presbyters who were before us and who lived with the apostles. For when I was still a child, I saw you with Polycarp; you shone at the imperial court, and endeavoured to gain his approbation. Indeed I remember better those times than recent events. For the things one learns when one is young become one with the soul and unite themselves with it, so that I can say in what place the blessed Polycarp used to sit in order to speak, how he came in and went out, what was the character of his life, his physical appearance, the talks he had with people, how he told of his relations with John and with the others who had seen the Lord, how he reported their words and all that he had learnt from them concerning the Lord, His miracles and His teaching; all this Polycarp had gathered from those who had seen the Word of Life, and he related it all, in conformity with the Scriptures. I carefully listened to all these things then, by the grace of God given me; I have kept them in memory, not on paper but in my heart. Continually, by God's grace, I recall them faithfully, and I can testify before God that if this blessed and apostolic presbyter had heard things such as these, he would have cried out and stopped his ears, saying as he often did: 'O good God, unto what times hast thou reserved me, that I should endure all this!' And whether he was sitting or standing, he would have fled from the place where he had heard such words. This can be shown moreover by the letters which he sent to the neighbouring churches to strengthen them, and to certain brethren, to warn and exhort them" (Hist. Eccles., V, 20, 4-8).

This letter, written in the time of Pope Victor about 186, is one of the most interesting documents in the early history of the church of Asia; it shows the veneration which at the end of the first and the beginning of the second century surrounded the presbyters who had seen the Lord with their eyes and could repeat his words; and after them, the witnesses of that past generation, and amongst them all, Polycarp, "the blessed and apostolic presbyter." It shows us how this influence spread round him into the neighbouring churches, and above all it confirms what we know already of this faithful disciple, "firm as a rock." But this firmness did not make him unfeeling; he suffered, as did St. Ignatius and St. John, when anything divided and troubled the Church: "O good God, to what times has thou reserved me!" All this is confirmed again by the testimony full of veneration that Irenæus gave to his master.[4]

St. Polycarp in Rome

In this passage, Irenæus recalls the journey made to Rome by St. Polycarp under the pontificate of St. Anicetus; he speaks of it more fully in a letter he wrote later to Pope Victor:

"The blessed Polycarp paid a visit to Rome under Anicetus; there were between them some differences of little importance, and they quickly came to agreement; on this question (of the Pasch) they did not desire to quarrel. Anicetus was unable to persuade Polycarp not to observe what he had always observed with John the disciple of Our Lord and the other apostles whom he had known; Polycarp, on his side, could not persuade Anicetus, who said to him that he was obliged to retain the custom of the presbyters who had preceded him. This being so, they remained in communion with each other, and with the Church. Anicetus gave the Eucharist to Polycarp, evidently out of respect, and they parted in peace, and in the Church all were at peace, whether they retained the observance or not" (*Hist. Eccles.*, V. 24, 16-17).[5]

---

[4] *Haer.*, III, 3, 4 (Migne, *P.G.*, VII, 851-855), reproduced by Eusebius, *Hist. Eccles.*, IV, 14: "Not only was Polycarp a disciple of the apostles, who had lived with several of those who had seen the Lord, but also he was appointed by the apostles as bishop in the church of Smyrna, for Asia, and we ourselves saw him in our childhood. . . ."

[5] On this incident, cf. G. Bardy, *L'Eglise romaine sous le pontificat de saint Anicet*, in *Recherches de Science religieuse*, Vol. XVII, 1927, pp. 481-511, especially pp. 496-501.

We shall return later to this Easter question, and the peacemaking intervention by St. Irenæus; what we note here is the part played by St. Polycarp in this matter, his attachment to tradition, his care for the unity of the Church, and lastly, the veneration with which he was regarded.

This veneration, which surrounded the old bishop at Rome, was still more marked at Smyrna. In the account of his martyrdom, we read how the bishop removed his clothes and bent down to take off his shoes: "He did not usually do this himself, for on every occasion the faithful contended for the honour of touching him, so great was the veneration accorded to him, even before his martyrdom, because of the holiness of his life" (*Mart.*, XIII, 2).

Martyrdom of St. Polycarp

The year which followed his visit to Rome [6] saw the martyrdom of St. Polycarp. All Asia was roused; the church of Philomelium asked for an account of his death. The Church of Smyrna entrusted Marcianus, one of its members, with the writing of the account, and sent it round to all the churches. This is "the earliest hagiographical document we possess, and all agree that there does not exist a more beautiful one. It is enough to read it and to weigh each phrase to be convinced that this account is what it claims to be, the work of a contemporary who knew the martyr, saw him in the midst of the flames, and touched the remains of the saint's body with his own hands." [7]

Other martyrs had already been tormented; one only had yielded, a Phrygian named Quintus, who had denounced himself, a practice

---

[6] On the date of the martyrdom of St. Polycarp, cf. Lightfoot, *op cit.*, Vol. I, pp. 644-722; Harnack, *Chronologie*, Vol. I, pp. 334-356: "There is scarcely a date in the early history of the Church which is so universally accepted as that of the martyrdom of Polycarp, the 23rd February, 155" (p. 334); Corssen. *Das Todesjahr Polycarps*, in *Zeitschrift für N. T. Wissensch.*, 1902, pp. 61-82, confirms this conclusion. We read in the *Acts*, XXI: "The martyrdom of the blessed Polycarp took place . . . on the seventh of the kalends of March, on a great sabbath day . . . under the proconsulate of Statius Quadratus." The proconsulate of Quadratus is dated, according to the speech of Aelius Aristides and an inscription at Ephesus, in the years 154-155; the 7th of the Kalends of March fell on a sabbath day in the year 155.

[7] Delehaye, *Les Passions des Martyrs*, pp. 12-13. This beautiful account has often been translated: by Racine, when staying in 1662 with his uncle, the chanoine Sconin at Uzès; by Lelong in *Textes et Documents*, 1910; by Dom Leclercq, *Les Martyrs*, Vol. I, p. 65.

disapproved by the Church; the others had been wonderfully constant. Amongst the spectators, some were moved with pity (*Mart.*, II, 2), but others, exasperated by the courage displayed, cried out: "Away with the atheists! Go and find Polycarp!" (*ibid.*, III, 2).

The bishop had, at the urgent request of the faithful, withdrawn to the country. He was betrayed by a young lad, saw the soldiers coming, and would not flee; he made them eat, and asked to be allowed to pray to God; "he was so full of the grace of God that for two hours he could not cease, and those who heard him were struck with admiration" (*ibid.*, VII, 3). He was taken away; Herod the *irenarch* or "High Sheriff," took him into his carriage and endeavoured to persuade him. Eventually Polycarp said: "I will do nothing of what you advise me to do"; and he was brutally thrown out of the carriage. He arrived at the stadium; a heavenly voice was heard by the Christians: "Courage, Polycarp, play the man!"

The proconsul, Statius Quadratus, tried again to shake him, and finally called upon him to curse Christ. Polycarp replied: "For eighty-six years now I have served Him, and He has never done me any ill. How could I blaspheme my King and my Saviour?" He was thereupon declared to be a Christian, and at the request of the populace, he was condemned to be burnt alive. In this way was to be verified the prophetic vision he had had three days earlier: he had seen his pillow on fire, and turning towards the faithful he had said to them: "I am to be burnt alive."

The crowd, mainly of Jews, hastened to prepare the fire; Polycarp was bound on it, "like a holocaust acceptable to God." He raised his eyes to heaven, and prayed:

"O Lord, God Almighty, Father of Jesus Christ, Thy well beloved and blessed Son, who has taught us to know Thee, God of angels, powers, and of all creation and all the race of the just who live in Thy presence! I bless Thee because Thou hast thought me worthy of this day and of this hour, worthy to take part amongst the martyrs in the chalice of Thy Christ, to rise again to eternal life of body and soul in the incorruptibility of the Holy Spirit. May I be this day admitted amongst them in Thy presence, as a fatted and acceptable victim, the destiny which thou hast prepared for me and made me to see in advance, and which Thou bringest about now, O God who liest not, true God! For this grace and for all things I praise Thee, I bless Thee, I glorify Thee through the eternal and heavenly High Priest, Jesus Christ Thy well beloved Son. Through Him may glory be to Thee, with Him and the Holy Spirit, now and for ever, Amen." [8]

The fire was lit, and the flames surrounded the martyr's body; it seemed as though it was "not flesh that was burning, but bread that was being baked, or an ingot of gold or silver that was being purified in a furnace; and we smelt a delightful odour, like that of incense or some other precious perfume." The *confector* killed Polycarp with a dagger; from the wound blood flowed so abundantly that it extinguished the fire. When the faithful went to remove the body from the fire, it was taken away from them, at the instigation of the Jews; who said: "Christians would be capable of leaving the Crucified to give worship to Polycarp! They did not realise that we could never give up Jesus Christ, who suffered for the salvation of those who are saved in the whole world, the innocent for the guilty, and that we could not give worship to another. For Him we adore as being the Son of God; as for the martyrs, we love them as disciples and imitators of the Lord, and they are worthy of it because of their supreme attachment to their King and their Master." [9]

But the Christians could at least gather the bones of the martyr, and put them in a suitable place. "There we meet together, as far as the Lord permits, in joy and gladness, to celebrate the anniversary day of the martyrdom." [10]

The Lessons of the Martyrdom

This account is not only one of the most moving in early Christian literature, but also one of the most instructive. It shows us the attitude, at once prudent and firm, recommended by the Church to the faithful in face of persecution. The opinion of pagans was still on the whole violently hostile: the courage of the martyrs called forth pity from some spectators, but in the case of the majority, hatred was increased and exasperated: it was the crowd that clam-

[8] On this prayer, cf. *Histoire du Dogme de la Trinité*, Vol. II, p. 197-200.
[9] Cf. *Histoire du Dogme de la Trinité*, Vol. II, pp. 204 *et seq.*
[10] The Church of Smyrna continued faithful to the celebration of this anniversary, even in the worst days of the persecutions: it was on the day of this feast that the priest Pionius was arrested with several other Christians in 250, during the persecution of Decius: *Acts*, II, 1, ed. Knopf, p. 59.

oured for the arrest of the bishop, and then for his condemnation to death by fire. Amongst these opponents, the Jews were the most bitter: the death of the martyr did not satisfy them, they demanded that his body should be destroyed.[11]

The martyr sought his strength only in prayer; Polycarp, prepared so long for this desired hour, did not tire of prayer, but continued in it when the officers arrested him, when he was bound to the fire, and when he was waiting for death: at this supreme moment his prayer was already an act of thanksgiving, and spontaneously the liturgical formulas which he had so often pronounced came back to his lips. The Christian populace which was so deeply attached to him venerated him still more when sanctified by martyrdom; and yet there is an impassable gulf between him and Christ; no text reveals better than this profession of faith, so full of adoration, what Christ is to His believers: "Him we adore as the Son of God; as for the martyrs, we love them as disciples and imitators of the Lord."

§4. THE CONTROVERSY WITH THE JEWS AND THE LETTER OF BARNABAS

The writings which we have studied in the preceding sections have brought before us great bishops, Clement, Ignatius and Polycarp. They have deserved our study: in the person of these leaders, the Christian Church itself appears before us. The other documents which we find, under the names of apostles, have not the same origin, and do not bring us the same knowledge: the letter of Barnabas is a spurious work; Hermas is an unknown person; the *Didache* is an anonymous work. The Church no longer appears in the person of its great men, but it is still present; these writers are unknown or without interest, but the books themselves are witnesses which enable us to see the Christian people, their struggles, their aims, and their prayers.

[11] This request was addressed to the governor by "Nicetas, father of Herod and brother of Alce" (XVII, 2). This Alce seems to be the one mentioned by Ignatius, *Smyrn.*, XIII; *Polyc.*, VIII. Cf. Lightfoot, *op. cit.*, Vol. I, p. 366. Christianity had therefore penetrated into the family of the irenarch; the reaction of hatred was only the more violent.

The letter of Barnabas will not detain us long.[1] This little book is set forth modestly and humbly without the author's name: "As for me, it is not as a doctor, but as one of yourselves that I will give you some instructions."[2] This anonymous and modest doctor was, especially at Alexandria, identified with St. Barnabas;[3] this apostolic attribution gained for some time great credit for this little work; the confusion has been long dispelled, and for ever, but the epistle is nevertheless not without its interest.

It was composed, it seems, at Alexandria, probably shortly before the revolt of Barkokeba (130-131).[4] It comprises two parts of unequal length and importance: the four last chapters (XVIII-XXI) contain a moral exhortation in which we find the distinction between the two ways of good and evil, presented in the form in which we find it in the *Didache*. The first part, much longer (ch. I-XVIII) is also much more original, and gives the letter its chief interest: it is a controversal work against Judaism; not a scholastic dissertation, but a moving exhortation in face of a great and pressing danger:[5] "The days are evil; the enemy is active and powerful" (ch. II, 1). "The great scandal spoken of in Scripture has come nigh" (ch. IV, 3). "I therefore beg you, I who am one of you, and who love you more than my own life: take care of yourselves, and be not like some people who heap sins upon sins, and who say that the Testament belongs to those (Jews) as to ourselves. It is ours, but those have lost it for ever" (ch. IV, 6-7). We hear in this work not the peaceful speculations of a

---

[1] This letter is contained in two MSS., both discovered in the nineteenth century: the *Sinaiticus*, discovered by Tischendorf in 1859 and the Jerusalem MS. discovered by Bryennios in 1875. Edited by Gebhardt-Harnack; Funk-Bihlmeyer; Oger, Paris, 1907; Windisch, Tübingen, 1920. In this last work is an abundant annotation; also in the translation by Veil, *Apocryphes du N. T.* by Hennecke, Tübingen 1904, and 1923. The theological teaching has been studied in *Histoire du Dogme de la Trinité*, Vol. II, pp. 332-345. Literary study in Puech, *op. cit.*, Vol. II, pp. 22-31.

Quotations in text follow the French edition. An English translation by Lightfoot of the whole letter will be found in *Excluded Books of the New Testament*, London, 1927.

[2] I, 8; cf. IV, 6 and 9; VI, 5.

[3] This identification appears already in Clement of Alexandria; cf. Harnack, *Gesch. d. altchristl. Literatur*, Vol. I, p. 60, and *Histoire du Dogme de la Trinité*, Vol. II, p. 344, n. 4; it was adopted by Origen, and also explains why it finds a place in the *Sinaiticus* after the New Testament.

[4] Cf. *Histoire du Dogme de la Trinité*, Vol. II, p. 332, n. 3.

[5] Cf. the just comments by Veil (*Handbuch*, p. 208, and *Neutestamentl. Apokryphen*, 1924, p. 503).

catechist, but "the cry of alarm by the shepherd." This alarm gives the letter its great interest, and also accounts for the exaggerations in which the controversialist indulges.

Symbolical Interpretation of the Law

In order to preserve his correspondents, whose peril moves him so deeply, the writer defends the radical thesis which the Church never approved, and the danger of which will soon be revealed by Marcion, that the old alliance never existed as a positive law willed by God subjecting the Jewish people to certain practices or cere-monies; it had only a symbolical value, which the Jews failed to realise, in attaching themselves to the letter: the circumcision demanded by God was not a carnal circumcision (ch. IX, 4); the alimentary prescriptions were only allegories (ch. X); the true sab-bath is the rest of God after six thousand years, inaugurating a new world (ch. XV). The only Temple acceptable to God is not an edifice in stone such as the Temple of Jerusalem, which God interdicted through His prophets, but the spiritual temple of our souls (ch. XVI).

All this is not only weak, but dangerous, as will soon appear; but it must not be overlooked that Barnabas was only following the example of numerous Jewish exegetes, who likewise allegorised the Law;[6] in utilising this weapon of allegorical exegesis he thought he could defend the Church and save it from Judaism; in reality he was destroying the historical facts on which the Church was based; the Church has rejected this allegory, this gnosis to which Barnabas invites the faithful.[7] The apologetic argument of Barnabas contains another feature, however, of permanent value: the divinity of the Son of God, and the infinite value of His Passion.

[6] Philo, *De migr. Abrah.*, 89 (I, 450). Philo rejects this allegory, which sees only the symbol and denies the reality, and certainly Barnabas goes beyond Philo, but only by travelling further, along the same road. Cf. Heinisch, *Der Einfluss Philos auf die älteste christliche Exegese*, Münster, 1908, especially pp. 60, 106, 262.

[7] I, 5: "I am writing to you briefly in order that, together with the faith, you may have a perfect gnosis." IX, 8-9: "What says the gnosis? Learn it. It says: 'Hope in him who must manifest himself to you in the flesh, Jesus. For man is a land which suffers. . . .'" The gnosis is here presented by Barnabas as a gift deposited by God in the soul of the master, and communicated by the latter to those who are worthy; it is in the light of this gnosis that the author develops his allegorical exegesis. Cf. *Histoire du Dogme de la Trinité*, Vol. II. pp. 344-345.

Theology

To the disciples of Barnabas, as to those of St. Paul, the Passion of Jesus appeared first of all as a scandal; the apologist effaces nothing, but on the contrary brings it out into full light, and shows the divine power of it:

"If the Lord endured that His flesh should be given up to destruction, this was in order to purify us by the forgiveness of sins, which takes place through the sprinkling of His blood" (V, 1).

"If the Lord endured to suffer for our souls, though He is the Lord of the whole world, and the one to whom God said at the foundation of the world: 'Let us make man to our image and likeness,' how could He endure to suffer at the hand of man? Learn this. The prophets, receiving grace from Him, prophesied about it, and it is in order to abolish death, and to manifest the resurrection from the dead, that He endured to suffer, for He had to appear in the flesh in order to fulfil the promise given to our fathers, and to prepare for Himself a new people, and to show while still upon earth that it is He who will bring about the resurrection, and will judge" (V, 5).[8]

He recognises also in the Incarnation a manifestation of God: our minds, incapable of sustaining the immediate vision of the godhead, are able to contemplate it veiled in flesh (ch. V, 10). By these great theological ideas, Barnabas is linked up with the most authentic Christian tradition; he echoes St. Paul, and prepares the way for St. Irenæus.[9] By his anti-Jewish polemic, he testifies, not indeed to the deep thought of the Church, but at least to the danger which Judaism constituted for it, and the Church's reaction to the danger.

This fact must be borne in mind by the historian: the violence and success of the Marcionite propaganda will be understood better if Barnabas has been read: the condemnations imprudently formulated in this epistle against the Jewish legalism, will be pronounced by Marcion against the very author of the Law; not only the Jews will be affected, but also their God. The excessive character

---

[8] This passage calls up numerous reminiscences in the literature of the second century and those which followed: Irenæus, *Demonstr.*, VI and XXXVIII; G. Hippolytus, *Anaphora of the Apostolic Tradition*, etc. Cf. *Histoire du Dogme de la Trinité*, Vol. II, p. 339, n. 2.

[9] E.g., in his doctrine of the "recapitulation"; we find in Barnabas (V, 11) the verb ἀνακεφαλαιῶ, familiar to St. Paul (*Rom.* xiii, 9; *Ephes.* i, 10) and to St. Irenæus, but not found elsewhere in the apostolic Fathers or apologists.

of these exaggerations will show the Church the danger in this unwise apologetic, and will keep her clear of it once and for all.[10]

§5. THE MORAL REFORM AND PENANCE IN THE ROMAN CHURCH. THE SHEPHERD OF HERMAS[1]

The Book and the Author

Of all the writings of the Apostolic Fathers, there is none more instructive than the *Shepherd* of Hermas, but there is none more difficult to interpret. In this first half of the second century which is so obscure to us, this book presents in simple and sincere pictures, not indeed high theological doctrines, but Christian life in its simplest, commonest, and at the same time its deepest form. While arousing our curiosity in this way, it also presents as many arduous problems as it offers aspects: its date, its composition, its character, its doctrine—all are matter for discussion. It is not that the style is difficult—it is simple and abrupt, like that of a man of the people; but the thought is often incomplete, often also obscured by additions: the writer was evidently not quite satisfied with what he had said, but instead of effacing it, he added to it new developments which often agree ill with the first text.

This explains the fortune of this work: it was accepted almost everywhere with great favour in the second century; in the third,

[10] We must remark in conclusion that this Jewish danger, and the strong reaction against it, can be explained by what we know of the great influence of the Jews at Alexandria: previous to the Christian preaching this great influence is shown by the life and work of Philo; in the first centuries of the Christian era it continued and threatened the Church: it was at Alexandria above all that the apocryphal Gospels, with their Judaising tendencies, were read.

[1] Editions: Hilgenfeld, Leipzig, 1866; Gebhardt-Harnack, 1877; Funk, Tübingen, 1881; Lelong, 1912; German translations and notes by Weinel, *Neutestamentl. Apokryphen*, pp. 217-229; Dibelius, Tübingen, 1923. On the old Latin translation, see Turner in *Journal of Theol. Studies*, XXI, 1920, pp. 193-209. A quarter of the Greek text has been found in a fourth-century papyrus, cf. C. Bonner, *A papyrus Codex of the Shepherd of Hermas*, University of Michigan, 1934.
    Chief studies: T. Zahn, *Der Hirt des Hermas*, Gotha, 1868; A Stahl, *Patristische Untersuchungen*, Leipzig, 1901, pp. 223-359; d'Alès, *L'édit de Calliste*, 1914, pp. 52-113; Puech, *op. cit.*, Vol. II, pp. 71-95; Lebreton, *Histoire du Dogme de la Trinité*, Vol. II, pp. 346-387. [Good discussion also in Cayré, *Manual of Patrology*, Paris, 1936, pp. 83-96. English translation by Lightfoot in *Excluded Books of the New Testament*, London, 1927.—Tr.]

the West rejected it, and in the East it kept its place only in Egypt; from the fourth century it disappeared very quickly.[2] What the early Fathers loved in it was not its theology, but its moral teaching, its conception of the Christian life; that constitutes its value, and that is why it calls for our attention here.

The Book of Hermas as we have it consists of a series of five Visions, ten Commandments, and ten Parables or Similitudes; the writer himself suggests another division which corresponds better to his plan: in a first part, the Church appears under various symbols, in four successive Visions; the second part, the longer and more important, contains the revelation of the Shepherd: after a Vision which constitutes an introduction, the Shepherd teaches Christians their duties and exhorts them to penance; this is the theme of the Commandments and the Parables.

This short outline already enables us to realise the character of the book: it is an apocalypse, full of visions and revelations; but at the same time it is an autobiography. The writer calls himself Hermas; he was a slave freed by Rhoda, became rich, married a shrewish woman, and had several children who turned out badly; they apostatised, denounced their parents, and ruined them. Hermas had, it seems, been brought up in Christianity, but he had been only a poor kind of Christian; when he was ruined, he was converted.[3] It was his anxiety for his children that led him to preach; he had the joy of seeing them converted (*Sim.*, VII, 4), and the angel revealed to him the re-establishment of his fortune. To these details in the book itself, the *Muratorian Canon* adds another: Hermas was a brother of Pope Pius (about 140-154). This last indication would put the composition of the book in about the end of the first half of the second century.[4] The work indeed

[2] On all this tradition cf. *Histoire du Dogme de la Trinité*, Vol. II, pp. 346-348, and above all Harnack, *Gesch. der Literatur*, Vol. I, pp. 51-58.

[3] *Vis.*, III, 6, 7: "When thou wert rich, thou wert good for nothing; now thou canst serve, thou art fit for life."

[4] This is also the date suggested by the book itself: the description of the persecution, which applies better to the system inaugurated by Trajan than to the procedure of Domitian (Lelong, *op. cit.*, pp. xxix-xxxii), and the new Gnosticism, not yet a great danger (*ibid.*, p. xxxvii). Against this date there is the mention of Clement (*Vis.*, II, 4, 3). This is certainly difficult to explain, but this difficulty cannot prevail against the arguments on the other side; it can be solved if we suppose that the first visions belong in Greek text to the time of Clement and were put forth under Pius. Cf. Lightfoot, *Clement*, Vol. I, pp. 359-360; Turner, in *Journal of Theol. Studies*, Vol. XXI, pp. 193-194.

was not all composed at once; the different parts which go to make it up are separated by fairly large intervals, and reveal great changes in the state of the Church and the preoccupations of the author. At the beginning of the work, a violent persecution is in progress; in the second, we have the after-effects of this trial, the reconciliations which the apostates implore and the Church grants or refuses. At the beginning the author has in view the final catastrophe; later on it is penance that preoccupies him, the conditions it requires, the renewal to which it should lead: in the family of Hermas himself, the situation is different, and the apostate children have repented.

This succession of episodes rather loosely linked together is the cause of a certain lack of consistence in the book, and a lack of coherence in the doctrine, which it is difficult to unify; but it has for a historian the interest of a film which is slowly projected before his eyes, and brings out through the witness of a freedman of Rome the moral preoccupations of Christianity.

Moral Reform

That is indeed what we must look for in the first place: Hermas has no theological training, and speculative questions do not interest him; we are not surprised to find that from the doctrinal standpoint he is extremely inconsistent; but he is a sincere and fervent Christian, very much occupied with the moral problems arising out of life around him; he sets them forth as he sees them; we could not desire a more sincere witness.

Like all moralists, Hermas is a righter of wrongs, and the first impression he gives us is a severe one: the Church first of all appears to him in the guise of an infirm old lady seated in a chair; but from the second vision onwards she regains her powers, and in the third vision she is "young, beautiful and gay": the message of the Lord has been heard, hearts have revived, and have taken new life.[5] From so rapid a transformation it will be inferred that the evil was less deeply rooted than it seemed. This impression is strengthened in the course of the book; we find there under various forms and symbols the examination of conscience of the Roman Church; this examination shows us that the majority of Christians

[5] *Vis.* III, 11-13.

are good people who have never lost their baptismal innocence, and have no need of penance.[6]

Thus in the eighth parable, we have a great willow tree which represents the Law or the Son of God; the archangel Michael has detached some branches from this tree and given them to mankind: this is the law taught to the faithful; the branches which they have received and carry represent symbolically the state of their consciences. Several bring back branches which are split, dried up, or at least have lost their leaves; these are those Christians who are sinners or negligent. "Others carry their branches green and as they had received them from the angel; this is the case with most people."[7] The just are therefore a majority in the Church.

Strength and Weakness

This statement has all the more weight because of the delicate nature of Hermas's conscience: the scene with which the book opens (*Vis.*, I, 1), the remorse arising from a look or a desire, shows that the Christian ideal was strong within him, with all its exigencies.

Yet this Church has also its weaknesses; we find the details in the third vision, and in the eighth and ninth parables. The general impression is well set forth in *Vision*, III, 11:

"Why did the woman appear to thee in the first vision as old, and seated in a chair? It was because thy mind was aged, already exhausted and without power, because of thy softness and thy doubts . . . (she was seated in a chair) because every infirm person by reason of his weakness sits in a chair in order to support his weakened body."[8]

Thus, the most widespread and serious fault is hesitation, or discouragement, such as that of old men who have no more hope,

---

[6] Cf. Lelong, *op. cit.*, p. lviii; Duchesne, *Hist. ancienne de l'Eglise*, Vol. I, p. 229.

[7] *Simil.*, VIII, 1, 16. Hermas himself interprets this symbol thus (*ibid.*, 3, 8): "Those who have given back the branches as they received them, are the saints and the just, who have lived in perfect purity of heart and in the faithful observance of the commandments of the Lord." Above these again Hermas distinguishes those who have brought back branches covered with new shoots, or even with fruits: these are the confessors and martyrs.

[8] In *Vis.*, II, 4, 1, Hermas explained this aged character of the Church by saying that she is the oldest of creatures; there he was considering rather the transcendent Church; here the Church Visible.

who ask "if all this is real or not" (*Vis.*, III, 4, 3). Hence the great aim of the first chapters is to strengthen hope, and this not so much by the preaching of penance as by the announcement of the end: "The Tower will be quickly built" (*ibid.*, III, 8, 9). In the rest of the work, the perspective widens and the effort is directed more and more towards penance.

Riches

The softening and lukewarmness arises above all from contact with the world: the Church has numerous members, it gathers them from all ranks of society; the rich are particularly liable to deteriorate:

"Those who brought back their branches with one half green and the other dried up are men occupied with business, and who have become almost foreign to the society of the saints" (*Sim.*, VIII, 8, 1).

"Those who have brought branches with two-thirds dried up and the other green are men who, after embracing the faith, have amassed riches and won the esteem of the pagans. This has been a source of great pride, and they have become haughty; they have abandoned the truth, and left the society of the just in order to share in the life of the pagans, finding this way easier. Nevertheless they have not denied God, but have persevered in the faith, although they do not the works of the faith . . ." (*ibid.*, IX, 1).

"From the third mountain, which is covered with thorns and thistles, there come these believers: some are rich, the others are men full of the bustle of affairs. The thistles represent the rich; the thorns, those who are entangled in the multiplicity of affairs. These last, those who are hampered by a mass of business of all kinds, do not frequent the servants of God, but walk at a distance, at random, stifled as they are by their occupations. As for the rich, these have little to do with the servants of God, lest these should ask something from them. Such men will enter only with difficulty into the kingdom of God" [9] (*ibid.*, IX, 20, 1).

In the persecution, "their business and their riches lead them to deny their Master"; they will enter into the Tower when they will have been deprived of their riches; "thy own example will bring this truth home to thee: when thou wert rich, thou were good for nothing; now thou canst serve, thou art fit for life" (*Vis.*, III, 6, 5-7). This last trait confirms the impression we get from

[9] Cf. *Vis.*, III, 11, and *Sim.* 1.

the others: the rich whom Hermas criticises are those of his own circle: prosperous merchants, absorbed by business, and puffed up by their quickly won fortunes, but upset by persecution, unless this saves them by despoiling them. Even apart from these times of crisis, these rich people run the risk of feeling out of their element in the midst of the lowly folk who surround them in the Christian community; they are always obsessed by the fear that they are going to be called upon to give something; they are inclined to regret their fine pagan surroundings, and to cast an envious glance over the wall of the Church towards the world outside.[10]

Ambition

Another evil which Hermas strongly denounces is ambition, with the dissensions to which it gives rise. In the maternal exhortation the Church addresses to all her children, she especially warns the leaders, and those who occupy the first places: "Take care, my children, that your divisions do not lead you to loss of life!" (Vis., III, 9, 7). In the parable of the willow tree, the Shepherd emphatically points out the same danger:

"Those who have brought back their branches green, but slit, are men who have always remained faithful and good, but quarrel bitterly amongst themselves for the first places and for honours. They are foolish thus to dispute for priority. But at heart these men are good; thus, as soon as they have become aware of my commandments, they have purified their hearts and have hastened to do penance. Accordingly they have been allowed to dwell in the Tower; but if ever one of them should fall again into discord, he will be expelled from the Tower and lose his life" (Simil., VIII, 4-5).

[10] We may recall here what St. James had already written concerning the attentions sometimes multiplied to the rich, to the despite of the poor: "If there shall come into your assembly a man having a golden ring, in fine apparel, and there shall come in also a poor man in mean attire, and you have respect to him that is clothed with the fine apparel, and shall say to him: 'Sit thou here well'; but say to the poor man: 'Stand thou there, or sit under my footstool': Do you not judge within yourselves, and are become judges of unjust thoughts? Hearken, my dearest brethren: hath not God chosen the poor in this world, rich in faith, and heirs of the kingdom? . . . But you have dishonoured the poor man" (James ii, 2-6). The rich St. James has in mind are also merchants who go from town to town, promising themselves great profits, and boasting of their riches (IV, 13-17). On the penetration of the rich into the Church, cf. Harnack, Mission und Ausbreitung, pp. 559 et seq.

These last words show that the evil is much less serious at Rome than it was at Corinth; [11] Clement could then give to the ring-leaders no other counsel than to leave the country; at Rome, exhortations have sufficed, and there is peace.

Many other vices are rebuked by Hermas, especially in the Parables VIII (6, 4 *et seq,*) and IX (15, 3 and 19 *et seq.*); but they are less characteristic of the state of the Roman Church at this time. What is most interesting to observe is the persecution, the dangers it creates, the terrible trial it represents, and the results it brings.

Persecution

In the Visions, the Church appears as threatened by an imminent persecution; a great tribulation is expected, to be followed, it is hoped, by a definitive triumph.[12] The second part of the book carries us a few years further on; the persecution has struck the Church; not the fiscal inquisition inaugurated by Domitian, but the persecution of the Christian name, as determined by the pro-cedure laid down by Trajan; this name is the pride of the Christian and the reason for his martyrdom. The martyrs appear in the ninth parable; they are the believers who come from the eleventh mountain:

"These are the men who have suffered for the name of the Son of God, and who have displayed all the eagerness and generosity of their hearts in suffering and sacrificing their lives. . . . All those who have suffered for the Name are glorious before the Lord, and have seen all their sins blotted out. . . . All those who, when haled before the magistrates and subjected to the questioning, have not denied but have suffered willingly, rejoice before the Lord with a much greater glory. . . . But there are others who showed themselves timid and hesitant; only after debating in their hearts whether they ought to deny or confess did they decide to suffer; these last have as their symbol the less beautiful fruits, because of this thought which arose in their hearts" (*Sim.*, IX, 28, 2).

Fear has not been entirely removed; the persecution still threat-ens the Church; the parable ends with an ardent exhortation:

[11] Lelong accordingly exaggerates when he writes (*op. cit.*, p. xxxvi): "There took place at Rome in the time of Hermas what had taken place at Corinth at the time of Clement."

[12] *Vis.*, II, 2, 7: III, 4; and above all *Vis.*, IV, the sea-monster.

"You who suffer for the Name, ought to give thanks to God that He has judged you worthy to bear this name, and to receive the healing of all your sins. Consider yourselves therefore happy; indeed, think that you have done a great work when you suffer for God. The Lord gives you life, and you do not think of this. For your sins have weighed you down, and if you had not suffered for the name of the Lord, they would have made you dead to God. It is to you I speak, you who know not whether you ought to deny or confess; confess that you have a Master, if you do not wish to be cast into prison as renegades. If the pagans punish a slave who has denied his master, what, think you, will the Lord, who is the Master of all things, do to you? Cast these thoughts out of your heart, in order that you may live always for God" (*Sim.*, 28, 5).

Turning over the pages of this book, we seem to mingle with the crowd of Christians in Rome; we feel ourselves constrained by the bitterness of the persecutions, but we also realise the pride and power of the faith in the hearts of these neophytes.

The Hierarchy

If we try to find in the Shepherd some indications of the constitution of the Church, we note first of all that the monarchical episcopate is not directly mentioned; but we shall not overlook the fact that the writer was brother to the Bishop of Rome.[13] He speaks on several occasions of the heads of the Church, presbyters and pastors;[14] he does not spare them from rebuke; he warns them above all against love of first places, vanity, ambition;[15] he stigmatises the untruthful deacons who have dissipated the goods of widows;[16] but he praises the charitable bishops who open wide their houses to the brethren, who maintain widows, and who lead

---

[13] Turner (*art. cit.*, p. 194) rightly says: "As the *Shepherd* was published by Hermas during his brother's tenure of the see, and as it seems probable that in Mandate IX he is intending to glance at conditions actually prevailing within the Roman community, then the conclusion is natural that Hermas comes before the public at this particular time both because his relationship to the bishop will attract attention to his revelations, and because in his capacity as a seer he can do something to assist his brother in the difficulties of his position."

[14] Presbyters: *Vis.* II, 2, 6; III, 9, 7; II, 4, 2-3; pastors, IX, 31, 5-6. He uses the titles "presbyter" and "bishop" in the same sense: *Vis.*, III, 5, 1; cf. the notes by Funk, and Lelong, p. lxxxii.

[15] *Vis.*, III, 9, 7; *Simil.*, VIII, 7, 4.

[16] *Simil.*, IX, 26, 2.

a holy life.[17] We find traces still of the rivalry which at the end of the first century occasionally broke out between the prophets and the presbyters (*Vis.*, III, 1, 8), and already we notice a struggle between the martyrs and the hierarchy (*ibid.*, 9); this will be more pronounced in the third century, in the time of Cornelius and Cyprian.

The Church the Mother of the Christian

Beyond all these human inequalities, faults and virtues in the leaders of the Church, Hermas contemplates the Church herself, the Mother of the Christian.[18] Like a mother, the Church exhorts her Christian children:

"Hear me, my children; I have brought you up in great simplicity, innocence and holiness, thanks to the mercy of the Lord, who has poured out justice upon you. . . . Make peace to reign amongst you, so that I also may be able to go joyfully before the Father to give an account of all of you to your Lord" (*Vis.*, III, 9, 1).

We see from these last words that the office of the Church towards the Christian is the same as the office of Christ, that of a mediator with the Father; [19] this is because the Church is one with Christ. Hermas expresses this by the symbol of the Tower which is the Church, and the rock which is Christ: "The Tower was formed as of one single stone; no join could be seen in it; one would have said that the stone had been drawn from the Rock itself; the whole gave me the impression of a monolith" (*Simil.*, IX, 9, 7). "Thou seest," he says again, "that the Tower forms one mass with the Rock." [20]

[17] *Ibid.*, 27, 2. Other features in this indication of the hierarchy will be found in *Vis.*, II, 2, 6; III, 5, 1; IV, 3; IX, 7. Cf. Dobschuetz, *Urchristl. Gemeinden*, p. 233; Weinel, *Neutest. Apokryphen*, p. 330.

[18] On this belief, so dear to the Christians of the second century, cf. Lebreton, *Mater Ecclesia*, in *Recherches de Science religieuses*, 1911, pp. 572-573.

[19] See also *Simil.*, X, 2, 2: "Et hic (Pastor) apud me de his bene interpretetur et ego apud dominum."

[20] Cf. Durell, *The Historic Church* (Cambridge, 1906, pp. 99 *et seq.* This affirmation of the identity between the Church, the body of Christ, and its head, could appeal to the teaching of St. Paul, and will remain dear to all Christians. Hermas also affirms that the Church was the first of all creatures to be created, and that the world was formed for her (*Vis.*, I, 4, 1); this conception reappears in a more definite form in the II*a Clementis*. Cf. *Histoire du Dogme de la Trinité*, Vol. II, p. 388, 392.

Penance

Of all the moral problems dealt with by Hermas, there is one which dominates all the others, that of penance and reconciliation. This is the chief object of the message transmitted to the Roman Church.[21]

This message is set forth with great energy; but it formulates at the same time two theses which at first sight are impossible to harmonise: there is no other penance than baptism, and yet another penance is offered. Hermas is himself aware of this contradiction, at least apparently, and sets it forth clearly:

"I have heard, O Lord, some masters teach that there is no other penance than that which we made when we descended into the water and there received the pardon of our previous faults." "Thou has well understood, it is so. For he who has received the forgiveness of his sins ought to sin no more but remain in innocence. But since thou wishest to know the last word of all, I will discover also this to thee: . . . For those who were called before these days, the Lord established this penance, and set me over it. But I say to thee that if any one should, after this great and solemn call, yield to a temptation of the devil and sin, there is a penance; but if he falls again indefinitely, to do penance again, let him hope not for fruit; his salvation is indeed compromised." "I revive," I cried, "after the very precise explanations you have just given me, for I know that, if I do not commit new sins, I shall be saved." "Thou wilt be saved," he said to me, "as also will those who act thus" (*Command.*, IV, 3).

The last words of this passage reveal its significance: what causes Hermas anxiety is the danger in which are those believers who have sinned after their baptism, and amongst these he includes himself. Are these lost beyond recall? They would be, if one had to adhere rigorously to the principle laid down at first: there is only one penance, baptism; but the Lord, knowing "the weakness of man and the malice of the devil," has instituted another penance, and has set the Shepherd over it. This merciful institution, which remedies past faults, must not encourage future sins: to those, then, who have not yet received baptism, or who have just received

---

[21] Cf. A. d'Alès, *L'édit de Calliste*, 1914, pp. 53-113. In the *Shepherd,* three portions especially concern the question of penance: the third Vision: the construction of the Tower (d'Alès, *op. cit.*, p. 54); the fourth Commandment: chastity; there is no other penance besides baptism (*ibid.*, p. 67); the eighth and ninth Parables: the branches, the twelve mountains, and the Tower (*ibid.*, p. 87).

it, the principle is repeated: there is no other penance besides baptism. Does this mean that the penance preached by Hermas is, so to speak, a Jubilee, which will never be repeated? Certainly not; [22] and the proof is that later on the same promise of reconciliation will be made, accompanied by the same warning: this is the last pardon.[23] In all these texts we see the pressing exhortations of a preacher, and we must not look for the precision of a canonist.

What we note above all is the strength of the Christian ideal: a grave fault after baptism is an unworthy falling back; an indefinite perspective of such faults cannot be considered, but since unfortunately these falls have taken place in the past, the guilty ones are restored, with the warning that such a fault must never be repeated.[24]

This reparation of sin is regarded and can only be regarded as a return into the Church; [25] this is already the teaching of the third Vision: one can be saved only by entering into the Tower; and "the Tower which you see being built is Myself, the Church." [26]

Theology

The problems we have so far studied are the constant subject of the preoccupations of Hermas; but we have noticed therein more than one obscure point, especially in the question of penance and the reconciliation of sinners. If we pass from moral problems to theological conceptions, we must be prepared for more serious confusion: these high speculations are entered upon by Hermas only occasionally, in order to illuminate the moral questions which occupy him: thus in the fifth parable he preaches the meritorious character of fasting and works of supererogation; in order to explain this he sets forth to Christians the example of Christ, and doubtless

[22] This comparison of the Jubilee, first advanced by Batiffol, *Etudes de théologie positive*, Vol. I, p. 57, has been adopted by Lelong, *op. cit.*, p. lxiv, but is rightly rejected by d'Alès, *op. cit.*, p. 79.
[23] *Simil.*, IX, 26, 5.
[24] There is no reference in the *Shepherd* to the three unpardonable sins (apostacy, adultery, homicide) which will appear as such in Tertullian.
[25] This essential point is misunderstood by Lelong, *op. cit.*, pp. lxxiii-lxxv, but is well established by d'Alès, *op. cit.*, pp. 104 *et seq.*
[26] In the eighth Parable, VIII, 6, 6, we see penitent believers who are admitted into "the external precincts" of the Tower: in this symbol we probably have the situation of those who cannot be readmitted into the Church but who remain on the threshold in penance and prayer; cf. d'Alès, *op. cit.*, pp. 111 *et seq.*

nothing is more excellent, but, too anxious about the moral lesson, he forgets theology: Jesus appears to him as a faithful servant who, having been charged by God to care for his vineyard, did more than his duty, more than the Master of the vineyard had asked of him: ordered to surround it with a fence, he dug it, weeded it, and cleaned it of noxious plants; the Master of the vineyard, touched by this zeal, made his servant a co-heir with his son.

This may lead to very useful moral resolutions, but it is difficult to harmonise with the Christian Faith. Hermas himself sees this and perhaps hears those around him saying: "Why, O Lord, is the Son of God represented as a servant in the parable?" He feels the objection strongly, and to parry it, he has recourse to his usual procedure; he does not strike out, but he adds; he tries to enunciate more correctly the mystery of the Incarnation, and above all he hastens to draw from the new interpretation he presents a new moral lesson: just as the flesh, that is, the humanity of Christ, served in all faithfulness and purity the divinity it bore within itself, so also the Christian must keep without stain the spirit which dwells in him: the moralist is pleased with this useful instruction; the theologian is less satisfied with the theological conception it suggests.[27]

Anyone who is familiar with the *Shepherd,* and the embarrass-ment of thought, and still more of expression, in which the writer is involved, will not be too surprised at these obscurities and in-coherences, and above all he will take care not to hold the official teaching of the Church responsible for the awkwardness of this amateur theologian; what we must gather above all from the fifth Parable is the uneasy protest of the Christian conscience: the Son of God is not a servant; and also the firm affirmation of his redemp-tive office and his lordship:

"God created his people, and entrusted them to his Son; and the Son established angels over the people to guard them; and He Himself has washed away their sins with many tears and labours. Having thus washed away the sins of the people, He has shown them the ways of life, giving to them the law He had received from His Father. Thou

[27] If the parity proposed by this interpretation were pressed, the divinity of Christ would be reduced to a sanctification similar to that accorded to all Chris-tians; this would do violence to the thought of Hermas just as much as to Christian doctrine; hence we must be careful not to interpret too strictly the imprudent expressions of the writer. Cf. *Histoire du Dogme de la Trinité* Vol. II, p. 372.

seest that He is the Lord of the people, having received all power from His Father" (*Simil.*, V, 6, 2-4).

But what we must notice above all is that the points still vague in the fifth Parable are taken up again and firmly treated in the two last, the eighth and the ninth. The seer contemplates an immense Rock, in which a door has recently been hewn:

"What is the rock, and the door?" "This rock and this door, is the Son of God." "How then, O Lord, is the rock old, and the door new?" "Hear and understand, O man who understandest nothing. The Son of God was born before all creation, so that He was the counsellor of His Father in His creative work. That is why He is old." "But why, O Lord, is the door new?" "Because it is in the last days of the world that He has been manifested; that is why the door is new (and it has been made) in order that those who must be saved shall enter through it into the kingdom of God. . . . None will enter the kingdom of God if he has not received the name of the Son. . . ." (*Simil.*, IX, 12, 1.)

The Son of God, born before all creation, counsellor of His Father in the work of creation, is both rock and door; "His name is great, infinite, and upholds the whole world"; [28] "He manifested Himself" [29] by the Incarnation; He is the door: "He is the only entrance that gives access to the Lord; hence no-one will have access to Him if he goes not through His Son." The highest angels, even, can find access to God only through the Son: "Of these glorious angels not one will have access to God without Him; whosoever has not received His name will not enter into the kingdom of God." (*Simil.*, IX, 12, 6.)

On the rock a tower is built: this is the Church. It is formed of one single stone, and there is no join to be seen; it seems to have been hewn from the rock, and the whole, tower and rock, gives the impression of a monolith (*ibid.*, IX, 9, 7): the Church is one, Christ and the Church are only one Body. And the parable develops, manifesting the indispensable mediation of the Son of God; it concludes by pressing exhortations to martyrdom, fidelity and penance.

It is this deep and sincere Christian faith which made the *Shepherd* in the second century a book dear to very many Christians; and the same character still makes us look upon Hermas as

[28] *Simil.*, IX, 14, 5: Hermas here repeats *Hebr.* i, 3.
[29] This expression is much more correct than that of "habitation" found in the fifth Parable.

a Christian worthy of sympathy and respect, in spite of the incertitudes and weaknesses in his theology.

§6. PRAYER IN THE PRIMITIVE CHURCH[1]

The Example and Teaching of Christ

The reading of the Gospels and the writings of the apostles have revealed to us the fundamental importance of prayer in the individual life of all Christians and in the social life of the Church. Jesus Christ our leader is, in this as in all things, also our model. It was by prayer that He prepared Himself for the great mysteries and great events in His life: His baptism, the choice of the apostles, the confession of St. Peter, the Transfiguration, and above all His Passion.[2] It was in prayer that He sought repose and power;[3] it was also by prayer that He desired His apostles to prepare themselves for the great trials and works which awaited them.[4]

This teaching of the Master was not forgotten; prayer was for the apostles their chief and indispensable duty; when the increasing number of the faithful made their task too heavy, they instituted deacons so as to transfer to them a part of their ministry, reserving themselves for "prayer and preaching" (*Acts*, VI, 4). St. Paul asks "incessant prayer" from his faithful (*I Thess.* v, 17); similarly St. Ignatius from the Ephesians (x, 1) and from Polycarp (i, 3).

This prayer of the Christian, the first of his religious duties, and at the same time his consolation and his power, is something so great that God alone can teach it. The apostles understood this: from Judaism they had received a religious teaching, and the custom of prayer; most of them again had been trained in prayer by John the Baptist; and yet they felt that they had everything to

---

[1] Cf. on prayer and worship in the Antenicene Church, *Histoire du Dogme de la Trinité*, Vol. II, pp. 174-247; Dom Cabrol, *The Prayer of the Early Christians*, London, 1930; Bardy, *L'Eglise à la fin du Ier siècle*, pp. 47-76.

[2] Prayer at the baptism, *Luke* iii, 21; at the choosing of the apostles, vi, 12; at Cæsarea Philippi, ix, 18; at the Transfiguration, ix, 29; the sacerdotal prayer, *John* xvii; prayer at the Agony in the Garden, *Matt.* xxvi, 39, and parallel verses; prayer on the Cross, *Luke* xxiii, 34, 46.

[3] *Mark* i, 35; *Luke* v, 16.

[4] *Matt.* xxvi, 41; *Mark* xiv, 38; *Luke* xxii, 46.

learn and when one day they saw Jesus praying, they said to him: "Lord teach us to pray." It was then that Jesus taught them the *Our Father* (*Luke* xi, 1-4); but oral teaching, even that of Christ, was not sufficient; the Christian needed also the interior inspiration of the Holy Spirit: "We know not how to pray as we ought; but the Spirit himself pleadeth in our behalf with unutterable groanings." [5]

This teaching of the Master and the Apostles will enable us to understand the prayer of the Church as it is revealed in the writings of the end of the first and the beginning of the second centuries.

Jewish and Christian Prayer

If we consider the matter in general, the first thing we note is that Christian prayer resembles and echoes Jewish prayer in several ways: these resemblances appear in the Gospel canticles, the *Magnificat*, the *Benedictus*, and even in the *Lord's Prayer*.[6]

We find them again in the writings of the Apostolic Fathers, St. Clement, and the *Didache*. There is nothing here which should surprise a Christian: the God of Abraham, Isaac and Jacob is also the Father of Christ; the books of the Old Testament belong to the Church, which is the true Israel. But while the Church appears to Hermas as "the first of creatures" (*Vis.*, II, 4, 1), older than Moses and the patriarchs themselves, she is also the Spouse of Christ, eternally young, and rejuvenating all she touches.

This youthfulness, which the Church receives from the Holy Spirit, appears in her prayer: we feel there a spontaneity, a freshness, and above all a joyful and assured trust which makes the

[5] *Rom.* viii, 26, Westminster version. Père Lagrange thus comments on this text: "This prayer is one which is powerless, which feels its powerlessness but is not ignorant of its aim; a prayer which is already that of the Christian conscious of his end, as is shown by the context. But what can one say to God to touch his heart, how approach Him, and in what dispositions? Jesus had taught this by the *Our Father*, the official prayer of the faithful, but this does not wholly dissipate the difficulty of mental prayer. Wearied by its efforts, and dissatisfied with what it finds to say, the soul says nothing definite, and it is the Spirit who prays within her."

[6] Cf. *Histoire du Dogme de la Trinité*, Vol. II, p. 177; on the *Our Father*, see *Life and Teaching of Jesus Christ*, Vol. II, pp. 60-78.

traditional themes vibrate in an entirely new way. Thus, we have
in the Eucharistic prayers in the *Didache*:

"We give Thee thanks, O our Father, for the holy vine of David
thy servant, which Thou hast made known to us through Jesus, Thy
servant.[7] Glory be to Thee for ever! . . . We give Thee thanks, O our
Father, for the life and knowledge Thou hast made known to us
through Jesus Thy servant. Glory to Thee for ever! Thine is the glory
and the power, through Jesus Christ, for ever." (*Didache*, IX, 2-5.)

The blessings the Church receives from God are those asked for
by the Synagogue;[8] but they are better understood and more firmly
hoped for; the Church relies on the all powerful intercession of the
Son of God, and all her prayer is transformed accordingly. This
new spirit which animates the Christian soul is felt in the short
exclamations of the *Didache;* we feel it also in the long prayer of
Clement, and we do not possess for the period we are studying here
any liturgical document comparable to this. Half a century later,
St. Justin, describing the Sunday liturgy, writes: "When we have
finished praying, bread is brought, with wine and water; he who
presides sends up to heaven prayers and thanksgiving, according
to his ability, and all the people reply by the acclamation 'Amen.' "[9]
He who prayed thus did not create his prayer entirely; being full of
the Scriptural hymns, he echoed them, as Mary did in the *Magnificat,* and Zachary in the *Benedictus;* but all these traditional
themes were enriched by a new inspiration. These improvised
prayers, full of Scriptural reminiscences, are our earliest liturgical
documents; they were not conserved in books, and most of them
have disappeared; those which have survived are all the more
precious to us; such is the last prayer of St. Polycarp, transcribed
above; such also the great prayer of St. Clement. Towards the end

___

[7] Here, as in many of these early documents, Jesus is called $\pi\alpha\hat{\iota}\varsigma\ \theta\epsilon o\hat{\upsilon}$; this term
signifies both "servant of God" and "Son of God."

[8] Thus, in this eucharistic prayer, the Christian asks "that the Church may be
gathered together from the ends of the earth into thy kingdom"; this is the prayer
of the Jews, but transposed by a new hope: what is hoped for is no longer the
land of Israel, but heaven.

[9] *Apol.,* I, 67. Similarly, in the Christian meetings of the agapes, at the end of
the second century and in the third, those present either sang hymns from memory
or improvised them: "Post aquam manualem et lumina, ut quisque de scripturis
sanctis vel de proprio ingenio potest, provocatur in medium Deo canere" (Tertullian, *Apol.,* 39). "Sonet psalmos convivium sobrium: et ubi tenax memoria est,
vox canora, aggredere hoc munus ex more" (Cyprian, *Ad Donatum,* XVI). Cf.
Histoire du Dogme de la Trinité, Vol. II, p. 186.

of his letter, the bishop of Rome, after exhorting the faithful at Corinth, concludes his homily, as was his custom, by a prayer:

Prayer of St. Clement

May the Creator of the universe keep intact in the whole world the fixed number of His elect, through His well beloved Son Jesus Christ, through whom He has called us from darkness to light, from ignorance to the knowledge of the glory of His name, so that we may hope in Thy name, the principle whence proceeds every creature.

Thou hast opened the eyes of our hearts in order that they may know Thee, the sole Most High in the highest (heavens), the Holy in the midst of holy ones; who humblest the insolence of the proud, who destroyest the imaginations of the nations, who exaltest the humble and humblest the great, who makest rich and makest poor, who killest and savest and makest alive. Sole benefactor of spirits, and God of all flesh; who beholdest the bottom of abysses, who searchest the works of man; help of those who are in danger, saviour of those in despair, Creator and Watcher (Bishop) of all spirits. Who multipliest the nations on the earth, and hast chosen in the midst of all, those who love Thee, through Jesus Christ Thy well beloved Son, by whom Thou hast instructed, sanctified and honoured us.

We pray Thee, O Master, be our help and our support. Save us who are oppressed, take pity on the humble, raise up those who have fallen, show Thyself to those who are in want, heal the sick, bring back those who have wandered from Thy people, feed the hungry, free our prisoners, restore those who languish, console the fearful; let all peoples know that Thou art the only God, that Jesus Christ is Thy Son, that we are Thy people and the sheep of Thy fold.

For Thou by Thy works hast manifested the everlasting constitution of the world. Thou, O Lord, hast created the earth, Thou who art faithful in all generations, just in Thy judgments, wonderful in Thy power and magnificence, Thou who createst with wisdom, and establishest with prudence what Thou hast created, Thou who art good in things visible, and faithful towards those who trust in Thee, merciful and compassionate, forgive us our sins and our injustices, our falls and our wanderings. Reckon not up the sins of Thy servants, but purify us by Thy truth, and direct our steps so that we may walk in holiness of heart and do that which is good and acceptable in Thine eyes and in the eyes of our governors. Yea, Master, make Thy face to shine upon us, so we may enjoy good things in peace; cover us with Thy mighty hand, deliver us from all sin by Thy strong arm, save us from those who hate us unjustly. Give concord and peace to us and to all the inhabitants of the earth, as Thou didst give it to our fathers when they called upon Thee reverently in faith and truth, so that we may be subject to the supreme power and excellence of Thy name, to our governors, and to those who rule us on earth.

Thou, O Master, hast given them the royal power, through Thy magnificent and unspeakable might, so that, knowing the glory and honour which Thou hast given them, we may be subject to them and may not oppose Thy will. Grant them, O Lord, health, peace, concord, stability, so that they may exercise without hindrance the sovereignty Thou hast entrusted to them. For Thou, O Master, heavenly king of ages, givest to the sons of men glory, honour and power over the things of the earth. Direct Thyself, O Lord, their counsel, according to that which is good and acceptable in Thy sight, so that, exercising piously, in peace and meekness, the power Thou hast entrusted to them, they may find Thee propitious.

Thou alone hast the power to do this, and to give us still greater blessings; we praise Thee through the High Priest and Protector of our souls, Jesus Christ, through whom be glory and greatness to Thee, now and from generation to generation, and for ever and ever, Amen" (ch. LIX-LXI).

In this prayer, so similar in many features to Jewish prayers, we already perceive the traditional characteristics which will mark the Christian liturgy; [10] we find them also in other parts of this letter, which also have the tone of the primitive liturgy, and which are already related to the liturgies of the fourth century, as for instance to the prayers of the *Apostolic Constitutions*.[11]

This permanence in liturgical characteristics confirms what we said about the composition of these prayers; they were improvised by the bishop, but on a traditional theme, nourished with memories of the psalms, prophets, Gospels, and apostolic writings.

[10] Duchesne, *Origines du culte chrétien*, 1920, p. 55: "It is sufficient to remark that the liturgical language of which St. Clement gives us so early and authoritative an example, and the ritual presented by St. Justin as generally used in Christian assemblies, are altogether similar to those we shall meet with three centuries later, in a time when documents are plentiful. On the contrary, the liturgy described in the *Didache* has all the appearance of an anomaly; it will provide a few features for later compositions, but on the whole it is outside the stream of the general line of development, both for the ritual and for the style."

[11] Such are ch. XX, XXXIII, XXXIV in the letter of Clement; they may be compared with the prayer of thanksgiving found in the liturgy of baptism (*Const. Apost.*, VII, 34) and the anaphora (*ibid.*, VIII, 12, 9 *et seq.*). Cf. *Histoire du Dogme de la Trinité*, Vol. II, pp. 256-260.

Prayers to the Father and to Christ

It is to the Heavenly Father that liturgical prayer is usually addressed: the Church follows in this matter the teaching and example of her Master, as set forth in the *Our Father* and in the sacerdotal prayer of Christ (*John* xvii). This prayer is addressed to the Father in the name of His Son Jesus Christ our Lord, through His intercession, and through His ministry as High Priest.[12] These features are manifest in the prayer of Clement; they similarly appear in most of the documents of this time. But it would be a mistake to see in this liturgical usage an absolute rule, or to regard prayers addressed to Christ as merely late deviations, or alterations of the primitive liturgy. To Christ are addressed the earliest hymns we possess: the morning hymn, and the evening hymn;[13] about the year 113, at the beginning of the second century, Pliny in his letter to Trajan thus describes Christian worship: "The Christians are accustomed to meet together on certain days before dawn, and to sing in alternating ranks hymns in honour of Christ."[14]

We can go still further back, and read once more in the *Apocalypse* the heavenly canticles which are in the epistles of St. Paul echoed by voices on earth:

"The Lamb that was slain is worthy to receive power, and divinity, and wisdom, and strength, and honour, and glory, and benediction" (*Apocalypse*, V, 12).

"Rise thou that sleepest, and arise from the dead, and Christ shall enlighten thee" (*Ephes.*, V, 14).

"Great is the mystery of godliness,
which was manifested in the flesh,
was justified in the spirit,

[12] Cf. *Histoire du Dogme de la Trinité*, Vol. 11, pp. 175 *et seq.*

[13] Cf. *Histoire du Dogme de la Trinité*, Vol. II, pp. 220-222; the morning hymn is the *Gloria in excelsis*, which we sing in the Mass; in its primitive form this is a hymn to Christ. Cf. *Recherches de Science religieuse*, 1923, pp. 322-329; D. Casel, in *Theol. Revue*, 1927, col. 64. The evening hymn in the φῶς ἱλαρὸν: "Joyous light of the holy and immortal glory of the heavenly Father, holy and blessed Jesus Christ. The hour of sunset has come, and seeing the evening star appear, we sing of the Father, Son and Holy Spirit of God. Thou art worthy at all times to be praised by holy voices, O Son of God, who givest life; therefore the world glorifies thee." Cf. E. Smothers, in *Recherches de Science religieuse*, 1929, pp. 266-283.

[14] Pliny the Younger, *Epist.*, X, 96.

> appeared unto angels,
> hath been preached unto the Gentiles,
> is believed in the world,
> is taken up in glory."
>
> (*I Tim.*, iii, 16)

The Eucharistic Liturgy

What thus appears in Christian worship as a whole is still more manifest in the heart of the liturgy, that is, in the celebration of the Eucharistic mystery.

It is to the Father that the Eucharistic Sacrifice is offered; the Son of God, Jesus Christ our Lord, is the priest and the victim. The earliest Eucharistic prayers we possess are those found in the *Didache* (IX-X):

"As to the Eucharist, give thanks thus:

"First for the chalice: We give Thee thanks, O our Father, for the holy Vine of David Thy servant, which Thou hast made known to us through Jesus Thy servant. Glory be to Thee for ever!

"For the broken bread: We give Thee thanks, O our Father, for the life and knowledge Thou hast made known to us through Jesus Thy servant. Glory be to Thee for ever.

"As the elements of this bread, scattered upon the mountains, have been gathered together to become one whole, so also may Thy Church be gathered together from the ends of the earth into thy Kingdom. For Thine is the glory and power, through Jesus Christ, for ever.

"After you have been filled, give thanks thus:

"We give Thee thanks, O holy Father, for Thy holy name which Thou hast made to dwell in our hearts, and for the knowledge, faith and immortality which Thou hast revealed to us through Jesus Thy servant. Glory be to Thee for ever.

"Thou, O almighty Master, hast created the universe for the glory of Thy name, and hast given to men food and drink, that they may enjoy them and give Thee thanks; but to us Thou hast given spiritual food and drink, and eternal life through Thy servant. Above all we give Thee thanks because Thou art mighty. Glory be to Thee for ever!

"Remember, O Lord, to deliver Thy Church from all evil and to make it perfect in Thy love. Gather it together from the four winds, this holy Church, into Thy Kingdom which Thou hast prepared for it. For Thine is the power and the glory for ever.

"May grace come, and this world pass away. Hosanna to the God of

David. If any one be holy, let him come. If he is not, let him repent. Maranatha! Amen." [15]

In this text, if we leave provisionally on one side the acclamations and the final monitions, we can distinguish two chants, each of three strophes: each of the two first strophes ends in a short doxology: "Glory be to Thee . . . ," and the whole chant by a fuller doxology: "For Thine is the glory . . ." The first chant precedes the communion, the second follows it. These prayers call to mind in more than one feature Jewish prayers, but they are inspired above all by the New Testament, and chiefly by the Johannine and Pauline writings.

These prayers have left little trace in later liturgical tradition. It is quite otherwise with the acclamations and the final monitions. We read, for instance, in the *Apostolic Constitutions*, VIII, 13, 12-14:

"The bishop, addressing the people, says: 'Holy things to the holy!' And all the people reply: 'One only holy, one only Lord, Jesus Christ . . . Hosanna to the Son of David. Blessed is he who cometh in the name of the Lord. God is Lord, and He has appeared amongst us. Hosanna in the highest.' And after that, the bishop communicates, and then the priests and the deacons. . . .'"

In this fourth century text we find in a more developed form the same liturgical elements found in the *Didache*: monitions to the faithful, acclamations in honour of the Son of David who comes among his people.

The author of the *Didache* ends by saying:

"As to the prophets, let these give thanks as much as they will."

The Eucharistic Liturgy according to St. Justin

Half a century later, a text of an entirely different character makes known to us, not now the eucharistic prayers, but the Christian mystery: the apologist St. Justin, in order to refute pagan calumnies, gives the emperors Marcus Aurelius and Lucius Verus a description of the Mass as Christians celebrated it; he does this on

[15] These prayers have often been studied: by the editors of the *Didache*, and also by J. A. Robinson, *Barnabas, Hermas and the Didache*, London, 1920, pp. 94-97; *Histoire du Dogme de la Trinité*, Vol. II, pp. 193-195, Lietzmann, *Messe und Herrenmahl*, pp. 230-238.

two occasions, explaining first the baptismal liturgy, and then the Sunday Mass. We reproduce here the first text, which is the more explicit:

"LXV. When we have washed the one who has made a profession of faith and who has become one of us, we lead him to the place where are assembled those whom we call our brethren. Together we make fervent prayers for ourselves, for the baptised, and for all others in whatsoever place they may be, in order to obtain, after the knowledge of the truth, the grace to practise virtue and to keep the commandments, that we may arrive at eternal salvation. When the prayers are concluded, we give to each other the kiss of peace. Then one brings to him who presides over the assembly of the brethren, bread, and a cup of wine and water. He takes them, and praises and glorifies the Father of the universe through the name of the Son and the Holy Spirit, and he makes a long thanksgiving ('eucharist') for these good things that we have received from Him. When he has finished the prayers and the thanksgiving, all the people present reply by the acclamation: Amen. 'Amen' signifies in the Hebrew language 'So may it be.' When he who presides has made the thanksgiving, and all the people have replied, the ministers whom we call deacons distribute the consecrated bread and wine to all those present, and they take some to the absent.

"LXVI. We call this food 'eucharist,' and none may partake of it if he believes not in the truth of our doctrine, has not received the washing for the forgiveness of sins and regeneration, and lives not according to the precepts of Christ. For we do not take this food as common bread and common drink, but just as our Saviour Jesus Christ, incarnate by the power of the Word of God, took flesh and blood for our salvation, so the food consecrated by the prayer formed of the words of Christ, this food which is to nourish our blood and our flesh by being assimilated, is the flesh and blood of the incarnate Jesus: such is our teaching. For the apostles, in their memoirs called Gospels, report that Jesus gave them these instructions: he took bread, and having given thanks, said: 'Do this in memory of me, this is my body'; he likewise took the cup, and having given thanks he said: 'This is my blood'; and he gave it to them only. This the evil spirits have imitated by instituting the mysteries of Mithra; for you know, or may know, bread and a cup of water are given in the ceremonies of initiation, and certain formulæ are pronounced."

This description of the baptismal Mass is followed by a chapter dealing with the liturgy of Sunday. It is shorter, but in some details it completes the one we have just read:

"LXVII, 3. On the day called Sunday, all, in town or country, gather together in one and the same place; the memoirs of the apostles and the writings of the prophets are read, as much as the time will permit. When the reader has finished, he who presides gives a discourse, to instruct, and to encourage the imitation of these beautiful teachings. Then we all rise up together and pray. Next, as we have said above, when we have finished praying, bread, wine and water are brought; he who presides sends up to heaven prayers and thanksgivings as much as he is able, and all the people reply by the acclamation: Amen. Then takes place the distribution and partaking of each of the things consecrated, and their sending to the absent by the ministry of the deacons."

This important text suggests to a historian many useful points. What we infer from it in the first place is that the discipline of the secret was not yet enforced: we shall find it at the end of this second century in Tertullian, but Justin shows no knowledge of it. He expounds to the pagans the eucharistic liturgy and the Christian belief in the presence of the body of Christ: this intention to hide nothing is clearly inspired by the desire to refute calumnies, and indeed this exposition was the most effective of apologies.[16]

Origin and Development of this Liturgy

This frank description enables us to reconstitute, at least in its general features, the primitive liturgy. In presence of all the assembled Christians, there were read first "the memoirs of the apostles and the writings of the prophets." The Synagogue service comprised two readings from holy Scripture; the first was taken from the Pentateuch, and the second from the prophets. We find similarly two readings in the Christian liturgy, but one is from the New Testament, and the other from the Old.[17]

In the case of the Jews, these Scriptural readings were followed by a homily; the same takes place in the Christian liturgy. After

[16] It is evident that the reception of the Eucharist is reserved to believers, as it will be always; Justin says so explicitly (LXVI, 1), and so also the *Didache*, IX, 5. It is supported by the words of the Lord (*Matt.* vii, 6), on which will later be based the law of the secret (Tertullian, *De præscr.*, XLI, 2). But though the pagans have not the right to receive the Eucharist, they have a right to know the rite and the mystery.

[17] Of the New Testament, Justin mentions here only the Gospels; but the epistles were equally read; we see even from the letter of Dionysius of Corinth (cf. *supra*, p. 410, n. 6) that the letter of Clement of Rome and that of Soter were read at Corinth during the Sunday office. Of the Old Testament, the prophets were chiefly read by Christians, because they gave a more evident testimony to Christ, but the veneration felt for them did not lead the Pentateuch to be overlooked, or the Psalms.

the homily, all those present rise for common prayer; the letter of St. Clement shows us how the bishop passed from exhortation to prayer, leading all his people.

Readings, homily and prayers together form only a preparatory liturgy. When they are ended, the Eucharist commences: bread, wine and water are brought, then "he who presides sends up to heaven prayers and thanksgivings ('eucharists') as much as he can"; there is as yet no eucharistic form officially adopted by the Church and imposed by her upon bishops and priests; the officiant improvises the form of this prayer, and continues it "as much as he can." [18] At the same time, this eucharistic prayer develops according to a liturgical theme; it praises the blessings received from God, creation, redemption, and above all the mysteries of the life of Christ; it stresses the Supper, and repeats the words of consecration, which Justin explicitly sets forth; it recalls the death and resurrection of the Lord; it prays for the Church and the faithful; and ends with a doxology. Such is the theme which we shall find developed at the beginning of the third century in the anaphora of St. Hippolytus; that liturgy displays in more than one point the personal impress of its author, but it was not wholly created by him; it was the codification of a previous usage, the terminus of a long tradition.[19]

After the anaphora, the Communion is distributed to those present and carried to the absent. It is at this moment, immediately before the Communion, that we find in many early liturgies the acclamations which we have already read in the *Didache*; we also find, but more rarely, eucharistic prayers expressing the desire of the believer; thus in the *Acts of Thomas*:

"O Jesus, who hast given us the grace of being participants in the Eucharist of Thy holy body and Thy blood, behold we dare to approach Thy Eucharist, and to invoke Thy holy name. Come and communicate unto us." [20]

[18] We have seen a similar expression in the *Didache*, X, 7: "Let the prophets give thanks as much as they wish."

[19] On this anaphora, cf. the next book.

[20] *Acts of Thomas*, XLIX. The long eucharistic prayer which follows (ch. L) is clearly of Gnostic origin; the text transcribed above would seem not to come from a Gnostic source (cf. W. Bauer in the collection of *N. T. Apokryphen* of E. Hennecke, 1923, p. 257); but the whole book is too suspect in origin and character to be presented with full assurance as an authentic witness of the Catholic faith.

To these sentiments of adoration and love were often joined, especially from the fourth century, sentiments of reverential fear in presence of the majesty of the eucharistic mystery.[21]

The Baptismal Liturgy

In this passage of St. Justin, we have so far considered the testimony it gives to the eucharistic liturgy, and it is this that gives it its chief interest. But we must also notice the baptismal liturgy; it appears as a solemn rite in which the whole Church takes part. We are no longer in the very beginnings, which the *Didache* showed us: baptism is no longer conferred as it was then, with such means as circumstances permitted; the Church has constructed piscinas for the use of its neophytes; but first of all, before the baptism, there is a profession of faith followed by prayers and fasts in which all the faithful join; [22] then the neophytes "are conducted by us to the place where the water is, and there, in the same way that we ourselves were regenerated, they are regenerated in their turn; for it is in the name of the Father and Master of the universe, and of Jesus Christ our Lord, and of the Holy Spirit that they are then washed in the water." [23]

At the end of this chapter, Justin returns once more to the baptismal initiation. A little later on, St. Irenæus once more sets forth the baptismal rite in his *Demonstration of the Apostolic Preaching*:

"When we are regenerated by the baptism given to us in the name of the three Persons, we are enriched in this second birth with the good things which are in God the Father by means of His Son, with the Holy Spirit. For those who are baptised receive the Spirit of God, who gives them to the Word, that is, to the Son; and the Son takes and offers them

---

[21] These sentiments are very marked in St. Cyril of Jerusalem (*Cat. myst.*, V, 4, Migne, *P. G.*, XXXIII, 1112, cf. 1116), and still more in St. John Chrysostom; on the other hand, we do not find them in the Cappadocian Fathers. There is a like difference in the liturgies; these sentiments do not appear in the Anaphora of Serapion, nor in the *Apostolic Constitutions;* on the other hand they are very marked in the liturgy of St. James, somewhat less, but still very noticeable, in that of St. Basil and of St. John Chrysostom. Cf. Dom. Connolly, *Fear and Awe attaching to the Eucharistic Service, Texts and Studies*, VIII, pp. 92-97; Nicolas Cabasilas, *Liturgiæ expositio*, 1 (Migne, *P. G.*, CL, 369).

[22] Justin, *Apol.*, I, 61, 2.

[23] *Ibid.*, 3.

to His Father, and the Father communicates to them incorruptibility. Thus without the Spirit one cannot see the Word of God; and without the Son none can arrive at the Father; for the knowledge of the Father is the Son, and the knowledge of the Son of God is obtained by means of the Holy Spirit; but it is the Son who, by office, distributes the Spirit according to the good pleasure of the Father, to those whom the Father wishes, and as the Father wishes.[24]

We see from this fine passage that the baptismal formula prescribed by Christ, "baptize in the name of the Father and of the Son and of the Holy Spirit," was not only faithfully repeated, but it planted in the hearts of the faithful belief in the Trinity, and the rite which accompanied the formula again stressed its significance: for the neophyte was washed three times, either by immersion or by infusion.[25]

On coming out of the baptismal piscina, the neophytes were conducted to the assembly of the faithful, and then came common prayers, and the kiss of peace. In the course of the second and third centuries, the catechumenate took shape; the baptismal liturgy, reserved for the vigils of Easter and Pentecost, became more solemn; but already in the first half of the second century its essential features were already fixed, and then more than ever its social bearing was felt. At that time, when persecutions unceasingly threatened the Church and martyrdoms were common, the entrance of the neophyte into the Christian community was a heroic step, and one marked by a fraternal charity the striking fervour of which people loved to recall later on. In the following century, towards the end of a long period of peace, Origen will call up these memories in one of his homilies:

"If we judge things according to truth . . . we must recognise that we are not faithful. Then people were truly faithful, when martyrdom came at our birth (into the Church); when, returning from the cemeteries whither we had accompanied the bodies of the martyrs, we re-entered the assemblies, when the whole Church was there, unshakeable,

---

[24] *Demonstr.*, ch. vii, cf. ch. iii.

[25] The triple infusion is prescribed in the *Didache*, ch. VII. Triple immersion is explicitly attested by Tertullian, *Adv. Praxeam.*, xxvi: "Nec semel, sed ter, ad singula nomina in personas singulas tinguimur." We see also from this chapter that the Monarchian heretics, who had abandoned belief in the Trinity, still had a triple immersion; this proves that they had received this from the custom of the Church, previous to their heresy. Cf. *Histoire du dogme de la Trinité*, Vol. II, pp. 134-141.

when the catechumens were catechised in the midst of the martyrdoms and deaths of Christians who confessed the truth to the end, and when these catechumens, surmounting these tests, attached themselves without fear to the living God. Then we were aware of having known astonishing and wonderful marvels. Then the faithful were few in number, doubtless, but they were really faithful, treading the straight and narrow way which leads to life." [26]

§7. THE APOSTLES' CREED [1]

The study of the baptismal liturgy has shown us that in the history of Christian doctrine and particularly of the dogma of the Trinity, the formulæ and rites of baptism played a most important part: they were the expression and the safeguard of the dogma; this is true especially of the baptismal creed, which we must study more closely.

Profession of Faith in Apostolic Times

Already in apostolic times, neophytes were admitted to baptism only after a profession of faith.[2] Philip the deacon required it already from the Ethiopian eunuch (*Acts* viii, 37); St. Paul required it from all his converts: they had to confess with the mouth that Jesus is Lord, and believe with the heart that God raised Him up from the dead (*Rom.* x, 9); all the candidates for baptism had to accept the traditional catechesis as we find it recalled, for example, in the first epistle to the Corinthians (*I Cor.*, XV, 3 *et seq.*).

The faith proposed by the Church to the neophytes and professed by them was thus the faith of the apostles, which the apos-

[26] *Hom. in Jerem.*, IV, 3; ed. Klostermann, p. 25; Migne, *P.G.*, XIII, p. 288-289.

[1] The most detailed study of the history of the Apostles' Creed is that of F. Kattenbusch, *Das Apostolische Symbol*, Leipzig, 1894-1900. The texts are conveniently collected together in A. Hahn, *Bibliothek der Symbole*, Breslau, 1897. Research and hypotheses have been multiplied in recent years. We mention above all J. Haussleiter, *Trinitarischer Glaube und Christusbekenntnis*, Gütersloh, 1920; A. Nussbaymer, *Das Ursymbolum nach der Epideixis des hl. Irenæus und dem Dialog. Justins*, Paderborn, 1921; H. Lietzmann, *Symbolstudien*, articles published in *Zeitschr. f. N. T. Wissensch.*, 1922-1927; Dom B. Capelle, *Le Symbole romain au IIe siècle*, in *Recherches de Théol. anc. et med.*, Vol. II, 1930, pp. 5-20; Lebreton, *Histoire du Dogme de la Trinité*, Vol. II, pp. 141-173; *Les origines du symbole baptismal*, in *Recherches de Science religieuse*, 1930, pp. 97-124.

[2] Cf. *supra*, p. 342.

tles themselves had received from Christ. This is brought out into full light by Tertullian, in his treatise *De præscriptione contra hæreticos*. After transcribing in its entirety the "rule of faith," he adds:

"Such is the rule which Christ instituted—as I will prove—and it can give rise to no questions amongst us other than those raised by heresies and heretics" (ch. xiii).

A little later he links up this baptismal creed with the formula of baptism, and shows that this teaching of Christ was entrusted by him to the apostles, who in their turn taught it to the Church; thus is assured the chain of tradition which links us through the Church to the apostles, through the apostles to Christ, and through Christ to God.[3]

We cannot infer from this that this teaching communicated by Christ to the apostles must, according to Tertullian, consist in the formula of the Creed, but it remains true that this Christian and apostolic faith has its "rule" in the baptismal creed, and that this creed is based on the baptismal formula which Christ prescribed; this is what Tertullian himself teaches when, speaking of the replies given by the neophyte to the baptismal questions, he writes: "We reply by a formula somewhat longer than that which the Lord gave us in the Gospel" (*De Corona*, iii).

We have here not only theological theses of great importance, but also some fruitful historical statements. The Christian liturgy was determined by the initiative of Christ; the whole anaphora is based on the narrative of the Institution and on the words of the Lord, "This is My body . . . this is My blood . . . do this in memory of Me." Similarly the baptismal liturgy is determined by the commandment of Jesus: "Go, teach all nations, baptizing them in the name of the Father, and of the Son, and of the Holy Ghost." By repeating these words over the head of the baptized person, the Church consecrates him to the God whom Jesus Christ has revealed

---

[3] "One of the apostles having been expelled, He commanded the eleven others . . . to go and teach the nations and to baptize them in the name of the Father, Son and the Holy Spirit. . . . It was in Judea that they first established the faith in Jesus Christ and founded churches; then they set out across the world, and announced to the nations the same doctrine and the same faith" (XX, 3-4). "It is clear that every doctrine which is in agreement with that of these churches, mothers and sources of the faith, must be regarded as true, since it evidently contains that which these churches received from the apostles, the apostles from Christ, and Christ from God" (XXI, 4).

to us; she at the same time calls upon the neophyte to consecrate himself to God, and to make an act of faith in Him.

The Baptismal Creed

For a long time, until after the middle of the second century, we shall not as yet find a liturgical formula imposed authoritatively in the name of the Church: this conclusion, to which we are led by the study of the eucharistic liturgy, is also suggested to us by the study of the baptismal liturgy, and in particular of the Creed; but at the same time we note in the Creed as in the anaphora, through the accidental variations of a still plastic formula, the affirmation of the same dogma: the Creed, basing itself on the baptismal formula, confesses God in three Persons, Father, Son and Holy Spirit. The earliest forms of the Creed are very short; the *Epistle of the Apostles,* a Christian apocryphal work written about 180, gives us this formula:

> I believe in the Father Almighty,
> in Jesus Christ our Saviour,
> and in the Holy Spirit, the Paraclete;
> in the Holy Church, in the forgiveness of sins.[4]

The papyrus of Der-Balizeh, which contains an Egyptian ritual of the end of the second century, presents the following text:

> I believe in God the Father Almighty,
> and in His only Son Our Lord Jesus Christ,
> and in the Holy Spirit;
> in the resurrection of the flesh, in the holy Catholic Church.[5]

About the same date, or a little later, we find more developed texts, as for instance, this of St. Irenæus:

The Church, although spread throughout the universe as far as the ends of the earth, has received from the apostles and their disciples the faith in one God, the Father Almighty, who made heaven and earth and the seas, and all that is in them; and in one only Christ Jesus, the Son of God, who was incarnate for our salvation; and in one Holy Spirit, who through the prophets announced the dispensation, the coming, the virginal birth, the passion, the resurrection from the dead, and the bodily

[4] Cf. C. Schmidt, *Gespräche Jesu mit seinen Jüngern.,* p. 32; cf. p. 400.
[5] Cf. B. Capelle, *art. cit.,* p. 6.

ascension into heaven of the well beloved Christ Jesus Our Lord, and His second coming, when in the heavens He will appear at the right hand of the Father, to restore all things and to raise up all flesh and all humanity, in order that before Christ Jesus Our Lord, God, Saviour and King, every knee may bend in heaven, hell, on earth, and every tongue confess Him, and He may give to all a just judgment. . . .[6]

This statement is not a literal transcription but a brief commentary on the Creed; at the same time it must be noted that this commentary is wholly formed of traditional formulæ which will remain living in tradition.[7]

Before appearing here in Irenæus, these expressions were familiar to Barnabas, and Justin; they will be more familiar still to Hippolytus and Tertullian; we shall find them again in the *Apostolic Constitutions*, the Creeds of Antioch, Cæsarea, Jerusalem and Sirmium. We see by this example how liturgical usage came to be formed, and how in turn it reacted on theological literature, passing on to it its formulæ and giving a priestly and solemn character to its style.

These precisions which tend to determine still further the formula of faith will multiply in the course of the centuries; to the denials of heresy the Church will oppose the professions of faith in her Creeds; against Arius, Nestorius, Eutyches, and all the teachers of error she will define ever more and more explicitly the dogmas she sets forth to her faithful. This is apparent to us already in the second century in Tertullian, Irenæus, and in the first years of the century, in Ignatius of Antioch:

Shut your ears, then, to the speech of those who do not speak to you of Jesus Christ, born of the race of David, born of Mary, who was really generated, really ate and drank, really suffered persecution under Pontius Pilate, was really crucified and died, in the sight of heaven, earth, and the lower regions; who was really raised up from the dead. . . .[8]

We find in this fragment some formulæ already traditional, and which are echoed in the majority of the Creeds, in particular the passion, dated under Pontius Pilate, the crucifixion, death, and resurrection. Ignatius had to oppose those who taught Docetism;

---

[6] *Adv. hær.*, I, 10, 2. Cf. *Demonstr.*, c. VI, quoted and commented on in *Histoire du Dogme de la Trinité*, Vol. II, p. 152, and *Recherches de Science Religieuse*, 1930, p. 102.

[7] Cf. Lietzmann, *Zeitschr. f. N. T. Wiss.*, XXVI (1927), p. 93.

[8] *Trall.*, IX; cf. *Smyrn.*, I; *Magn.* XI.

he set against them these great facts of the life of Christ, and stressed with energy their reality.

These progressive precisions of the Creed affect Christology above all: to the profession of faith in the Trinity is added the profession of faith in the principal mysteries of the life of Christ.[9]

The Roman Creed

If we wish to sum up this account, and to separate it from the hypotheses and discussions which weigh it down, we can reduce it to these main points. After the formulæ of faith of the apostolic age, we find at Rome from the first half of the second century a baptismal creed professing faith in God the Father Almighty, in Jesus Christ His Son, and in the Holy Spirit; the mention of the Holy Spirit was followed by those of the Holy Church and the resurrection of the flesh.

This brief formula, similar to those we have mentioned above,[10] is enriched from the time of St. Justin with a profession of faith in the principal mysteries of the life of Christ. The Christological formulæ, joined sometimes to the third article,[11] will find their definitive place in the second article, as is natural. Thus from the end of the second century or the first years of the third, the Creed will be subject only to a few literary retouches of little or no importance.[12]

[9] This Christology has not the same place in the different creeds of the second century: in the text of Irenæus quoted above (Hær., I, 10, 2) it is joined to the third article of the Creed, which has as its subject the Holy Spirit; so also in St. Justin, Apol. I, LXI, 10-13. On the other hand, in the Demonstration of St. Irenæus, c. vi, it occupies in the second article the place which it will henceforth retain in the Creed. From this fact it is not unreasonably inferred that the Christological formulæ, first of all isolated, took their definitive place in the Trinitarian symbol only towards the end of the second century. Cf. Histoire du Dogme de la Trinité, Vol. II, pp. 160 et seq., Recherches de Science Religieuse, 1930, p. 107 et seq.

[10] Cf. supra, pp. 471-472.

[11] As we have seen from the texts of Justin and Irenæus, this position is due to the mention of the prophecies: to the prophetic Spirit is joined all these mysteries which it foretold.

[12] Cf. Dom Capelle, Rech., p. 19. The same author, speaking of the texts of Tertullian and Hippolytus, reconstitutes thus the Roman creed of the last years of the second century (Revue bénédictine, 1927, p. 39):

"I believe in one God almighty, creator of all things,

"And in Christ Jesus, the Son of God, born of the Holy Spirit and of the Virgin Mary, crucified under Pontius Pilate, dead and buried; raised from

In this progressive elaboration of the baptismal creed, the part played by the Church of Rome was decisive; [13] it was she above all who assured throughout the whole Christian world that unanimity of faith which St. Irenæus attested towards the end of the second century with such force:

"It is this preaching that the Church has received, this faith, as we have said; and although she is scattered through the whole world, she keeps it carefully, as if she dwelt in one single house, and she believes it unanimously, as if she had but one soul and one heart, and with perfect accord she preaches it, teaches it, and transmits it, as though she had only one mouth. Doubtless the languages on the surface of the world are different, but the force of tradition is one and the same. The churches founded in the Germanies have not another faith or another tradition; nor the churches founded amongst the Iberians, or the Celts, or in the East, or in Egypt, or in Lybia, or in the centre of the world; but just as the sun, that creature of God, is one and the same in all the world, so also the preaching of the truth shines everywhere and enlightens all men who wish to come to know it" (*Adv. hær.*, I, 10, 2).

The Rule of Faith

What assures this uniformity in the teaching of the Church is above all the living magisterium which conserves, transmits and develops the deposit received from Christ and the apostles; but this living magisterium utilises the Creed in order to express its faith and to give it the official formulation which maintains all its force, which opposes it to error, and which determines for all people and all time its immutable doctrine. When the Arian heresy will arise, the Church gathered together in council at Nicæa will define its faith in a Creed; she will not create it entirely; she will base herself on a baptismal Creed, contenting herself with adding to it some new precisions aimed at the new heresy.

---

the dead the third day; ascended into heaven; seated at the right hand of the Father; who will come to judge the living and the dead;

"And in the Holy Spirit, the Holy Church, the resurrection of the flesh."

For some details, this reconstitution is conjectural: thus the omission of the word "Father" in the first article seems insufficiently guaranteed in view of the texts of Tertullian (*De bapt.*, VI, *Adv. Prax.*, II) and of Hippolytus (Capelle, p. 36). On the other hand, the omission of "the forgiveness of sins" in the third article seems well established (p. 42).

[13] Cf. Kattenbusch, *op. cit.*, Vol. I, p. 80 (dependence of the other Western creeds); Vol. I, p. 380 *et seq.* (dependence of the Eastern creeds).

During the three centuries which precede Nicæa, there was no universal council; the Church had nevertheless to conquer many heresies: Gnosticism, Marcionism, Monarchianism, Modalism; it opposed to these not conciliar definitions, but the baptismal creed, the solemn expression of the apostolic faith. This faith, sworn to by the Christian at baptism, is his most precious treasure, and at the same time his password, or *tessera*, which will lead to his being recognised everywhere as a son of the Catholic Church, and as one of Christ's faithful. He may, like St. Irenæus, be born and grow up at Smyrna, live in Rome, and evangelise the Gauls: he will find everywhere the same faith, and will be everywhere illumined by the same sun of God.

CHAPTER XI

ECCLESIASTICAL ORGANISATION IN THE FIRST TWO CENTURIES[1]

In the conditions, apparently so precarious, in which the Church found itself in the Roman Empire in the first two centuries, what was its organisation?

§1. THE PRIMITIVE CHURCH

Charity and Fraternity

The Church is an organic collectivity, and not a mere juxtaposition of men thinking and acting in the same way on certain points regarded by them as fundamental; there is a bond uniting them which makes them a society with an externally visible organisation.

Yet in the very earliest days, this organisation shows itself only in a few somewhat ill-defined features. The Church, the society of the friends of Christ, that is, of those who love Him and are loved by Him, and who for love of Him love one another, form above all a brotherhood and a "charity," ἀγάπη. This is the term of St. Ignatius of Antioch,[2] who was indeed a man consumed by the love of God and of men's souls for God's sake. This charity is inseparable from unity: if this unity does not yet find its explicit expression in certain organs having its maintenance and manifestation for their special function, primitive Christianity has nevertheless a passion

---

[1] Bibliography.—Besides the works indicated in the General Bibliography, one may consult for the matters treated in this chapter: A. Michiels, *L'origine de l'épiscopat*, Louvain, 1900; C. De Smedt, *L'organisation des églises chrétiennes jusqu'au milieu du IIIe siècle*, 1re partie, in *Revue des questions historiques*, 1888, pp. 329-384; J. Zeiller, *La conception de l'Eglise aux quatre premiers siècles*, in *Revue d'histoire ecclés.*, Vol. XXIX, 1933, pp. 571-585 and 827-848; Bartoli, *The Primitive Church and the Primacy of Rome*, London, 1909; F. Mourret, *La Papauté (Bibliothèque des Sciences religieuses*, Paris, 1929); E. Caspar, *Die römische Bischofsliste*, in *Schriften den Königsberger Gelehrten Gesellschaft Geisteswissenschaftliche Klasse*, 2 Jahr. Heft 4, 1926, and *Geschichte des Papsttums*, Vol. I, Tübingen, 1930, the theories in which are discussed below: F. X. Seppelt, *Der Aufstieg des Papsttums. Geschichte der Päpste des von Anfangen bis zum Regierungsantritt Gregors des Grossen*, Leipzig, 1931; J. Turmel, *Histoire du Dogme de la Papauté des origines à la fin du IVe siècle*, Paris, 1908.

[2] *Epistola ad Romanos, inscr.*

for deep unity, inseparable in fact from the existence of a hierarchy;[3] the ἀγάπη is a consensus, the realisation itself of the *sint
unum* which is the object of the prayer of Christ in the Gospel of
St. John.[4]

The sense, will, and consciousness of this unity shine forth in the
letters of St. Ignatius, which make us realise so well that all the
churches are but one, and that all Christians make only one single
body, or better, one soul. But this unity is not merely imposed
by a commandment. It remains essentially based on charity, it is
the fruit of the union of those who love one another, as well as one
of the reasons for this love; they love one another because they are
all one, and they are one because they love one another, Christ
being the bond of this unity and the centre of this love.

Unity

Being one single body throughout the world in which they are
scattered, not a federation of distinct groups but the one society of
Christ's faithful spread in many places, they constitute one single
whole in each place. The Christian community in each city—for
Christianity shows itself as a religion of cities and not one of cor-
porations—appears as one whole which is not at first divisible into
various sections. "From the first generation, wherever it was established, and for instance in a great city such as Antioch or Rome,
Christianity did not constitute synagogues distinct from one another, as," it seems, at least in the absence of proof, and in spite of
certain contrary theories,[5] "the synagogues of the Jews were in
Rome, nor did it constitute autonomous colleges, such as the pagan
collegia. It had as its meeting place the house of some particular
Christian. All the Christians of the city, however great it may have
been, formed one single confraternity or ἐκκλησία, which bore the
name of this city. A cult like that of Mithra developed by cells or
brotherhoods, dividing up regularly when the number of the devo-
tees of the god increased: the law of Christianity, a law which was
constant long before the principle of the monarchical episcopate
was everywhere in force, was that there is only one church in each

---

[3] On the infant church as a hierarchical society, as shown in the Gospels, Acts
and St. Paul cf. above, p. 346 *et seq.*

[4] xvii, 11.

[5] Cf. Bk. I, pp. 33-34.

city, and similarly, that no church in the world is isolated from the others." [6]

Nevertheless, each church lived its own life, without any regular intervention by the action of directing centres through clearly defined organs. Intercommunion for a long time manifested itself above all by the exchange of letters, just as, in the quite primitive time, the great founders of churches, Peter, Paul or John, had assured the nascent tradition and the unity of minds by their letters to so many churches in Asia, Macedonia, Greece or Italy. The letters of Clement of Rome, Ignatius of Antioch, Polycarp of Smyrna, and of the Church of Lyons after the tragedy of 177, played a similar part in the general life of the Church.

§2. THE EPISCOPATE AND THE PRESBYTERATE

The Origins of the Episcopate

But each community, however simple it may have been in constitution in the primitive period, had from the first the essential elements of a real organisation. A council of presbyters or elders governed it, subordinated, in the apostolic period, to the apostle-founder, or his representatives, who were at first itinerant.[1] The fixation of this superior authority is the beginning of the episcopate such as we know it. This is distinctly found quite early in many places. It is evident at Jerusalem from the beginning in the episcopate of James;[2] we find it in Crete with Titus, Paul's disciple, shortly afterwards;[3] the letters of Ignatius show it in existence at Antioch about the year 100;[4] nothing shows that it did not exist at Rome already in the time of the first successors of Peter.

Collegiate or Unitary Episcopate

The collegiate organisation of ecclesiastical government which characterised most of the known churches in primitive times did not, then, exclude the unity of the directing authority. Some have

[6] P. Batiffol, *L'Eglise naissante et la catholicisme*, 1st edn., Paris, 1909, pp. 41-42.
[1] Cf. Bk. I, pp. 33-34.
[2] Cf. Bk. I, p. 300.
[3] *Epist. ad Titum*, i, 5.
[4] Cf. *supra*.

thought that towards the end of the first century Roman Christianity was still governed according to the collegiate system, for when the letter of St. Clement was written to the Church of Corinth in the reign of Domitian, its writer seems to appear therein rather as the chief mandatory of the Church of Rome, in the name of which the epistle is sent, rather than as its head properly so called. The collegiate character, if not of the episcopate itself, at least of the ecclesiastical organisation of Rome in early times, may seem to be confirmed by the tradition registered in the *Liber pontificalis*, according to which the two persons usually presented as the first successors of Peter, Linus and Anacletus, began to preside over the destinies of the Roman Church already in his lifetime. But this tradition is perhaps not anterior to the third century, and even if well founded, it would follow also from it that there was in the college itself a definite hierarchy, for Peter the apostle and his co-adjutors could obviously not be put on the same plane as the others. After Peter, the college of presbyters still had a head, and the great reputation enjoyed by Clement makes it impossible to doubt that if he wrote the letter to the Corinthians, it was not merely as secretary to the Church, as has too easily been inferred from a slightly later work, the *Shepherd* of Hermas,[5] but as its best qualified representative. The early episcopal lists of Rome, moreover, make no difference between the first representatives of the Roman Church and those of the time when the existence of the monarchical episcopate admits of no question. Moreover, a college must always have a president, and it is easily understandable that there was a swift passage from an apparently plural episcopate to a unitary one.

One might indeed think to find an attestation of the existence of the unitary episcopate in the letter of St. Clement itself, for it borrows from the Greek version of the Old Testament the significant terms ἀρχιερεύς and ἱερεύς, and seems to apply these to two kinds of dignitaries, who would be none other than the governors of the Christian communities, the bishop, ἐπίσκοπος and the priests, πρεσβύτεροι. But some question whether Clement had in mind in these passages any hierarchy other than the Mosaic one. Even so, this is figurative of the new. But the distinction between the

---

[5] The *Shepherd* (*Vis.*, II, 4, 3) says that it was Clement's office to correspond with the other churches. There is nothing here which would reduce him necessarily to the functions of a secretary; inter-ecclesiastical relations are the province of the head of a church.

bishop and the presbyteral body, even if not made in works such as the letter of Clement or the *Shepherd* of Hermas, is affirmed in a most striking way almost at the same time in the letters of St. Ignatius of Antioch to the churches of Asia. It is incontestably the monarchical episcopate that these letters proclaim, with a clearness which leaves nothing to be desired, as existing in the greatest metropolis of the East. And they do not speak of it as a new institution, or one which met with any difficulties or opposition in its introduction. The *Muratorian Fragment*, about 150, speaks of Pius the brother of Hermas who wrote the *Shepherd*, as the one bishop of the Church of Rome, and moreover, an ecclesiastical organisation similar to that of Antioch appears in the course of the second century, sooner or later in very different countries, and hence there is reason to believe that if this ecclesiastical organisation did not exist everywhere as such from the beginning, at least it was not something fundamentally unlike the collegiate organisation, and that the latter, under a different appearance, already contained the germ of the future development, from which this naturally and very quickly arose.

It has indeed been suggested that the monarchical episcopate was not really founded until after the middle of the second century, and that its development was connected with the general movement of reaction in the Church against Marcionism,[6] and that the Church only then defined against this heresy its dogmas, its Scriptural canon, and even its hierarchy, concentrating this in the episcopal authority. The theory makes light of the testimony of Ignatius, and requires the inauthenticity of the Ignatian letters. But these letters say nothing of Marcion and the resulting controversy, and the episcopate is represented in them as in possession: how then can they be explained by the anti-Marcionite controversy, or as a defence of an institution which they do not represent as being contested?

The truth is rather, as we have already said, that the explicit distinction between the presbyteral college, and its head the bishop, was made more or less rapidly in different places; towards the middle of the second century it was an accomplished fact almost everywhere.

[6] On the exaggerations of the "Pan-Marcionism" of some contemporary writers, see the next volume. One of the most recent refutations, dealing essentially with the formation of the Scriptural canon, is that of Père Lagrange, *Saint Paul ou Marcion*, in *Revue Biblique*, 1932, pp. 5-30.

The Question of Alexandria

An apparent exception is presented by the Church of Alexandria, where, until about the middle of the third century, the bishop would seem to have been really only the *primus inter pares* in the presbyteral body, the members of which consecrated him. The testimony of the patriarch Eutyches seems definite in this respect.[7] It would follow from this that the Church of Alexandria retained the primitive regime longer than others, and that the distinction between the presbyteral college and its head was less marked than it became subsequently.[8] This peculiarity might be explained by the fact that, until the third century, there was no other bishop in Egypt besides that of Alexandria. Demetrius (189-232), was the first to establish others, for he set up three outside the metropolis. Until then, the sole bishop of Egypt, who had his seat of Alexandria, could not have been consecrated by other members of an episcopate which he alone represented; he would seem to have been consecrated by the co-participants of the apostolic authority residing in the college, the members of which had more power than simple priests have to-day, while those of the bishop were less exclusively concentrated in his person. Things would no longer be the same after Demetrius. A memory of this situation would seem to exist in a passage in the fourth century treatise of uncertain authorship called the *Ambrosiaster,* which mentions the right to confirm, *consignare,* as possessed by the priests of Egypt in default of the bishop.[9]

Similarly the period, vague in duration, in which in Rome also the distinction between the bishop and the presbyteral college would seem to have been less explicit than it was later on, might correspond to the period in which there was no other bishop in Italy besides that of Rome, i.e., down to the middle of the second century. When other episcopal sees were instituted, the holder of one of them consecrated the bishop of Rome, and such would be the origin of the traditional custom by which a newly elected pope, if not already a bishop, is even to-day consecrated by the bishop of Ostia, the first of the suburbican bishops of Rome.[10]

[7] Migne, *P. G.,* CXI, 982.

[8] Thus Timothy, to whom St. Paul entrusted the church of Ephesus, received the imposition of hands of the college of presbyters (*I Tim.,* iv, 14).

[9] *Ambrosiaster,* Eph. 4, 11 *et seq.*

[10] On all this cf. K. Mueller, *Kleine Beiträge zur alten Kirchengeschichte,* in *Zeitschrift für neutestamentliche Wissenschaft,* Vol. XXVIII, 1929, pp. 273-305.

But in reality, how many conjectures are involved in all this! The text of the *Ambrosiaster* has not much weight, for the instances of priests invested with the power to confirm are not rare. The testimony of the patriarch Eutyches is very late, seeing that it belongs only to the tenth century. St. Jerome, much closer to the facts, who also speaks in a letter of the office of the priests in the nomination of the bishop of Alexandria, does not explain whether he is referring to the election or the consecration. Finally, Origen, a compatriot and contemporary of Demetrius, and therefore also of the change of discipline said to have taken place in the mode of consecration of the Alexandrian bishop, makes no allusion whatever to it in his homilies at Cæsarea on the duties and privileges of bishops.[11] It is quite possible, in fine, that the later tradition has here confused election with consecration.

From the moment when the episcopate as we know it was organised everywhere, the bishop appears universally as the authentic head of a church; he is its pastor *par excellence*, its essential priest, without whom the liturgy cannot be celebrated in its integrity, its guide in the faith, its director in discipline, its administrator in the matter of its collective interests, and its representative to those outside.

Priests

The presbyteral college, from which the bishop is not in early days always explicitly distinguished, is composed of the priests, πρεσβύτεροι, or elders. These form the bishop's council, and help him in his liturgical and teaching functions; they take his place when necessary, and particularly when the see is vacant.

In all the churches at the head of which we see in the course of the second century a bishop in action, he seems to be almost everything, and the office of the priests is not, so far as we can judge, comparable with what it becomes later on, except in large Christian communities or where the ineluctable law of the division of labour calls for a more positive collaboration by them.

Certain texts even give the impression that the second order of collaborators of the bishop, inferior in dignity to the priests, namely, the deacons, διάκονοι, servants, had then, if not more real authority,

[11] *In Num., Hom.* 22. Cf. also *Contra Celsum*, VIII, 75.

at least a more effective ministry.[12] The priests will have more importance when the extension of the Christian communities will bring about their division into sections which will be called parishes, παροικίαι, at the head of which certain priests will be placed.

§3. THE OTHER ECCLESIASTICAL ORDERS

The Deacons

The diaconate, the third rank in ecclesiastical order, clearly goes back to the apostolic age. We have seen that it was instituted by the Apostles themselves when, according to the account in the *Acts* (vi, 2 *et seq.*) they chose the seven who were to "serve tables," διακονεῖν τραπέζαις, and laid hands on them. Very soon the care of the poor, which had so greatly preoccupied the Church from its birth, was also entrusted to them.

Hence we get the two fold ministry of deacons in the first centuries: they were the active liturgical auxiliaries of the Church, distributing the Eucharist and conferring baptism with the authorisation of the bishop, and assisting the latter in his administration, particularly in seeing to the interests of the community. This explains why, at a time when practically the whole of the priesthood properly so called was still concentrated in the bishop, the diaconate stood out in greater relief than the priesthood.

Inferior orders were to be created later on, in order to relieve the deacons of a certain number of functions of lesser importance. But they were completely organised only in the third century.

Deaconesses

On the other hand, we note the early disappearance of an institution the existence of which is clear in apostolic times, that of deaconesses, mentioned in the epistle to the Romans (xvi, i), who are probably not distinct from the widows referred to in *I Tim.* (v, 3 *et seq.*), although there must have also been some who were

[12] St. Ignatius, in his letter to the church of the Magnesians, VI, 1, in a symbolical interpretation of the ecclesiastical hierarchy, says that the bishop presides in place of God, the priests in place of the college of the apostles, and the deacons are charged with the ministry of Jesus Christ. The *Didascalia Apostolorum* (see next book) attributes an absolute right to the portion of the oblations not distributed to the faithful to the bishop and the deacons only.

virgins: they devoted themselves to the care of the sick, and the
unfortunate, and to the education of children.

They are mentioned still in the letter of Pliny, who tells Trajan
that he had put two *ministræ* to the torture, to get confessions
from them.

Doctors

Certain Churches, amongst them the greatest such as Rome and
Alexandria, also had teachers or *didascaloi,* who devoted themselves
to religious teaching. The Acts of the Apostles (xiii, 1) and the
epistles of St. Paul (*I Cor.* xiii, 28-31; *Ephes.* iv, 11-12) already
mention them. The *Shepherd* of Hermas refers several times to the
activity of the teachers in the Roman community towards the
middle of the second century. St. Justin the philosopher and other
personages taught about the same time. But in their schools a
teaching was given for which the ecclesiastical authority did not
take the responsibility, though it certainly did not disinterest itself
in it. The Roman schools of the second century were in fact only
private institutions, due to personal initiatives. It is not till a little
later that we find an ecclesiastical school functioning at Alexandria.
This was an advanced school of catechetics whose mission it was to
teach the truths of the faith, not merely to children, but to adult
and educated converts, and placed as it was under the direct control
of the Church, it became an official institution.[1]

Prophets

The Primitive Church had also known "prophets," whom St.
Paul treated with honour; the *Acts* mention the daughters of Philip
as having received the gift of prophecy. But already the *Didache*
seems to mistrust the prophets: they were itinerant preachers, destined to disappear fairly soon, inasmuch as they doubled the existing
hierarchy, and the nature of their ministry involved the risk of
opening their ranks to persons of unequal worth. Thus, although
the *Didache,* while warning readers against the false prophets,
displays a great veneration for those inspired by the Spirit of God,
and although the *Shepherd* of Hermas puts prophets above priests,[2]

[1] On the *didascaloi* cf. *infra,* pp. 545 *et seq.,* and next book.
[2] *Visio,* III, 1, 8.

they very quickly ceased to play a recognised part. Montanism was in the second half of the second century an attempt to restore the reign of prophets in the Church; in spite of its local success in Asia and some sympathy elsewhere, mainly in Africa, it collapsed in presence of the firm resistance of the hierarchy.[3]

Clergy and Laity

The bishop, the presbyteral college and the deacons, then, alone constituted the clergy properly so called, forming in each church a group separate from the rest of the faithful. The separation is not so sharp as it will be later between layfolk and clerics,[4] but the distinction is already shown by the exercise of functions to which in fact not all can aspire. They call for a certain number of particular qualities in those who desire them. The pastoral epistles (II Tim. iii, 21-23; Titus i, 5-9) already excluded those with two wives, i.e., who had married more than once. According to the Didascalia Apostolorum, the episcopate could be received only by those fifty years old, and the priesthood only by those who were thirty. On the other hand, there was no thought in the first two centuries of the obligation of celibacy. The preferences of St. Paul (I Cor. vii, 7, 32-34) for this state are manifest, and he might have appealed to the words of Jesus Himself (Matt. xix, 12) about spiritual eunuchs. But the esteem for continence, however real it may have been in the primitive epoch, did not go so far as to impose it even on those who aspired to holy orders. A married man could receive them without being obliged to renounce conjugal life. On the other hand, quite early—for the practice was established by the third century—ordination deprived one who was then celibate of the right to marry subsequently, at least unless he renounced the exercise of ecclesiastical functions. But from the second century the state of virginity was in high honour in the Church,[5] and it is not surprising that the idea spread of calling to the priesthood by preference those Christians who were disposed to keep to this state and who were regarded as more perfect.

[3] Cf. next book.

[4] The expression ἄνθρωπος λαικός is already found in the letter of St. Clement (XI, 5).

[5] Cf. St. Justin, Apologia, I, 15; Athenagoras, Legatio pro Christianis, 33; Minucius Felix, Octavianus, 31.

Choosing Clerics; Bishops Elected by the Churches

The choice of the first clerics belonged almost exclusively to the Apostles, and the choice of their successors and of new ecclesiastical recruits to the successors of the Apostles. But the opinion of the ordinary faithful was not without its influence upon this choice, and after the death of the first heads of communities, the latter designated their new pastors. In other words, the bishops were elected by the Churches, but they were usually proposed by the clergy of the episcopal city, and it was for the Christian people then to confirm their choice. The transmission of the episcopal character took place only by the consecration of the new elect by a bishop already in office, allowing for the possibility of survivals of the collegiate episcopate which would explain episcopal consecrations made by a presbyteral body like that of Alexandria, if the existence of such a usage were proved.

§4. ECCLESIASTICAL GEOGRAPHY

Were the forms of religious life and ecclesiastical organisation we have just described found wherever Christians existed?

Episcopal Sees

The answer is in the affirmative, generally speaking, but there were exceptions. Very small Christian nuclei could not constitute themselves into communities possessing all the organs found in more important communities. And in particular, there could not be as many bishops as there were Christian centres.

From the fourth century, the almost general rule will apparently be that to each *civitas* in the Empire in which the faith is solidly established there will correspond an episcopal see. In the second century Christian penetration was not sufficiently advanced to bring this about, and there are reasons for thinking that in a country like Gaul, for example—apart from Narbonne—there was, until the third century, no episcopal see other than that of Lyons, whereas according to the martyrological traditions, the Gospel had been previously preached and received beyond the Gallic metropolis in a degree surpassing that of the ecclesiastical dioceses of the later epoch. For no other bishopric is mentioned then, and other sees seem from the episcopal lists not to go back before the third century. This state of things lasted perhaps longer than is sometimes allowed; [1] it was the most probable in the second century.

The Future Metropolises

At a time when not every city possessed a bishop, the grouping of bishops into ecclesiastical provinces such as it would be later on did not yet exist. But geographical proximity and common traditions already established a natural solidarity between sees in the same region, and we can thus speak of an Asiatic Church, formed by the various Churches of this province, which comprised numerous episcopal cities like Ephesus, Smyrna or Sardis.

It is probable that already in the groups thus constituted, the more venerable antiquity of a particular Church, and sometimes its apostolic foundation, itself not altogether unconnected with the previous importance of the city, gave it a particular prestige and thereby also a particular authority. This was the case with Ephesus, Antioch and Alexandria.

§5. THE ROMAN CHURCH

The Roman Church in the 1st Century

Still more did the Church of Rome enjoy from the first a special position. Because it was the centre of the Greco-Latin world, Rome had attracted the head of the apostolic college and also the Apostle *par excellence* of the Gentiles. Inasmuch as Rome was the last residence of Peter, hallowed for ever by his martyrdom and that of Paul, and occupied the incomparable place of the capital city, whatever sentiments some Christians may have entertained concerning the Empire itself, the Roman Church appears as the senior member of the great Christian family from its first manifestation in history after the deaths of Peter and Paul, although in

---

[1] We shall return in the next book to this question of the Gallic sees before the middle of the third century. It has been the subject of an interesting discussion between Mgr. Duchesne, *Fastes épiscopaux de l'ancienne Gaule*, Vol. I, pp. 29-59, and Harnack, *Mission und Ausbreitung des Christentums*, 2nd edn., Vol. II, pp. 373-397.

fact other Churches may have been older. In the Apostolic period, and so long as James the Lord's brother, who presided over the destinies of the Christian community at Jerusalem, was alive, this latter church, although it never exercised any special authority after the departure of Peter, remained nevertheless the Mother Church, venerated and assisted by the others. On all sides collections were made to give help to its members, who had voluntarily deprived themselves of their possessions by the communal system instituted in the enthusiasm of the first days. But that lasted only for a time. After the catastrophe of A.D. 70, Jerusalem temporarily ceased to exist. The Church which continued that which had been in the Holy City rapidly became isolated in the particularism of the Jewish Christians, and the churches as a whole soon ceased to look towards her. Rome quite naturally came to inherit to the full this spiritual succession, as a more vigorous branch substitutes its strength for that of a trunk which the sap no longer nourishes.

Thus the history of the Church of Rome very quickly overflows its own boundaries, and either by its spontaneous action or by reason of the recourse had to her, she becomes very closely concerned in the happenings in the Church universal.

St. Clement

We see this almost at once after the death of St. Peter. His immediate successors Linus and Anacletus, if they were not, as certain traditions seem to indicate,[1] merely his auxiliaries, did not in any case stand out in much relief; Linus is honoured as a martyr, but we do not know his title to this veneration. But we feel ourselves in the presence of a person of some importance when we come to the one who may be regarded as the real successor of Peter, St. Clement,[2] whose intervention in the ecclesiastical affairs of another Christian community, that of Corinth, and the almost canonical character attributed thereupon to the letter written by him on this occasion, show clearly the prestige and authority of his church.

Let it suffice to recall briefly the facts already set forth.

The community at Corinth, the most important, apparently, at

[1] Cf. *supra*, p. 478.
[2] On the personality of Clement, cf. *supra*, p. 389.

that time in Roman Greece, of which this famous city was the metropolis, was disturbed by serious internal disagreements in the reign of Domitian: some members of the presbyteral college, appointed by the Apostles themselves, were set at nought by a party of young people with a readiness which even gave some scandal to those outside.

The Church of Rome, acting as though from its origin it had been conscious of a mission which, as the sequel shows, was not denied, considered it its duty to make its voice heard. It had itself hardly emerged from a difficult time—for we know that it had been hard pressed towards the end of the reign of Domitian, when about the year 95 it sent to the Church of Corinth three of its members, Claudius Ephebus, Valerius Bito and Fortunatus, to make representations, and to take a letter from Clement, written in Greek, then the language of the Church, recommending fraternal charity and respect for authority.

This letter is truly a noteworthy document, very Roman in character, in which we perceive a kindly Christianity, in no wise hostile to the society in which it is developing, a valuable example of "the wise and positive spirit which ever since those far-off times has animated Roman piety." [3] It is strange that some modern writers see here nothing more than a reflection of the Jewish mentality.[4] Speaking of the evil effects of indiscipline, and the value of obedience, Clement sets forth the ecclesiastical ministry as coming from the Apostles and Christ, and therefore as having the right to be obeyed. Consequently, the guilty faithful of Corinth ought to repent, and certain of them should depart, if peace should require it. "Is there amongst you someone generous, compassionate, and filled with charity? Let such a one say: 'If I am the cause of the sedition . . . I will leave the country, I will go wherever it is desired . . . but let the flock of Christ live in peace with its constituted presbyters!' He who will act thus will gain great glory in Christ, and he will be well received everywhere." [5] The Church will pray for these repentant Christians, and Clement thereupon utters a prayer in which we may see "a specimen of the way in

---

[3] L. Duchesne, *Hist. anc. de l'Eglise*, Vol. I, p. 221.

[4] Bousset, *Kyrios Christos*, Göttingen, 1st edn., 1913; 2nd edn., 1921, pp. 291 et seq. Cf. *supra*, p. 417, n. 1.

[5] 54.

which the leaders of the Christian assemblies developed at that time the theme of the eucharistic prayer." [6] The letter ends with a last exhortation, and salutations.[7]

There is no indication at all that this Roman initiative gave rise to any discontent or surprise at Corinth. True, we do not know how the Corinthian crisis was settled. But the success of Clement's initiative is shown by the fame of his letter, for it was put by its recipients with the books read together with the Scriptures in the Sunday assemblies.

The Testimony of St. Ignatius of Antioch

Shortly afterwards, the pre-eminence of the Roman Church was proclaimed, as we have already seen,[8] by St. Ignatius of Antioch. In a letter he addressed in August, 107, to the Roman Church, he calls it "president of the charity" or "brotherhood," προκαθημένη τῆς ἀγάπης,[9] and this name "agape" was at that time a synonym for the Christian union, or in other words, the Church itself.[10] This presidency was no mere honorary one: Ignatius adds that Rome, which heard the very words of the Apostles Peter and Paul, has the right to guide the other churches in the faith: "You have never deceived anyone; you have taught others; I desire that all that you prescribe by your teaching may remain incontested." [11]

The Testimony of St. Irenæus

The end of the second century echoed its beginning, the West echoed the East, Irenæus, Bishop of Lyons echoed Ignatius of Antioch when, in his *Adversus hæreses*, written under the pontifi-

[6] L. Duchesne, *ibid.*, p. 222.
[7] The best editions of the *Prima Clementis*, thus named to distinguish it from a second apocryphal letter, are those of Lightfoot, *Apostolic Fathers*, Part I, London, 1890, and of Funk, *Patres Apostolici*, Vol. I, Tübingen, 1901. Cf. *supra*, p. 409, n. 4.
[8] Cf. above, pp. 425-426.
[9] *Rom.*, inscr. On the sense of these words, see Lelong's edn. in *Les Pères Apostoliques*, III, Paris, 1910, pp. 54-55.
[10] The translation of προκαθημένη τῆς ἀγάπης as "which presides over charity," i.e., which is superior by its works of charity, is, although in harmony with the facts, to be rejected. Προκαθημένη requires a concrete complement, designating a place or a collectivity. And we know besides that St. Ignatius currently uses ἀγάπη in the sense of ἐκκλησία (cf. Trall., XIII, i; Phil., XI, 2).
[11] *Rom.*, III, 1.

cate of Pope Eleutherius (175-189) he attributed to the Roman Church a superior pre-eminence, *pontentior principalitas,* which he likewise connected with its foundation by the Apostles Peter and Paul, and by reason of which the other churches ought to be in agreement with it, *convenire.*[12]

The Epitaph of Abercius

Lastly, let us add that a well known text, the epitaph of Abercius, Bishop of Hierapolis in Phrygia Salutaris, under Marcus Aurelius, also gives, in the form of a symbolism which has given rise to many discussions but the sense of which seems now to be beyond question, a witness to the majesty of the Roman Church, the Queen of the Christian world.[13]

Nevertheless, apart from the striking intervention of St. Clement in the affairs of Corinth, the Church of Rome, from the end of the first century to the end of the second, remained like others, modest in its external action, and of the majority of its heads, from St. Clement to Pope Victor, the contemporary of Irenæus, we know very little.

The Roman Pontiffs as Guardians of Doctrine and as Heads of the Church

But that would certainly not be a sufficient reason to deny that the Roman Church had heads at that time. We have said above that the possible survival, perhaps more apparent than real, of the collegiate episcopate during a time difficult to determine, would not contradict it.[14] On the other hand, a rather strange theory has been advanced in connection with the Roman episcopal lists by a

---

[12] *Adv. hær.,* III, 3, 2 (Migne, P. G., VII, 848-849). [On the interpretation of this passage see Fortescue, *Early Papacy,* London, 1920, pp. 55-7. More detailed discussion in *Dictionnaire de Théologie Catholique,* s.v. Irenée.—Tr.]

[13] "I am the disciple of a holy shepherd, who feeds his flocks of sheep on the mountains and in the plains, who has great eyes whose vision extends everywhere. It is he who taught me the Scriptures worthy of belief. It is he who sent me to Rome to contemplate the royal majesty, and to see a queen in golden vestments and golden sandals." The text of the epitaph, with a summary of the discussion it has aroused, and the literature of the subject down to 1907 will be found in the article *Abercius* in the *Dictionnaire d'archéologie chrétienne* of Dom Cabrol. [Text, translation and photograph of the grave stone are given in S.P.C.K.'s *Texts for Students,* No. 11.—Tr.]

[14] Cf. pp. 478-480.

recent historian of the Papacy, Erich Caspar. Before the publication of the first volume of a *Geschichte des Papsttums*[15] he had written a work entitled *Die ältere römische Bischofliste*[16] in which he maintained that the Roman episcopal list, conserved with more or less important variations in catalogues such as the Philocalian and Liberian and the Chronicle of Eusebius, is the list not so much of heads of the Roman Church as of personages regarded as the guardians of the authentic tradition, whose names could be opposed to those of the heretics; going back as far as St. Peter, they would oppose the innovators by the antiquity of the true doctrine as taught by the Apostles.

This is attractive if it be regarded as an affirmation of the essentially doctrinal character of the ecclesiastical magisterium, but hardly an acceptable thesis if it implies a dissociation of the governing authority and the teaching authority: the list of the popes of the first two centuries would in that case be, not a list of heads of the Church, but of leaders of thought, or hardly more. But those who represented doctrinal tradition had thereby doctrinal authority also, and authority as such could not exist apart from it.

[15] Vol. I: *Römische Kirche und Imperium romanum*, Tübingen, 1930.
[16] In *Schriften der Königsberger gelehrten Gesellschaft*, Jahr 2, 1926, Heft 4.

CHAPTER XII

THE VARIOUS CHURCHES IN THE SECOND CENTURY[1]

§1. THE ROMAN CHURCH

The Episcopal Succession in Rome established from Apostolic Times

However little may be our knowledge of the history of the popes of the first two centuries, we know more of the Roman episcopate than of that of any other Church, for the Roman Church alone has its episcopal succession established without a gap from its apostolic founders.

---

[1] Bibliography.—On the churches of the various parts of the Christian world, consult: F. Lanzoni, *Le origini delle diocesi antiche d'Italia* (*Studi e testi*, 35), Rome, 1923, 2nd edn. under the title: *Le diocesi d'Italia dalle origini al principio del secolo VII*, 2 vols., Faenza, 1927,; F. Savio, *Gli antichi vescovi d'Italia dalle origini al 1300 descritti per regioni. La Lombardia*, 1st part, Bergamo, 1898, 2nd part, 1929 and 1932; F. Ughelli, *Italia sancta*, Re-edited by J. Colegi, 10 vols., Venice, 1717-22; S. A. Morcelli, *Africa cristiana*, 3 vols., Brizen, 1816-7; P. Monceaux, *Histoire littéraire de l'Afrique chrétienne depuis les origines jusqu'à l'invasion arabe*, 7 vols. so far, Paris, 1901-23; Dom A. Leclercq, *L'Afrique chrétienne*, 2 vols., Paris, 1904, 2nd edn. of Vol. I; A. Audollent, *Carthage romaine*, Paris, 1901; A. Toulotte, *Géographie de l'Afrique chrétienne*, 4 vols., Rennes-Paris, 1892 (1); Montreuil-sur-Mer, 1894 (II and III); Rennes-Paris, 1894 (XIV); J. Mesnage, *L'Afrique chrétienne, Evêchés et ruines antiques d'après les manuscrits de Mgr. Toulotte*, Paris, 1912; E. Le Blant, *Inscriptions chrétiennes de la Gaule*, 2 vols., Paris, 1856-65; *Nouveau recueil des inscriptions chrétiennes de la Gaule*, Paris, 1892; *Gallia christiana*, by Dom Denis de Sainte-Marthe and the Benedictines of St. Maur, 13 vols., Paris, 1715-85, completed by B. Hauréau, 3 vols., Paris, 1856, 1860 and 1865; the 13 first volumes reprinted by Dom Piolin, 1870-5; Mgr. L. Duchesne, *Fastes épiscopaux de la Gaule*, 3 vols., Paris, 1894, 2nd edn., 1907, 1910 and 1915; T. Scott Holmes, *Origin and Development of the Christian Church in Gaul during the first six centuries of the Christian Era*, London, 1911; C. Jullian, *Histoire de la Gaule*, Vol. IV: *Le gouvernement de Rome*, Paris, 1914 (ch. xi is devoted to the Christians in Gaul); J. Zeiller *Les origines chrétiennes de la Gaule*, in *Revue d'histoire de l'Eglise de France*, Vol. XII, 1926, pp. 16-34; Dom. L. Gougoud, *Les chrétientés celtiques*, Paris, 1911; Huerner, *Inscriptiones Hispaniæ christianæ*, Berlin, 1871, Supplement, 1900; L. Garcia Villada, *Historia ecclesiastica de Espana*, I, *El cristianesimo durante la dominacion romana*, Madrid, 1929, 2 vols.; Huerner, *Inscriptiones Britanniæ christianæ*, London and Berlin, 1876; Dom H. Leclercq, *L'Espagne chrétienne*, Paris, 1900; Le Quien, *Oriens christianus*, 3 vols., Paris, 1740; V. Chapot, *La province romaine d'Asie*, Paris, 1904; ch. vii deals with the Christian

The Popes of the First Century

But its chronology remains uncertain. A catalogue, the first form of which may go back to the time of Pope Eleutherius,[2] who was a contemporary of the Emperor Commodus, and who died in 189, gives, if St. Peter was really martyred in 64, a total of 125 years for the pontificates of his first twelve successors.

We have already had occasion to say [3] that the first two, Linus and Anacletus, are almost unknown; they were perhaps first the auxiliaries of Peter in the government of the Roman Church, and the transposition to the time of Peter of the twelve years of episcopate attributed to each of them might be the origin of the tradition of the twenty-five years of the Roman episcopate of the Prince of the Apostles. St. Clement, the first successor of Peter who is well known, was a contemporary of Domitian.

The Popes of the Second Century

Next come Evaristus, Alexander, Xystus and Telesphorus, almost all bearers of Greek names, contemporaries of the emperors Nerva, Trajan and Hadrian. Telesphorus alone is known, because of his martyrdom under the reign of Hadrian.[4] Hyginus and Pius, the latter mentioned in the *Muratorian Fragment* about 150, perished under Antoninus.[5]

Anicetus, who succeeded Pius, received in 154 a visit from the illustrious bishop of Smyrna, St. Polycarp. Soter next, under Marcus Aurelius, may have heard in Rome the story of the prodigy of the Thundering Legion.[6] He was replaced by the old deacon

---

church; H. Grégoire, *Recueil des Inscriptions grecques chrétiennes d'Asie Mineure*, in course of publication, Paris, 1922; Heckel, *Die Kirche von Agypten, Ihre Anfänge, ihre Organisation und ihre Entwicklung, bis zur Zeit des Nicenum*, Strassburg, 1918; G. Hanotaux, *Histoire de la nation égyptienne*, Vol. III, 2nd part, *L'Egypte romaine*, by V. Chapot, and 3rd part, *L'Egypte chrétienne et byzantine*, by C. Diehl, Paris, 1933; F. J. A. Hort, *Judaistic Christianity*, London, 1894.

[2] The list of Roman bishops is given by St. Irenæus in the third book of his treatise *Against Heresies*. It is reproduced by Eusebius, *Hist. Eccles.*, V, 6, 1. But it did not indicate the length of each pontificate. On the various catalogues, cf. the article *Listes episcopales* in the *Dictionnaire d'Archéologie chrétienne*.

[3] Cf. *supra*, pp. 479, 488.

[4] Cf. *supra*, p. 394.

[5] Cf. *supra*, p. 397.

[6] Cf. *supra*, pp. 402-403.

of his predecessor, Eleutherius, who became pope before the death of Marcus Aurelius and received the letter from Dionysius of Corinth to the Church of Rome which forms one of the links in the chain of testimonies concerning the Roman apostolate of St. Peter; [7] Eleutherius received also a visit from Irenæus, the envoy of the Church of Lyons,[8] illustrious then because of its martyrs, and whence the Gospel was to spread over a whole portion of Gaul; he was requested to define his position in the matter of Montanism.[9] His pontificate ended only in 189, nine years after the coming of Commodus to the throne.

But it was only his successor, Pope Victor, who saw the pardon granted by the emperor to those condemned to the Sardinian mines, and the precarious but unquestionable improvement in the relations between the Church and the Empire which marked the reign of the last of the Antonines.

§2. THE OTHER CHURCHES IN THE WEST

The Churches of Italy

Besides Rome, several Christian communities in Italy have left traces of their existence before the end of the second century.

We have already spoken of those of Puteoli and of Pompeii, known already in the first century.[1] Christian cemeteries have been discovered at Naples and elsewhere which may go back to the second century. But only two episcopal sees, other than Rome, can claim such great antiquity, and these are Milan and Ravenna.

The seventh bishop of Milan, Mirocles, was present at the synods of Rome and Arles in 313 and 314, and the twelfth bishop of Ravenna took part in the Council of Sardica in 343, and hence the respective founders of these two churches, or at least their first titular bishops, must have lived between 150 and 200. The traditions concerning an apostolate of St. Barnabas at Milan belong to the sphere of legend, like that which makes St. Apollinaris, the Apostle of Ravenna, a disciple of St. Peter.

Also, we know hardly anything more about the history of these

---

[7] Eusebius, *Hist. Eccles.*, II, 25, 8, and IV, 23, 9. Cf. Bk. I, pp. 287-9.
[8] Eusebius, *Hist. Eccles.*, V, 4, 2.
[9] Cf. next book.
[1] Cf. *supra*, p. 360.

Churches before the fourth century besides the fact of their existence and the names of the pastors who ruled them. We must add,
however, so far as Ravenna is concerned, that its Christian community arose in the port of Classe, as is shown by the first episcopal
tombs which are at some distance from the town. Here Orientals
were numerous; [2] and here, as in many other places, they evidently
provided Christian propaganda with its first agents and its first
recruits. But as to the progress which it then made, or its penetration into other parts of Italian territory before the third century,
we are so far unable to say anything. In fact, until that time, the
history of the Church in Italy reduces itself practically to the history
of the Roman Church.

Africa

In Africa before this date we know only of the martyrdom of
the Scillitans and what the catacombs of Hadrumetum suggest
concerning a Christian life which must have begun a long time
previously.[3] But the writings of Tertullian, which are a little later
in date, show African Christianity occupying already such a position in the time of the Severi that it must have counted for something before the end of the Antonines.

Spain and Gaul

In Spain the position is obscure, as we have said. In Gaul, a very
old inscription preserved at Marseilles, and which seems to allude
to martyrs,[4] might well constitute a positive testimony to the diffusion of Christianity on the coasts of Provence before the foundation
of the Church of Lyons. On this church the martyrs in the persecution of Marcus Aurelius bestow an incomparable splendour in the
middle of the second century. St. Irenæus, successor to St. Pothinus,
will bring it a new glory.[5] But from Lyons we know little as to

[2] On these beginnings of the sees of Milan and Ravenna, cf. F. Lanzoni, *Le
origini delle diocesi antiche d'Italia* (Studi e testi, 35, Rome, 1923), pp. 452-75
and 543-60).
[3] Cf. pp. 367-368, 404-405.
[4] Inscription called the Volusian, *C.I.L.*, XII, 480.
[5] Cf. next book.

the progress of the Gospel and Christian life in Gaul down to the period of the Severi.[6]

Britain

Of Roman Britain [7] we know nothing in this period, and the same remark applies to the Illyrian countries. But it is otherwise with the Mediterranean East.

§3. THE CHURCHES OF THE EAST

Greece

We have enumerated above [1] the already numerous churches which have left proofs of their existence in Greece in the first and second centuries. Eusebius has handed on the illustrious name of the first bishop of one of these, Dionysius the Areopagite, the convert of St. Paul, who was put at the head of the Christian community of Athens.[2]

As to their internal life, we know the famous episode which caused the intervention of Clement of Rome at Corinth in the last years of the first century.[3] Some seventy years later, we find at the head of this same Church of Corinth a very prominent personage, Dionysius, who had succeeded a bishop named Primus. Dionysius was consulted from all sides, and his letters were so well thought of that they were collected together.[4] This collection contains amongst others the letter to the Church of Rome, the importance of which we have already pointed out,[5] another to the Church of Sparta, and another to the Church of Athens, which had just passed through a serious crisis. Following the persecution which had removed the bishop Publius in the reign of Marcus Aurelius, the Christians of

[6] Cf. O. Hirschfeld, *Zur Geschichte des Christentums in Lugdunum vor Constantin* (*Sitzungsberichte* of the Berlin Academy, 1895, pp. 381-409) and next book.
[7] The origins of British Christianity are discussed in the next book.
[1] Cf. pp. 364-365.
[2] Eusebius, *Hist. Eccles.*, IV, 25.
[3] Cf. pp. 488-490.
[4] Eusebius, *Hist. Eccles.*, XVIII, 23.
[5] Cf. Bk. I. pp. 286-9.

Athens had almost abandoned their faith; but their new bishop, Quadratus, brought them back once more to the straight path.

Two other hellenic Christian communities, both in Crete, appear also in the correspondence of Dionysius of Corinth: that of Knossos, which had for its bishop Pinytos, an ascetic, and that of Gortyna, whose bishop was called Philip.

These testimonies are all the more valuable because we know little otherwise concerning Christian Greece in the second century. Indeed, it seems that at this time, as in the following century, its history was hardly so full as that of Greek Asia. Perhaps Christianity made slower progress there; it would not be surprising that its propaganda found greater difficulty in overcoming resistance in a country in which the lower classes were most fully penetrated by the traditions of the old Mediterranean polytheism, and whose upper classes were most inclined to rationalistic criticism. Even so, Christian Greece produced in the second century besides Dionysius of Corinth, two apologists,[6] the Athenian Marcianus Aristides, and Athenagoras, perhaps of the same town.[7]

Asia Minor

Asia Minor was more speedily and more thoroughly won to the new faith. The testimony of Pliny the Younger concerning Bithynia in the time of Trajan was repeated half a century later under the pen of Lucian, through whom we learn of the anger of the famous pseudo-prophet Alexander of Abonouteiches at the great number of Christians in Pontus.[8]

Some illustrious personages shed the light of their martyrdom or of their activity as theologians or as preachers on the Asiatic Churches in the second century. Let it suffice to mention the names, most of them already met with, or to appear later on, of St. Polycarp of Smyrna, Papias of Hierapolis, Melito of Sardis, the apologists Quadratus, Apollinaris and Miltiades, Ammias of Philadelphia, Papirius the successor of Polycarp, Sagaris of Laodicea, Thraseas, bishop of Eumenia in Phrygia, martyred at Smyrna.

[6] Cf. *infra*, ch. xiv.

[7] The Athenian origin of Athenagoras is indicated only by Philip of Sidon, whose statement is too late to call for an unreserved acceptance. [But the title of the *Apology* states that Athenagoras was "an Athenian, Christian philosopher." —Tr.]

[8] *Alexander seu Pseudomantis,* 38.

Syria and Palestine

To the south of Asia Minor, Syria occupied a position in the front rank in the Church until the second century. It was at Antioch that Christianity had freed itself from Judaism. We might almost say that the Church became truly what it ought to be only on the day when Paul, joining with Barnabas, the founder of the community at Antioch, organised with him the first distant mission, and when the supreme authorities in the Apostolic college, Peter, John and James, the brother of the Lord, accepted their view and admitted the recruits from the Gentiles without imposing circumcision upon them. The temporary establishment of St. Peter at Antioch confirmed the new state of things. In order to take his place when his own apostolate called him elsewhere, he left there Evodius,[9] who had as his successor St. Ignatius.

Syria from that time, like the Palestinian communities which are naturally grouped with it, figured prominently in the universal Church, with its martyrs, its bishops and its writers.

Aelia Capitolina, the Roman city built in Hadrian's time on the ruins of Jerusalem, had very soon a group of believers mainly of Gentile origin;[10] they had in the middle of the second century a bishop named Marcus;[11] one of his successors, Narcissus, was celebrated in the time of Commodus because of his longevity, his miracles and his sanctity. But whereas the first Christian Church of Jerusalem had always been regarded as the Mother Church, that of Aelia had from its commencement neither particular prerogative nor prestige, and when later on there was established in the Church the provisional organisation which raised the metropolises above ordinary bishoprics, its bishop depended for some time on that of the civil metropolis of the province, Cæsarea in Palestine.

Palestine, like Syria, could boast of illustrious martyrs. St. Simeon of Jerusalem and St. Ignatius of Antioch had laid down their lives out of fidelity to Christ almost at the same time. In the second century, Palestinian Christianity had above all to suffer from the Jews, instigated by Bar Kokhba under Hadrian (132-5).[12]

But it is by the work of religious teaching on the part of several of their members, clerical and lay, that the Syro-Palestinian

---

[9] Eusebius, *Chronicon*, ann. 43; *Hist. Eccles.*, III, 22.
[10] Cf. Bk. I. p. 309.
[11] Eusebius, *Chronicon*, ann. 135.
[12] Cf. *supra*, pp. 389, 395.

Churches left most traces in history in the second century: not to mention the unknown authors of the *Didache* and the *Epistle of Barnabas*, the origin of which is uncertain—it might be Egyptian— Ariston of Pella, St. Justin, born at Flavia Neapolis in Samaria, from whence he went to Rome, Tatian, Theophilus of Antioch and Hegesippus all bear their witness.[13]

Egypt

Christian Egypt was also to shine particularly in the theological domain, and from the second half of the second century, the Catechetical School of Alexandria, destined to become so famous, had begun to function. We know less about the other aspects of the history of the Church in Egypt at the same time. We can only say that Christianity made rapid progress there, for from the beginning of the following century we find it spread over a great part of the valley of the Nile.

§4. THE JUDEO-CHRISTIAN CHURCH

The Christian Community of Pella

There was one ethnic group which retained a character all its own in the Church of the first two centuries: this was that of the Christians who had come from Judaism, known as Judeo-Christians. We know [1] that some of the faithful of Judea who had constituted the community at Jerusalem had taken refuge at Pella in the course of the war which ended in the destruction of the Holy City.[2] But neither this separation nor the disappearance of the Temple were able to break their links with Judaism, and they continued to unite with the practice of the religion of Christ that of a certain number of ancient observances, which they reverently maintained.

Characteristics of the Judeo-Christian Church

This Christian community was, however, not able to retain the prestige possessed by that of Jerusalem: governed by James, the

---

[13] Cf. ch. XIV.
[1] Cf. Bk. I, pp. 306-7.
[2] Eusebius, *Hist. Eccles.*, III, 5.

Lord's brother, until the Sanhedrin had him stoned in 62, and next by Simeon, another near relative of Jesus, the Mother Church had attracted the regard and consideration of all the others. When the sale of the possessions of its first members with a view to the common use of the proceeds soon rendered its material existence difficult, alms poured into it; if the Roman *plebs*, unaccustomed to work and fed by the care of its rulers, lived on the rest of the world, compelled to feed it, this mother of the Churches lived mostly on the charity of the others, but they were free offerings, and it was thought natural to send them.

The situation changed after 70, when Simeon, in presence of the imminent prospect of the ruin of Jerusalem, headed the exodus of his flock towards Pella.

Pella could not claim the prestige of the Holy City, and the particularism of its little Church tended speedily to isolate it. Some few of its members returned, it is true, to Jerusalem, which did not remain a pure desert after 70.[3] It was only after the repression of Bar Kokhba that the history of the old Jerusalem came to a definite end. But the reconstruction of the city under the name of Aelia Capitolina by Hadrian was far from bringing about a general return, the Emperor having forbidden Jews to stay there, and so the Jewish Christians had under these circumstances to keep away. But it is possible, nevertheless, that their pacific spirit, which kept them outside the insurrection, in spite of the assaults of the revolutionaries, and which was calculated to tranquillize the Roman authority, won for some the authorisation to return, or to remain in their ancient city. But the majority remained outside. Some migrated to Kokhaba in Transjordania, to Nazareth in Galilee, and even to Berea (Aleppo) in Northern Syria.[4]

The spirit of these communities continued with its particular characteristics. The representatives of the family of Christ were always held in honour among them. The sons of Jude, the Lord's

[3] St. Epiphanius, *On weights and measures amongst the Jews*, 14-15, ed. Dindorf, IV, 17, says that the fugitives returned from Pella, and that there was once more a small Christian community at Jerusalem, where St. Simeon certainly seems to have been martyred. According to Eusebius, *Chronicon*, ann. 131, this community would seem to have had a certain importance in the time of Hadrian. Cf. Schlatter, *Die Kirche Jerusalem von 70-130*, Gütersloh, 1898, who has utilised rabbinic texts on this subject, and J. Jeremias, *Golgotha*, in ΑΓΓΕΛΟΣ, *Archiv fur neutestamentliche Zeitgeschichte und Kulturkunde*, Beihefte, Leipzig, 1926.

[4] Epiphanius, *Hær.*, XXIX, 7.

brother, who according to the historian of the Judeo-Christian communities, Hegesippus,[5] had had to appear before Domitian, "presided then over the churches"; perhaps one of them succeeded to Simeon, martyred under Trajan. In the third century there were still in the Judeo-Christian centres some of these Δεσπόσυνοι, members of the Lord's family, regarded with great respect.[6]

The Judeo-Christians had their own Gospel, which received the name of the *Gospel according to the Hebrews*. It was related mainly to that of St. Matthew, but differed from it in some ways.[7]

The Judeo-Christian Church, which soon appeared somewhat singular in the group of churches, ended by occupying a border-line position. Thus almost immediately after the death of James, the Lord's brother, a section which was more Judaistic, to the point of claiming to impose the legal observances even on converts from paganism, had opposed to Simeon a rival named Tebuthis: "He began in the people," says Hegesippus,[8] "the work of corruption arising from the seven Jewish sects to which he himself belonged." But the other part of the Judeo-Christians came also to be regarded as a sect, that of the Ebionites, from which it had nevertheless been quite distinct at the beginning of the second century;[9] the name of "Ebionites" took the place or was added to that of "Nazarenes," formerly used to designate the Judeo Christians. This name "Ebionite," which meant "poor," became theirs, either because they were really poor, in accordance with the tradition of the old community of Jerusalem, or else they themselves took this name because of the merit attributed to poverty in the Gospel. But some ecclesiastical writers speak of a certain Ebion as their founder.[10] Whatever may have been the origin of the word, their designation by a particular term making them Christians apart was not unreasonable; the survival amongst them of the Judaism of the early times in a backward state eventually made them a veritable sect. Using only one gospel, and rejecting the epistles of St. Paul,

[5] Cf. Bk. I, pp. 307-8.

[6] Eusebius, *Hist. Eccles.*, I, 7; III, 19 and 20.

[7] On this Gospel, cf. Harnack, *Chronologie*, p. 631, and James, *Apocryphal New Testament.*

[8] Quoted in Eusebius, *Hist. Eccles.*, IV, 22, 5.

[9] Cf. Bk. I, pp. 307-8, and this bk., pp. 389-90, for the circumstances of the martyrdom of Simeon, a victim of heretics, amongst whom the Ebionites must have had their place.

[10] Cf. Tertullian, *Liber de carne Christi*, c. 14; Eusebius, *Hist. Eccles.*, III, 27; Epiphanius, *Contra hæreses*, Hær., XXX.

who was in their eyes an apostate from Judaism, a part of them came to repudiate in addition the belief in the virginal conception of the Lord, and towards the latter part of the second century they already appeared as separated from the great Church.[11]

They gradually grew less in numbers. They existed still as a distinct group in the fourth century, when several Fathers of the Church speak of them in not very favourable terms.[12] They were regarded with curiosity by scholars such as St. Jerome, or students of heresies such as St. Epiphanius, but none regarded their Church as quite pure in doctrine. Yet a certain reunion seems to have taken place between them and the Great Church, and there was doubtless some fusion in the end, "but by individual action. None of the Judeo-Christian communities entered as such"[13] into the ecclesiastical system of the East. It is possible on the other hand that some portions may have been re-absorbed by Judaism.

"Thus ended Judeo-Christianity, obscurely and miserably. The Church, in the measure in which it developed in the greco-roman world, had left its cradle behind it. It had had to emancipate itself from Judeo-Christianity, just as it had had to do from Judaism itself."[14]

[11] Cf. Origen, *In Johannem*, I, 1.

[12] Cf. St. Augustine, *Contra Faustum*, XIX, 4, 17; *Contra Cresconium*, I, 31; St. Jerome, *Epist. ad August.*, 89; Epiphanius, *Hæreses*, XXIX, who regards them frankly as heretics.

[13] Duchesne, *Hist. anc. de l'Eglise*, Vol. I, pp. 127-8.

[14] *Ibid.*, p. 128.

CHAPTER XIII

CHRISTIAN LIFE IN THE FIRST TWO CENTURIES[1]

THE characteristics of various Churches may differ, but the Christian life is one in its essence, and the same signs reveal the Christian everywhere.

§ I. CHRISTIANS AND ORDINARY LIFE

Christians Share in Civil Life

Their name distinguishes Christians sufficiently for them to appear not to be like all the world, yet it did not make them strangers in the city, although some have maintained this.

The author of the valuable work of the end of the second century, the *Letter to Diognetes*,[2] insists [3] that Christians do not differ from their contemporaries either in vesture or in housing or in food,

[1] Bibliography.—Besides the works mentioned in the General Bibliography and those cited in the notes to the preceding chapter, the following may be consulted: G. Bardy, *L'Eglise à la fin du Ier siècle*, Paris, 1932; J. Lebreton, *La vie chrétienne au Ier siècle de l'Eglise*, Paris, 1932; C. Guignebert, *Tertullien, Etude sur ses sentiments à l'égard de l'Empire et de la société civile*, Paris, 1901; G. Boissier, *La fin du paganisme*, I, Paris, 1913, 5th edn., Paris, 1907; Martin-Doisy, *Histoire de la charité chrétienne pendant les six premiers siècles*, Paris, 1848; F. Allard, *Les esclaves chrétiens depuis les premiers temps de l'Eglise jusqu'à la fin de la domination romaine en Occident*, 5th edn., Paris, 1914; *Dix leçons sur le martyre*, Paris, 1913; E. Le Blant, *Les persécuteurs et les martyrs aux premiers siècles de notre ère*, Paris, 1893; H. Delehaye, *Martyr et confesseur*, in *Analecta Bollandiana*, Vol. XXXIX, 1921, pp. 20-49 and 50-64; *Les origines du culte des martyrs*, 2nd edn., Brussels, 1933; A. Harnack, *Der Vorwurf des Atheismus in den drei ersten christlichen Jahrhunderten*, Leipzig, 1905; C. M. Kaufmann, *Handbuch der christlichen Archeologie*, Paderborn, 1905, and *Handbuch der christlichen Epigraphik*, Freiburg in Bresgau, 1917; P. de Labriolle, *La réaction paienne, Etude sur la polémique antichrétienne du Ier au VIe siècle*, Paris, 1934; Dom H. Leclercq, *Manuel d'archéologie chrétienne*, Paris, 1907, 2 vols.; O. Marucchi, *Manuale di Archeologia cristiana*, 4th edn. revised by G. Belvederi, Rome, 1933; *Le catacombe romane*, posthumous work published by E. Josi, Rome, 1933; J. Martigny, *Dictionnaire des Antiquités chrétiennes*, 3rd edn., Paris, 1889; J. Wilpert, *Die Malereien der Katakomben Roms*, Vol. I, Text, Vol. II, Plates, Freiburg in Bresgau, 1903, and *I sarcofagi cristiani antichi*, 2 vols. in 4 (text and plates), Rome, 1929-32.

[2] Cf. *infra*, pp. 538-540.

[3] V. 1, 4.

although the interdiction of things strangled and of the blood of animals, derived from the Jews, may have persisted in some communities until this time;[4] in all these matters which concern earthly life, they conform themselves to the customs of their countries. Tertullian, who began to write at the end of the second century, and who describes Christian life as the contemporaries of the last of the Antonines would have seen it, says in his *Apologeticus*, written about 195, addressing the pagans: [5] "We others, Christians, do not live apart from this world; we like you frequent the forum, the baths, the workshops, the shops, the markets, the public places; we follow the professions of sailor, soldier, planter, merchant, we put at your service our labour and our industry."

A typical detail in the martyrological history of the second century confirms these statements of Tertullian: the letter of the Church of Lyons concerning the persecution of 177 narrates that when the population, roused against the Christians, began to molest them in all kinds of ways pending the intervention of the authorities, they expelled them from the baths and the forum, which proves that they had not deserted the public places.

Christians Did Not Object to Military Service

The episode of the Thundering Legion,[6] even if religious enthusiasm had transformed it into an imaginary miracle due to the prayers of Christian soldiers, would even so suffice to prove the existence of Christians in the armies in the Antonine period. After all, had not St. Clement in his letter to the Corinthians in the preceding century spoken of "our legions" and of "our generals," from the standpoint of a Roman?

Tertullian also confirms that the Christian faith did not exclude the calling of a soldier. His own mind may have changed on this point, and the opposite idea and the conduct it leads to will find its disciples. But until the end of the second century, a "conscientious objection" against bearing arms is no more a theme of discussion in literature than it is a current fact in Christian practice.

---

[4] One of the martyrs of Lyons answers the accusation of cannibalism made against Christians by saying that it is strange to accuse of eating human beings those who abstain even from the blood of animals (Eusebius, *Hist. Eccles.*, V, 24).

[5] *Apol.*, 42.

[6] Cf. *supra*, p. 402-403.

§2. CHRISTIANS AND SOCIAL LIFE

Christians and the Life of the Ancient City

Nevertheless, the disagreement which might arise between the duty of the believer and certain obligations of the citizen was the difficult point in the situation of Christians in the city. The close union in the ancient State between civic activity and religious acts unacceptable to those who adored the one God, or of customs which the Gospel morality reproved, such as the combats in the circus, compelled the Christians to renounce a part of social life; it put them in a certain measure on the boundaries of the city. This was a moral semi-secession, incontestable and inevitable, which may have been aggravated by the apocalyptic tendencies of some inclined to prophesy, if not to desire or to prepare for the more or less proximate collapse of the ancient order. But the legitimate authorities of the Church and the most qualified representatives of Christian thought in the first two centuries did not at all stand for this extremism. Only it must be said that for Christians preoccupations of a terrestrial order went to the background, and that there existed among them, in degrees varying according to individual temperaments, a relative lack of interest in social matters, which might well prove a difficulty one day.

But in the second century their number was relatively too small for this partial abstentionism to have much effect, although it already deprived the Roman State of the active concourse of some of its best subjects, in limited domains.

Christian Asceticism

But on the other hand, the Christians made up for this civic failing by providing the example of a conduct better calculated than that of other men to give to human life all its dignity, which is that of a life according to the spirit. For as the Letter to Diognetus says again,[1] Christians live in the flesh, but not according to the flesh. If they avoid spectacles, combats of gladiators and wild beasts, and all the distractions of a similar nature which seem so natural to pagan society, it is because of the cruelty or immodesty of such things and all the disorders inseparable from them.[2]

[1] V, 8, 9.
[2] Cf. Tertullian, De spectaculis.

Christians also showed themselves indifferent to the advantages of riches, or at least they refused to enjoy them selfishly: the good things of the earth are only a means for heaping up better treasure in heaven, and they spend them liberally in the service of those deprived of them. "We who once loved gain," writes St. Justin in his First Apology,[3] "now distribute all we possess, and give to all the needy." Thus Christians condemned unnecessary expenditure, renouncing splendour and luxury in dress, although doubtless some of them allowed themselves a certain licence in this matter. Tertullian [4] criticises the liking, excessive in his view, that too many Christian women retain for the care of the person and the choice of dresses. Rigorists like him go as far as to forbid the use of flowers in the hair, as well as in the ornamentation of tombs.[5]

Circumspection in the personal use of the goods of the world, and also in moral conduct: these are two characteristics distinctive of the true Christian. Alone amongst all the religions, Christianity, maintaining inexorably the law of the apostolic assembly of Jerusalem, has always regarded sexual relations outside marriage as a grave fault. There were even amongst a few a tendency to condemn second marriages. Nevertheless, St. Paul had not only tolerated these, but recommended them for young widows: "I will that the younger should marry, bear children, be mistresses of families, give no occasion to the adversary to speak evil." [6] But the Church did not view a second marriage with a very favourable eye, and she made it an impediment for the reception of holy orders.

§3. CHRISTIAN PRACTICES

Prayer

Pure in their morals, and using earthly goods only for the satisfying of their essential needs and for the benefit of their neighbours, if they really lived according to the Gospel ideal, Christians also gave a large place in their daily life to prayer. Apart from worship properly so called, which was celebrated in common,[1] the faithful

[3] I, 14.
[4] *De cultu feminarum.*
[5] Tertullian, *De corona militis.* Cf. Minutius Felix, *Octavius,* 12, 38; Clement of Alexandria, *Pædagogus,* II, 8.
[6] *I Tim.,* v, 14.
[1] Cf. *supra,* ch. vi.

Christian, in accordance with the Gospel precept,[2] prayed to his heavenly Father in secret. Following the Master, Tertullian recommends the use of the *Lord's Prayer*.[3] The Psalter was also utilised as a prayer book. Prayer was made more particularly in the morning and evening, as also at the third, sixth, and ninth hour (9 A.M., noon and 3 P.M.). This is the origin of the offices of Prime, Terce, Sext, None and Vespers.[4] We must also pray, says Tertullian, before meals and before a bath.[5]

Fasts

The Christian who unites his soul to God in prayer also mortifies his body, the appetites of which endanger this union. He gives himself to penance as well as to prayer. Fasting, the practice of which associates him with the voluntary mortification of Christ in the desert, is the chief ascetical practice.[6]

In the first two centuries, the faithful fasted twice a week, on Wednesdays, perhaps in reparation for the treason of Judas, and on Fridays, in memory of the Passion; these fasts were called stational, from the Latin word "statio," which designated the guarding by soldiers of a military post. To the stational fast there began to be added towards the end of the second century a paschal fast, mentioned by St. Irenæus, which extended to the days immediately preceding the feast of Easter, and particularly Good Friday and Holy Saturday; the fast of forty days in Lent will be a later extension of this practice. These fasts consisted in abstention from all food and even all drink until the ninth hour, that is, until the middle of the afternoon.

Charity

Mortified in his personal life in memory of Christ and to keep in check the ever dangerous pressure of his lower passions, the Christian worthy of this name sought only the good of his neighbour.

Each member of the community was at the service of all, and the

---

[2] *Matt.* vi, 6.
[3] *De Oratione.*
[4] *Ibid.*
[5] *Ibid.*
[6] Cf. Hermas, *Shepherd;* Tertullian, *De jejunio;* Clement of Alexandria, *Strom,* VII, 14.

fulfilling of this duty of charity went from almsgiving, which prevented death from hunger, to encouragement to martyrdom. The Christians of Lyons gave amongst others a very moving example of this.[7] Such mutual love struck the pagans: "See how they love one another," they said,[8] and this is perhaps among the various traits of Christian life, and in spite of all the prejudices which slandered it, the one which was most perceptible, and which people could not help admiring. The chief argument put forward by the apologists of the first centuries in favour of Christianity is, in fine, the exemplary conduct of its followers.

A pure life, a solid piety, a perfect loyalty, and a boundless charity have perhaps done more for the extension of the reign of the Gospel than the most eloquent discourses intended to convert the pagans.

§4. CHRISTIANITY AND HUMANITY

Christianity and Slavery

This unique charity renewed the relations between men to such a degree that it began by a radical transformation of a social institution which seemed to be inherent in ancient society, but the principle of which was nevertheless incompatible with the spirit of Christianity, so that the latter was bound to lead to its disappearance by the extension of its domination. We refer to slavery. St. Paul had already said in the beginning [1] that in the Church there is "neither bond nor free," any more than one can distinguish before God the Jew from the Greek, or man from woman. Physiological, ethnical and juridical distinctions may continue to exist between human beings; but morally they fade away, and all, being equally children of God and "clothed with Christ," [2] "form now only one person in Jesus Christ," and those who had ceased to belong to themselves by reason of their social condition as slaves, recover their liberty in order to give themselves, like the others, to Jesus Christ, who has made them free in making them His. In the eyes of the Church there are no slaves in reality, for the person of a man cannot belong to another man, and it was this ownership of man by man that constituted slavery.

[7] Cf. supra, pp. 399-402.
[8] Tertullian, Apologeticus, 39, 7.
[1] Gal. iii, 28.
[2] Gal. iii, 27.

Nevertheless, in the political and social sphere, the Church did not begin by condemning an institution which she found established, and which as a system of social and economic organisation seemed then quite natural, if not necessary, to almost all the world.

Some Stoic philosophers, rising to a conception hitherto unknown of the value of human personality and of the natural equality of all may well have thought and said that slavery was opposed to them, but these were only theoretical views. Christianity said less, but it spoke in a different tone,[3] and it did more. There was no condemnation for long centuries of the institution, but an implicit denial of its basis, in the doctrine of the divine sonship as St. Paul formulated it. Together with a *de facto* acceptance of the existing social regime there was brought into being a moral system which undermined its basis. In ancient law, the slave, not being a complete person, could not exercise personal prerogatives: the slave, for instance, could not contract a veritable marriage, and the caprice of his master could break up his union. The Church did not sanction such an inferiority, and condemned such abuses of power. Furthermore, she made such an appeal to a charity which, for a true Christian, has all the exigencies of justice, that the master, in his relations with the slave, will renounce the exercise of rights which hitherto had constituted him the veritable master of a person, and not merely of his services.

The slave of a Christian master was doubtless compelled, unlike a servant of our days, to remain in his service; he might receive orders from him, or even severe treatment, which domestic service has known even down to a time near our own, but even so he was a man, towards whom the master had duties higher and more imperious than those dictated by his own interests or those of the city.[4] The day would come when the pressure of this sentiment of

[3] ". . . Let us contrast the doctrine of the Stoics, for instance, with Christian morality. They proclaim themselves citizens of the world, and they add that all men are brothers, having come from the same God. The words were almost the same, but they did not find the same echo, because they had not been spoken in the same tone" (H. Bergson, *Les deux sources de la morale et de la religion*, Paris, 1932, p. 58).

[4] "There are institutions the fruits of which are modified by the very fact that their spirit is improved. Slavery in the house of Pliny or in that of a Christian was similar only in name to slavery in the house of Epaphroditus or of Vedius Pollio. The legal position had not changed: the slave remained theoretically the property of his master, but for the former he was a possession that was prized and protected; he remained for the others a possession, which one used and enjoyed." (O. Lemarié, *Précis d'une sociologie*, Paris, 1933, pp. 91-2.)

the obligation of a master towards one whom circumstances had made subject to him would be so strong that it would bring about the slave's enfranchisement.[5] Enfranchisement multiplied in the last ages of the Roman Empire. Earlier on it was only a counsel and more rare. But this counsel was given very soon, or at least it corresponded to the implicit desire of the Christian spirit.

In any case, both masters and slaves were reminded from the commencement that they ought never to forget in their mutual relations that they are children of the same God, but to fulfil their reciprocal duties one to the other: careful service and submission on the one hand, and kindness on the other. St. Peter, it is true, exhorts the slaves of evil masters—doubtless pagan masters—to a higher virtue: "What glory is it if committing sin and being buffeted for it, you endure? But if doing well you suffer patiently, this is thankworthy before God."[6]

The Epistle to Philemon

We also see St. Paul intervening, with great delicacy, but also with a calm assurance of being heard, in order to obtain the pardon of a slave, Onesimus, who had fled from the house of his master Philemon, a Christian of Colossæ, and had taken refuge near the Apostle, who had converted him. "Perhaps," writes Paul, "Onesimus therefore departed for a season from thee, that thou mightest receive him again for ever, not now as a slave, but instead of a slave, a most dear brother, especially to me, but how much more to thee both in the flesh and in the Lord? . . . Trusting in thy obedience I have written to thee, knowing that thou wilt also do more than I say."[7]

That was an exceptional case, or at least one relatively rare. But the prestige which surrounded the little slave Blandina in the midst of the martyrs of Lyons, and as we shall see later, the sentiments of the Carthaginian matron Perpetua for her slave Felicitas[8] bear

---

[5] "How could the new conception fail eventually to react on the institution itself, to lessen its abuses, and finally to dissolve it? The breathing of a new spirit into a society renders all its rules flexible, and predisposes it to modify their tenor. This first reform, wholly moral, is in fine a change in the inmost recesses of individual wills. Morals are changed before laws" (*ibid.*, p. 92).

[6] I Pet., ii, 20.

[7] *Philemon*, i, 15-21.

[8] See next book.

eloquent witness to the fact that the Church was unaware of any distinction between master and slave in spiritual matters. "Both received from her the same means of personal sanctification, saw opening before them the same possibility of ecclesiastical honours, and underwent the same penances for their sins." [9] The attitude of the Church towards slavery, like the exquisite and magistral note of St. Paul to Philemon, show what was in fact the powerful action of the Gospel which, regenerating men's souls and proclaiming the universal brotherhood of all men in Jesus Christ, created a new society without overturning social institutions.

This universalism is again one of the characteristics of the Christian conception. It was to extend to the whole world: it embraces all humanity, and the immense domain of the Roman Empire was itself transcended. The Church was made for all the earth, whence its name Catholic, which we find already in St. Ignatius [10] about the year 100.

§5. THE PAGAN ATTITUDE TOWARDS CHRISTIANITY

Pagan Hostility

Such is the Christian ideal, in all its grandeur—an ideal evidently, and one which will not be realised by all those who aim at it. Christians, even at a time very close to the "primitive fervour," had their faults, and the earliest writings of Christian literature blame their weaknesses. Christians nevertheless gave to pagans an example of a life surpassing that which usually characterised nature left to itself, good enough for them to notice it, and either to admire it or else to be disturbed by it.

The Accusations by the Populace

"See how Christians love one another," they said; and on more than one occasion, when public calamities happened, they were able to see that Christian charity put itself at the service of all, whether believers, indifferent, or opponents. But principles of living in

[9] Funk-Hemmer, *Histoire de l'Eglise,* Vol. I, p. 312.
[10] *Ad Smyrn.,* VIII, 2.

some respects so new, and which were in so great a contrast with the easy characteristics of current morality as well as contrary to the customs of social conformity, could not fail to lead to an unfavourable reaction on the part of pagan society.

Not only did political authority condemn Christians as men who did not worship the gods of the Empire, and the higher and cultivated classes tend to despise them as groups in which the lower classes predominated and in which culture and refinement were not preponderant, but also the mass of the people, in spite of their admiring wonder provoked by the spectacle of a superhuman charity or of unheard of heroism, suspected almost inevitably, those who followed a life apart, separated from the common religion, of faults and vices, and even of secret crimes, and from suspicion to belief and then on to accusation, the passage was easy.

Atheism, since Christians did not render the homage due by all to the gods of Rome; magic, since they celebrated ceremonies which were known little or not at all; and cannibalism, and by extension, child murder, arising perhaps out of a wrong idea people had of the communion in the Body of Christ; scandalous indecencies again, for that is a charge easily hurled against those whose lives one does not like; such were the current imputations, combined moreover with less dangerous criticisms affecting the cultural practices attributed to Christians through unexpected confusions, such as the supposed adoration of a god with an ass's head—an ancient calumny of which the Jews had been the first victims and which was now revived against the Christians.[1] Who has not heard of the famous *graffito* of the Palatine, a chance inscription traced perhaps at the beginning of the Antonine era, by a sorry jester and representing one crucified with an ass's head, accompanied by the words: "Alexamenos adores his god"? To which the Christian thus teased by a fellow disciple of the imperial pedagogium replies with this tranquil affirmation of his faith: "Alexamenos fidelis." [2]

---

[1] On this, cf. P. de Labriolle, *La réaction paienne*, Paris, 1934, pp. 193-9, which gives more complete data on the question. Complementary indications in C. Cecchelli, *Noterelle sul cristianesimo africano* (*Estratto dal volume 'Studi dedicati alla memoria di Paolo Ubaldi'*; Pubblicazioni dell' Universita cattolica del Sacro Cuore, Ser. V: Scienze storiche, Vol. XVI, Milan, 1937), pp. 197-9.

[2] This very precious relic is conserved in the Kircher Museum in Rome. Bibliography on the subject in *Dictionnaire d'archéologie chrétienne* of Dom Cabrol and Dom Leclercq, Vol. I, p. 2041 *et seq.*

514 THE HISTORY OF THE PRIMITIVE CHURCH

The Prejudices of the Intellectuals

Educated people entertained less inexact ideas about Christianity. Even so we know only too well the readiness with which men and women of the world at all times will believe the most unlikely stories about people who profess ideas which do not square with their own.

But, apart from excessive partiality or credulity, the sentiment entertained on the whole in the high social circles in the Empire in the second century concerning the Christians, most of whom were of humble condition, in spite of the existence of converts from higher levels, and without any claim to intellectual elegance, was one of contempt, tempered sometimes with a little pity, sometimes also with astonishment, like that which Marcus Aurelius felt in view of their desire for martyrdom.[3]

The *literati*, orators or philosophers in high repute under the Antonines, many of whom attained to honours, a Herod Atticus, a Fronto, a Claudius Severus, were also very ill disposed.

The polemic of Celsus, known to us by the refutation which Origen wrote of his pamphlet [4] in the next century, reflects in a way very instructive for posterity the complex sentiments entertained for a long time in the circles of imperial society with regard to Christians, sentiments in which a lack of understanding of the spiritual realities of the Christian life play a large part. Celsus especially criticises Christianity as being "a barbarous and absurd doctrine, suitable for people without culture," [5] and as finding most of its recruits from people of that kind.

Contempt on the part of the aristocracy of mind if not of birth certainly occupies a large place in this anti-Christian prejudice. To this is to be added that of the philosophers, for whom the Christian beliefs lower the Divinity, or are against reason. But Celsus also criticises Christians because "they separate themselves from other men, despise the laws, customs, and culture of the society in which they live," [6] as also knowledge itself. Far from allowing that the improvement in individual morality is in the last analysis good for the State, he sees in the Christian "chimera" only a public danger, for it attacks on points regarded as vital the social edifice, and "the

[3] Marcus Aurelius, *Meditations*, XI, 3.
[4] *Contra Celsum.*
[5] P. de Labriolle, *La réaction païenne*, p. 112.
[6] *Ibid.*, p. 118.

civilisation to which it remains deeply attached." [7] The numerous pagans who, animated with the same spirit as Celsus, continued to put the State, "the defender of the national traditions, and administrator of material goods, in the first place in their preoccupations" [8] could not agree with an affirmation of the superiority of the invisible world over the visible. Such a doctrine was to them unhealthy and even seditious.

It is not to be wondered at, then, that being thus in agreement with a public opinion inspired by mistrust, contempt, or open hostility, the severe legislation which denied to Christians the right to exist and held over their heads a constant threat of death maintained itself so long.

§6. MARTYRDOM

The Frequency of Martyrdom

This explains also why Christians were always thinking of a possible martyrdom, and why we find among them a voluntary preparation for its calm or even joyful acceptance, and amongst many a positive desire for it. These characteristics constituted a definite feature of the life of the Church of the first centuries, and one which was none the less disconcerting to those outside, as it still is for many in our own day.

But in point of fact, during these two first centuries in which, by virtue of the principles of the Neronian decree as interpreted by Trajan, persecution was never more than temporary and sporadic, though in periods of greater frequency and length, martyrdom was not the lot of the majority of the disciples of Christ. Nero made a veritable massacre of Christians at Rome; the executions in Bithynia, in spite of the natural moderation and kindness of Pliny the Younger, made numerous victims, in proportion to the great number of conversions which had taken place in that region; apostasies were likewise not rare there. Lastly, the reign of Marcus Aurelius and the first years of Commodus undeniably constituted a particularly severe phase in the history of the development of Christianity, for in it we see hatred and severities increased against members of the Church in Asia, Greece, Italy, Gaul, and Africa.

[7] *Ibid.*, p. 168.
[8] *Ibid.*, p. 169.

But apart from these critical moments, though the danger never ceased for Christ's faithful, surrounded as they were by an atmosphere of hatred or suspicion, and threatened by an implacable law, yet the passage from hostile intentions to acts which set the law in motion took place only occasionally.

The Number of the Martyrs

Were the martyrs in fact very numerous or not? This has been much discussed. For the first two centuries, when the Church lived under the sign of the Neronian *Non licet,* applied in the sense of Trajan's commentary, and did not suffer from general persecutions but only sporadic attacks many times repeated, the reply to the question is particularly difficult.

Out of the total number of martyrs attested by documents of relatively good standing, such as the *Hieronymian Martyrology,* it is not possible for us to say which ones belonged to these two centuries, for many of them are of unknown or uncertain date. The *Passions* which, for the most part, deal with martyrs appearing in the *Martyrology,* provide only a weak supplement for the historical information contained in the latter, as there is so much in them that has nothing to do with history.

On the other hand, it is at least to be supposed that everywhere there were some Christians who perished for the faith, from the time of Nero to that of Commodus, though their names have not come down to us. We may add that if we could count up all the martyrs, which would certainly be most helpful, this absolute figure would possess its complete significance only if it were accompanied by a relative figure, that is, if we could evaluate the proportion of the martyrs in relation to the total number of Christians. But this figure remains equally beyond our knowledge, and moreover it happily never ceased to vary, since we can affirm—and it is the only affirmation we can make here—that it was ever increasing.

Even so, very different estimates have been given. There is evidently a strong dose of rhetoric in the oft quoted passage in the *Apologeticus* of Tertullian: [1] "We are of yesterday, and we fill your cities, your islands, fortified towns, country towns, centres of meeting, camps, tribes, classes of public attendants, the palace, the

[1] 37.

Senate, the forum; we leave you only the Temples. If we were to withdraw from amongst you, you would be aghast at your solitude." To this has been opposed another statement, made later by Origen, who seems to say that Christians were very insignificant in the midst of the tens of millions of men who peopled the Empire, πάνυ ὀλίγοι.[2]

We also get the impression, when reading the history of the martyrs of Lyons, for instance, of a little flock lost in a great hostile multitude. But how many of the Christians of Lyons were seized by the authorities and sent to their death? The Church of Lyons continued to exist, for it shortly afterwards addressed letters to those in Rome and Asia; a new bishop, Irenæus, took over its government, and the Christian life continued in the capital of the Gauls. It had therefore taken deeper and wider root there than one would be tempted to infer from the account of the persecution.

Moreover, the same Origen who wrote πάνυ ὀλίγοι also uses in another place in the same treatise *Contra Celsum,* the contrary expression, οὐκ ὀλίγοι[3] and Tacitus had already called the Christians of Rome *multitudo ingens.*[4] The singularly rapid progress of Christianity in some regions, as in at least a part of the Asiatic provinces, cannot be doubted, since unbiased pagans such as Pliny the Younger testified to it,[5] and the declarations of Tertullian himself in his *Apologeticus* would have seemed to his readers somewhat of a mockery if the Christians in the western provinces of which he spoke from experience, namely, Italy and Africa, had been only a handful of men.

But the martyrs? We have seen that they shed their blood in all the countries of the Empire, intermittently, without doubt, sometimes in this place only, sometimes in that. At the same time, every imperial kingdom, or almost every one, and every province had its own. And at times, as under Marcus Aurelius, we find some in so many different places that we might almost think that there was then a generalised persecution, even though this was not really the case. All these groups of distinct martyrs together form a total which demands respect.

Besides, it is no mere conjecture that there were also a number,

[2] *Contra Celsum,* VIII, 69.
[3] I, 26.
[4] Cf. *supra,* p. 373.
[5] Cf. *supra,* pp. 391-2.

perhaps a large number, of unknown victims. What liturgical, literary or lapidary text has conserved the name of a single one of the martyrs of Bithynia under Trajan? "How many times already has an archeologist not deciphered on a piece of marble sticking in the earth the names of martyrs that no parchment has conserved?" [6] De Rossi wrote sixty years ago: "The more I continue the study of history and of the monuments of the centuries of persecution, the more I am persuaded that the number is very great of martyrs whose names have not come down to us, and whose anniversaries are not indicated even in the rich and ancient compilation of the *Hieronymian Martyrology*." [7] The ancient inscriptions themselves allude to these anonymous heroes, whose names are known to God, *quorum nomina Deus scit.*

Lastly, this strong sentiment of expectant martyrdom, in which the Christian generations of the first centuries lived, could not be explained if the threat of death, following on denunciations which were at all times possible, had not only overshadowed them but also had over and over again been realised. This is perhaps the most decisive argument in favour of the thesis of the great number of the martyrs, that is, of a relatively very high proportion of Christians compelled to choose between confessing Christ and saving their lives. And that before this terrible choice, confessors were in a great majority over apostates, is a natural inference from accounts such as the Letter of the Church of Lyons on the persecution of 177. The letter of Pliny to Trajan certainly gives a different impression; without saying anything precise as to the respective number of the fearless and the weak amongst the crowd of accused persons brought before his tribunal, he says explicitly that he had succeeded in persuading many to return to the ancient religion, though this does not prevent him from expressing regret at the number of condemnations, still too numerous in his view, which he had had to pronounce. We may believe that the proportion of apostasies in the course of the first centuries and in the various parts of the Roman Empire was so much the higher as the Christian community put to the test was itself more numerous; there is generally more active energy and persevering courage in minorities.

[6] Paul Allard, *Histoire des persécutions pendant les deux premiers siècles*, 3rd edn., Paris, 1903, p. 477.
[7] *Bollettino di archeologia cristiana*, 1875, p. 179.

§7. THE VOLUNTARY EFFACEMENT
OF CHRISTIANS

Christians Compelled to Lead a Retired Life by Pagan Hostility

The constant threat under which they lived during the first centuries certainly had its effect in the voluntary partial withdrawal of Christians from the social life of the time. Causes and effects then, as often, reacted on one another.

Cut off by their beliefs and the precepts they obeyed from a certain number of practices inseparable from public or private life, the Christians appeared to be suspect; this suspicion involved their condemnation by public opinion and the law; this condemnation ended by relegating them to the borders of Society, for sometimes it caused their expulsion, as we see in the popular movements which expelled them from public places, and at others they themselves sought to separate and withdraw themselves from inquiries or dangerous curiosity.

Nevertheless Christians Were Still Found Everywhere

Yet that is only one aspect of things, which may have seemed more striking at certain moments. The reality is often more complex and more resilient than the principles which seem to govern it; and we should be mistaken were we to picture the Christians as reduced to live like hunted animals, and the pagans as always ready to fall upon them.

If Christians were found even close to the throne, in the Palace and the Senate, amongst the representatives of the most prominent families and amongst the philosophers who taught in the Forum, such as the Flavian princes, Apollonius, Justin, and many others, the periods of respite for the various groups of faithful must have lasted for some time, and further, it is clear not only that people did not on every occasion seek for an opportunity to denounce them, but also that the authorities themselves, knowing over and over again the position of various individuals, intentionally shut their eyes to this.

This *de facto* toleration was accompanied by attitudes which were the exact opposite of a lack of interest in Society and public matters.

If Apollonius sat in the Senate, if Justin argued in the Forum, and if other disciples of Christ sat in the municipal curiæ, they evidently did not live as strangers to their city and their times. The statement of Tertullian as to the presence of Christians in all the spheres of general activity thus seems to be confirmed by a certain number of facts.

It remains true, nevertheless, that the rigour of the laws, the hostility of the crowds, or the sarcasms of the upper classes were constantly directed against men whose religion, which admitted no compromise on its doctrine and morality, kept them apart from their fellow citizens. In presence of the ever-threatening danger of an outburst of hatred and violence, and in spite of the acceptance in advance of martyrdom, which the most ardent went so far as to desire, but which the religious authority would not allow to be voluntarily brought about by provocative acts capable of leading to an unhappy increase in official measures against Christianity, it was necessary, if not always to dissimulate, at least not to advertise oneself. In particular, for reasons also of reverence towards the sacred mysteries, it became the custom not to celebrate religious services except when free from indiscreet curiosity.

§8. THE CATACOMBS

Christian Worship in Private

Thus is explained the organisation by Christians of a part of their existence, at least in some places, away from the light, which they must nevertheless have loved like other men. They consented to spend underground the time they devoted to honouring God, so as to keep to themselves, and in periods of greater danger they spent more time there. But we must avoid a serious misunderstanding here: the usage made by Christians of catacombs at Rome and several other places, at Naples,[1] and Sicily,[2] in Tuscany,[3] in Africa,[4]

[1] The catacombs of Naples are among the largest which have been explored, after those of Rome. There are those of St. Vitus, St. Gaudiosus, St. Severus, St. Euphebus, and St. Januarius. In the last mentioned, in addition to numerous inscriptions, paintings have been discovered some of which go back perhaps to the second century. Cf. Schultze, *Die Katakomben von S. Gennaro*, Jena, 1877, and *Bollettino di archeologia cristiana*, 1871, pp. 37-8 and 155-8, the account of the latest excavations by A. Bellucci, *Atti del III Congresso internazionale di Archeologia cristiana*, Rome, 1934, p. 327 *et seq.*, and above all H. Achelis, *Die Katakomben von Neapel*, Leipzig, 1936.

at Alexandria,[5] and in Asia Minor [6] was not at first due to a care for personal safety on the part of people who no longer dared to live in daylight, and it was only progressively that such use became frequent at Rome, if not almost habitual in times of crisis.

Christians had used private houses as their first places of worship, and apart from exceptional cases they were able to continue peacefully until the time of the great persecutions. The fairly numerous conversions among the aristocracy, particularly in Rome, resulted relatively quickly in their putting at the disposition of the Church some of their great houses which, with the atrium, peristyle and long chamber called the tablinum, lent themselves very well to the carrying out of the Christian rites. Penitents could there be separated, as well as catechumens from the faithful; if it was thought desirable, one side could be reserved for men and another for women, and the clergy could be installed in the *alæ* or wings. The use of private houses as places of worship lasted until after the second century, but other places were then also utilised.

The Origin of Catacombs as Cemeteries

The Christian catacombs, which go back to the beginnings of the Church, were not always used for this purpose of worship. They were at first cemeteries.

Christians, who like the Jews always buried their dead and did not cremate them, had two kinds of cemeteries: those in the open air, usually in the East and in Africa, and subterranean cemeteries, which are found above all in the other Western provinces; these were given the name of crypts, *hypogea* or catacombs. This last term, used especially for the underground cemeteries of Rome, which were by far the largest of all, originated in one of them, situated in the neighbourhood of the actual Church of St. Sebastian, a few miles to the south-east of Rome, near to a depression in the ground which had caused it to be named in the Greek language, the official language of the Roman Church until the end of the

---

[2] Chiefly at Syracuse, where the catacombs are still more extensive than those of Naples.

[3] Cf. the nomenclature of the Italian catacombs other than those of Rome, in the *Dictionnaire d'archéologie chrétienne*, Vol. II, 1910, col. 2443-5.

[4] On the catacombs of Hadrumetum, cf. *supra*, p. 367, n. 26.

[5] *Dictionnaire d'archéologie chrétienne*, Vol. II, col. 2442-3.

[6] *Ibid.*, col. 2442.

second century, κατὰ κύμβην, that is, in Latin, *ad catacumbas*. This underground cemetery "of the catacomb" was the only one opened in the Middle Ages, and its name was extended to all the others when these began to be rediscovered in the period that opens with the fifteenth century.[7]

The usage of underground cemeteries was not peculiar to Christians. The Egyptians and Phœnicians had already adopted it, and they had been copied by the Jews. In Italy, the Etruscans, whose eastern origin seems to be more and more clear, had left not far away from Rome numerous necropolises which in their deep caves and neatly hewn passages resembled small catacombs. Lastly, in Rome itself, where the practice of cremation was neither primitive nor general, and where certain families had retained or returned to the practice of burial, there existed some sepulchres which recalled on a smaller scale those of the East; such was the tomb of the Scipios. And the Jews, a large colony of whom had settled in Rome even before the Empire, also had underground burial places which were still more important.

It is not surprising that the Christians of Rome, whose first nucleus had been recruited from amongst the Jews, followed the same usages, and that those of Campania or Sicily did the same. But the Christian catacombs, especially at Naples, Syracuse and Rome, speedily attained to a much greater extension: in Rome, or rather round about it, for the ancient cemeteries were outside the cities, there was a veritable underground city, *Roma sotterranea*, which gradually grew larger, a city of the dead which began at the walls

---

[7] The first methodic explorer of the catacombs in modern times was Bosio, in the seventeenth century. His researches were continued in the second half of the nineteenth century by J. B. de Rossi, whose *Roma Sotterranea cristiana* (2 vols. and 2 vols. of plates, Rome, 1864-7) is still the chief work on the Roman catacombs. An abridged adaptation was published in English by J. Spencer Northcote and W. B. Brownlow in 1879. More recently, several volumes of popular information on the catacombs have been published: A. Perate, *L'Archéologie chrétienne* (the study of the Catacombs forms only a part of this), Paris, 1892; M. Besnier, *Les catacombs de Rome*, Paris, 1909; H. Chéramy, *Les catacombes romaines*, Paris, 1932; J. P. Kirsch, *Le catacombe romane*, Rome, 1933. The important works of Mgr. Wilpert on the paintings in the catacombs and on the sarcophagi, a certain number of which belong to them, are mentioned in the bibliography to this chapter.

Several reviews in various languages published by the different national groups of Friends of the Catacombs give information nowadays on the discoveries and researches which are always being made in the catacombs of Rome and other places.

of the living city, and extended away into the country to limits which we shall probably never know completely.

This extraordinary extension is explained both by the state of the Christians and by their faith. Christians, who believed firmly in the resurrection, had learnt from St. Paul that the body which is to rise again will be a spiritual body, compared to which the body of our earthly life is, as he himself says, like the seed as compared with the future plant. But nevertheless they had a profound respect for the remains of the dead. Such was the origin of the cult of relics, as also of the custom of going to pray near the dead, to meet at their tombs, and even to celebrate a sacred repast there. This was, it is true, merely the continuance of the pagan rite of the funeral banquet, which also implied a belief in another life. Thus Christians possessed a first motive for frequenting their cemeteries, namely, to meet together there and celebrate rites.

The Catacombs become Places of Worship

The insecurity in which they lived, which was at least relative, and sometimes terrible, provided them with another. The friendly houses in which they met in the first period to celebrate divine service doubtless ensured a secrecy which seemed sufficient at first, and also safeguarded those taking part. But though respect for private property was great in Rome, it had to give way to the requests of the public authority. Arrests could be made even in private dwellings.

Amongst the private properties, some were especially sacred, namely, the burial properties. The respect with which Roman law surrounded the dead has received a new proof in the rescript of Augustus, reproduced in a Palestinian inscription recently published,[8] which lays down very severe penalties against the violators of tombs. Now, tombs were, at Rome and many other places at the beginning of Christian history, family properties: great families put their funeral grounds at the disposition of their brethren. The latter knew that not only would their dead be free from profanation there, but also that they themselves would, so to speak, be protected there by the dead. Thus when the Christians descended into the catacombs to celebrate their religious rites, this was not at first in order to hide themselves, although the catacombs provided a

[8] Cf. Bk. I, p. 292, n. 27.

material shelter, but it was both to honour their dead and to put themselves under their protection, which their sepulchres legally offered them, as a moral rather than a material shelter.

Development of the Catacombs

Hence the great development of the catacombs, which soon underwent a tremendous extension.

Their use must have begun from the very first days of Roman Christianity, if we are to believe the tradition according to which St. Peter himself exercised his ministry in the Ostrian cemetery, near the present Church of St. Agnes outside the Walls, on the Via Nomentana.[9] We may, it is true, wonder whether, before they were disturbed, the Christians really adopted the cemeteries as meeting places. But even if the words of Peter did not resound in its galleries, the Ostrian cemetery is undeniably very ancient. The neighbouring catacomb, that of St. Priscilla, on the Via Salaria, the origins of which are linked with the mausoleum of the Acilii Glabriones, likewise goes back to the earliest Christian times.[10]

But others again have a no less venerable past: the Vatican crypt, in which were buried not only St. Peter, but many of his successors down to the end of the second century; the cemetery of Commodilla, on the Ostian Way, in which St. Paul was buried; the cemetery called that of Domitilla, from Flavia Domitilla, niece of Domitian,[11] on the Via Ardeatina; the crypts of Lucina on the Appian Way, put perhaps at the disposition of the young Church by the illustrious convert made by her in the time of Nero from among the high Roman aristocracy, Pomponia Græcina, and which were the starting point of the cemetery of Callistus, the official cemetery of the Roman Church in the third century, where numerous popes were buried. The cemetery of Prætextatus was utilised · in the second century, and the body of a son of St. Felicitas, martyred under Marcus Aurelius, was placed there. Perhaps the first Christian tombs in the catacomb of St. Sebastian are not much less ancient.

[9] Tradition transmitted in a fourth century Passion, the *Acta Marcelli.*
[10] The identification of the cemetery "where Peter baptized," *ubi Petrus baptizabat, ad nymphas sancti Petri,* with the very ancient catacomb of Priscilla, proposed by O. Marucchi, has not received much support. Cf. J. Zeiller, *A propos de l'inscription damasienne de Saint-Sebastien,* in *Bulletin des Amis des Catacombes romaines,* 1933, pp. 272-7.
[11] Cf. *supra,* pp. 383-384.

§9. THE ART OF THE CATACOMBS

The Decoration of the Catacombs

Christians did not content themselves with depositing their dead in tombs, *loculi*, hollowed out from the walls of the long galleries of the catacombs, and framed sometimes in an arcade, *arcosolium*, under which a *mensa* or altar table enabled the Holy Sacrifice to be offered: the catacombs became veritable places of worship, and efforts were made to adorn them.

The paintings with which they were gradually covered count amongst the most precious sources of information left to us by Christian antiquity on the faith and religious life of the first ages of the Church.[1]

Purely Decorative Paintings

At first, these paintings were purely decorative. The pagans, Egyptians, and Greeks, Etruscans and Romans, decorated the underground chambers in which their dead rested. The Jews themselves, so opposed to pictorial ornamentation, set to work at Rome to enliven with paintings the caves of their catacombs. It seemed quite natural for Christians to do the same, and as the decorative motifs of the pagan tombs were much the same as those of their houses, so also was it at first with the Christians. The decorative artists of the houses of the great Roman families which created the first Christian cemeteries were called upon to decorate the catacombs, and they introduced there the then traditional motifs, inherited from Greek art, which we find in many houses at Pompeii, graceful and symmetrical lines, birds, flowers and vases, forming very pleasant wholes, but with nothing specifically Christian.

The same may be said of another kind of painting, full of interest moreover, and equally ancient, portraits and scenes from real life, such as the famous portrait of the fossor Diogenes, or a picture of the distribution of wheat to the people, executed in the catacomb of Domitilla for the college or corporation of the employés of the *annona*, that is, of the victualling service. In another part of

[1] The chief work on the paintings in the catacombs is that by Mgr. Wilpert, *Die Malereien der Katakomben Roms.* We must also mention, concerning the origins of Christian art, W. Elliger, *Zur Entstehung und frühen Entwicklung der altchristlichen Bildskunst*, Leipzig, 1934.

the same cemetery we see the Tiber market, at the foot of the Aventine Hill, but also Christ and the Apostles, in one and the same decoration. Were the artists who executed these works Christians? We cannot say so definitely. But at any rate the inspiration which guided them was at least respectful towards the Christian faith.

Religious Paintings

The paintings of the catacombs soon manifested a more religious inspiration, and the Christian crypts began to reflect the ideas of the first Christians: the religious art, truly original, which arose in the catacombs, came from the piety of the faithful. But this piety, though deep and tender, remained for a long time discreet and, as it were, restrained; during the first centuries it expressed itself only with a pious and perhaps timid reserve and in a veiled manner; it abstained from setting forth always clearly the mysteries with which it dealt, and just as Christ had given a great part of his teaching in the form of parables, which were in fact transparent, so also it expressed itself by symbols, derived in part from traditions anterior to Christianity.

It is thus that in the second century, and still more in the third, Jesus was personified sometimes by the figure of the Good Shepherd, carrying, like the Creophore Hermes, a lamb on his shoulders, at other times by Orpheus, the ideal singer, who had descended to the lower regions and had returned thence. The lamb, who represented first of all the believer, the soul saved by Christ and led to paradise, soon became the divine victim, in accordance with the two evangelical symbols: "Behold the Lamb of God," and "Feed my lambs" (*John* i, 20 and xxi, 15).

Another symbol is the *Orante,* a female figure which, with its eyes upturned towards heaven and its arms raised, seems to implore mercy from God or to thank Him for His benefits; it symbolises also the human soul praying or entering into a blessed immortality, and it remains the most constant and the most traditional representation.

Numerous other representations, always connected with the work of salvation, were in use in the decoration of the catacombs: some, still borrowed from pagan symbolism, like the peacock, the emblem of immortality; the phœnix, the emblem of the resurrection; and the dove, the bird of the goddess of love but now the emblem either of the Holy Spirit or else of the soul; others again ingenious Christian inventions: the dolphin curled round a trident, a deliberate transformation of the cross or *Tau*, under which is also hidden the sign of the Redemption; the fish, whose name in Greek with its five letters forms the acrostic Jesus Christ, Son of God, Saviour; and again the ship, a figure of the Church, and the lighthouse which guides the ship to the harbour, and the anchor, which expresses Christian hope.

Lastly, in addition to symbolic figures, Christian art very soon shows traces of a veritable religious iconography. This primitive art did not confine itself to the one theme of hope in the future life, as though it had the essentially funerary character which was wrongly attributed to it at first. "A more careful interpretation of the paintings in the Roman catacombs as a whole has modified this point of view. From the end of the second century, in the cemetery of Callistus, the Chamber of the Sacraments presents themes which funerary symbolism no longer suffices to explain: what are figured are the essential doctrines of Christianity. . . . Already in the second century the figures appear which are destined to become the very centre of religious iconography: that of Christ and that of the Virgin." [2] Christ here is no longer the Christianised Orpheus or the Good Shepherd of the allegorical paintings; in the cemetery of St. Prætextatus, in which we see him healing the woman with an issue of blood, He has the appearance of a young beardless man with curly hair, clothed in a tunic over which is thrown a pallium enveloping the left arm, leaving the right arm free, and with bare feet.

The figure of the Virgin is fixed equally early. "A celebrated painting in the cemetery of St. Priscilla, which may go back to the middle of the second century, shows the Virgin seated, carrying on her knees the Infant Jesus. . . . Before her a man standing up and draped in a pallium is drawing a star. This scene has been interpreted as a representation of the prophecy of Isaias (ix, 2), who compares the coming of the Messias to the rising of a star." [3]

Other themes in the decoration of the catacombs, directed also towards the religious instruction of the living rather than towards the solace or the commemoration of the souls of the dead, Biblical

[2] L. Bréhier, *L'art chrétien*, 2nd edn., Paris, 1928, pp. 27 and 40.
[3] *Ibid.*, p. 40.

or evangelical episodes, or illustrations of sacramental doctrine, will become frequent, especially a little later on. But already in the end of the first century we can see in the gallery of the Flavians in the cemetery of Domitilla, Daniel in the den of lions, which we find again in the next century in the crypt of Lucina; and in the Capella Græca in the cemetery of Priscilla besides Daniel we have the history of Noel and the sacrifice of Abraham. The history of Adam and Eve painted on the vault of the vestibule of the cemetery of St. Januarius in Naples is of no less antiquity. The same is true of the baptism of Christ in the crypt of Lucina, the resurrection of Lazarus in the Capella Græca, the meeting between Jesus and the Samaritan woman, and the healing of the woman with an issue of blood at St. Prætextatus; and the twofold miracle of the marriage at Cana and the multiplication of the loaves, prefiguring the Eucharist, in a catacomb at Alexandria.[4]

The Sarcophagi

Lastly although the reproduction of the human figure in stone was at first forbidden amongst Christians, as in Judaism, and because of a similar aversion for idolatry, the sarcophagi which were put in the underground caves of the catacombs were finally ornamented with bas reliefs. But the first examples of this Christian sculpture are not met with before the third century. Until then the Christians, reduced like all the world to utilising commercial models from pagan workshops, contented themselves with a plain ornamentation, usually of simple strigils. Very exceptionally they accepted sometimes an Orpheus or an Aaron, or even a Ulysses, attached to the mast of his vessel so as not to give way to the call of the sirens, in which we might see an allegory of the temptation.[5]

As for a Christian architecture, there was no question of such then, for the only places of worship were private houses or the catacombs.

---

[4] A German scholar, P. Styger, in a quite recent work, *Die römischen Katakomben*, Berlin, 1933, thinks it possible to give a much later date for a number of Christian cemeteries in Rome. These would go back only to the third, or more often only to the fourth century, and he thinks that many of their paintings, such as the Eucharistic Banquet, are only the representations of pagan scenes, without religious signification. But that seems to run counter to the evidence.

[5] Cf. J. Wilpert, *I sarcofagi cristiani antichi*, Vol. I, Rome, 1929, pp. 1*-2*.

§10. CHRISTIAN ECONOMY

The Contributions of the Faithful to the Material Life of the Church

During the first two centuries, the Church had for its upkeep only what the faithful put at her disposition. The Christian cemeteries remained private property, which their owners opened to their brethren living or dead. There was as yet no ecclesiastical ownership of property. But we may suppose that it was not the same in the case of goods of other kinds and of money. From the first, the Christian communities had their charitable treasury, filled by the offerings of the faithful. The *Didache* and the *Didascalia* mention the custom, possibly peculiar to the East, of taking to the Church and putting into the hands of the bishop the first fruits of the harvest. The *Didascalia* speaks of tithes. This contribution, which was subsequently to become obligatory, was first of all voluntary, and it does not seem to have been general even in the third century, much less in the second.

The End of the Second Century Marks the End of an Epoch in the History of the Church

But in the history of ecclesiastical property, as in that of the condition of Christians in the Roman Empire, the end of the second century is also the end of an epoch. The reign of the last of the Antonines was marked, for the first time since Nero, by an act of toleration towards the Church, although the previous legislation was not withdrawn. With the Severian dynasty, other initiatives will be taken, which will modify the regime to which the Church is subject. The relations between the Church, which does not cease to make progress, and the Empire, which goes through a deep internal crisis, will be different in the third century from what they were in the second.

CHAPTER XIV

CHRISTIAN APOLOGETICS IN THE SECOND CENTURY[1]

§1. THE ORIGINS OF CHRISTIAN APOLOGETICS

APOLOGETICS, understood in its widest sense, is as old as Christianity; from the first, those who came to preach the good news did their best to prove its truth and answer the objections made against it. Many of the discourses of Christ, especially those He pronounced at Jerusalem and which are reported by St. John, are apologetical; as also are those of St. Peter, St. Stephen, and St. Paul, which we read in the *Acts*. Amongst the writings of the apostolic age, the *Epistle of Barnabas* has a plainly apologetic character. But it was above all in the course of the second century that this class of literature developed, and this calls for a special study.

The Pagan Calumnies

The history of the persecutions suffices to make us realise the necessity of an apologetic effort. Christianity, spreading throughout the Empire, met everywhere with hostility, not only on the part of the authorities, but also that of public opinion. Already in the persecution under Nero, the Christians were regarded by the populace as wretched people who deserved the worst punishments. In the *Acts of St. Polycarp* we find the populace taking the initiative in the measures against the bishop; when he appeared, they called for his death; a similar spectacle took place at Lyons in 177. This hatred had its origin in the calumnies spread everywhere, and

---

[1] Bibliography.—Editions: Dom Maran, 1742, edition reproduced in Migne's *Patrologia Græca*, VI; J. C. T. de Otto, *Corpus apologetarum christianorum sæculi secundi*, Jena, 1847-72, 9 vols. Literary studies: A. Puech, *Les Apologistes grecs du IIe siècle de notre ère*, Paris, 1912; A. Puech, *Histoire de la Littérature grecque chrétienne*, Paris, 1928, Vol. II, pp. 109-234. Theological studies: J. Tixeront, *La théologie anténicéenne*, Paris, 1905, pp. 221-46; J. Lebreton, *Histoire du Dogme de la Trinité*, Vol. II, Paris, 1928, pp. 395-516. Dictionaries: E. Goodspeed, *Index Apologeticus*, Leipzig, 1912. Bibliographical indications special to each author will be given in the course of the chapter.

which for a long time were blindly believed.[2] The deadly and ever-present danger of denunciation compelled the Christians to hide themselves and to conceal from hostile eyes their meetings and their mysteries; but this very reserve caused mistrust; all kinds of suspicion were entertained about them. It was said that in the eucharistic supper a child was butchered in order to drink his blood, and that in the agapes they gave themselves up under cover of darkness to all sorts of disorders; even the terms "brothers" and "sisters" evoked in the pagan imagination the idea of incestuous unions. Minucius Felix in the first part of his *Octavius* sets out to reproduce these accusations, basing himself perhaps on Fronto; this indictment is too long to be given here in its entirety, but it will be useful to give some of its points. We must remember that the pagan into whose mouth Minucius puts his words belongs to the best Roman society and is speaking to Christian friends:

"How can we witness without pain the attacks against the gods made by this miserable, unlawful and fanatical faction? They collect from the scum of the populace ignorant and credulous folk and make them fellow-conspirators; in their nocturnal meetings, after solemn fasts and unnatural repasts, they bind themselves together, not by an oath but by a sacrilege; they are a race which hides itself, and flies from the light, silent in public, loquacious in their retreats. . . . They recognise each other by secret signs, and love each other almost before knowing each other; they are united together by a religion of debauchery, they all call one another brother and sister. . . . It is said that by some unheard-of-folly they adore the head of a filthy animal (of an ass): a fine religion, and one well worthy of them! . . . Their rites of initiation are as detestable as they are known. A child covered with flour, to deceive the uninstructed, is presented to the one to be initiated; the latter, seeing only a floury mass, and thinking his blows harmless, strikes the unseen child and kills him. And then these wicked people greedily drink his blood; they unite themselves together by this sacrifice, and bind each other mutually to silence by complicity in this crime" (*Octavius*, VIII, 3).

These calumnies seem to us as foolish as they are odious, but in the second century they were spread everywhere, even in the most

---

[2] These calumnies, which are reproduced in all the literature of this period, have often been set forth, e.g., by H. Leclercq, article *Accusations contre les chrétiens*, in *Dictionnaire d'Archéologie chrétienne*; Harnack, *Mission und Ausbreitung*, pp. 513 *et seq.*

cultivated circles, and there was no apologist who did not have to refute them.

Anti-Christian Literature

The pagan literature of the second century enables us to follow the progress of this anti-Christian propaganda; by contrast it marks the stages of the Christian conquest penetrating gradually all the classes of greco-roman society and there encountering an opposition which became more violent every day. The Christian Church in its beginnings was recruited above all from the lower classes: "See your vocation, brethren, that there are not many wise according to the flesh, not many mighty, not many noble" (I Cor. i, 26). The little flock kept this appearance for a long time; at the end of the second century again, Christians recognised it and pagans urged it against them.[3] Nevertheless from this date educated circles had been reached by Christian propaganda: this penetration became evident in the reign of Hadrian, and much more so in the second half of the second century.

Pagan literature, which had long adopted a contemptuous attitude, began then to be alarmed: we find about 120 some references in Epictetus, then in Marcus Aurelius, Galen, and Aelius Aristides.[4] From the reign of Marcus Aurelius we get organised attacks: that of Fronto, the tutor to the emperor;[5] in 167 Lucian published his Peregrinus, in which he attacked mainly the Cynics, but also the Christians;[6] about 178 Celsus composed his True Discourse;[7] and all these writers were only the advance guard; behind them the historian sees an army of controversialists: Porphyry, Hierocles, Julian, and hosts of others. The fight continued without respite: it is still going on around us.

Against all these calumnies and attacks, Christians had to defend themselves; they felt the fearful weight of public opinion against

[3] Minucius, Octavius, V. viii, xii; Celsus, apud Origen, I, 27; III, 18, 44; VIII, 75.

[4] Cf. Harnack, Mission, pp. 254 et seq., 517; P. de Labriolle, La réaction paienne, Etude sur la polémique antichrétienne du Ier au VIe siècle, Paris, 1934.

[5] Cf. P. de Labriolle, op. cit., pp. 87-94.

[6] Cf. Zahn, Ignatius, pp. 517-28.

[7] The work has perished, but we find in Origen the whole process of reasoning, and even a great part of the text of Celsus. Cf. on Celsus P. de Labriolle, op. cit., pp. 111-169. On this conflict between the apologists and educated people, cf. Histoire du Dogme de la Trinité, Vol. II, pp. 396-400.

them, but they felt also the tremendous force of a pure doctrine and a holy life. And they did not confine themselves to defence; they attacked the immorality and the superstitions of the pagans.

Jewish Apologists and Pagan Controversialists

In this task they had had forerunners; the Jews first of all who had also defended monotheism and attacked idolatry.[8] Amongst the pagans themselves the apologists could find many criticisms of idolatry and superstitions, to be utilised in their polemic.[9] Thus this polemic is the least original and least solid part in the work of the apologists; but on the contrary, their defence of Christianity is directly based on life; this is what gives it its persuasive force and, to a historian, constitutes the value of its testimony. The first Christian writers felt that they were despised by the educated world around them; but they were aware that they possessed a force which was worth more than all literature, namely, life. "Non eloquimur magna, sed vivimus." [10]

Apologetic of the Martyrs

The martyrs, when called to appear before their judges, endeavoured always to defend before them the cause for which they were to die. Jesus Himself had done the same before Pilate, Stephen before the Sanhedrin, and Paul before Festus; the Acts of the martyrs show that these great examples were duly followed. But this apolgetic, powerful because of the testimony which guaranteed it, could scarcely be developed: the judge usually cut short the words of the prisoner [11] and moreover circumstances did

[8] Cf. M. Friedlander, Geschichte der Jüd. Apologetik als Vorgeschichte des Christentums, Zurich, 1903; in this very full work the most interesting features are taken from Philo and Josephus; for instance, p. 289, Philo, De Cherubim; pp. 154 et seq.: the contrast between the religious festivals of the Jews and those of the pagans.

[9] J. Geffcken devoted himself especially to seek out these pagan sources in the work he has written on Aristides and Athenagoras: Zwei griech. Apologeten, Leipzig, 1907; a learned study, but marred by the author's antipathy against the Christian apologists.

[10] These words are from Minucius Felix (Octav., XXXVIII, 6); they were repeated by St. Cyprian, De bono patientiæ, III.

[11] Thus in the Acts of Justin, the Scillitan martyrs, etc., Apollonius had a certain amount of freedom to expound his belief, and he profited by it; but he was a Roman senator, interrogated by the prætor, and treated by him with consideration which ordinary Christians did not receive.

not permit long speeches. It was therefore opportune and even necessary to compose works which could make known to well disposed pagans the Christian life and teaching. These expositions are of great value for the historian: he finds, for instance, in Aristides, in the *Letter to Diognetus,* or the *Apology* of Justin, excellent descriptions of Christian customs; Justin introduces him into the intimacy of liturgical assemblies, and there he is able to follow all the ceremonies of baptism and the Eucharist.[12] The sincerity of these pages is evident. At the same time, the desire to gain attention and sympathy is not without danger, especially in the exposition of the Christian doctrine: in order to render it, if not acceptable, at least intelligible to the pagans, there will occasionally be a temptation to modify it somewhat; we know how in Josephus the desire to defend Judaism in pagan eyes led more than once to altering its sense, by transforming the Pharisees into Stoics, the Sadducees into Epicureans, etc. The Christian apologists were more circumspect and more sincere, but they were exposed to the same danger, and the historian must bear this in mind.[13]

The Apologies, Their Destination and Their Object

Several of these apologies are addressed to the emperors; it certainly seems that this was not a mere conventional formula, but that the writers of these books had in fact a hope, which may indeed seem chimerical to us, to be read by the emperors, to gain their attention and even their sympathy for Christianity. This desire enables us to understand the effort made by Justin above all in his second Apology, to set forth in Stoic language the Christian theology of the Word, and to make himself thus the more easily understood by the Emperor Marcus Aurelius;[14] hence also in the apology of Athenagoras the delicate flatteries addressed to Marcus Aurelius and Commodus;[15] these first apologists did not adopt towards the emperors the attitude of Tertullian; in the midst of

[12] These descriptions of the Christian liturgy have been reproduced and studied above, p. 463 *et seq.*

[13] Cf. *infra,* p. 560, and *Histoire du Dogme de la Trinité,* Vol. II, pp. 400 *et seq.*

[14] Cf. *Histoire du Dogme de la Trinité,* Vol. II, p. 437 and note 2.

[15] Cf. Puech, *Les apologistes grecs,* p. 5: "When Justin asked the emperors to give the official stamp to his Apology (II, 14), he did not think in his simple mind that such a request was absolutely chimerical, however bold it may have seemed. . . . Why should Athenagoras have multiplied as he did his delicate flatteries of Marcus Aurelius and Commodus, and why should he have insisted on

persecution they believed in the reconciliation of Church and Empire, and worked for it.

Nevertheless, though this official audience was really in view, it was above all the public in general that was to be enlightened. The apologists had come from its ranks, they knew its prejudices and also its miseries, they wished to help it to become Christian, and realised what light and power they could bring to it; that is why they lay so much stress on the holiness of Christian morals, and the moral transformation which comes from Christianity.[16] In this great pagan populace, apologists after Justin single out the philosophic and educated public, and endeavour to reach it. They themselves have so long and so laboriously sought for religious truth; now they have passed from darkness to this wonderful light; they are aware that they possess a truth which the most exalted minds around them had sought but had failed to find; they realise through their personal experience how precious and indispensable this revelation would be to so many troubled minds, and they set it forth to them. This presentation may sometimes seem somewhat clumsy, but too much will not be made of this: it is not the talent of the writer which constitutes the value of these works, but the moral value of the witness; from this standpoint most of them [17] still draw the attention of the reader and please him.

Quadratus

The earliest apologist we know of is Quadratus. He addressed an *Apology* to Hadrian (117-38); we possess of it only a fragment of a few lines, transmitted to us by Eusebius.[18]

---

their justice, their enlightened mind, their philosophy, if he had not had some hope of being read, if not by them, at least by some of the magistrates who persecuted in their name? For such dreams to be abandoned, and for Tertullian to write that the very idea of a Christian Cæsar or of an imperial Christian was an absurdity (*Apol.*, XXI, 24), a progressive disillusionment was required. Not Quadratus or Aristides, not Justin or Athenagoras could have given that trenchant statement of an inexorable conflict; however dark may have been the horizon in their day, their ideas were less proud and more confident."

[16] Justin, *Apol.*, I, xiv, 2; *Aristides*, XV, xvii; *Athenagoras*, XI, xxxiii; *Theophilus*, III, ix-xv; *Minucius Felix*, xxxviii; *Diognetus*, vi.

[17] All of course are not on the same level: one cannot compare Justin with his pupil Tatian, whose defection followed so soon after his *Apology*, which already contained indications of it; but Tatian is an exception in this group of early apologists; the others, so far as we know, remained faithful to the Church.

[18] *Hist. Eccles.*, IV, iii, 2: "The works of our Saviour have always lasted, for they were real: the sick He cured and the dead He raised were not seen merely

Aristides

In the same chapter, Eusebius [19] mentions an apology by Aristides. This work, addressed to Antoninus,[20] was long unknown; it has been rediscovered, in whole or in part, first in an Armenian translation, then in Syriac, and lastly in its original text, in the Lives of SS. Barlaam and Joasaph, in which a Byzantine hagiographer had inserted it.[21]

Aristides begins his work with an exposition of belief in God; a high and pure theodicy, but one which stays on the ground of natural philosophy.[22] Then, setting out to explain the religious beliefs of humanity, he distinguishes four races of men: the Greeks, the barbarians, the Jews and the Christians. This leads him to describe the Christian life, which he does in a beautiful and affecting way: [23]

"Christians are nearer than other people to the truth. For they know God and believe in Him, Creator of heaven and earth, in whom are all things and from whom are all things; who has no other god as com-

---

on the day of their cure or resurrection, but also subsequently; they continued to live during the earthly life of the Saviour, and even after his death they lived a considerable time, so that some of them have continued until our own time."

[19] IV, iii, 3. Eusebius seems however not to have read it: he is mistaken in saying that it was addressed to Hadrian.

[20] Antoninus reigned from 138 to 161; in 147 he associated Marcus Aurelius in the government; the apology of Justin will be addressed to the two emperors; that of Aristides, addressed to Antoninus alone, is therefore previous to 147; this date is moreover confirmed by the description of the Christian life, which seems to indicate a relatively peaceful period, and also by the mention made (viii, 7) of great famines; this last fact seems a reference to the reign of Hadrian (cf. Spart., Had., 21).

[21] An Armenian fragment was discovered in 1878 by the Mechitarists of Venice; the Syrian translation in 1889 by Rendel Harris in the monastery of St. Catherine on Sinai; J. A. Robinson, associated with the publication of this Syrian text, recognised the original in the Lives of Barlaam and Joasaph, ch. 26 and 27 (Migne, P.G., XCVI, 1108-24); this Greek text had indeed been fairly freely translated by the hagiographer; the comparison with the Syriac reveals notable omissions in it. The *editio princeps*, by Robinson and Harris, appeared in 1891 in *Texts and Studies*, I, 1, Cambridge; 2nd edn. without change in 1892. Ed. Hennecke, *Texte und Untersuchungen*, IV, 3, 1893; De Geffcken, 1907. A fair-sized portion found in the Oxyrhynchus papyrus has enabled the chief lacuna in the Greek text to be filled. This fragment was published by H. J. M. Milne in *Journal of Theological Studies* XXV (1923), pp. 73-7; it is translated above.

[22] This philosophy owes much to Stoicism, and also resembles Philo closely.

[23] This picture, which the Syriac version contains in its entirety, was shortened by the Greek hagiographer; the papyrus mentioned above contains the whole of the Greek text except the first lines, and confirms the testimony of the Syriac version.

panion; from whom they have received these commandments which they have graven in their minds and which they keep in the hope of the world to come.

Because of that, they commit no adultery or fornication; they bear no false witness; they deny not the deposits they have received; they covet not that which is not theirs; they honour their father and mother; they do good to their neighbour, and when they judge they judge justly. They adore no idols in human form; whatever they wish not that others do to them they do not to anyone; they eat no food offered to idols because it is impure.

Those who injure them they succour and make their friends; they do good to their enemies; their daughters are pure and are virgins, and avoid prostitution; the men abstain from all unlawful alliances and from all impurity; the women are similarly chaste, in the hope of the great reward in the next world; as for their slaves, if they have any, and their children, they persuade them to become Christians because of the love they have for them, and when they have joined them they call them simply brethren. They adore no strange gods; they are gentle, good, modest, sincere; they love one another; they do not despise the widow, they save the orphan, he who has gives without murmuring to him who has not. When they see strangers, they make them enter into their houses and rejoice at it, recognising them as true brethren, for they call brethren not those who are so according to the flesh, but those who are so according to the spirit.

When a poor man dies, if they know of it, they contribute according to their means to his funeral; if they learn that some are persecuted or put in prison or condemned for the name of Christ, they put their alms in common and send them what they need, and if possible they deliver them; and if there is a slave or a poor man (to be helped) they fast two or three days, and the food which they had prepared for themselves is sent to him, for they consider that they rejoice themselves just as they have been called to joy.[24]

They observe carefully the commandments of God, living holily and justly as the Lord God has instructed them; they give Him thanks every morning and at all hours, for all food and drink and all other goods. And if a pious man dies amongst them they rejoice, they give thanks, they pray for him, and they accompany him as if he were setting out on a journey. And if a child is born to one of them, they give thanks to God, and if the baby dies they give thanks still more for that he has departed without sin. And if a man dies in sin they weep as for one who is gone to receive his punishment.

[24] These two lines are lacking in the Syriac; Milne corrects $\kappa \epsilon \kappa \lambda \hat{\eta} \sigma \theta \alpha \iota$ into $\kappa \epsilon \kappa \lambda \eta \mu \acute{\epsilon} \nu o \iota$ (art. cit., p. 76).

Such are, O king, their laws. What good things they should receive from God they ask from Him, and thus they go through this world until the end of time, because God has subjected all to them. Therefore they are grateful to Him; it is for them that the whole universe has been made, and the creation."

We have purposely translated this beautiful passage here; [25] it is a precious document. Doubtless it has not the literary charm of the *Epistle to Diognetus*; its style is without art, its composition loose and embarrassed; but beneath its somewhat awkward simplicity the Christian life appears pure and sincere, as the Christians made a point of practising it. Tending towards the great reward which God promises them in the other world, they strive to live here below without sin, in joy and gratitude towards God, and in charity towards man. This last feature is particularly striking: in this pagan world "without affection, without mercy (*Rom.* i, 31), what a revelation and what an attraction is this spectacle of a life so full of affection and devotion! [26] Lastly, let us note its first lines: these reveal the source of this very holy life: if Christians live thus it is because they "know God and believe in Him." [27]

The Letter to Diognetus

To this early *Apology* we must join a document the date of which cannot be exactly determined, but which belongs without doubt to the end of the second century, or perhaps to the beginning of the third: the *Letter to Diognetus*.[28] In order to answer the questions

[25] We have translated it from the Greek text of the papyrus; in more than one point the Syriac, which the translators have generally followed, glosses it fairly freely.

[26] But to realise this programme there had to be, especially in the rich, a wonderful fervour; if this enthusiasm died down, it was quickly felt that this duty of assistance was a heavy burden; it is this weakness which was condemned by Hermas, *Shepherd,* Parable ix, 20, 2.

[27] Cf. Puech, *Apologistes,* p. 43: "The best propaganda was the purity and charity of the primitive churches. The best apology was the depicting without rhetoric of these sweet and innocent virtues. We feel ourselves still very close to the apostolic age; we understand that primitive Christianity appears less as a new doctrine than as a new way of spiritual life, and a tremendous hope; and there is so little egotism in this way of speaking of oneself that Aristides succeeded in the most difficult thing in the world: the praise of oneself without surprising anyone."

[28] This epistle was found in one single manuscript, the *Argentoratensis,* 9, of the thirteenth or fourteenth century, burnt with the library of Strassburg on August 24th, 1870. It was put under the name of Justin, together with the

of his correspondent, Diognetus, the unknown author of this little work explains what Christianity is, what are its titles, and why it has appeared so late. The Christian life is described in a page which won the admiration of Renan [29] and of which Tillemont already praised the "magnificent and eloquent style." [30] In the construction of the work, with its parallel and antithetical members, we recognise the influence of St. Paul; [31] we find it still more in the exposition of God's plan, suffering for a long time the injustice of men, and repairing it finally by the incarnation of His Son:

"God . . . conceived a great and ineffable thought, and communicated it only to His Son. While He kept and hid His wise design in mystery, He seemed to forget and to neglect us. When He revealed by His beloved Son and discovered what He had prepared from the beginning, He gave us all things at the same time. . . . Having therefore disposed all things in Himself in union with His Son, He left us to walk as we wished until the present time, in a disordered manner, led on by our pleasures and our passions; not at all that He rejoiced at our faults, but because He bore with them; not that He took pleasure in times past, those times of injustice, but because He was preparing the present time, the time of justice, in order that, having been convinced

---

Discourse to the Greeks. There is a lacuna at the end of chapter 7 and at the end of chapter 10, in the conclusion; chapters 11 and 12 are not authentic. This opusculum is found in the editions of the Apostolic Fathers, or in collections of the apologists.

[29] *Marc-Aurèle*, p. 424. He who could not forgive Christians for having been persecuted by Marcus Aurelius sees nevertheless in the author "an eloquent anonymous but fairly good writer, who reminds us at times of Celsus and Lucian": two unexpected comparisons, which are made mainly for the sake of contrast. For the rest, Renan recovers himself very soon, and after transcribing chapters 5 and 6, he draws from them an argument against the Christians: "When a society of men takes up such an attitude in the midst of the great society, when it becomes in the State a republic apart, even if composed of angels, it is a plague . . ." (p. 428).

[30] *Mémoires*, II, p. 371. Cf. Puech, *Apologistes*, p. 255.

[31] See for instance ch. V: ". . . They (the Christians) live on earth, but are citizens of heaven. . . . They love everyone, and they are persecuted by everyone. They are despised and condemned and put to death, and this ensures their life. They are poor, and they enrich others. They lack all things, and superabound. They are covered with insults, and by insult they attain to glory. They are calumniated, and a moment later they are proclaimed to be just. When harmed, they bless; they answer insult by respect. Doing only good, they are punished like malefactors; when punished they rejoice, as if life were bestowed on them. . . ." (Puech., p. 255). Cf. *II Cor.* vi, 9-10: "(We are regarded) as deceivers, and yet true; as unknown, and yet known; as dying, and behold we live; as chastised, and not killed; as sorrowful, yet always rejoicing; as needy, yet enriching many; as having nothing, and possessing all things."

in the past by our own works that we do not deserve life, we might be judged worthy of it now through the goodness of God, and that having shown that of ourselves we are incapable of entering into the Kingdom of God, we might become capable of it by the power of God. When our injustice was complete, and it had been conclusively proved that the reward in store for it was punishment and death, then came the moment which God had reserved in order to manifest His goodness and His power." [32]

We have here the reply of the apologist to one of the questions put by Diognetus: why did Christianity appear so late? What the author had said before (VII, 2) about the Word sent into the hearts of men seemed to prepare for another solution, that which Justin loved to develop: [33] our apologist has left it on one side, and to this difficult question he knows only the answer of St. Paul: "All have sinned, and do need the glory of God. Being justified freely by His grace, through the redemption that is in Christ Jesus. Whom God hath proposed to be a propitiation, through faith in His blood, to the shewing of His justice, for the remission of former sins, through the forbearance of God, for the shewing of His justice in this time, that He Himself may be just, and the justifier of him who is of the faith of Jesus Christ." [34] This Paulinism is worthy of note in view of the circumstances and the date. [35]

We note on the other hand that, though the apologist speaks of the incarnation of the Word, he does not name Jesus Christ, and says nothing of His life, His miracles, His passion and resurrection. This silence is not peculiar to our author; most of the apologists follow a similar course, reserving doubtless to a later Christian instruction all the Gospel teaching. St. Justin departs from this reserve: while the other apologists stop on the threshold, he enters into the sanctuary of faith and takes his reader with him; for this reason and many others he deserves a specially careful study; it is he above all who will show us not only by his teaching but by the history of his conversion and by his martyrdom, what could be the place and work of an apologist in the second century.

[32] Ch. viii and ix (Puech, p. 258).
[33] Cf. *infra*, p. 551.
[34] *Rom.* iii, 23-26; cf. viii, 32; *Ephes.* i, 7; *I Tim.* ii, 6.
[35] We do not find it elsewhere in the group of apologists; and in the second century, in the Catholic Church, we can hardly recognise this Pauline influence except in Irenæus. But it would be an abuse of language to call the author of our epistle for this reason "a Catholic Marcion," as has been done by Harnack, in his preface to his edition of the Apostolic Fathers, p. 152.

§2. ST. JUSTIN[1]

Life of St. Justin

Of all the Greek apologists, St. Justin is by far the best known. Quadratus and Aristides are nothing more than names; Athenagoras and St. Theophilus do not appear much in their works; Tatian is less in the shadow, but he is known as a restless spirit who after defending the Church became the leader of a sect. Justin on the contrary is revealed in his works; he crowned his life by martyrdom, and his confession is known to us by authentic *Acts*; his friends and disciples, especially St. Irenæus, have testified to his merits and helped us to appreciate his importance. Not only is Justin one of the best known Christians of the second century, but also his apologetic work is the most complete that this period has left to us: the two *Apologies* addressed to the emperors are completed by the *Dialogue with Trypho;* besides the controversy with the pagans we can study the controversy with the Jews, and see in this way not only another side of Christian apologetic, but also another point of view on Christianity.

"Justin, son of Priscos, son of Baccheios, of Flavia Neapolis in Palestinian Syria"; that is how he presents himself in the first line of his *Apology*. He was therefore born of pagan parents, in a pagan city, but in a country which retained many vestiges of its Jewish past, and many memories. Justin left Palestine and went to stay some time at Ephesus; that is where he places his dialogue with Trypho; he dates it in the time of the war of Bar Kokhba (132-5); he was then a Christian; his conversion thus goes back at the latest to about the year 130.

His Conversion

The motives of this conversion have been set forth by Justin himself: in the first pages of his *Dialogue* he narrates his philo-

[1] Editions: Dom P. Maran, Paris, 1742, reproduced in Migne, *Patrologia Græca*, VI; Otto, *Corpus apologetarum sæculi secundi*, I-V, Jena, 1875-1881; L. Pautigny, *Justin, Apologies*, Paris, 1904; G. Archambault, *Justin, Dialogue avec Tryphon*, Paris, 1909, 2 vols. Chief studies: A. Puech, *Les apologistes grecs.*, pp. 46-147; *Histoire de la littérature grecque chrétienne*, Vol. II, pp. 131-70; G. Bardy, art. *Justin* in *Dict. de Théol. Cath.*, especially cols. 2242-62; J. Lebreton, *Histoire du Dogme de la Trinité*, Vol. II, pp. 405-84, and in Cayré, *Manual of Patrology*, Engl. tr., pp. 114 *et seq.* A more complete bibliography will be found in these works.

sophical Odyssey: pressed by the desire to know God, he put himself first of all in the school of a Stoic; but very soon he found that his master "knew nothing about God, and even maintained that this knowledge was not at all necessary." A Peripatetic gladly welcomed him, but very soon asked him for honoraria; a Pythagorean required as an indispensable preparation the study of music, astronomy and geometry. A Platonist who then came upon the scene, fascinated the young man: by considering incorporeal things and contemplating the ideas, Justin thought himself quite ready to attain to the vision of God. But one day when he was walking by the side of the sea, he met a mysterious old man who destroyed his illusions and showed him that the human soul cannot attain by its own powers to the contemplation of God, but that it must be led thereto by the prophets.

Clearly we must not regard this famous page as an autobiography: there is here, as in the recollections of Goethe, "poetry and truth," [2] all in it is not "truth," but also all is not "poetry"; the experiences of Justin are presented as an Odyssey through all the schools of philosophy in order to show their weakness, and to lead the reader to the Christian revelation. But the efforts made by the young Justin cannot be denied; this frequentation of the philosophers who had fascinated him for awhile had not left him merely with the memory of lost illusions; he understood, having once shared it, the enthusiasm of these philosophers, and especially of the Platonists, for the contemplation of the ideal world; he rejected their claim to attain to God by ecstasy, but he did not despise their aims or their endeavours.[3] From the first line of the *Dialogue*, Justin

[2] This is the title which Zahn has given to his study of these chapters: *Dichtung und Wahrheit in Justin's Dialog.*, in *Zeitschrift für Kirchengesch.*, Vol. VIII, 1885-6, pp. 37-66.

[3] Engelhardt (*Das Christentum Justins des Martyrers*, Erlangen, 1878), and still more Aubé (*Saint Justin philosophe et martyr*, Paris, 1861) regarded Justin as a half-converted philosopher who continued to teach within the Church Platonist and Stoic speculations. This is most unfair to Justin. Without going so far as that, P. Pfættisch (*Der Einfluss Platos auf die Theologie Justins*, Paderborn, 1910) thinks that his theology was seriously affected by his Platonist formation; but this thesis also is an exaggerated one. Justin quite realised the fundamental lack of power in Platonism to elevate the soul to the contemplation of God, and the indispensable necessity of the Christian revelation in order to attain to it. It remains true that on some important questions such as those of the transcendence of God and the generation of the Word, he sometimes allows his theology, anxious to utilise Greek philosophy for apologetic ends, to be drawn on to the ground of his opponents. Cf.*Histoire du Dogme de la Trinité*, Vol. II, pp. 422-8, 449, 452-5.

presents himself under their mantle; that is not a disguise, serving to draw to Christianity the Jew Trypho or others; Justin remains a philosopher, but the philosophy he professes has been learnt by him from Christ and the prophets, who in turn received it from God:

"That which we teach, after learning it from Christ and the prophets who preceded him, is the only true doctrine, and more ancient than that of all your writers, and if we ask you to accept it, it is not because it resembles the latter, but because it is true" (*Apol.*, I, xxiii, 1).

The ascendancy of religious truth was revealed to Justin not only by the theology of the prophets, but also by the life of the Christians. This other aspect of his conversion and of his apologetic is hidden in the *Dialogue*, but is brought out in the *Apologies*:

"I myself, when I was a disciple of Plato, hearing the accusations made against the Christians, and seeing them fearless in face of death and of what men dread, I said to myself that it was impossible that they should be spending their lives in sin and in the love of pleasure" (*Apol.*, II, xxii, 1).

These autobiographical fragments complete each other: the *Apologies* show us Justin convinced by the sanctity of Christian morals (*Apol.*, I, xiv), the *Dialogue* presents him as persuaded by the divine truth of Christian doctrine. These are the two great proofs which convinced him, and which he utilises in his turn in order to convert the Jews and the pagans.

St. Justin in Rome

Justin lived at Ephesus apparently for a fairly long time. He went to Rome on two occasions, as he later on tells the prefect of Rome in the interrogatory which preceded his martyrdom; he lived "near to the Baths of Timotheus, with a man named Martin." There he had his school; six of his disciples were arrested and condemned at the same time as himself, about 165, by the prefect Rusticus, their names were Chariton, Charito, Evelpistos, Hierax, Pæon and Liberianus. They were slaves, or poor people, and the school of Justin was never so brilliant as that of Epictetus, or the conferences of Plutarch; it had no such influence as that of Clement of Alexandria or Origen. Yet it is of great interest to the church historian; it throws some light on an important subject of which we know little: the organisation of Christian teaching in the second century.[4]

If this organisation was a slow process, this arose in great part from the character of Christian conversion: "Fiunt, non nascuntur christiani," wrote Tertullian. It was men already formed who came to the faith . . . those born in a believing family were rare, and also those who from their tender infancy received the seal of spiritual regeneration."[5] They were certainly rare, but not exceptional. In the interrogation of Justin's companions, Rusticus said to them: "Was it Justin who made you Christians?" Hierax answered: "I was already a Christian, and I will remain one"; Pæon said: "It was from our parents that we received this splendid profession of faith." Evelpistus replied: "I heard with pleasure the teaching of Justin, but it was from my parents that I also learnt to be a Christian."

These disciples were thus not catechumens; neither were they children: they were grown men who had received the Christian faith from their parents, and wanted to know it better. The instruction moreover was not reserved to Christians; it was offered to all: "to whomsoever was willing to come to me I communicated the doctrine of truth" (Acts, 3). Close to this house of Martin in which Justin lived, a Cynic philosopher named Crescentius likewise held a school. He was jealous of his neighbour the Christian master, and Justin expected to be denounced by him, as in fact happened.[6] Meanwhile he went on arguing: there was a public discussion between the two masters; the report of this had been kept, and in Justin's view it revealed the complete ignorance of Crescentius. The apologist asks the Emperors, if they have not seen the account of the debate, to have the latter renewed in their presence (Apol., II, iii, 4). The challenge was not taken up, and the only testimony the Roman authorities were to receive from Justin was that of his blood.

[4] Cf. Bardy, L'Eglise et l'enseignement pendant les trois premiers siècles, in Revue des sciences religieuses, 1932, pp. 1-28: "The Christian writers of the first three centuries rarely deal with these problems, and leave us almost completely ignorant of the way in which the children of Christian families were brought up and instructed," p. 1.
[5] Bardy, ibid.
[6] Apol., II, iii, 1; Tatian, xix.

The Schools of Rome

These incidents show how Christianity could then be taught, what were its fruits, and also what were its dangers. The latter did not terrify the Christians: in the midst of persecution, Hermas shows us the activity of the teachers in Rome; [7] in the middle of the second century Justin continued their work and extended it. His martyrdom did not destroy the teaching of Christian doctrine; Tatian, a disciple of Justin, continued it.[8] Very soon Tatian fell into heresy and left Rome; Rhodon, his disciple, carried on the teaching. He not only argued with the Marcionites: he also commented on the Hexaemeron and continued the exegetical researches begun by Tatian.[9]

The heretics also taught in Rome: the Marcionites had several schools there, in which divergent teaching was given: Apelles, who acknowledged only one divine principle, was opposed to Syneros who admitted three; [10] then the disciples of Noetus established themselves in Rome, first Epigonus and then his pupil Cleomenes.[11] These schools which sprang up on all sides show the interest aroused in the Church and outside it by theological problems. The bishop of Rome did not fail to interest himself in these matters: some Christians, desirous of following the teaching of Cleomenes, asked permission from Pope Zephyrinus to do so.[12]

It is difficult to determine the subject matter of this second-century teaching, and especially that of Justin. At Alexandria thirty or forty years later, Clement gave to his pupils an encyclopædic formation, and an introduction to all the sciences, sacred and profane. Origen adopted the same method, first at Alexandria and

---

[7] These *didascaloi* were mainly teachers of morals, or at least it was that part of their teaching which appealed to Hermas: *Mand.*, IV, iii, 1; cf. *Vis.*, III, v, 1; *Parables* IX, xv, 14; IX, xvi, 5; IX, xxv,2.

[8] Irenæus, *Hær.*, I, xxviii, 1, quoted by Eusebius, *Hist. Eccles.*, IV, xxix, 3.

[9] *Hist. Eccles.*, V, xiii, 1-8. In this chapter Eusebius quotes some extracts from the polemic of Rhodon against Apelles; he adds (8, cf. 1) that Rhodon admitted that he had been a disciple of Tatian; he mentions a work of his master entitled *Problems;* it dealt with obscurities in the Scriptures. Rhodon promised to solve these problems. This chapter, in spite of its brevity, reveals the nature of Rhodon's teaching: controversy with heretics, and biblical exegesis. These will also be the chief preoccupations of Origen.

[10] *Hist. Eccles.*, V, xiii.

[11] Hippolytus, *Philosoph.*, IX, 7, ed. Wendland, p. 240.

[12] Hippolytus, *loc. cit.*

then at Cæsarea. There is no proof that Justin gave such fulness to his teaching, and it seems hardly likely. It is more probable that he directed all his efforts towards demonstrating and defending the Christian religion; apologetics aiming at converting the Pagans and Jews, and controversy refuting the theses of the heretics, and in particular of Marcion. That is at any rate what we gather from the works of Justin, those which are still extant, those the titles of which are mentioned in ancient writers, and a few fragments. We shall examine this literature shortly, but we must stop a moment more at this little school. Justin was its first master, and he had sufficient influence around him to affect a disciple as independent and presumptuous as Tatian.[13] If we bear in mind again the veneration which a great theologian like Irenæus retained for the Roman master, we shall be careful not to despise the apologist-philosopher.

Works of Justin

We possess only three works of Justin of unquestioned authenticity: the two *Apologies* and the *Dialogue with Trypho*. These works have come down to us only in a single manuscript, which is very imperfect, and contains considerable gaps.[14] This very poor manuscript tradition shows the lack of attention paid for a long time to the antenicene apologists. The controversy which they carried on against the pagans and the Jews seemed pointless later on, and attention was turned by preference towards books with an explicit and richer theology.[15]

Fortunately, this single manuscript has conserved what is of greatest value to us,[16] the apologetic work of Justin. Here we can

[13] Cf. Puech, *Apologistes*, p. 149: "Those who are inclined to despise over much the Christian philosopher of Naplouse should not forget that one who was able to attract to himself a disciple like Tatian must certainly have played a fairly prominent part in Rome, and to have exercised a real influence in some circles."

[14] This is the *Parisinus*, gr. 450, completed on September 11th, 1364. The *Dialogue* should be preceded by a dedicatory letter to Marcus Pompeius and probably also by an introduction; both are lacking. In ch. lxxv there is lacking a fairly large portion, containing the end of the first book and the beginning of the second.

[15] On this manuscript tradition of the apologists, cf. A. Harnack, *Die Ueberlieferung der griech. Apologeten. Texte und Untersuchungen*, I, i (1883).

[16] Among the other works of Justin, he himself mentions (*Apol.*, I, xxvi, 8) a "Treatise against all the Heresies." St. Irenæus mentions (*Hær.*, VI, 2) a treatise against Marcion, which was perhaps only a part of the preceding work. The *Sacra Parallela* have conserved for us some fairly large fragments of a *Treatise on*

study the most interesting and the most complete examples of the great effort of exposition and defence made by the Church in the second century: the *Dialogue* happily completes the *Apologies,* and shows us another aspect of the Christian demonstration.

In the manuscript, the three works present themselves in the following order: *Second Apology, First Apology, Dialogue.* Dom Maran (Paris, 1742) re-established the original order, and all later editors have followed him: [17] the two *Apologies,* or rather the single *Apology* composed of the book first written and of the appendix called the *Second Apology,* were written between 153 and 155.[18] The *Dialogue* is certainly later than the *Apology;* it seems prior to the death of Antoninus (161).[19] All this work thus belongs to the last years of the life of Justin. We find in it all the fruit of his teaching, and better still, the Christian apologetic as it was set forth in Rome towards the middle of the second century. We will now proceed to study this, without attempting to follow the books of Justin in detail.[20]

---

the *Resurrection* (Migne, *P.G.,* VI, 1572-92). This work seems to be attributed to Justin by Methodius; it was probably utilised by Irenæus and Tertullian. Its authenticity appears, if not certain, at least quite probable. Bardenhewer (I, 228) regards it as quite certain; cf. Rauschen-Altaner, *op. cit.,* p. 75; Puech (*Littérature,* Vol. II, pp. 169-70) hesitates.

[17] This order cannot be doubted: the first *Apology* is quoted in the second (IV, 2; VI, 5; VIII, 1). For the rest, this second *Apology* is not a complete and independent work; it forms rather an appendix to the first: as something new became known to Justin, he decided to make use of it without rewriting his work.

[18] Christ was born 150 years previously (I, xlvi, 1); Marcion had already spread his error everywhere (I, xxvi, 5); Felix, the prefect of Egypt (I, xxix 2), was in office in September, 151, probably since 150, and until 154 (Grenfeld-Hunt, *Oxyrhynchus Papyri,* Vol. II, p. 163, cf. p. 175).

[19] The *Dialogue* (xii) mentions the *Apology* (I, xxvi). It seems from this passage that the emperors to whom the *Apology* was addressed were still alive.

[20] Justin's method of composition is rather loose; it is difficult to give an analysis of his books following out all their deviations. We may summarise them thus:

First Apology (cf. Veil, *Justinus des Phil. Rechtfertigung,* Strasburg, 1894):

I-III, Justin explains his object: to enlighten the emperors, to discharge his responsibility, and place it on them.

IV-XII: 1st part or Introduction: the procedure of the persecutors is wicked: they persecute a name (IV-V); Christians are neither atheists nor criminals (VI-VII); they allow themselves to be slain rather than deny their God (VIII); they refuse to adore idols (IX, XIII); conclusion (XII).

XIII-LXVII: 2nd part: Exposition and Demonstration of Christianity. Christians adore God the Creator and Christ crucified (XIII); Christ is their Master; His moral precepts (XIV-XVII); the future life and the judgment (XVIII-XX); Christ is the Incarnate Word (XXI); comparison with pagan heroes

The Knowledge of God

Before his conversion, what Justin sought for everywhere, in all the philosophical sects, was the knowledge of God. When he became a Christian, he found this knowledge there, and strove to possess it more fully and to give it to others. This must be our starting point in our study of his religious thought.

Of the philosophies he had passed through, only one had attracted him: Platonism. This had given him some idea of God, and had promised to reveal Him:

"Plato said that the eye of the soul is thus made, and has been given us in order that we might, through its own transparency, contemplate that true Being who is the cause of all the intelligible beings, who has neither colour nor form, nor size, nor anything of what the eye perceives, but is a being beyond every essence, ineffable and inexpressible, but the solely beautiful and good, and who appears suddenly in well born souls because of an affinity of nature and a desire to see Him." (*Dial.*, IV).

We note first of all in this text a statement of the divine transcendence. This affirmation will always remain an essential element

(XXI-XXII); superiority of Christianity; hatred of men and devils (XXIII-XXVI); purity of Christian morals (XXVII-XXIX); Christianity proved by the prophecies (XXX-LIII); two digressions: freedom and the prophecies (XLIII-XLIV); philosophy considered as Christianity before Christ (XLVI); the similarities we notice between Christianity and the philosophies or pagan mysteries coming from the devils (LIV-LX); description of Christian worship: baptism (LXI); the Eucharist (LXV-LXVI); the Sunday liturgy (LXVII).

Second Apology: injustice of the prefect Urbinus (I-III). Why God allows these evils; providence, freedom, judgment (IV-XII).

The *Dialogue* is much longer than the two Apologies (Migne, *P.G.*, VI, 328-469; 472-800).

I-IX: Introduction: History of his philosophical formation and conversion; the knowledge of God; the immortality of the soul.

X-XXX: The Law. Trypho criticises Justin for not observing the Law. Reply: The prophets teach that the Law has been abrogated; it was given to the Jews only because of their hardness of heart; superiority of the Christian circumcision, necessary for the Jews themselves.

XXXI-CVIII: The Law given by Christ. Christ's two comings (XXXI); the Law a figure of Christ (XL-XLV); divinity and pre-existence of Christ proved especially by the theophanies (LVI-LXII); the Incarnation and virginal conception (LXV-); his death foretold (LXXXVI); his resurrection (CVI).

CVIII-end: Christians; the conversion of pagans foretold by the prophets (CIX-); Christians a more holy race than the Jews (CXIX); the subject of promises (CXXI); figured in the Old Testament (CXXXIV). Final exhortation for conversion (CXL).

in Justin's theology. We see there also the bold claim of Platonism to attain to God by the sole powers of nature; this claim will be rejected by Justin as an illusion. He himself once entertained it,[21] but Christianity corrected him. This is the theme of the first chapters of the *Dialogue*.

If we wish to understand the strength and danger of these illusions, we may recall a few statements by contemporaries of Justin. Apuleius, for instance, says:

"Plato . . . has often repeated that this one Being, by reason of the unbelievable and ineffable greatness of His majesty, cannot be grasped by any speech in any degree, so poor is human language; and that wise men themselves, when they have by great efforts separated themselves from their bodies as far as this is possible, conceive some idea of this God only as a flash of lightning, or the instantaneous bursting forth of a strong light in the midst of the deepest darkness." [22]

"The sovereign Good cannot be explained, but as a result of much intercourse He becomes present to the soul, and suddenly as a spark from a fire, a light shines forth in the soul." [23]

What these philosophers sought for and promised was the vision of God, which was suddenly to shine forth in the soul like a flash of lightning illuminating the night. Such was also the pretension of the mystery religions, but in the mysteries it was the rites of initiation that illumined the initiate; the Platonists thought to arrive at the same result by the desire and energy of the soul. The soul, they said, can attain to this because it has a natural affinity with the Deity (*Dial.*, IV).

It is on this point that Christianity as interpreted by Justin is clearly opposed to Platonism: the human intellect cannot see God unless it is clothed with the Holy Ghost (*ibid.*, IV, 1).

It must be noted, moreover, that what Justin excludes from the natural powers of the soul is the vision of God, not all knowledge of God. The old man who converted Justin to Christianity said to him: "I agree with thee on this point, that souls can know that

[21] "The intelligence of incorporeal things quite enraptured me; the contemplation of the ideas gave wings to my spirit, so that after a little while I thought I had become a wise man; I was even foolish enough to hope that I was going to see God immediately, for such is the aim of the philosophy of Plato" (*Dial.*, ii, 6).

[22] *De deo Socratis.*

[23] *Apud Orig.*, VI, 3. The same hopes are set forth by Maximus of Tyre to whomsoever desires to rise to God: Conference XVII, 9-11; texts quoted in *Histoire du Dogme de la Trinité*, Vol. II, pp. 74-76.

there is a God, and that justice and virtue are beautiful." (IV, 7).

But this knowledge does not suffice for our religious life: what this requires is to know God as one knows a person, not as one knows a science: "to know a man, or to know God, is not the same as to know music, arithmetic and astronomy"; one attains to these sciences "by study or by exercise"; one knows a person "only by seeing him" (III, 6).

But how can we see God? The Platonist philosophers claimed to lead us to ecstasy by the simple play of our natural powers. That is an illusion. Must we then renounce any personal knowledge of God, and consequently, any religious life?

Divine Revelation

This problem, which seemed insoluble, has been answered by God: He revealed Himself to the prophets, and the prophets have made Him known to us:

"There were of old, in earlier times than those of these pretended philosophers, men who were happy, just, and dear to God, who spoke by the Holy Spirit, and uttered oracles concerning the future which are being fulfilled now; they are called prophets. . . . They did not speak with logical proofs; above all such proofs they were worthy witnesses of the truth; and past and present events compel belief in their word. Moreover, the wonders they worked gave them the right to be believed, since they glorified the Author of the universe as God and Father, and announced the Christ who comes from Him, His Son. That, the false prophets filled with the spirit of error and impurity have not done, and do not now; they have the audacity to perform wonders to fill men with amazement, and they glorify the spirits of error and the devils. But above all, pray that the gates of light may be opened to thee; for no one can see or understand if God and His Christ do not give him understanding" (Dial., vii).

This important passage sums up the whole apologetic of Justin: it explains the function of prophecy and miracle, and above all of grace. But before studying more closely the preparation for faith, we must consider for a moment this theory of religious knowledge. It is the first time we find in Christian theology so clear an explanation of the difference which separates divine revelation from human speculation; Justin recognises, as he should, that the human mind can arrive by its natural powers at a knowledge of God; but he shows well that our religious life cannot feed on an abstract knowledge; man must enter into personal relations with God, and if he himself has neither seen nor heard Him, at least he must enter into contact with Him through the intermediary of those who are His witnesses, and the depositaries of His revelations.

This divine origin gives to Christian doctrine an authority which no other teaching can claim:

"That which we teach, after learning it from Christ and the prophets who preceded Him, is the only true doctrine, and more ancient than that of all your writers, and if we ask you to accept it, it is not because it resembles the latter, but because it is true." [24]

Christianity and Philosophy

These categorical affirmations express a very definite aspect of Justin's thought: if he himself has accepted Christianity, and if he presses his readers to accept it in their turn, it is not because Christianity can claim the patronage of philosophers, but because it comes from God, and because it is true in consequence. At the same time, he delights, especially in the *Apology*, to show that the philosophers often resemble Christians by their life, by the persecutions they have undergone, and even by the doctrine they have professed:

"Those who have lived according to the logos are Christians, even though they have been regarded as atheists: such were among the Greeks, Socrates, Heraclitus and their like; amongst the barbarians, Abraham, Ananias, Azarias, Misael, and many others whose names and actions we know, but it would take too long to recall here" (*Apol.*, I, xlvi, 3).

To explain this propagation of Christian principles within paganism, Justin points out first of all that the Word of God enlightens all men.[25] All share in the truth which He teaches; but the Chris-

[24] *Apol.*, I, xxiii, 1. With these texts of the *Dialogue* and the *Apology* we can compare this fragment of the *Treatise on the Resurrection*: "The doctrine of truth is open and free, and does not agree to submit itself to examination. . . . The truth is God Himself, it is from Him that this doctrine comes, and consequently, this freedom is not insolence." Of course, Christian doctrine does not seek to withdraw from examination the proofs of its divine origin, but once this origin has been recognised, the human mind must submit itself to the revelation of God.

[25] "We say that Christ was born a hundred and fifty years ago. . . . It is objected that all those who lived before him were irresponsible; we hasten to resolve this difficulty: Christ is the first-born of God, His Word, in which all men share" (*ibid.*, xlvi, 1-2; cf. II, viii, 1).

tians alone possess it in its fulness; hence the transcendence of their doctrine:

"Our doctrine surpasses every human doctrine, because we have the whole of the logos: Christ, who appeared for us, body, word and soul. For all that the philosophers and legislators have said or managed to discover, they were able to discover and contemplate it thanks to a partial influence of the logos. But because they have not known the whole of the logos, who is the Christ, they have often contradicted themselves" (*ibid.*, II, x, 1-3).

Thus "all that has ever in the whole human race been well said belongs to us Christians (II, xiii, 4); the contradictions and errors which disfigure these truths come from human weakness, which apart from Christianity has received from the Word only a partial communication, and has mixed corruptions with it.[26]

These principles explain and justify Justin's attitude of great sympathy and great independence towards Greek philosophy; he delights to see in its most illustrious masters, Heraclitus, Socrates and above all Plato, disciples of the Word; but no one is a master for him; he will repeat with the old man who converted him: "I do not trouble about Plato or Pythagoras" (*Dial.*, vi, 1). He knows that he has received in Christianity the complete revelation of the Word, of whom the greatest among the pagans received only a partial communication; he delights to discover these portions in them; but he will not be envious of them, knowing that he himself possesses the whole.[27]

The explanation which we have just reproduced enables us to

[26] "I am a Christian and I confess that all my desire and effort is to be recognised as a Christian. Not that the teachings of Plato are wholly foreign to those of Christ, but they are not wholly like them, any more than are those of the others, Stoics, poets and writers. Each of them, indeed, thanks to a partial participation of the divine seminal logos, well realised what was in conformity with (the partial logos he possessed); but as they contradict one another on very important matters, it is clear that they do not possess infallible science and irrefutable knowledge" (II, xiii, 2-3). The conception of the "seminal logos" to which Justin appeals, especially in the second *Apology*, in order to explain this participation, is of Stoic origin; coming from a materialistic and pantheistic philosophy, it retains its impress; Justin does violence to it in order to adapt it to his Christian faith; but he could not entirely succeed. Cf. *Histoire du Dogme de la Trinité*, Vol. II, pp. 434-9.

[27] Amongst the criticisms which the old man makes of philosophy as Justin represents it before his conversion is this: "Is it then the discourse that thou lovest, and not action or truth? Hast thou not a desire to act rather than to reason?" (*Dial.*, iii, 3).

understand the origin of the truths scattered in paganism; it also at the same time reveals the deepest thought of Justin. Yet more than once the apologist has recourse to a hypothesis which the Jews had employed and which Christians had often borrowed from them: if we discover more than one similitude between the doctrines and rites of the pagans and those of the Christians, it is because of conscious or unconscious plagiarism on the part of the pagans. Plato said that God fashioned formless matter in order to make the world; it was from Moses that he learnt this (*Apol.*, I, lix, 1-5). The same applies to the final conflagration, affirmed by the Stoics, after Moses (*ibid.*, lx, 8); "it is not we who reproduce what the others have said, but the others who copy what we say" (*ibid.*, x).[28]

This hypothesis of plagiarism was decidedly weak; Justin received it from his predecessors; he reproduced it, but at least he enriched it with a remark which gives it more value: "Amongst ourselves one can hear and learn these things from those who do not know even how to write; these are ignorant people, barbarous in language, but wise and faithful in spirit . . . and we see well that we have here not a work of human wisdom, but of divine power" (*ibid.*, lx, 11).

Whence comes this transcendence of Christian truth, affirmed with such certitude in face of all the philosophies? Justin affirms that "we alone prove what we affirm." What are these proofs?

The Argument from Prophecy

The fundamental proof for Justin, as for the other apologists of this period, is prophecy. We have already noted this in the preface to the *Dialogue;* the *Apology* is no less explicit. Here is the way in which the argument from prophecy is set forth to the pagans:

"There were amongst the Jews prophets of God, by whom the prophetic Spirit announced in advance future events. The kings who reigned over the Jews in the time of the prophets kept the prophecies as they had been pronounced, in books written in Hebrew by the prophets themselves. Now when Ptolemy, King of Egypt, wished to found a library in which he could gather together the works of all writers, he became aware of these prophecies. He sent to ask Herod,

[28] "The evil spirits have imitated the institution of the Eucharist in the mysteries of Mithra" (lxvi, 4).

who reigned then in Judea, to send him these books. King Herod sent them to him written, as I have said, in Hebrew. As the Egyptians did not understand this language, Ptolemy asked him for men capable of translating these books into Greek. The work was carried out; the books are still to-day in the hands of the Egyptians, and everywhere in the hands of the Jews; but the Jews read them without understanding them. They look upon us as their enemies and opponents, and like you they kill and persecute us when they can. And yet, in the books of the prophets, we see it foretold that Jesus, our Christ, is to come, to be born of a virgin, to arrive at man's age, to heal all sickness and all infirmity, to raise the dead, to be hated, misunderstood, crucified, to die, to rise again, to ascend to heaven. We read that He is, and that He is called Son of God, that men sent by him will preach these things to the whole human race, and that it will be above all the gentiles who will believe in him. These prophecies were made long before his coming, some five thousand years before, others three thousand, others again two thousand or a thousand or eight hundred years; for the prophets succeeded one another from generation to generation" (*Apol.*, I, xxv).

We will not dwell on the strange anachronism which makes King Herod the contemporary of Ptolemy Philadelphus,[29] but we note the value attached by Justin, and by all Christian apologists as well, to the Septuagint translation: In relation to the Jews and pagans it is a very effective instrument; being prior to Christianity and established by the Jews, this Greek text gives to Christian reasoning an incontestable starting point. It is still more important to notice how Justin understands prophecy: he seeks it not only in the books which the Jews recognise as having been written by the prophets, Isaias, Jeremias and others; he finds it throughout the Bible, and first of all in the books of Moses, the "first of the prophets," and the one whom in fact he most frequently quotes. The texts he quotes are not only formal predictions, but quite as often stories the symbolical signification of which refers to Christ. The prophetic argument understood in this way does not depend on a few passages in the Bible, but on the Bible whole and entire; histories, poems, prayers, all tend towards Christ. This conception, inspired by St. Paul, is legitimate and fruitful; in Justin it will sometimes be weakened by questionable interpretations and by un-

[29] On the Septuagint translation and the progressive development of the legend concerning it, see Tramontano, *La Lettera di Aristea a Filocrate*, 1931, pp. 122 *et seq.*

satisfactory arguments, but these faults of detail cannot seriously compromise the value of the whole.

The great importance which the apologist attaches to this argument appears first of all in the way in which he develops it. He devotes to it more than a third of the *Apology* (ch. xxx-liii) and almost the whole of the Dialogue. The form of the argument varies from one work to the other, according to the dispositions of the opponent in view. The pagans do not recognise the Bible as a book inspired by God, and so Justin cannot draw from it an argument from authority as he will do in the case of the Jews; he contents himself, as we have seen, with showing them that the books of the prophets are much anterior to Christ, that the authenticity of the text and the correctness of the translation are guaranteed by the Jews, and that these writings contain prophecies concerning the life of Christ and the expansion of his teaching which can be explained only by their divine origin. It must be remembered that most pagans were very susceptible to this kind of argument; many believed in the oracles of the Greek or Latin religions, and thus were not inclined to reject *a priori* all prophecy.[30]

Certainly the distance was great between these pagan oracles and the Biblical prophecies; and the difference was not less profound between the Stoic divination and the Christian theology of inspiration. But both sides agreed in recognising the reality of the predictions, and the action of God in them. And once the pagans had been led to admit the reality of the prophecies of Israel, it was not difficult to lead them on to acknowledge the doctrine preached by the prophets.

In the *Dialogue,* Justin is arguing with the Jews, and can take for granted the divine origin of the revelation and the sacred character of the Biblical writings. Strong in this belief, and enlightened by the light of Christ, he seems sometimes to regard his arguments as irresistible for those of good faith: "Pay attention to the testimonies I am going to quote: they need no commentary, it suffices

[30] For the Stoic philosophers, the effectiveness of divination was one of the best loved theses, and the evidence seemed to them so irresistible on this point that they preferred to prove thereby the existence of a divinity and a Providence (Cicero, *De natura deorum,* II, v, 13; lxv, 162; *De divinatione,* I, v, 9; xxxviii, 82). Marcus Aurelius, the emperor addressed by Justin and later on by Athenagoras, has left us in his *Meditations* (IX, 27) an expression of his belief in dreams and divination. Plutarch equally believed in them (*De defectu oracul.,* IX; *De Pyth. orac.,* XVII, XX), and sought the explanation of phenomena he did not dream of denying in the activity of spirits or emanations from the earth.

to hear them" (*Dialogue*, lv, 3). But often also he shows that this interpretation is difficult to grasp: "Thou sayest, and we also agree, that all the words and actions of the prophets have a symbolical and typical signification, so that most of them are not easily understood by all, because the truth is hidden in them, and those who seek it must make many efforts in order to find and understand it" (*ibid.*, xc, 2).

He even holds that the prophecies as a whole have been understood only since Christ, and thanks to Him, and for this reason he calls Him the interpreter of hidden prophecies (Apoc., I, xxxii, 2; cf. *Dial.*, c, 2). The teaching given by the Master does not suffice for this, any more than his example and his life: there are required also in a man moral dispositions, and the grace of God. Those only can understand the prophets who are ready to suffer what the prophets suffered. "Ask above all," says the old man to Justin, "that the gates of light may be opened to thee, for none can see or understand these things if God and His Christ do not give him the grace to do so" (*Dial.*, vii, 3; cf. xxix, 5). And again: "If anyone has not received from God a great grace in order to understand what has been said and done by the prophets, it will be useless to read their words or the accounts of their works, for he will not be able to explain them" (xcii, 1).

The Argument from Miracles

Together with prophecies, Justin presents miracles as a proof of the Christian revelation. We have found this already in the passage quoted above (*Dial.*, vii, 3) concerning the wonders wrought by the prophets in testimony of their doctrine. The mission of Christ was likewise confirmed by His works, and by the marvels which are still being performed in His name (xxxv, 8). Justin returns to this later on with more emphasis:

"Christ healed those who according to the flesh were blind, deaf or lame from birth, making them to see, hear, or walk by His word. Indeed, He even raised some from the dead and brought them back to life; and by His works He confounded His contemporaries and called upon them to recognise Him, but they, seeing all these things, attributed them to a magical power, for they dared to call Him a magician and seducer. He Himself performed these works also in order to show those who were to believe in Him that if anyone has a bodily infirmity,

He will make him perfectly whole again at His second coming by raising him up and freeing him from death, corruption and pain" (lxix, 6-7).

It must be recognised that in Justin and the other apologists of that period, the form of the argument is quite different from that of our own time, and supposes different preoccupations.

All our effort nowadays is directed to obtaining the recognition of a fact (a cure, resurrection, or prophecy) as supernatural; in the second century this point was not the most difficult to get recognised; people found no great difficulty in allowing an activity superior to that of natural agents, but the whole problem was to discern the origin of these supernatural activities.

It was the period in which Alexander of Abonouteichos deceived Marcus Aurelius himself by his illusions, and married Rutilianus the consul to a daughter whom he claimed to have had from the moon.[31] It was also the time when the Gnostic Mark was multiplying the feats of magic related by St. Irenæus (I, xiii), and which astonished the faithful.

Moreover, the apologists found no difficulty in recognising the extraordinary power of the evil spirits. Tatian explains thus, according to St. Justin, the marvellous cures they brought about:

"The evil spirits do not cure, they captivate men by cunning, and the excellent Justin has rightly said that they are comparable to brigands. For as the latter are accustomed to make captives and to give them back afterwards to their relatives in exchange for a ransom, so also these pretended divinities slip into the members of certain men, then by dreams make them believe in their power, command their sick to appear in public in the sight of all, and after enjoying the praises given to them, they fly out of the bodies of their sick, putting an end to the malady which they had themselves caused, and re-establishing the men in the primitive condition" (XVIII).[32]

[31] Lucian, *Alexander*, XLVIII, XXXV.

[32] So also St. Irenæus, when combating the disciples of Simon and Carpocrates, insists on showing that their marvels have not the same character as the miracles of Christ and of Christians: "They cannot give back sight to the blind, or hearing to the deaf; they cannot expel evil spirits, save perhaps those they have themselves introduced; they cannot heal the sick, the lame, the paralytics, the cripples. . . . As for resurrections, they are so far from being able to do it that they do not think it in any way possible. But the Lord did this, as also did the apostles by their prayers, and often, amongst the brethren, in cases of necessity, the whole Church of the place prays, fasts and beseeches, and the spirit of the dead man comes back, and the man is restored at the prayers of the saints" (II, xxxi, 2).

The superiority of Christ over the evil spirits is shown especially by the exorcisms: the pagans were struck by this, and the apologists recall it with insistence. Thus Justin, in his Second *Apology* (VI, 5-6):

"Christ became man, and was born, by the will of God the Father, for the salvation of believers and the destruction of evil spirits; now you can still convince yourselves of this by what happens beneath your eyes. In the whole world, and in your own city, there are many demoniacs whom neither adjurations nor enchantments nor philtres have been able to cure: many of our Christians, adjuring them in the name of Jesus Christ crucified under Pontius Pilate, have cured them and still cure them to-day, by mastering and expelling the evil spirits who possess them."

Christian Morals

But of all these miraculous works, that on which Justin dwells for preference, and which is indeed the most clearly divine, is the moral transformation brought about by Christianity. He himself, we recall, had been won to the Christian faith by the heroism of the martyrs (*Apol.*, II, xii, 1). He never tires in his *Apology* of offering to the pagans this decisive proof of the holiness of his religion. He presents Christians to them as men who do not fear death,[33] who prefer truth to life, and who at the same time wait without anticipating the hour when God will call them;[34] they are devoted to their children (*Apol.*, I, xxvii); they are chaste;[35] they are peaceful

---

The apologist of the *Clementine Recognitions* (III, lx) stresses still more the beneficial character of true miracles; he makes St. Peter speak thus: "Tell me, what is the use of making statues walk, dogs of bronze or stone bark, mountains leap and fly in the air, or a thousand other marvels of this kind, which you attribute to Simon? But the works of him who is good have for their object the well being of men, like the works which Our Lord did, making the blind to see, the deaf to hear, curing the sick and the lame, putting to flight the maladies and evil spirits, raising the dead, and doing many other things which you see me also doing." Cf. Athenagoras, *Legat.*, xxiii; Tertullian, *Apol.*, xxii; Minucius Felix, *Octav.*, xxvii.

[33] *Apol.*, I, ii, 4; xi, 1-2; xlv, 6; II, ii, 14; *Dial.*, xxx, 2.

[34] *Apol.*, II, iv.

[35] *Apol.*, I, xxix: "If we marry, it is to bring up our children; if we renounce marriage, it is in order to keep perfect continence." This exigence and this virtue of Christianity appear in the fact which gave rise to the Second *Apology*: a woman had lived in vice with her husband; she was converted to Christianity, and "considered that it was an impiety to share the couch of a man who sought by all

(I, xxxix, 3); they love their enemies and endeavour to save them (I, lvii, 1; *Dial.*, cxxxiii, 6); in persecution they are patient, they pray, they love all men.[36] Hence it is useless to persecute them unto death; the Church flourishes like a vine that is pruned:

"We are beheaded, we are crucified, we are delivered to wild beasts, to chains, to the fire, and to all torments, and you see that we do not renounce the profession of our faith; on the contrary, the more we are persecuted, the greater becomes the number of those who, through the name of Jesus, become faithful and pious. When people cut off from a vine the branches that have borne fruit, other shoots appear, flourish, and bear fruits; it is the same with us. The vine planted by Christ, God and Saviour, is his people" (*Dial.*, cx, 4).

This pure morality, this fruitful life, have their source in the teaching and grace of Christ:

"Previously we took pleasure in debauchery; now chastity constitutes our whole delight; once we practised magic, now we are consecrated to the good and unbegotten God. We were greedy for money and possessions; now we put in common what we possess, and share it with whoever is in want. Hatred and murders opposed us to each other; difference in manners prevented us from receiving the stranger in our homes; now, after the appearance of Christ, we live together, we pray for our enemies, we try to win our unjust persecutors, in order that those who live in conformity with the sublime doctrine of Christ may hope for the same rewards as us from God, the Master of the world" (*Apol.*, I, xiv, 2-13).

And he continues, quoting abundantly the moral precepts of Jesus, especially the Sermon on the Mount (*ibid.*, xv-xviii).

Thus is developed this apologetic demonstration, modest and restrained yet strong in a tranquil and irresistible assurance. Justin has not the sarcastic liveliness of Tatian, nor the passionate eloquence of Tertullian. To the odious calumnies spread against Christians he sometimes replies, like the other apologists, by taking the offensive, and reproaching the pagans for their immorality (*Apol.*, I, xxvii; II, xx, 4-5); but he does not dwell on these obscenities; the interlocutor in the *Dialogue* protests that he does not believe

means, pleasures contrary to the natural law and to justice"; she tried in vain to convert her husband; finally she separated from him. She was then denounced by him as a Christian (*Apol.*, II, ii).

[36] *Dial.*, xciii, 3.

in the stories told about the Christians (x, 2); the friends who accompany Justin and who disturb the discussion by their noisy protestations and loud laughter are asked to go away, "so that we may continue our discussion in peace" (ix, 2). In the *Apology* (II, iii, 2) Crescentius is severely recalled to the reserve which befits a philosopher; he forgets it by seeking to please the misguided multitude. Justin, who despises this hostile crowd, has no appetite to oppose it, nor the strength to dominate it; he continues his argumentation before his little circle of chosen hearers, men who are capable of following an argument and of being reached by an idea.

What gives these modest speeches their persuasive force is the assurance of a faith which is based upon God Himself and which is capable of facing death.

This apologetic demonstration is the whole work of Justin, at least all that we possess. It has in addition the advantage of making known to us, as the end to which it leads, the theological doctrine which the apologist professes, and towards which he leads his hearers. We shall not enter here into the details of this theology; [37] it will be sufficient for us to give its main outlines.

Theology

The study of this theology is more difficult than that of the Apostolic Fathers or of Irenæus. The doctrinal teaching is presented, as we have said, as the goal to which the apologist leads his reader; he has not yet arrived there, he ascends towards it, and as much as possible by a path along which his interlocutor can follow him without difficulty. This aim leads him, not indeed to falsify the doctrine he sets forth, but to represent it in a light which will enlighten the neophyte without blinding him. The apologist makes use for this end of analogies, sometimes more apparent than real, which are suggested by the religious conceptions familiar to his reader; if he is trying to convert a Platonist, he will insist on the conception he entertains of the intelligible world and the divine world; if he is addressing a Stoic, he will dwell on the theory of the logos, and in particular of the seminal word, or again on the belief in the final conflagration of the world. Approaching the

[37] We have studied and discussed this in *Hist. du Dogme de la Trinité*, Vol. II, pp. 411-84.

Christian mystery by this familiar path, the interlocutor will feel more at home.

But this apologetic advantage is not without its disadvantages; by stressing apparent analogies, one runs the risk of imprudently effacing profound doctrinal divergences, or again of disconcerting the reader to whom there suddenly appears, in familiar terms, a quite new and unexpected dogma. This last impression will be obtained by anyone who studies in the second *Apology* the account which Justin gives of the theory of the seminal word as applied to Christ.[38]

On this point, moreover, the silence which Justin maintains in all the rest of his work is a sufficient indication that this conception of the seminal word has not for him the importance which he seems to attribute to it in his *Apology* addressed to the emperor-philosopher. This influence was not very dangerous for Justin, who had in fact little sympathy for Stoicism. But Platonism had once dominated his thought, and continued to attract him; this attraction constituted a danger; he will keep himself from it nevertheless, and will maintain on the essential points the independence of his religious thought.[39] Other apologists will be less prudent and less firm.

The anti-Jewish controversy will also have its dangers. Justin will be able to find arguments he can utilise in defending the Christian religion in the writings of Jews, in the rabbinical literature and above all in the apocalypses, but only too often these arguments defend Christianity only by misrepresenting it.

Of all these arms which apologists derive from their opponents the most effective, but also the most dangerous, is the theory of intermediaries. Between the supremely pure God and the matter which is unworthy of contact with Him, there must be an intermediate agent, without which creation cannot be understood. Similarly the revelation of the supreme God can reach man only by the influence of the intermediaries who propagate it. These conceptions, very widespread in Greek philosophy and in Judaism, provided the apologists with an argument, but at the same time constituted a danger for them.

To understand this, we can start with this rule of interpretation put forward by Tertullian when arguing against the Marcionites:

[38] Cf. *ibid.*, p. 436.
[39] Cf. *ibid.*, p. 481.

"All that you require as being worthy of God you will find in the Father: He is invisible, beyond reach, tranquil, and so to speak, the God of philosophers. All that you single out as unworthy of God, will be attributed to the Son: He is seen, met with, He is the agent of the Father and His Minister, combining in Himself man and God: in His greatness He is God, in His infirmities, man; giving to man all that He takes from God; in a word, all that you regard as unworthy of God, is the mystery of the salvation of humanity" (*Marc.*, II, xxvii).

If we consider the supreme God, this exegetical rule might lead to striking out of the Bible all that is thought unworthy of his transcendence, that is to say, all his personal interventions; one will see in him, as Tertullian says, nothing more than "the God of philosophers." The theology of the Son of God is likewise in great danger: "all that one judges unworthy of the supreme God will be attributed to the Son"; this is a very dangerous rule; one may justify it, as Tertullian does here, by imputing these weaknesses not indeed to the divine nature of the Son, but to His humanity; at the same time there is more than one point in which this interpretation will not work.

The Word in Creation

The first problem which arises is that of the creation. Christian theology taught clearly that God had made all things by His Word; the Greek philosophers were disposed to receive this teaching, but understanding the Word to be an intermediary between the supreme God and matter. The Jews also admitted this conception, which they applied either to Wisdom, or else to the Law.[40]

The apologists made the most of this present offered them by their opponents, but sometimes they allowed themselves to be drawn on to their ground. We read in Justin:

Apol., II, i, 2. "His Son, the only one who is properly called Son, the Word, who before all creatures was with Him and had been generated when in the beginning the Father made and ordered all things by him. . . ."

Dial., lxi, 1. "As a beginning, before all creatures, God generated from himself a Power which was the Word. . . . This can receive all

[40] Cf. *Hist. du Dogme de la Trinité*, Vol. II, pp. 456-8.

names because He carries out the plans of the Father and is born of the Father by will."

Ibid., lxii, 4: "This Son, really sent forth before all creatures, was with the Father, and with Him the Father converses, as is shown by the sacred text of Solomon: this same being is the beginning before all creatures, and was generated by God as His Son, and it is He whom Solomon calls Wisdom."

These texts recall that of St. John:

"In the beginning was the Word, and the Word was with God, and the Word was God. The same was in the beginning with God. All things were made by Him, and without Him was made nothing that was made."

But the Gospel text has a firm touch which is lacking in the apologist: in St. John the divine life, and the generation of the Word, is wholly independent not only of all the external operations of God, but also of all his plans: from the beginning, eternally, the Word was, and was with God, and was God; when God willed it, He created the world by His Word, but this external and contingent action had no influence on the inner life of God; this was eternally and necessarily what it was, in the simplicity of its essence, and in the Trinity of its persons.

In Justin, on the contrary, at least in the *Apology*, the generation of the Word is closely linked up with the creation of the world; this connection is not without danger: it runs the risk of drawing the eternal and necessary generation of the Word into the temporal and contingent sphere of creation.[41]

The inexact translation given to the classical text in *Proverbs*

---

[41] This danger of contamination is still more manifest in other apologists. Thus Tatian says: "By the will of his simplicity, there comes forth from Him the Word, and the Word, which does not go forth into the void, is the first work of the Father. It is he, as we know, who is the beginning of the world" (*Discourse*, v).

Athenagoras: "If, in your high wisdom, you wish to know who is the Son, I will tell you in a few words: He was the offspring of the Father, not that He was made, for God being an eternal intellect from the beginning, had with Him His Word, so that in all the material things, which were like a formless nature or a sterile earth . . . He was amongst them idea and energy, having come from without" (*Leg.* x).

St. Theophilus: "When God willed to make what He had decided, He generated this uttered Word, the first born of the whole creation, not depriving Himself of the Word, but generating the Word, and speaking constantly with His Word" (II, xxii). On all these passages, cf. *Hist. du Dogme de la Trinité*, Vol. II, pp. 453-5. On the theory of the twofold state of the Word, internal and uttered, see *ibid.*, pp. 449 *et seq.*

(viii, 22) led in the same direction: the apologists, like the Jews of their times, did not translate this text as: "The Lord has formed me at the beginning of His ways, before His works," but "The Lord has formed me as a beginning of His works." Thus one is tempted to regard the Word as the first of the works of God, and that was how the rabbis contemporary with Justin regarded the Law.[42] Justin will resist this temptation, safeguarded by his firm belief in the generation of the Word; his unfortunate and unfaithful disciple Tatian will be less vigilant, and while saying that the Word is "generated by the Father," he will also say that he is "the first work of the Father" (*Discourse*, v).

The Divine Appearances

As in the case of the problem of creation, that of the relation between God and the world suggested to the apologists a solution both tempting and dangerous. The Old Testament contains many accounts of theophanies: God appearing to Abraham, Jacob and Moses. The explanation proposed is that it is not God the Father who appears thus, but the Son of God, and thus all these Scriptural texts are so many arguments which enable the apologist to distinguish in God two distinct persons. This is how the argument is presented in the *Dialogue*:

"The ineffable Father and Lord of the universe goes nowhere nor walks, nor sleeps, nor gets up, but remains in His own place wherever this may be; He is endowed with a penetrating sight and hearing, not by eyes or ears, but by an unspeakable power; He sees all, He knows all, and not one of us escapes Him; He does not move, and no place can contain Him, not even the whole world, for He was before the world was made. How, then, could this God speak to anyone, or show Himself to anyone, appear in a small corner of the earth, whereas on Sinai the people had not the strength even to see the glory of the one He sent, and Moses himself could not enter into the tent he had made because it was filled with the glory which came forth from God? . . . Thus neither Abraham nor Isaac nor Jacob nor any other amongst men saw the Father and the ineffable Lord of all things absolutely and of Christ Himself, but only Him who according to the will of God is God, His Son and Angel inasmuch as He is the Minister of His plans. It is He whom God willed to be born man of a virgin, He who became

[42] Cf. the treatise *Pesachim*, 54 a, Bar.: "Jahveh created me as the beginning of his ways, as the first of his works," and this is understood of the Law. Cf. *Hist. du Dogme de la Trinité*, Vol. II, pp. 457-8.

fire formerly to speak with Moses from the bush. For if we do not thus understand the Scriptures, it will follow that the Father and Lord of the universe was not then in heaven, whereas it was said through the mouth of Moses: 'The Lord rained on Sodom fire and brimstone from the Lord from the height of heaven' " (*Dial.*, cxxvii).[43]

From the apologetic point of view, this exegesis presented great advantages: the Platonist philosophers could follow it, for they themselves likewise held that the supreme God is invisible and inaccessible, and manifests Himself to men only by the ministry of secondary gods; [44] the Palestinian Jews, represented by Trypho,[45] thought that in the theophanies it was not God Himself who appeared, but an angel; to refute them it sufficed to prove to them that the personage seen by Abraham or Moses was divine.

While the apologist could feel pleased at this exegesis, the theologian had to suffer from it: not only was he led to represent God as dwelling above the world, and having there His place and His throne,[46] but above all it compromised the consubstantiality of the Father and the Son. At the time of which we speak, the Trinitarian controversies had not yet arisen, and there was less danger in these imprudences, but the Arian crisis would reveal them.[47] To remove them in a decisive manner, St. Augustine will reject the interpretation of the theophanies developed by the apologists: in these appearances it is not the Son alone who is showing Himself to men, but either the Father, or the Son, or the Spirit, or the whole Trinity.[48]

What we have just said will show how far we must recognise

[43] Cf. *Hist. du Dogme de la Trinité*, Vol. II, p. 426; we may consult other similar but less explicit passages in Justin: *Dial.*, lxi, 2; *Apol.*, I, lxiii, 11.

[44] Maximus of Tyre, quoted *ibid.*, p. 665.

[45] It is fairly generally said that Justin is referring to Philo; this is an error (cf. *ibid.*, pp. 667 *et seq.*). The opponents represented by Trypho are the Palestinian Jews; their exegesis and their theology cannot be identified with those of Philo.

[46] Cf. *ibid.*, p. 427.

[47] The Arians, according to St. Phoebadius, will argue as follows: God the Father is invisible, immutable, perfect, eternal; the Son on the contrary is visible, since He was often seen by the patriarchs; He is subject to change, for He appeared under various forms; He is therefore not of the substance of the Father (*De Filii divinitate*, viii; Migne, *P.L.*, XX, 45). Cf. Augustine, *De Genesi ad litteram*, VIII, 27, 50; Migne, *P.L.*, XXXIV, 392. Cf. *Saint Augustin théologien de la Trinité*, in *Miscellanea Agostiniana*, Vol. II, pp. 821-36.

[48] St. Irenæus, while reserving these appearances to the Son of God, avoids the danger by presenting these theophanies as preludes to the Incarnation. Cf. *Hist. du Dogme de la Trinité*, Vol. II, pp. 594-8.

Subordinationist tendencies in Justin, and what were their origin. We must recognise a deviation in his theology on two important points: the generation of the Word and His action in the world; His generation is put in too close a relation with the creation of the world, and thereby His necessity and His eternity are compromised; [49] in the manifestations He appears as the envoy or servant of the supreme God rather than the Son of God, equal and consubstantial with His Father.

This deviation is noteworthy, but it does not affect the theology of Justin as a whole, and what is still more important, it did not originate in an earlier tradition which led Christian thought in this direction; we find no trace of it in the Apostolic Fathers, Clement or Ignatius; we shall not find it either in Irenæus. In the apologists it is explained by the preoccupations of controversy: a foreign element has affected the doctrine of Justin, and has made it sometimes go astray.

In any case, we must not exaggerate this inexactitude: when we study carefully the weak points in the theology of the apologists, at least of the greatest amongst them, we realise that they did not give themselves up blindly to the Platonist or Jewish influences which attracted their attention; they resisted them. This resistance was of varying strength, certainly, in the different apologists, and also differed in perspicacity, but it manifested always the same Christian reaction against the same danger, Jewish or pagan.[50]

Personality of the Word

Having pointed out, as we had to do, these weaknesses in the theology of Justin and the other apologists, we must emphasise the traditional data which Justin maintains firmly and defends with energy.

[49] We note sometimes a too close bond between the generation of the Word and the creation of the world (*Apol.*, II, vi, 2), but more often Justin affirms emphatically the absolute anteriority of the Word in relation to all creation: *Apol.*, II, vi, 3; *Dial.*, lxi, 1; lxii, 4; c, 2 and 4; cxxxix, 4.

[50] Cf. *Hist. du Dogme de la Trinité*, Vol. II, p. 459. These apparently opposed elements in the theology of the apologists have provided arguments for the historians who have attacked or defended their orthodoxy. This question has often given rise to keen discussion: in the seventeenth century, by Petavius and Huet; then by Jurieu and Bossuet in France; in England by Bull and S. Clarke; and towards the end of the last century by Duchesne and Newman. Cf. *ibid.*, pp. 499-500.

The Word is really distinct from the Father. This is one of the fundamental theses of the *Dialogue*. Thus we read in chapter lvi, 11:

"I will endeavour to convince you that He who appeared to Abraham, Jacob and Moses and who is described as a God, is other than the God who made all things, I mean other in number, not in thought; for I affirm that He did nothing and said nothing else but what the Creator of the world, He above whom there is no other God, willed Him to do and to say."

Several other texts are invoked in the same sense, in particular, the account of creation. In saying, "Let us make man . . ." the Creator addressed Himself to "someone who was numerically distinct from Him, and who by nature was the Word." The same conclusion is deduced from this other text of *Genesis*: "Behold Adam is become as one of us"; "By saying 'as one of us' he indicates a number of beings together, and who are at least two" (lxii, 2 and 3).

Later on, in commenting on the theophanies, the apologist encounters the exegesis of certain Jewish doctors who saw in the divine Being appearing to the patriarchs a Power which radiated from God but which was inseparable from Him and was reabsorbed into Him. Justin categorically rejects this interpretation:

"It has been proved that this Power which the prophetic text calls God, and angel, is not only nominally distinct (from the Father), as light is distinct from the sun, but that it is something numerically distinct." [51]

The same thesis is defended again by the text of *Proverbs* (viii, 21-25):

"This text shows that He whom the Father thus generated was generated absolutely before all creatures; now that which is generated is numerically distinct from the one who generates, as all will agree" (*Apol.*, cxxix, 4).

Divinity of the Word

That which is thus generated by the Father is "an intelligent being" (*Apol.*, lxii, 2), "an intelligent power" (lxi, 1); in other

[51] *Dial.*, cxxviii, 4. By a strange mistake Vacherot attributes to Justin the theory which he refutes (*Hist. de l'Ecole d'Alexandrie*, Vol. I, p. 230).

words, a person. And this person is divine. This essential dogma of Christianity is demonstrated in the *Apology*, but above all in the *Dialogue*. And what gives to these affirmations all their value is the religious faith which animates them. In the *Apology* Justin repeats to the pagans: "We must adore God only" (I, xvi, 6); "we adore only God" (xvii, 3). And yet he also says: "We adore and we love, after God, the Word born of the unbegotten and ineffable God" (II, xiii, 4). And in the *Dialogue,* he thus concludes a long process of reasoning:

"Thus then He is adorable, He is God, He is Christ; He who made all that we see gives testimony of this, and these texts say so clearly" (lxiii, 5).

And again, lower down:

"David has shown that, being Christ, He is a strong and adorable God" (lxxvi, 7).

We thus find ourselves in presence of two series of equally categorical affirmations, to which the martyr's death will give a force of irresistible conviction: We adore only God; we adore Christ. The great disciple of Justin, Irenæus, has shown the intimate union of these two theses; he quotes first of all from the work of Justin against Marcion this peremptory declaration:

"I would refuse my faith to the Lord Himself if He preached to us a God other than the Demiurge."

And then he adds:

"But because it is from the one God who made the world, who created us and who governs all, that the one Son has come to us . . . my belief in Him is assured, and my love towards the Father is unshakeable" (IV, i, 2).

We find here already the answer which the Fathers of the fourth century will develop against the Arians: our faith is given to the Son without disturbing our love for the Father, for the Son was generated by the Father; our homage and our adoration are not scattered over several gods, for the source of the Godhead is one.

The Generation of the Son of God

This dogma of the generation of the Son of God is brought out splendidly by Justin.[52] The apologist does so in contrasting the origin of the Word of God with that of creatures; the world has come from matter, the Word has come from God;[53] the other beings are works of God, ποιήματα, creatures, κτίσματα;[54] the Word is the bud of God, γέννημα, His child, τέκνον, His only Son, the only one who is really Son.[55]

The significance of these affirmations is confirmed by the numerous texts in which Justin endeavours to describe, or at least to hint at, the origin of the Word: it is like an emission,[56] a going out,[57] a springing forth;[58] it is a fire lit by another fire;[59] a Word which, without amputation or diminution, the Father generates from Himself:

"Is it not something like what takes place in ourselves? When we utter some word, we generate a word, and we utter it not by an amputation which diminishes the word which is in us. Again it is like a fire lit at another fire: the one at which it is lit is not diminished, but remains the same; and the one which is lit there is seen to be quite real, without diminishing that from which it was lit" (Dial., lxi, 2).

It goes without saying that these are only far-off comparisons—such are the only ones which can be found to throw light on the mystery of God—but at least they turn the mind towards a correct conception of the dogma: the Son of God is not a creature, He is born of the Father. This decisive affirmation opposes beyond any question the theology of Justin and the other apologists to what will later be the Arian heresy. From this fruitful principle bequeathed by the apostolic tradition, the apologists did not know

[52] Loofs, who sees in this doctrine a deviation from the primitive faith, writes: "Certainly, as we see from Hermas and Barnabas, it was not the apologists who were first responsible for this deviation; at the same time, so far as we know, no Christian theologian before Justin laid as much stress as he did on the divine sonship" (Paulus von Samosata, p. 315).

[53] Apol., I, x, 2; Dial., lxi, 1.

[54] Apol., II, vi, 3; Dial., lxii, 4; lxxxix, 2; Dial., lxi, 1; c, 2; cxxv, 3; cxxix, 4.

[55] Apol., I, xxi, 1; Dial., lxii, 4; cxxix, 4; cxxv, 3; cv, 1; Apol., II, vi, 3. Cf. Hist. du Dogme de la Trinité, Vol. II, p. 444.

[56] Dial., lxii, 4; lxiv, 1.

[57] Dial., c, 4.

[58] Dial., cxxviii, 3.

[59] Dial., cxxviii, 4.

how to draw all the consequences it implied; the Church will find the principle in their works, and will know how to draw all these conclusions which flow from it, even those which had escaped these early apologists.

Martyrdom

"No one believed Socrates so far as to die for what he taught, but for Christ's sake even working people and ignorant folk have despised fear and death" (*Apol.*, II, x, 3). The apologist was to confirm this proud word by his own death. Together with his companions, he was summoned to appear before the prefect of the city, Rusticus the philosopher and master of Marcus Aurelius.[60]

Justin tried to expound his faith; the prefect allowed him to say a few words:

"The true doctrine which we Christians follow piously, is belief in only one God, the Creator of all things visible and invisible, and in the Lord Jesus Christ, the Son of God, foretold by the prophets as the messenger of salvation for the human race and the master of good disciples. And I, who am but a man, cannot speak worthily of his infinite divinity; I confess (that this requires) a prophetic power; and the prophets have announced the coming of Him who is as I have said the Son of God. For I know that long ago the prophets foretold his coming amongst men."

We recognise in this brief exposition Justin's apologetic, the argument from prophecy on which he dwelt by preference. Rusticus did not reply: he pressed on the interrogation of Justin first and then of his companions. Lastly, turning once more to the apologist, he tried to shake him:

"Listen, thou who art said to be eloquent and who pretendest to know the true doctrine: if I have thee scourged and then beheaded, dost thou believe that thou shalt then ascend into heaven?" "I hope," replied Justin, "to receive the reward, if I suffer that which thou hast announced to me. For I know that those who have thus lived will keep the divine favour until the end of the world." "Thou fanciest, then," said Rusticus, "that thou wilt ascend to heaven to receive a reward?" "I do not fancy it, I know it, and I am fully persuaded of it." "Let us come back to realities. Come, all of you, and sacrifice together to the

[60] The *Acts* are in the *Corpus apologetarum* of Otto, III, 2, 262-75 (1879), and in Knopf, pp. 17-20.

gods." "No sensible man abandons piety to fall into impiety." "If you do not obey, you shall be tormented without mercy." "All our desire is to suffer for Jesus Christ our Lord and to be saved. This will be our salvation and our assurance at the fearful and universal judgment of our Master and Saviour." The other martyrs said likewise: "Do what thou wilt. We are Christians, and we do not sacrifice to idols." The prefect Rusticus pronounced the sentence: "Those who have refused to sacrifice to the gods and to obey the order of the emperor will be scourged and taken away to undergo the capital penalty in conformity with the laws.

"The holy martyrs, glorifying God, were led to the ordinary place of execution; their heads were cut off, and they consummated their martyrdom in the confession of the Lord."

§3. THE GREEK APOLOGISTS OF THE END OF THE SECOND CENTURY

Tatian [1]

St. Justin deserved an attentive study, the other apologists will not keep us so long. The first we meet with was a disciple of St. Justin; he spoke of his master only with veneration,[2] but he was little like him. Candid and boastful, he wrote at the beginning of his *Discourse*: "We have detached ourselves from your wisdom, and yet I was one of the most eminent of its representatives." Born in the land of the Assyrians (ch. xli) about the year 120, he went to Rome, and there doubtless he was converted, and became a disciple of Justin. As long as his master lived, he was faithful to the Church; "but after the martyrdom of Justin he fell away; he was exalted and puffed up by his title of master, thought himself superior to the others, and founded a new school." St. Irenæus, from whom we take this statement, adds: "He imagined invisible sons, like those we find in the fables of Valentine; like Marcion and Saturninus, he called marriage a corruption and a debauchery; and

[1] Cf. A. Puech, *Recherches sur le Discours aux Grecs de Tatien*, Paris, 1903; id., *Les Apologistes grecs*, ch. v, pp. 148-71. Edition of the *Discourse* by Schwartz, *Texte und Untersuchungen*, IV, 1.

[2] *Discourse*, xviii and xix. This fidelity to the memory of Justin does honour to Tatian; it also shows the prestige of the master, and all the more because of the very deep differences between the two men, and because the exaggerations of Tatian seem to have made him less likely to be influenced by a balanced mind like that of Justin.

finally, it was he who conceived the idea that Adam was not saved." [3] This judgment of so eminent a man, who had personally known Justin and doubtless Tatian himself, confirms the impression the *Discourse* gives us: we do not yet find a heretic therein, but we are repelled by the presumptuous assurance of a writer who jeers at and despises his opponents, and who airily settles all the questions he deals with.

Three quarters of the work (ch. i-xxx) are devoted to polemics; the apologist violently attacks the pagan philosophers, pagan wisdom, and pagan religion. In his defence, it has been said that "he borrows from the Greeks the arms with which he combats the Greeks." [4] That is true, but we must add that such arms could only wound; [5] it was not by such arguments that Tatian himself had been converted. [6] A few other apologists, especially Tertullian, imitated him; to excuse them it is recalled that they echoed what they heard proclaimed around them, and that they were glad to reply thus to the calumnies urged against the Christians. But it is to be noted that the most violent polemical writers were two who themselves abandoned the Church, Tatian and Tertullian, and one is glad to register that the best amongst the Christians remained foreign to such methods. [7]

Justin, when giving a reason for the resemblances between the pagan philosophy and Christian doctrine, explains them by preference by the action of the seminal Word, and sometimes also by the theory that the Greeks borrowed from the Jews. In Tatian the former explanation has disappeared save for a slight trace (ch.

---

[3] *Hær.*, I, xxviii, 1, quoted by Eusebius, *Hist. Eccles.*, IV, xxix, 3. Eusebius, *ibid.*, 6-7, adds some information concerning Tatian, his *Diatesseron* and his *Discourse.*

[4] Puech, *Recherches*, p. 40.

[5] We may quote, as an example, this series of anecdotes on the philosophers: "Diogenes, who advertised his independence by the bragging of his tub, ate an octopus quite raw, and seized with colic, died from his intemperance. Aristippus, who paraded with his mantle of purple, gave himself up to debauchery with an air of gravity; the philosopher Plato was sold by Dionysius because of his gluttony, and Aristotle was guilty of the extreme folly of flattering Alexander, the wild young fool who, quite in accordance with the Aristotelian principles, put in a cage like a bear or a panther his friend who was not willing to adore him, and had him thus drawn after him. . . ."

[6] He narrates that he was converted by the reading of Holy Scripture (xxix).

[7] It must be put to Tatian's credit that in his attacks on pagan religion, he dwells less than others on mythology, and deals above all with the superstitions, which were in fact most dangerous: astrology (ch. ix-xi), magic (xvii-xx), the Mysteries (xxix). Cf. Puech, *Recherches*, p. 43.

xiii); all the effort of the apologist is directed to establishing the priority of the prophets over the philosophers, and to infer therefrom that the Greeks are plagiarists (ch. xxxi *et seq.*). This argument was not original,[8] it will often be repeated and it will not enrich Christian apologetic.

Christian Doctrine

Tatian's exposition of Christian doctrine would be more interesting to a historian than his polemics, but unfortunately his testimony in this matter is difficult to gather: the statement is often obscure,[9] and the thought generally confused. In the theology of the Word, Tatian retains some of the essential points in the Christian dogma, as Justin had set them forth; the Son is born of the very substance of the Father; this is signified by the illustration of the torches, lit one from the other; Justin had given this (*Dial.*, lxi); Tatian repeats it (v), and after him Tertullian, Lactantius,[10] the Nicene Fathers in their Creed. This image is clearly opposed to what the Arians will maintain when they make the Word a creature of God, formed from nothing, and not His Son, born of His substance. We must note again that, for Tatian as for all the apologists, it is not the Incarnation which makes the Word the Son of God, but the divine generation. At the same time it must be recognised that in Tatian the conception of this divine generation is less firm than in Justin;[11] it is moreover obscured by the dangerous distinction between the twofold state of the Word, first latent, and then uttered.[12]

[8] Cf. Puech, *Recherches*, pp. 82-9.

[9] This obscurity is not always due to Tatian; the most important text (ch. v) has been clearly altered. Already in the tenth century, Archbishop Arethas, to whom we owe the best manuscript of Tatian, added a marginal note in which he accused Tatian of Arianism; the scribe probably had the same impression, and attempted a correction. This text has been studied in *Histoire du Dogme de la Trinité*, Vol. II, p. 450.

[10] Tertullian, *Apol.*, xxi; Lactantius, *Inst. div.*, IV, xxix.

[11] The Word is called "the first born work of God," a contradictory formula combining the idea of creation with that of generation.

[12] "The master of all things, who is himself the substantial support of the universe was alone in this sense that creation had not yet taken place; but in the sense that all the power of things visible and invisible was in him, He included all things in Himself by means of His Word. By the will of his simplicity, the Word came forth from Him, and the Word, who went not out into the void, is the first-born work of the Father. He, as we know, is the beginning of the world. He comes from a distribution, not from a division. . . ." (v).

On the subject of the human soul, Tatian confusing eternity and immortality, considered that the soul is by nature mortal, but that if it has known God, after it has been dissolved for a time it will live again, to die no more.[13] Elsewhere he rather imprudently makes use of Platonist conceptions [14] or Gnostic ones.[15]

All these contaminations show the weakness of a mind which thought itself strong because it was severe, and which allowed itself to be affected by the most unsound elements of the philosophies it despised.

The Defection of Tatian

This *Discourse* was doubtless written very shortly before the defection of Tatian.[16] It was in the twelfth year of Marcus Aurelius, 172-3,[17] that Tatian abandoned the Church. He had, it seems, already left Rome for the East; he lived for a few years more at Antioch, in Cilicia, in Pisidia. The small sect of Encratites which he had founded lasted a long time, but did not spread much; most of his works, which seem to have been fairly numerous, disappeared

[13] "The human soul, in itself, is not immortal, O Greeks, it is mortal; but this same soul is capable also of not dying. . . . It does not die, even if it be dissolved for a time, if it has acquired a knowledge of God." We find in Justin (*Dial.*, v) the germ of this confusion: the Platonists commonly held that there was between the human soul and God an affinity of nature; this for them implied immortality. Justin rejects all that, recognising in the soul only an immortality accorded by a grace from God. Tatian goes further, making all souls die, but granting to the souls of the just a kind of resurrection. On these confusions, fairly frequent at this time, cf. Bainvel, art. *Ame aux trois premiers siècles*, in *Dict. de théol. cath.*

[14] "The wing of the soul is the perfect spirit, which she loses by sin; after which she keeps close to the ground like a young chicken, and having fallen from her conversation with heaven, she desires to participate in lower things" (xx).

[15] This above all in his theory of the spirit. Tatian distinguishes between two spirits: an inferior spirit which animates and differentiates the stars, angels, men and animals; and a superior and divine spirit, which he identifies with Light and the Word; if the soul unites itself to this spirit, it forms with it a syzygy or couple, according to the will of God: ch. xiii and xv. Cf. Puech, *Recherches*, pp. 65 and 68.

[16] Harnack, *Literatur*, II, i, 284 *et seq.*, dates the *Discourse* in Justin's lifetime. It would then be a manifesto of the newly converted Tatian; R. C. Kukula, *Tatiens sogenannte Apologie*, Leipzig, 1900, maintains on the contrary that the *Discourse* is an opening lecture in the heretical school founded by Tatian, delivered in Asia Minor about 172 (p. 52). These two extreme theses have found no echo: what Tatian says about Justin is better understood if Justin was already dead; on the other hand, the heresy is not yet declared but it is threatened.

[17] This date is given us by Eusebius in his *Chronicle*, an. 2188.

quickly.[18] Apart from the *Discourse,* only one had a great and wide diffusion: the *Diatessaron.* This is a harmony of the four Gospels, the first, apparently, to be composed. It was long in use in the Syrian Church; it is known to us to-day through Arabic and Armenian translations, and also by Latin and Flemish Gospel harmonies.[19]

Athenagoras

Four or five years after the *Discourse* of Tatian, there appeared the *Apology* of Athenagoras.[20] The author is quite unknown; [21] but

[18] *Hist. Eccles.,* IV, xxix 7: "He left a great number of works." Eusebius speaks of them, apparently, only from hearsay. Clement of Alexandria (*Strom.,* III, 12) mentions a book by Tatian on *Perfection according to Christ;* Rendel Harris thinks he has rediscovered this in an Armenian translation.

[19] Theodoret, *Hær. fab. comp.,* I, 20 (Migne, P.G., LXXIII, 372) writes: "Tatian also composed the Gospel called *Diatessaron,* suppressing the genealogies and everything which shows the Lord to have been born of David according to the flesh. And this book is in use not only by those of his sect, but also by those who follow the doctrine of the apostles, and who do not perceive the malice of this composition, and who find it more convenient to make use of this summary. I myself found more than two hundred copies of this book in honour in our churches; I collected them all and put them aside, and substituted for them the four gospels of the evangelists." Theodoret was Bishop of Cyr on the borders of the Syrian world; this explains the diffusion of the work in his diocese. For a long time, in fact, the work was in great honour in the Syrian Church. Aphraates quotes it, and Ephrem comments on it; at the beginning of the fifth century its use was forbidden. Cf. Zahn, *Forschungen. Geschx. des N. T. Kanons,* Vol. I, Erlangen, 1881, pp. 1-328; Vol. II, 1883, pp. 286-99; *Gesch. d. N. T. Kanons,* II, 2 (1892), pp. 530-56. Latin translation of the Armenian version: G. Moesinger, *Evangelii concordantis expositio in Latinum translata,* Venice, 1876; Arabic: A. S. Marmardji, O.P., *Diatessaron de Tatien,* Beyrouth, 1935.

The Latin text of Victor of Capua is not so much a translation as a revision of the *Diatessaron* (Migne, P.L., LXVIII, 255-358). A Flemish translation has been found and studied by D. Plooij, *A Primitive Text of the Diatessaron,* Leyden, 1923. This publication has led to a great number of articles and studies. Cf. *Recherches,* 1924, pp. 370-1; *Revue Biblique,* 1924, pp. 624-8.

[20] The *Apology* is dedicated to the emperors Marcus Aurelius Antoninus and Lucius Aurelius Commodus. Commodus was associated in the government of the empire on November 27th, 176; Marcus Aurelius died on March 17th, 180; the book was thus written between these two dates. The description of a profound peace in chapter 1 must refer to the time before the war of the Marcomans, which broke out in 178; there is no trace either of the Lyons persecution; note especially what is said about slaves (xxxv): "none of them has been denounced"; the apologist would not have spoken thus after 177. All this takes us back, then, to the end of 176 or the beginning of 177.

[21] The only references we find to Athenagoras in Antiquity are, in Methodius, one explicit citation (*De Resurrect.,* xxxii, quoting *Apol.,* xxix), and two allusions; in addition, a fragment attributed to the lost history of Philip of Sidon

the two books of his which we possess, the *Apology* and the *Treatise on the Resurrection,* are well worth reading; it is a joy for one who has just read the invectives of Tatian to find himself here once more in contact with a truly Christian soul, tranquil and pure.

From the first words, the *Apology* displays a reserve and courtesy in expression. The whole Empire enjoys a profound peace; Christians alone are persecuted: what is the reason? If we are convicted of a crime, we accept the punishment; but if we are persecuted only for a name, we appeal to your justice. Three accusations are discussed: Christians are reproached for being atheists, for eating human flesh, and practising incest; these two last calumnies are refuted briefly; the accusation of atheism is discussed at length (ch. iv-xxx); Athenagoras sets forth Christian dogma and the Christian life in a valuable section from which we can quote here only a few fragments.[22] After expounding the essential features of Christian theology, the apologist continues:

"Allow me to raise my voice and to speak frankly, as before philosopher-kings: is there one among those who resolve syllogisms, who dissipate amphibologies . . . who has a soul sufficiently pure to love his enemies instead of hating them, to bless those who curse him instead of replying to them at least by insulting words, to pray for those who aim at taking his life? . . . But amongst ourselves you will find poor people, working men, old women, who are doubtless incapable of proving by argument the value of our doctrine, but who prove it by their actions; they do not recite harangues, but they show good actions; when they are struck they do not return the blows; when they are robbed they do not take proceedings; they give to those who ask from them; they love their neighbour as themselves" (*Apol.,* xi).

Here we have the theme, so dear to all the apologists, of the superiority of life over discourse; *Non eloquimur magna, sed vivimus,* as Minucius Felix will shortly say. It is also the argument which Origen will take up powerfully against Celsus: Christianity alone has been able to transform and raise to the highest virtue these working people, these poor folk, whom philosophy had never

(Migne, *P.G.,* VI, 182); this fragment is full of obvious errors: the author says that Athenagoras addressed his apology to Hadrian and Antoninus; he adds that "his disciple was Clement, the author of the *Stromateis,* and Pantænus the disciple of Clement." Nothing can be made of this.

[22] Longer citations and some comments will be found in *Histoire du Dogme de la Trinité,* Vol. II, pp. 494-505.

reached. And the source of all this is the Christian faith, and the goal it sets before us:

"Will those who take as their motto in life, 'Let us eat and drink, for to-morrow we die' . . . be regarded as pious folk? And are we to be regarded as impious, we who know that the present life is short, and worth little, who are animated by the sole desire to know the true God and His Word, (to know) what is the unity of the Son with the Father, what is the communion of the Father with the Son, what is the Spirit, what is the union and distinction of these terms united to each other, the Spirit, the Son, the Father, we who know that the life we await is greater than we can say, provided always we leave the world pure of every stain, we who love mankind so much as to love not only our friends . . . ? Once more, will it be believed that we are impious, we who are such, and who lead such a life to escape the judgment?" (*Apol.*, xii).

Written at this date, on the eve of the massacres at Lyons, this page is very moving; it reveals the profound source of Christian life; nothing can dry it up or repress it. It also shows what dogma is for the Christian, and in particular, the dogma of the Trinity, which the pagan readers of Athenagoras regarded merely as a speculation like their own; the apologist shows them that it is the term towards which tends the whole life of faith; there is no more expressive commentary on the words of Jesus: "This is eternal life, to know Thee, the only true God, and Him whom Thou hast sent."

Of Athenagoras we possess, besides the *Apology,* a *Treatise on the Resurrection of the Body*. The doctrine defended therein is one of those which the pagans found greatest difficulty in accepting; we see this already in the discourse of St. Paul at Athens (*Acts* xvii, 32); it is also one of those which were most dear to Christians. At this time of persecutions, when the body was constantly menaced with the worst torments and with death, the belief in the glorious resurrection was a great consolation. Also, the pagans took all possible steps to remove the remains of the martyrs, not only to prevent the survivors from getting relics, but also in the vain hope of making the resurrection impossible.[23] It is easy to understand the importance of this doctrine for the apologists: Justin had defended it in a treatise of which we possess only some fragments;[24]

[23] E.g., at Lyons, *Hist. Eccles.*, V, i, 63.
[24] The attribution of this treatise to Justin is not certain, but it is likely. Cf. *supra*, p. 546, n. 16.

THE HISTORY OF THE PRIMITIVE CHURCH

and we have a treatise by Athenagoras on the same subject. This

Section heading "St. Theophilus"

The footnote is "25 The death of Marcus Aurelius is mentioned (III, xxvii, xxviii); these three books seem to belong to the first years of Commodus (182-3)."

and we have a treatise by Athenagoras on the same subject. This little book has the same character as the *Apology*; it is a gentle and lucid discussion; addressed to philosophers, it keeps altogether on their ground; it is thereby deprived of some decisive arguments, namely, those which are based on the positive dispositions of God, the Incarnation and Resurrection of Christ. Here as in the *Apology*, the method to which Athenagoras confines himself made this sacrifice necessary: these two works are impoverished in consequence.

St. Theophilus

Five or six years after the *Apology* of Athenagoras there appeared the three books *To Autolycus*.[25] The author, Theophilus, is known as "the sixth bishop of Antioch after the Apostles" (*Hist. Eccles.*, IV, xx); he stands out in the group of apologists because of his pastoral charge, for he was a bishop. He did not address his work to the emperors, nor to pagan opinion in general, but, like the writer of the *Letter to Diognetus*, to a pagan he wished to convert, Autolycus; a real or fictitious personage, we do not know which.

From the beginning (I, ii) he stresses the necessity of a moral preparation:

"If thou sayest to me, 'Show me thy God,' I answer: 'Show me what sort of man thou art, and I will show thee what sort is my God. Show me if the eyes of thy soul see clearly, and if the ears of thy heart know how to listen. . . . God is seen by those who are capable of seeing him, when they have the eyes of their soul open. All men, indeed, have eyes, but some have eyes that are troubled and blind, insensible to the light of the sun; but from the fact that there are blind people it does not follow that the light of the sun is not shining. Let the blind acknowledge the facts, and let them open their eyes. Similarly, O man, thou hast eyes which are troubled by thy faults and thy bad actions. One must have a soul which is pure like a well-polished mirror. If there is rust on the mirror, it will not reproduce the image of a man; in the same way, when sin is in a man, the sinner is not capable of seeing God."

We recognise here one of the theses familiar to the apologists as also to the martyrs. In 177, the aged bishop of Lyons, St. Pothinus was asked by the proconsul: "What is thy God?" "Thou shalt

[25] The death of Marcus Aurelius is mentioned (III, xxvii, xxviii); these three books seem to belong to the first years of Commodus (182-3).

learn this," he replied, "if thou art worthy of it" (*Hist. Eccles.*, V, i, 31). Again under Commodus, the martyr Apollonius said to the prefect Perennius: "The word of the Lord, O Perennius, is perceived only by the heart which sees, just as light by the eyes which see, and it is in vain that a man speaks to fools, or that light shines for the blind" (*Acts*, ed. Knopf, n. 32).

After a long and involved reasoning, in which there is question not only of God but of the resurrection of the body (viii, xiii), and of the evil doings of the gods of Olympus (ix, x), Theophilus ends his first book by saying that he himself once did not believe, and that he was converted by the reading of the prophets. He exhorts his friend to read them in his turn. The second book is for the most part devoted to the exposition of the teaching of the prophets; in the third, the apologist demonstrates the priority of Holy Scripture over pagan literature.

Theophilus has no sympathy for Hellenism; he condemns it wholly and in all its representatives: Homer, Hesiod, Orpheus, Aratus, Euripides, Sophocles, Menander, Aristophanes, Herodotus, Thucydides, Pythagoras, Diogenes, Epicurus, Empedocles, Socrates and Plato. The death of Socrates, which Justin loved to recall as that of a just man persecuted by the wicked, is judged severely: "Why did he decide to die? What recompense did he hope to receive after death?" (III, ii). In this summary condemnation we recognise the moral preoccupation which is so strong in Theophilus; we recognise its sincerity, but regret its narrowness.[26]

Very much on guard against Hellenism, the bishop of Antioch was in contact with Judaism, and sometimes was subject to the influence of its traditions or its legends.[27] Above all he had for the

---

[26] The chronology is very weak, but is presented with great assurance: from the Creation down to the day on which he is writing, 5,698 years have elapsed, plus a few months and days; Theophilus is proud of this reckoning: what historian has gone back so far? (III, xxvi). This demonstration might appeal to minds to whom all Antiquity appeared venerable, and Theophilus himself takes it very seriously. Still less importance will be attached to the etymologies in which he delights: the cry Evan (Evoe) is inspired by Satan, who deceived Eve (II, xxviii); Noe was called Deucalion because he said to men: Come, God calls you (δεῦτε, καλεῖ ὑμᾶς ὁ θεός) (III, xix), etc. We find similar fantasies in the *Cratylus*, but Plato did it for amusement, whereas Theophilus regarded them as proofs.

[27] Whereas he rejects all Greek philosophy, he regards the Sibyls as prophets (II, ix *et seq.*). He is probably following some *haggada* when he writes that shed blood coagulates and cannot penetrate the earth, because the earth has a horror for it since the murder of Cain (II, xxix). Similarly, when he affirms that the priests who resided in the Temple cured leprosy and every illness (II, xxi).

Old Testament a profound veneration; he wrote against Marcion a treatise which has not come down to us;[28] he thus opened the way to those courageous Eastern bishops who down to the fifth century had to defend their churches against the Marcionite propaganda.

§4. MINICIUS FELIX[1]

The Octavius

Minucius Felix is doubtless the last in date of the apologists known to us,[2] but he is one of the first in charm of style: Theophilus took us to the Eastern world, to the frontiers of the Hellenic and Syrian churches; the reading of the Octavius brings us back to the West, and for the first time, puts us in presence of a Latin text.[3]

This little treatise is written in a very attractive style, and all the humanists admired it. "When we read," says Boissier,[4] "this charming work, which goes back to the Phaedrus by way of the Tusculans, and seems illumined by a ray of light from Greece,

[28] This work is mentioned by Eusebius (Hist. Eccles., IV, xxiv), as well as a work against the heresy of Hermogenes. Loofs (Theophilus v. Antiochien adv. Marcionem, Leipzig, 1930) thinks he has found the substance of the treatise against Marcion in the work of Irenæus, Adversus Hæreses, and he has devoted a mass of learning and ingenuity in order to prove this thesis. But it cannot be upheld. Cf. Recherches de Sc. Relig., 1931, pp. 596-601. On the theology of Theophilus, cf. Histoire du Dogme de la Trinité, Vol. II, pp. 508-13.

[1] The Octavius, conserved in a manuscript of the ninth century (Parisius, 1661) was edited in the Vienna Corpus by Halm in 1867, also with a French translation and commentary, by Waltzing (Louvain, 1903). English translation by Freese, published by S.P.C.K. Cf. Boissier, La fin du paganisme, Vol. I, pp. 261-89; Monceaux, Histoire littéraire de l'Afrique chrétienne, Vol. I, pp. 463-508; P. de Labriolle, Histoire de la littérature latine chrétienne, Vol. II, pp. 147-75.

[2] This date is much discussed; between the Octavius and Tertullian's Apologeticus, which dates from 197, we find striking resemblances; to explain them, the hypothesis of a common source has been given up, and there remain two rival theses: Tertullian is prior (Boissier, Monceaux, De Labriolle); Minucius is prior (Schanz, Ehrhard, Waltzing, Moricca). Fifteen years ago, Dom de Bruyne wrote (Revue bénédictine, October, 1924, p. 136): "This question bids fair to take its place amongst the tedious and insoluble problems raised periodically by some courageous seekers." We shall study the Octavius briefly without referring again to this discussion.

[3] Pope Victor is said to be the first Christian writer in Latin, but what he wrote has not come down to us. The Acts of the Scillitan martyrs begin Latin Christian literature for us; the first work in Latin is Tertullian's Apologeticus or else the Octavius, according to the side taken in the debate on the relative priority of these two works.

[4] G. Boissier, op. cit., p. 289.

we see well that the writer imagined a kind of smiling and sympathetic Christianity which ought to penetrate into Rome without making a noise, and renew it without shock." The Church historian, whose curiosity is more exigent, will find something to regret in this charming work, which is after all only a distant introduction to the faith.

Octavius Januarius, the friend of Minucius, meets him in Rome in September; after long conversations, they profit by the fact that the law courts are closed for the holidays and go to Ostia, taking with them a pagan friend, Cæcilius. Perceiving a statue of Serapis, Cæcilius salutes it according to the custom by throwing a kiss to it. Octavius turns to Minucius and says: "Really it is not good, my dear friend, to give up to the vagaries of common ignorance a man who loves you and never leaves you, and to let him address homage one fine day to stones, especially when you know that you are equally responsible with him for his shameful error." Cæcilius is saddened by this incident, and as soon as they arrive at the end of the mole they sit down and the discussion begins.

Cæcilius, who defends paganism, is a philosopher of the Academy; in human things, everything is doubtful and uncertain; we meet with probabilities rather than with truths; hence it is a strange presumption for the ignorant to pretend to know God; we are wiser, we who, in the midst of such uncertitude, believe our ancestors and respect our Roman traditions. Those who reject them are intolerable, and Christians more than all others. And here Cæcilius, in his indignation and contempt, echoes all the calumnies uttered against all Christians.[5]

The Apologetics of Minucius Felix

Octavius answers him by stressing in the first place the contradiction between this sceptical philosophy and this intolerant paganism. There is only one God: the spectacle of the world convinces us of this, and popular belief tends to its spontaneously;[6] the poets and philosophers proclaim it; it is the belief of Christians. By contrast, how silly are the pagan fables, and how shameful are the pagan mysteries! Your calumnies against Christianity can bring

[5] Cf. *supra*, p. 531.
[6] We find here (xviii) the arguments developed by Tertullian in his little book on the *Testimony of the Soul*.

a blush only to those who invent them: amongst us everything is simple and pure:

"Is it necessary to raise statues to God, if man is His image? Why should one build temples to Him, seeing that the universe which He formed with His hands is not able to contain Him? How can one enclose this immensity in a small chapel? It is our souls which must serve as a dwelling place for Him, and He wants us to consecrate our hearts to Him. Of what use is it to offer victims to Him, and would it not be an ingratitude, when He has given us all that is born on earth for our use, to give back to Him the presents He has given us? Let us realise that He requires of us only a pure heart and an upright conscience. To conserve one's innocence is to pray to God, to respect justice is to honour Him. We win His favour by abstaining from all fraud, and when one saves a man from danger, one offers Him the sacrifice He prefers. Those are the victims, and that is the worship we offer to Him. Amongst us, he is the most religious who is the most just." [7]

This brilliant page reveals the attractiveness but also the inadequacy of this *Apology*: if Christianity were only that, it would be only a philosophy. Octavius moreover is aware of this, for he promises to return elsewhere to the discussion which he begins here (ch. xxxvi). The only argument he pursues to the end is the spectacle of Christian virtues, especially in martyrdom:

"What a fine spectacle for God is that of a Christian who fights against pain, who vindicates his liberty in face of kings and princes, yielding only to God to whom he belongs, who surmounts, triumphant and victorious, the magistrate who condemns him. . . . This is because the soldier of God is not abandoned in pain, not destroyed by death. A Christian may seem to be unhappy, but he is not. . . . Do you not realise that no one would wish without reason to expose himself to such torments, and could not support them without God? . . . Peaceful, modest, certain of the goodness of our God, we uphold the hope of future happiness by faith in His ever present majesty. Thus we rise again to a happy life, and already here below we live in the contemplation of the future. (We despise the disdain of the philosophers) whom we know to be corrupters, adulterers, tyrants, of an inexhaustible loquaciousness against what are their own vices. But we, who make a show of wisdom not by our mantle but by our soul, the greatness of

[7] Ch. xxxii, 3.

which is not in speech but in our life, we glory because we have grasped what these men have striven to find with such great efforts and have never succeeded. . . . We wish superstition to be driven back, impiety to be expiated, and the true religion to be respected" (ch. xxxvii-xxxviii).

This discourse made a deep impression on the two friends. Finally Cæcilius broke the silence and declared himself converted; he only asked for a further instruction, which was promised him for the next day.

This brilliant *Apology* is then only an introduction to the faith, and this explains its silences: Minucius wished to reach the educated public, and arouse a sympathetic curiosity in favour of Christianity. At the same time we may wonder whether a less reserved exposition would not have been more effective, and thereby wiser. We may well think so; but having said that, we must allow that the *Octavius* has a great charm and a great strength. We do not find in it the vigour or originality of Tertullian; the borrowed elements are numerous, but they are utilised with a very sure and very personal touch; the introduction itself is not a mere addition, but it aims at showing the readers that Christians can be, like them, cultivated people and of good standing, lawyers who profit by the court vacations in order to discuss amongst themselves the most elevated problems. The discussion confirms the impression of the beginning: in Cæcilius's exposition, so vigorous and sometimes so brutal, the pagans would recognise their own objections, in the very form they gave to them or would wish to give them; the defence of Octavius would appeal to them, there is not one objection made against the Christians which is not turned back against the paganism they knew so well and which they excused by habit or by tradition, but which a moment of reflection would lead them to despise. Philosophy would give way in its turn; some of its most elevated theses confirm the Christian doctrines or at least dispose the mind in favour of them; on the other hand, it will acknowledge its inability to uphold life, and this will be done by those who give the most brilliant exposition of it. In face of it, we have Christianity, which it despises, but the moral beauty of which is so simple, so sincere, and so widespread, and which surpasses it in every way. With this description the *Octavius* finishes; it can be understood that its attraction was very great indeed.

Christian Apologetics in the Second Century

If we consider it as a whole, the apologetics of the second century makes known to us in the first place the opposition which Christianity encountered, and which the apologists endeavoured to lessen. At first it was the pagan cults the Apostles found opposing them, as was the case with St. Paul at Athens; their aim was then to combat polytheism and idolatry, and to establish the belief in one only God, in order to pass on to the mission of Christ. Very soon other opponents came on the scene and occupied the first place; these were the philosophers, who gave to Hellenism its consistence; the pagan cults and their mysteries sufficed to deceive and to lull religious needs, but they could not justify themselves before the intellect unless they were transformed and spiritualised by philosophy; the philosophers moreover were not content merely to defend paganism, they attacked the new religion. More and more the combat was taken up by two teams of thinkers, those of the Church, and those of Philosophy.

The issue of this combat could not be doubted; from the time we are considering, it was plain: Hellenism could maintain its empire over men's souls only by deliberate combinations and compromises: philosophy of itself resulted only in a barren speculation and one which was generally uncertain; it had to rest on the pagan cults in order to obtain the force or at least the illusion of a religious energy, but in order to derive from these cults some semblance of life, it had to purify them, elevate them, and transform them; in spite of all these endeavours, it could not give them an objective truth which their whole contents excluded.

Christianity, on the contrary, was everything combined: a belief, a cult, and a moral code; all was in one system, with the same solidity throughout: all that philosophy had anticipated was consecrated by a divine revelation, and this natural theology was continued in mysteries which illumined the present life and prepared for the one to come. All this gave to the apologists a tone of certitude which was calm, sincere and deep, a tone philosophy could not imitate, and which was irresistible; to this must be added the spectacle of the fruits which this religion produced, in its martyrs first of all, and also in the whole mass of its followers, even the most humble; here above all Christianity displayed an evident and decisive superiority over Hellenism.

Such was truly the essence of the debate, and on these questions the affirmations of the apologists of the second century had a lasting value. Besides that, many secondary questions, raised in the course of the discussion, received solutions which were not always the best: Christianity, necessary to mankind, appeared very late; why was this? To this puzzling question the *Letter to Diognetus* replied by affirming the providential plan which will draw salvation from general misery; St. Justin showed the action of the seminal Word which reveals at least some of the indispensable religious truths; Tertullian spoke of the naturally Christian soul; Justin, Tatian and others added that the philosophers have copied from the Bible. Is Christianity a unique revelation, or was it prepared for by a revelation given to all men, or at least to the Jews? This question is closely linked with the preceding one; it was answered only incompletely. The Jewish revelation was imperfectly understood; prophecy was well brought out into the light, but we do not yet find in the apologists the idea of the progressive education of mankind which St. Irenæus will set forth in a masterly way. Whence comes the transcendence of Christian doctrine? Justin saw plainly and said with truth that its source is the divine revelation. There is more incertitude in the exposition of this revealed teaching; the apparent similarities between this theology and the Platonist or Stoic philosophy sometimes hide from the apologists the fundamental opposition between these two systems; hence the dangerous inexactitudes we have pointed out. We must note, moreover, that the apologists undertook their task of their own initiative; the Church was pleased with their zeal, but it did not wish to cover with its authority their sometimes too tolerant philosophy. Very soon, moreover, towards the end of this second century, the struggle against the heretics will force the Church to give to the rule of faith more rigour, to the liturgy more unity, and to the ecclesiastical government a more effective power.

CHRONOLOGICAL TABLE OF POPES AND EMPERORS

Emperors		Popes	
Augustus ... died in	14		
Tiberius	14- 37		
Caligula	37- 41		
Claudius	41- 54		
Nero	54- 68	St. Peter	30 ?- 64
Galba, Otho, Vitellius	68- 69	St. Linus	64 ?- 76 ? [1]
Vespasian	69- 79	St. Anacletus	76 ?-88 ? [1]
Titus	79- 81	St. Clement	88 ?-about 100
Domitian	81- 96	St. Evaristus	?- ?
Nerva	96- 98	St. Alexander	?- ?
Trajan	98-117	St. Sixtus	?-?
		St. Telesphorus	?- about 136
Hadrian	117-138	St. Hyginus ... about 136- about 140	
Antoninus the Pious ...	138-161	St. Pius ... ... about 140- before 154	
		St. Anicetus ... from 154- ?	
		St. Soter ... ... before 175-175	
Marcus Aurelius ...	161-180	St. Eleutherus	175-189
Commodus	180-192		

[1] The dates of Linus and Anacletus are unknown. We might attribute to each the twelve years given to them in the tradition enshrined in the *Liber Pontificalis*. Cf. above p. 479.